Testimonials from Lily

"The five-element cosmic system, as elaborated in the Meng, has proven to be an invaluable aid in my personal and professional life. Knowing how the elements work, I am better prepared to schedule my work flow, weigh my decisions, and interact with my clients on a more effective level."

— *Lillian Ng*

"I have tested the theories of the Meng for the last two years and have been amazed at how the flows of water and fire affect the lives of my family. I have become a more effective parent to my son … this is one of the few investments with happy returns!"

— *Jenny Hong*

"[The Meng is] a powerful tool for analyzing the cosmic strengths of my children. Through the process of testing and verification, I have found out how certain elements benefit or adversely affect their lives.

— *Mabel Dang*

"I have learned to preserve my energy by avoiding useless efforts. Without this knowledge, I would still be stumbling in constant frustration.

— *Henry Low*

About the Author

Lily Chung was born and raised in Hong Kong. She has a B.A. degree from Chinese University of Hong Kong, and a Ph.D. from the University of Minnesota. She taught college in the United States (Wisconsin and Pennsylvania) from 1969 to 1971, in Hong Kong from 1972 to 1974, and recently retired from teaching Chinese metaphysics at City College of San Francisco. Lily hosts a talk show on Chinese Astrology for Sinocast, a Chinese radio station. She is a consultant and tutor in Chinese metaphysics, and occasionally gives personal Meng readings. Her published articles include a regular column in *Asian Week* since 1992, which provides lunar year predictions for the twelve cosmic animals.

To Write to the Author

If you wish to contact the author or would like more information about this book, please write to the author in care of Llewellyn Worldwide, and we will forward your request. Both the author and publisher appreciate hearing from you and learning of your enjoyment of this book and how it has helped you. Llewellyn Worldwide cannot guarantee that every letter written to the author can be answered, but all will be forwarded. Please write to:

Llewellyn Worldwide Ltd.
P.O. Box 64383, Dept. K133-3, St. Paul, MN 55164-0383, U.S.A.
Please enclose a self-addressed, stamped envelope for reply, or $1.00 to cover costs.
If outside U.S.A., enclose international postal reply coupon.

The Path to Good Fortune

The Meng

Lily Chung, Ph.D.

1997
Llewellyn Publications
St. Paul, Minnesota, 55164-0383, U.S.A.

FIRST EDITION
First Printing, 1997

All interior figures are the original works of Lily Chung
Cover design by Tom Grewe
Cover photo from Digital Stock Corp.
Editing and layout by Deb Gruebele
Book design and project coordination by Connie Hill

Library of Congress Cataloging-in-Publication Data
Chung, Lily, 1937–
    The path to good fortune : the meng / Lily Chung
      p.   cm.
    ISBN 1–56718–133–3 (trade pbk.)
    1. Fate and fatalism. 2. Divination—China. 3. Yin—yang.
I. Title.
BJ1461.C53   1997   97-2437
133.3'3—dc21   CIP

Printed in the United States of America.

Llewellyn Publications
A Division of Llewellyn Worldwide, Ltd.
St. Paul, Minnesota 55164-0383, U.S.A.

Table of Contents

List of Figures

CHAPTER 1

Introduction to The Meng

This book is dedicated to enhancing the quality of human life. The key to achieving this goal is to gain control of our individual lives. It is not an easy task. Gaining control of our lives takes more than hard work, intelligence, competence, or education. Even the most gifted and ambitious among us can become confused and frustrated over unforeseeable and uncontrollable events. More than we care to admit, we can be victims of circumstance.

Attempts to Foretell Events

To fully control life, we need to be able to foretell events and prepare for them. Throughout history, humans have struggled to control the invisible elements in our destiny. The earliest attempts probably took place in China where, as early as 2800 B.C., the emperors studied turtle shells to aid them in making decisions on affairs of the state. Among the ancient Greeks, unmarried young men and women sought to foretell the name of a future spouse by counting rose petals or onion layers.

The Babylonians tried to forecast events by reading the pattern of flour dropped in boiling water. Other forms of divination include card reading, tea leaf reading, palmistry, and crystal ball gazing. If we include all the rituals in Africa and Asia, the list would be practically endless.

Today, the most popular pursuit is horoscope reading, which originated in Greece. Horoscope columns, which are carried by almost ninety percent of the current newspapers in the United States, attract more than twenty-six million regular readers. Their popularity demonstrates our persistent desire to control our life!

Stubbornly Perplexing Questions

Control starts with understanding. Most of us know our strengths and weaknesses; the clear-thinking have a complete inventory of personal assets, both tangible and intangible. Is this enough? No. There is a missing link in this approach. The most fundamental factor controlling our lives is never accounted for in our normal problem-solving analysis.

Many of us must have noticed a pattern of energy flow in the timing of our daily activities. We work best during certain hours, days, months, and perhaps seasons. These "best moments" vary from person to person. Some enjoy being an early bird; others prefer to be a night owl. We also have favorite months or seasons. Don't we all have some good years and some bad ones?

The sensitive and the aware among us must also have noticed that the events of our lives occur in patterns. Certain activities tend to crowd together at certain periods of time. Examples include our visits to doctors or dentists, social engagements, and work schedules. Is there a reason? Don't we also experience a periodic change of luck? How do we explain these changes?

We have all been through ups and downs in the course of our lives; we all tend to accept these as a fact of life. But why does a person whose endowments don't change go through a life of ups and downs with dramatically different luck at different times? Why are these changes beyond our control? Don't they have a relationship in terms of time and space? What is it? How does it work?

Why do some people have more luck than others? Why don't intelligent and diligent people always succeed? Why do some people have a magic finger turning everything they touch into gold? Why do we feel so compatible with one person and clash with somebody else? Why do our lucky events always seem to be associated with the same kind of people and our happy experiences with certain places?

The Search for an Answer

The lucky few who have enough foresight to gain a precise sense of destiny succeed in life. The rest of us attribute this phenomenon to one word: *luck*. What is luck? It is basically doing the right thing at the right time in the right place. Is creating luck the sole privilege of the divine? Not necessarily. In order to create or to enhance luck, we must properly bring together the factors of time, place, and action. How to do so is the theme of this book.

This is not a new topic. Practically all Chinese people are aware of this concept, although only a few are knowledgeable about it. The study is called *Meng*. Literally, Meng means life. It implies destiny. Ancient Chinese scholars generally agreed that no one could live a full life without knowing one's destiny. Their ultimate goal was to attune their lives to their destiny, making it error-free.

The above arguments lead to one conclusion: There is an invisible element controlling our life. We call this controlling element the *ultimate truth*. Knowing the ultimate truth is the only way to set ourselves free.

Cosmic Flows Are the Answer

Is there a perfect answer? The search for the ultimate truth continues to the present day. Some have promised a partial answer, but of all the attempts that have been made until now, the one developed by the ancient Chinese seems to offer the most fundamental answer to our perplexing question. It is not perfect; it needs more testing and revision, but it is the most plausible answer offered until now.

The Chinese answer is called *cosmic flow*, a mysterious natural force that governs the cosmos. It follows a constant order and changes periodically in a closed-ended cycle that repeats itself. It interacts with all lives in the universe and affects them in many different ways. Those who are favorably affected have good luck; those who are negatively affected have bad luck. Since the nature of the flows changes periodically and the cycle of flows repeats itself, we all periodically experience a change of luck, better or worse.

The person who first discovered the order of cosmic flow was the legendary culture hero, Fu Hsi. He formulated the cosmic order into a system that became the foundation of the Chinese lunar calendar. Incorporating the system into Chinese divination was the concerted effort of a few geniuses in China, whom we call the sages. They were born in the two most prosperous dynasties in Chinese history near the area where the civilization of China was first born. That is, at the most prosperous time and in the most prosperous place.

There is no birth data for these sages that would allow us to trace the cosmic influence in greater detail. One fact that stands out is that since Meng divination was first established, for more than a thousand years there has been no change or expansion in the field. Regardless of its popularity, all publications on the subject have been on the level of testing theories. Perfect timing is never repeated.

Sorting out the order of the vast mosaic of the universe solely through the efforts of one's own mind takes unique perceptual powers. Understanding it and putting it to work for divination requires tremendous contemplation, which only a few can afford. As a result of its mysterious nature and high complexity, divination has been regarded as superstition.

No one should waste time or effort on superstition. We have to clear the air on this matter before we can move on. What is superstition? According to Webster's Dictionary, it is a practice or belief resulting from the ignorance and fear of the unknown, based on unfounded facts. How do we prove that the study of Meng divination does not fall into this category? After all, the force is invisible and its influence cannot be tested in a physical laboratory.

Meng Divination

Meng divination is not superstition; it is systematic knowledge originally developed by a unique set of minds. For over a thousand years it has been tested on a huge population all over China. This long-term laboratory has provided an immensely powerful testing ground for its theories. Its validity has been supported by a continuous accumulation of consistent observations among the population. Its popularity has grown over time. It is a combination of metaphysics, science, and statistics incorporated into the deep-rooted philosophy of the Chinese people.

Cosmic flow is cyclical and closed-ended. The cycle repeats, patterns can be identified, making it possible to put together a picture of the cosmic whole that reveals the conditions affecting our luck. This particular feature makes it a unique and most valuable tool for divination.

Cosmic flow affects every substance and life in the universe by constantly interacting and interchanging with individual energy systems. When, at any given moment, the interaction happens to be mutually supporting, the possibility of great fortune is created. When the flows clash, great misfortune results. The momentum of interaction, which depends on the timing and the nature of flows, determines the magnitude of luck. At any given point in time, people are affected by countless different types of luck as a result of this interaction.

How do we discover the order and how it affects our luck? How do we reduce this big picture to serve our goal? A few sages in ancient China have provided us with the answer. It is the single most valuable component of Chinese civilization, one that sets the Chinese apart from other nations. They have crafted a unique world for all people. It is, of course, not perfect. Its greatest merit is that it offers us a rich insight into life that surpasses any other means available with our current technology. This insight offers us a powerful tool for exploring our potential in greater depth.

Despite its popularity, only a few full-time professional astrologers have mastered a small portion of the Meng. Despite its solid footing as a divination tool, it has rarely been tested outside of China, except for a few attempts at analyzing some western celebrities. Meng divination is derived from I Ching and puts its idea into practice. While the I Ching has attracted global attention in the academic world, Meng divination has never traveled beyond the borders of China.

It is the purpose of this book to introduce Meng methodology to the public outside China, testing it for the first time in a global laboratory. This book serves only as an introduction; the complexity of the subject cannot be covered in a single book.

How Do We Benefit from the Study?

The methodology of the Meng enables us to derive a full account of ourselves: our endowments, strengths, limitations, and the key events covering our entire lifetime. It leads us to the fundamental force that accounts for our outlook and most of our achievements. It is a valuable and highly functional tool. It does not promise miracles, but offers us ample alternatives to enhance our lives.

However, we have to remember and accept the fact that destiny cannot be abolished. For the world to function as a unit, it is necessary for every person to be created different and to perform a specific role in order to keep the world functioning properly. Our social role might be to a large extent predetermined, but it is not fixed once and for all; moreover, the means of getting to our goal is open. For instance, there are sad beggars and happy beggars! Knowing our destiny, we try to make the best out of what we have. How we choose to sail our course makes a difference, and may affect our level of achievement.

It is true that we have no choice of our parents, siblings, kin, citizenship, and the place of our birth. However, within the framework of our kin and our living environment, we can choose our friends and how we relate to our kin. How to relate is a matter of our decision, which is not controlled by destiny. Within the framework of our endowments, we have free will and can choose how to use them.

By being aware of destiny, we can maximize our endowments and minimize negative impacts on our system. According to Meng, no destiny is strictly set; there are dozens of different formulas of development for a given life. Just consider all the people born at the same time and how differently their lives turn out! In other words, the possibilities for achievement are wide open within the same framework of destiny. With a good understanding of how the system works, we can steer our life course in compliance with the cosmic flows. "Sailing with the wind!" is the only easy way to win.

Having benefited from destiny awareness myself, I earnestly want to share my experience and knowledge with you. Of course, there are a chosen few who enjoy life to the fullest extent because their birth coincided with those few perfect moments that guarantee a perfect life. They are not the concern of this study.

The great majority are like myself, who struggle frantically to achieve a goal and find themselves going in circles. We have so much frustration and so many questions about life that prompt us to look for the ultimate truth.

For you, the reader, this book offers a shortcut. It is the first attempt in human history outside China to explore destiny in a systematic way. There are many publications on the study of Meng written in Chinese, but none of them incorporate the idea of the cosmic flows in a systematic discussion. None of them elaborate on the idea of attracting luck by attuning ourselves to the cosmic flow. Most important, there is no English version on the subject at all!

However, I do not pretend to be a magician. As the subject is so intricate, no one should expect to master the tools by reading a few books on the subject. Valuable knowledge carries a high price tag. It takes a serious, open mind and determination to master the tools. I have personally tested the validity of the Meng theories with my life events. After practicing these theories with hundreds of people around the world, I am fully convinced that those who know how to use them have an edge over those who do not. The missing link in our problem-solving process in life has to be connected before we can arrive at a valid conclusion. This connection has to be made with these tools.

The Structure of the Study

This study covers the basics of Meng divination, its fundamental components, methodology, and theories, and shows readers how to attune themselves to the cosmic flows. The theories are illustrated with real life examples of different types. There are charts, tables, and summaries to help you grasp the essence of the theories.

The study is organized in four parts. Part One, which includes Chapters 2, 3, and 4, covers the origins of Meng divination, the structure of cosmic flow, and the procedure of defining our cosmic system. Part Two, which includes Chapters 5 and 6, discusses theories on the interaction of cosmic flows and the procedure of analyzing cosmic systems.

Part Three, which includes Chapters 7 and 8, focuses on illustrations of model cosmic systems. It offers some guidelines for readers to analyze their cosmic systems by selecting the model closest to their own. Part Four, which is the concluding chapter, outlines a foolproof procedure for determining how certain cosmic flows affect our lives, and suggests ways to attune to such flows.

A unique feature of this book is the inclusion of the lunar calendars in the appendix, which provide a daily guide on cosmic flows. Once we work out our cosmic system, we can determine our energy level and luck, any time throughout our lifetime, by referring to the appendix without further calculation or help from a professional astrologer. It is a lifetime reference book.

Analyzing cosmic systems is an intellectual pursuit that requires substantial effort. However, the skill can be attained at three different levels. Busy readers are encouraged to share the fun and benefit of using some of these valuable tools by spending a few hours with the book.

Level One is straightforward. Readers can get a general picture of their cosmic strengths by using a few simple charts in Chapters 2 and 4. The serious-minded can also test their findings and attune their lives to the flows by following the suggestions outlined in Chapter 9.

Ambitious readers can move to Level Two, where they learn how to work out their cycle of luck changes so they can predict their future course. The procedure takes some simple but painless calculations. The step-by-step instructions are explained with a real life illustration. This level can be attained by reading Part One and Part Four.

Advanced readers can move to Level Three, where they develop an indepth understanding of all cosmic signs and a rich insight in the analysis of cosmic systems. The objective is achieved by learning all the theories and browsing through all the illustrations in the book.

Once all the concepts, theories, and methodologies have been learned, this book can be used as reference book. The appendix provides a daily guide on cosmic flows for years to come. As we move along in our daily practice of attuning ourselves to the flows, occasionally checking for answers from the book, we'll gradually build up our insight on the subject and move to the next level. In any event, all beginners will benefit by Level One skill with a few hours of time and a little effort.

CHAPTER 2

The Origin of Chinese Divination

Chinese divination is part of Chinese philosophy. Its theories are derived from the spatial concepts of ancient Chinese people. It is a complex subject, but can be boiled down to two basic aspects: Tao and spatial order.

The Essence of Tao

Ancient Chinese people believed there was an ultimate law under which the universe operated, including the creation and sustenance of all life in all forms at all times. They called this law the Tao. The mechanism of the Tao is the interaction between two fundamental opposite forces known as *yang* and *yin*. These forces contrast each other in nature and function to maintain the check-and-balance state of the universe.

Yang, of the masculine gender, is the expression of all things in the masculine category. Examples, to name a few, are males, the sun, day, summer, all odd numbers, and all bright colors. In nature, it is forward-going and virile.

Yin, of the feminine gender, is the expression of retreating and being docile, gentle, subtle, and submissive. Examples are females, the moon, night, winter, all even numbers, and most subtle and dark colors. Regardless of their contrasting nature, yang and yin forces are equally powerful.

To illustrate the interaction between yang and yin, let us use some examples. Many great generals and kings (yang force) who conquered the world, in turn succumbed to the charm of a queen or other woman (yin force). A saying claims that behind every great man there is a woman. Stories such as the race between a hare and a tortoise, and how an elephant was killed by a mouse, convey the same theme. The hare, being a yang force (more powerful in momentum), lost the race because it failed to perceive the relentless perseverance of the subtle yin force in the tortoise.

Yang and yin always co-exist. Whatever we do, in whatever situation, there is always an interacting opposite force, either yang or yin. Anyone who, at any point, fails to properly perceive the other force is inviting trouble. For instance, we might jeopardize our health or social relationships by pushing our ambitions too far; a tyrant (yang force) might encounter revolution (yin force) from suppressed subjects when his or her control goes unchecked.

The most ideal state is to keep both forces in perfect balance, which is equilibrium. Achieving equilibrium (perfect life) is the ultimate goal for all of us. Equilibrium guarantees success, happiness, and all good things. The Tao shows us how to achieve this goal. All wise Chinese desperately try to understand the Tao and behave accordingly. Conscientious teachers and parents struggle to pass the message of Tao to the next generation.

It pays to push our ambition to success. However, wise people proceed in a manner so as not to create destructive competition or to ruin their health or social relationships. A wise dictator tries hard to keep his or her subjects happy in order to stay in power. To maintain a happy marriage, husband and wife should stay in their own domain of power. We should keep in mind that there is always a counter force nearby.

Yang and yin always take turns reigning. Examples are sunrise and sunset (the rotation of day and night), and the change of seasons. As the saying goes, there is no lasting glory or misery. Prudent people always prepare for rainy days; downtrodden people should look forward to better days. All happenings follow a natural sequence, alternating ups and downs; perseverance is the key to victory. This is why a periodic change of luck cycle is the key feature of Chinese divination. Wise Chinese people judge others on their potential rather than their current state. Change, the operating law of the universe, is the soul of Chinese philosophy.

All of us are subject to the interplay of the yang and yin forces, and this partly explains why we have ups and downs in our lives. Understanding the Tao enriches our insight on our destiny and is the sure way to happiness. However, the Tao is subtle. The line separating yang and yin forces is fine, and it shifts from time to time and from point to point. It takes a clear mind and a clean soul to properly identify the Tao and act accordingly. Regular meditation and certain exercises are practiced by some Chinese to sharpen their mind and clean their soul. Success comes to those who have a strong will to implement their clear vision.

The Spatial Order

The universe, as the Chinese perceived it, is a space composed of five components known as the five elements: wood, fire, metal, water, and earth. Each element has its own domain, and all five interact in a specific manner.

The Domain

The domain of each of the five elements is ordered as follows: wood/east, fire/south, metal/west, water/north, earth/center. See Figure 2A on page 12. This order is close to the geographic reality of China, where there is woodland in the east, a warm climate in the south, abundant minerals in the west, cold land and big rivers in the north, and a fertile flood plain at the center.

These elements take turns ruling the universe. The lunar calendar, on which the Meng is based, begins in spring. Wood reigns in spring, when all vegetation thrives, dominantly visible, taking in plenty of water and penetrating into the earth, making it hollow. Metal gives way to spreading roots. Water dwindles as tree roots absorb so much of it. Wood is the king of the universe.

As summer approaches, fire takes its turn. The sun is bright and its fire strong. Heat is universally felt. Days get longer. The sun's fire evaporates water, cracks the earth, melts down metal, and burns wood and forest. Fire enjoys super power.

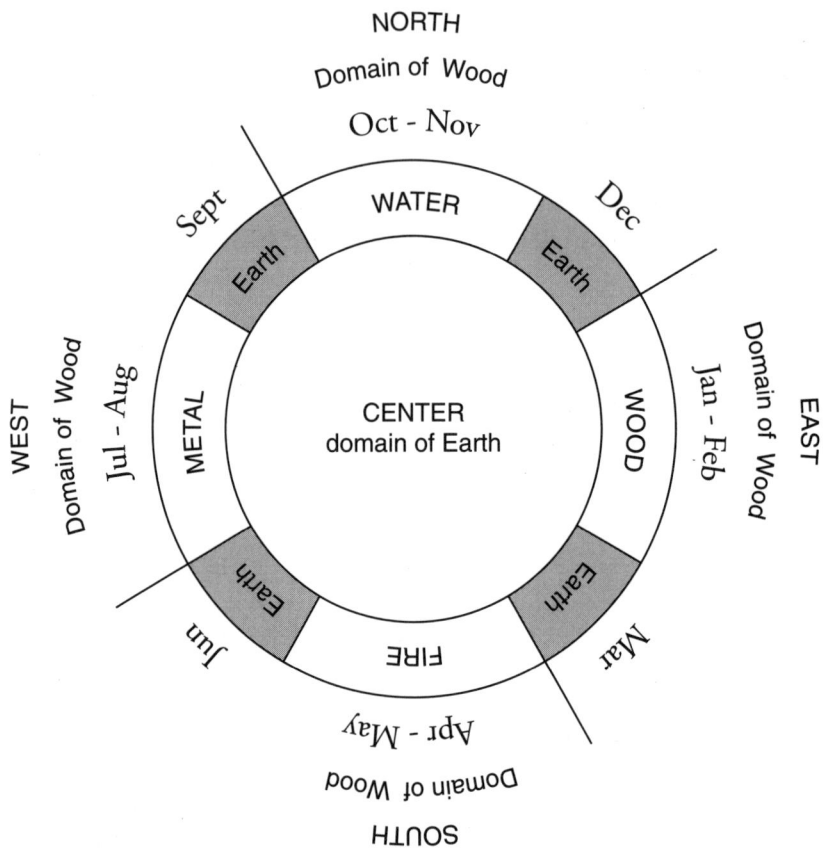

Figure 2A. The Elements and Their Domains

Metal matures in fall. It becomes solid and shiny, perfect for turning into great tools. It undermines the earth and chops down wood. Fire, which is weakening, cannot harm the massive solid ore. Metal influence produces little sensory effect. It is only subtly and mysteriously felt by the perceptive. To ease any doubt, let us quote some findings on metal. Unofficial figures indicate that gold prices tend to peak between August and mid-September. People whose favorable element happens to be metal experience a surge of energy and unusual good luck during autumn. This theory has been backed up by my personal experience.

Water rules in winter. This idea reflects the geographic reality of central China, where the study of Meng was first developed. It rains in the winter there! This raises some controversy, as summer rain is globally prevalent. However, summer rain is offset by great heat and is not as visible as the drizzle, snow, and icy landscape of a lengthy winter. Misty winter also tends to create a perception of permanent moisture. During winter, water threatens fire, soaks up earth, uproots trees, and undermines metal. It controls the fate of the other four elements.

In the last month of each season, the dominant element wanes in power, leaving a gap for earth to fill in. Earth dominates the months of March, June, September, and December in the lunar calendar, which are approximate to April, July, October, and January in the western calendar.

Earth influence also produces little sensory effect. It is, however, manifested in communication blocks, traffic jams, drought, soaring property values, and increasing sand deposits in streams. For instance, during 1988, when earth ruled the universe, there was a substantial increase in property values throughout the United States, Japan, and Hong Kong. A great drought took place in the western United States. Major ship-sinking incidents around the world are associated with dominant earth. Earth's influence can be felt by those whose lives are greatly affected by it. In any given year, those whose cosmic system is benefited by earth will experience better luck during the four months ending each season. On the other hand, those who dread earth suffer during those months.

This rotating dominance between the five elements also applies to monthly and daily changes. The order of change remains constant and follows a system that will be discussed later in this chapter. How do the five elements affect us? It depends on where and when we were born, and where we live. Those who live in the north will be substantially affected by cosmic water. Water enhances the luck of those who need it and aggravates those who dread it. Such people should consider moving or making some other adjustment. The same logic applies to other elements.

Interaction Between the Five Elements

While the position and rotation of the five elements determines the spatial order of the universe, the interaction between them sets its tempo of change. The five elements interact with themselves in a closed-ended cycle and are responsible for all energy flows and all forms of life in the universe. There are numerous kinds of interactions, but there are two basic *ways* the elements interact: interbreeding and interruling.

To *breed* is to produce and to support. Water breeds wood because it supports its growth, producing more wood. Wood breeds fire because it fuels it. Fire breeds earth by providing warmth to keep organisms in the soil alive, which consequently creates living and productive soil.

Earth provides the home base for all metals, so earth breeds metal. Without earth, no metal can grow. Metal breeds water. This idea was the observation of our sages, although it raises some doubt. The logic is that metal produces the tools used to dig ditches for irrigating farm fields. This interaction is summarized in Figure 2B.

To *rule* is to control. Wood rules earth, as it can penetrate into the soft soil. Earth controls water by absorbing or blocking it. Water extinguishes fire; fire melts down metal; metal tools chop down wood. This interaction is summarized in Figure 2C on page 15.

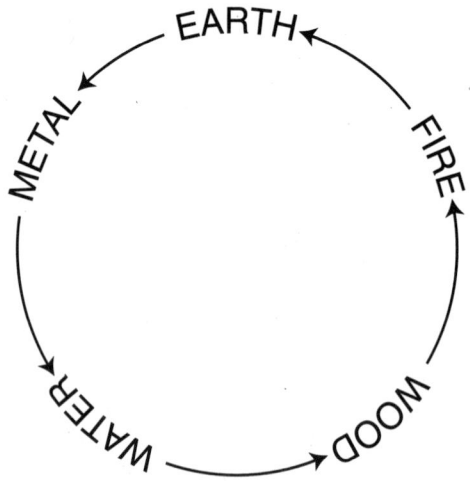

Figure 2B. The Interbreeding of the Five Elements

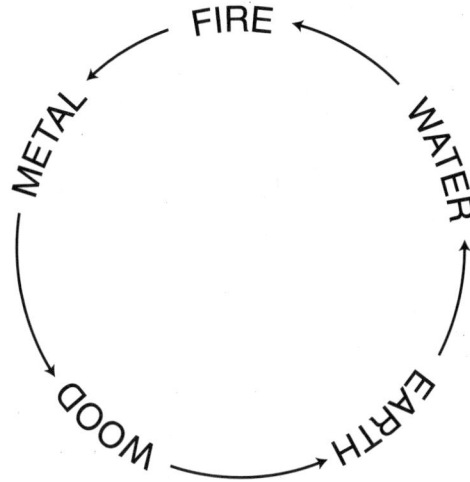

Figure 2C. The Interruling of the Five Elements

Basically, every element has equal opportunities to rule and to breed. However, there are exceptions. For example, a rusty axe fails to chop down a tree; resistant hard wood could break an axe; water yields to a fierce blaze; stiff earth can collapse a plant; a feeble fire cannot shape a massive metal; a great flood can destroy an earth embankment.

The same is true in the breeding process. An element has to be in good condition to breed. A drying well or river does not provide much irrigation to breed the crop; damp wood does not burn; barren or stiff earth does not nurture metal; soggy or loose earth cannot stop flooding or nurture vegetation.

The interaction of the five elements, guided by the joint force of yang and yin, constitutes the cosmic flows. This interaction is constant and cyclical. All life and all matters in the cosmos are products of the five elements; each constitutes a cosmic system of its own. People with dominant metal in their system will be the natural superior of those with dominant wood. Dominant metal, in turn, has to watch out for dominant fire. This is one of the reasons we feel so compatible with some people and clash with others.

The nature of luck, again, depends on the nature of the flows and interactions. Someone whose birth captured the perfect moment of interaction could command the world; another could suffer total disaster. This is basically how our destiny is determined.

Defining the Cosmic System

Our gracious sages devised a functional scheme to express the order of these interactions. To identify the flow of these interacting elements, twenty-two signs were invented—ten for their spatial distribution and twelve for their temporal changes. There are two signs for each element—one for yang and one for yin. The spatial signs are known as *stems* and the temporal signs as *branches*.

Each sign is represented by a Chinese character. We'll replace these characters with letters of the alphabet. Each element is assigned the same letter in both groups: upper case letters for yang elements and lower case letters for yin elements.

The Ten Stems

The ten spatial signs, or stems, are listed below and in Figure 2D on page 17 in their constant order—yang and yin alternate each other, as in the list.

T   t   **F**   f   **E**   e   **M**   m   **R**   r

The Twelve Branches

There are twelve branches, representing the temporal changes. They appear below in their constant order.

R   g   **T**   t   **W**   f   **F**   d   **M**   m   **H**   r

The branch group represents the same five elements as the stem group, following the pattern of alternating yang and yin. The major difference is that there are four earth signs, two for each gender—yang and yin. They are **g**, **W**, **d**, and **H**. See Figure 2E on page 18. The other eight signs, representing the other four elements, are equivalents of their counterparts in the stem group.

We use a different set of signs for the four earth branches for two reasons. First, there are four of them, all different from each other in nature and function. Second, they are different from their stem counterparts in their unique function. Each of these four earth signs is influenced by two of the other four elements.

Branches also represent the twelve months of the lunar year, and the twelve hours of a day. Most branches include more than one element in the same sign. Their associated elements and temporal order for the lunar months are listed in Figure 2F on page 19.

You will notice from Figure 2F that, in a lunar year, spring always begins in lunar January. The lunar calendar is approximately forty-five days ahead of the western calendar. There are four seasons in a lunar year, each consisting of three months. The corresponding season and domain for each branch are also listed in the table.

T:	yang wood, standing for trees, forest, or lumber; being erect, strong, and protective; symbolizing honesty, kindness, and fairness.
t:	yin wood, standing for the branches of a tree, plants, shrubs, and bushes; being gentle and flexible; symbolizing honesty and kindness.
F:	yang fire, standing for the sun or great heat; being strong, bright, and hot; symbolizing courtesy, integrity, and quick wit.
f:	yin fire, standing for man-made fire of any form; being warm, bright (intelligent), and gentle, yet strong enough to melt or to burn.
E:	yang earth, standing for massive dry earth such as embankment and blockage, the supporting base for most life; symbolizing stability, reliability, and integrity.
e:	yin earth, being moist or muddy, supporting vegetation and metal; excellent in absorbing heat.
M:	yang metal, standing for metal ore and heavy metal tools; symbolizing justice, decisiveness, and a sharp mind.
m:	yin metal, standing for refined metal, small tools, or ornaments; being shiny, sleek, elegant, polished, and delicate.
R:	yang water, standing for rivers, lakes, or other ground water sources; being elongated, flexible, and changing; symbolizing wisdom, creativity, and flexibility.
r:	yin water, standing for a changed form of water, such as rain, drizzle, snow, fog, or mist; symbolizing wisdom, elegance, and creativity.

Figure 2D. The Ten Stems

g:	moist earth (yin), rain (**r**), and metal (**m**); its function varies according to circumstances; it is associated with the domain of north, or water.
W:	dry earth (yang), wood/plants (**t**), and rain (**r**); its function depends on the situation; it is associated with the domain of east, or wood.
d:	moist earth (yin), man-made fire (**f**), and wood/plants (**t**); it produces a great fire when joining a fire sign, due to its rich wood content; it is associated with the domain of south, or fire.
H:	dry earth (yang), metal (**m**), and man-made fire (**f**); it is hot and dynamic; it is associated with the domain of west, or metal.

Figure 2E. The Four Earth Branches

The cosmic influence of the lunar month plays a vital role in Chinese divination. *In the analysis of cosmic systems in this book, all months referred to are lunar months.* It is important to remember this. A brief guide on the climate of each lunar month and how to interpret the lunar calendars appears on page 161 at the beginning of the appendix, *The Lunar Calendars*. It is a good idea to read and learn the information in this guide before reading on.

The twenty-two signs representing the elements are paired to define the cosmic condition of any given time period. Each year, month, day, and hour is defined by a *pair* of signs—always one sign from the stem group and one from the branch group, in the given order.

What makes the pairing tricky is the unequal number of signs in each group. In each round of pairing, two signs in the branches are left without a mate. These two ending branches from the first round become the matching mate of the first two stems in the second round (underlined in Figure 2G on page 20). The process repeats in each round. After five rounds, or repetitions, the branches left out add up to ten. By the sixth round, there are exactly ten signs in each group, a complete match.

This process completes one cycle and defines the cosmic condition of the time period, whether year, month, or day. Identical pairs reappear every sixty cycles. The yearly cycle repeats every sixty years; the monthly cycle, every sixty months; the daily cycle, every sixty days. Reading these signs takes skill and experience. We will discuss the method and rules later in this chapter and in Chapter 4.

Branch	Stem Equivalents	Lunar Month	Season	Domain	Hours	Animal
R	r rain	November	Winter	North	11 P.M. – 1 A.M.	Rat
g	e moist earth r rain m metal	December	Winter	North	1 – 3 A.M.	Ox
T	T trees F sun E dry earth	January	Spring	East	3 – 5 A.M.	Tiger
t	t plants	February	Spring	East	5 – 7 A.M.	Rabbit
W	t plants E dry earth r rain	March	Spring	East	7 – 9 A.M.	Dragon
f	F sun E dry earth M metal ore	April	Summer	South	9 – 11 A.m.	Snake
F	f man-made fire e moist earth	May	Summer	South	11 A.M. – 1 P.M.	Horse
d	t plants e moist earth f man-made fire	June	Summer	South	1 – 3 P.M.	Ram
M	E dry earth M metal ore R ground water	July	Fall	West	3 – 5 P.M.	Monkey
m	m metal	August	Fall	West	5 – 7 P.M.	Rooster
H	m metal E dry earth f man-made fire	September	Fall	West	7 – 9 P.M.	Dog
r	R ground water T trees	October	Winter	North	9 – 11 P.M.	Boar

Figure 2F. The Branches and Their Stem Equivalents

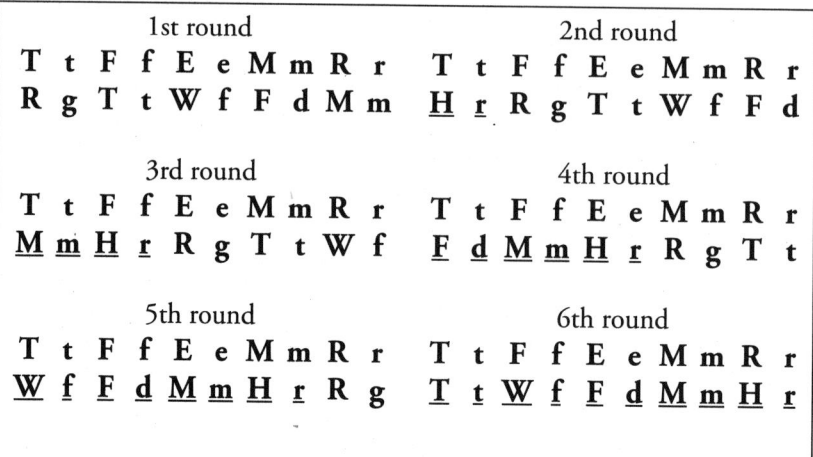

Figure 2G. The Six Rounds of Pairings

Thus, all time units are defined by two signs: one stem and one branch. Each pair is called a *pillar*. In a horizontal display of pillars, stems are always on the left and branches on the right. In a vertical display, stems are always above branches. It is important to remember this.

T stem   **TW**
W branch   stem ╱   ╲ branch

A pillar of two yang symbols is always followed by a pillar of two yin symbols—a constant order. This pattern is clearly displayed in the lunar calendars in the appendix, the basic tool in the analysis of Chinese divination. The lunar calendar is also a daily guide of cosmic flows, a tool for assessing our cosmic strength.

How do we define an hour? The twenty-four hours of a day are divided into twelve zones. Each two-hour zone is defined by one of the twelve branches, as illustrated in Figure 2H on page 21. The cycle begins with **R** for the zone from 11 P.M. to 1 A.M., **g** for the zone from 1 A.M. to 3 A.M., and so forth. This is why older generations of Chinese identify the hour as **R**-hour, **g**-hour, etc. Each hour zone is then paired with one of the stems in the pairing order previously discussed.

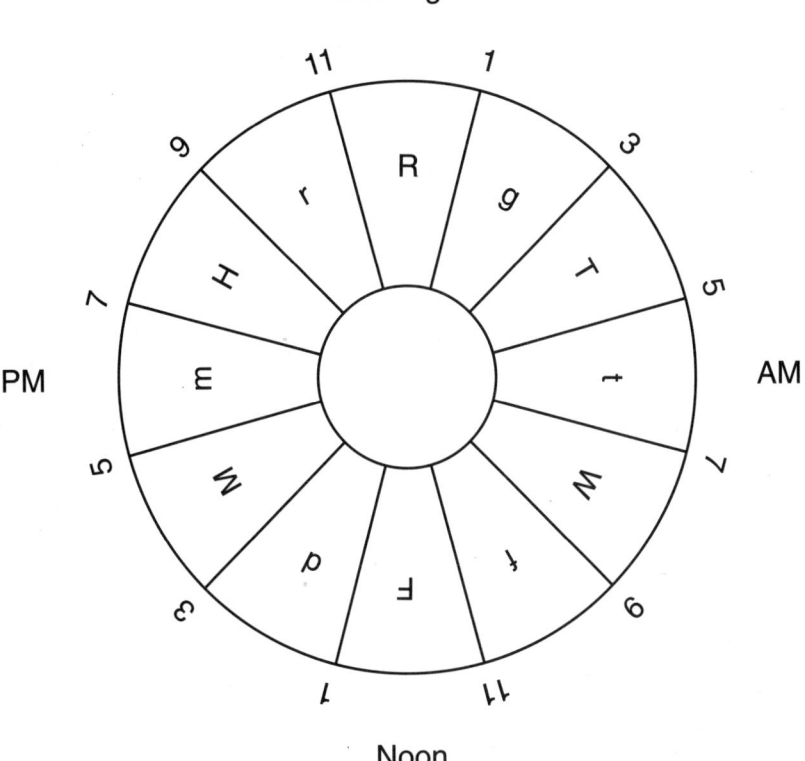

Figure 2H. The Hour Zones

The Development of Chinese Divination

Creating a divination tool from the idea of cosmic flows was a slow process. It began in the Chin Dynasty (221–207 B.C.), when cosmic flows became a popular subject among scholars. Studies concluded that every life was a mini-cosmic system consisting of the five elements, each constantly interacting with the grand cosmic system of the universe. The trend intensified during the following Han dynasty, when great prosperity in the country provided scholars with ample leisure to pursue metaphysics.

A breakthrough was achieved by Chung-shu Tung (179–104 B.C.), a high-ranking government official and great scholar. He discovered and documented the recurring pattern of human response to the cosmic flows in the universe. This monumental discovery set the stage for the study of Meng divination in China.

During the Tong dynasty, another sage, Hsu-chung Li (762–813 A.D.), extended the idea into a methodology on divination. He noted the difference in human response to cosmic flows between males and females, and among various age groups. Through his relentless observations, he was able to incorporate the ideas of yang and yin, and birth data, into a divination tool.

By the beginning of the ninth century, a hermit named Tzu-Ping Hsu had modified Li's methodology in a manuscript. It became the infallible gospel of Chinese divination. This study is often referred to as Tzu-Ping Divination.

Hsu's work gained great popularity during the Ming and Ching Dynasties. Hzu developed thousands of formulas to analyze the cosmic systems of human beings. These formulas were vigorously tested on different strata of population in the palace, and gradually on the general public. The process of development of all these mysterious ideas took place in Central China, mainly between the latitudes of thirty and forty degrees north. The analysis thus tends to be more accurate for people born within these latitudes globally.

California, which is located in comparable latitudes, offers an interesting testing ground for this tool. In fact, the findings based on a few samples have been very encouraging so far. The method does not apply to births in the Southern Hemisphere, where the atmospheric condition at any given point is in contrast to the north.

In China, it has been a common practice for parents to have their children's birth dates analyzed by a professional astrologer. If something seriously unfavorable is detected, a remedy is identified. The most common practice is to select an unusual name, which will make up for the missing link or unfavorable situation. For instance, if a person's cosmic system is in need of wood, the person might be named after a forest or flower. Some complicated remedies may involve rearranging furniture, moving one's residence, or relocating the tomb of an ancestor.

Analysis of Cosmic Signs

Making sense out of the cosmic pillars requires experience and practice. There are some basic rules for beginners to follow when learning the system. The fundamental rule: Stems define the first half of the time period, and branches the latter half. However, the line between the first half and second half is not clear-cut, leaving a gray area in which both signs offset each other's influence. This rule applies to all year, month, and day pillars, but is not as clear when defining hours.

Determining the nature of the signs is relatively easy, as spelled out in the first part of this chapter. The biggest challenge is assessing the strength of each sign. The following rules are our basic guides. All rules assume that the season is the same for all the elements.

Rule One:	Everything equal, a yang sign is more powerful than a yin sign.
Rule Two:	A pillar with two signs of the same element is stronger than a pillar with two different elements.
Rule Three:	Any sign supported (being bred) by a pillar mate is stronger than one not being bred.
Rule Four:	A sign mated with a ruling element is the weakest of all.

Figure 21. The Rules of Interaction

The following pillars in each element are listed by strength in descending order, strongest to weakest. In all examples, the season is the same and the pillars are not influenced by other pillars in their environment.

Water: **RR, rr, RM, rm, RW, rg**

As we can see from the order, **RR** is before **rr** (Rule One); **RR** is before **RM** (Rule Two); **RM** is before **RW** because the **R** in **RM** is supported by a water breeder, **M**, and the **R** in **RW** is not (Rule Three); **rm** is before **rg** because the **r** in **rm** has no earth (ruler) to dissipate its strength (Rule Four).

Wood: **TT, tt, TW, td, tr, TR**

Again, the rules apply. However, the nature of wood is different than that of water. **td** is before **tr** because **d** is earth influenced by wood; **tr** is before **TR** because **tr** is actually **tTR**, adding more wood to the pillar (remember that the stem equivalent of branch **r** is **TR**).

Fire: **FF, fd, FT, ft, FH, ff**

The order of all yang pairs is quite clear. **FF** comes first (Rule One); **FT** is before **FH** because it has more wood, which fuels fire. The order of the yin pillars is a little confusing because of the unique nature of yin fire. The strength of yin fire depends entirely on wood. Between the three yin pillars, **fd** is first because **d** has fire and plenty of wood; **ft** is next because it is influenced by yin wood, **t**; and **ff** is last for having no wood influence at all.

Earth: **EF, ed, EH, ef, EW, eg**

EF is yang earth bred and supported by yang fire. **ed** is yin earth supported by earth and fire, fueled by wood. Why is **ed** stronger than **EH**? **H** contains metal, which tends to undermine the strength of the earth. Why is **ef** behind **ed**? **f** also contains metal. **W** and **g** both contain water, which tends to dilute earth.

Metal: **MM, mm, MW, mg, MH, mf**

The order of metal is rather straightforward. The first two pillars are two of a kind. The middle pairs are supported by moist earth, and the last two pillars have dry earth, which does not breed metal.

The above discussion refers only to a normal situation. Signs do align with other signs to become powerful alliances. When that happens, the rules of the game change. We'll discuss sign transformation in Chapter 5.

To fully understand the cosmic condition of any day, the pillars of the year, month, and day must be taken into consideration at the same time. The order of description goes from year to month to day, and so does the order of the strength of the signs. That is, the cosmic influence of the year far outweighs that of the month or day.

When a year is denoted as **FF**, great heat and drought is in store for the entire year; **ff** indicates a similar condition, but of less intensity, as yin is less powerful than yang. **RR** denotes a very wet year, possibly flooding; **rr** symbolizes wetness, but of less magnitude. **RF** means the first part of the year will be wet, and the latter part dry; however, since the signs offset each other, the strength of both is mutually mitigated. The result would be moderately wet weather the first few months, moderately hot weather the last few months, and a long cloudy period in between.

Weatherwise, these rules apply to months and days, but not so much to specific hours. In analyzing the condition for a particular day, try to take the year and month pillars into consideration. It follows that an **rr** day in an **FF** year and an **FF** month will be hot and dry, as the influence of the day is minimal compared to the year and the month. On the other hand, an **RR** day in an **RR** month and **RR** year will be torrential. There is no straightforward formula. The Tao is subtle and mysterious! How valid is this device? Chinese farmers have relied on the calendar for thousands of years. Let us test its validity outside of China by looking at some current events.

1983 was the year of **rr**, two yin water signs. The United States had a very wet period from the end of 1982 to 1983, with prevailing floods over most of the country, particularly in the Midwest and in the delta region of the South. Mud slides in California resulted in great disasters. In fact, 1983 was the wettest in ten years.

1986 was the year of **FT**, a yang fire supported by abundant yang wood. It was a hot, dry year with wars and violence. What happened? Marcos exited the Philippines as a result of civil revolt. The United States had a very hot, dry year, particularly in the Southeast, the domain of fire and wood. There were numerous widespread forest fires. The northern states sent hay to southern farmers for their livestock. Being in the domain of water, the north was a lot better off.

1988 was the year of **EW**, double yang earth, super strong. Great drought, communication blocks, traffic jams, and soaring property values dominated the year. Property manifests earth. Yang earth absorbed so much water that it created drought.

Remember when gold prices reached $800 an ounce and silver reached $50? That was 1980, the year of **MM**. A powerful metal flow was ruling the universe. The following year was **mm**, double yin metal. Metal prices dropped significantly, but silver remained relatively high at $25, and gold at $600. As water influence replaced metal in the following years, the price of metal plummeted.

How accurate is this book? Unfortunately, there are no statistics. However, there are some interesting findings. June 21, 1989 was a very hot day in the San Francisco Bay area of California, and the temperature at the airport reached 109 degrees Fahrenheit. The cosmic condition of the day was, from year to day: **ef**, **MF**, **RR**. There was no rain on that **RR** day. Why? The **ef** year (branch **f** contains **F**, **E**, and **M**) had tremendous earth and fire influence, making the year dry as a whole; the **MF** month was the hottest in the year. Its enormous influence of earth and fire over-ruled the water influence of one particular day.

It rained the evening of January 31, 1989. Let us examine the cosmic condition: **EW**, **TR**, **MM**. The latter half of the year was reigned by **W**, which is a reservoir, making the atmosphere moist. The month was branch **R**, a rainy month. The double yang metal for the day was a pow-erful water breeder. Evening of any day is dominated by metal influence. The strong influence of moisture, rain, and metal contributed to the rain that day.

Why did California have five years of drought from 1986 to 1991? Our lunar calendar gives a good reason. The first two years were influ-enced by very strong fire, which evaporates water. The following two years were very strong in earth, which absorbs water. 1990 was the year of **MF**, a yang metal sitting on fire. **M**, as a water breeder, should be able to pro-duce some water. However, it is not strong enough when controlled by a branch fire. Moreover, the fire sign is in the latter half of the year, our rainy season; it dissipated the rain and the drought continued.

1991 was the year of **md**, a yin metal and an earth sign mixed with fire and wood. For similar reasons, the water-breeding power of **m** is weak. The mixture of fire, wood, and earth enervates the formation of rain.

Our big relief came in 1992. Why? It was the year of **RM**, yang water sustained by another water sign and a water breeder, **M**. It turned out to be a rainy year. The year pillar was supported by the month pillars— November was **mr**, a water breeder sustained by water; December was **RR**, two yang water signs in one pillar; January was **rg**, a yin water mixed with wet earth. Rainfall continued, but eased off in the latter half of the month. California's drought was over!

While our weather forecast can predict change in short range data only, this book offers prediction for years ahead. It would be fascinating to test it as a supplement to the weather forecast.

The Five Elements and Human Destiny

How do we apply these principles to human beings? According to the theories of Meng, all lives are embraced by the five elements. Each of us has a cosmic system that is a function of the cosmic condition at the time our life was created. It is registered in our birth time and becomes our life structure. This framework determines how we are going to respond to, or interact with, the universal energy flow. The outcome of the interaction determines our luck.

Since we are the product of the five elements, our outlook, disposition, and abilities reflect their nature. Our behavioral patterns and interactions with our counterparts in the community are determined by the same principles of the five elements, over which we have very little control. Our birthday and birthplace establish the basic framework for the analysis of our destiny. Studying the Meng will help you determine your own destiny, learn how to balance the elements that make up who you are, and anticipate your best and most challenging periods of luck.

CHAPTER 3

The Five Elements and Chinese Culture

In the preceding chapter, we covered just the fundamental concepts of the five elements. This much is usually taught in Chinese literature courses in high school, basically covering the names of the elements and how they are used to show the climate in the lunar calendar.

The twenty-two characters in the calendar are used exclusively to express the cosmic flow. They are seldom used by the public. The ten stems are sometimes used by older generations of Chinese to express grades, like the A, B, C, D, and F used in American schools.

As a matter of fact, except for a knowledgeable few who learned it for professional reasons, hardly anyone understands what the five elements stand for and how they work. The great majority can't even name the twelve lunar months in the calendar. Regardless of public ignorance, the concept of the five elements is amazingly far-reaching in Chinese culture due to the hard work of a few avid and intelligent leaders. Let us discuss how the elements work in the following aspects.

Social Mentality

Basically, the concept of the five elements embraces the total physical and social environment, being the basic ingredient of all lives. Practically everything in the world is categorized into one of the five big element groups. Every thing and every situation in the environment is classified as an entity or composite of the five elements.

At any time, in any state, when the elements are in perfect harmony, when all the elements are in a check-and-balance state, an equilibrium is created that represents all good things, such as happiness, good health, and prosperity. As equilibrium rarely exists, achieving it is the ultimate goal of every one of us in everything we do. The concept is ingrained in the mentality of the general public. Equilibrium is highly valued as a desired state for the individual and between family members. There are quite a few traditional formulas designed to achieve this goal.

Chinese cuisine is known for variety dishes, combining several vegetables with meat in one dish. The mixture of vegetables follows a certain pattern, and the kind of meat that goes with the vegetables follows certain rules. Yet hardly anyone cares to know why, even though they follow the recipe faithfully. The practice has a long tradition, reflecting the concept of harmony between the five elements. The Chinese are also great lovers of soup, in which they can blend a variety of ingredients with contrasting nature to counterbalance the function of each one. The idea is to produce a harmony of the five elements in order to promote good health, with great consideration for good taste as well, of course.

There are exercises incorporating the concept of yang and yin that regulate the flow of energy through our physical system to achieve maximum health benefits. Each geographical direction—north, south, east, and west—is also designated by one or two elements. Knowledgeable people design their residence to attract favorable flows.

In the field of medicine, the practice is even more complicated. First, a Chinese doctor has to know the element classification of herbs, all human organs, and every part of the body, such as the limbs, blood, and flesh. He or she also has to be familiar with the function of each element. For instance, those in the water category will clean up the toxins in our system; the fire group will stimulate metabolism, while earth will thwart infection. Each herb in the group takes care of certain parts of the body.

After discovering the problem, the doctor should be able to classify it as an entity of the five elements and be able to tell what interaction between the elements led to such a problem. Upon the diagnosis, he or she should be able to prescribe a remedy to achieve harmony in the patient's system. The sickness is cured as soon as equilibrium is restored.

This procedure refers to the authentic, effective doctor who truly understands how the five elements work. Such an ability involves some psychic power, which is basically inborn. This is one of the reasons Chinese medicine has made little progress in the field, although some Chinese doctors have achieved miracles beyond any explanation. Examples abound and are well-documented. The majority just copies formulas.

Social Value

On the social front, the five elements represent the five basic Chinese virtues: kindness (wood), justice (metal), courtesy (fire), wisdom (water), and integrity and reliability (earth). These five virtues, as the Chinese believed, are crucial for keeping the country intact. Each should perform in its own domain, while at same time checking and enhancing the other four elements to produce equilibrium, keeping the country healthy.

Before we discuss how these five elements work as a unit, let us go through the logic of how the virtues are assigned to each element. In ancient China, wood (green) formed the base for all food, clothing, medicine (herbs), furniture, and transportation (horse carts and boats)—practically all the needs in every aspect of life. It was fundamental and visible. Such generosity is very kind indeed!

Metal (white), in ancient China, represented all metal tools, such as knives, swords, and axes. Metal chops, prunes, trims, and conquers. To achieve justice, it prunes and chops troublemakers, keeping everybody in the system in line. It punishes criminals and protects the innocent.

Fire (red) includes all natural light, heat, and all man-made fire, such as stoves, candles, and torches. It cooks food, keeps people warm, and faithfully guides everyone through darkness, always obliging, never imposing. Candles and torches are indispensable symbols of celebration and solemn events, providing a gracious service. Fire praises, encourages, sympathizes, and consoles. What a courtesy to perform!

Water (black) washes, cleans, shines, and opens blockages. It subtly sustains all life in various manners. What a great problem solver! It is flexible and changeable, existing in many forms and colors. Only the very wise can perform so many miracles.

Earth (brown) is anchored to the ground, rarely moving or changing. It provides the base for all plants, metals, and water (rivers, lakes, etc.). It is stable and reliable, which constitutes integrity.

To show how these virtues work, let us begin with wood. When there is too much kindness in the nation, such as an overly generous welfare system, dependence and fraud are encouraged, damaging the integrity of the people. This is how wood (kindness) rules or hurts the earth (integrity). Also, those who make too many sweet promises are not to be trusted because they are unlikely to keep them.

In such a case, metal (justice) comes into play to stop the wood from going too far. A visionary leader should be able to implement a policy to ensure that handouts properly go to the needy in just the right amount to tide them over until they become independent. Productive citizens should not be burdened with unfair taxes. On the other hand, if the policy becomes too rigid, brutality could result, as some can never make it on their own without generous assistance. Justice (metal) is then hurting wood (kindness). Under such circumstances, fire is called in to help, exercising courtesy to stop brutality.

As courtesy goes unchecked, spreading benefits to everyone without discrimination, it hurts justice (metal). When that happens, water marches forward to correct the situation. It tells the fire to use wisdom with courtesy. It helps run society efficiently and it makes people creative and productive.

However, when water runs too freely, it deviates from its channel, meandering, branching into tributaries, or overflowing. It then creates disasters. When wisdom is carried to the extreme, it creates selfish people engaging in conspiracy without regard for courtesy. Thus, water (wisdom) extinguishes fire (courtesy).

When water does not perform properly, earth steps in to help. Depending on the circumstance, it either absorbs the excessive water or blocks the entire flow, keeping the water within its channel. Earth restores integrity and reliability, which is essential for building business and friendship.

Stem		Cosmic Identity	Social Value	Color
Wood	**T**	All trees, forests, and wood furniture.	Kindness, honesty, scholarship, oral skill.	Green
	t	All plants, branches of trees, herbs, fabrics, and paper.		
Fire	**F**	All natural fire (the sun, light, great heat).	Courtesy, intelligence, honesty.	Red, orange, bright yellow.
	f	All man-made fire (stoves, lamps, candle light).		
Earth	**E**	Dry earth and all objects constructed of earth.	Integrity, reliability, patience.	Brown, all other earth tones.
	e	Moist earth for cultivation.		
Metal	**M**	Metal ore, metal, all heavy duty tools, and appliances.	Justice, decisiveness, quick-mindedness.	White, silver.
	m	Refined metal, ornaments, and small metal tools.		
Water	**R**	All forms of ground water (rivers, creeks, lakes, wells).	Wisdom, talent in the arts, writing.	Black, gray, navy.
	r	All forms of water above the ground (rain, snow, fog).		

Figure 3A. The Stems and Their Symbolization

However, when earth gets too strong, blocking the free flow of water, it chokes creativity and innovation. Then wood is the natural candidate to correct the situation. Its roots branch out to loosen up the earth, enabling water to flow freely.

The greatest challenge for a national leader in keeping a country in order is to properly draw the boundaries between the five elements. It takes sharp vision, which is basically inborn. An average leader can sharpen his or her vision with exercises such as meditation. What is most important is constant devotion to fair play. Practicing the principles of fair play is the sure way to maintain equilibrium. Extensive reading, especially a good knowledge of world history, is a big plus.

Astrology

The best and only way to understand how the five elements actually work is to study Chinese astrology, which has three or four schools, depending on how one classifies it. The most popular is the Tzu-Ping school, which is based solely on the interactions of the five elements. Others focus on the interactions of many stars, each classified as one of the five elements. The principles of interruling and interbreeding between the elements also apply in analysis of the stars.

Since the Tzu-Ping school is the subject of this book, we'll touch on some of its basic concepts to provide some background for later discussions. Like everything else in the cosmos, each person is classified as one of the five elements by one's birth time; each element interacts with the other elements in a specific cosmic environment also defined by the birth time.

The concepts of the five virtues apply to people as well. The quality of the virtue demonstrated by the individual depends on the person's cosmic environment. Let us explain with an example. A person classified as earth is not necessarily always going to act with integrity or be reliable. Sand dunes, tundra, or soggy mud (earth) do not support life; they are not reliable. A person born as earth in an environment crowded with wood, metal, and water will never develop integrity because these elements hinder the growth of firm soil. Instead, he or she is cunning, as there is no substance behind his or her earthy look. Fire is needed to melt some of the metal, evaporate some of the water, and burn up some of the wood in order to firm the soil and restore its integrity. That is how fire breeds earth.

On the other hand, when the earth is surrounded by loads and loads of additional earth in the cosmic environment, all heavily packed together, the person's rock-solid integrity is no good to anyone. The soil is too stiff to produce and no one can rely on it for crops. People having excessive earth in their system also tend to be overweight, stubborn, and closed-minded. Only good earth, with the proper combination of elements surrounding it, is reliable, demonstrating the quality of integrity.

These ideas apply to other elements as well. It all boils down to common sense. The study has thousands of formulas to analyze the characters, abilities, and chances of success for people born at various times and environments. Chapters 5 through 8 touch on many of these formulas.

However, being born at the wrong time and in the wrong place is not the end of the world. Our cosmic system changes periodically, introducing a different game with additional elements. For instance, when a team of metal and wood enters the system of someone with compact, stiff earth, the earth will loosen up. As a result, it will produce abundant crops. This person would suddenly become rich and successful, restoring his or her integrity.

However, no theory is one-hundred-percent correct. The earth might be too hard for the wood, which would break before it even entered the earth. Thus, the introduction of wood into a life of thick earth may not make the person rich. Instead, it might create pain and illness as the wood keeps poking and pounding the earth (person), trying so hard to enter without success.

Metal, on the other hand, could do a good job. Its growing process within the earth is gradual and subtle, yet constant. Its effort is barely felt, never causing pain, and it is very effective in loosening up the earth. As soon as the earth becomes porous, trees can poke through to speed the process. Trees and metal can work together, but metal has to do the first part. Deciding the right time to introduce wood to the earth so as to create luck is a tricky decision. Our worksheet and discussion in Chapter 9 will help you perform the necessary tests to determine your best times for creating luck.

This is a simplified case, but the idea applies to other elements as well. There are thousands of formulas to account for the interactions between the five elements, and to predict the outcome of such interactions. Chapters 5 through 8 in this book touch on many of them.

What are we to do when we are confronted with the luck of a poor system like thick earth without metal to rescue us? We should attract more metal into our system. First and foremost, try to select a good name to amend the system. Knowledgeable Chinese people genuinely believe that our name plays a more important role in our fate than our birth time. Some even consult a professional. Others labor over the most authoritative dictionary, picking the lucky characters that have strokes falling in the lucky number group. Naming people and businesses is an independent field of study in China, as well as in some other parts of the world.

The next step is to stay, if possible, in the domain of metal, the west of our environment, which will surround us with metal force. Moving to a city or street with a name in the metal category could also help. When a move is not feasible, we should orient our activities toward the west. Choosing a metal-related career is a big plus. Wearing gold jewelry will also help. The concluding chapter discusses solutions for problems with various elements.

When the earth is too thin, we have to do the opposite, avoiding wood and metal, and attracting more earth into our system in order to become a stronger earth. We should focus on brown colors and pick an earth-related career. Again, choosing a good name always comes first.

This example gives us a general picture of how the Tzu-Ping school of astrology works. This system allows us to map out our cosmic composition and its changes over our life path. It is the only way under current technology to discover the fundamental truth of our life. Knowing the truth, we can target the turning points of our life and behave accordingly, being aggressive in an upswing cycle and keeping a low profile in a down turn. There are also ways to amend the system, enhancing luck.

Best of all, the study was based on the well-documented lunar calendar, which registers the cosmic flows by day, month, and year, and can be extended indefinitely. All theories of the study can be tested and verified before we apply them to our life. Once we determine the key element that turns our life around, and its supporting elements, we can refer to the calendar on a regular basis to determine our luck.

There are some drawbacks, of course. The subject is mind-boggling, requiring substantial patience and some knowledge of the Tao. After all, astrology of all kinds involves the elements of mystery and has never been an easy subject. This book does one more great thing, which hardly any other astrology book does: it provides a hand-holding guide, every step of the way, to finding out the truth, taking responsibility to serve our readers' needs.

Discovering your key element is a big challenge; it is like finding the key to success. Those born in an extreme cosmic environment, like the example of Crystal in Chapter 4, will have a clear-cut system that is easy to analyze. Those born in a transitional period will find their system more confusing at times. Understanding simply requires more testing.

A profound understanding of the Tao is a big plus in the study of astrology, especially for our subject, which is basically a matter of achieving equilibrium. The Tao means fair play, and a person who constantly plays fair in all aspects of life will find it easier to see the Tao. Playing fair at all times enables us to accurately draw a line between the yang and yin forces and view the truth from the proper perspective.

CHAPTER 4

Defining the Cosmic System

Each of us has a miniature cosmic system. Although the grand cosmic system of the universe was neatly defined by our gracious sages, as we discussed in Chapter 2, it is up to us to define our own. Defining our own cosmic system requires precise birth data, including the birth year, month, day, and hour.

The method applies only to those born in the Northern Hemisphere. It consists of two parts: the birth composite and the luck cycle.

The Birth Composite

Charting your birth composite is simple. To do so you need:

- The date and hour of your birth.

- A calendar for the lunar year of your birth.

- The hour zone and hour stem charts (see Figure 2H on page 21 and Figure 4A on page 42) to determine the signs of your birth.

- A worksheet (see page 41).

Lunar year charts can be found in the appendix, preceded by a guide to reading and interpreting them. If you haven't already, read this guide before proceeding. When reading the pillars, remember that the stems, or spatial symbols, are on the top or the left; branches, or temporal symbols, are on the bottom or to the right.

We can best illustrate the process of charting the birth composite with an example. Suppose we have a female named Crystal, born in China on July 3, 1937 at noon. Our first task is to assign a cosmic sign to each element of her birth year, month, day, and hour. To do this, we locate the lunar calendar for year 1937 in the appendix. On top of the calendar, next to the year number, is the cosmic year pillar, **fg**, and an animal name. The animal name is not our concern in this book. **fg** is the cosmic description for the year of our example, 1937.

The corresponding lunar month for July 3 is May, for which the cosmic sign is **FF**. The cosmic sign for the day pillar is next to July 3, and it is **mt**. The equivalent lunar birthday of July 3 is May 25. Copy these signs onto the worksheet on the following page. The procedure is summarized in Model A (See Figure 4C on page 49).

Pay particular attention to the stem of the day pillar. This is the key to the birth composite; the Chinese call it the *self,* for it is the sign that represents the person whose birthday is being interpreted. It tells us about the basic character of that person. In our illustration, Crystal's day stem is **m**, which means that her basic character is that of yin metal. Since there are ten possible stems, there are also ten possible selves. Every person in the world can be categorized by one of the ten selves.

We find the cosmic sign for the hour in two steps. From Figure 2H on page 21, we locate the branch of the hour pillar. In our example, Crystal's hour of birth is noon. It falls, therefore, into the zone between 11 A.M. and 1 P.M., so its sign is **F** (branch). To find a matching hour stem, we need Figure 4A on page 42. From the cross section between column **m** and row **F**, we locate the matching stem hour as **T**. Thus, the hour pillar is **TF**, which we can now copy onto the worksheet. The complete cosmic description of Crystal's birthday looks like this:

Hour	Day	Month	Year
T	m	F	f
F	t	F	g

Meng Worksheet

Name _____   Gender: M   F

Birthday _____ Time of Birth _____ Birth Place _____

Birth Composite   Hour   Day   Month   Year

_____   _____   _____   _____   Stems

_____   _____   _____   _____   Branches

1. Find your year pillar at the top of the lunar calendar in the appendix for the year of your birth and fill in the year pillar.
2. Find the pillar for the lunar month of your birth and fill in the month pillar.
3. Find the pillar for the lunar day of your birth and fill in the day pillar.
4. Use Figure 2H to find the sign for your time of birth and fill in the hour branch.
5. Use Figure 4A to find the sign that intersects the column of your day stem and the row of your hour branch, and fill in the hour stem.

Luck cycle   ___ ___ ___ ___ ___ ___ ___   Your ages

___ ___ ___ ___ ___ ___ ___   Stems

___ ___ ___ ___ ___ ___ ___   Branches

1. Find the calendar of your birth year.
2. If your year pillar is yin, and you are female, begin with the pillar of the month you were born and add the pillars of the six months *following* it. If you are male, begin with the pillar for the month just before the lunar month you were born and add the seven *preceding* months.
3. If you are female, count the number of days from your lunar day of birth to the day of the *next* climate divider. If you are male, count the number of days from your lunar day of your birth to the day of the *previous* climate divider.
4. Divide the number by three, round your answer to a whole number, and fill in your age at your first luck cycle.
5. Add ten to the age of your first luck cycle to arrive at the age of your second luck cycle, and so on.

Note: When the year stem is yang, reverse the procedure for female and male in steps 2 and 3. Simply substitute female for male and vice versa. Continue with steps 4 and 5 to complete the chart.

In Chinese, the birth composite is often called The Four Pillars. For all birth composites, the order of pillars is always from year to hour, starting from right to left. In our subsequent discussion on birth composites, we will omit the labels. To follow the analysis, you should learn this fixed format.

Self〳Hour	T	t	F	f	E	e	M	(m)	R	r
R	T	F	E	M	R	T	F	E	M	R
g	t	f	e	m	r	t	f	e	m	r
T	F	E	M	R	T	F	E	M	R	T
t	f	e	m	r	t	f	e	m	r	t
W	E	M	R	T	F	E	M	R	T	F
f	e	m	r	t	f	e	m	r	t	f
(F)	M	R	T	F	E	M	R	(T)	F	E
d	m	r	t	f	e	m	r	t	f	e
M	R	T	F	E	M	R	T	F	E	M
m	r	t	f	e	m	r	t	f	e	m
H	T	F	E	M	R	T	F	E	M	R
r	t	f	e	m	r	t	f	e	m	r

Figure 4A. The Hour Stems

Understanding the Birth Composite

The birth composite defines a person's living environment, which in turn determines one's ability, character, and opportunities. In Chinese, it consists of eight characters. That is why it is common for Chinese to refer to life as "eight-word." In this book, the Chinese characters are replaced by letters of the alphabet.

A good living environment provides a comfortable and successful life. How is the environment for Crystal? Refer to the definitions of the signs on page 17 in Chapter 2. Crystal is a piece of refined metal (**m**), surrounded by moist earth (**g**), four fires (three **F** and one **f**), and two woods (**T** and **t**). Remember, May 25 in the lunar calendar is summer, so the fire in Crystal's composite is summer fire, the strongest of the year. It is clear that the environment is too hot and burning for a small piece of metal. But exactly how bad is it?

To find out in greater detail, we need some guidelines. Chapters 7 and 8 provide an elaborate discussion on how various signs affect each of the ten selves. Each self category is described by season and divided into twelve model groups according to birth month. Altogether there are 120 model selves, which cover practically all birthdays. These models are illustrated with real-life examples, with crucial elements for each model summarized in charts for the ten selves at the end of each chapter.

To check the guidelines for Crystal, let us turn to the section on the **m** self in Chapter 8 (page 131) and the summary of crucial elements for the **m** self at the end of that chapter (Figure 8D on page 146). The birth month is determined by the branch of the month pillar in the birth composite. In Crystal's case, this is **F**, lunar May (note that the branch sign of a month pillar is always the same, regardless of the year).

We know **m** selves born in the summer dread fire, which gives them a hectic life. Crystal needs a lot of water to offset the summer fire and a substantial amount of moist earth to absorb the heat. At the same time, she needs to be very strong to fight the surrounding enemy (fire). Her best friend is a more powerful metal, which would act like a big brother. Her crucial elements are water, moist earth, and the more powerful yang metal. The signs for these elements are **R**, **r**, **e**, and **M**. Unfortunately, none of these signs is found in her birth composite.

Crystal will live a very hectic and poor life unless a remedy is available. Her metal could be melted down early, resulting in premature death.

Let us look further by examining Crystal's branch signs. Recall that most branches contain more than one element. By going back to the figure of the stem equivalents of branch signs (Figure 2F on page 19), we find that year branch **g** contains **r**, **e**, and **m**. It has three of Crystal's crucial elements, and therefore becomes her lifesaver. However, due to its limited strength, branch **g** is like a lonely soldier who has to fight very hard to keep the fire in check, to achieve its goal.

The other branch signs are of little help. The water could evaporate quickly and the moist earth could dry up and lose its shielding effect. Nevertheless, the picture has changed somewhat. Crystal will still have a hectic life due to the surrounding enemy, but the hardship will be harmless. She will be protected in her struggle along the way and will eventually turn her hard lessons into functional wisdom and achievement. The bottom line: She will have a difficult struggle to attain her goal unless extra cosmic help is provided.

By using Crystal's example as a model, you can understand how the principle of favorable elements applies to your own life. Any elements that improve our living environment bring us good luck and become our favorable elements. To clearly determine the crucial elements for a good life takes elaborate testing by each individual. Chapter 9 provides a procedure for the task.

The Social Standing of the Signs

In a birth composite, each of the seven signs other than the self plays a different social role, with stems representing the male, and branches, except for the day branch, representing the female.

Pillar	Social Standing
Year	Grandparents, distant relatives, aunts, uncles, in-laws
Month	Parents, older brothers and sisters
Day stem	Self
Day branch	Spouse
Hour	Children, younger brothers and sisters, friends

What these signs represent depends on the self. We find their meaning by keeping careful records of the events in our lives, and drawing conclusions from them.

In any composite, there are good signs and harmful signs responsible for the luck of the self. Good signs in the year and month pillars indicate supportive parents and relatives, and inherited wealth; the self is most likely from a good family; some are born with a silver spoon, as the saying goes. Most succeed early in life. Good signs in the day and hour pillars indicate a good spouse, good children, and friends; the self is a self-made person, succeeding late in life. Super lucky people have good signs throughout their birth composite.

Harmful signs in the year and month pillars signify a difficult start in life or poor relationships with the immediate family. In the hour pillar, harmful signs indicate a miserable life in later years and/or bad children.

The four pillars also represent the four different stages of the self's life.

Pillar	Stage
Year	First quarter
Month	Second quarter
Day	Third quarter
Hour	Fourth quarter

Each sign reigns about seven and one-half years, with some overlapping periods. A complete cycle takes sixty years. The cycle repeats as life continues. The initial age of the cycle is determined by the first year of the luck cycle (see next section).

If you have charted your cosmic system and followed all the steps up to this point, you have discovered your cosmic sign, your favorable and negative elements, and your life's general picture. It should answer some of your questions about your life. If Crystal wondered why her life has been so hectic, and why she has had so many harsh bosses, she has found an answer through a smooth and painless procedure.

We'll summarize the steps to analyze a birth composite:

- Circle the self sign and note the element of each of the other signs.

- Go to the relevant self section in Chapter 7 or 8, and try to understand the nature of your cosmic sign.

- Pay special attention to the examples given for your birth month.

- Go to the end of the chapter and locate your cosmic sign by birth month on the relevant calendar.

- Copy your crucial elements onto your worksheet.

- Search for signs of the crucial elements in your birth composite, including the hidden stem equivalents in the branches.

Attuning Yourself to the Cosmic Flows

How do we benefit from our findings? Truth sets us free. We accept with grace what we cannot change, conserving our energy by avoiding fruitless struggles. On the other hand, where changes to improve our lives are possible, we should try our best to make them.

In Crystal's case, it is clear that she should avoid fire as much as possible and attract all the water, metal, and/or earth she can find. She can accomplish this goal in two ways:

1. Attune to the grand cosmic flows.

2. Seek out the source of her crucial elements and attune herself to them.

To attune yourself to the cosmic flows, you need to apply what you learned in Chapters 2 and 3 about the nature and strength of cosmic signs, and be able to use the appendix. Remember that the cosmic flows are constant. Each time period is dominated by a cosmic flow that is represented by several signs (review how to read signs in Chapter 2). We have better luck under favorable cosmic influences. Naturally, all the time periods designated by our favorable elements are our lucky days; those with our negative elements are bad days.

In our example, Crystal would have a very comfortable and peaceful life in a cosmic year of **RR**, **rr**, or **EW**, when abundant water and/or earth from the cosmos fight her enemy for her. She will achieve more, and/or make more money, during **MM** or **mm** years, when she becomes mentally and physically stronger. An **MM** month in an **RR** year would be her super month. At such times she should be exceedingly aggressive in pursuing her goals.

In years dominated by fire, she should expect a more hectic life and frequent ailments, like a sore throat, coughing, infection, or toothaches, disruptions in her daily chores, and financial loss or setbacks in her career. During the hard times, she should keep a low profile, such as minimizing all unnecessary activities, putting important projects on hold, adjusting her diet by drinking ample fluids, and avoiding hot places. This is just a partial list. Chapter 9 demonstrates an elaborate procedure for checking our favorable elements and attuning ourselves to their flows.

The identification of lucky or favorable times can also be charted on an hourly level. Figure 2H on page 21 is the correct guide. Compare your energy level and mental power with the hours of your favorable and harmful elements. Note the difference. Do this for a few weeks to test its consistency.

How can Crystal discover the sources of her crucial elements? Where can she find **g**, her lifesaver? It is on the year branch of her birth composite, the location for relatives on the maternal side, which includes grandparents, aunts, and cousins.

What is her strategy in this regard? She should search the events in her past life to determine exactly which group or person actually benefited her and in what way. In fact, in Crystal's case, it happened to be her maternal aunts and cousins. They showed up in time to save her from heat strokes on several occasions during her childhood. Their advice also helped her make some financial gains during her adulthood.

It is sad when your most favorable sign represents your remote relatives. If **g** had been part of Crystal's month branch, it would have signified a helpful mother. Life would have been a lot easier, since help would have been so much more accessible. The ideal position for a favorable element is on the day branch, since this position is most accessible to the self and also represents a supportive spouse.

What about Crystal's negative signs? Since they are spread among her other relatives, there is no way she can ignore them. She just has to learn to be self-reliant and independent.

At this point, readers should be able to do the following:

- Identify cosmic flows on a timely basis using the appendix.

- Chart their birth composite.

- Locate their crucial signs and source of influence.
- Understand their cosmic system.
- Attune to the cosmic influence so as to enhance their life.

This is achievement Level One. For beginners, this should be an exciting discovery. You have discovered the invisible, yet most fundamental, factor influencing your life. This should offer some rewarding experiences for those who can't afford any further effort or time on the subject. Those of you who are able and willing can proceed to Level Two, the luck cycle.

The Luck Cycle

The birth composite is not the final picture of our life. Our cosmic system, like the universe, is influenced by cycles of periodic change. It follows a system that is called the luck cycle.

Charting the Luck Cycle

Determining the luck cycle requires some simple calculation. The procedure varies with the gender of the self and its year pillar of the birth composite. There are two models, which are illustrated on separate worksheets (see page 49 for Model A and page 50 for Model B). To chart your luck cycle, select the model matching your cosmic system.

Model A		Model B	
Self	Year Pillar	Self	Year Pillar
Female (yin)	Yin	Male (yang)	Yin
Male (yang)	Yang	Female (yin)	Yang

Figure 4B. Luck Cycle Models

Luck Cycle Models

If you match Model A, your luck cycle will be determined by the pillars of the seven months *following* your lunar birth month. If you match Model B, your luck cycle will be determined by the pillars of the seven months *prior to* your lunar birth month.

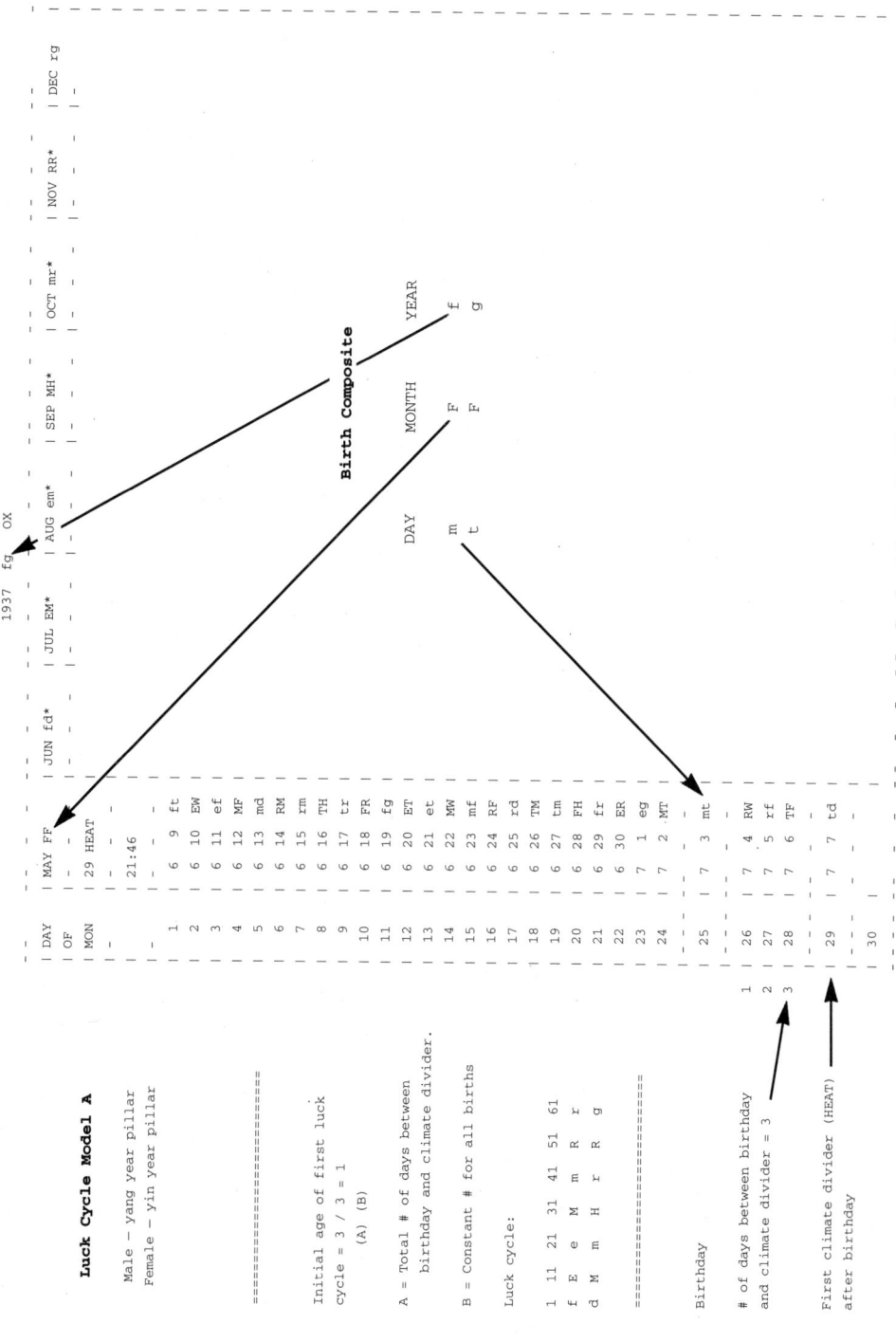

Figure 4C. Luck Cycle Model A

1936

OCT er*	NOV MR*	DEC mg*	JAN RT*	FEB rt*	MAR TW*	APR tf*	DAY OF MON

1937 fg OX

MAY FF
29 HEAT
21:46

Luck Cycle Model B

Male — yin year pillar
Female — yang year pillar

================================

Initial age of first luck
cycle = 26 / 3 = 9 (round figure)
          (A)   (B)

A = Total # of days between birthday and climate divider.

B = Constant # for all births

Luck cycle:

9	19	29	39	49	59	69
t	T	r	R	m	M	e
f	W	t	T	g	R	r

================================

Total # of days between birthday & climate divider = 26

(From July 2 to June 7)

Birthday

First climate divider preceding birthday (lunar April 28, GRAIN).

Birth Composite

DAY	MONTH	YEAR
m	F	f
t	F	g

APR tf*
28 GRAIN
11:23

DAY OF MON			
1	5	10	fm
2	5	11	EH
3	5	12	er
4	5	13	mn
5	5	14	mg
6	5	15	RT
7	5	16	rt
8	5	17	TW
9	5	18	tf
10	5	19	FF
11	5	20	fd
12	5	21	EM
13	5	22	em
14	5	23	MH
15	5	24	mr
16	5	25	RR
17	5	26	rg
18	5	27	TT
19	5	28	tt
20	5	29	FW
21	5	30	ff
22	5	31	EF
23	6	1	ed
24	6	2	MM
25	6	3	mm
26	6	4	RH
27	6	5	rr
28	6	6	TR	26
29	6	7	tg	26
30	6	8	FT	25

	MAY FF		
24	6	9	ft
23	6	10	EW
22	6	11	ef
21	6	12	mn
20	6	13	md
19	6	14	RM
18	6	15	rm
17	6	16	TH
16	6	17	tr
15	6	18	FR
14	6	19	fg
13	6	20	ET
12	6	21	et
11	6	22	MW
10	6	23	mf
9	6	24	RF
8	6	25	rd
7	6	26	TM
6	6	27	tm
5	6	28	FH
4	6	29	fr
3	6	30	ER
2	7	1	eg
1	7	2	MT
	7	3	mt
	7	4	RW
	7	5	rf
	7	6	TF
	7	7	td

Figure 4D. Luck Cycle Model B

We'll illustrate the procedure using Crystal's birthday. She is a female, and the year pillar of her birth composite is **fg**, a yin sign, so her cosmic system matches Model A. Her birthday is July 3, which converts to lunar May 25. To determine her luck cycle, we copy each of the seven month pillars after her birth month, starting with June, all the way to December. These become the luck cycle pillars of the self. Each pillar represents ten years. The stems determine the luck for the first five years in the cycle, and the branches the latter five years. The dividing line is not clear-cut; there is a zone of transition in which both signs exercise some influence.

The next step is to calculate the initial age of the first pillar. To do this, follow these steps:

1. On the second row of the lunar calendar (1937 for Crystal), locate the first climate divider after the birthday (July 3; May 25), which is May 29, titled Heat (corresponding to July 7 of the western calendar).

2. Count the days between the birthday and the climate divider (three in Crystal's case).

3. Divide the total number of days by three, which is constant for all births. The quotient, one, is the age at which the first luck pillar begins.

4. Add ten to your age at the first pillar to get your age at the second pillar.

5. Keep adding ten to the previous pillar's age to get the other six ages.

This process results in the luck cycle for Crystal shown below:

1	11	21	31	41	51	61
f	E	e	M	m	R	r
d	M	m	H	r	R	g

There is no fixed rule for how far the cycle can go. For convenience of presentation, we use seven pillars for most births.

Gender is a crucial factor in Chinese divination. A male and a female with the same birthday will have different luck in their lifetime. For a male with Crystal's birthday, the calculation follows Model B, with his luck cycle calculated in descending order (see Model B on page 50). We use the first climate divider before his birthday, which is Grain (second row on the calendar), on lunar April 28 (June 6 on the western calendar). To complete the luck cycle, follow steps 2, 3, 4, and 5 in the Model A illustration. The luck cycle is indicated on the worksheet.

To reinforce the method of working out the birth composite and the calculation of the luck cycle, we'll illustrate with a male born at 7:30 P.M. on March 15, 1924. On the calendar for 1924, we obtain the first three pillars, for the year, month, and day. From Figure 2H on page 21, *The Hour Zones*, we see that 7:30 P.M. falls in hour zone **H**. From Figure 4A on page 42, *The Hour Stems*, we locate the cross section of the row for hour branch **H** and the column for self **r**, and obtain the hour stem of **R**. The complete birth composite is as follows:

R	r	f	T
H	f	t	R

This is a male with a yang year pillar in the birth composite, so the calculation of his luck cycle falls in Model A. The only difference is the number of days between his birthday and the climate divider, which is twenty. As a result, the starting age of the luck cycle is seven. His luck cycle:

7	17	27	37	47	57	67
E	e	M	m	R	r	T
W	f	F	d	M	m	H

The above method covers most birthdays. For borderline cases, such as for people born very close to a climate divider, the beginning of a new year, or a few minutes before the next day, adjustment might be necessary, involving more vigorous testing of the formulas.

The Role of the Luck Cycle

In Level One, we learned how our birth composite interacts with the grand cosmic system of the universe, and how changing flows in the cosmos affect our luck. This is only a partial interaction. The luck cycle plays a major role. As you have seen, the influence of each sign in the luck cycle lasts five years; each sign gathers momentum over the course of its governing period, and so does its impact. On the other hand, each dominant flow in the universe lasts about six months, barely gathering momentum.

In any given year during our life, three sets of factors interplay: the cosmos, our birth composite, and our luck cycle. How do we determine the playing schedule of the signs in the birth composite? Each of the eight signs governs seven and one-half years of a person's luck, starting with the year stem, then the year branch, all the way to the hour branch. The starting age follows the initial age of the first luck cycle. The cycle repeats as life continues.

The full interaction of these signs is discussed in Chapter 5. For the moment, simply bear in mind that the influence of each sign in our luck cycle, or in our birth composite, is never isolated; each sign may dominate our life for a given period, but our birth composite sets the framework for how we live most of our life. For instance, the driving force from Crystal's fire is always present. She might enjoy more peace and comfort, or make more money, with the onset of water in her life, but she should never expect an idle moment. We were all born to perform a specific role, which is constant; our luck cycle changes only the quality of our life. *The purpose of studying Meng divination is to attune to, not to change, our destiny.*

With your birth composite and luck cycle worked out, you can follow the example in Chapter 9 and prepare a worksheet that, when completed, will allow you to:

- Precisely identify your favorable and negative elements and signs.

- Predict trends and changes in your future.

- Plan your action table to maximize your luck and minimize negative impact on your life.

Those who clearly know their favorable and negative elements should be able to determine the schedule of their upcoming luck without following the approach in Chapter 9. In Crystal's case, her life will begin to improve at age forty-one, and the momentum of her good life will intensify during the period between ages fifty-one and seventy-one, as all her favorable elements come to her rescue. Determining the nature of the luck requires some other formulas, which are beyond the scope of this book.

We can also identify the climax of Crystal's luck during her good luck period using her luck cycle. All we need to do is flip through the lunar calendar and pinpoint the years dominated by her favorable elements. As she benefits by all the water and metal she can get, any additional water from the cosmos definitely enhances her luck.

Advanced Topics

At this point, you have completed Level Two. If your cosmic system happens to be simple and you are happy with knowing only your system, you might choose not to read any further. The interplay between signs in many of our cosmic systems, however, involves complicated rules. Not knowing these rules can cause us to sometimes miss our target. The remainder of this chapter is devoted to explaining some of the rules that affect the functional characteristics of the signs.

By now it should be second nature for us to know that the day stem of the birth composite is the sign of the self. The seven other signs relate to the self functionally as opportunities in the environment. The ideal environment is rich with balanced opportunities to both rule and support others, and to be ruled and supported by the leadership of someone else.

Among the five elements, the one controlling the self becomes our boss, symbolizing our driving force; this sign is referred to as our *ruler*. Remember that water is the ruler of fire, which in turn becomes the ruler of metal; metal rules wood; wood is the ruler of earth, which then rules water (refer to Figure 2C on page 15 to review the interruling of the five elements). The ruler in a woman's composite also represents her spouse.

A ruler disciplines, creating high achievers, which is crucial for fame and power. Strong rulers in one's system create a hard worker. However, too many rulers can kill the self unless they are under proper control. The Tao says: "Moderation is the best policy," which translates to "just right."

How do we know how much is just right? The formulas could fill a book. Some guidelines are provided in Chapters 6, 7, and 8. In Crystal's case, the rulers are definitely excessive. There are four strong rulers (fire) for one piece of refined metal (the **m** self). It is like having four fierce tyrants to control a child.

The element the self controls becomes its possession and is called the *money sign*. Fire can melt and shape metal into ornaments that can be sold for a profit. Thus, metal is the money sign of fire. To follow the principle further, fire is the money sign of water, water the money sign of earth, and so forth.

A money sign simply represents money-making opportunities. Having no money sign in one's cosmic system is apparently bad. Having too many money signs could be worse. It is like being tempted with many money-making schemes, and being unable to focus on any. The result is hard work for nothing. A good money sign makes a person rich. The money sign in a man's composite represents his spouse, so a good money sign means a good wife who is rich and capable. A truly rich man always respects his wife. A Chinese myth claims that anyone who abuses his wife is never rich. It is like abusing wealth; he loses what he abuses.

It is best to have only one strong money sign; it signifies lasting, immense wealth acquired with little effort. Too many money signs for a strong self means getting rich with excessive effort; the person is tempted by too many insignificant money-making opportunities to succeed at any of them. For a weak self, too many money signs does more harm than good. One works too hard for too little, and the other for nothing at all. Poorly positioned money signs do more harm than good. We will touch on this in case studies later in this book.

The element that breeds the self is called the *grantor*, for its supporting effort. The grantor for a wood self is water, as water supports the growth of plants. Like any other sign, a grantor has to be well-positioned and right for the person. When a plant is properly watered, it thrives. When there is no water, it withers and dies. When there is too much water, it gets sick and eventually dies too.

The need for a grantor varies with the nature and the strength of the self. A weak self needs a powerful grantor. A strong self with too much support is a disaster. The person tends to indulge in vices and ends up unhappy. Too many grantors is never good for anyone. It is the same idea as "too much tender care spoils the child." This is another manifestation of the Tao.

An element the self breeds becomes its descendant, which is called the *offspring*. Fire is the offspring of wood, as wood fuels fire; wood is the offspring of water, as water feeds wood and helps it grow. An offspring can be compared to a new birth from a pregnant woman. It releases the desire to create and express; it symbolizes wisdom. Poets, artists, and those who engage in vocal professions have good offspring in their systems. Offspring are also essential for acquiring high position.

An element that is the same as the self becomes its sibling and is called *kin*. The kin of an **M** self is metal, and that of an **R** self is water. A weak self needs kin so that he or she is helped, just as in a poor family brothers and sisters work together to help one another. A strong self, however, does not need kin. Competing kin only create disasters, such as social and financial disputes among siblings, as in a rich family where brothers and sisters fight for the family's possessions.

Functional relationships between the self and the twelve branches are more complicated. Since most of the branches contain more than one element, a branch can perform several functions at one time. Let us take the **m** self as an example. Stems **M** and **m** are its kin since they are all metal. Branch **M**, however, is a kin, an offspring, and a grantor, since it contains metal, water, and earth. Branch **t** functions only as a money sign, as it has only one stem equivalent, **t**.

Stems / Self	**T, t** Wood	**F, f** Fire	**E, e** Earth	**M, m** Metal	**R, r** Water
T, t	kin	offspring	money	ruler	grantor
F, f	grantor	kin	offspring	money	ruler
E, e	ruler	grantor	kin	offspring	money
M, m	money	ruler	grantor	kin	offspring
R, r	offspring	money	ruler	grantor	kin

Kin—the same element as the self
Ruler—the element controlling the self
Grantor—the element breeding or supporting the self
Offspring—the element supported by the self
Money—the element being subdued by the self

Figure 4E. The Interrelation Between the Five Elements

CHAPTER 5

Interactions Between Cosmic Flows

Cosmic flows represented by the twenty-two signs and their various combinations interact with each other constantly. Our lives change because the flows in our birth composite and luck cycle are constantly interacting with the changing flows in the cosmos. The outcome of their interaction with each other is determined by two basic factors: the strength of the signs and the rules of the interaction.

The Strength of the Signs

There are several factors affecting the strength of each sign. One factor, the fundamental pillar structure, was discussed in Chapter 2. Other factors in the strength of a sign are growth cycle and cosmic environment.

Growth Cycle

Each element has its own growth cycle. For example, wood shows its greatest strength in spring, gradually declines in summer, and reaches dormancy in the winter. Fire is strongest in mid-summer and dies in late winter. These are just some general observations. The growth cycles designed by our sages are more detailed. There are twelve stages in a growth cycle.

Birth: The stage for new life, new hope, and positive changes. Any favorable sign in this stage is fortunate. When the self sign is in the birth stage, long life and good health are indicated. A money sign in this stage represents growing wealth. An offspring in the birth stage brings wisdom.

Childhood: A period of slow development, immaturity, and playfulness. A self born at this stage lacks motivation. A spouse sign in the childhood stage is associated with sickness.

Adolescence: An intense growth period and preparatory stage for achievement. In terms of strength, it is above average.

Adulthood: A stage for independence and fulfillment. A self born in this stage will be assertive and highly motivated to succeed in life. Any other sign in this stage is also likely to bring good fortune.

Prime: The peak stage, when a person is mature, established, and wise. Great fortune is associated with this stage. However, there is also great potential for downfall due to the law of change. The self born in this stage is healthy and capable, but unlikely to keep his or her good fortune for very long. All other signs in this stage are powerful, but unstable.

Decline: A stage of thinking, planning, and apprehension. The self is cautious as he or she anticipates upcoming negative development. Other signs in this stage reflect similar traits. Luck comes from hard work and planning.

Aging: Similar to the Decline stage, but of greater intensity. There is, of course, less luck.

Death: Extreme inactivity and low vitality. It is very unfortunate to have an important sign in this stage. A self in this stage will have a stagnant life, or a dull and rigid personality. A money sign here causes stagnant income over a lifetime. A career sign in the Death stage indicates lack of promotion.

Dormancy: A stage of complete inactivity. The luck associated with this stage is worse than in the Death stage. However, it also means recuperation, which under some circumstances could ignite high energy and good luck, bringing the potential to rebound.

Void: Complete emptiness. The strength of this stage is close to zero. The self needs a lot of help from kin. Any favorable signs in this category will have no strength. However, unfavorable signs in this position will bring no harm. A spouse in this stage could mean an unmarried life, a brief marriage, or a long but empty marriage.

Embryo: The beginning of a new cycle, signifying new hope and new potency. Any sign in this stage will grow in strength, and the self will tend to be forward-looking.

Pregnancy: The initial developmental stage of a new life, an extension of the previous stage, but with greater strength.

The most powerful stages are adolescence, adulthood, and prime. They are categorized as blooming stages. The worst stages are void, dormancy, aging, death, and decline; these form the contracting stage. Those in between—embryo, pregnancy, birth, and childhood—make up the growing stage.

There are ten growth cycle patterns for the five elements because the growing cycle of yang elements is different from the growing cycle of yin elements. The growth cycles of the ten stems are shown in Figure 5A on page 60.

The stage of the signs in your own cosmic system can be determined by looking at this chart. First, look up the sign in question among the ten stems in the first row. Second, along the column of the given stem, look for the element matching the birth month of the given birth composite, and then read the name of the stage from the same row.

Cycle \ Stems	T	t	F	f	E	e	M	m	R	r
Birth (BH)	r	F	T	m	T	m	f	R	M	t
Childhood (CD)	R	f	t	M	t	M	F	r	m	T
Adolescence (AE)	g	W	W	d	W	d	d	H	H	g
Adulthood (AD)	T	t	f	F	f	F	M	m	r	R
Prime (PE)	t	T	F	f	F	f	m	M	R	r
Decline (DE)	W	g	d	W	d	W	H	d	g	H
Aging (AG)	f	R	M	t	M	t	r	F	T	m
Death (DH)	F	r	m	T	m	T	R	f	t	M
Dormancy (DY)	d	H	H	g	H	g	g	W	W	d
Void (VD)	M	m	r	R	r	R	T	t	f	F
Embryo (EO)	m	M	R	r	R	r	t	T	F	f
Pregnancy (PY)	H	d	g	H	g	H	W	g	d	W

Figure 5A. The Growth Cycles of the Stems

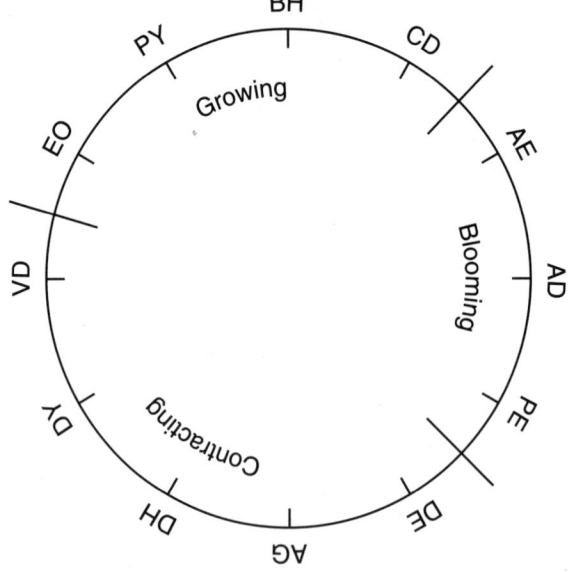

Figure 5B. Growth Stages by Strength

To illustrate, let us use the example of Big River.

r	**R**	f	**M**
t	**H**	r	**W**

The sign for the month of birth is always the month branch in the birth composite. In Big River's case, it is **r**, lunar October. This **r** determines the growth stage for every sign in the birth composite. Let us begin with the self, day stem **R**. In the column for stem **R**, **r**, representing the branch in the month pillar, falls into the stage of adulthood, which is the blooming stage. From this, we know the self is very strong. Using the same procedure, we list the growth stage of each stem, beginning with the year pillar.

Stem	Growth Cycle	Stage/Strength
M	aging	contracting stage
f	embryo	growing stage
r	prime	blooming stage

The Growth Stages for Big River's Stems

Identifying the growth cycle for the branches is more complicated, as they contain more than one sign. We have to convert them into stem equivalents before we can use the chart. Let us list each with their stem equivalents.

Branch	Stem Equivalents	Growth Cycle	Stage/Strength
W	t	death	contracting
	E	void	contracting
	r	prime	blooming
r	T	birth	growing
	R	adulthood	blooming
t	t	death	contracting
H	m	childhood	growing
	E	void	contracting
	f	embryo	growing

The Growth Stages for Big River's Branches

The strength of each sign must be evaluated in terms of its cosmic environment, which we will discuss next.

Cosmic Environments

Signs in the same growing cycle, and with the same pillar structure, may perform differently in different cosmic environments. To show how a cosmic environment can affect the strength of signs, let us illustrate with two birth composites.

M	**T**	**t**	**r**
F	**T**	**t**	**g**

Birth Composite A

r	**T**	**e**	**M**
m	**T**	**t**	**F**

Birth Composite B

Both birth composites have a wood self, **T**, and the same self pillar structure, and both are in the growth stage. However, **T** in Composite A is stronger, as there are three wood signs supporting the self. **T** in Composite B has one less wood sign and slightly more metal influence, which tends to curtail the strength of wood. In other cases, additional supporting signs, such as water for wood, also make a difference. We'll cover many more cases in our illustrations in Chapters 6, 7, and 8.

Using the rules we learned in Chapter 2 (Figure 2I on page 23), let us evaluate the strength of the signs in Big River's birth composite:

r	**R**	**f**	**M**
t	**H**	**r**	**W**

The self, **R**, was born in the stage of adulthood, supported by powerful kin, **r**, and a grantor, **M**. She is much too strong for her own good. She is too confident to take precautions or advice, and so motivated to succeed that she works too hard at seeking vanity. This creates frustration.

The super energy flow also makes her restless and listless. She cannot focus on meaningful endeavors.

Rules of Interaction

Signs interact in specific ways in the cosmic environment. *Pairing* is the union of two signs. Certain signs always pair up and function as one unit, each losing its original nature and function. There are five such pairs in the stem group:

Te   tM   Fm   fR   Er

As shown, each pair is composed of one yang sign and one yin sign, one ruling the other. However, once paired, their interruling nature changes to a supporting role.

When a pair does not include the self sign, both signs can lose most of their function, depending on the strength of the signs. A weak sign can lose its entire function, while a strong sign will retain half of its influence. There is no formula for precise assessment. As a result, variable fortune is created. Losing a good sign deprives the self of good fortune, while losing a bad sign elevates the self from some bad luck. On the whole, pairs indicate success, good social skill of the self, harmony, and good fortune. They also mean an active social life. Let us illustrate with the example of Rain Drop:

E	r	F	e
F	r	T	r

The self in this birth composite is yin water (rain). Ideally, water should be clear. Clear water is healthy and intelligent (clear-minded). The worst element for the self in this composite is the yin earth (moist earth) on the year stem, as it muddies the water. Muddy water creates a confused mind and physical disorder. The best way to lessen its effect is to pair it with a **T** (tree), which would thrive in the moist earth and keep the mud out of the water.

Unfortunately, there is no **T** in Rain Drop's composite or luck cycle. Yet she is not entirely out of luck. Her lucky break came in 1984, the cosmic year of **TR**. Rain Drop had a wonderful year, with a good career promotion and a lengthy overseas trip on which she met her future spouse.

What happened? The **T** from the cosmic year pillar of 1984 paired with the **e** in the stem of Rain Drop's year pillar, clearing up the water and creating good luck. Of course, there was another important process contributing simultaneously to the event of marriage. This will be discussed later in this chapter.

When a pairing involves the self, either easy financial success or congenial relationship is indicated. In reality, when the selves of a couple, or any two individuals, happen to be one of the five stem pairs, a compatible and rewarding relationship is likely to develop, resulting in good fortune.

The Five Stem Pairs

Te is the union of a tree and moist earth, an enduring and mutually supporting relationship. Just imagine a tree without soil or with barren soil! **e** is the money sign for a **T** self, since wood controls the earth. This union means easy financial success for the self. The source of wealth depends on the location of the sign. When **e** happens to be the self, **T** becomes the ruler of the self. The self has a supporting boss and perhaps a successful career.

Here is an example to illustrate how a lucky pairing created a great fortune of easy money for Goodearth.

E	e	T	E
W	f	R	H

The self is **e**, yin earth. There are five other earth signs, representing his siblings. There is only one money sign, **R**. This is a scenario of siblings battling for the family wealth! Goodearth managed to inherit most of the wealth and the only family title. How?

Goodearth's money sign is located on his month branch. Since it is in the prime stage, it manifests tremendous wealth. It is in the parent position, indicating great wealth from the parents. This wealth happened to be under stem **T**, Goodearth's natural pairing partner, and the position representing his father as well. His father always sided in his favor, so naturally, Goodearth became the sole beneficiary of the wealth.

tM is the union of plant and metal. The supporting relationship is less enduring, as there is only mutual liking, no interdependence. It creates less fortune.

Fm is yang fire paired with yin metal, a relationship between a superior and a subordinate. There is harmony as long as the fire enjoys the power and the metal enjoys the loving protection. For an **F** self, **m** indicates automatic access to money—a wealthy wife, a permissive parent, or an obedient child—depending on the position of the sign. Very often, it also indicates the self's indulgence in vices.

When the self happens to be **m**, **F** becomes the ruler, as fire controls metal. The self expects a good and protecting boss, or a good career, and for the female, a supporting and protecting spouse. This also indicates a congenial relationship with parents, children, or spouse, depending on the position of the sign.

fR is the pairing of yin fire and yang water, the strongest bonding pair among the five pairs. A couple in such a pair will sacrifice anything for emotional gratification; they are great lovers. Other principles of the above pairing apply.

E and **r** pair up for mutual need; emotional involvement between the two signs is not strong. This pair usually creates odd couples with contrasting disposition or a large gap in age; but there is always harmony and a mutual bond between them. The same principle applies to other social relationships. The principles of easy money apply here as well.

When there are two or more of the same sign trying to pair with one sign, there is conflict. In reality, this denotes legal, social, or financial disputes. For example, a female **f** with two **R** signs is likely to have affairs or romantic entanglements. This is called jealous pairing. Stems can also pair with some stem equivalents in the branches. We will illustrate some of the ideas with a few examples.

T	M	m	F
M	F	t	F

In this birth composite for Wild Ore, **F** pairs with **m**. Since the self is not involved, both signs offset each other and lose most of their function. **F** is the ruler of the **M** self, a driving force that disciplines her. **m** is a kin and is more accessible to **t** (her money sign); **m** is competing for the money, and is more likely to win. Let us examine how the pairing process changes all the rules.

Wild Ore has a very protective and permissive father who has shielded her from all hardships and discipline in life. Her father is the **m**, as it sits in the male parent position. **m** absorbs the power of **F** by pairing with it. Wild Ore turned out to be unorganized, indulgent in vices, and willful.

On the other hand, **m** disappeared from the scene (being the weaker sign) after pairing with **F**, leaving the money, **t**, intact. The **M** self can therefore pair with **t**, making her a legal beneficiary of the source of wealth. Wild Ore received a substantial insurance payment when her mother died (branch **t** is in the mother position). She was not the only child; the payment was a result of some unusual arrangement by a relative. It was a matter of destiny!

Our next illustration explains how pairing affects social relationships. Easy Penny's birth composite:

f	M	t	r
r	F	t	d

Self **M** is pairing with **t** on the month pillar, signifying a strong parental bond. Easy Penny relates beautifully to her parents. She and three other siblings in their middle age live happily under the same roof. Since **t** is Easy Penny's money sign, she has also been enjoying career promotions and salary increases without much effort.

The following example offers some interesting observations on how a ruler pairing affects career.

f	e	T	R
t	t	W	T

This is the birth composite of Treegarden, a professional secretary, highly disciplined and well-mannered. She has too many rulers (four wood signs), imposing too much discipline in her life. Most of her bosses have been women (**t**, yin wood, representing a female boss) she could not get along with. However, all the male bosses she has had have been congenial and supporting. Why?

Treegarden's yang ruler, **T**, on the month stem, representing her male bosses, pairs with her **e** self. Besides getting along well with male bosses, she always had her parent's support at home whenever she fought with her siblings. The **T** in the parent position of her composite acts as a natural and constant protective judge. All her yin rulers represent her female bosses; they are oppressors.

The Six Branch Pairs

The pairing process also takes place in the branches. There are six pairs:

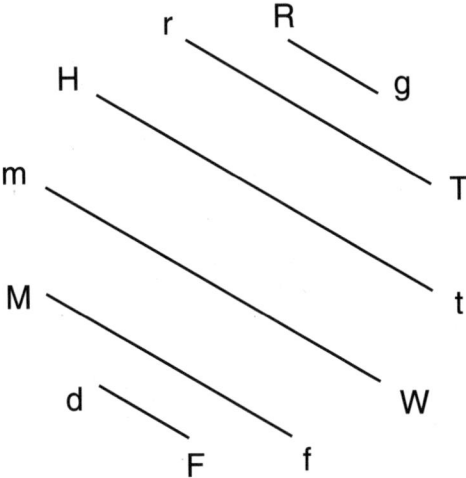

Figure 5C. The Six Branch Pairs

The pairing of branches never involves the self, since the self is represented by a stem. Branch pairing can be complicated, as some pairings involve more than one element in one sign. They do *not*, however, involve the stem equivalents of the branches. During the branch pairing process, each sign in the pair merges with, and functions as, one sign. See Figure 5D on page 68.

Pair	Changed Form
Rg	Earth
Tr	Wood
tH	Fire
Wm	Metal
fM	Water
Fd	Fire

Figure 5D. The Branch Pairs Transformed

Let us explain with an example.

M	**e**	**T**	**r**
F	**r**	**T**	**d**

The **e** self, being born in misty January, is soggy. Unfortunately, there are two more water signs, **r**, in the birth composite, disintegrating the earth and weakening the self. However, the pairing between branches **T** and **r** turns the whole situation around.

The **Tr** pairing changes the most damaging sign, **r**, into a powerfully favorable wood team with **T**, causing **r** to lose its original function as water. Instead of drowning the environment, it drains the water, making the environment more livable. This fortunate pairing becomes a great problem solver. In fact, the cosmic system belongs to a high achiever.

Tri-union

The *tri-union* process applies only to the branches and occurs when three branches merge to form a new element. There are two ways in which branches merge—the *con-trio* and the *trio*.

The Con-trio

The first type of tri-union, as demonstrated in Figure 5E on page 69, is called a con-trio. It involves three signs associated with the same cardinal direction, or domain—north, south, east, or west—in the branch group.

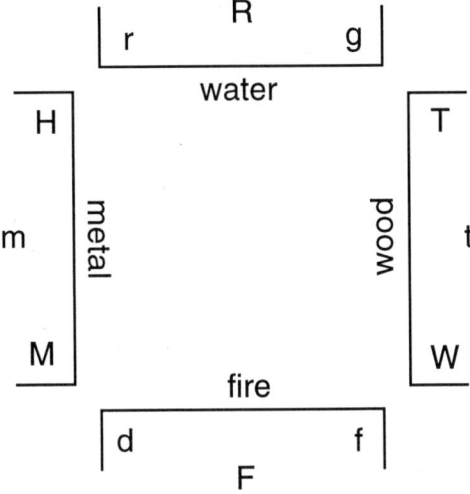

Figure 5E. The Con-trios

There is no earth con-trio, as earth's domain is the center. The four earth branches combine with the element of the domain with which each is associated.

Domain	Con-trio	Changed Form
North	**rRg**	Water
South	**fFd**	Fire
East	**TtW**	Wood
West	**MmH**	Metal

Figure 5F. The Con-trios Transformed

A con-trio becomes the most powerful sign, as there are three similar signs working together. As in pairing, the process can involve signs from the composite, the luck cycle, or the cosmos at any given time. The duration of the effect varies. When all the signs are from the birth composite, the effect lasts a lifetime; when one of the signs is from the luck cycle, the effect lasts for the five years ruled by the element involved; when the cosmic year pillar is involved, the effect lasts the entire year.

Let us illustrate the process with Sinky's cosmic system.

	f	M	f	M		
	g	W	r	W		

E	e	M	m	R	r	T
R	g	T	t	W	f	F

There is the potential for a con-trio of water, as two of the three signs, **r** and **g**, are found in the birth composite. The merger took place during the branch **R** period, resulting in a big flood. This created a great misfortune. Sinky is a piece of metal born in a wet and cold winter. He needs all the fire he can get to survive. Such powerful water destroyed his fragile, crucial fire, **f**. Sinky struggled to stay afloat in a freezing pool. He had a very miserable childhood with a prolonged illness. Amazingly, he recovered and stayed healthy after the con-trio period.

The Trio

The second type of tri-union involves three branches in the same growth stage. This is simply called a trio. The merging signs and their transformations are illustrated in Figures 5G and 5H.

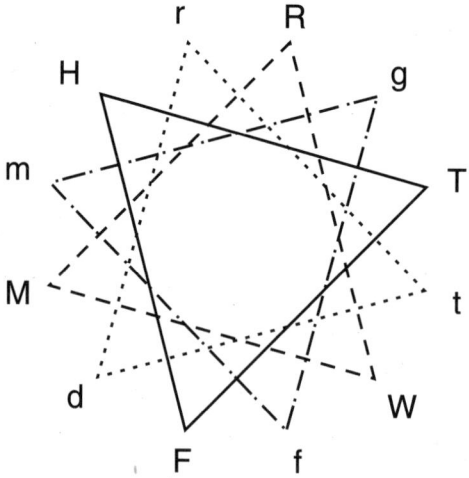

Figure 5G. The Trios

Domain	Trio	Changed Form
North	**MRW**	Water
South	**TFH**	Fire
East	**rtd**	Wood
West	**fmg**	Metal

Figure 5H. The Trios Transformed

A trio functions basically as a con-trio. The major difference is that any two branches can form a partial trio, which is, of course, less powerful. These partial trios are called an *alliance.*

The development of a favorable trio at a given time can indicate marriage, a new birth, promotion, or success in a project. A favorable trio in a birth composite indicates a fortunate life. Great leaders tend to have a favorable pairing or trio in their cosmic system. Let us illustrate these ideas with an example.

R	F	R	M	
W	R	F	H	

r	T	t	F	f	E	e
d	M	m	H	r	R	g

There is a water alliance formed by **W** and **R** in the composite. It became a complete trio of water during the **M** period of the luck cycle. The self was under a powerful water influence during that five-year period. The influence of this trio gradually subsided as the self moved into the **t** period.

Branches **F** and **H** remain an alliance until the missing **T** dominates the grand cosmic flows. A fire trio of **T**, **F**, and **H**, would exist for the duration of that year. The self would then experience more fire influence.

Let us put our knowledge to work in the next example, finding the climax of luck in Weak Fire's life.

m	f	r	r
r	t	r	t

R	m	M	e	E	f	F
H	m	M	d	F	f	W

From the discussion on the **f** self in Chapter 7 (page 109), we know that Weak Fire needs a lot of wood to sustain his life (the self being fire) and to drain off the excessive water. His most crucial element is wood; the more the better. It follows that the formation of a wood trio would bring him the best luck. Our job is to search the lunar charts for the time when such a development occurs.

Weak Fire is lucky to have two wood alliances already formed by **t** and **r** in his birth composite. He is a tough (able to turn damaging water into lucky wood) and resourceful person (double-edged protection). Searching his luck cycle, we know for sure he would reach his climax of luck during the **d** period, as one of his wood alliances would turn into a wood trio. In fact, he became the prime minister of his country during that time.

Clashing

Clashing is confrontation between two signs. The process creates disruption or misfortune in a person's life, such as sickness, financial loss, marital problems, or social conflicts. It is a significant process between branches. There are six clashing pairs.

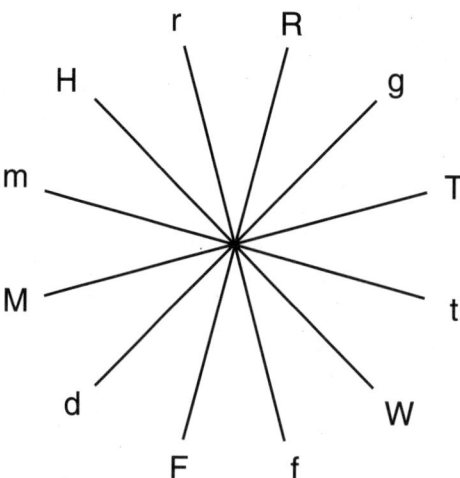

Figure 51. The Clashing Branches

The clashing process can occur between the signs in the birth composite (stem or branch), the luck cycle, or the cosmos. When the clashing signs are equal in strength, there will be lasting battles during the clashing period, creating disruption or loss to the self. Otherwise, a stronger sign can oust a weaker one, resulting in good fortune when the ousted sign is harmful, and bad luck when the ousted sign is favorable. In all cases, there are some conflicts of various nature. Clashing creates an eventful life, pleasant or otherwise. In the following illustrations, we'll touch upon some of these aspects.

Coldrain's birth composite:

F	r	t	r
W	r	t	m

3	13	23	33	43	53	63
T	r	R	m	M	e	E
T	g	R	r	H	m	M

There is a clash between stem **t** and **m** in the composite. Since it takes place in the parent and relative position, it indicates conflict, turbulent relationships, or loose bonds between parents and relatives. How do we determine the strength of the battling signs? **t** is clearly the stronger sign, for two reasons. First, **t** is in its stage of adulthood, blooming. By contrast, **m** is in its void stage, the weakest. Second, **t** is supported by three grantors (**r** in both stems and branch) and two kin signs (there is a **T** hidden in branch **r**), while **m** is alone; it is a battle between a soldier and an army. Thus, **m** is ousted.

How does real life turn out in this case? Coldrain was born into a large family. His father had three wives. The third wife, Coldrain's natural mother, had little control over her children. Losing his father at age five, Coldrain was under the loose guidance of his older brother, a child from the first wife, as males dominated the society in China. There was substantial conflict and rivalry between the wives and their children. Finally, Coldrain and his full-blood siblings moved out of the family home. Later, he left for college overseas and never returned.

How do we relate the theories and the events? Clashing signs in this case created loose bonds and conflicts between relatives. The ousted **m** signifies, in this case, other mothers and their children. The process of clashing caused Coldrain's departure from home and his rejection of his relatives.

During the **H** period of his luck cycle, between ages forty-eight and fifty-three, when **H** clashed with **W**, the position of children, Coldrain had daily battles with his two children, a big contrast to their normal relationship. Amazingly, the quarrels quieted down after the **H** period.

What happened during the branch **m** period of the luck cycle? There were two yin metal signs clashing with **t**. How to assess the strength of this metal team? The **m** in the luck cycle was bred by moist earth on the stem, very well sustained, and it gathered strong momentum during the five-year period. Coldrain had frequent conflicts with his siblings, and some of his children left home.

Clashes involving the spouse sign usually indicate problems in the marriage, such as a late or unhappy marriage, or divorce. The following example illustrates some of these principles.

F	r	e	M
W	m	t	F

This is the birth composite of a smart, pretty, and hard-working woman, divorced after a brief marriage. She always wanted a lasting relationship. Her life did not turn out the way she had chosen. She had gone to three fortune-tellers, unable to find the truth. No one would disclose such a fatal truth to a young woman.

Her spouse sign, **m**, is very unstable, as it clashes with **t**. **t**, in its blooming stage, is far stronger, ousting **m**. **m** also pairs with **W**, loses its identity, and stops functioning as a spouse sign. In any event, **m** is doomed to be out of the picture. Thus, the chance for the self to have a permanent spouse is slim. She had two wonderful children, however.

What is the use of knowing such truth? The self has a choice, depending on her priorities. Knowing the truth, she won't waste time pursuing the impossible. Her viable options are focusing on her career and her children, and strengthening the ties between her relatives.

Sign transformation plays a vital role in changing the nature and role of signs. After identifying your self sign, identify and outline your sign transformations in conjunction with your luck cycle and the cosmic flows.

Up to this point, we have covered the basic theories of the analysis of cosmic systems. The rest of the book is designed to help you with the application of these theories.

CHAPTER 6

Assessing the Strength
of the Self

Equipped with the knowledge of cosmic signs and the rules of their inter-action, we are able to analyze a cosmic system. We'll begin with the birth composite, which basically consists of two parts: the self and its birth environment. The self is defined by the day stem. The other seven signs define the self's opportunities and challenges in the environment.

While the self's life depends on the environment, its abilities also determine how it responds to the quality of the environment. Different people thrive in different environments. Capable people welcome a chal-lenging environment. Others enjoy a simple life in a stable habitat. Some simply succumb to a harsh challenge. A lucky few were born in a perfect world, into which they fit naturally, and enjoy a perfect life.

People succeed when their opportunities are commensurate with their abilities, and suffer when the environment deprives them of their needs. The same logic applies to the analysis of our cosmic system. We'll first determine what makes the self thrive, and secondly, how the environment measures up to those needs.

Since the self and the environment are interrelated, our strategy is to classify the selves according to the environment in which they were born. Within each category, we'll assess how the different types of selves, with different strengths, respond to opportunities. Our cosmic environments can be broadly divided into two types: equilibrium and non-equilibrium, or faulty. Both types are described in the next sections.

The Equilibrium Environment

An equilibrium environment has all five elements in perfect harmony. It is like having all nations or peoples of the world in a check-and-balance state, in which people enjoy equality, stability, and prosperity. It is the best life, in which all good things are in the right proportion.

Being born in the equilibrium state is super lucky and very much blessed. Such people could be super intelligent and capable, or just plain ordinary. However, they all succeed naturally in all aspects of their lives, always doing the right thing at the right time and in the right place. There are two kinds of such environments.

Interlocking Equilibrium

This is a rare state in which all five elements interbreed each other in a natural sequence with almost equal strength. It is a naturally permanent equilibrium. This perfect environment creates the most competitive, and the most blessed, people in the world. We will illustrate with a typical example.

$$\uparrow \quad \begin{matrix} \mathbf{F} & \leftarrow & \mathbf{T} & \leftarrow & \mathbf{r} & \leftarrow & \mathbf{m} \\ \mathbf{T} & \leftarrow & \mathbf{R} & & \mathbf{f} & \rightarrow & \mathbf{g} \end{matrix} \quad \uparrow$$

This is the birth composite of a prime minister in ancient China. He lived to be ninety years old at a time when the average life span was thirty. He had many children and grandchildren, all good, and some very successful. He was super rich and highly respected as a great and effective civil leader with vision and high integrity.

All five elements are included in his birth composite in an interbreeding, sequential order starting from branch **f**, to **g**, **m**, **r**, **T**, and **F**, as indicated by the arrows. The inclusion of all five elements signifies all inclusive blessings in the world. Since all elements are sequentially interbreeding, the blessings are well-bonded and forever mutually-sustained. Best of all, the first element, fire, is repeated at the end, signifying repetitive cycles and endless blessings lasting generations.

Such people are born to succeed naturally in everything they do, and to be tremendously blessed in all aspects of life. Having such a cosmic system is like winning a big lotto!

Equilibrium by Dominant Element

There are times when a dominant element gains full control of an environment, such as at the climax of a season. The mechanism for the equilibrium depends on the super control of one single element over all other elements. Since there is no bond such as mutual support or interdependence among them, the equilibrium is fragile. Its duration is brief and subject to a downturn.

While the equilibrium brings great fortune, its tilt causes as much disaster. Any change in the luck cycle or the cosmos can change the condition and topple the equilibrium. Such a system creates an exciting life, with frequent ups and downs. Basically, it produces two extremely different kinds of selves: the super strong and the super fragile. To qualify as an equilibrium system, the birth composite should have at least one trio or alliance involving the dominant element in the branch group. We'll illustrate below.

Equilibrium by Dominant Self

When the self happens to be the dominant element, it controls the environment. A dominant self commands great luck as long as the equilibrium lasts. The self is like a powerful dictator, setting up its own rules to control its destiny. The cosmic system of Allfire illustrates the structure of the dominant self. The self is yang fire and there are two fire alliances in the branches. We'll see how his luck shifted with changing conditions in the environment.

| | T | | F | | T | | F |
| | F | | H | | F | | H |

| t | F | f | E | e | M | m |
| d | M | m | H | r | R | g |

Allfire was a great general. He was born as yang fire, the sun, in lunar May, the hottest month (the climax) of summer. There are six fire signs in his composite fueled by two woods. Four of the fire signs form two small teams. Clearly, fire dominates the environment, and the self is a part of this dominance. This fierce fire created the most stable dominant equilibrium. He was a super man who set his own rules to achieve his goal. However, the equilibrium was subject to tilt under external force.

Let us examine how Allfire's luck shifted with the changing environment. During the **td** period of his luck cycle, he was an excellent student in the military academy. Additional fire and wood reinforced the equilibrium to create good fortune. During the **F** period, he was promoted to general. Again, the extra fire enhanced the equilibrium.

However, the equilibrium toppled during the **M** period. Water from branch **M** confronted the fire, weakening its force. Allfire was seriously ill for a few years.

During the **f** period, as fire replaced water, reinstating the equilibrium, Allfire resumed his normal life. Can you explain why his bad luck recurred during the **m** period? It is because **m** is a water breeder, so it challenged fire's dominance. Luckily, it was yin metal, which is less forceful than **M**. Allfire suffered only a demotion and some other minor setbacks.

Allfire had three lucky periods and two downturns in a span of thirty years. He finally grew wiser, learning how to keep his equilibrium in tact. How do we know? The next three periods were **E**, **H**, and **e**, all earth, blocking water from confronting the fire. Earth is the offspring of a fire self, symbolizing wisdom. Such a system produced a mellow survivor. Allfire died in a battle at the beginning of an **r** (water) period—a natural course!

Equilibrium Through Helpless Self

When the dominant element in the environment is different from the self element, a reverse situation occurs. The self is controlled by the dominant element, like a hostage who survives only by totally surrendering to the kidnapper, the controlling element. On the other hand, as the ruling (dominant) element needs the victim to secure a ransom, it has to take good care of the helpless self. This means good life by entitlement for the self. The mechanism of the equilibrium relies on the self's total surrender to the dominant element. As long as the ruler maintains complete control, the equilibrium remains and the self is entitled to a good life.

However, any time the helpless self tries to get help from his or her folks, the ruling element is angered and subsequently topples the equilibrium. Help comes from the participation of either a kin or a grantor. It follows that any time such a sign from the luck cycle or the cosmos interplays in the system, disasters will take place, as the equilibrium topples. Let us illustrate with the life of Obeyan.

t	t	m	m
m	m	g	f

Obeyan was a plant (yin wood) born in a contracting period, surrounded by a metal trio (formed by **f**, **m**, and **g**) and three other metal signs, which were all his rulers. The other **t**, his kin, was of no help, as it was tightly controlled by another metal. This is an equilibrium of fragile wood controlled by a metal team.

Obeyan's only way to survive is to surrender. His total loyalty entitled him to a wonderful life. However, this was not a permanent situation. Let us see how the equilibrium changed during his luck cycle.

M	e	E	f	F	t	T
R	r	H	m	M	d	F

Obeyan received a series of good promotions in his career during the **EH** period, when strong earth bred the metal, reinforcing the equilibrium. During the next twenty years, his life remained stagnant, as the fire and metal offset each other in the **fm** and **FM** periods, producing little significant impact. However, Obeyan lost his position during the **t** period, when an additional kin came to his assistance, angering the rulers. The self was punished.

The line between a weak self, which is discussed in the next section, and a helpless self is very fine. While a helpless self dreads kin or grantors, a weak self welcomes both. In a real life situation, how often does a kidnapped victim and his or her family know exactly what to do? The involvement of the police sometimes frees the victim; other times, the victim is killed.

Other helpless selves include those controlled by offspring or the money sign. All command great fortune. In such cases, the same concepts of equilibrium apply.

Non-Equilibrium Systems

The composition of the elements in non-equilibrium environments is always askew, with either excessive or deficient elements that are never in harmony. The selves in such environments are in constant struggle to correct the fault and achieve equilibrium. However, they lead the most exciting lives! Being faulty makes these environments challenging and fulfilling. They produce great achievers. In fact, the greatest satisfaction in life comes from succeeding in solving difficult problems.

The fault of these systems is one of two extremes: the self is either too strong or too weak. A strong self is born in a blooming stage supported by kin, grantors, or both. Such a person is overly energetic and needs extra opportunities to expend his or her energy.

If this blooming self has several kin, there are fewer positions left in the composite for career, money, and power, since the number of signs in the birth composite is fixed. As a result, the self will have fewer opportunities for his or her extra energy, and will be unproductive.

A weak self is born in a contracting stage without support from kin or grantors. In contrast, the other signs in the composite, which represent the environment, are too strong and provide more opportunities than his or her limited energy can handle. Poor health or low ability prohibits the self from using available resources. Imagine a very sick person who can't reach any of the abundant money spread over the floor; a wasteful life!

At this point, we need to clear up some possible confusion. An overly strong person is a common person, different from the super strong. While the super strong person in an equilibrium environment can command his or her fortune without help from others, common people have to abide by the law and rely on the environment for support. The same idea applies to the "helpless" and the "weak." While a helpless child is entitled to parental provisions, the weak adult has to struggle for a living among fierce competitors.

What to do when the self gets too strong? The ideal solution involves two methods. First, to avoid confrontation, it is essential to calm the self by gradually channeling its excessive energy. This is the job of an off-spring. For instance, when a water self has too much water (additional kin or grantors in the birth composite), he or she needs wood (the offspring of water) to slowly consume the excessive water. The self can then gradually and surely achieve his or her equilibrium. Wood becomes the remedial element for an overly-strong water self.

The same idea applies to the selves of other elements, with different remedial elements, of course. For easy reference, the remedial elements for each self type are listed in Figure 6A.

Type of Self	Too Strong	Too Weak
Wood	Fire to calm; metal to curtail.	Water to grow; wood to help the team.
Fire	Yin earth to calm; water to curtail.	Wood to breed; fire to help the team.
Earth	Metal to calm; wood to curtail.	Fire to breed; earth to help the team.
Metal	Water to calm; fire to curtail.	Yin earth to breed; metal to help the team.
Water	Wood to calm; earth to curtail.	Metal to breed; water to help the team.

Figure 6A. Remedial Elements for the Selves

The effect of an offspring is slow. The self needs some drive to focus its efforts for action. This is the job of a ruler. For instance, yang earth (ruler of water) can confine the spreading water to a proper channel. Thus, the self, being on track, can focus on production.

An overly strong self with both remedial elements working in the environment can easily become a high achiever. Those with offspring alone are likely to lead a peaceful life, but lack the drive to excel. Those with a ruler alone tend to overact or become ruthless.

What to do when the self is too weak? He or she needs helping hands (kin) and protection (grantors). To elaborate, a wood self born in the contracting stage needs a couple of other wood signs, or a strong water sign, or both, in the composite, to prosper in life.

A faulty system amended by the right remedial elements becomes a perfect system, enabling one to effectively solve problems and turn adversity into good fortune. Having remedial elements in one's birth composite is the most ideal situation, creating a lifetime of good luck. Having them in the luck cycle creates ups and downs in one's life. The onset of a remedial element will bring a surge of good luck, depending on the nature and the force of the sign.

The position of the remedial elements in the composite also makes a difference. They should be close to the self. The day branch is the best position, being closest to the self. The month or hour pillars are the next best positions, and the year pillar is the least effective position. Remedial elements in the day and hour pillar create a self-reliant person, and in the year and month positions indicate family support.

Great achievers usually have a system with a serious fault amended by the right remedy, creating the powerful ability to conquer mounting obstacles. A very ordinary person usually has a mixed-up system, in which no distinctive fault can be identified. Consequently, no remedy is available, and no significant success is expected. Those with great fault and no remedy, of course, fare the worst—a lifetime of unrewarding struggles!

In evaluating a faulty system, the first thing we do is identify the fault and then search for the remedy. The remedial element becomes the self's favorable element, while the element that reinforces the fault becomes the negative element. The former brings good fortune and the latter causes bad luck. This is the basic approach to analyzing the Meng. Faulty selves can be categorized as overly strong or weak.

The Overly Strong Self

An overly strong self is created under the following conditions:

1. Born in a blooming or growing stage, surrounded by grantors and kin.

2. Born at the beginning of a contracting stage, surrounded by strong grantors and strong kin.

These people are usually healthy and ambitious, and tend to be self-centered. Many of them are great leaders or self-employed. Unfortunately, their kin and/or grantors take up so much of the birth composite that there is no room for the elements that would bring challenge and opportunity for the self's excessive energy. Without remedial elements, these people might become listless. Some could even find their current life totally meaningless and choose to be a hermit. However, with remedial elements, they become competitive and productive people. Let us illustrate with examples.

T	F	t	F
F	R	d	H

Bigfire was born in June (month **d**), at the beginning of the contracting stage (see Figures 5A and 5B on page 60). Let us count his kin and grantors. There are three additional fires supported by two woods. This is an overly strong self. Since there is no fire trio or alliance, the self does not qualify as dominant. This is, therefore, a faulty system. We need to identify the fault.

Undoubtedly, there is too much fire; the self is too strong. What is the remedy? From Figure 6A on page 83 we know that the remedy for a strong fire self is moist earth to absorb heat, or powerful water to curtail it. Unfortunately, there are no such elements in Bigfire's composite. There is no remedy! Consequently, Bigfire is very hot-tempered, conceited, thoughtless, and has achieved very little in life.

In the following example, let us find out how a remedial element changed Goodfire's life.

e	F	T	F
g	F	F	F

Goodfire was born in May during a blooming stage. Thus, by birth, he was already strong. With three more fire signs supported by a wood, he had even more energy than Bigfire. However, he was calm, confident, and above all, rich and famous. As part of his fire nature, he was also strict and dignified, fair, and honest.

Type of Self	Criteria	Remedy
Dominant	1. Born in blooming cycle. 2. With trio of self element. 3. Without rulers or tyrants.	Offspring to calm the excessive load, no interruling element to challenge the dominant element.
Overly-strong	1. Born in blooming cycle with grantor and/or kin. 2. Born in growing cycle with strong grantor, or a few strong kin.	Offspring to calm the excessive energy, tyrants or rulers to discipline the self.
Overly-weak	1. Born in contracting cycle, without kin or grantor. 2. Born in contracting cycle with too many offspring and/or tyrants.	Grantors to protect the self, kin to help. In the case of too many tyrants, offspring to mitigate the rulers or tyrants.
Weak	1. Born in contracting cycle with weak kin or weak grantor. 2. Born in growing cycle with too many tyrants or too many offspring.	The above principles apply.
Helpless	1. Born in contracting cycle without kin or grantor. 2. With all tyrants or rulers.	No kin or grantor to challenge the tyrants or rulers.
Competitive	1. Born in blooming cycle with no grantor or kin. 2. Born in growing cycle with strong grantor or kin. 3. Born in contracting cycle with kin and grantor.	No remedy necessary. Need challenge and opportunity for achievement.

Figure 6B. Types of Selves by Strength

What makes the difference? The moist earth in the hour pillar. There are two of them in one pillar, double insurance, which is very effective. These elements steadily absorb and dissipate his great heat. Their calming effect promotes clear thinking, which guides him in decision-making. He was a self-made millionaire.

Moist earth is always the most effective remedy for excessive fire. This golden rule is also supported by the cosmic system of an acquaintance of mine. He is an electrical engineer who happens to have excessive fire in his system. For a few years, he had several jobs in the electronics field and was constantly miserable. Finally, he lost all the jobs. With his excessive fire, an electrical job is the wrong career for him.

In despair, he changed to real estate, which is an earth career. Earth in the bay area of San Francisco is wet land—moist earth! To his surprise, his life took a positive turn after a few months. Both his boss and his clients were super supporting. His income increased by leaps and bounds. Within less than a year, he purchased a house, and he continues to prosper. This happened during his moist earth luck period—the onset of his remedial element brought surging luck.

The Weak Self

A weak self is one that is unable to command luck. Some are physically weak; others could be physically strong, but are not able to do the right thing at the right time. These people fall into the following categories:

1. Born in a contracting stage without grantors or kin, or with too many offspring.

2. Born in a growing stage with too many rulers.

Being weak and without help is miserable. Such lives are usually associated with birth defects, poor health, low mental ability, or a poor background. However, a weak self with proper remedial elements can become as competitive as a strong self. Many great people fall into this category. In the following section we will illustrate this idea with a few examples.

The Weak Self Without Remedial Elements

Consider the life of Feeble, who is yang metal, **M**, born in January in the void stage, the weakest stage in the growth cycle.

F	M	T	r
H	F	T	t

Feeble is very fragile and needs a lot of help from kin (metal signs), and grantors (moist earth). However, there are no such signs in his birth composite. It is a faulty system without remedy. Instead, there is a fire trio (formed by branches **H**, **F**, and **T**) constantly burning beneath him—very oppressive rulers.

Feeble had crippled feet and lived in great poverty all his life. Strong fire from below melted the metal in his environment, weakening his feet. The fault in Feeble's composite was too overwhelming to be corrected by his luck cycle or the cosmos. Any lucky break was slight and brief.

The Average Self with Too Many Rulers

A self born with average cosmic strength can become a weak self when there are too many rulers in the composite. These ruling elements can take many forms—a harsh environment, abusive bosses, or tremendous and unrewarding responsibility.

Let us illustrate with the cosmic system of Dry River.

R	R	E	F
T	F	H	W

2	12	22	32	42	52	62
f	F	t	T	r	R	m
m	M	d	F	f	W	t

Dry River was born in September, in the growth stage of adolescence, the beginning of the blooming stage, with a kin in the next pillar. Basically, she is a capable person. With only a few years of schooling, Dry River managed to read and write fluently all her life. At one point, she even started her own business from scratch in a foreign country and supported her family. However, except for a few short breaks, she has had a very difficult life.

To find out why, let us first count the earth signs—her rulers and oppressors, the driving force behind her hard work. There are three of them, **E**, **H**, and **W**, clustered in one spot as a team, with fire at both ends breeding them. Unity is power! Dry River's ruling team is super powerful and oppressive. In addition, there is a fire alliance formed by branches **F** and **T**, evaporating the water (self) and draining her energy. This is a seriously faulty system without remedy. Dry River needs a water team and strong wood to fight the earth influence. She is out of luck.

Let us examine how the events in Dry River's life support the theories of Meng. She lived in a Chinese village. Her poor parents forced her to marry at eighteen. After her marriage, her spouse left to study in a boarding school outside the village. She lived with her in-laws, shouldering the major farming tasks, working daily with bleeding fingers. Her life got even more difficult after the births of her three children. In addition to the work of raising young children, she had to nurse her spouse, who had become chronically ill. The ruler in her parental pillar signifies harsh parents. The fire on her spouse branch drained her energy.

Dry River experienced her worst luck when she turned thirty-seven, during the **F** period of her luck cycle. This additional fire literally evaporated her, until she weighed only sixty pounds. She was virtually sucked up into the air by a strong gale during one incident. Finally, one of her lungs collapsed into her ribs, and she was hospitalized for about six months.

Let us see how the onset of water in her luck cycle changed her life. During her **r** period, her sick spouse died, releasing her from the burden of nursing him. At the same time, her grown-up children became self-supporting. They turned out to be loving children, even though they were unable to provide for her.

Her best luck took place in her early fifties, during her **R** period, which was powerful for two reasons—the influence of yang water supported by a reservoir, **W**. During that time, she immigrated to Canada with her children and enjoyed a peaceful retirement.

The Weak Self With Remedy

A weak self with the proper remedy will gain the strength to prosper. Let us illustrate with Kinny's system.

r	**F**	**R**	**r**
f	**T**	**H**	**d**

23	33	43
t	F	f
g	T	t

Kinny is a sun, **F**, born in the contracting stage, surrounded by three rulers (water signs), and two offspring (earth signs). A sun in late fall is weak. However, she has good kin, the fire alliance formed by **T** and **H**, concerted support from her spouse and parents. Thus, she has a good system, with remedy to amend the fault.

The remedy is good for a comfortable life, but not powerful enough to create prosperity. While there is no shortage of money signs (metal, her money sign, is hidden in branches **H** and **f**), the self is simply too feeble to grasp the opportunity.

Kinny's lucky break came at age thirty-three, during her **FT** period, when she started an eyeglasses business with her spouse. Business exploded for the next few years and she became rich. The momentum lasted twenty years. The joint effort of a kin and a grantor made a winning team for Kinny.

Summary

The procedure for analyzing the strength of the self is summarized below.

1. Classify the cosmic environment as either in equilibrium or faulty.

2. In an equilibrium system:
   a. Determine the status of the self as either dominant or helpless.
   b. Identify the signs that would tilt or reinforce the stability.
   c. Pinpoint those signs in the luck cycle or the cosmos so as to determine the self's upcoming luck.

3. In a faulty system:
   a. Determine the self's strength using Figure 6B on page 86.
   b. Identify the fault in the composite.
   c. Determine the remedial signs.
   d. Search for those signs in the birth composite, luck cycle, and cosmos to determine upcoming luck.

Following the above procedure does not guarantee success in identifying a faulty system. Many cosmic systems do not show a pattern, and some respond minimally to cosmic changes. Readers confronted with such systems must conduct more tests. To guide readers through the process, we have provided an illustration in Chapter 9. Readers need at least twenty-four years of life experience and a very good record of life events to verify their system analysis. The more data one has, the more valid the conclusion will be.

CHAPTER 7

Wood and Fire
Selves

We are now ready to analyze a cosmic system. The analysis includes how the self relates to the other seven signs in the birth composite, the key elements required to change one's luck, and how the onset of signs from the luck cycle and cosmos changes the picture of one's life.

To do this, we need a framework and some guidelines. As discussed in Chapter 4, people of the world are categorized into ten groups according to the day stem in the birth composite. People within the same group tend to share some common traits in their outlook and in the way they respond to their environment.

Each of these groups can be further divided into twelve sub-groups according to the month of birth; this is the most crucial factor in differentiating one person's system from another's. There are 120 models of cosmic systems. By matching your day stem and birth month to one of these models, you can identify the model that will serve as the framework for the analysis of your cosmic system. We'll divide these models into two chapters, with fire and wood selves covered in this chapter.

For each model, we'll guide our readers through the analysis by listing the crucial elements for a good life, and explaining why and how they affect our luck, with real-life examples. To begin the analysis, choose the proper framework and follow the guidelines. By comparing the structure of your cosmic system to the guidelines, you should be able to measure how far you fall short of the ideal model. The crucial elements contributing to a good life for each model are summarized and listed in a chart at the end of the chapter.

Bear in mind that the study of Meng does not account for the genetic factor, which plays an important role in the process of interchange. That is why people born at exactly the same time and place do not share the same destiny. However, they do have a lot in common.

The author happens to know two women who were born at the same time in different places. Both have a comfortable life. One obtained her wealth by marriage and has a retarded adult child, her only child. The other had a mediocre spouse, but is well-provided for by some of her wealthy children. They are both kind and generous, and love to knit and sew. They enjoyed a congenial relationship at their first encounter without knowing why until they disclosed their birthdays to each other.

Another example involves two men born at the same time in China, one a great general and the other, his servant. Regardless of the great difference in status, they had a wonderful relationship. The servant was treated as a family member and shared many of the good things in the general's life.

On the whole, a good cosmic system is associated with good life, which, according to the ancient Chinese, includes power, wealth, fame, longevity, good health, and above all, good male heirs.

A poor cosmic system is, of course, associated with bad luck and a poor life. By Chinese standards, some typical examples of bad luck are poverty, premature death, permanent or chronic ailments, an unsettling life in both career and family, and worst of all, infertility, or not having a male heir.

Remember that the same element creates different luck for different selves, and people prosper only in the right environment. Our job is to search for the key element that creates the ideal environment to bring us luck, and target its onset so as to predict our upcoming luck. In each model, we'll show you how to search for your key elements.

The T Self

Yang wood is a tree or lumber. Since a tree is normally erect and straight, a **T** self will ideally reflect this nature, which is honest, fair, and trim. Wood also symbolizes kindness and utility. The goal of a tree is to produce good lumber for tools and furniture. A well-grown tree brings good luck.

What produces a good tree? Good soil, the proper amount of water, sunlight, and above all, good tools for shaping and harvesting. Sunlight creates brightness, which equals intelligence and fame. It makes the leaves shine and the tree erect, representing glamour and power.

Metal creates tools, an axe (yang metal) or a trimmer (yin metal). The line is not clear-cut between yang and yin metal, and yang metal can function in an all-inclusive manner, depending on its strength, which varies with the time factor. To shape a tree is to educate, refining the self into a high achiever.

Successful wood selves are mostly scholars. Those with abundant fire are great lecturers or lawyers; those with metal in addition to fire are great authors. A well-coordinated wood system produces a kind, intelligent, and fair person. Let us go through the various models.

Spring

January, being very cold and misty, is the budding stage for plants and trees. It is spring in the lunar year. Being very delicate and sparing in branches and leaves, the budding tree needs abundant sunlight and rain to grow. Thus, sunlight and rain become the crucial spatial factors. However, since rain blocks sunlight, the two signs in the birth composite must be separated to avoid an offsetting effect. Otherwise, a frustrating life is indicated.

A **T** self born in January meets the above conditions, is like a well-grown tree—happy and likely to succeed. An earth sign in the composite, to anchor the plant, creates the best life. When sun and rain are substituted by river and man-made fire, success by means of hard work is indicated, since a greenhouse and irrigation require extra effort. Without fire or water, hard life is in the picture, regardless of how hard the person works. It is like growing plants in the arid arctic land.

Metal creates disasters. The trees are too young and feeble to stand the trimming or cutting. To survive, the trees have to struggle to grow more new leaves and branches to protect themselves from being destroyed. This means a life of unrewarding struggles or premature death, depending on the amount and strength of the metal. However, when there is sufficient fire to curtail the metal, success after hard work is indicated. A great problem solver is created.

February is warmer and trees are getting stronger. Heat and water are still basic, but not as crucial, and metal is welcome to trim the trees. The bottom line: February is a lot better timing for wood than January, and the self is strong enough to cope with less favorable spatial factors. Sunlight and rain remain important for a good life; but without them, the self can still survive.

March is the beginning of a warming trend. The tree is full-grown. Sunlight and water are secondary. Metal has become the most important element for harvesting the tree. Without metal, the tree is shapeless and will never be harvested. There are no opportunities for its talent, and consequently there is no achievement. A shapeless tree is aimless. We will illustrate how these spatial factors affect the life of Abletree.

	T	T	M	m		
	R	F	T	f		

4	14	24	34	44	54	64
e	E	f	F	t	T	r
g	R	r	H	m	M	d

Abletree was born in January, a blooming stage, with two kin signs, and is very competitive. With a wood team, he is a good fighter, capable and tenacious.

Let us examine his environment. There is a fire in the year branch and a fire alliance (formed by branches **F** and **T**) furnishing welcome sunlight and heat. Ideally, sunlight should be from the sky (the stems). Abletree has branch fire, or man-made heat, which also serves the goal, but less effectively, of course. Water is found in branch **R**, which is the equivalent of **r** in the stem, so there is rain. He has the essential ingredients for success. There are also earth signs hidden in branches **f**, **T**, and

F to anchor the tree. He is able to establish his roots in society. Good life is in order.

However, there is too much metal too close by for a young tree. Is there enough fire to control the metal? Remember, it is chilly in January and it takes a lot of heat to warm the environment. There is not enough fire in Abletree's composite to curtail the metal. The metal signs are the major fault. The key element to turn his luck around is additional fire from his luck cycle or the cosmos.

Abletree's negative signs on the year and month stems indicate poor family background and great pressure to succeed from parents who are not supportive. His favorable signs, on the day branch and in the hour position, indicate success through his own effort.

This is the life of a college professor, a great scholar, hard-working and bright. Regardless of a poor background, he fought his way single-handedly to become a professor of a prestigious university. He is always busy, trying to achieve, reflecting the constant and strong shaping effect from the metal in his system.

Let us examine the role of fire in Abletree's life. His greatest success took place during the luck period of **FH**, from age thirty-four to forty-four. Why? Stem **F** adds more sunlight to his life, while branch **H** joined **T** and **F** to form a fire trio, his most welcome breakthrough. The trio curtailed the fierce metal, creating a comfortable life.

Abletree was promoted to professor, and published about ten books during that period, becoming a celebrity in the community. He also received a few visiting professorships overseas. With the metal in his system under control, he had a very good life, with great popularity in the community, a circle of congenial and supporting friends, ample leisure, a luxurious apartment, and a nice European car.

After that period, his academic achievement quieted down, his position was threatened by some adverse political development, his health took a downturn, the number of good friends dwindled, and he was in constant apprehension over the uncertainty of his well-being in the future. Without the strong fire effect, more unrewarding hard work was on the way.

Summer

During summer, when fire dominates, sunlight is not needed. Extra water, however, is the most crucial element, to offset the heat. Metal is crucial for two reasons: To generate water and to trim the growing trees. Without metal, the tree grows aimlessly. Without water in any form, slow growth and hard life is expected. We will provide two examples of summer wood to illustrate the roles of water and fire.

T	**T**	**F**	**f**
R	**T**	**F**	**f**

This is the birth composite of Sumtree, a civil official in China. Born in a contracting stage, assisted by two kin signs, he should be tenacious and capable. Let us examine his opportunities to succeed in life.

There is only one water sign and it is weak. There is too much fire to offset the water; and, unfortunately, it is more accessible to his kin, another **T**, which needs the same crucial element to survive. His next best alternative would be a strong metal sign, which would breed some water and trim the tree. Unfortunately, there is only a small amount hidden in branch **f**.

On the other hand, there are four negative fire signs, the element Sumtree dreads most. By birth composite alone, he will have a tough life. His system has a serious fault.

Yet Sumtree was not completely out of luck. He prospered during the stem **r** period of the luck cycle. The magic touch of rain boosted his energy and curtailed the fire. It moistened the earth and nurtured the metal, which could then start trimming. As a result, he progressed in his career.

The next birth composite of a summer tree has a similar living environment with the same great need for additional water. Unfortunately, this person was influenced by additional fire during his luck cycle and became a beggar as a result.

F	**T**	**r**	**F**
T	**R**	**f**	**F**

Fall

During fall, trees mature and metal is full-grown, abounding in the cosmos. The timing is perfect for a wood self—the tree is ready to serve society and the powerful metal provides opportunities by turning the tree into furniture.

However, this is also a very delicate situation. Excessively powerful tools could result in ruthless cutting, turning the trees into useless pieces and creating frustration. Thus, the right amount of fire is needed to curtail the metal. Too much fire, on the other hand, would burn the tree.

Water is essential during September, but it has to be just right so as not to hamper the fire. The requirements vary with the system. Vigorous testing is needed to determine the key elements.

Overall, July has a more balanced environment for wood selves. August wood selves need more fire, as the metal is full-grown. September is dominated by earth, which tends to offset the influence of water. Additional water in any form is, therefore, important.

Let us illustrate how these elements work together with the birth composite of Primtree, who was the prime minister in the Ming Dynasty of China.

M	T	M	R
f	F	H	F

Primtree was born in September, well-grown and strong, ready to be harvested and to serve the community. There are two metal signs to do the job, each being sharpened and also checked in power by a yin fire in the next pillar, constantly keeping the tree in good shape, refining the self to perform, and at the same time keeping it from ruthless cutting. Water is sustained by metal to nurture the self. There is earth to support its growth. Primtree had a successful political career all his life.

With all the elements in a check-and-balance state, this system is close to equilibrium. An ideal environment produces a happy person!

To illustrate the role of fire in creating powerful metal, let us use two other extreme examples. The first belongs to Augwood, who was born in August, when metal is in its most powerful stage.

T	T	e	R
R	M	m	W

In this birth composite, **W** pairs with **m**, becoming a metal partner, and joins branch **M** to create a team, full-grown and supported by moist earth. There is not a trace of fire to curtail this powerful force. The self is constantly under ruthless cutting! He had a very frustrating life, switching frequently from job to job, and suffering from family problems. He died in his forties.

Unchecked powerful rulers often create extreme characters. Augwood was very timid. Others could be very violent. Let us examine the following example, the birth composite of Wood Dust.

R	T	T	M
M	M	M	M

This is a wood self surrounded by powerful metal in July. Wood Dust had a very frustrating life and eventually became a violent robber. Why do two similar systems turn out two opposite personalities? The dividing line depends on the strength of the self.

A weak self remains timid and hard-working. A super-strong self becomes a great achiever. Someone in the middle, boosted by favorable circumstances, might rebel. It is like being pushed into a corner. Wood Dust became a robber when strong water force from his luck cycle boosted his strength.

Winter

Winter is wet and cold. As strong water could uproot trees, extra earth is critical at this time to safeguard the tree. During November and December, in addition to yang earth, sunshine is critical to shine on the leaves, dry the moist earth, and warm the environment. Without sun, the tree ages, but hardly grows. We will explain with a typical case, the life of Wetfeet, who is a poor servant.

r	T	f	e
m	W	g	g

Wetfeet was born in December. By birth cycle, she is strong, tenacious enough to struggle and to undertake hardship. However, she doesn't have a rewarding environment.

Let us search for her two most crucial elements: yang earth and sunshine. There is a yang earth hidden in **W**, but it is soaked with water from the same sign. There is no sunshine. The yin fire, being surrounded by three moist earth signs, is too weak for any good. Instead, there is strong water at the hour stem, in the blooming stage and well-sustained. It is soaking up the earth. Wetfeet is getting all the wrong elements in a bundle!

The moist earth signs, spread all over Wetfeet's system, are rotting her roots and making her life rootless. There is no remedy for the fault! Wetfeet has no problem-solving skills. Her environment is too poor to be significantly remedied by her luck cycle or cosmic influence.

While fire is associated with intelligence, Wetfeet is not expected to be smart. The tree has dull leaves and dripping branches. She has to put up with all her problems without solution because there is no remedy. Without stable roots, she constantly worries about her livelihood, which makes her an obedient servant. The tree ages, but barely grows. There is no progress in her life. The end result is an unskilled and lowly person.

The next example, in contrast to the above, illustrates how a remedy element can change one's life.

E	T	M	F
W	H	R	M

Oak Tree was also born in a cold, wet month. The sunshine, **F**, is far from enough: it is too close to the water and too far from the self. However, there is plenty of dry earth, **E** and **H**, to block the water; and as a bonus, both elements are right next to the self—the right things in the right places—effective protection. The environment created a determined problem solver.

Oak Tree was able to maintain a comfortable life, but to prosper, he needed more help. He suddenly became a multi-millionaire during the luck period of fire and wood, which provided what he needed. The self became strong and intelligent, fulfilling Oak Tree's potential.

The t Self

Yin wood is a plant or the branches of a tree. The ultimate goal of a plant is to bloom and grow luxuriant leaves. The contributing factors are sunshine and water; the amounts needed vary with the birth time. Metal is not important, as discipline is reserved for the male, or yang wood selves.

Sunlight shines on the leaves of the yin plant, creating fame, and is crucial for all **t** selves born at any time. Without sunlight, **t** selves cannot excel. Water provides the necessary food. Rain is natural food, indicating easy success. Yang water requires irrigation, meaning that success comes from hard work. Without water in any form, hard life or pre-mature death is likely.

Spring

Spring is the season for fast growth, and the misty chilly weather makes sunlight crucial, far more important than water. This is particularly true for January and February births. As March approaches, rain is more important than sunlight. Let us illustrate with the life of Planty.

e	t	r	f
t	m	t	r

10	20	30	40	50	60	70
T	t	F	f	E	e	M
W	f	F	d	M	m	H

Planty was born in February, a blooming stage. Surrounded by three other kin signs, she is super tenacious. Is her environment supportive? There is enough water, as there are two water signs, and they are well-positioned, one right next to the self. There is also some earth to anchor the plant. Sunshine, the crucial element, is missing, however. It is the biggest fault in Planty's system.

She can survive as a competent self, hard-working, tenacious, resilient, and resourceful. Without remedy, though, she is a crawling plant in a dense bush, struggling relentlessly to reach for sunlight, with no hope to shine.

Luckily, there is great remedy on the luck cycle. Planty's crucial element, sunlight, showed up when she was thirty, as two yang fires on the same pillar, very powerful. During that ten-year period, she had a series of great, unexpected promotions in her civil service position and became the head of a division in a big city. All the glamour and power of life in the fast lane came along easily.

However, at the end of the period, the sunlight dwindled to a minimum. The cosmic year was **EW**. Powerful cosmic earth dissipated the last trace of her fire and paired with stem **r**, the water that was so crucial for her well-being. With the fire and water gone, the plant lost the essentials for a good life, and Planty became unemployed.

The next period of her luck cycle was **fd**, which is like a greenhouse for a plant. In contrast to the **FF** period, during which blessings came naturally and abundantly, as though in a valley of sun, Planty's greenhouse period brought good things on a much smaller scale after far greater effort. She had to make a humble living by working very hard.

Summer

Summer is dominated by fire. Water is the most crucial element to maintain equilibrium. Metal is needed to sustain water. In fact, summer rarely produces successful wood selves. The following illustration of Rainless indicates the importance of water for a summer plant.

e	t	m	E
t	t	f	T

7	17	27	37	47
R	r	T	t	F
F	d	M	m	H

Rainless was born in April, a growing stage. With three kin signs, he seems super strong. However, there is no water. The soil loses its support as it cracks; the plant has to struggle just to survive, without a chance to grow. This is a seriously faulty system without remedy; one of the worst. Luckily, there are two water signs in the luck cycle. We don't have to extend the luck cycle beyond the **FH** pillar. Why? It would be almost impossible for Rainless to survive the additional fire from the **FH** period.

We know Rainless can count on about ten years of good luck during the **R** and **r** periods. Remember that the magnitude of luck varies from year to year as a result of the interacting flows from the cosmos. That is, within the period, a rainy year will bring him additional good luck while an earth or fire year will strip some of his good luck.

Has Rainless's life been compatible with our theory? He was from a good family and had a happy adolescence, but he struggled through the rest of his life. Rainless was strong enough to be tenacious, surviving the good and bad times, like a desert plant, but it was a difficult and stagnant life.

Fall

Fall is not a good time for delicate plants, which have to face the threat of powerful metal. For a comfortable life, two signs are important: fire to curtail the metal, and water to mediate its excessive power. These two signs have to be positioned separately in the birth composite to avoid offsetting each other. Let us explain with the life of Fallplan.

F	**t**	**m**	**E**
R	**d**	**m**	**R**

Fallplan, a great general in China, was born in August, a contracting stage. Luckily, he had a helping kin sitting right below, and two grantors. With the right help in the right place, he became a tenacious problem solver.

However, he faced a big threat: two metal signs piled up in a pillar, in their prime stage, right next to the self. This is the basic fault in Fallplan's system. A strong fire is the best remedy, and it is not found in his birth composite.

As a result of the missing element, Fallplan remained ordinary during a large part of his life, regardless of his great ability and strong discipline. It wasn't until the **FT** and **ft** periods of his luck cylce that he achieved great fame and power. The strong fire released him from the bondage of the metal, making him free to achieve. In fact, he did become rich and famous.

Winter

Winter is a terrible time for plants. Yang earth and sunlight are both essential for comfort. Kin are welcome to share the hardship, such as absorbing the excessive water or anchoring the soggy soil. The following birth composite of Coldplant illustrates these principles.

m	t	r	R
f	t	g	F

Coldplant was born in cold December, a contracting stage. Supported by a kin close by, he was doing fine. However, his environment was too wet. He needed plenty of fire and yang earth to make a comfortable home. He was lucky enough to have both crucial elements in branch **f**, which contains **E** and **F**, and another fire in branch **F**. He had the right elements for a good life; but to prosper, his signs had to be more powerful. He settled as a small town mayor.

The F Self

Yang fire is the sun, or great heat. Its job is to heat and to shine. To be able to shine is to succeed. Since no one is comfortable staring at the glare of the sun, the best way to display its glory is through the reflection of water. Thus, yang water is the crucial element for all **F** selves to succeed.

The ideal environment for a fire self is moist and calm. A hot or windy environment could trigger a burning fire, which hurts everybody, including the self. However, moisture or water is different from rain, which blocks the sun. The sun does not shine on a rainy day or in a cloudy sky, which creates a frustrating and disappointing life for an **F** self.

A good **F** self is honest, quick-witted, and bright. Such people are also obliging, benevolent, and conforming. Many successful **F** selves are scientists and scholars, where integrity is essential. Excessive fire makes them hot-tempered and brutal. On the other hand, weak fire selves tend to be rude and obnoxious, as they try frantically to avoid attack in order to survive; there is simply no room for courtesy.

Spring

In Spring, yang fire is in its birth stage, so it is mild and growing. With wood dominating the cosmos, it is well-fueled and therefore competent enough to meet challenges. We need two other crucial elements to make a lucky system: yang water and yang metal. The job of the metal is to breed water and provide financial opportunities.

The best life is having both **R** and **M** in the stems. Having either one as stem and the other as branch is the next luckiest. With both as branches, or having only one of them, good life is likely, but there is no fame. Without water or metal in any form, one is likely to have a hard life.

During March, when powerful moist earth, **W**, dissipates heat, weakening the self, extra wood, **T**, is needed to curtail the earth. Metal must be avoided, as it hinders the function of wood. Water remains important. Let us illustrate with an example.

t	F	M	m				
d	R	T	r				

e	E	f	F	t	T	r	
g	R	r	H	m	M	d	

This system belonged to Gladfire, a prime minister in ancient China. As usual, our first step is to evaluate the self. He was born in the growing stage, fueled by two wood signs—a very competitive self. Was he born in the right place too? The two crucial signs, water and metal, are spread between stem and branch. He got the second best system for a very good life.

However, it was not perfect. Since the environment was too cold for the water to evaporate, there was no need for extra water, **r**. Metal could be excessive too, as there was no need to refill the water.

Gladfire's life events testify to our hypothesis. He greatly prospered during his **fr** and **FH** periods, when additional wood and fire curtailed the water and metal, and received high promotions.

Summer

During summer, the **F** self tends to be overly strong. It needs at least two water signs to offset the fire. Metal is important for two reasons. First, it generates water to ensure a constant supply. Second, a fire self's money sign is metal, so it is welcomed by the overly strong self.

On the other hand, summer fire can easily develop equilibrium as dominant fire. In such cases, water must be avoided, as it topples the equilibrium. In any event, a sufficient amount of moist earth would ensure a comfortable life. It mellows and inspires the fire. The competent fire also welcomes plenty of financial opportunities from the metal.

Summer **F** selves are more likely to become rich than famous, since water, the fame factor, is dwindling. Some lucky ones might get help from the luck cycle. Let us find out how water and metal affect the luck of Starlit, a successful movie star in Hong Kong.

F		**F**		e		e
M		**W**		f		f

M	m	**R**	r	**T**	t	**F**
F	d	**M**	m	**H**	r	**R**

The self is definitely overly strong, being in the blooming stage with three kin. Fortunately, remedy is on the way. There is plenty of moist earth to dissipate the excessive heat. Water signs are hidden in both **M** and **W**; metal is hidden in three of the branches—a lifetime of wealth-building potential. However, we suspect the strength of the self is ahead of its opportunities. While the number of fire signs equals those from the water and metal group, they are far different in strength. Starlit needs more water and metal to make up the difference. Her favorable elements are water and metal. Her luck cycle is predominantly water and metal. That is what we call good luck.

Fall

Fall is the contracting stage for **F** selves. Fall fire needs help from wood and other fire. Water remains important for fame, but there should be no shortage of it, as water begins to gather momentum in fall. When water becomes excessive, yang earth is needed to block it. Fall is not a good time for **F** selves to prosper. Let us find out how Hifire struggled his way to the hall of fame.

R	F	E	R
W	M	M	H

Hifire was the chief historian in China who was responsible for documenting the national history, an honorable post requiring high integrity and excellent scholarship. He was honest—his entire system consists of yang signs (remember the nature of yang flows). He was also a great problem solver. Being a weak fire self surrounded by abundant water, he achieved fame. Why and how?

Hifire possessed the key element, yang earth, which blocks the water. Its strategic location made it super effective. **E** was surrounded by year stem **R** and two **M** branches, exercising central control over the various water fronts. It created a hard-working intellectual, sophisticated in allocating resources. Branch **H** was more powerful, but less effective, due to its peripheral location. However, it was a big help, making Hifire a resourceful problem solver.

Winter

Winter is the toughest time for **F** selves, being cold, wet, and windy. It takes plenty of fire and wood, and possibly yang earth, to create a good life. One of the few favorable systems is illustrated below. It belongs to Winfire.

M	F	e	t
T	T	g	f

6	16	26	36	46	56	66
E	f	F	t	T	r	R
R	r	H	m	M	d	F

Winfire was a great general in China. Born in a contracting stage, without helpful kin, he was a weak self. He had plenty of wood, but only a little fire. There was metal to chop wood for fuel. He had all the means to make a living the hard way. To prosper, he needed additional fire from his luck cycle.

Winfire was sent to study overseas on government funds during the **F** period of his luck cycle. He graduated and worked for the government during his **H** and **t** periods. Except for a few setbacks during the **m** period, he received good promotions throughout his career and was promoted to top-ranking general during his **T** period.

The f Self

A good man-made fire is gentle, intense, and elegant; it can melt down any metal and it sharpens all tools. An ideal yin fire has to be intense, steady, and ongoing. It needs a constant fuel supply to maintain such conditions. Yang wood is always the most ideal source of fuel. Yet a tree does not burn well unless it is chopped into pieces by metal. It follows that **M** and **T** are the crucial elements for a yin fire self. For the best life, the two signs have to stand side by side at all times.

Yin wood and yin metal can also do the job, but they produce a weak and erratic fire. The self has to look for additional fuel constantly, which means hard work and a hard life. The situation is worse when there is no wood or metal at all.

Spring

During gloomy and misty spring, yin fire needs a lot of help. With **M** and **T** in proper proportion, working side by side, a sustained fire is guaranteed. During the end of the season, when fire begins to dominate the cosmos, water is needed to check the fire. The following system illustrates the subtle relationship between wood and metal.

m	f	F	T
g	m	T	M

f	E	e	M	m	R	r
t	W	f	F	d	M	m

This cosmic system belonged to Exfire, a famous prime minister who created revolutionary tax reform in China. Born in the contracting stage, he had all the help he needed. With powerful tools chopping abundant wood to fuel his life, he brilliantly lighted the tunnel, leading his people out of political chaos. His reform was a brilliant and monumental proposal. However, he never succeeded with it. His project was destroyed by his opponents.

Why didn't his good signs bring permanent success? There was too much metal chopping up the wood at high speed and fueling a fierce fire for only a brief period of time. When the wood was gone, the fire was out. For the lucky one, this should not be the end. Sadly, Exfire had a poor luck cycle.

There was no yang wood in Exfire's luck cycle. Instead, he got additional metal during the most critical period in his political career. Branch **f** and **F** provided some relief, of course. He was burned out after the **F** period, though, and his luck had run out for the rest of his life. He was stripped of power, and retired.

Summer

During summer, yin fire is vulnerable to burning itself up. Water becomes crucial to moisten the environment and keep the fire in place, providing a stable and comfortable life. Abundant metal will create great wealth, since the self is extremely competitive, able to gain in any challenge. Wood is still essential, but it should be in a moderate amount.

Additional requirements vary slightly with the months. During April, water is preferable on the branches so that it moistens the ground but doesn't extinguish the fire. During May, water is paramount in any form, as the yin fire is super strong. As it cools in June, wood resumes its important role as a source of fuel; it also checks the power of earth.

The following birth composite of Firor is a typical one.

r	f	T	F
t	m	F	R

Firor was a famous scholar, extremely brilliant. Born in May, the prime stage, with two kin, he was super competitive and overly strong. There is water in various forms to keep him in place so he can focus on achievement. He had a permanent fuel supply from **T** and tools from **m**. He had everything for a successful life, except that his tools were small. He needed to work hard.

Fall

Fall is the contracting cycle for yin fire. It needs **M** and **T** to ensure a fuel supply, and possibly **E** as the water gathers momentum. Kin is also welcome to offer a helping hand. With all these signs in proper position, good life is in order. Let us examine how they work to create a great life for Warmglow.

F	f	**m**	r			
F	g	**m**	**m**			

R	r	**T**	t	**F**	f	**E**
H	r	**R**	g	**T**	t	**W**

Warmglow is another successful movie star in Hong Kong. Being born in a growing stage, assisted by two kin, she was competitive. However, there is no wood to sustain her fire, but there is plenty of powerful metal (in the prime stage). The fault in Warmglow's system is that there are too many financial opportunities for an aging fire. Her remedy comes from the luck cycle.

It is a super luck cycle. Count the number of her most needed element, wood. There are four, a full score in a sixty-year cycle. As a bonus, they are crowded in her prime stage of life, when life's battles are toughest!

As a matter of fact, Warmglow started to prosper at the beginning of her **T** period, and increased her momentum for a long time. She had a long career as both a movie star and a singer.

Winter

Winter is the toughest time for a yin fire. It takes fire, wood, and yang earth to make a good life. We will illustrate how these elements changed the life of Unifire, a scholar with a successful and versatile career.

M	f	M	F
R	d	R	F

13	23	33	43	53	63	73
R	r	T	t	F	f	E
T	t	W	f	F	d	M

Unifire was born in November, in the void stage, and so was very weak. He survived on the assistance of kin. Wood, the most crucial element, was in limited amount, hidden in **d**, far from enough to keep a good fire burning. The key to prosperity is missing. Unifire was a competent person in a harsh environment! Only an improved environment could improve his life.

Unifire also got a full score of both wood and fire signs in his luck cycle, all crowded in his prime stage of life. A super remedy brings super luck! Let us see how his life events correspond to these signs.

Unifire was raised in a well-to-do family (good signs in the year pillar). He got a masters degree from an Ivy League school in the United States and married the daughter of a Chinese diplomat.

Right after his graduation, he worked as the state secretary in a provincial government office, and later as a diplomat. All these events happened in his period of wood (branch **t** and stem **T**), between the ages of twenty-eight and thirty-five. He benefited tremendously from the wood, enjoying a brilliant career.

Things began to take a big dive during his **W** period, when the Sino-Japanese War took place. Unifire fled to his hometown, poor and unemployed. **W** joined **R** in his birth composite to form a water alliance, flooding his base and creating more misery.

During the **t** stem period, after Japan was defeated, he moved back to the city and his life began to improve. With a few ups and downs in later years, he had a prominent career as a successful bank executive for almost thirty years, mostly under the influence of fire. His ups and downs in life can be attributed to the lack of yang wood in his birth composite to provide permanent support.

Unifire became seriously ill during his stem **E** period and the year of **ed**, when powerful earth dissipated his energy. He passed away during the winter of the same year, when water joined the hostile earth team. The feeble fire simply succumbed to fate!

Conclusion

From the above discussion, we have learned some criteria for evaluating a cosmic system. It is important to pinpoint the key element that would turn our luck around. This is the only way to accurately predict our future. Older readers have the advantage of having more life events to test the validity of such elements; younger readers have to take detailed notes during their life for a more thorough analysis. In any event, we'll strengthen our skills by moving to the next chapter.

*Figure 7A. The **T** Self*

Lunar Birth Month	*Your Crucial Elements	Explanation
T January	**F, r**	Sunlight and rain to nurture young plants; substituted with **f** and **R**: success by hard work.
t February	**M, e, r**	Metal to trim growing trees, earth to support extending roots; rain essential.
W March	**M, f, r**	Man-made fire to sharpen the tool for trimming the growing branches; rain to water roots.
f April	**r, f, M**	More rain to counter the hot weather; sharp tools important for trimming growing branches.
F May	**r, f, M**	Principles of month **f** apply.
d June	**r, f, M**	Principles of month **f** apply.
M July	**M, f, R**	Sharp tool to trim mature trees; rain no longer important; **R** to channel excessive metal.
m August	**f, F, M**	Extra fire to curtail excessive metal from ruthless cutting; sharp tool for proper harvesting.
H September	**M, f, R**	Sharp tool for trimming; ground water to sustain wood.
r October	**f, F, M**	Water abundant in cosmos; extra fire to offset the cold weather.
R November	**f, F, M**	Principles of month **r** apply.
g December	**f, F, M**	Principles of month **r** apply.

* All signs refer to stems or their equivalents in the branches.

*Figure 7B. The **t** Self*

Lunar Birth Month	* Your Crucial Elements	Explanation
T January	**F, r**	Sunlight and rain to nurture young plants; **r** to promote wealth; **F** to promote fame.
t February	**F, r**	Principles of month **T** apply.
W March	**r, F**	Rain is more important than sunlight as the weather gets warmer.
f April	**r, m**	Rain and metal work together to offset the influence of increasing fire and earth.
F May	**r, F**	Rain and sunlight to nurture growing crops, but the two signs must be separated.
d June	**r, F**	Principles of month **F** apply.
M July	**F, r, E**	Extra fire to curtail growing metal influence and to protect plants; rain remains important.
m August	**r, f, F**	Rain remains important; extra fire to curtail the metal.
H September	**r, m**	Environment is hot and dry, so rain remains important; **m** to ensure water supply.
r October	**F, E**	Sunlight to counter the cold winter weather; **E** to keep floods from uprooting plants.
R November	**F, E**	Principles of month **r** apply.
g December	**F, E**	Principles of month **r** apply.

* All signs refer to stems or their equivalents in the branches.

*Figure 7C. The **F** Self*

Lunar Birth Month	* Your Crucial Elements	Explanation
T January	**R, M**	**R** is basic for all **F** selves; **M** to chop the abundant wood to fuel the fire.
t February	**R, M**	Principles of month **T** apply.
W March	**R, T**	Additional **T** to keep dominant earth from blocking the fire; **R** to reflect sunlight.
f April	**R, M**	**R** to provide a moist environment to prevent **F** from burning; **M** to ensure watersupply.
F May	**R, M**	Principles of month **f** apply.
d June	**R, M**	Principles of month **f** apply.
M July	**R, E**	**R** to reflect sunlight; **E** to keep excessive water from flooding.
m August	**R, F**	**R** to reflect sunlight; kin to boost the energy of the contracting fire.
H September	**T, R**	**T** to check the strong earth; **R** to reflect the sunlight.
r October	**T, E** **M, R**	**T** and **M** to fuel the waning fire; **E** to check the excessive water; **R** to reflect the sunlight.
R November	**R, E**	**R** to reflect sunlight; **E** to guide the water and block flooding.
g December	**R, T**	**R** to reflect sunlight; **T** to check the earth influence.

* All signs refer to stems or their equivalents in the branches.

*Figure 7D. The **f** Self*

Lunar Birth Month	* Your Crucial Elements	Explanation
T January	**T, M**	Metal to chop trees to fuel the yin fire.
t February	**T, M**	Principles of month **T** apply.
W March	**T, M**	Additional **T** to offset strong earth influence; **M** remains important.
f April	**T, M**	Extra metal to function as both a tool and money sign for the strong yin fire.
F May	**R, M, r**	Principles of month **f** apply; extra water to moisten the super hot environment.
d June	**T, M, R**	Extra wood to offset the earth influence and provide fuel; **R** to moisten dry summer earth.
M July	**T, M** **F, E**	**T** and **M** to provide fuel; **F** to add energy to the weak fire; **E** to check excessive water.
m August	**T, M** **F, E**	Principles of month **M** apply.
H September	**T, M, E**	Principles of month **M** apply; no F needed as environment is hot.
r October	**T, M**	**T** and **M** to provide fuel.
R November	**T, M, E**	Principles of month **r** apply; **E** needed in case of excessive water.
g December	**T, M, E**	Principles of month **R** apply.

* All signs refer to stems or their equivalents in the branches.

CHAPTER 8

Earth, Metal, and Water Selves

In this chapter we will analyze earth, metal, and water selves, providing models of each.

The E Self

Yang earth is dry by nature. Mixed with water, it is also moist. Good earth is productive, and it should be moist, warm, rich in nutrients and organisms, and porous enough for roots to breathe and water to circulate. To achieve this goal, the system first requires water and fire. Creating porous soil requires tree roots and minerals (metal). Tree roots comb through the earth; mineral crystals create pores in the soil and enlighten it, representing inspiration and education.

Plants grow slowly without sunlight, while excessive sunlight kills the plants. The result is poverty. Excessive water also destroys the plants, as it separates the roots from the soil, depriving it of access to food. Dry and barren soil results in very hard life, with no hope of succeeding. The need of the soil varies with the months, which we will discuss below.

Spring

During January and February, as fast-growing tree roots loosen the soil, weakening it, kin are welcome to keep the soil intact. In this season, when trees are growing, metal must be avoided, as it, too, loosens the earth with its crystals and minerals. Too much wood and metal together would loosen the earth too much. Sunlight is needed to warm the cold earth. Rain is not critical.

March is rich with earth, so the self is strong (remember that earth rules the last month of each season). Kin must be avoided to protect the self from overloading. Sunlight is essential to enliven the earth. Extra trees are welcome to comb the thick soil. Rain is beneficial, but not critical. The birth composite of Great Earth illustrates how these principles interact.

M	**E**	**M**	**F**
M	**W**	**T**	**T**

Born in a growing stage, with a kin right below and three yang fires (two hidden in branch **T**) as grantors, the self was very competitive. How challenging is the environment for this able earth?

There are plenty of trees and metal spread all over the birth composite to enlighten the soil, indicating a lifetime of educational opportunities. Fire (two hidden in **T**) keeps the earth warm, while water in branches **M** and **W** moisten the soil. Our next question: Are the signs in the right proportion?

Wood seems to be excessive, as there are two of them in the prime stage. Luckily, there is plenty of metal to keep them in check. Is metal in oversupply too? It could be, since there are three of them. However, there are three fire signs too. Is fire getting too strong? There is moist earth and water. A state of interlocking balance exists, providing a secure base for steady progress and creating great fortune.

Summer

During summer, substantial water is needed to offset the great heat. Earth selves born in summer can take in water in all forms—rain (from the stem) or irrigation (from the branch). The compact heavy earth of June prefers rain, as it does not respond well to irrigation. Stiff earth also needs combing. Since metal is super weak during the hot season, wood is more desirable. Sunshine should be moderate. Let us illustrate with the birth composite of Primearth, a prime minister of China.

R	E	T	m
R	T	F	d

Born in the prime stage, supported by a powerful grantor, **F**, and assisted by three hidden kin signs in branches **T**, **F**, and **d**, Primearth is compact and stiff, not wise enough. Luckily, there is a remedy—plenty of trees and some metal to enlighten him, and water from both stem and branch to moisten the earth. And, best of all, the most crucial element, water, is far away from the strong summer fire to avoid evaporation, and it is most accessible to the self. This system commands great fortune. Primearth was born at the right hour!

Fall

During fall, as metal abounds in the cosmos, there is no need for additional metal. Wood is not important for July or August births. As the weather gets cooler, sunshine gradually resumes its importance. Rain is preferred. September births need more trees. Let us illustrate.

	E		E		R		T
	F		W		M		R

m	M	e	E	f	F	t
d	F	f	W	t	T	g

This was the life of Earthwin, a female movie star in Taiwan. Born in the contracting stage, assisted by a grantor and kin, she should be strong. However, there is an unfortunate development. Branches **R**, **M**, and **W** form a water trio, turning her kin, **W**, into water. The environment is close to flooding—it spells hard life.

Earthwin needed additional earth to block the flood, wood to channel the excessive water, and a lot of fire to firm the earth and warm up the environment. Luckily, she got strong support from her luck cycle. Starting with branch **F**, all the way to the end, every sign is either earth, wood, or fire, her most needed elements. She was a self-made achiever.

Winter

Winter births need plenty of sunlight and trees. Additional yang earth is welcome to keep it intact. Only firm earth can achieve fame. Without any of these elements, hard life is in the picture. Let us see how the elements work together in Cold Earth's system.

E	E	m	f			
F	R	r	f			

M	e	E	f	F	t	T
H	m	M	d	F	f	W

Cold Earth was born in the contracting stage. With a kin and some fire to firm him up, he had help. He could make a good living with hard work, but his environment was too wet. There are two water signs, in their prime stage, defeating the two feeble fire signs (remember that fire is weakest in winter). He definitely needed more fire.

Cold Earth remained unproductive for a long time, wasting his time just fighting to stay intact. His life began to improve during the **fd** period, when extra fire and wood (**d** and **r** formed a wood alliance) boosted his energy. His greatest luck, however, started with the onset of the powerful fire pillars, **fd** and **FF**. Those twenty years were a rapid wealth-building process for Cold Earth.

A powerful remedy for a serious fault always brings great luck. It is always a blessing to have a distinctively faulty system amended by the right remedy.

The e Self

Yin earth is moist and lumpy. Like yang earth, it needs sunlight, tree roots, and metal to stay productive. Sunlight is almost always crucial for all births, except those in mid-summer. Yang water is to be avoided at all times, as it might disintegrate the delicate yin earth. Any birth composite with a yang water sign has to be checked by trees or yang earth. The requirements vary with the seasons. We will discuss this below.

Spring

In January and February, when soil is soaked with water, yin earth needs sunshine to firm it up and metal to curtail wood from hurting it. During March, as earth builds up, trees become the most important.

The following cosmic system of Right Earth, a cabinet head in China, meets most of the requirements.

	T		e		F		T	
	R		g		T		R	
f	E		e		M	m	R	r
t	W		f		F	d	M	m

Born in January, in the contracting stage, assisted by kin **g**, and helped by grantor **F**, he was doing fine. In his environment, we find crucial fire supported by two yang wood signs, strong and steady. There is no yang water for him to worry about. Branch **R** is actually rain (remember that the stem equivalent of branch **R** is **r**). Metal, hidden in **g**, educates the self. Right Earth had all the essential elements to be a productive person.

Basically, this is a good system, except that water seems to be excessive. Right Earth could take in more fire, wood, and earth to enhance his environment. Fortunately, his luck cycle provides what he needs. He progressed easily to his ultimate goal: becoming a cabinet head.

Summer

Rain is most important for summer births, as cracking soil is not productive. When the self has to rely on metal alone to breed rain, the person has to work very hard for small gain. The life of Lady Luck, who married a top-ranking civil official, was close to ideal.

t	e	r	**F**
r	**r**	**f**	**M**

Born in the prime stage, assisted by a hidden kin and two powerful summer fire signs, her grantors, Lady Luck was very strong. However, she had a matching environment for her energy. There were two metal signs in the year and month branches (one hidden in **f**) and three wood signs (two hidden in each **r** branch). We can be sure Lady Luck had opportunities for education. There were three water signs moistening the dry soil, enriching her.

Lady Luck was mellow, wise, and graceful. She effortlessly maintained her good life with sophistication. As a bonus, her ruler, **T**, is found in branch **r** (which contains **R** and **T**), and is well-sustained by water, indicating a prosperous and progressing spouse (remember that in a woman's chart, the ruler represents the spouse). It is also in the right spot, the day branch, where one's spouse should be. Since this sign also happens to contain her favorable elements, a wealthy and supportive spouse is indicated.

Fall

During fall, as weather gets cooler, sunshine resumes its importance. While the soil is already porous as a result of powerful metal influence, extra metal could do more harm. September births, as usual, need extra wood to check the thick earth. With every element in order, perfect life is likely.

Earth selves born in the fall tend to be very smart, as full-grown metal is extremely enlightening. Unchecked, a person could become very cunning. Holloway's system is a typical example of overwhelming metal influence.

	T	e	**R**	e			
	H	m	**M**	f			
m	**M**	e	**E**	f	**F**	t	
d	**F**	f	**W**	t	**T**	g	

Holloway was very cunning and ambitious. However, he was too clever for his own good. Born in a time when a king was required to be the heir of a king, he dreamed of making himself one without birthright. To fulfill his goal, he harmed and destroyed many innocent civil officials who were loyal to the king. He even threatened the life of the emperor. His scheme, however, was not supported by his luck cycle, and he was finally executed by the emperor.

Let us examine how the elements in Holloway's system interplayed to create such a life. He was born in a growing stage with four kin signs (three hidden in the branches) scattered throughout the birth composite—it was a troop, able to meet great challenges. Strong selves are aggressive and ambitious.

However, Holloway's environment did not support his ambition. There was a powerful metal trio, plus more metal in the **f** branch, severely undermining him. There was not enough fire or water to check the metal, and its overwhelming and inspiring effect produced a passion for conspiracy. This metal produced a very secretive, cunning, and manipulative person, forever engaging in conspiracy. Holloway enjoyed prolonged success because he had a long period of good luck, starting with branch **F** all the way to stem **f**—all signs were exclusively earth or fire, supplying extra help and energy.

With the disappearance of fire and earth, he failed to maintain his equilibrium. He died in the **t** period when the additional wood collapsed the hollow earth shell.

Winter

During the wet winter months, water in any form is to be dreaded, as it dilutes the earth and eventually destroys it. Sunshine is crucial to warm and firm up the soggy soil. Wood is essential to channel the excessive water. Yang earth might be needed to block the oncoming water in severe cases. Let us find out how sunlight changed the life of Wetearth.

T	e	r	R
H	g	g	M

Born in a contracting stage, surrounded by three kin signs, Wetearth was patient, tenacious, and able to endure hardship. However, the environment was too wet, soaking Wetearth and disintegrating his system. There was no hope for succeeding without additional help.

His crucial elements are on the hour pillar, making him a late bloomer. Wetearth finally prospered during the sunlight period. Wise Chinese do not judge people by their current status!

The M Self

Yang metal includes metal ore, finished metal, metal appliances, and heavy tools such as an axe. It is also the source of yin metal. Ideal yang metal is shiny, sharp, and solid. What makes metal shine is the flushing effect of running water—stem **R**. What sharpens metal into a good tool is yin fire, intense heat—stem **f**, also hidden in some branches, of course. A solid **M** self is mature or well-grown. There are several ways to produce solid yang metal. The most ideal way is to be born in the blooming stage. Otherwise, solid metal must be well-bred and well-nourished, such as being sustained by a good grantor (moist earth) or kin.

Wood signifies the money sign for metal, since the axe can chop down trees for trade; it therefore makes a competitive **M** self rich. The proper amount of yin fire in the system is the ticket to fame, since it sharpens the sword, which conquers! A birth composite with such elements in good order brings good fortune.

M selves possessing the above crucial elements should reflect the following qualities: being erect and having a somewhat square face and vibrating voice resembling the sound issued by a piece of vibrating metal. They are also fair and obliging, with high integrity, and are quick and sharp in decision making. They are loyal friends and make wonderful executives and generals.

Overly strong metal selves without water or fire to check them can become brutal and abusive in power, and indulgent in vices. Most are big spenders. Those overloaded with earth tend to have respiratory problems or dizziness, and will never shine. Weak metal with plenty of wood is likely to labor for nothing because their feeble tool can never chop down anything, regardless of how hard they try.

Spring

In January, the cold soil does not nurture metal, and the best survival tactic for **M** selves is to reach out for sunlight. To do this, there must be tree roots, **T**, creating as much open space in the soil as possible. Sunlight, **F**, is equally important. Without **T**, the metal will be buried in a poor environment, and a lowly life is certain. Without **F** to provide a livable base, metal will not grow.

In February, as **M** gets stronger, three elements must work together to make the metal a strong tool: **T**, **M**, and **f**. Extra **M** chops the trees to make fire. A birth with these elements in the stems will be rich and famous. When **f** is replaced by **F**, success comes by hard work, as winter sunlight is not intense enough to make sharp tools. When wood and metal dominate the birth composite, great wealth is possible.

Being strong and being sharp are different. Being a strong and competitive metal self, one can diligently chop down plenty of wood and sell it to accumulate wealth. However, to chop down the hard wood of exceptional quality, the tool has to be sharp. Without an intense flame, the task can never be achieved.

Yang wood is the best friend of people with March births. Trees loosen the strong March earth so water can run clearly over the metal, cleaning it and making it shine. **T** represents the effort in striving for advancement. As a matter of fact, a March **M** self with a **T** is a great problem solver. **f** helps to acquire fame. The life of Big Coin illustrates some of these principles.

t	**M**	t	r
m	**W**	t	**f**

Big Coin is a multi-millionaire in Asia. Born in the growing stage, assisted by two kin signs (one hidden in branch **f**), and a grantor, **W**, he is super healthy and competitive. There are three wood signs in the blooming stage, spread over the composite. They provide a lifetime of rich financial opportunities. Money comes easily and naturally to Big Coin from various sources, as plants, **t** (the money sign for **M**), surround the self and create a fortunate pairing, **tM**, with the self.

Big Coin also has a tendency to sacrifice fame for financial gain. How can we tell? There is no yin fire to sharpen the tool. The only fire sign, branch **f**, joins his kin to form a metal alliance, making more metal tools. He does not have the patience for sharpening the tool. All he wants to do is use the available tools to chop all the wood at his disposal, as much and as quickly as possible, to accumulate wealth.

Summer

Summer is the toughest time for metal, as great heat can melt it down. Shielding from this great heat is of top priority to maintain a comfortable life. Moist earth, the natural shield for metal, is hard to come by in dry summer, so water is necessary to moisten the earth. Kin are welcome to share the hardship.

During June, trees are needed to loosen the earth for metal to breathe and shine. Moderate heat is welcome as the weather gets cooler and the metal gets stronger.

The life of Hot Iron, a great general, illustrates how the crucial elements enhance one's luck.

	E	M	F	R	
	T	T	F	F	
f	E	e	M	m	R	r
d	M	m	H	r	R	g

There are three blooming fires in this birth composite, too much for a weak summer metal. Poor Hot Iron had a miserable life! All the earth hidden in the branches is dry, and the water sign is not strong enough to moisten it. The key for survival is more water and moist earth.

Luckily, Hot Iron got the right remedy for the fault. He has an amazingly supportive luck cycle. Except for a relatively difficult childhood, and a few years in the **H** period, he got protection from additional metal and moist earth. His best luck, of course, started with branch **r** and continued all the way to the end of his life.

Hot Iron, however, always had to work hard to earn everything. In fact, this is the typical system of a hard worker.

Fall

Fall is the prime stage for metal, when it is well-grown and solid, the best quality for the best tool. It can take in plenty of strong yin fire and some wood to sustain the fire. Such a combination is the ticket to success. Excessive water would hamper the fire in sharpening the tool, rendering the self an ordinary person.

However, when fire is not strong enough to make a tool, water becomes the next best alternative—to shine the metal. Such a self could shine (by holding a high position), but never conquer (will have no great achievement). Without fire or water, the self could be restless, indulging in vices and becoming useless.

As the weather gets cooler in August, sunlight is needed in addition to the yin fire to warm the environment. In September, more trees are needed to check the earth power. We will illustrate the effects of these elements with a perfect example from Super Ore.

F	M	f	m
R	F	m	t

F	t	T	r	R	m	M
M	d	F	f	W	t	T

Super Ore was a great emperor in the Ching dynasty. He reigned for forty years in great prosperity and peace. He had a wonderful life and great fun. There were, of course, some unique features in his birth composite responsible for such great fortune, which are too advanced for this book. Its basic structure, however, verifies our theory.

Being born in a prime stage and assisted by two kin signs, the self was super strong. However, the perfect remedy was right in the birth composite itself. Water, in moderate amount, calmed the overloaded metal self without putting out the fire he needed; sunshine was right next to him, warming him. Best of all, there were two yin fires (one in branch **F**) right next to Super Ore to sharpen him into a marvelous tool.

This marvelous tool could conquer any and all the wood. Thus, his next crucial element was wood. Except for a brief time during the **RW** period, his entire life was supported by good luck, with all the wood and fire signs he needed most. Super Ore did have some hard times, including a fight against the invasion of the barbarians, but overall he had a super life.

Winter

The power of metal declines as winter approaches. More hard work is needed to succeed. Sunshine comes first in order to provide a warm home. Yang wood is always welcome. Yang earth might be needed to block roaring water, and it should be in the branch.

Let us see how sunshine, the magic ingredient, made a world of difference in Frident's life. The following cosmic system belongs to a president in the western world.

F	M	r	R	
H	T	g	R	

9	19	29	39	49	59	69
T	t	F	f	E	e	M
T	t	W	f	F	d	M

Like most great men, Frident was a great problem solver. Such people usually have a faulty system with the key remedy appearing sometime in their life. Most of them also tend to have a poor start and gradually achieve their goal.

Frident was yang metal born in a cold, wet environment. Water, the last thing he needed, came in a team of three, in the blooming stage, all ganged up in one spot. Unity is strength! Poor Frident was constantly washed by icy water.

However, there was a solution to turn his luck around—two fortunate pairings in the branches. **R** and **g** become earth, eliminating one water and adding more earth to the environment to fight the water. **T** and **H** become a fire alliance, maximizing the fire he needed. The best remedy to a messy problem.

With fire warming his environment and a strong grantor (the earth team) protecting him from the cold water, Frident was able to grow in a relatively comfortable environment and put up a good fight against all his problems. He needed a lot more fire to prosper.

Frident's luck cycle rewarded his hard work. The first thirty years of his life, with dominant wood gradually draining the excessive water in his environment, was a tedious process of problem solving. He was slowly improving his life, but was never sharp enough to chop the wood for financial gain. There was simply not enough fire.

Starting with the **FW** period, with extra fire, his career took an upward swing. It gathered momentum during the following period, **ff**, beginning at the age of thirty-nine. The additional man-made fire made him a sharp sword. He became the vice president of the country.

Frident reached the peak of his career during the branch **F** period, when yang fire joined with **T** and **H** in the birth composite to form a fire trio, the most powerful fire he could get. This magic fire turned him into a super sword. He was elected president. Frident retired during his branch **d** period, when the fire dwindled and more earth entered his system.

The m Self

Yin metal is refined metal, such as ornaments and small tools. Good yin metal is sleek, shiny, and solid. Many **m** selves are trim and elegant people. Since the refining process is not needed, yin fire is not important. In fact, it does more harm than good, particularly for summer births. Excessive yin fire spells a hectic life.

The remedy for excessive fire is moist earth. It absorbs the heat and shields the metal. This remedy makes the self a very disciplined and capable person, able to turn adversity into achievement and challenges into blessings. However, the challenge will never be easy.

Yin fire is welcome only when there is too much metal in the birth composite, causing competition between siblings. Yin fire in this case keeps the kin in control so that the resources are kept intact for the self, an effective way to safeguard assets.

Yang water, such as rivers and cascades, is the best element to shine yin metal. Yin water, such as rain, comes next. Without water, yin metal can never hold high positions. Sunlight is necessary to warm the living base during cold months.

Regardless of how essential an element is, the amount must be right, and it must be in the right position. Excessive water will sink delicate metal; excessive earth buries it, creating premature death or frustrating life, depending on the amount of earth. Excessive sunlight creates hectic life.

Spring

During spring, weak yin metal needs sunlight and earth to nurture it. Yang metal, like a big brother, is welcome for support, checking the growth of trees as well.

The following birth composite, of an opera singer, came close to the requirements. There is plenty of earth in **d** and **E**, and some hidden in branch **T**, to nurture the metal. Sunshine is sufficient to warm the environment. Branch **M** contains the yang water necessary for fame, and is also kin for additional help.

The fault is having too much wood undermining the growing base and not enough metal to check it. There are too many financial opportunities for the weak self.

F	m	E	t
M	d	T	t

Summer

The biggest enemy of summer selves is heat. It is worst in April, when yin fire reaches its climax. Water in all forms is most welcome. **M** is also a big plus.

As June approaches, extra trees are needed to counter the overwhelming earth. **M** is still desirable, as it adds a fighting edge, but it has to be positioned separately from **T** to avoid hurting the wood. Yin earth is to be dreaded for two reasons: the cosmos already has an excessive amount, and it has a tendency to pair with **T**, eliminating its function.

Let us examine how these elements interact in Talentie's career.

R	m	T	m
W	m	F	m

She was a rich and famous movie star with a long entertainment career that included singing and acting. She was born in May, the climax of summer. Fortunately, she had only one fire sign in her system. She was nurtured by moist earth, **W**. Her fame factor, **R**, is accessible and strong. With the help of three kin signs, she is very tenacious and determined to succeed.

This is a well-coordinated system. However, it could use some enhancement. As an entertainer, she needs more water to shine and to be creative. The metal is too strong, depriving her of more financial opportunities.

Fall

Yin metal becomes super competitive in fall. Its biggest enemy is earth, which keeps the mature metal from getting off the ground to serve society. Earth also muddies the water, depriving the metal of a clean and much-needed bath.

On the other hand, water begins to gather momentum in fall, and it tends to become excessive. Its constant shining process can create a wasteful life. The self tends to aim high without ever accomplishing anything. The effort ends in vanity unless there is yang earth to check the water. Wood provides great financial opportunities, which are the most welcome blessing for mature metal. A fall metal succeeds easily in life.

Julmet was one in the lucky group. He was a state governor in China, competent and well-respected. Born in July as mature metal, he was super competitive.

r	m	R	T
f	t	M	F

With three water signs (one hidden in branch **M**), Julmet had more water than he needed to achieve fame. There were two wood signs to channel the slightly excessive water, correcting the fault. Fire, one at each end of the environment, was enough to warm his base.

Yin wood, his money sign, was right below the self, accessible and under control. It also indicated a rich spouse, as it was sitting in the spouse position. Yang wood on the year stem indicates a wealthy and supporting family. Julmet's water was crystal clear and clean; the environment was warm. He was both self-reliant and well-supported by his family. He had a good life.

Winter

During winter, when water dominates, no extra water is needed by the **m** self. Sunshine, however, is most important to maintain a comfortable life. It is terrible to be washed constantly by freezing water. Yang earth and strong wood are needed to check the water. Kin are also welcome.

The following cosmic system, Big Hat's, illustrates the importance of sunshine for a winter metal.

	F		**m**		**e**		**t**	
	M		**r**		**g**		**d**	

E	**f**	**F**	**t**	**T**	**r**	**R**
R	**r**	**H**	**m**	**M**	**d**	**F**

Big Hat was a prime minister who held a powerful position in two different dynasties. Born in the growing stage, he was fortunate to have three grantors and a kin, making him very competitive. There was wood to stabilize the earth and channel the water. Sunshine was present, but it was not enough, as it was not supported.

This is the system of a capable person in an uncomfortable environment. He had all the right elements, but his environment was too cold for him to be happy. Big Hat's peak achievement took place during the **FH**, **tm**, and **TM** periods, when fire provided the warmth he needed to improve his home and kin boosted his fighting edge. He enjoyed a long period of high position and prosperity. His downturn came during the water period. Additional earth and water dissipated his limited sunshine, his key for good luck. Big Hat retired in his hometown. He was, however, offered another high position from the government in the new dynasty during the branch **F** period, providing a very happy ending to his life.

The R Self

Water flows, moves, takes many forms, and comes in many colors. Yang water includes all forms of ground water, such as oceans, rivers, and wells, to name a few. Yin water is basically rain. Its colors include different shades of blue, green, gray, and black. It can be dynamic and powerful, or deadly tranquil. The bottom line: water is amazingly flexible, changeable, and creative—a symbol of wisdom!

Ideal water is free-flowing, clear, glittering, and delightfully warm. Free-flowing water is creative—it indicates a good artist or writer. Clean water is intelligent (a clear mind). Glittering water is associated with fame. Because of their flexibility, water selves make good managers.

Stagnant or frozen water is unproductive. Roaring water rolls aimlessly, resulting in a restless life. Muddy water creates a confused mind, distractions, frustration, and/or physical disorder.

How do we create good water? Sunshine keeps water aglitter, warm, and alive. Yang wood calms roaring water. Yang earth guides the flow and blocks flooding.

The biggest challenge for water selves is to stay clear and clean. Their biggest enemy is yin earth, which muddies the flow. Metal and wood are the basic elements for creating clear water. Tree roots anchor the earth, while metal crystals filter the water.

Spring

Metal is most important for spring births, as dominant wood absorbs too much water, weakening the self. Metal, a water breeder, is essential for replenishing the water supply. Sunshine is crucial for comfort. Yang earth is crucial for confining the flow into one channel, as weak water tends to meander or develop tributaries in soggy soil—it helps the self focus on a goal.

Let us illustrate how these flows created a good life for Lucky Flow, a prime minister in China.

m	R	R	f
f	W	T	r

Lucky Flow, born in January, a contracting stage, was lucky to have helpful kin to provide additional water supply, making him very competitive.
There was yang earth, hidden in branch **f**, to guide the flow and keep it
from meandering. Fire on both ends of the environment, and hidden in
T, produced warm and glittering water. **m**, on hour stem and hidden in
branch **f**, performed a filtering effect.

With all the crucial elements working together, the water was clear,
free-flowing, well-guided, and glittering. It produced a healthy, intelligent,
disciplined, and competitive self, capable of achieving fame and wealth.

Summer

Summer is rich in fire. As excessive fire evaporates water, additional water
is most welcome; the more the better. Metal, a crucial element, is of little
help, as it is too weak in the summer. During June, trees are needed to
check the earth. Throughout the season, earth must be avoided, as it
hampers the movement of water.

Summer births rely heavily on the luck cycle for success in life. The
water or metal from the luck cycle does not reflect the nature of the season;
its strength depends on pillar structure only. By all means, these elements
in the luck cycle are always stronger than the summer water or metal found
in the birth composite.

Let us see how abundant water made Riverfull a great leader. He was
a great governor, leading his people through a long period of prosperity
and peace.

| | R | R | F | R | |
| | T | W | F | W | |

| f | E | e | M | m | R | r |
| f | M | m | W | r | R | g |

Born in the hottest month with two fires in one pillar, Riverfull had abundant opportunities for wealth and fame. Was he capable of capitalizing on
such opportunities? It all depended on his strength. Let us count the water
signs. The self was sitting on a reservoir, well-supported. There are two

more water signs on the stems (excluding the self), and one more hidden in the year branch. They are spread all over the birth composite, indicating a lifetime of luck with the right help. Riverfull was a capable self with commensurate opportunities for achievement. Is his a perfect system?

There was an obvious drawback: there are two earth signs he did not need, and there is not sufficient wood to check it. Any additional earth from the luck cycle or the cosmos would put him off guard, unable to make good decisions.

As a result, he had quite a few disastrous setbacks in his life, including a brief, wrongful imprisonment. He was able to turn things around as a result of his dynamic ability. His mind, however, is not constantly clear, being particularly vulnerable when earth dominates the cosmos and hinders him from clear thinking.

Fortunately, he had a supportive luck cycle dominated by water and metal, which helped filter the water. The **mr** period, with both metal and wood (**T** in branch **r**) purifying his system, became the best part of his life. His vulnerable periods were **e** and **W**.

Fall

During fall, water begins to grow and metal matures. A fall water self is, therefore, likely to be clear-minded and competitive. Additional wood and metal would make a perfect life.

The birth composite of Roaring Water illustrates the coordinated effects of these elements. He was one of the few contributing founders of modern China—dynamic, dedicated, and visionary.

R	R	E	R
T	T	M	F

Born in a growing stage with three kin signs, all strong, and a powerful grantor, Roaring Water was overly strong. He was healthy and energetic, and tended to overact at times. To help correct this fault, **E** exercised central control over the three water signs (one in branch **M**)—strenuous and effective. There was plenty of wood to calm the self, and luckily, no moist earth to muddy the clean flow. The system produced a balanced self with high integrity.

Winter

During winter, water dominates the cosmos. **T** or **t**, as a rule, is always welcome to channel the excessive water. Yang earth is needed to guide the flow. Sunlight is the ticket to success; it keeps the water aglitter, and above all, moving. Freezing water spells stagnant or confined lives. We will explain how these principles work together with an example.

t	R	R	R
f	W	R	W

3	13	23	33	43
r	T	t	F	f
g	T	t	W	f

This is the composite of Icy River, a great general in the Sino-Japanese War. Born in the prime stage with three kin, the self was overly strong. He needed plenty of wood, yang earth, and sunlight for a good life. His system had the crucial elements, but all were of limited strength. A yang earth, hidden in branch **f,** struggled alone to fight a strenuous battle against the roaring water. Sunlight, also hidden in branch **f,** was too feeble to bring prosperity. His only wood was not well-sustained. He relied heavily on his luck cycle.

The best part of Icy River's life was between ages thirteen and thirty-eight, during the periods of **TT**, **tt**, and **F**. His peak achievement was accomplished during the **F** period, when strong sunlight melted the freezing water for action, resulting in a series of great promotions in his military service.

Icy River was stripped of military power during his **W** period, in the year of **rm**. Moist earth muddied the water, producing confusion and setbacks. Additional water from the cosmos created floods in his life, which translated into disasters. After a temporary setback, Icy River had a very comfortable retirement during the **ff** period, when fire replaced earth and water.

The r Self

Yin water includes rain, drizzle, snow, fog, and other forms of moisture from the atmosphere. Like yang water, it has to be clean, clear, free-flowing, and warm. Sunshine is still the fame factor. Most yin water selves are also artists. A healthy yin plant in the birth composite is the ticket to success in art.

Spring

During spring, when bountiful plants drain the earth's water supply, yang metal becomes most crucial. It does two important things: replenishes the water supply and reduces plants by pairing up with some of them to keep the water intact. Sunshine is important for comfort. As March approaches, more trees are essential for keeping the earth from muddying up the water. We will illustrate with Rainy's system below.

M	r	e	M
M	m	t	R

Rainy was born in February, a growing stage. With two kin signs and a few good grantors, he was doing fine. There is wood to check the earth and metal to filter the water. In fact, Rainy was very healthy, capable, and intelligent. How do we identify all these qualities? A well-supported self is healthy (one more **R** in branch **M**). An **r** self with strong yin wood is likely to be wise and talented. Rainy's water was very clear (three **M** and one **m**).

However, Rainy's **e**, which could muddy the water, is too close by. Luckily, he had the right remedy in the right position: **t**, in its blooming stage, is keeping a tight control on the earth, making Rainy a great problem solver.

Rainy's next urgent problem was the absence of sunlight. The water did not glitter. Luckily, help was on the way. He became a cabinet head in the national government during his fire period—a big success created by the right remedy.

Summer

Summer births, like yang water, need plenty of help from both water and metal. However, there are a few rare optimal moments, which have produced a few great **r** selves. Lukrain was one of the lucky few. He was a general.

T		r		e		T	
T		g		f		F	

M	m	R	r	T	t	F
F	d	M	m	H	r	R

At first sight, this looks like a poor birth composite. Lukrain was born at such a hard time, and instead of all the water he needed, he got wood, fire and worst of all, two moist earth signs. How could the feeble water survive?

There were some magic formulas at work. Year stem **T** paired up with **e**, eliminating one moist earth. In the branches, **g** and **f** formed a metal alliance, which became a powerful water breeder. At the same time, both fire and earth signs lost their original natures and functions. There was no more moist earth left, and less fire to deal with.

Lukrain had the best solution for most of his problems, but he was not ready to prosper. The lessons he learned from his fight against adversity would bring him success. He became a great general during the periods of **RM** and **rm**, when additional metal and water boosted his winning edge. The case clearly illustrates the importance of kin and grantors for a summer water. Wise men judge people on their potential!

Fall

Water begins to grow during fall. With its grantor, metal, maturing, the **r** self has great potential to succeed. Sunlight resumes its importance. As September approaches, the self needs more wood to check the earth. The life of a president of modern China sheds some light on these principles.

F		r		F		t
W		m		H		t

t	T	r	R	m	M	e
m	M	d	F	f	W	m

Bright Rain was born in September, when earth dominates; he needed help. There was sufficient wood and metal to clear the water. Sunlight was abundant, providing ample financial opportunities. However, there was no kin or grantor. Bright Rain had more opportunities than he could handle.

Fortunately, he had a very supportive luck cycle—starting with branch **M**, all the way to stem **M**—it was mostly metal and water, which he needed most. Remember that branch **F** in the luck cycle pairs with **H** in the birth composite, turning into fire and eliminating the earth; and branch **f** pairs with **m** in the birth composite, changing into metal. There were some difficult years in between, of course. Bright Rain's successful political life started at period **r** and peaked at stem **M**, when he became the president. He was ousted during the beginning of the **W** period, when additional earth messed up his system.

Winter

Abundant fire is essential to keep winter rain from freezing. Yang earth is needed to block the flood in case of excessive water. Water selves can be intelligent without fire, but no one can succeed without it.

The system of a great Chinese poet testifies to our theory.

t	r	m	F
t	r	g	R

R	r	T	t	F	f	E
T	t	W	f	F	d	M

Snowdrift was born in a blooming stage with strong kin; the water was very dynamic and powerful. A trio formed by branches **R**, **g**, and **r** eliminated his worst enemy, moist earth. There was metal to clear the water and two wood signs to calm him and encourage thinking, creating a very talented writer.

Fire, the magic ingredient for fame, was, however, far from enough. There was also no yang earth to confine the dynamic water, which would allow Snowdrift to focus on a goal. He spent most of his life writing poems without recognition. He served as an official in the government for a brief period during the last part of his life, in the **FF** and **fd** periods. Snowdrift was finally recognized, after his death, as one of the top few genius poets in China. His work was extremely popular in literary circles and was recited with great passion for generations. Sadly, he didn't live to enjoy his fame.

*Figure 8A. The **E** Self*

Lunar Birth Month	* Your Crucial Elements	Explanation
T January	**F, T, r** or **R**	**F** to provide sunlight; **T** to loosen soil; **r** to water plants.
t February	**F, T, r** or **R**	Principles of month **T** apply.
W March	**T, F, r**	**T** is most crucial to loosen soil for growing plants; **F** to provide sunlight; **r** to water plants.
f April	**T, F, r**	Principles of month **W** apply; both **W** and **f** have dominant earth influence.
F May	**R, T, F**	**R** to provide irrigation for dry soil; **T** to loosen stiff, dry soil; **F** for sunlight.
d June	**r, T, F**	**r** replaces **R** as heat begins to subside; **T** to curtail strong earth; **F** for sunlight.
M July	**F, T, r**	Similar to month **d**; sunlight more important than rain as the weather cools.
m August	**F, r**	Similar to month **M**; wood not needed, as strong metal influence loosens the soil.
H September	**T, r, F**	**T** to loosen stiff, thick earth; **r** to water plants; **F** for sunlight.
r October	**T, F**	**T** to channel excessive water; **F** for sunlight.
R November	**F, T**	**F** very crucial for cold and soggy soil; **T** to channel excessive water.
g December	**F, T**	Principles of month **R** apply.

* All signs refer to stems or their equivalents in the branches.

*Figure 8B. The **e** Self*

Lunar Birth Month	* Your Crucial Elements	Explanation
T January	**F, M**	**F** is crucial to warm the soggy soil; **M** to curtail excessive wood.
t February	**F, T, r**	**F** to warm the soil; **T** to loosen the earth, making it easier for new plants to emerge.
W March	**F, r, T**	**F** to warm the soil; **r** to water growing plants; **T** to curtail strong earth influence.
f April	**r, F**	**r** to offset growing summer heat (if no **E** to pair with **r**); **F** for sunlight; must be separate.
F May	**r, F**	Principles of month **f** apply.
d June	**r, F**	Principles of month **f** apply.
M July	**F, r**	**F** for sunlight; **r** to curtail strong and growing metal influence (if no **E** to pair with **r**).
m August	**F, r**	Principles of month **M** apply.
H September	**T, F, r**	**T** to curtail earth influence; **F** for sunlight; **r** to water plants (if no **E** to pair with **r**).
r October	**F, E, T**	**F** crucial for cold winter soil; **E** to block water from soaking moist earth; **T** to channel water.
R November	**F, E, T**	Principles of month **r** apply.
g December	**F, E, T**	Principles of month **r** apply.

* All signs refer to stems or their equivalents in the branches.

*Figure 8C. The **M** Self*

Lunar Birth Month	* Your Crucial Elements	Explanation
T January	**T, F, R**	Earth is deprived of nutrients; **M** must be exposed to breathe. **T** loosens soil; **F** warms soil; **R** shines.
t February	**f, F, M, T**	**f** to shape **M** into tool; **M** to chop trees to fuel the fire; **F** warms the soil.
W March	**T, f, R**	**T** to curtail strong earth influence; **R** to flush the metal; **f** to shape the metal.
f April	**R, E, f**	**R** to moisten and cool the earth; **f** to shape the metal into a tool.
F May	**R, r, m**	**R** and **r** to offset the powerful fire and to moisten the earth; **m** to help.
d June	**R, f, T**	**R** to cool and moisten the soil; **f** to shape the tool; **T** to loosen the soil.
M July	**f, T, t**	Self is very competent, able to turn any wood into wealth; **f** to sharpen the tool.
m August	**f, F, T**	**f** to sharpen the solid metal into a good tool; **T** to provide money-making potential.
H September	**T, R**	**T** to loosen the earth; **R** to shine the metal.
r October	**f, F**	**f** to shape the tool; **F** to warm the soil.
R November	**f, F, T**	Principles of month **r** apply; **T** to sustain the fire.
g December	**F, T, f**	Principles of month **R** apply; **T** is before **f** because the earth is thicker and needs loosening.

* All signs refer to stems or their equivalents in the branches.

*Figure 8D. The **m** Self*

Lunar Birth Month	* Your Crucial Elements	Explanation
T January	e, M, R	Earth and metal are weak in spring; extra **e** to nurture the metal; **R** to wash/shine; **M** to help.
t February	e, R	Principles of month **T** apply; **M** not needed because of its nature to pair with **t**.
W March	T, R	**T** to curtail strong earth influence; **R** to shine.
f April	R, r	Plenty of water to moisten the earth to nurture the metal; **R** to shine **m**.
F May	R, r, M, e	Principles of month **f** apply; **M** to help counter growing fire; additional earth to shield from fire.
d June	R, T, M	**R** to shine; **T** to check the earth; **M** to help.
M July	R, T, E	**R** to shine mature metal; **T** to provide financial opportunities; **E** is optional.
m August	R, T	Principles of month **M** apply.
H September	R, T	Principles of month **M** apply. Extra yang wood checks the earth.
r October	R, F	**R** to clean the metal; **F** to warm the home base.
R November	F, R E, T	Principles of month **r** apply; **E** and **T** to check the growing water.
g December	F, R, E, e	Principles of month **R** apply; extra earth to block the water.

* All signs refer to stems or their equivalents in the branches.

*Figure 8E. The **R** Self*

Lunar Birth Month	* Your Crucial Elements	Explanation
T January	**M, E, F**	**M** to generate water; **E** to guide the flow; **F** to warm.
t February	**E, M, m**	**E** to keep weak water from meandering; plenty of metal to generate water supply.
W March	**T, M**	**T** to curtail strong earth influence; **M** to generate water; must be separate.
f April	**R, M** **m, r**	Kin and grantors to help the weak self counter the dominant fire and earth of April.
F May	**r, M, m**	Principles of month **f** apply; heat is fierce.
d June	**m, T, r**	**m** to generate water; **T** to check strong earth; **r** to replenish water supply.
M July	**E, f**	**E** to guide the roaring flow of growing water; **f** to warm and light up the water.
m August	**T or E, F**	**T** to channel the excessive water; **E** if **T** not available; **F** to warm and shine.
H September	**T, F**	**T** to check strong earth influence; **F** to warm and enhance glittering water.
r October	**E, F, M**	**E** to guide roaring water; **F** to warm and reflect; **M** to keep the **T** in month **r** away from **E**.
R November	**T, F**	**T** to channel roaring water; **F** to warm and reflect.
g December	**F, T, f**	Principles of month **R** apply; extra fire to counter increasingly cold weather.

* All signs refer to stems or their equivalents in the branches.

Figure 8F. The r Self

Lunar Birth Month	* Your Crucial Elements	Explanation
T January	**m, F**	**m** to generate water to compensate for loss from plant consumption; **F** for sunlight.
t February	**M, m**	**M** to pair with **t** (plants) to keep water intact; **m** to generate more water to protect the self.
W March	**F, m, T**	**F** to warm the water; **m** to generate more water; **T** to curtail strong earth influence.
f April	**m** or **M**	Metal to generate water to offset the fire and earth influence in **f** month.
F May	**M, R, r**	**M** to generate water; water in all forms needed to counter the heat.
d June	**M, R, m**	Principles of month **F** apply; **m** replaces **r** to curtail earth influence.
M July	**f**	**f** to provide heat and serve as a source of wealth.
m August	**m, F**	**m** to clear the water; **F** to warm.
H September	**m, T, R**	**m** to generate water; **T** to check the earth influence; **R** to breed **T** and strengthen the self.
r October	**M, m,** or **E, f**	Metal to check possible excessive wood; or **E** to check excessive water; **f** needed for both.
R November	**F, m**	**F** crucial for comfort; **m** to check the influence of wood.
g December	**F, f**	Plenty of fire needed to help the self counter the cold weather.

* All signs refer to stems or their equivalents in the branches.

CHAPTER 9

Attuning to the Cosmic Flows

So far we have covered the basic theories of the Meng. Knowledgeable readers who have clear-cut systems should have a clear picture of their cosmic strength. However, there are special cases that require advanced theories not included in this book. There are also borderline or mixed-up systems that do not respond to the flows in a standard manner. The solution to such cases is vigorous testing. This concluding chapter will elaborate on the procedure of such testing.

Testing the Flows

Using life events to test your system is foolproof. Our interaction with a given element is almost constant. How we interacted with certain flows in the past can be studied to determine our response to the repeated pattern in the future. Even though identical cosmic conditions are rarely repeated, similar cosmic patterns do occur from time to time. Our positive life events should correspond to the occurrence of our favorable elements in the cosmos or in our luck cycle. Likewise, our negative life events should correspond with the occurrence of the elements we now know we want to avoid.

At any given point in our life, three sets of flows are interacting in our system: the flows in the cosmos, in our birth composite, and in our luck cycle. We'll use a year as the unit of time in our testing in order to get a good, overall picture of our response to the flows throughout our life. Start with the worksheet on pages 151 and 152. There are five columns: one for the year, one for the cosmic pillar for that year, one for the element ruling the corresponding luck cycle, one for the element in the birth composite representing the corresponding stage of your life (see page 45 in Chapter 4), and one for a summary of your significant life events.

The purpose of such a design is to identify how a specific cosmic sign corresponds to specific life events, either positively or negatively. We'll use Crystal's system again as an example. A copy of her worksheet can be found on pages 153 and 154. In Chapter 4, we assumed Crystal's system was faulty for convenience of illustration. In fact, according to the theories in Chapters 5, 6, and 7, this is a borderline case, shifting between faulty and equilibrium.

Since Crystal's birth year is 1937, we begin the test worksheet with 1938, her first year of life, and progress all the way to 1989, a period of fifty-one years. In the second column, the cosmic signs for each year are copied from the lunar calendars in the appendix. In the luck cycle column, we write the sign from her luck cycle that ruled each year, beginning with stem **f** (remember that each sign in the luck cycle rules for five years).

The birth composite represents a cycle of sixty years, with each sign reigning seven and one-half years, beginning with the stem of the year pillar. *The starting year always matches the beginning year of the luck cycle.* In that order, we write each sign seven and one-half times in the birth composite column. Crystal's starts with stem **f**. Bear in mind that every sign in our birth composite plays a role in our luck throughout our life. The choice of significant life events to write in the last column is personal and subjective.

Crystal's data filled two worksheets. First, let us identify two broad patterns: positive and negative events. Her most successful period was from 1964 to 1973. The dominant player was metal. From 1964 to 1967, branch **m** from the luck cycle joined with **g** in the birth composite to form a metal alliance, functioning like an ore mine—powerful, boosting Crystal up like a metal giant. At the same time, fire was strong, fiercely

Luck Cycle Worksheet				
Cos = Cosmic pillar; L.C. = Luck Cycle period; B.C. = Birth Composite period				
Year	Cos	L.C.	B.C.	Significant Life Events

| Luck Cycle Worksheet |||||
| Cos = Cosmic pillar; L.C. = Luck Cycle period; B.C. = Birth Composite period |||||
Year	Cos	L.C.	B.C.	Significant Life Events

				Crystal's Luck Cycle Worksheet
				Cos = Cosmic pillar; L.C. = Luck Cycle period; B.C. = Birth Composite period
Year	Cos	L.C.	B.C.	Significant Life Events
38	ET	f	f	Happy childhood under caring and well-to-do
39	et	f	f	parents from age 1–4.
40	MW	f	f	
41	mf	f	f	
42	RF	f	f	Fled from Hong Kong to a village in China during
43	rd	d	f	the Sino-Japanese War; lived in poverty behind
44	TM	d	f	war zone 1942–45.
45	tm	d	f, g	
46	FH	d	g	Returned to Hong Kong after the war.
47	fr	d	g	Began grade school; excellent student; very happy
48	ER	E	g	school life through 1954.
49	eg	E	g	
50	MT	E	g	
51	mt	E	g ·	
52	RW	E	G	
53	rf	M	F	
54	TF	M	F	
55	td	M	F	Became seriously ill in June; quit school for a year;
56	FM	M	F	returned to school in September, 1956.
57	fm	M	F	Remained a very good student through college.
58	EH	e	F	
59	er	e	F	
60	MR	e	F, F	
61	mg	e	F	
62	RT	e	F	Graduated from college with first honor.
63	rt	m	F	Finished teacher training; began teaching.
64	TW	m	F	Teaching; dating; applying for overseas study.
65	tf	m	F	Taught until July; moved to U. S. in September.

				Crystal's Luck Cycle Worksheet
				Cos = Cosmic pillar; L.C. = Luck Cycle period; B.C. = Birth Composite period
Year	Cos	L.C.	B.C.	Significant Life Events
66	FF	m	F	Graduate study on assistantship until 1967; happy.
67	fd	m	F	M.A. degree in June; started Ph.D. program.
68	EM	M	m	Received special grant to research for thesis.
69	em	M	m	Finished course work; taught college; September.
70	MH	M	m	Passed exam; relocated to teach college.
71	mr	M	m	Taught until June; began field work on thesis.
72	RR	M	m	Received Ph.D.; continued college teaching.
73	rg	H	m	Busy teaching, publishing, and giving speeches.
74	TT	H	m	Lost job in June; completed writing textbook.
75	tt	H	m, t	Married; unemployed.
76	FW	H	t	Started career at a bank; continued working
77	ff	H	t	until 1978; very little career progress.
78	EF	m	t	
79	ed	m	t	Unemployed most of the year.
80	MM	m	t	Good progress at job; promoted three grades.
81	mm	m	t	Steady work; purchased property.
82	RH	m	t	Very hectic work; co-worker on disability.
83	rr	r	T	Good boss; extra income on O.T.; good health.
84	TR	r	T	Occasional minor conflicts with new boss
85	tg	r	T	until 1985.
86	FT	r	T	Easy work; extra income; long paid vacation.
87	tt	r	T	Rewarding working life; good summer.
88	EW	R	T	Very easy working life; writing manuscript.
89	ef	R	T	Hectic work starting second half of year.

shaping her into a sharp tool, allowing her to easily achieve her goals. After sending out just two applications, she was awarded an assistantship from a university in the United States, which paid more than double what she was making as a full-time teacher in Hong Kong.

During her graduate study, she frequently got crucial help from strangers, and successfully completed all the programs on target, to her surprise.

From 1968 to 1972, yang metal replaced the metal alliance and the momentum of metal force kept building, with more significant accomplishments on the way.

Now let us single out the climax of this lucky period. The fall of 1965 was a banner period, when Crystal received the award and set out for the United States. There was a metal trio formed by **f** (cosmic), and the alliance of **m** and **g**, the most powerful union of all.

Another climax occurred in 1970, when her income was the highest in her life. Three metal flows, including two yang metals, combined to bring her luck. In fact, Crystal's income had been steadily increasing since 1968, with the onset of more metal in her system. She can be sure that metal is her top crucial element, and it is also her money sign, as it empowers her to make use of the financial opportunities in her environment.

To reassure her finding, Crystal also found that 1980 and 1981, when strong metal flows dominated the cosmos, were also good years for money. She received good promotions and purchased property. The finding was being verified.

What happened in 1972 and 1973? Crystal achieved her ultimate goal and began teaching college in Hong Kong, actively engaged in publishing articles, giving speeches, and participating in television commentaries and community functions. She achieved some fame, but her income was far behind the level of 1970. The dominant interplaying signs were metal and water. Water shines the metal and becomes her fame factor. Only fire can sharpen metal, which then conquers and possesses! Metal that is shiny only, and not sharp, does not conquer. Crystal had no financial gains from her fame.

The other good period in Crystal's life was during her school years; she was an excellent student. The dominant signs were **g**, **e**, and **E**, all earth, shielding her from danger so she could grow.

Now let us move to the negative periods. Basically, they include her wartime childhood and her bank career. The dominant signs were fire and wood (keep in mind that **H** and **d** contain plenty of fire). There were a few exceptions. 1983 was wonderful, with substantial income increase, new congenial friends, a good boss, and plenty of happiness. That was a very wet year! Abundant rain makes Crystal happy.

1986 was an even better year, ruled by a fierce fire sign. Why? It created an equilibrium of dominant fire. The fire from the cosmic year was fierce. The **r** from Crystal's luck cycle joined **T**, losing its water nature and forming an alliance of wood, fueling the blaze. For a change, the self became helpless, entitled to effortless blessings. She had a paid vacation for three months (the hottest months, reinforcing the fire-dominant equilibrium), very light work for the rest of the year, extra income, and a good raise. Such equilibrium also occurred during the first four years of her childhood.

What are Crystal's worst signs? Let us single out the worst years. They include the second halves of 1943, 1955, and 1979. The sign persistently dominating these years was **d**. By nature, **d** contains plenty of fire and wood, something Crystal dreads. However, the worst comes from the unique ability of **d** to clash with **g**, Crystal's only grantor and life saver, exposing her to dangers and attacks.

She was seriously ill in 1943 and 1955, and had a significant dental bill in 1979 when she was mostly unemployed.

The same **d** influence in 1967 did not cause disaster because the **g** allied with **m**, making it difficult for **d** to influence it. Regardless, there were minor setbacks. What happened in 1991 when **d** ruled again? Crystal lost two teeth and had four gum surgeries. She also had some major confrontations with her boss and barely kept her job.

With these findings, Crystal can learn how to attune to the flows, attracting the good flows and avoiding the bad flows. She should be aggressive on good days, and on bad days, keep a low profile and prepare for possible disasters. We'll elaborate on the approaches she can take to achieve this goal.

Enhancing Our Luck

Before we start, we should be able to categorize everything in the universe into one of the five elements. For instance, **t** can be a plant, herb, grass, flower, or vegetable. It is also the basic material in paper, fabrics, clothing, and drugs (in ancient China). **M** includes all metals (raw or refined), tools, appliances, vehicles, and some furniture. Stem **F** is basically the sun, but is also heat, fire, and light. Earth includes soils, property, and all chinaware. Water includes all forms of moisture and all bodies of water in the world. The list is endless.

Armed with our knowledge of the five elements, we can approach our goal in the following areas: people, activity space, activity schedule, career and investment planning, and predicting the future.

People

We need to associate with people who have a substantial amount of our favorable elements in their cosmic system. Try to associate with these people and follow their lead as much as possible.

How do you know if someone has your favorable elements in their system? The surest way, of course, is to check their cosmic system. However, this might not always be practical. People experienced with the Meng can tell by a person's outlook, or personality, which is practically the imprint of our cosmic system. Some Chinese business people try to master the art of face-reading.

For Crystal, all people rich in metal and water are her benefactors. People with strong fire and wood influence are a different story. As a rule, she should avoid people in this group. However, in rare periods when a fire equilibrium occurs, she should attract more of these elements to enhance the equilibrium.

Activity Space

Our activity space includes all the environments in which we perform our daily activities. To improve our luck, we need to orient our activities to the sectors of our favorable elements. To do this, we need Figure 2A on page 12, which indicates the cardinal directions associated with the twelve branches.

For Crystal, west (the sector of metal) is her top choice; north (water) comes next. The sector for **g**, being earth and metal, is also good. She should avoid the south and southeast (fire and wood).

Within our space, we can move our desk, bed, and other frequently used furniture in such a way that we are facing the sectors of our favorable elements. The resourceful among us can, of course, choose a favorable city in the world, select a compatible site in the city, and build a home with the main door and windows opening toward the most ideal sectors.

We can also surround ourselves with furnishings that signify our favorable elements. For example, Crystal may want some paintings of rain, rivers, waterfalls, or gold mines.

Colors also play a vital role. Fire colors include all reds, oranges, and reddish purples; wood colors are all greens; water colors are black, gray, and ocean blue; metal colors are whites; earth colors include all brown tones.

Activity Schedule

Since each element dominates space in rotation, we can anticipate our good times in terms of hour, day, month, year, and luck cycle. We want to be aggressive in our good hours. Figure 2H on page 21 can be used to schedule hourly activities, and the lunar calendars in the appendix serve as our daily guide.

By knowing how specific signs affect us, and by mastering the skill of reading the lunar calendars, we can more effectively plan our schedules for vacations, meetings, interviews, or shopping.

Career and Investment Planning

Ancient Chinese believed that having a wrong mate or a wrong career were among the biggest disasters in one's life. Most of us logically plan our career, but how many of us are genuinely happy with our choice? Many of us must have had the frustration of trying something and failing, and then, all of a sudden, succeeding easily in something we had never dreamed of. It is a matter of doing the right things at the right time.

When we understand our cosmic strengths, we can save frustration by planning ahead. To succeed, we have to know the right *time* to do the right things. Our career should be associated with our favorable elements. Those who need earth should work with construction or property management in order to prosper.

Your lucky elements can be found in the nature of a job, or the name of a firm. When making career decisions, evaluate the nature of the job, the location, and name of the firm—the entire package.

On the investment front, the same principles apply. Choose stocks or funds that correspond to your favorable elements, again considering the entire package—nature, location, name, etc. However, there is something more you must consider: the timing. This takes effort. Use Figure 5A on page 60 on the growth cycles of the ten stems as your guide. After you select a stock, study the curve of its past performance to check out whether it conforms to the growth cycle theory. Upon positive findings, note the peaks and valleys, and time your trading schedule accordingly. That is, buy in the contracting stage and sell in the blooming stage.

This author experimented with this procedure with several stocks associated with metal and earth, her favorable elements, with some success. The high price of the metal stock sold in lunar September did not repeat until the next fall. The high price for the moist earth stock sold in June was the highest for the entire year. Such testing takes patience.

Those who can benefit from earth should invest in real estate. Someone with excessive water should work with or invest in wood, fabrics, or paper. Such investments would involve garments, decorating, carpentry, or publishing. It follows that for negative elements, we use the same procedure and try to avoid them as much as possible.

There was a joke among the Chinese in Hong Kong. It claimed that the wealthy Chinese who play the stock market do not study the crazy stock fundamentals. All they need to do is study the face of the Chief Executive Officer of the company. If the CEO is in a favorable luck cycle, the company stock goes up. Otherwise, it dives. There is some truth in this. A good astrologer masters both the art of the Meng and face reading.

Predicting the Future

To predict the future course of our lives, we simply extend the worksheet and find the patterns of luck over the years ahead. In anticipation of upcoming good luck, we can launch important projects. Otherwise, we focus on daily routines and work on details, patiently waiting for the right time instead of blindly pushing for fame and success. By so doing, we can avoid setbacks and conserve our energy for enjoying a happy family life.

Let us all sail with the cosmic wind and win!

The Lunar Calendars 1920–2030

Each page of the appendix represents one lunar year calendar. The cosmic sign of the year, and its cosmic animal, appear at the top next to the calendar year. The twelve lunar months, with their cosmic signs, appear on the first row. Each month has twenty-nine or thirty days, which are indicated in the column marked "Day of Mon" (Mon for month).

The corresponding months and days in the western calendar are listed in each month column with the cosmic sign for each day. For instance, on the calendar for 1931 on page 176, lunar January 1 is February 17 in the western calendar, and the cosmic sign for that day is **rt**.

Climate Dividers

There are twelve climate dividers in each lunar year, one falling into each month, indicating significant climatic changes between the two adjacent periods. These are listed in the second row, each with a preceding number indicating the initial day of the new climatic period in that lunar month. For instance, on the calendar for 1931, the first climate divider is WARM. It falls on January 18 (March 6 in the western calendar). The time at which the change begins is indicated in the third row.

161

As a result of lunar influence, the beginning or ending climate divider of one particular year can fall into the preceding or the following year, resulting in one year with thirteen dividers and the other with eleven. Years with two SPRINGs are favorable years. The climate dividers, described briefly below, are important guides for farmers when scheduling their activities.

SPRING   indicates the first day of the spring season, and the new lunar year as well. This is the beginning of a reviving fire cycle. For those whose cosmic strength depends on fire, life begins to improve.

WARM   is the beginning of a long frost-free period. Animals and insects emerge from their dormancy. Wood begins its thriving cycle.

CLEAR   is the beginning of a clearing trend. Mist is replaced by light showers and subsequent clear skies, which promote vegetation growth.

SUMMER   is the first day of summer, the beginning of a reviving earth cycle. Prior to this day, earth was dead. People depending on earth for good luck see new hope.

GRAIN   is the beginning of a fruit-bearing period. The strength of fire and earth begins to gather momentum.

HEAT   marks the beginning of a dominating yang fire (the sun). Trees are well-grown. The strength of water is at its lowest.

FALL   marks the first day of autumn. Metal becomes well-grown, solid, and shiny. Water begins to revive its growing cycle.

DEW   is the beginning of a cooling trend. Metal strength has reached its climax. Those who benefit from metal influence have a surge of good luck or good health.

COLD DEW   is the beginning of an intense cooling period when precautions are necessary to protect crops from bad weather. Metal starts its contracting cycle.

WINTER   is the first day of winter. Water is in control of the cosmos.

SNOW   denotes the coldest and darkest period of the year. Water strength is at its climax. Snow prevails. People born during this period need a lot of fire or wood to sustain a good life.

CHILL   is the transitional period between cold winter and spring. Snow is still possible. Fire is still dead.

Since some months have only twenty-nine days, and no month has more than thirty days, there are fewer than 365 days in any given year. These missing days add up to one month every three years. This additional month is added to the third year, making it a thirteen-month year. This additional month is called the leap month. For instance, 1933 had two months of May; the second May was an extension of the first May, and it shares the same cosmic signs. In fact, they can be treated as the same month, with its length doubled.

In figuring our luck cycle, the repeating month is treated as an extension of the previous month; its cosmic pillar is used only once. There is no other change in the procedure. If a birthday falls into the leap month, use the cosmic signs of the preceding month as the month pillar.

The Climate of the Lunar Months

The order of lunar months is different from their counterparts in the western calendar. Spring always begins in January in a lunar year, while it starts in March in the western calendar. Since all formulas of Chinese divination are based on the order of a lunar calendar, it is important to become acquainted with the climate of each lunar month.

January (**T**):   Ruled by wood; cool and misty; soil soggy from winter rain.

February (**t**):   Ruled by wood; cool and misty; soil soggy from winter rain.

March (**W**):   Ruled by strong yang earth and wood; warm and clear; soil firm.

April (**f**): Ruled mostly by fire, and some earth and metal; the beginning of summer; water at its weakest.

May (**F**): Ruled by fire; the hottest month of the year; climax of summer; earth gathering momentum.

June (**d**): Ruled by strong, dry earth, plenty of wood, and some fire; a dry month.

July (**M**): Ruled by yang water and strong yang metal; the beginning of autumn; a cooling trend, with water growing in strength.

August (**m**): Ruled by very strong metal; intensifying cooling trend.

September (**H**): Ruled by very strong dry earth, some fire and metal; a very dry month.

October (**r**): Ruled by water and wood; the beginning of winter; water gathers momentum; very chilly.

November (**R**): Ruled by the strongest water; wet, with prevalent snow.

December (**g**): Ruled by wet earth; cloudy; very cold and wet.

1920 MM MONKEY

JAN ET	FEB et	MAR MW	APR mf	MAY RF	JUN rd	DAY OF MON	JUL TM	AUG tm	SEP FH	OCT fr	NOV ER	DEC eg
16 WARM	17 CLEAR	18 SUMMER	20 GRAIN	22 HEAT	24 FALL		26 DEW	27 C DEW	28 WINTER	28 SNOW	28 CHILL	27 SPRING
4:51	10:15	4:12	9:03	19:19	5:29		7:27	23:33	1:05	17:31	4:34	16:21

JAN ET	FEB et	MAR MW	APR mf	MAY RF	JUN rd	DAY/MON	JUL TM	AUG tm	SEP FH	OCT fr	NOV ER	DEC eg
2 20 EM	3 20 fg	4 19 fd	5 18 FR	6 16 tf	7 16 tr	1	8 14 TW	9 12 rm	10 12 rm	11 11 rm	12 10 RT	1 9 RM
2 21 em	3 21 ET	4 20 EM	5 19 fg	6 17 FF	7 17 FR	2	8 15 tf	9 13 TH	10 13 TH	11 12 TH	12 11 rt	1 10 rm
2 22 MH	3 22 et	4 21 em	5 20 ET	6 18 fd	7 18 fg	3	8 16 FF	9 14 tr	10 14 tr	11 13 tr	12 12 TW	1 11 TH
2 23 mr	3 23 MW	4 22 MH	5 21 et	6 19 EM	7 19 ET	4	8 17 fd	9 15 FR	10 15 FF	11 14 FR	12 13 tf	1 12 tr
2 24 RR	3 24 mf	4 23 mr	5 22 MW	6 20 et	7 20 et	5	8 18 EM	9 16 fg	10 16 fd	11 15 fg	12 14 FF	1 13 FR
2 25 rg	3 25 RF	4 24 RR	5 23 mf	6 21 MH	7 21 MW	6	8 19 em	9 17 ET	10 17 EM	11 16 ET	12 15 fd	1 14 fg
2 26 TT	3 26 rd	4 25 rd	5 24 RR	6 22 mf	7 22 mr	7	8 20 MH	9 18 et	10 18 em	11 17 et	12 16 EM	1 15 ET
2 27 tt	3 27 TM	4 26 TM	5 25 rd	6 23 RF	7 23 RF	8	8 21 mr	9 19 MW	10 19 MH	11 18 MW	12 17 em	1 16 et
2 28 FW	3 28 tm	4 27 tm	5 26 TM	6 24 rg	7 24 rd	9	8 22 RR	9 20 mf	10 20 mr	11 19 mf	12 18 MH	1 17 MW
2 29 ff	3 29 FH	4 28 FH	5 27 tm	6 25 TT	7 25 TM	10	8 23 rg	9 21 RF	10 21 RR	11 20 RF	12 19 mr	1 18 mf
3 30 EF	3 30 fr	4 29 fr	5 28 FH	6 26 tm	7 26 tm	11	8 24 TT	9 22 rd	10 22 rd	11 21 rd	12 20 RR	1 19 RR
3 31 ER	3 31 EF	4 30 EF	5 29 ff	6 27 FW	7 27 FH	12	8 25 tt	9 23 TM	10 23 TM	11 22 TM	12 21 rg	1 20 rd
3 1 MM	4 1 eg	4 31 ER	5 30 EF	6 28 ff	7 28 fr	13	8 26 FW	9 24 tm	10 24 tt	11 23 tm	12 22 TT	1 21 TM
3 2 mm	4 2 MT	5 1 eg	6 31 eg	6 29 ER	7 29 ER	14	8 27 ff	9 25 FH	10 25 FW	11 24 FH	12 23 tt	1 22 tm
3 3 RH	4 3 mt	5 2 MT	6 1 MT	6 30 ed	7 30 eg	15	8 28 EF	9 26 fr	10 26 ff	11 25 fr	12 24 FW	1 23 FH
3 4 rf	4 4 RH	5 3 mt	6 2 mt	7 31 MM	8 31 MM	16	8 29 ed	9 27 ER	10 27 EF	11 26 ER	12 25 ff	1 24 fr
3 5 TR	4 5 rf	5 4 RH	6 3 RH	7 1 mt	8 1 mt	17	8 30 MM	9 28 eg	10 28 ed	11 27 eg	12 26 EF	1 25 ER
3 6 tg	4 6 TF	5 5 rf	6 4 rf	7 2 RH	8 2 RW	18	8 31 mm	9 29 MT	10 29 MM	11 28 MT	12 27 ed	1 26 eg
3 7 FT	4 7 td	5 6 TF	6 5 TR	7 3 rf	8 3 rf	19	9 1 RH	9 30 mt	10 30 mm	11 29 mt	12 28 MM	1 27 MT
3 8 ft	4 8 FM	5 7 td	6 6 tg	7 4 TF	8 4 TF	20	9 2 rr	10 1 RW	10 31 RH	11 30 RW	12 29 mm	1 28 mt
3 9 FM	4 9 fm	5 8 FM	6 7 FT	7 5 td	8 5 TR	21	9 3 TR	10 2 rr	11 1 rr	12 1 RH	12 30 RH	1 29 RW
3 10 fm	4 10 EH	5 9 fm	6 8 ft	7 6 FT	8 6 FM	22	9 4 tg	10 3 TF	11 2 TR	12 2 rr	12 31 rr	1 30 rf
3 11 EW	4 11 er	5 10 EH	6 9 EH	7 7 ft	8 7 fm	23	9 5 FT	10 4 td	11 3 tg	12 3 TF	1 1 TR	1 31 TF
3 12 ef	4 12 MR	5 11 er	6 10 ef	7 8 EW	8 8 EH	24	9 6 ft	10 5 FM	11 4 FT	12 4 td	1 2 tg	2 1 td
3 13 MF	4 13 mg	5 12 MR	6 11 MF	7 9 ef	8 9 er	25	9 7 EW	10 6 fm	11 5 ft	12 5 FM	1 3 FT	2 2 FM
3 14 md	4 14 RM	5 13 mg	6 12 mg	7 10 MF	8 10 MR	26	9 8 ef	10 7 EW	11 6 EW	12 6 fm	1 4 ft	2 3 fm
3 15 RM	4 15 RT	5 14 RM	6 13 RM	7 11 md	8 11 rr	27	9 9 MF	10 8 er	11 7 ef	12 7 EH	1 5 EW	2 4 EH
3 16 rm	4 16 TW	5 15 rt	6 14 rt	7 12 mg	8 12 RT	28	9 10 md	10 9 MF	11 8 MF	12 8 er	1 6 ef	2 5 er
3 17 rt	4 17 tf	5 16 TH	6 15 TW	7 13 RM	8 13 rt	29	9 11 RM	10 10 md	11 9 md	12 9 MF	1 7 MF	2 6 MR
3 18 tr	4 18 FF	5 17 tr		7 14 rm		30		10 11 RM	11 10 RM		1 8 md	2 7 mg
3 19 FR				7 15 TH								

165

1921 mm ROOSTER

JAN MT	FEB mt	MAR RW	APR rf	MAY TF	JUN td	DAY OF MON	JUL FM	AUG fm	SEP EH	OCT er	NOV MR	DEC mg
27 WARM	27 CLEAR	29 SUMMER		1 GRAIN	4 HEAT		5 FALL	7 DEW	9 C DEW	9 WINTER	10 SNOW	9 CHILL
10:46	16:09	10:05		14:42	18:31		11:17	13:10	5:22	7:58	0:07	10:17
2 8 RT	3 10 RM	4 8 mg	5 8 md	6 6 MR	7 5 ef	1	8 4 er	9 2 EW	10 1 fm	10 31 ft	11 29 FM	12 29 FT
2 9 rt	3 11 rm	4 9 RT	5 9 RM	6 7 mg	7 6 mg	2	8 5 MR	9 3 ef	10 2 EH	11 1 EW	11 30 fm	12 30 ft
2 10 TW	3 12 TH	4 10 rt	5 10 rm	6 8 RT	7 7 md	3	8 6 mg	9 4 MF	10 3 er	11 2 ef	12 1 EH	12 31 EW
2 11 tf	3 13 tr	4 11 TH	5 11 TH	6 9 rt	7 8 RM	4	8 7 RT	9 5 md	10 4 MF	11 3 MF	12 2 MF	1 1 ef
2 12 FF	3 14 FR	4 12 tf	5 12 tr	6 10 TW	7 9 rm	5	8 8 rt	9 6 RM	10 5 mg	11 4 md	12 3 MR	1 2 MF
2 13 fd	3 15 fg	4 13 FF	5 13 FR	6 11 tf	7 10 TH	6	8 9 TW	9 7 rm	10 6 RT	11 5 RM	12 4 mg	1 3 md
2 14 EM	3 16 ET	4 14 fd	5 14 fg	6 12 FF	7 11 tr	7	8 10 tf	9 8 TH	10 7 rt	11 6 rm	12 5 RT	1 4 RM
2 15 em	3 17 et	4 15 EM	5 15 ET	6 13 fd	7 12 FR	8	8 11 FF	9 9 tr	10 8 TW	11 7 TH	12 6 rt	1 5 rm
2 16 MH	3 18 mf	4 16 em	5 16 et	6 14 EM	7 13 fd	9	8 12 fd	9 10 FR	10 9 tf	11 8 tr	12 7 TW	1 6 TH
2 17 mr	3 19 mf	4 17 MH	5 17 MW	6 15 em	7 14 ET	10	8 13 EM	9 11 fg	10 10 FF	11 9 FR	12 8 tf	1 7 tr
2 18 RR	3 20 RF	4 18 mr	5 18 mf	6 16 MH	7 15 et	11	8 14 em	9 12 ET	10 11 fd	11 10 fg	12 9 FF	1 8 FR
2 19 rg	3 21 rd	4 19 RR	5 19 RF	6 17 mr	7 16 MW	12	8 15 MH	9 13 et	10 12 EM	11 11 ET	12 10 fd	1 9 fg
2 20 TT	3 22 TM	4 20 rg	5 20 rd	6 18 RR	7 17 mf	13	8 16 mr	9 14 MW	10 13 em	11 12 et	12 11 EM	1 10 ET
2 21 tt	3 23 tt	4 21 TT	5 21 TT	6 19 rg	7 18 RF	14	8 17 RR	9 15 mf	10 14 MH	11 13 MW	12 12 em	1 11 et
2 22 FW	3 24 FH	4 22 tt	5 22 tm	6 20 TT	7 19 rg	15	8 18 rg	9 16 RF	10 15 mr	11 14 mf	12 13 MH	1 12 MW
2 23 ff	3 25 fr	4 23 FW	5 23 FW	6 21 tt	7 20 TT	16	8 19 TT	9 17 rd	10 16 RR	11 15 RF	12 14 mr	1 13 mf
2 24 EF	3 26 ER	4 24 ff	5 24 ff	6 22 FW	7 21 tm	17	8 20 tt	9 18 TM	10 17 rg	11 16 rd	12 15 RR	1 14 RF
2 25 ed	3 27 eg	4 25 EF	5 25 EF	6 23 ff	7 22 FH	18	8 21 FW	9 19 tm	10 18 TT	11 17 TM	12 16 rg	1 15 rd
2 26 MM	3 28 MT	4 26 ed	5 26 eg	6 24 EF	7 23 ff	19	8 22 ff	9 20 FH	10 19 tt	11 18 tm	12 17 TT	1 16 TM
2 27 mm	3 29 mt	4 27 MM	5 27 MT	6 25 ed	7 24 ER	20	8 23 EF	9 21 fr	10 20 FW	11 19 FH	12 18 tt	1 17 tm
2 28 RH	3 30 RW	4 28 mm	5 28 mt	6 26 MM	7 25 eg	21	8 24 ed	9 22 ER	10 21 ff	11 20 fr	12 19 FW	1 18 FH
3 1 rr	3 31 rf	4 29 RH	5 29 RW	6 27 mm	7 26 MT	22	8 25 MM	9 23 eg	10 22 EF	11 21 ER	12 20 ff	1 19 fr
3 2 TR	4 1 TF	4 30 rr	5 30 rf	6 28 RH	7 27 mt	23	8 26 mm	9 24 MT	10 23 ed	11 22 eg	12 21 EF	1 20 ER
3 3 tg	4 2 td	5 1 TR	5 31 TF	6 29 rr	7 28 RH	24	8 27 RH	9 25 mt	10 24 MM	11 23 MT	12 22 ed	1 21 eg
3 4 FT	4 3 FM	5 2 tg	6 1 td	6 30 TR	7 29 rr	25	8 28 rr	9 26 RW	10 25 mm	11 24 mt	12 23 MM	1 22 MT
3 5 ft	4 4 fm	5 3 FT	6 2 FM	7 1 tg	7 30 TR	26	8 29 TR	9 27 rf	10 26 RH	11 25 RW	12 24 mm	1 23 mt
3 6 EW	4 5 EH	5 4 ft	6 3 fm	7 2 FT	7 31 tg	27	8 30 tg	9 28 TF	10 27 rr	11 26 rf	12 25 RH	1 24 RW
3 7 ef	4 6 er	5 5 EH	6 4 EH	7 3 ft	8 1 FM	28	8 31 FT	9 29 td	10 28 TR	11 27 TF	12 26 rr	1 25 rf
3 8 MF	4 7 MR	5 6 ef	6 5 er	7 4 EH	8 2 fm	29	9 1 ft	9 30 FM	10 29 tg	11 28 td	12 27 TR	1 26 TF
3 9 md		5 7 MF			8 3 EH	30			10 30 FT		12 28 tg	1 27 td

JAN RT / 8 SPRING / 22:07	FEB rt / 8 WARM / 16:34	MAR TW / 9 CLEAR / 21:58	APR tf / 10 SUMMER / 15:53	MAY FF / 11 GRAIN / 20:30	MAY FF / 14 HEAT / 7:13	JUN fd / 16 FALL / 17:05	DAY OF MON	JUL EM / 17 DEW / 19:07	AUG em / 19 C DEW / 11:11	SEP MH / 20 WINTER / 13:47	OCT mr / 20 SNOW / 5:11	NOV RR / 20 CHILL / 16:15	DEC rg / 20 SPRING / 4:01
1 28 FM	2 27 FT	3 28 td	4 27 tg	5 27 td	6 25 TR	7 25 TF	1	8 23 rr	9 21 RW	10 21 RH	11 19 mt	12 19 mm	1 17 MT
1 29 fm	2 28 ft	3 29 FM	4 28 FT	5 28 FM	6 26 tg	7 26 td	2	8 24 TR	9 22 rf	10 22 rr	11 20 RW	12 20 RH	1 18 mt
1 30 EH	3 1 EW	3 30 fm	4 29 ft	5 29 fm	6 27 FT	7 27 FM	3	8 25 tg	9 23 TF	10 23 TR	11 21 rf	12 21 rr	1 19 RW
1 31 er	3 2 ef	3 31 EH	4 30 EW	5 30 EH	6 28 ft	7 28 fm	4	8 26 FT	9 24 td	10 24 tg	11 22 TF	12 22 TR	1 20 rf
2 1 MR	3 3 MF	4 1 er	5 1 ef	5 31 er	6 29 EW	7 29 EH	5	8 27 ft	9 25 FM	10 25 FT	11 23 td	12 23 tg	1 21 TF
2 2 mg	3 4 md	4 2 MR	5 2 MF	6 1 MR	6 30 ef	7 30 er	6	8 28 EW	9 26 fm	10 26 ft	11 24 FM	12 24 FT	1 22 td
2 3 RT	3 5 RM	4 3 mg	5 3 md	6 2 mg	7 1 MF	7 31 MR	7	8 29 ef	9 27 EH	10 27 EW	11 25 fm	12 25 ft	1 23 FM
2 4 rt	3 6 rm	4 4 RT	5 4 RM	6 3 RT	7 2 md	8 1 mg	8	8 30 MF	9 28 er	10 28 ef	11 26 EH	12 26 EW	1 24 fm
2 5 TW	3 7 TH	4 5 rt	5 5 rm	6 4 rt	7 3 RM	8 2 RT	9	8 31 md	9 29 MR	10 29 MF	11 27 er	12 27 ef	1 25 EH
2 6 tf	3 8 tr	4 6 TW	5 6 TH	6 5 TW	7 4 rm	8 3 rt	10	9 1 RM	9 30 mg	10 30 md	11 28 MR	12 28 MF	1 26 er
2 7 FF	3 9 FR	4 7 tf	5 7 tr	6 6 tf	7 5 TH	8 4 TW	11	9 2 rm	10 1 RT	10 31 RM	11 29 mg	12 29 md	1 27 MR
2 8 fd	3 10 fg	4 8 FF	5 8 FR	6 7 FF	7 6 tr	8 5 tf	12	9 3 TH	10 2 rt	11 1 rm	11 30 RT	12 30 RM	1 28 mg
2 9 EM	3 11 ET	4 9 fd	5 9 fg	6 8 fd	7 7 FR	8 6 FF	13	9 4 tr	10 3 TW	11 2 TH	12 1 rt	12 31 rm	1 29 RT
2 10 em	3 12 et	4 10 EM	5 10 ET	6 9 EM	7 8 fg	8 7 fd	14	9 5 FR	10 4 tf	11 3 tr	12 2 TW	1 1 TH	1 30 rt
2 11 MH	3 13 MW	4 11 em	5 11 et	6 10 em	7 9 ET	8 8 EM	15	9 6 fg	10 5 FF	11 4 FR	12 3 tf	1 2 tr	1 31 TW
2 12 mr	3 14 mf	4 12 MH	5 12 MW	6 11 MH	7 10 et	8 9 em	16	9 7 ET	10 6 fd	11 5 fg	12 4 FF	1 3 FR	2 1 tf
2 13 RR	3 15 RF	4 13 mr	5 13 mf	6 12 mr	7 11 MW	8 10 MH	17	9 8 et	10 7 EM	11 6 ET	12 5 fd	1 4 fg	2 2 FF
2 14 rg	3 16 rd	4 14 RR	5 14 RF	6 13 RR	7 12 mf	8 11 mr	18	9 9 MW	10 8 em	11 7 et	12 6 EM	1 5 ET	2 3 fd
2 15 TT	3 17 TM	4 15 rg	5 15 rd	6 14 rg	7 13 RF	8 12 RR	19	9 10 mf	10 9 MH	11 8 MW	12 7 em	1 6 et	2 4 EM
2 16 tt	3 18 tm	4 16 TT	5 16 TM	6 15 TT	7 14 rd	8 13 rg	20	9 11 RF	10 10 mr	11 9 mf	12 8 MH	1 7 MW	2 5 em
2 17 FW	3 19 FH	4 17 tt	5 17 tm	6 16 tt	7 15 TM	8 14 TT	21	9 12 rd	10 11 RR	11 10 RF	12 9 mr	1 8 mf	2 6 MH
2 18 ff	3 20 fr	4 18 FW	5 18 FH	6 17 FW	7 16 tm	8 15 tt	22	9 13 TM	10 12 rg	11 11 rd	12 10 RR	1 9 RF	2 7 mr
2 19 EF	3 21 ER	4 19 ff	5 19 fr	6 18 ff	7 17 FH	8 16 FW	23	9 14 tm	10 13 TT	11 12 TM	12 11 rg	1 10 rd	2 8 RR
2 20 ed	3 22 eg	4 20 EF	5 20 ER	6 19 EF	7 18 fr	8 17 ff	24	9 15 FH	10 14 tt	11 13 tm	12 12 TT	1 11 TM	2 9 rg
2 21 MM	3 23 MT	4 21 ed	5 21 eg	6 20 ed	7 19 ER	8 18 EF	25	9 16 fr	10 15 FW	11 14 FH	12 13 tt	1 12 tm	2 10 TT
2 22 mm	3 24 mt	4 22 MM	5 22 MT	6 21 MM	7 20 eg	8 19 ed	26	9 17 ER	10 16 ff	11 15 fr	12 14 FW	1 13 FH	2 11 tt
2 23 RH	3 25 RW	4 23 mm	5 23 mt	6 22 mm	7 21 MT	8 20 MM	27	9 18 eg	10 17 EF	11 16 ER	12 15 ff	1 14 fr	2 12 FW
2 24 rr	3 26 rf	4 24 RH	5 24 RW	6 23 RH	7 22 mt	8 21 mm	28	9 19 MT	10 18 ed	11 17 eg	12 16 EF	1 15 ER	2 13 ff
2 25 TR	3 27 TF	4 25 rr	5 25 rf	6 24 rr	7 23 RW	8 22 RH	29	9 20 mt	10 19 MM	11 18 MT	12 17 ed	1 16 eg	2 14 EF
2 26 tg		4 26 TR	5 26 TF		7 24 rf		30		10 20 mm		12 18 MM		2 15 ed

1923 rr BOAR

Month	Code	Marker	Time
JAN	TT	19 WARM	22:25
FEB	tt	21 CLEAR	3:46
MAR	FW	21 SUMMER	21:39
APR	ff	23 GRAIN	2:15
MAY	EF	25 HEAT	13:01
JUN	ed	26 FALL	22:25
JUL	MM	29 DEW	1:41
AUG	mm	29 C DEW	17:00
SEP	RH		
OCT	rr	1 WINTER	19:30
NOV	TR	1 SNOW	11:05
DEC	tg	1 CHILL	22:06

JAN	FEB	MAR	APR	MAY	JUN	DAY OF MON	JUL	AUG	SEP	OCT	NOV	DEC
2 16 MM	3 17 eg	4 16 ed	5 16 eg	6 14 EF	7 14 ER	1	8 12 ff	9 11 fr	10 10 FW	11 8 tm	12 8 et	1 6 TM
2 17 mm	3 18 MT	4 17 MM	5 17 MT	6 15 ed	7 15 eg	2	8 13 EF	9 12 ER	10 11 ff	11 9 FH	12 9 FW	1 7 tm
2 18 RH	3 19 mt	4 18 mm	5 18 mt	6 16 MM	7 16 MT	3	8 14 ed	9 13 eg	10 12 EF	11 10 fr	12 10 ff	1 8 FH
2 19 rr	3 20 RW	4 19 RH	5 19 RW	6 17 mm	7 17 mt	4	8 15 MT	9 14 MT	10 13 ed	11 11 ER	12 11 EF	1 9 fr
2 20 TR	3 21 rf	4 20 rr	5 20 rf	6 18 RH	7 18 RW	5	8 16 mm	9 15 mt	10 14 MM	11 12 eg	12 12 ed	1 10 ER
2 21 tg	3 22 TF	4 21 TR	5 21 TF	6 19 rr	7 19 rf	6	8 17 RH	9 16 RW	10 15 mm	11 13 MT	12 13 MM	1 11 eg
2 22 FT	3 23 td	4 22 tg	5 22 td	6 20 TR	7 20 TF	7	8 18 rr	9 17 rf	10 16 RH	11 14 mt	12 14 mm	1 12 MT
2 23 ft	3 24 FM	4 23 FT	5 23 FM	6 21 tg	7 21 td	8	8 19 TR	9 18 TF	10 17 rr	11 15 RW	12 15 RH	1 13 mt
2 24 EW	3 25 fm	4 24 ft	5 24 fm	6 22 FT	7 22 FM	9	8 20 tg	9 19 td	10 18 TR	11 16 rf	12 16 rr	1 14 RW
2 25 ef	3 26 EH	4 25 EW	5 25 EH	6 23 ft	7 23 fm	10	8 21 FT	9 20 FM	10 19 tg	11 17 TF	12 17 TR	1 15 rf
2 26 MF	3 27 er	4 26 ef	5 26 er	6 24 EW	7 24 EH	11	8 22 ft	9 21 fm	10 20 FT	11 18 td	12 18 tg	1 16 TF
2 27 md	3 28 MR	4 27 MF	5 27 MR	6 25 ef	7 25 er	12	8 23 EW	9 22 EH	10 21 ft	11 19 FM	12 19 FT	1 17 td
2 28 RM	3 29 mg	4 28 md	5 28 mg	6 26 MF	7 26 MR	13	8 24 ef	9 23 er	10 22 EW	11 20 fm	12 20 ft	1 18 FM
3 1 rm	3 30 RT	4 29 RM	5 29 RM	6 27 md	7 27 mg	14	8 25 MF	9 24 MR	10 23 ef	11 21 EH	12 21 EW	1 19 fm
3 2 TH	3 31 rt	4 30 rm	5 30 rt	6 28 RM	7 28 RT	15	8 26 md	9 25 mg	10 24 MF	11 22 er	12 22 ef	1 20 EH
3 3 tr	4 1 TW	5 1 TH	5 31 TW	6 29 rm	7 29 rt	16	8 27 RM	9 26 RT	10 25 md	11 23 MR	12 23 MF	1 21 er
3 4 FR	4 2 tf	5 2 tr	6 1 tf	6 30 TH	7 30 TW	17	8 28 rm	9 27 rt	10 26 RM	11 24 mg	12 24 md	1 22 MR
3 5 fg	4 3 FF	5 3 FR	6 2 FF	7 1 tr	7 31 tf	18	8 29 TH	9 28 TW	10 27 rm	11 25 RT	12 25 RM	1 23 mg
3 6 ET	4 4 fd	5 4 fg	6 3 fd	7 2 FR	8 1 FF	19	8 30 tr	9 29 tr	10 28 TH	11 26 rt	12 26 rm	1 24 RT
3 7 et	4 5 EM	5 5 ET	6 4 EM	7 3 fg	8 2 fd	20	8 31 FR	9 30 FF	10 29 tr	11 27 TW	12 27 TH	1 25 rt
3 8 MW	4 6 em	5 6 et	6 5 em	7 4 ET	8 3 EM	21	9 1 fg	10 1 fd	10 30 FR	11 28 tf	12 28 tr	1 26 TW
3 9 mf	4 7 MH	5 7 MW	6 6 MH	7 5 et	8 4 em	22	9 2 ET	10 2 EM	10 31 fg	11 29 FF	12 29 FR	1 27 tf
3 10 RF	4 8 mr	5 8 mf	6 7 mr	7 6 MW	8 5 MH	23	9 3 et	10 3 em	11 1 ET	11 30 fd	12 30 fg	1 28 FF
3 11 rd	4 9 RR	5 9 RF	6 8 RR	7 7 mf	8 6 mf	24	9 4 MW	10 4 MH	11 2 et	12 1 EM	12 31 ET	1 29 fd
3 12 TM	4 10 rg	5 10 rd	6 9 rg	7 8 RF	8 7 RF	25	9 5 mf	10 5 mr	11 3 MW	12 2 em	1 1 et	1 30 EM
3 13 tm	4 11 TT	5 11 TM	6 10 TT	7 9 rd	8 8 rd	26	9 6 RF	10 6 RR	11 4 mf	12 3 MH	1 2 MW	1 31 em
3 14 FH	4 12 tt	5 12 tm	6 11 tt	7 10 TT	8 9 TT	27	9 7 rd	10 7 rg	11 5 RF	12 4 mr	1 3 mf	2 1 MH
3 15 fr	4 13 FW	5 13 FH	6 12 FW	7 11 tm	8 10 tt	28	9 8 TM	10 8 TT	11 6 rd	12 5 RF	1 4 RF	2 2 mr
3 16 ER	4 14 ff	5 14 fr	6 13 ff	7 12 FH	8 11 FW	29	9 9 tm	10 9 tt	11 7 TM	12 6 rd	1 5 rd	2 3 RR
	4 15 EF	5 15 ER		7 13 fr		30	9 10 FH			12 7 TT		2 4 rg
						31						

1924 TR RAT

Month	Code	Solar term	Time
JAN	FT	1 SPRING	9:50
FEB	ft	2 WARM	4:13
MAR	EW	2 CLEAR	9:34
APR	ef	3 SUMMER	3:26
MAY	MF	5 GRAIN	8:02
JUN	md	6 HEAT	18:30
JUL	RM	8 FALL	4:13
AUG	rm	10 DEW	7:30
SEP	TH	10 C DEW	21:53
OCT	tr	12 WINTER	1:26
NOV	FR	11 SNOW	16:54
DEC	fg	12 CHILL	3:54

DAY OF MON

JAN

2	5	TT
2	6	tt
2	7	FW
2	8	ff
2	9	EF
2	10	ed
2	11	MM
2	12	mm
2	13	RH
2	14	rr
2	15	TR
2	16	tg
2	17	FT
2	18	ft
2	19	EW
2	20	ef
2	21	MF
2	22	md
2	23	RM
2	24	rm
2	25	TH
2	26	tr
2	27	FR
2	28	fg
2	29	ET
3	1	et
3	2	MW
3	3	mf
3	4	RF

FEB

3	5	rd
3	6	TM
3	7	tm
3	8	FH
3	9	fr
3	10	EF
3	11	eg
3	12	MT
3	13	mt
3	14	RW
3	15	rr
3	16	TF
3	17	td
3	18	FM
3	19	fm
3	20	EH
3	21	er
3	22	MR
3	23	mg
3	24	RT
3	25	rt
3	26	TW
3	27	tf
3	28	FF
3	29	fd
3	30	EM
3	31	em
4	1	MH
4	2	mr
4	3	RR

MAR

4	4	rg
4	5	TT
4	6	tt
4	7	FW
4	8	ff
4	9	EF
4	10	ed
4	11	MM
4	12	mm
4	13	RH
4	14	rr
4	15	TR
4	16	tg
4	17	FT
4	18	ft
4	19	EW
4	20	ef
4	21	MF
4	22	md
4	23	RM
4	24	rm
4	25	TH
4	26	tr
4	27	FR
4	28	fg
4	29	ET
4	30	et
5	1	MW
5	2	mf
5	3	RF

APR

5	4	rd
5	5	TM
5	6	tm
5	7	FH
5	8	fr
5	9	ER
5	10	eg
5	11	MT
5	12	mt
5	13	RW
5	14	rf
5	15	TF
5	16	td
5	17	FM
5	18	fm
5	19	EH
5	20	er
5	21	MR
5	22	mg
5	23	RT
5	24	rt
5	25	TW
5	26	tf
5	27	FF
5	28	fd
5	29	EM
5	30	em
6	1	MH

MAY

6	2	RR
6	3	rg
6	4	TT
6	5	tt
6	6	FW
6	7	ff
6	8	EF
6	9	ed
6	10	MM
6	11	mm
6	12	RH
6	13	rr
6	14	TR
6	15	tg
6	16	FT
6	17	ft
6	18	EW
6	19	ef
6	20	MF
6	21	md
6	22	RM
6	23	rm
6	24	TH
6	25	tr
6	26	FR
6	27	fg
6	28	ET
6	29	et
6	30	MW
7	1	mf

JUN

7	2	RR
7	3	rg
7	4	TT
7	5	tt
7	6	FW
7	7	ff
7	8	EF
7	9	ed
7	10	MM
7	11	mm
7	12	RH
7	13	rr
7	14	TR
7	15	tg
7	16	FT
7	17	ft
7	18	EW
7	19	ef
7	20	MF
7	21	md
7	22	RM
7	23	rm
7	24	TH
7	25	tr
7	26	FR
7	27	fg
7	28	ET
7	29	et
7	30	MW

JUL

8	1	RR
8	2	rg
8	3	TT
8	4	tt
8	5	FW
8	6	ff
8	7	EF
8	8	ed
8	9	MM
8	10	mm
8	11	RH
8	12	rr
8	13	TR
8	14	tg
8	15	FT
8	16	ft
8	17	EW
8	18	ef
8	19	MF
8	20	md
8	21	RM
8	22	rm
8	23	TH
8	24	tr
8	25	FR
8	26	fg
8	27	ET
8	28	et
8	29	MW

DAY OF MON: 1, 2, 3, 4, 5, 6, 7, 8, 9, 10, 11, 12, 13, 14, 15, 16, 17, 18, 19, 20, 21, 22, 23, 24, 25*, 26, 27, 28, 29, 30

AUG

8	30	mf
8	31	RF
9	1	rd
9	2	TM
9	3	tm
9	4	FH
9	5	fr
9	6	ER
9	7	eg
9	8	MT
9	9	mt
9	10	RW
9	11	rf
9	12	TF
9	13	td
9	14	FM
9	15	fm
9	16	EH
9	17	er
9	18	MF
9	19	mg
9	20	RM
9	21	rm
9	22	TH
9	23	tr
9	24	FF
9	25	fd
9	26	EM
9	27	em
9	28	MH

SEP

9	29	mr
9	30	RR
10	1	rg
10	2	TT
10	3	tt
10	4	FW
10	5	ff
10	6	EF
10	7	ed
10	8	MM
10	9	mm
10	10	RH
10	11	rr
10	12	TR
10	13	tg
10	14	FT
10	15	ft
10	16	EW
10	17	ef
10	18	MF
10	19	md
10	20	RM
10	21	rm
10	22	TH
10	23	tr
10	24	FR
10	25	fg
10	26	ET
10	27	et

OCT

10	28	MW
10	29	mf
10	30	RF
10	31	rd
11	1	TM
11	2	tm
11	3	FH
11	4	fr
11	5	ER
11	6	eg
11	7	MT
11	8	mt
11	9	RW
11	10	rf
11	11	TF
11	12	td
11	13	FM
11	14	fm
11	15	EH
11	16	er
11	17	MR
11	18	mg
11	19	RT
11	20	rt
11	21	TW
11	22	tf
11	23	FF
11	24	fd
11	25	EM
11	26	em

NOV

11	27	MH
11	28	mr
11	29	RR
11	30	rg
12	1	TT
12	2	tt
12	3	FW
12	4	ff
12	5	EF
12	6	ed
12	7	MM
12	8	mm
12	9	RH
12	10	rr
12	11	TR
12	12	tg
12	13	FT
12	14	ft
12	15	EW
12	16	ef
12	17	MF
12	18	md
12	19	RM
12	20	rm
12	21	TH
12	22	tr
12	23	FR
12	24	fg
12	25	ET

DEC

12	26	et
12	27	MW
12	28	mf
12	29	RF
12	30	rd
12	31	TM
1	1	tm
1	2	FH
1	3	fr
1	4	ER
1	5	eg
1	6	MT
1	7	mt
1	8	RW
1	9	rf
1	10	TF
1	11	td
1	12	FM
1	13	fm
1	14	EH
1	15	er
1	16	MR
1	17	mg
1	18	RT
1	19	rt
1	20	TW
1	21	tf
1	22	FR
1	23	fd

1925 tg OX

JAN ET	FEB et	MAR MW	APR mf	APR	MAY RF	JUN rd	JUL TM	AUG tm	SEP FH	OCT tr	NOV ER	DEC er
12 SPRING	12 WARM	13 CLEAR	14 SUMMER	16 GRAIN	18 HEAT	19 FALL	21 DEW	22 C DEW	22 WINTER	22 SNOW	22 CHILL	22 SPRING
15:37	10:00	15:23	9:18	13:57	0:25	10:08	12:40	3:48	7:16	23:26	9:55	21:39

170

1926 FT TIGER

JAN MT	FEB mt	MAR RW	APR rf	MAY FF	JUN td	DAY OF MON	JUL FM	AUG fm	SEP EH	OCT er	NOV MR	DEC mg
22 WARM	23 CLEAR	25 SUMMER	26 GRAIN	29 HEAT			1 FALL	2 DEW	3 C DEW	4 WINTER	4 SNOW	3 CHILL
16:00	21:19	15:09	19:42	6:06			15:45	19:07	9:25	13:05	5:16	15:45
2 13 rm	3 14 RT	4 12 md	5 12 mg	6 10 MF	7 10 MR	1	8 8 MF	9 7 er	10 7 ef	11 5 EH	12 5 EW	1 4 EH
2 14 TH	3 15 rt	4 13 rm	5 13 RT	6 11 md	7 11 mg	2	8 9 md	9 8 MR	10 8 MF	11 6 er	12 6 ef	1 5 er
2 15 tr	3 16 TW	4 14 rm	5 14 rt	6 12 rm	7 12 RT	3	8 10 rm	9 9 mg	10 9 md	11 7 MR	12 7 MF	1 6 MR
2 16 FR	3 17 tf	4 15 TH	5 15 TW	6 13 rm	7 13 rt	4	8 11 rm	9 10 RT	10 10 rm	11 8 mg	12 8 md	1 7 mg
2 17 fg	3 18 fd	4 16 tr	5 16 tf	6 14 TH	7 14 TW	5	8 12 TH	9 11 rt	10 11 rm	11 9 RT	12 9 rm	1 8 RT
2 18 ET	3 19 EM	4 17 FR	5 17 FF	6 15 tr	7 15 tf	6	8 13 tr	9 12 TW	10 12 TH	11 10 rt	12 10 rm	1 9 rt
2 19 et	3 20 em	4 18 fg	5 18 fd	6 16 FR	7 16 FF	7	8 14 FR	9 13 tf	10 13 tr	11 11 TW	12 11 TH	1 10 TW
2 20 MW	3 21 MH	4 19 ET	5 19 EM	6 17 fg	7 17 fd	8	8 15 fg	9 14 FF	10 14 FR	11 12 tf	12 12 tr	1 11 tf
2 21 mf	3 22 mf	4 20 et	5 20 em	6 18 ET	7 18 EM	9	8 16 ET	9 15 fd	10 15 fg	11 13 FF	12 13 FR	1 12 FF
2 22 RF	3 23 RF	4 21 MW	5 21 MW	6 19 et	7 19 em	10	8 17 et	9 16 EM	10 16 fd	11 14 fd	12 14 fg	1 13 fd
2 23 rd	3 24 RR	4 22 mf	5 22 mr	6 20 MW	7 20 MW	11	8 18 MW	9 17 em	10 17 et	11 15 EM	12 15 ET	1 14 EM
2 24 TM	3 25 rg	4 23 RF	5 23 RR	6 21 mf	7 21 mr	12	8 19 mf	9 18 MH	10 18 MW	11 16 em	12 16 et	1 15 em
2 25 tm	3 26 TT	4 24 rd	5 24 rg	6 22 RF	7 22 RR	13	8 20 RF	9 19 mr	10 19 mf	11 17 MH	12 17 MW	1 16 MH
2 26 FH	3 27 tt	4 25 TM	5 25 TT	6 23 rd	7 23 rg	14	8 21 rd	9 20 RR	10 20 RF	11 18 mr	12 18 mf	1 17 mr
2 27 ff	3 28 FF	4 26 tm	5 26 tt	6 24 TM	7 24 TT	15	8 22 TM	9 21 rg	10 21 rg	11 19 RR	12 19 RR	1 18 RR
2 28 ER	3 29 ff	4 27 FH	5 27 FW	6 25 tm	7 25 tt	16	8 23 tm	9 22 TT	10 22 TM	11 20 rg	12 20 rg	1 19 rg
3 1 eg	3 30 EF	4 28 fr	5 28 ff	6 26 FH	7 26 FW	17	8 24 FH	9 23 tt	10 23 tm	11 21 TT	12 21 TT	1 20 TT
3 2 MT	3 31 ed	4 29 ER	5 29 EF	6 27 fr	7 27 ff	18	8 25 fr	9 24 FW	10 24 FH	11 22 tt	12 22 tt	1 21 tt
3 3 mt	4 1 MM	4 30 eg	5 30 ed	6 28 ER	7 28 EF	19	8 26 ER	9 25 ff	10 25 fr	11 23 FW	12 23 FH	1 22 FW
3 4 RW	4 2 mm	5 1 MT	5 31 MT	6 29 eg	7 29 ER	20	8 27 eg	9 26 EF	10 26 ER	11 24 fr	12 24 fr	1 23 fr
3 5 rf	4 3 RH	5 2 mt	6 1 mm	6 30 MT	7 30 MM	21	8 28 MT	9 27 ed	10 27 ed	11 25 EF	12 25 ER	1 24 EF
3 6 TF	4 4 rr	5 3 RW	6 2 RH	7 1 mt	7 31 mm	22	8 29 mt	9 28 MM	10 28 MT	11 26 ed	12 26 eg	1 25 ed
3 7 td	4 5 TR	5 4 rf	6 3 rr	7 2 RW	8 1 RH	23	8 30 RW	9 29 mm	10 29 mt	11 27 MM	12 27 MT	1 26 MM
3 8 FM	4 6 tg	5 5 TF	6 4 TR	7 3 rf	8 2 rr	24	8 31 rf	9 30 RH	10 30 RW	11 28 mm	12 28 mt	1 27 mm
3 9 fm	4 7 FT	5 6 td	6 5 tg	7 4 TF	8 3 TR	25	9 1 TF	10 1 rr	10 31 rf	11 29 RH	12 29 RW	1 28 RH
3 10 EH	4 8 ft	5 7 FM	6 6 FT	7 5 td	8 4 tg	26	9 2 td	10 2 TR	11 1 TF	11 30 rr	12 30 rf	1 29 rr
3 11 er	4 9 EW	5 8 fm	6 7 ft	7 6 FM	8 5 FT	27	9 3 FM	10 3 tg	11 2 td	12 1 TR	12 31 TF	1 30 TR
3 12 MR	4 10 ef	5 9 EH	6 8 EW	7 7 fm	8 6 ft	28	9 4 fm	10 4 FT	11 3 FM	12 2 tg	1 1 td	1 31 tg
3 13 mg	4 11 MF	5 10 er	6 9 ef	7 8 EH	8 7 EW	29	9 5 EH	10 5 ft	11 4 fm	12 3 FT	1 2 FM	2 1 FT
		5 11 MR		7 9 er		30	9 6 er	10 6 EW		12 4 ft	1 3 fm	2 2 ft
												2 3 EW

171

JAN RT	FEB rt	MAR TW	APR tf	MAY FF	JUN fd	DAY OF MON	JUL EM	AUG em	SEP MH	OCT mr	NOV RR	DEC rg
4 SPRING	3 WARM	5 CLEAR	6 SUMMER	8 GRAIN	10 HEAT		11 FALL	14 DEW	14 C DEW	13 WINTER	15 SNOW	14 CHILL
3:31	21:51	2:57	20:54	1:25	11:50		21:32	0:06	15:16	17:57	11:05	21:32
2 2 ft	3 4 fm	4 2 FT	5 1 td	5 31 tg	6 29 TF	1	7 29 TR	8 27 rf	9 26 rr	10 25 RW	11 24 RH	12 24 RW
2 3 EW	3 5 EH	4 3 ft	5 2 FM	6 1 FT	6 30 td	2	7 30 tg	8 28 TF	9 27 TR	10 26 rf	11 25 rr	12 25 rf
2 4 ef	3 6 er	4 4 EW	5 3 fm	6 2 ft	7 1 FM	3	7 31 FT	8 29 td	9 28 tg	10 27 TF	11 26 TR	12 26 TF
2 5 MF	3 7 MR	4 5 ew	5 4 EH	6 3 EW	7 2 fm	4	8 1 ft	8 30 FM	9 29 FT	10 28 td	11 27 tg	12 27 td
2 6 md	3 8 mg	4 6 MF	5 5 er	6 4 ef	7 3 EH	5	8 2 EW	8 31 fm	9 30 ft	10 29 FM	11 28 FT	12 28 FM
2 7 RM	3 9 RT	4 7 md	5 6 MR	6 5 MF	7 4 er	6	8 3 ef	9 1 EH	10 1 EW	10 30 fm	11 29 ft	12 29 fm
2 8 rm	3 10 rt	4 8 RM	5 7 mg	6 6 md	7 5 MR	7	8 4 MF	9 2 er	10 2 ef	10 31 EH	11 30 EW	12 30 EH
2 9 TH	3 11 TW	4 9 rm	5 8 RT	6 7 RM	7 6 mg	8	8 5 md	9 3 MR	10 3 MF	11 1 er	12 1 ef	12 31 er
2 10 tr	3 12 tf	4 10 TH	5 9 rt	6 8 rm	7 7 RT	9	8 6 RM	9 4 mg	10 4 md	11 2 MR	12 2 MF	1 1 MR
2 11 FR	3 13 FF	4 11 tr	5 10 TW	6 9 TH	7 8 rm	10	8 7 rm	9 5 RT	10 5 RM	11 3 md	12 3 md	1 2 mg
2 12 fg	3 14 fd	4 12 FR	5 11 tf	6 10 tr	7 9 TH	11	8 8 TH	9 6 rt	10 6 rm	11 4 RT	12 4 RM	1 3 RT
2 13 ET	3 15 EM	4 13 fg	5 12 FF	6 11 FR	7 10 tf	12	8 9 tr	9 7 TW	10 7 TH	11 5 rt	12 5 rm	1 4 rt
2 14 et	3 16 em	4 14 ET	5 13 fd	6 12 fg	7 11 FF	13	8 10 FR	9 8 tf	10 8 tr	11 6 TW	12 6 TH	1 5 TW
2 15 MW	3 17 MH	4 15 et	5 14 EM	6 13 ET	7 12 fd	14	8 11 fg	9 9 FF	10 9 FR	11 7 tf	12 7 tr	1 6 tf
2 16 mf	3 18 mr	4 16 MW	5 15 em	6 14 et	7 13 EM	15	8 12 ET	9 10 fg	10 10 fg	11 8 FR	12 8 FR	1 7 FR
2 17 RF	3 19 RR	4 17 mf	5 16 MH	6 15 MW	7 14 em	16	8 13 et	9 11 EM	10 11 ET	11 9 fd	12 9 fg	1 8 fd
2 18 rd	3 20 rg	4 18 RF	5 17 mr	6 16 mf	7 15 MH	17	8 14 MW	9 12 em	10 12 et	11 10 EM	12 10 ET	1 9 EM
2 19 TM	3 21 TT	4 19 rd	5 18 RR	6 17 RF	7 16 mr	18	8 15 mf	9 13 MH	10 13 MW	11 11 em	12 11 et	1 10 em
2 20 tm	3 22 tt	4 20 TM	5 19 rd	6 18 rd	7 17 RR	19	8 16 RF	9 14 mr	10 14 mf	11 12 MH	12 12 MW	1 11 MH
2 21 FH	3 23 FW	4 21 tm	5 20 TM	6 19 TM	7 18 rg	20	8 17 rd	9 15 RR	10 15 RF	11 13 mr	12 13 mf	1 12 mr
2 22 fr	3 24 ff	4 22 FH	5 21 tm	6 20 tm	7 19 TM	21	8 18 TM	9 16 rg	10 16 rd	11 14 RR	12 14 RF	1 13 RR
2 23 ER	3 25 EF	4 23 fr	5 22 FH	6 21 FH	7 20 tm	22	8 19 tm	9 17 TT	10 17 TM	11 15 rg	12 15 rd	1 14 rg
2 24 eg	3 26 ed	4 24 ER	5 23 fr	6 22 fr	7 21 FH	23	8 20 FH	9 18 tt	10 18 tm	11 16 TT	12 16 TM	1 15 TT
2 25 MT	3 27 MM	4 25 eg	5 24 ER	6 23 ER	7 22 fr	24	8 21 fr	9 19 FW	10 19 FH	11 17 tt	12 17 tm	1 16 tt
2 26 mt	3 28 mm	4 26 MT	5 25 eg	6 24 eg	7 23 ER	25	8 22 ER	9 20 ff	10 20 fr	11 18 FW	12 18 FH	1 17 FW
2 27 RW	3 29 RH	4 27 mt	5 26 MM	6 25 MT	7 24 eg	26	8 23 eg	9 21 EF	10 21 ER	11 19 ff	12 19 fr	1 18 ff
2 28 rf	3 30 rr	4 28 RW	5 27 mm	6 26 mt	7 25 MM	27	8 24 MT	9 22 ed	10 22 eg	11 20 EF	12 20 ER	1 19 EF
3 1 TF	3 31 TR	4 29 rf	5 28 RH	6 27 RW	7 26 mm	28	8 25 mt	9 23 MM	10 23 MT	11 21 ed	12 21 eg	1 20 ed
3 2 td	4 1 tg	4 30 TF	5 29 rr	6 28 rf	7 27 RH	29	8 26 RW	9 24 mm	10 24 mt	11 22 MM	12 22 MT	1 21 MM
3 3 FM			5 30 TR		7 28 rr	30		9 25 RH		11 23 mm	12 23 mt	1 22 mm

172

1928 EW DRAGON

JAN TT	FEB tt	FEB tt	MAR FW	APR ff	MAY EF	JUN ed	DAY OF MON	JUL MM	AUG mm	SEP RH	OCT rr	NOV TR	DEC tg
14 SPRING	15 WARM	15 CLEAR	17 SUMMER	19 GRAIN	7 HEAT	23 FALL		25 DEW	25 C DEW	27 WINTER	26 SNOW	26 CHILL	25 SPRING
9:17	3:38	8:55	2:44	7:18	17:45	3:28		6:02	21:11	0:44	16:18	3:23	14:57
1 23 RH	2 21 mt	3 22 mm	4 20 MT	5 19 ed	6 18 eg	7 17 EF	1	8 15 fr	9 14 ff	10 13 FH	11 12 FW	12 12 FH	1 11 FW
1 24 rr	2 22 RW	3 23 RH	4 21 mt	5 20 MM	6 19 MT	7 18 ed	2	8 16 ER	9 15 EF	10 14 fr	11 13 ff	12 13 fr	1 12 ff
1 25 TR	2 23 rf	3 24 rr	4 22 RW	5 21 mm	6 20 mt	7 19 MM	3	8 17 eg	9 16 ed	10 15 ER	11 14 EF	12 14 ER	1 13 EF
1 26 tg	2 24 TF	3 25 TR	4 23 rf	5 22 RH	6 21 RW	7 20 mm	4	8 18 MT	9 17 MM	10 16 eg	11 15 ed	12 15 eg	1 14 ed
1 27 FT	2 25 td	3 26 tg	4 24 TF	5 23 rf	6 22 rf	7 21 RH	5	8 19 mt	9 18 mm	10 17 MT	11 16 MM	12 16 MT	1 15 MM
1 28 ft	2 26 FM	3 27 FT	4 25 td	5 24 TR	6 23 TF	7 22 rr	6	8 20 RW	9 19 RH	10 18 mt	11 17 mm	12 17 mt	1 16 mm
1 29 EW	2 27 fm	3 28 ft	4 26 FM	5 25 tg	6 24 td	7 23 TR	7	8 21 rf	9 20 rr	10 19 RW	11 18 RH	12 18 RW	1 17 RH
1 30 ef	2 28 EH	3 29 EW	4 27 fm	5 26 FT	6 25 FM	7 24 tg	8	8 22 TF	9 21 TR	10 20 rf	11 19 rr	12 19 rf	1 18 rr
1 31 MF	2 29 er	3 30 ef	4 28 EH	5 27 ft	6 26 fm	7 25 FT	9	8 23 td	9 22 tg	10 21 TF	11 20 TR	12 20 TF	1 19 TR
2 1 md	3 1 MR	3 31 MF	4 29 er	5 28 EW	6 27 EH	7 26 ft	10	8 24 FM	9 23 FT	10 22 td	11 21 tg	12 21 td	1 20 tg
2 2 RM	3 2 mg	4 1 md	4 30 MR	5 29 ef	6 28 er	7 27 EW	11	8 25 fm	9 24 ft	10 23 FM	11 22 FT	12 22 FM	1 21 FT
2 3 rm	3 3 RT	4 2 RM	5 1 mg	5 30 MF	6 29 MR	7 28 ef	12	8 26 EH	9 25 EW	10 24 fm	11 23 ft	12 23 fm	1 22 ft
2 4 TH	3 4 rt	4 3 rm	5 2 RT	5 31 md	6 30 mg	7 29 MF	13	8 27 er	9 26 ef	10 25 EH	11 24 EW	12 24 EH	1 23 EW
2 5 tr	3 5 TW	4 4 TH	5 3 rt	6 1 RM	7 1 RT	7 30 md	14	8 28 MR	9 27 MF	10 26 er	11 25 ef	12 25 er	1 24 ef
2 6 FR	3 6 tf	4 5 tr	5 4 TW	6 2 rm	7 2 rt	7 31 RM	15	8 29 mg	9 28 md	10 27 MR	11 26 MF	12 26 MR	1 25 MF
2 7 fg	3 7 FF	4 6 FR	5 5 tf	6 3 TH	7 3 TW	8 1 rm	16	8 30 RT	9 29 RM	10 28 mg	11 27 md	12 27 mg	1 26 md
2 8 ET	3 8 fd	4 7 fg	5 6 FF	6 4 tr	7 4 tf	8 2 TH	17	8 31 rt	9 30 rm	10 29 RT	11 28 RM	12 28 RT	1 27 RM
2 9 et	3 9 EM	4 8 ET	5 7 fd	6 5 FR	7 5 FF	8 3 tr	18	9 1 TW	10 1 TH	10 30 rt	11 29 rm	12 29 rt	1 28 rm
2 10 MW	3 10 em	4 9 et	5 8 EM	6 6 fg	7 6 fd	8 4 FR	19	9 2 tf	10 2 tr	10 31 TW	11 30 TH	12 30 TW	1 29 TH
2 11 mf	3 11 MH	4 10 MW	5 9 em	6 7 ET	7 7 EM	8 5 fg	20	9 3 FF	10 3 FR	11 1 tf	12 1 tr	12 31 tf	1 30 tr
2 12 RF	3 12 mr	4 11 mf	5 10 MH	6 8 et	7 8 em	8 6 ET	21	9 4 fd	10 4 fg	11 2 FF	12 2 FR	1 1 FF	1 31 FR
2 13 rd	3 13 RR	4 12 RF	5 11 mr	6 9 MW	7 9 MH	8 7 et	22	9 5 EM	10 5 ET	11 3 fd	12 3 fg	1 2 fd	2 1 fg
2 14 TM	3 14 rg	4 13 rd	5 12 RR	6 10 mf	7 10 mr	8 8 MW	23	9 6 em	10 6 et	11 4 EM	12 4 ET	1 3 EM	2 2 ET
2 15 tm	3 15 TT	4 14 TM	5 13 rg	6 11 RF	7 11 RR	8 9 mf	24	9 7 MH	10 7 MW	11 5 em	12 5 et	1 4 em	2 3 et
2 16 FH	3 16 tt	4 15 tm	5 14 TT	6 12 rd	7 12 rg	8 10 RF	25	9 8 mr	10 8 mf	11 6 MH	12 6 MW	1 5 MH	2 4 MW
2 17 fr	3 17 FW	4 16 FH	5 15 tt	6 13 TM	7 13 TT	8 11 rd	26	9 9 RR	10 9 RF	11 7 mr	12 7 mf	1 6 mr	2 5 mf
2 18 ER	3 18 ff	4 17 fr	5 16 FW	6 14 tm	7 14 tt	8 12 TM	27	9 10 rg	10 10 rd	11 8 RR	12 8 RF	1 7 RR	2 6 RF
2 19 eg	3 19 EF	4 18 ER	5 17 ff	6 15 FH	7 15 FW	8 13 tm	28	9 11 TT	10 11 TM	11 9 rg	12 9 rd	1 8 rg	2 7 rd
2 20 MT	3 20 ed	4 19 eg	5 18 EF	6 16 fr	7 16 ff	8 14 FH	29	9 12 tt	10 12 tm	11 10 TT	12 10 TM	1 9 TT	2 8 TT
	3 21 MM			6 17 ER			30	9 13 FW		11 11 tt	12 11 tm	1 10 tt	2 9 tm

173

1929 ef SNAKE

JAN FT	FEB ft	MAR EW	APR ef	MAY MF	JUN md	DAY OF MON	JUL RM	AUG rm	SEP TH	OCT tr	NOV FR	DEC fg
25 WARM	26 CLEAR	27 SUMMER	29 GRAIN		1 HEAT	1	4 FALL	6 DEW	7 C DEW	8 WINTER	7 SNOW	7 CHILL
9:32	14:52	8:41	13:11		23:32		9:09	11:40	3:55	5:28	21:57	9:03
2 10 FH	3 11 tt	4 10 tm	5 9 TT	6 7 rd	7 7 rg	1	8 5 RF	9 3 mr	10 3 mf	11 1 MH	12 1 MW	12 31 MH
2 11 fr	3 12 FW	4 11 FH	5 10 tt	6 8 TM	7 8 TT	2	8 6 rd	9 4 RR	10 4 RF	11 2 mr	12 2 mf	1 1 mr
2 12 ER	3 13 ff	4 12 fr	5 11 FW	6 9 tm	7 9 tt	3	8 7 TM	9 5 rg	10 5 rd	11 3 RR	12 3 RF	1 2 RR
2 13 eg	3 14 EF	4 13 ER	5 12 ff	6 10 FH	7 10 FW	4	8 8 tm	9 6 TT	10 6 TM	11 4 rg	12 4 rd	1 3 rg
2 14 MT	3 15 ed	4 14 eg	5 13 EF	6 11 fr	7 11 ff	5	8 9 FH	9 7 tt	10 7 tm	11 5 TT	12 5 TM	1 4 TT
2 15 mt	3 16 MM	4 15 MT	5 14 ed	6 12 ER	7 12 EF	6	8 10 fr	9 8 FW	10 8 FH	11 6 tt	12 6 tm	1 5 tt
2 16 RW	3 17 mm	4 16 mt	5 15 MM	6 13 eg	7 13 ed	7	8 11 ER	9 9 ff	10 9 fr	11 7 FW	12 7 FH	1 6 FW
2 17 rf	3 18 RH	4 17 RW	5 16 mm	6 14 MT	7 14 MM	8	8 12 eg	9 10 EF	10 10 ER	11 8 ff	12 8 fr	1 7 ff
2 18 TF	3 19 rr	4 18 rf	5 17 RH	6 15 mt	7 15 mm	9	8 13 MT	9 11 ed	10 11 eg	11 9 EF	12 9 ER	1 8 EF
2 19 td	3 20 TR	4 19 TF	5 18 rr	6 16 RW	7 16 RH	10	8 14 mt	9 12 MM	10 12 MT	11 10 ed	12 10 eg	1 9 ed
2 20 FM	3 21 tg	4 20 td	5 19 TR	6 17 rf	7 17 rr	11	8 15 RW	9 13 mm	10 13 mt	11 11 MM	12 11 MT	1 10 MM
2 21 fm	3 22 FT	4 21 FM	5 20 tg	6 18 TF	7 18 TR	12	8 16 rf	9 14 RH	10 14 RW	11 12 mm	12 12 mt	1 11 mm
2 22 EH	3 23 ft	4 22 fm	5 21 FT	6 19 td	7 19 tg	13	8 17 TF	9 15 rr	10 15 rf	11 13 RH	12 13 RW	1 12 RH
2 23 er	3 24 EW	4 23 EH	5 22 ft	6 20 FM	7 20 FT	14	8 18 td	9 16 TR	10 16 TF	11 14 rr	12 14 rf	1 13 rr
2 24 MR	3 25 ef	4 24 er	5 23 EW	6 21 fm	7 21 ft	15	8 19 FM	9 17 tg	10 17 td	11 15 TR	12 15 TF	1 14 TR
2 25 mg	3 26 MF	4 25 MR	5 24 ef	6 22 EH	7 22 FM	16	8 20 fm	9 18 FT	10 18 FM	11 16 tg	12 16 td	1 15 tg
2 26 RT	3 27 md	4 26 mg	5 25 MF	6 23 er	7 23 fm	17	8 21 EH	9 19 ft	10 19 fm	11 17 FT	12 17 FM	1 16 FT
2 27 rt	3 28 RM	4 27 RT	5 26 md	6 24 MR	7 24 EH	18	8 22 er	9 20 EW	10 20 EH	11 18 ft	12 18 fm	1 17 ft
2 28 TW	3 29 rm	4 28 rt	5 27 RM	6 25 mg	7 25 er	19	8 23 MR	9 21 ef	10 21 er	11 19 EW	12 19 EH	1 18 EW
3 1 tf	3 30 TH	4 29 TW	5 28 rm	6 26 RT	7 26 MR	20	8 24 mg	9 22 MF	10 22 MR	11 20 ef	12 20 er	1 19 ef
3 2 ff	3 31 tr	4 30 tf	5 29 TH	6 27 rt	7 27 rm	21	8 25 RT	9 23 md	10 23 mg	11 21 MF	12 21 MR	1 20 MF
3 3 fd	4 1 FR	5 1 FF	5 30 tr	6 28 TW	7 28 TW	22	8 26 rt	9 24 RM	10 24 RT	11 22 md	12 22 mg	1 21 md
3 4 EM	4 2 fg	5 2 fd	5 31 FR	6 29 tf	7 29 tf	23	8 27 TW	9 25 rm	10 25 rt	11 23 RM	12 23 RT	1 22 RM
3 5 em	4 3 ET	5 3 EM	6 1 fg	6 30 FF	7 30 FF	24	8 28 tf	9 26 TH	10 26 TW	11 24 rm	12 24 rt	1 23 rm
3 6 MH	4 4 et	5 4 em	6 2 ET	7 1 fd	7 31 fd	25	8 29 FF	9 27 tr	10 27 tf	11 25 TH	12 25 TW	1 24 TH
3 7 mr	4 5 MW	5 5 MH	6 3 et	7 2 EM	8 1 ET	26	8 30 fd	9 28 FR	10 28 FF	11 26 tr	12 26 tf	1 25 tr
3 8 RR	4 6 mf	5 6 mr	6 4 MW	7 3 em	8 2 et	27	8 31 EM	9 29 fg	10 29 fd	11 27 FR	12 27 FF	1 26 FR
3 9 rg	4 7 RF	5 7 RR	6 5 mf	7 4 MH	8 3 MW	28	9 1 em	9 30 ET	10 30 EM	11 28 fg	12 28 fd	1 27 fg
3 10 TT	4 8 rd	5 8 rg	6 6 RF	7 5 mr	8 4 mf	29	9 2 MH	10 1 et	10 31 em	11 29 ET	12 29 EM	1 28 ET
	4 9 TM			7 6 RR		30		10 2 MW		11 30 et	12 30 em	1 29 et

1930 MF HORSE

	JAN ET	FEB et	MAR MW	APR mf	MAY RF	JUN rd	JUN rd	DAY OF MON	JUL TM	AUG tm	SEP FH	OCT fr	NOV ER	DEC eg
	6 SPRING	7 WARM	7 CLEAR	8 SUMMER	10 GRAIN	13 HEAT	14 FALL		16 DEW	18 C DEW	18 WINTER	19 SNOW	18 CHILL	18 SPRING
	20:52	15:17	20:38	14:28	19:05	5:20	15:31		17:29	9:44	11:21	9:32	15:12	2:41
1	1 30 MW	2 28 em	3 30 et	4 29 em	5 28 ET	6 26 fd	7 26 fg	1	8 24 FF	9 22 tr	10 22 tf	11 20 TH	12 20 TW	1 18 rm
2	1 31 mf	3 1 MH	3 31 MW	4 30 MH	5 29 et	6 27 EM	7 27 ET	2	8 25 fd	9 23 FR	10 23 FF	11 21 tr	12 21 tf	1 19 TH
3	2 1 RF	3 2 mr	4 1 mf	5 1 mr	5 30 MW	6 28 em	7 28 et	3	8 26 EM	9 24 fg	10 24 fd	11 22 FR	12 22 FF	1 20 tr
4	2 2 rd	3 3 RR	4 2 RF	5 2 RR	5 31 mf	6 29 MH	7 29 MW	4	8 27 em	9 25 ET	10 25 EM	11 23 fg	12 23 fd	1 21 FR
5	2 3 TM	3 4 rg	4 3 rd	5 3 rg	6 1 RF	6 30 mr	7 30 mf	5	8 28 MH	9 26 et	10 26 em	11 24 ET	12 24 EM	1 22 fg
6	2 4 tm	3 5 TT	4 4 TM	5 4 TT	6 2 rd	7 1 RR	7 31 RF	6	8 29 mr	9 27 MW	10 27 MH	11 25 et	12 25 em	1 23 ET
7	2 5 FH	3 6 tt	4 5 tm	5 5 tt	6 3 TM	7 2 rg	8 1 rd	7	8 30 RR	9 28 mf	10 28 mr	11 26 MW	12 26 MH	1 24 et
8	2 6 fr	3 7 FW	4 6 FH	5 6 FW	6 4 tm	7 3 TT	8 2 TM	8	8 31 rg	9 29 RF	10 29 RR	11 27 mf	12 27 mr	1 25 MW
9	2 7 ER	3 8 ff	4 7 fr	5 7 ff	6 5 FH	7 4 tt	8 3 tm	9	9 1 TT	9 30 rd	10 30 rg	11 28 RF	12 28 RR	1 26 mf
10	2 8 eg	3 9 EF	4 8 ER	5 8 EF	6 6 fr	7 5 FW	8 4 FH	10	9 2 tt	10 1 TM	10 31 TT	11 29 rd	12 29 rg	1 27 RF
11	2 9 MT	3 10 ed	4 9 eg	5 9 ed	6 7 ER	7 6 ff	8 5 fr	11	9 3 FW	10 2 tm	11 1 tt	11 30 TM	12 30 TT	1 28 rd
12	2 10 mt	3 11 MM	4 10 MT	5 10 MM	6 8 eg	7 7 EF	8 6 ER	12	9 4 ff	10 3 FH	11 2 FW	12 1 tm	12 31 tt	1 29 TM
13	2 11 RW	3 12 mm	4 11 mt	5 11 mm	6 9 MT	7 8 ed	8 7 eg	13	9 5 EF	10 4 fr	11 3 ff	12 2 FH	1 1 FW	1 30 tm
14	2 12 rf	3 13 RH	4 12 RW	5 12 RH	6 10 mt	7 9 MM	8 8 MT	14	9 6 ed	10 5 ER	11 4 EF	12 3 fr	1 2 ff	1 31 FH
15	2 13 TF	3 14 rr	4 13 rf	5 13 rr	6 11 RW	7 10 mm	8 9 mt	15	9 7 MM	10 6 eg	11 5 ed	12 4 ER	1 3 EF	2 1 fr
16	2 14 td	3 15 TR	4 14 TF	5 14 TR	6 12 rf	7 11 RH	8 10 RW	16	9 8 mm	10 7 MT	11 6 MM	12 5 eg	1 4 ed	2 2 ER
17	2 15 FM	3 16 tg	4 15 td	5 15 tg	6 13 TF	7 12 rr	8 11 rf	17	9 9 RH	10 8 mt	11 7 mm	12 6 MT	1 5 MM	2 3 eg
18	2 16 fm	3 17 FT	4 16 FM	5 16 FT	6 14 td	7 13 TR	8 12 TF	18	9 10 rr	10 9 RW	11 8 RH	12 7 mt	1 6 mm	2 4 MT
19	2 17 EH	3 18 ft	4 17 fm	5 17 ft	6 15 FM	7 14 tg	8 13 td	19	9 11 TR	10 10 rf	11 9 rr	12 8 RW	1 7 RH	2 5 mt
20	2 18 er	3 19 EW	4 18 EH	5 18 EW	6 16 fm	7 15 FT	8 14 FM	20	9 12 tg	10 11 TF	11 10 TR	12 9 rf	1 8 rr	2 6 RW
21	2 19 MR	3 20 ef	4 19 er	5 19 ef	6 17 EH	7 16 ft	8 15 fm	21	9 13 FT	10 12 td	11 11 tg	12 10 TF	1 9 TR	2 7 rf
22	2 20 mg	3 21 MF	4 20 MR	5 20 MF	6 18 er	7 17 EW	8 16 EH	22	9 14 ft	10 13 FM	11 12 FT	12 11 td	1 10 tg	2 8 TF
23	2 21 RT	3 22 md	4 21 mg	5 21 md	6 19 MR	7 18 ef	8 17 er	23	9 15 EW	10 14 fm	11 13 ft	12 12 FM	1 11 FT	2 9 td
24	2 22 rt	3 23 RM	4 22 RT	5 22 RM	6 20 mg	7 19 MF	8 18 MR	24	9 16 ef	10 15 EH	11 14 EW	12 13 fm	1 12 ft	2 10 FM
25	2 23 TW	3 24 rm	4 23 rt	5 23 rm	6 21 RT	7 20 md	8 19 mg	25	9 17 MF	10 16 er	11 15 ef	12 14 EH	1 13 EW	2 11 fm
26	2 24 tf	3 25 TH	4 24 TW	5 24 TH	6 22 rt	7 21 RM	8 20 RT	26	9 18 md	10 17 MR	11 16 MF	12 15 er	1 14 ef	2 12 EH
27	2 25 FF	3 26 tr	4 25 tf	5 25 tr	6 23 TW	7 22 rm	8 21 rt	27	9 19 RM	10 18 mg	11 17 md	12 16 MR	1 15 MF	2 13 er
28	2 26 fd	3 27 FR	4 26 FF	5 26 FR	6 24 tf	7 23 TH	8 22 TW	28	9 20 rm	10 19 RT	11 18 RM	12 17 mg	1 16 md	2 14 MR
29	2 27 EM	3 28 fg	4 27 fd	5 27 fg	6 25 FF	7 24 tr	8 23 tf	29	9 21 TH	10 20 rt	11 19 rm	12 18 RT	1 17 RM	2 15 mg
30		3 29 ET	4 28 EM			7 25 FR		30		10 21 TW		12 19 rt		2 16 RT

175

1931   md   RAM

JAN MT	FEB mt	MAR RW	APR rf	MAY TF	JUN ed	JUL FM	DAY OF MON	AUG fm	SEP EH	OCT er	NOV MR	DEC mg
18 WARM	19 CLEAR	19 SUMMER	22 GRAIN	23 HEAT	25 FALL	27 DEW		28 C DEW	29 WINTER	29 SNOW	29 CHILL	29 SPRING
21:03	2:21	20:10	0:42	11:6	21:20	0:10		15:33	17:10	9:41	3:30	8:30
2 17 rt	3 19 rm	4 18 rt	5 17 RM	6 16 RT	7 15 md	8 14 mg	1	9 12 MF	10 11 er	11 10 ef	12 9 EH	1 8 EW
2 18 TW	3 20 TH	4 19 TW	5 18 rm	6 17 rt	7 16 RM	8 15 RT	2	9 13 md	10 12 MR	11 11 MF	12 10 er	1 9 ef
2 19 tf	3 21 tr	4 20 tf	5 19 TH	6 18 TW	7 17 rm	8 16 rt	3	9 14 RM	10 13 mg	11 12 md	12 11 MR	1 10 MF
2 20 FF	3 22 FR	4 21 FF	5 20 tr	6 19 tf	7 18 TH	8 17 TW	4	9 15 rm	10 14 RT	11 13 RM	12 12 mg	1 11 md
2 21 fd	3 23 fg	4 22 fd	5 21 FR	6 20 FF	7 19 tr	8 18 tf	5	9 16 TH	10 15 rt	11 14 TH	12 13 RT	1 12 RM
2 22 EM	3 24 ET	4 23 EM	5 22 fg	6 21 fd	7 20 FR	8 19 FF	6	9 17 tr	10 16 TW	11 15 TH	12 14 rt	1 13 rm
2 23 em	3 25 et	4 24 em	5 23 ET	6 22 EM	7 21 fg	8 20 fd	7	9 18 FR	10 17 tf	11 16 tr	12 15 TW	1 14 TH
2 24 MH	3 26 MW	4 25 MH	5 24 et	6 23 em	7 22 ET	8 21 EM	8	9 19 fg	10 18 FF	11 17 FR	12 16 tf	1 15 tr
2 25 mr	3 27 mf	4 26 mr	5 25 MW	6 24 MH	7 23 et	8 22 em	9	9 20 ET	10 19 fd	11 18 fg	12 17 FF	1 16 FR
2 26 RR	3 28 RF	4 27 RR	5 26 mf	6 25 mr	7 24 MW	8 23 MH	10	9 21 et	10 20 EM	11 19 ET	12 18 fd	1 17 fg
2 27 rg	3 29 rd	4 28 rg	5 27 RF	6 26 RR	7 25 mf	8 24 mr	11	9 22 MW	10 21 em	11 20 et	12 19 EM	1 18 ET
2 28 TT	3 30 TM	4 29 TT	5 28 rd	6 27 rg	7 26 RF	8 25 RR	12	9 23 mf	10 22 MH	11 21 MW	12 20 em	1 19 et
3 1 tt	3 31 tm	4 30 tt	5 29 TM	6 28 TT	7 27 rd	8 26 rg	13	9 24 RF	10 23 mr	11 22 mf	12 21 MH	1 20 MW
3 2 FW	4 1 FH	5 1 FW	5 30 tm	6 29 tt	7 28 TM	8 27 TT	14	9 25 rd	10 24 RR	11 23 RF	12 22 mr	1 21 mf
3 3 ff	4 2 fr	5 2 ff	5 31 fr	6 30 FW	7 29 tm	8 28 tt	15	9 26 TM	10 25 rg	11 24 rd	12 23 RR	1 22 RF
3 4 EF	4 3 ER	5 3 EF	6 1 fr	7 1 ff	7 30 FH	8 29 FW	16	9 27 tm	10 26 TT	11 25 TM	12 24 rg	1 23 rd
3 5 ed	4 4 eg	5 4 ed	6 2 ER	7 2 EF	7 31 fr	8 30 ff	17	9 28 FH	10 27 tt	11 26 tm	12 25 TT	1 24 TM
3 6 MM	4 5 MT	5 5 MM	6 3 eg	7 3 ed	8 1 ER	8 31 EF	18	9 29 fr	10 28 FW	11 27 FH	12 26 tt	1 25 tm
3 7 mm	4 6 mt	5 6 mm	6 4 MT	7 4 MM	8 2 eg	9 1 ed	19	9 30 ER	10 29 ff	11 28 fr	12 27 FW	1 26 FH
3 8 RH	4 7 RW	5 7 RH	6 5 mt	7 5 mm	8 3 MT	9 2 MM	20	10 1 eg	10 30 EF	11 29 ER	12 28 ff	1 27 fr
3 9 rr	4 8 rf	5 8 rr	6 6 RW	7 6 RH	8 4 mt	9 3 mm	21	10 2 MT	10 31 ed	11 30 eg	12 29 EF	1 28 ER
3 10 TR	4 9 TF	5 9 TR	6 7 rf	7 7 rr	8 5 RW	9 4 RH	22	10 3 mt	11 1 MM	12 1 MT	12 30 ed	1 29 eg
3 11 tg	4 10 td	5 10 tg	6 8 TF	7 8 TR	8 6 rf	9 5 rr	23	10 4 RW	11 2 mm	12 2 mt	12 31 MM	1 30 MT
3 12 FT	4 11 FM	5 11 FT	6 9 td	7 9 tg	8 7 TF	9 6 TR	24	10 5 rf	11 3 RH	12 3 RW	1 1 mm	2 1 RW
3 13 ft	4 12 fm	5 12 ft	6 10 FM	7 10 FT	8 8 td	9 7 tg	25	10 6 TF	11 4 rr	12 4 rf	1 2 RH	2 2 rf
3 14 EW	4 13 EH	5 13 EW	6 11 fm	7 11 ft	8 9 FM	9 8 FT	26	10 7 td	11 5 TR	12 5 TF	1 3 rr	2 3 TF
3 15 ef	4 14 er	5 14 ef	6 12 EH	7 12 EW	8 10 fm	9 9 ft	27	10 8 FM	11 6 tg	12 6 td	1 4 TR	2 4 td
3 16 MF	4 15 MR	5 15 MF	6 13 er	7 13 ef	8 11 EH	9 10 EW	28	10 9 fm	11 7 FT	12 7 FM	1 5 tg	2 5 FM
3 17 md	4 16 mg	5 16 md	6 14 MR	7 14 MF	8 12 er	9 11 ef	29	10 10 EH	11 8 ft	12 8 fm	1 6 FT	
3 18 RM	4 17 RT		6 15 mg		8 13 MR		30		11 9 EW		1 7 ft	

176

1932 RM MONKEY

JAN RT	FEB rt	MAR TW	APR tf	MAY FF	JUN fd	DAY OF MON	JUL EM	AUG em	SEP MH	OCT mr	NOV RR	DEC rg
30 WARM	30 CLEAR		1 SUMMER	3 GRAIN	4 HEAT		7 FALL	8 DEW	9 C DEW	11 WINTER	10 SNOW	11 CHILL
2:50	8:07		1:55	6:28	17:14		3:18	5:03	21:21	0:02	15:19	2:24
2 6 fm	3 7 ft	4 6 fm	5 6 ft	6 4 FM	7 4 FT	1	8 2 td	9 1 tg	9 30 TF	10 29 rr	11 28 rf	12 27 RH
2 7 EH	3 8 EW	4 7 EH	5 7 EW	6 5 fm	7 5 ft	2	8 3 FM	9 2 FT	10 1 td	10 30 TR	11 29 TF	12 28 rr
2 8 er	3 9 ef	4 8 er	5 8 ef	6 6 EH	7 6 EW	3	8 4 fm	9 3 ft	10 2 FM	10 31 tg	11 30 td	12 29 TR
2 9 MR	3 10 MF	4 9 MR	5 9 MF	6 7 er	7 7 ef	4	8 5 EH	9 4 EW	10 3 fm	11 1 FT	12 1 FM	12 30 tg
2 10 mg	3 11 md	4 10 mg	5 10 md	6 8 MR	7 8 MF	5	8 6 er	9 5 ef	10 4 EH	11 2 ft	12 2 fm	12 31 FT
2 11 RT	3 12 RM	4 11 RT	5 11 RM	6 9 mg	7 9 md	6	8 7 MR	9 6 MF	10 5 er	11 3 EW	12 3 EH	1 1 ft
2 12 rt	3 13 rm	4 12 rt	5 12 rm	6 10 RT	7 10 RM	7	8 8 mg	9 7 md	10 6 MR	11 4 ef	12 4 er	1 2 EW
2 13 TW	3 14 TH	4 13 TW	5 13 TH	6 11 rt	7 11 rm	8	8 9 RT	9 8 RM	10 7 mg	11 5 MF	12 5 MR	1 3 ef
2 14 tf	3 15 tr	4 14 tf	5 14 tr	6 12 TW	7 12 TH	9	8 10 rt	9 9 rm	10 8 RT	11 6 md	12 6 mg	1 4 MF
2 15 FF	3 16 FR	4 15 FF	5 15 FR	6 13 tf	7 13 tr	10	8 11 TW	9 10 TH	10 9 rt	11 7 RM	12 7 RT	1 5 md
2 16 fd	3 17 fg	4 16 fd	5 16 fg	6 14 FF	7 14 FR	11	8 12 tf	9 11 tr	10 10 TW	11 8 rm	12 8 rt	1 6 RM
2 17 EM	3 18 ET	4 17 EM	5 17 ET	6 15 fd	7 15 fg	12	8 13 FF	9 12 FR	10 11 tf	11 9 TH	12 9 TW	1 7 rm
2 18 em	3 19 et	4 18 em	5 18 et	6 16 EM	7 16 ET	13	8 14 fd	9 13 fg	10 12 FF	11 10 tr	12 10 tf	1 8 TH
2 19 MH	3 20 MW	4 19 MH	5 19 MW	6 17 em	7 17 et	14	8 15 EM	9 14 ET	10 13 fd	11 11 FR	12 11 FF	1 9 tr
2 20 mr	3 21 mf	4 20 mr	5 20 mf	6 18 MH	7 18 MW	15	8 16 em	9 15 et	10 14 EM	11 12 fg	12 12 fd	1 10 FR
2 21 RR	3 22 RF	4 21 RR	5 21 RF	6 19 mr	7 19 mf	16	8 17 MH	9 16 MW	10 15 em	11 13 ET	12 13 EM	1 11 fg
2 22 rg	3 23 rd	4 22 rg	5 22 rd	6 20 RR	7 20 RF	17	8 18 mr	9 17 mf	10 16 MH	11 14 et	12 14 em	1 12 ET
2 23 TT	3 24 TM	4 23 TT	5 23 TM	6 21 rg	7 21 rd	18	8 19 RR	9 18 RF	10 17 mr	11 15 MW	12 15 MH	1 13 et
2 24 tt	3 25 tm	4 24 tt	5 24 tm	6 22 TT	7 22 TM	19	8 20 rg	9 19 rd	10 18 RR	11 16 mf	12 16 mr	1 14 MW
2 25 FW	3 26 FH	4 25 FW	5 25 FH	6 23 tt	7 23 tm	20	8 21 TT	9 20 TM	10 19 rg	11 17 RF	12 17 RR	1 15 mf
2 26 ff	3 27 fr	4 26 ff	5 26 fr	6 24 FW	7 24 FH	21	8 22 tt	9 21 tm	10 20 TT	11 18 rd	12 18 rg	1 16 RF
2 27 EF	3 28 ER	4 27 EF	5 27 ER	6 25 ff	7 25 fr	22	8 23 FW	9 22 FH	10 21 tt	11 19 TM	12 19 TT	1 17 rd
2 28 ed	3 29 eg	4 28 ed	5 28 eg	6 26 EF	7 26 ER	23	8 24 ff	9 23 fr	10 22 FW	11 20 tm	12 20 tt	1 18 TM
2 29 MM	3 30 MT	4 29 MM	5 29 MT	6 27 ed	7 27 eg	24	8 25 EF	9 24 ER	10 23 ff	11 21 FH	12 21 FW	1 19 tm
3 1 mm	3 31 mt	4 30 mm	5 30 mt	6 28 MM	7 28 MT	25	8 26 ed	9 25 eg	10 24 EF	11 22 fr	12 22 ff	1 20 FH
3 2 RH	4 1 RW	5 1 RH	5 31 RW	6 29 mm	7 29 mt	26	8 27 MM	9 26 MT	10 25 ed	11 23 ER	12 23 EF	1 21 fr
3 3 rr	4 2 rf	5 2 rr	6 1 rf	6 30 RH	7 30 RW	27	8 28 mm	9 27 mt	10 26 MM	11 24 eg	12 24 ed	1 22 ER
3 4 TR	4 3 TF	5 3 TR	6 2 TF	7 1 rr	7 31 rf	28	8 29 RH	9 28 RW	10 27 mm	11 25 MT	12 25 MM	1 23 eg
3 5 tg	4 4 td	5 4 tg	6 3 td	7 2 TR	8 1 TF	29	8 30 rr	9 29 rf	10 28 RH	11 26 mt	12 26 mm	1 24 MT
3 6 FT	4 5 FM	5 5 FT		7 3 tg		30	8 31 TR			11 27 RW		1 25 mt

177

1933 rm ROOSTER

	JAN TT	FEB tt	MAR FW	APR ff	MAY EF	MAY	JUN ed	DAY OF	JUL MM	AUG mm	SEP RH	OCT ri	NOV TR	DEC tg
	10 SPRING	11 WARM	11 CLEAR	12 SUMMER	14 GRAIN	15 HEAT	18 FALL	MON	19 DEW	20 C DEW	21 WINTER	20 SNOW	21 CHILL	21 SPRING
	14:10	8:32	13:51	7:42	12:18	23:02	8:26		11:47	3:11	5:51	14:04	8:17	20:04
1	1 26 RW	2 24 mm	3 26 mt	4 25 mm	5 24 MT	6 23 MM	7 23 MT	1	8 21 ed	9 20 eg	10 19 EF	11 18 RR	12 17 ff	1 15 FH
2	1 27 rf	2 25 RH	3 27 RW	4 26 RH	5 25 mt	6 24 mm	7 24 mt	2	8 22 MM	9 21 MT	10 20 ed	11 19 eg	12 18 EF	1 16 fr
3	1 28 TF	2 26 rr	3 28 rf	4 27 rr	5 26 RW	6 25 RH	7 25 RW	3	8 23 mm	9 22 mt	10 21 MM	11 20 MT	12 19 ed	1 17 RR
4	1 29 td	2 27 TR	3 29 TF	4 28 TR	5 27 rf	6 26 rr	7 26 rf	4	8 24 RH	9 23 RW	10 22 mm	11 21 mt	12 20 MM	1 18 eg
5	1 30 FM	2 28 tg	3 30 td	4 29 tg	5 28 TF	6 27 TR	7 27 TF	5	8 25 rr	9 24 rf	10 23 RH	11 22 RW	12 21 mm	1 19 MT
6	1 31 fm	3 1 FT	3 31 FM	4 30 FT	5 29 td	6 28 tg	7 28 td	6	8 26 TR	9 25 TF	10 24 rr	11 23 rf	12 22 RH	1 20 mt
7	2 1 EH	3 2 ft	4 1 fm	5 1 ft	5 30 FM	6 29 FT	7 29 FM	7	8 27 tg	9 26 td	10 25 TR	11 24 TF	12 23 rr	1 21 RW
8	2 2 er	3 3 EW	4 2 EH	5 2 EW	5 31 fm	6 30 ft	7 30 fm	8	8 28 FT	9 27 FM	10 26 tg	11 25 td	12 24 TR	1 22 rf
9	2 3 MR	3 4 ef	4 3 er	5 3 ef	6 1 EH	7 1 EW	7 31 EH	9	8 29 ft	9 28 fm	10 27 FT	11 26 FM	12 25 tg	1 23 TF
10	2 4 mg	3 5 MF	4 4 MR	5 4 MF	6 2 er	7 2 ef	8 1 er	10	8 30 EW	9 29 EH	10 28 ft	11 27 fm	12 26 FT	1 24 td
11	2 5 RT	3 6 md	4 5 mg	5 5 md	6 3 MR	7 3 MF	8 2 MR	11	8 31 ef	9 30 er	10 29 EH	11 28 EH	12 27 ft	1 25 FM
12	2 6 rt	3 7 RM	4 6 RT	5 6 RM	6 4 mg	7 4 md	8 3 mg	12	9 1 MF	10 1 MR	10 30 ef	11 29 er	12 28 EW	1 26 fm
13	2 7 TW	3 8 rm	4 7 rt	5 7 rm	6 5 RT	7 5 RM	8 4 RT	13	9 2 md	10 2 mg	10 31 MF	11 30 MR	12 29 ef	1 27 EH
14	2 8 tf	3 9 TH	4 8 TW	5 8 TH	6 6 rt	7 6 rm	8 5 rt	14	9 3 RM	10 3 RT	11 1 md	12 1 mg	12 30 MF	1 28 er
15	2 9 FF	3 10 tr	4 9 tf	5 9 tr	6 7 TW	7 7 TH	8 6 TW	15	9 4 rm	10 4 rt	11 2 RM	12 2 RT	12 31 md	1 29 MR
16	2 10 fd	3 11 FR	4 10 FF	5 10 FR	6 8 tf	7 8 tr	8 7 tf	16	9 5 TH	10 5 TW	11 3 rm	12 3 rt	1 1 RM	1 30 RT
17	2 11 EM	3 12 fg	4 11 fd	5 11 fg	6 9 FF	7 9 FR	8 8 FF	17	9 6 tr	10 6 tf	11 4 TH	12 4 TW	1 2 rm	2 1 rt
18	2 12 em	3 13 ET	4 12 EM	5 12 ET	6 10 fd	7 10 fg	8 9 fd	18	9 7 FR	10 7 FF	11 5 tr	12 5 tf	1 3 TH	2 2 TW
19	2 13 MH	3 14 et	4 13 em	5 13 et	6 11 EM	7 11 ET	8 10 EM	19	9 8 fg	10 8 fd	11 6 FR	12 6 FF	1 4 tr	2 3 tf
20	2 14 mr	3 15 MH	4 14 MH	5 14 MW	6 12 em	7 12 et	8 11 em	20	9 9 ET	10 9 EM	11 7 fg	12 7 fd	1 5 FR	2 4 FF
21	2 15 RR	3 16 mf	4 15 mf	5 15 mf	6 13 MH	7 13 MW	8 12 MH	21	9 10 et	10 10 em	11 8 ET	12 8 EM	1 6 fg	2 5 fd
22	2 16 rg	3 17 RF	4 16 RR	5 16 RF	6 14 mr	7 14 mf	8 13 mr	22	9 11 MW	10 11 MH	11 9 et	12 9 em	1 7 ET	2 6 EM
23	2 17 TT	3 18 rd	4 17 rg	5 17 rd	6 15 RR	7 15 RF	8 14 RR	23	9 12 mf	10 12 mr	11 10 MW	12 10 MH	1 8 et	2 7 em
24	2 18 tt	3 19 TM	4 18 TT	5 18 TM	6 16 rg	7 16 rd	8 15 rg	24	9 13 RF	10 13 RR	11 11 mf	12 11 mr	1 9 MW	2 8 MH
25	2 19 FW	3 20 tm	4 19 tt	5 19 tm	6 17 TT	7 17 TM	8 16 TT	25	9 14 rd	10 14 rg	11 12 RF	12 12 RR	1 10 mf	2 9 mr
26	2 20 ff	3 21 FH	4 20 FW	5 20 FH	6 18 tt	7 18 tm	8 17 tt	26	9 15 TM	10 15 TM	11 13 rd	12 13 rg	1 11 RF	2 10 RR
27	2 21 EF	3 22 fr	4 21 ff	5 21 fr	6 19 FW	7 19 FH	8 18 FW	27	9 16 tm	10 16 tt	11 14 TM	12 14 TT	1 12 rd	2 11 rg
28	2 22 ed	3 23 ER	4 22 EF	5 22 ER	6 20 ff	7 20 fr	8 19 ff	28	9 17 FH	10 17 FW	11 15 tm	12 15 tt	1 13 TM	2 12 TT
29	2 23 MM	3 24 eg	4 23 ed	5 23 eg	6 21 EF	7 21 ER	8 20 EF	29	9 18 fr	10 18 ff	11 16 FH	12 16 FW	1 14 tm	2 13 tt
30		3 25 MT	4 24 MM		6 22 ed	7 22 eg		30	9 19 ER		11 17 fr			

1934 TH DOG

Month headers (month · sexagenary code · solar term · time):

Month	Code	Solar term	Time
JAN	FT	21 WARM	14:27
FEB	ft	22 CLEAR	22:44
MAR	EW	23 SUMMER	13:31
APR	ef	25 GRAIN	18:02
MAY	MF	27 HEAT	4:25
JUN	md	28 FALL	14:04
JUL	RM	30 DEW	17:36
AUG	rm		
SEP	TH	2 C DEW	7:45
OCT	tr	20 WINTER	11:41
NOV	FR	2 SNOW	3:53
DEC	fg	2 CHILL	14:03

Calendar grid (rows = DAY OF MON; cells = Gregorian month/day and day‑code):

DAY OF MON	JAN	FEB	MAR	APR	MAY	JUN	JUL	AUG	SEP	OCT	NOV	DEC
1	2/14 FW	3/15 tm	4/14 tt	5/13 TM	6/12 TT	7/12 TM	8/10 rg	9/9 rd	10/8 RR	11/7 RF	12/7 RR	1/5 mf
2	2/15 ff	3/16 FH	4/15 FW	5/14 tm	6/13 tt	7/13 tm	8/11 TT	9/10 TM	10/9 rg	11/8 rd	12/8 rg	1/6 RF
3	2/16 EF	3/17 fr	4/16 ff	5/15 FH	6/14 FW	7/14 FH	8/12 tt	9/11 tm	10/10 TT	11/9 TM	12/9 TT	1/7 rd
4	2/17 ed	3/18 ER	4/17 EF	5/16 fr	6/15 ff	7/15 fr	8/13 FW	9/12 FH	10/11 tt	11/10 tm	12/10 tt	1/8 TM
5	2/18 MM	3/19 eg	4/18 ed	5/17 ER	6/16 EF	7/16 ER	8/14 ff	9/13 fr	10/12 FW	11/11 FH	12/11 FW	1/9 tm
6	2/19 mm	3/20 MT	4/19 MM	5/18 eg	6/17 ed	7/17 eg	8/15 EF	9/14 ER	10/13 ff	11/12 fr	12/12 ff	1/10 FH
7	2/20 RH	3/21 mt	4/20 mm	5/19 MT	6/18 MM	7/18 MT	8/16 ed	9/15 eg	10/14 EF	11/13 ER	12/13 EF	1/11 fr
8	2/21 rr	3/22 RW	4/21 RH	5/20 mt	6/19 mm	7/19 mt	8/17 MM	9/16 MT	10/15 ed	11/14 eg	12/14 ed	1/12 ER
9	2/22 TR	3/23 rf	4/22 rr	5/21 RW	6/20 RH	7/20 RW	8/18 mm	9/17 mt	10/16 MM	11/15 MT	12/15 MM	1/13 eg
10	2/23 tg	3/24 TF	4/23 TR	5/22 rf	6/21 rr	7/21 rf	8/19 RH	9/18 RW	10/17 mm	11/16 mt	12/16 mm	1/14 MT
11	2/24 FT	3/25 td	4/24 tg	5/23 TF	6/22 TR	7/22 TF	8/20 rr	9/19 rf	10/18 RH	11/17 RW	12/17 RH	1/15 mt
12	2/25 ft	3/26 FM	4/25 FT	5/24 td	6/23 tg	7/23 td	8/21 TR	9/20 TF	10/19 rr	11/18 rf	12/18 rr	1/16 RW
13	2/26 EW	3/27 fm	4/26 ft	5/25 FM	6/24 FT	7/24 FM	8/22 tg	9/21 td	10/20 TR	11/19 TF	12/19 TR	1/17 rf
14	2/27 ef	3/28 EH	4/27 EW	5/26 fm	6/25 ft	7/25 fm	8/23 FT	9/22 FM	10/21 tg	11/20 td	12/20 tg	1/18 TF
15	2/28 MF	3/29 er	4/28 ef	5/27 EH	6/26 EW	7/26 EH	8/24 ft	9/23 fm	10/22 FT	11/21 FM	12/21 FT	1/19 td
16	3/1 md	3/30 MR	4/29 MF	5/28 er	6/27 ef	7/27 er	8/25 EW	9/24 EH	10/23 ft	11/22 fm	12/22 ft	1/20 FM
17	3/2 RM	3/31 mg	4/30 md	5/29 MR	6/28 MF	7/28 MR	8/26 ef	9/25 er	10/24 EW	11/23 EH	12/23 EW	1/21 fm
18	3/3 rm	4/1 RT	5/1 RM	5/30 mg	6/29 md	7/29 mg	8/27 MF	9/26 MR	10/25 ef	11/24 er	12/24 ef	1/22 EH
19	3/4 TH	4/2 rt	5/2 rm	5/31 RT	6/30 RM	7/30 RT	8/28 md	9/27 mg	10/26 MF	11/25 MR	12/25 MF	1/23 er
20	3/5 tr	4/3 TW	5/3 TH	6/1 rt	7/1 rm	7/31 rt	8/29 RM	9/28 RT	10/27 md	11/26 mg	12/26 md	1/24 MR
21	3/6 FR	4/4 tf	5/4 tr	6/2 TW	7/2 TH	8/1 TW	8/30 rm	9/29 rt	10/28 RM	11/27 RT	12/27 RM	1/25 mg
22	3/7 fg	4/5 FF	5/5 FR	6/3 tf	7/3 tr	8/2 tf	8/31 TH	9/30 TW	10/29 rm	11/28 rt	12/28 rm	1/26 RT
23	3/8 ET	4/6 fd	5/6 fg	6/4 FF	7/4 FR	8/3 FF	9/1 tr	10/1 tf	10/30 TH	11/29 TW	12/29 TH	1/27 rt
24	3/9 et	4/7 EM	5/7 ET	6/5 fd	7/5 fg	8/4 fd	9/2 FR	10/2 FF	10/31 tr	11/30 tf	12/30 tr	1/28 TW
25	3/10 MW	4/8 em	5/8 et	6/6 EM	7/6 ET	8/5 EM	9/3 fg	10/3 fd	11/1 FR	12/1 FF	12/31 FR	1/29 tf
26	3/11 mf	4/9 MH	5/9 MW	6/7 em	7/7 et	8/6 em	9/4 ET	10/4 EM	11/2 fg	12/2 fd	1/1 fg	1/30 FF
27	3/12 RF	4/10 mr	5/10 mf	6/8 MH	7/8 MW	8/7 MH	9/5 et	10/5 em	11/3 ET	12/3 EM	1/2 ET	1/31 fd
28	3/13 rd	4/11 RR	5/11 RF	6/9 mr	7/9 mf	8/8 mr	9/6 MW	10/6 MH	11/4 et	12/4 em	1/3 et	2/1 EM
29	3/14 TM	4/12 rg	5/12 rd	6/10 RR	7/10 RF	8/9 RR	9/7 mf	10/7 mr	11/5 MW	12/5 MH	1/4 MW	2/2 em
30		4/13 TT		6/11 rg	7/11 rd		9/8 RF		11/6 mf	12/6 mr		2/3 MH

1935　tr　BOAR

	JAN ET	FEB et	MAR MW	APR mf	MAY RF	JUN rd	DAY OF MON	JUL TM	AUG tm	SEP FH	OCT fr	NOV ER	DEC eg
	2 SPRING	2 WARM	4 CLEAR	4 SUMMER	7 GRAIN	8 HEAT		10 FALL	11 DEW	12 C DEW	13 WINTER	13 SNOW	12 CHILL
	1:49	20:11	1:27	19:12	0:06	10:06		19:48	23:25	13:36	17:30	9:43	19:47
1	2 4 mr	3 5 MW	4 3 em	5 3 et	6 1 EM	7 1 ET	1	7 30 fd	8 29 fg	9 28 fd	10 27 FR	11 26 FF	12 26 FR
2	2 5 RR	3 6 mf	4 4 MH	5 4 MW	6 2 em	7 2 et	2	7 31 EM	8 30 ET	9 29 EM	10 28 fg	11 27 fd	12 27 fg
3	2 6 rg	3 7 RF	4 5 mr	5 5 mf	6 3 MH	7 3 MW	3	8 1 em	8 31 et	9 30 em	10 29 ET	11 28 EM	12 28 ET
4	2 7 TT	3 8 rd	4 6 RR	5 6 RF	6 4 mr	7 4 mf	4	8 2 MH	9 1 MW	10 1 MH	10 30 et	11 29 em	12 29 et
5	2 8 tt	3 9 TM	4 7 rg	5 7 rd	6 5 RR	7 5 RF	5	8 3 mr	9 2 mf	10 2 mr	10 31 MW	11 30 MH	12 30 MW
6	2 9 FW	3 10 tm	4 8 TT	5 8 TM	6 6 rg	7 6 rd	6	8 4 RR	9 3 RF	10 3 RR	11 1 mf	12 1 mr	12 31 mf
7	2 10 ff	3 11 FH	4 9 tt	5 9 tm	6 7 TT	7 7 TM	7	8 5 rg	9 4 rd	10 4 rg	11 2 RF	12 2 RR	1 1 RF
8	2 11 EF	3 12 fr	4 10 FW	5 10 FH	6 8 tt	7 8 tm	8	8 6 TT	9 5 TM	10 5 TT	11 3 rd	12 3 rg	1 2 rd
9	2 12 ed	3 13 ER	4 11 ff	5 11 fr	6 9 FW	7 9 FH	9	8 7 tt	9 6 tm	10 6 tt	11 4 TM	12 4 TT	1 3 TM
10	2 13 MM	3 14 eg	4 12 EF	5 12 ER	6 10 ff	7 10 fr	10	8 8 FW	9 7 FH	10 7 FW	11 5 tm	12 5 tt	1 4 tm
11	2 14 mm	3 15 MT	4 13 ed	5 13 ed	6 11 EF	7 11 ER	11	8 9 ff	9 8 fr	10 8 ff	11 6 FH	12 6 FW	1 5 FH
12	2 15 RH	3 16 mt	4 14 MM	5 14 MT	6 12 ed	7 12 eg	12	8 10 EF	9 9 ER	10 9 EF	11 7 fr	12 7 ff	1 6 fr
13	2 16 rr	3 17 RW	4 15 mm	5 15 mt	6 13 MM	7 13 MT	13	8 11 ed	9 10 eg	10 10 ed	11 8 ER	12 8 EF	1 7 ER
14	2 17 TR	3 18 rf	4 16 RH	5 16 RW	6 14 mm	7 14 mt	14	8 12 MM	9 11 MT	10 11 MM	11 9 eg	12 9 ed	1 8 eg
15	2 18 tg	3 19 TF	4 17 rr	5 17 rf	6 15 RH	7 15 RW	15	8 13 mm	9 12 mt	10 12 mm	11 10 MT	12 10 MM	1 9 MT
16	2 19 FT	3 20 td	4 18 TR	5 18 TR	6 16 rr	7 16 rf	16	8 14 RH	9 13 RW	10 13 RH	11 11 mt	12 11 mm	1 10 mt
17	2 20 ft	3 21 FM	4 19 tg	5 19 tg	6 17 TR	7 17 TR	17	8 15 rr	9 14 rf	10 14 rr	11 12 RW	12 12 RH	1 11 RW
18	2 21 EW	3 22 fm	4 20 FT	5 20 FM	6 18 tg	7 18 tg	18	8 16 TR	9 15 TF	10 15 TR	11 13 rf	12 13 rr	1 12 rf
19	2 22 ef	3 23 EH	4 21 ft	5 21 fm	6 19 FT	7 19 FT	19	8 17 tg	9 16 td	10 16 tg	11 14 TF	12 14 TR	1 13 TF
20	2 23 MF	3 24 er	4 22 EW	5 22 EW	6 20 ft	7 20 fm	20	8 18 FT	9 17 FM	10 17 FT	11 15 td	12 15 tg	1 14 td
21	2 24 md	3 25 MR	4 23 ef	5 23 er	6 21 EW	7 21 EW	21	8 19 ft	9 18 fm	10 18 ft	11 16 FM	12 16 FT	1 15 FM
22	2 25 RM	3 26 mg	4 24 MF	5 24 MR	6 22 ef	7 22 ef	22	8 20 EW	9 19 EH	10 19 EW	11 17 fm	12 17 ft	1 16 fm
23	2 26 rm	3 27 RT	4 25 md	5 25 mg	6 23 MF	7 23 MR	23	8 21 ef	9 20 er	10 20 ef	11 18 EH	12 18 EW	1 17 EH
24	2 27 TH	3 28 rt	4 26 RT	5 26 RT	6 24 md	7 24 mg	24	8 22 MF	9 21 MR	10 21 MF	11 19 er	12 19 ef	1 18 er
25	2 28 th	3 29 TW	4 27 rt	5 27 rt	6 25 RM	7 25 RM	25	8 23 md	9 22 mg	10 22 md	11 20 MR	12 20 MF	1 19 MR
26	3 1 FR	3 30 tf	4 28 TH	5 28 TW	6 26 rm	7 26 rt	26	8 24 RM	9 23 RM	10 23 RM	11 21 mg	12 21 md	1 20 mg
27	3 2 fg	3 31 FF	4 29 tr	5 29 tf	6 27 TH	7 27 TW	27	8 25 rm	9 24 rt	10 24 rm	11 22 RT	12 22 RM	1 21 RT
28	3 3 ET	4 1 fd	4 30 FR	5 30 FF	6 28 tr	7 28 tf	28	8 26 TH	9 25 TW	10 25 TH	11 23 rt	12 23 rm	1 22 rt
29	3 4 et	4 2 EM	5 1 fg	5 31 fd	6 29 FR	7 29 FR	29	8 27 tr	9 26 tf	10 26 tr	11 24 TW	12 24 TH	1 23 TW
30			5 2 ET		6 30 fg		30	8 28 FR	9 27 FF		11 25 tf	12 25 tr	
31													

180

1936 FR RAT

Month header (month abbreviation · cycle code · FR‑calendar date & season · time)

Month	Code	FR date / season	Time
JAN	MT	13 SPRING	7:30
FEB	mt	13 WARM	1:50
MAR	RW	14 CLEAR	7:07
MAR	RW	16 SUMMER	1:14
APR	rf	17 GRAIN	5:31
MAY	FF	19 HEAT	15:59
JUN	td	22 FALL	1:43
DAY OF MON			
JUL	FM	23 DEW	5:13
AUG	fm	23 C DEW	19:33
SEP	EH	24 WINTER	23:19
OCT	er	24 SNOW	15:33
NOV	MR	24 CHILL	1:44
DEC	mg	23 SPRING	13:26

Daily grid (day‑of‑month + cycle code for each column)

JAN	FEB	MAR	MAR	APR	MAY	JUN	MON	JUL	AUG	SEP	OCT	NOV	DEC
24 tf	23 tr	23 TW	21 rm	21 rt	19 RM	18 mg	1	17 md	16 mg	15 MF	14 MR	14 MF	13 MR
25 FF	24 FR	24 tf	22 TH	22 TW	20 rm	19 RT	2	18 RM	17 RT	16 md	15 mg	15 md	14 mg
26 fd	25 fg	25 FF	23 tr	23 tf	21 TH	20 rt	3	19 rm	18 rt	17 RM	16 RT	16 RM	15 RT
27 EM	26 ET	26 fd	24 FR	24 FF	22 tr	21 TW	4	20 TH	19 TW	18 rm	17 rt	17 rm	16 rt
28 em	27 et	27 EM	25 fg	25 fd	23 FR	22 tf	5	21 tr	20 tf	19 TH	18 TW	18 TH	17 TW
29 MH	28 MW	28 em	26 ET	26 EM	24 fg	23 FF	6	22 FR	21 FF	20 tr	19 tf	19 tr	18 tf
30 mr	29 mf	29 MH	27 et	27 em	25 ET	24 fd	7	23 fg	22 fd	21 FR	20 FF	20 FR	19 FF
31 RR	1 RF	30 mr	28 MW	28 MH	26 et	25 EM	8	24 ET	23 EM	22 fg	21 fd	21 fg	20 fd
1 rg	2 rd	31 RR	29 mf	29 mr	27 MW	26 em	9	25 et	24 em	23 ET	22 EM	22 ET	21 EM
2 TT	3 TM	1 rg	30 RF	30 RR	28 mf	27 MH	10	26 MW	25 MH	24 et	23 em	23 et	22 em
3 tt	4 tm	2 TT	31 rd	1 rg	29 RF	28 mr	11	27 mf	26 mr	25 MW	24 MH	24 MW	23 MH
4 FW	5 FH	3 tt	1 TM	2 TT	30 rd	29 RR	12	28 RF	27 RR	26 mf	25 mr	25 mf	24 mr
5 ff	6 fr	4 FW	2 tm	3 tt	31 TM	30 rg	13	29 rd	28 rg	27 RF	26 RR	26 RF	25 RR
6 EF	7 ER	5 ff	3 FH	4 FW	1 tm	1 TT	14	30 TM	29 TT	28 rd	27 rg	27 rd	26 rg
7 ed	8 eg	6 EF	4 fr	5 ff	2 FH	2 tt	15	31 tm	30 tt	29 TM	28 TT	28 TM	27 TT
8 MM	9 MT	7 ed	5 ER	6 EF	3 fr	3 FW	16	1 FH	31 FW	30 tm	29 tt	29 tm	28 tt
9 mm	10 mt	8 MM	6 eg	7 ed	4 ER	4 ff	17	2 fr	1 ff	1 FH	30 FW	30 FH	29 FW
10 RH	11 RW	9 mm	7 MT	8 MM	5 eg	5 EF	18	3 ER	2 EF	2 fr	31 ff	1 fr	30 ff
11 rr	12 rf	10 RH	8 mt	9 mm	6 MT	6 ed	19	4 eg	3 ed	3 ER	1 EF	2 ER	31 EF
12 TR	13 TF	11 rr	9 RW	10 RH	7 mt	7 MM	20	5 MT	4 MM	4 eg	2 ed	3 eg	1 ed
13 tg	14 td	12 TR	10 rf	11 rr	8 RW	8 mm	21	6 mt	5 mm	5 MT	3 MM	4 MT	2 MM
14 FT	15 FM	13 tg	11 TF	12 TR	9 rf	9 RH	22	7 RW	6 RH	6 mt	4 mm	5 mt	3 mm
15 ft	16 fm	14 FT	12 td	13 tg	10 TF	10 rr	23	8 rf	7 rr	7 RW	5 RH	6 RW	4 RH
16 EW	17 EH	15 ft	13 FM	14 FT	11 td	11 TR	24	9 TF	8 TR	8 rf	6 rr	7 rf	5 rr
17 ef	18 er	16 EW	14 fm	15 ft	12 FM	12 tg	25	10 td	9 tg	9 TF	7 TR	8 TF	6 TR
18 MF	19 MR	17 ef	15 EH	16 EW	13 fm	13 FT	26	11 FM	10 FT	10 td	8 tg	9 td	7 tg
19 md	20 mg	18 MF	16 er	17 ef	14 EH	14 ft	27	12 fm	11 ft	11 FM	9 FT	10 FM	8 FT
20 RM	21 RT	19 md	17 MR	18 MF	15 er	15 EW	28	13 EH	12 EW	12 fm	10 ft	11 fm	9 ft
21 rm	22 rt	20 RM	18 mg	19 md	16 MR	16 ef	29	14 er	13 ef	13 EH	11 EW	12 EH	10 EW
22 TH		21 rm	19 RT	20 RM	17 mg	17 MF	30	15 MR	14 MF	14 er	12 ef	13 er	
		22 TH	20 rt		18 RT			16 mg	15 md		13 MF		

181

1937 fg OX

Month pillars / solar terms

Month	Pillar	Solar term	Day	Time
JAN	RT	WARM	24	7:45
FEB	rt	CLEAR	24	13:02
MAR	TW	SUMMER	26	7:02
APR	tf	GRAIN	28	11:23
MAY	FF	HEAT	29	21:46
JUN	fd	—	—	—
JUL	EM	FALL	3	7:26
AUG	em	DEW	4	11:01
SEP	MH	C DEW	6	1:12
OCT	mr	WINTER	6	5:09
NOV	RR	SNOW	5	21:22
DEC	rg	CHILL	5	7:32

Day of month table (cells show solar month/day and code)

DAY OF MON	JAN	FEB	MAR	APR	MAY	JUN	JUL	AUG	SEP	OCT	NOV	DEC
1	2/11 ef	3/13 er	4/11 EW	5/10 fm	6/9 ft	7/8 FM	8/6 tg	9/5 td	10/4 TR	11/3 TF	12/3 TR	1/2 TF
2	2/12 MF	3/14 MR	4/12 ef	5/11 EH	6/10 EW	7/9 fm	8/7 FT	9/6 FM	10/5 tg	11/4 td	12/4 tg	1/3 td
3	2/13 md	3/15 mg	4/13 MF	5/12 er	6/11 ef	7/10 EH	8/8 ft	9/7 fm	10/6 FT	11/5 FM	12/5 FT	1/4 FM
4	2/14 RM	3/16 RT	4/14 md	5/13 MR	6/12 MF	7/11 er	8/9 EW	9/8 EH	10/7 ft	11/6 fm	12/6 ft	1/5 fm
5	2/15 rm	3/17 rt	4/15 RM	5/14 mg	6/13 md	7/12 MR	8/10 ef	9/9 er	10/8 EW	11/7 EH	12/7 EW	1/6 EH
6	2/16 TH	3/18 TW	4/16 rm	5/15 RT	6/14 RM	7/13 mg	8/11 MF	9/10 MR	10/9 ef	11/8 er	12/8 ef	1/7 er
7	2/17 tr	3/19 tf	4/17 TH	5/16 rt	6/15 rm	7/14 RT	8/12 md	9/11 mg	10/10 MF	11/9 MR	12/9 MF	1/8 MR
8	2/18 FR	3/20 FF	4/18 tr	5/17 TW	6/16 TH	7/15 rt	8/13 RM	9/12 RT	10/11 md	11/10 mg	12/10 md	1/9 mg
9	2/19 fg	3/21 fd	4/19 FR	5/18 tf	6/17 tr	7/16 TW	8/14 rm	9/13 rt	10/12 RM	11/11 RT	12/11 RM	1/10 RT
10	2/20 ET	3/22 EM	4/20 fg	5/19 FF	6/18 FR	7/17 tf	8/15 TH	9/14 TW	10/13 rm	11/12 rt	12/12 rm	1/11 rt
11	2/21 et	3/23 em	4/21 ET	5/20 fd	6/19 fg	7/18 FF	8/16 tr	9/15 tf	10/14 TH	11/13 TW	12/13 TH	1/12 TW
12	2/22 MW	3/24 MH	4/22 et	5/21 EM	6/20 ET	7/19 fd	8/17 FR	9/16 FF	10/15 tr	11/14 tf	12/14 tr	1/13 tf
13	2/23 mf	3/25 mr	4/23 MW	5/22 em	6/21 et	7/20 EM	8/18 fg	9/17 fd	10/16 FR	11/15 FF	12/15 FR	1/14 FF
14	2/24 RF	3/26 RR	4/24 mf	5/23 MH	6/22 MW	7/21 em	8/19 ET	9/18 EM	10/17 fg	11/16 fd	12/16 fg	1/15 fd
15	2/25 rd	3/27 rg	4/25 RF	5/24 mr	6/23 mf	7/22 MH	8/20 et	9/19 em	10/18 ET	11/17 EM	12/17 ET	1/16 EM
16	2/26 TM	3/28 TT	4/26 rd	5/25 RR	6/24 RF	7/23 mr	8/21 MW	9/20 MH	10/19 et	11/18 em	12/18 et	1/17 em
17	2/27 tm	3/29 tt	4/27 TM	5/26 rg	6/25 rd	7/24 RR	8/22 mf	9/21 mr	10/20 MW	11/19 MH	12/19 MW	1/18 MH
18	2/28 FH	3/30 FW	4/28 tm	5/27 TT	6/26 TM	7/25 rg	8/23 RF	9/22 RR	10/21 mf	11/20 mr	12/20 mf	1/19 mr
19	3/1 fr	3/31 ff	4/29 FH	5/28 tt	6/27 tm	7/26 TT	8/24 rd	9/23 rg	10/22 RF	11/21 RR	12/21 RF	1/20 RR
20	3/2 ER	4/1 EF	4/30 fr	5/29 FW	6/28 FH	7/27 tt	8/25 TM	9/24 TT	10/23 rd	11/22 rg	12/22 rd	1/21 rg
21	3/3 eg	4/2 ed	5/1 ER	5/30 ff	6/29 fr	7/28 FW	8/26 tm	9/25 tt	10/24 TM	11/23 TT	12/23 TM	1/22 TT
22	3/4 MT	4/3 MM	5/2 eg	5/31 EF	6/30 ER	7/29 ff	8/27 FH	9/26 FW	10/25 tm	11/24 tt	12/24 tm	1/23 tt
23	3/5 mt	4/4 mm	5/3 MT	6/1 ed	7/1 eg	7/30 EF	8/28 fr	9/27 ff	10/26 FH	11/25 FW	12/25 FH	1/24 FW
24	3/6 RW	4/5 RH	5/4 mt	6/2 MM	7/2 MT	7/31 ed	8/29 ER	9/28 EF	10/27 fr	11/26 ff	12/26 fr	1/25 ff
25	3/7 rf	4/6 rr	5/5 RW	6/3 mm	7/3 mt	8/1 MM	8/30 eg	9/29 ed	10/28 ER	11/27 EF	12/27 ER	1/26 EF
26	3/8 TF	4/7 TR	5/6 rf	6/4 RH	7/4 RW	8/2 mm	8/31 MT	9/30 MM	10/29 eg	11/28 ed	12/28 eg	1/27 ed
27	3/9 td	4/8 tg	5/7 TF	6/5 rr	7/5 rf	8/3 RH	9/1 mt	10/1 mm	10/30 MT	11/29 MM	12/29 MT	1/28 MM
28	3/10 FM	4/9 FT	5/8 td	6/6 TR	7/6 TF	8/4 rr	9/2 RW	10/2 RH	10/31 mt	11/30 mm	12/30 mt	1/29 mm
29	3/11 fm	4/10 ft	5/9 FM	6/7 tg	7/7 td	8/5 TR	9/3 rf	10/3 rr	11/1 RW	12/1 RH	12/31 RW	1/30 RH
30	3/12 EH	—	—	6/8 FT	—	—	9/4 TF	—	11/2 rf	12/2 rr	1/1 rf	—

182

1938 ET TIGER

Lunar‑month columns (month label + month ganzhi):

Col	JAN	FEB	MAR	APR	MAY	JUN	JUL	AUG	SEP	OCT	NOV	DEC
Ganzhi	TT	tt	FW	ff	EF	ed	MM	mm	RH	rr	TR	tg

Solar‑term entries (day · term · time):

- 5 SPRING — 19:15
- 5 WARM — 13:34
- 5 CLEAR — 18:49
- 7 SUMMER — 12:36
- 9 GRAIN — 17:07
- 11 HEAT — 3:32
- 13 FALL — 13:13
- 15 DEW — 15:49
- 16 C DEW — 7:02
- 17 WINTER — 9:49
- 17 SNOW — 3:13
- 16 CHILL — 13:28
- 17 SPRING — 1:11

Conversion grid — for each lunar DAY OF MON (centre column), cells give the Gregorian date (M/D) and day ganzhi code:

DAY OF MON	JAN	FEB	MAR	APR	MAY	JUN	JUL	AUG	SEP	OCT	NOV	DEC
1	1/31 rr	3/2 rf	4/1 rr	4/30 RW	5/29 mm	6/28 mt	7/27 MM	8/25 eg	9/24 ed	10/23 ER	11/22 EF	12/22 ER
2	2/1 TR	3/3 TF	4/2 TR	5/1 rf	5/30 RH	6/29 RW	7/28 mm	8/26 MT	9/25 MM	10/24 eg	11/23 ed	12/23 eg
3	2/2 tg	3/4 td	4/3 tg	5/2 TF	5/31 rr	6/30 rf	7/29 RH	8/27 mt	9/26 mm	10/25 MT	11/24 MM	12/24 MT
4	2/3 FT	3/5 FM	4/4 FT	5/3 td	6/1 TR	7/1 TF	7/30 rr	8/28 RW	9/27 RH	10/26 mt	11/25 mm	12/25 mt
5	2/4 ft	3/6 fm	4/5 ft	5/4 FM	6/2 tg	7/2 td	7/31 TR	8/29 rf	9/28 rr	10/27 RW	11/26 RH	12/26 RW
6	2/5 EW	3/7 EH	4/6 EW	5/5 fm	6/3 FT	7/3 FM	8/1 tg	8/30 TF	9/29 TR	10/28 rf	11/27 rr	12/27 rf
7	2/6 ef	3/8 er	4/7 ef	5/6 EH	6/4 ft	7/4 fm	8/2 FT	8/31 td	9/30 tg	10/29 TF	11/28 TR	12/28 TF
8	2/7 MF	3/9 MR	4/8 MF	5/7 er	6/5 EW	7/5 EH	8/3 ft	9/1 FM	10/1 FT	10/30 td	11/29 tg	12/29 td
9	2/8 md	3/10 mg	4/9 md	5/8 MR	6/6 ef	7/6 er	8/4 EW	9/2 fm	10/2 ft	10/31 FM	11/30 FT	12/30 FM
10	2/9 RM	3/11 RT	4/10 RM	5/9 mg	6/7 MF	7/7 MR	8/5 ef	9/3 EH	10/3 EW	11/1 fm	12/1 ft	12/31 fm
11	2/10 rm	3/12 rt	4/11 rm	5/10 RT	6/8 md	7/8 mg	8/6 MF	9/4 er	10/4 ef	11/2 EH	12/2 EW	1/1 EH
12	2/11 TH	3/13 TW	4/12 TH	5/11 rt	6/9 RM	7/9 RT	8/7 md	9/5 MR	10/5 MF	11/3 er	12/3 ef	1/2 er
13	2/12 tr	3/14 tf	4/13 tr	5/12 TW	6/10 rm	7/10 rt	8/8 RM	9/6 mg	10/6 md	11/4 MR	12/4 MF	1/3 MR
14	2/13 FR	3/15 FF	4/14 FR	5/13 tf	6/11 TH	7/11 TW	8/9 rm	9/7 RT	10/7 RM	11/5 mg	12/5 md	1/4 mg
15	2/14 fg	3/16 fd	4/15 fg	5/14 FF	6/12 tr	7/12 tf	8/10 TH	9/8 rt	10/8 rm	11/6 RT	12/6 RM	1/5 RT
16	2/15 ET	3/17 EM	4/16 ET	5/15 fd	6/13 FR	7/13 FF	8/11 tr	9/9 TW	10/9 TH	11/7 rt	12/7 rm	1/6 rt
17	2/16 et	3/18 em	4/17 et	5/16 EM	6/14 fg	7/14 fd	8/12 FR	9/10 tf	10/10 tr	11/8 TW	12/8 TH	1/7 TW
18	2/17 MW	3/19 MH	4/18 MW	5/17 em	6/15 ET	7/15 EM	8/13 fg	9/11 FF	10/11 FR	11/9 tf	12/9 tr	1/8 tf
19	2/18 mf	3/20 mr	4/19 mf	5/18 MH	6/16 et	7/16 em	8/14 ET	9/12 fd	10/12 fg	11/10 FF	12/10 FR	1/9 FF
20	2/19 RF	3/21 RR	4/20 RF	5/19 mr	6/17 MW	7/17 MH	8/15 et	9/13 EM	10/13 ET	11/11 fd	12/11 fg	1/10 fd
21	2/20 rd	3/22 rg	4/21 rd	5/20 RR	6/18 mf	7/18 mr	8/16 MW	9/14 em	10/14 et	11/12 EM	12/12 ET	1/11 EM
22	2/21 TM	3/23 TT	4/22 TM	5/21 rg	6/19 RF	7/19 RR	8/17 mf	9/15 MH	10/15 MW	11/13 em	12/13 et	1/12 em
23	2/22 tm	3/24 tt	4/23 tm	5/22 TT	6/20 rd	7/20 rg	8/18 RF	9/16 mr	10/16 mf	11/14 MH	12/14 MW	1/13 MH
24	2/23 FH	3/25 FW	4/24 FH	5/23 tt	6/21 TM	7/21 TT	8/19 rd	9/17 RR	10/17 RF	11/15 mr	12/15 mf	1/14 mr
25	2/24 fr	3/26 ff	4/25 fr	5/24 FW	6/22 tm	7/22 tt	8/20 TM	9/18 rg	10/18 rd	11/16 RR	12/16 RF	1/15 RR
26	2/25 ER	3/27 EF	4/26 ER	5/25 ff	6/23 FH	7/23 FW	8/21 tm	9/19 TT	10/19 TM	11/17 rg	12/17 rd	1/16 rg
27	2/26 eg	3/28 ed	4/27 eg	5/26 EF	6/24 fr	7/24 ff	8/22 FH	9/20 tt	10/20 tm	11/18 TT	12/18 TM	1/17 TT
28	2/27 MT	3/29 MM	4/28 MT	5/27 ed	6/25 ER	7/25 EF	8/23 fr	9/21 FW	10/21 FH	11/19 tt	12/19 tm	1/18 tt
29	2/28 mt	3/30 mm	4/29 mt	5/28 MM	6/26 eg	7/26 ed	8/24 ER	9/22 ff	10/22 fr	11/20 FW	12/20 FH	1/19 FW
30	3/1 RW	3/31 RH	—	—	6/27 MT	—	—	9/23 EF	—	11/21 ff	12/21 fr	1/20 ff

1939 et RABBIT

	JAN FT	FEB ft	MAR EW	APR ef	MAY MF	JUN md	DAY OF MON	JUL RM	AUG rm	SEP TH	OCT tr	NOV FR	DEC fg
	16 WARM	17 CLEAR	17 SUMMER	19 GRAIN	22 HEAT	23 FALL	25 DEW	27 C DEW	27 WINTER	28 SNOW	27 CHILL	28 SPRING	
	19:27	0:38	18:21	23:19	9:19	19:04	20:39	14:05	15:40	9:02	19:24	7:08	
1	2 19 fr	3 21 ff	4 20 fr	5 19 FW	6 17 tm	7 17 tt	8 15 TM	9 13 rg	10 13 rd	11 11 RR	12 11 RF	1 9 mr
2	2 20 ER	3 22 EF	4 21 ER	5 20 ff	6 18 FH	7 18 FW	8 16 tm	9 14 TT	10 14 TM	11 12 rg	12 12 rd	1 10 RR
3	2 21 eg	3 23 ed	4 22 eg	5 21 EF	6 19 fr	7 19 ff	8 17 FH	9 15 tt	10 15 tm	11 13 TT	12 13 TM	1 11 rg
4	2 22 MT	3 24 MM	4 23 MT	5 22 ed	6 20 ER	7 20 EF	8 18 fr	9 16 FW	10 16 FH	11 14 tt	12 14 tm	1 12 TT
5	2 23 mt	3 25 mm	4 24 mt	5 23 MM	6 21 eg	7 21 ed	8 19 ER	9 17 ff	10 17 fr	11 15 FW	12 15 FH	1 13 tt
6	2 24 RW	3 26 RH	4 25 RW	5 24 mm	6 22 MT	7 22 MM	8 20 eg	9 18 EF	10 18 ER	11 16 ff	12 16 fr	1 14 FW
7	2 25 rf	3 27 rr	4 26 rf	5 25 RH	6 23 mt	7 23 mm	8 21 MT	9 19 ed	10 19 eg	11 17 EF	12 17 ER	1 15 ff
8	2 26 TF	3 28 TR	4 27 TF	5 26 rr	6 24 RW	7 24 RH	8 22 mt	9 20 eg	10 20 MT	11 18 ed	12 18 eg	1 16 EF
9	2 27 td	3 29 tg	4 28 td	5 27 TR	6 25 rf	7 25 rr	8 23 RW	9 21 MM	10 21 mt	11 19 MM	12 19 MT	1 17 ed
10	2 28 fm	3 30 FT	4 29 FM	5 28 tg	6 26 TF	7 26 TR	8 24 rf	9 22 mm	10 22 mt	11 20 mm	12 20 mt	1 18 MM
11	3 1 ft	3 31 ft	4 30 EH	5 29 FT	6 27 td	7 27 tg	8 25 TF	9 23 RH	10 23 rf	11 21 RH	12 21 RW	1 19 mm
12	3 2 EH	4 1 EW	5 1 er	5 30 ft	6 28 FM	7 28 FT	8 26 td	9 24 rr	10 24 TF	11 22 rr	12 22 rf	1 20 RH
13	3 3 er	4 2 ef	5 2 MR	5 31 EW	6 29 fm	7 29 ft	8 27 FM	9 25 tg	10 25 td	11 23 TR	12 23 TF	1 21 rr
14	3 4 MR	4 3 MF	5 3 mg	6 1 ef	6 30 EH	7 30 EW	8 28 fm	9 26 FT	10 26 FM	11 24 tg	12 24 td	1 22 TR
15	3 5 mg	4 4 md	5 4 RT	6 2 MF	7 1 er	7 31 ef	8 29 EH	9 27 ft	10 27 fm	11 25 FT	12 25 FM	1 23 tg
16	3 6 RT	4 5 RT	5 5 rt	6 3 md	7 2 MR	8 1 MF	8 30 er	9 28 EH	10 28 EH	11 26 ft	12 26 fm	1 24 FT
17	3 7 rt	4 6 rm	5 6 TW	6 4 RM	7 3 mg	8 2 md	8 31 MR	9 29 er	10 29 er	11 27 EW	12 27 EH	1 25 ft
18	3 8 TW	4 7 TH	5 7 tf	6 5 rm	7 4 RT	8 3 RM	9 1 mg	9 30 MR	10 30 MR	11 28 ef	12 28 er	1 26 EW
19	3 9 tf	4 8 tr	5 8 FF	6 6 TH	7 5 rt	8 4 rm	9 2 RT	10 1 mg	10 31 mg	11 29 MR	12 29 MR	1 27 ef
20	3 10 FF	4 9 FR	5 9 ET	6 7 tr	7 6 TW	8 5 TH	9 3 rt	10 2 RT	11 1 RT	11 30 mg	12 30 mg	1 28 MF
21	3 11 EM	4 10 fg	5 10 em	6 8 FR	7 7 tf	8 6 tr	9 4 TW	10 3 rt	11 2 rt	12 1 RM	12 31 RT	1 29 md
22	3 12 em	4 11 ET	5 11 MH	6 9 fg	7 8 FF	8 7 FR	9 5 tf	10 4 TW	11 3 TW	12 2 rm	1 1 rt	1 30 RM
23	3 13 MH	4 12 et	5 12 mr	6 10 ET	7 9 ET	8 8 fg	9 6 FF	10 5 tf	11 4 tf	12 3 TH	1 2 TW	2 1 rm
24	3 14 mr	4 13 MW	5 13 RF	6 11 et	7 10 em	8 9 ET	9 7 fd	10 6 FF	11 5 FR	12 4 tr	1 3 tf	2 2 TH
25	3 15 RF	4 14 mf	5 14 rd	6 12 MW	7 11 MH	8 10 et	9 8 EM	10 7 fd	11 6 fg	12 5 FR	1 4 FF	2 3 tr
26	3 16 rd	4 15 RF	5 15 rg	6 13 mf	7 12 mr	8 11 MW	9 9 em	10 8 EM	11 7 fd	12 6 fg	1 5 fd	2 4 FR
27	3 17 rg	4 16 rd	5 16 rg	6 14 RF	7 13 mr	8 12 mf	9 10 MH	10 9 em	11 8 EM	12 7 ET	1 6 EM	2 5 fg
28	3 18 TT	4 17 TM	5 17 TT	6 15 rd	7 14 RR	8 13 RF	9 11 mr	10 10 MH	11 9 em	12 8 et	1 7 em	2 6 ET
29	3 19 tt	4 18 tm	5 18 tt	6 16 TM	7 15 rg	8 14 rd	9 12 RR	10 11 mr	11 10 MH	12 9 MW	1 8 MH	2 7 et
30	3 20 FW									12 10 mf		2 8 MW

1940 MW DRAGON

Month	Ganzhi	Solar term	Time
JAN	ET	28 WARM	1:24
FEB	et	28 CLEAR	6:35
MAR	MW	29 SUMMER	0:16
APR	mf		
MAY	RF	1 GRAIN	5:07
JUN	rd	3 HEAT	15:08
JUL	TM	5 FALL	1:34
AUG	tm	7 DEW	3:30
SEP	FH	8 C DEW	19:54
OCT	fr	8 WINTER	21:27
NOV	ER	9 SNOW	13:58
DEC	eg	9 CHILL	1:04

DAY OF MON

Day	JAN	FEB	MAR	APR	MAY	JUN	JUL	AUG	SEP	OCT	NOV	DEC
1	2/8 mf	3/9 mr	4/8 mf	5/7 MH	6/6 MW	7/5 em	8/4 et	9/2 EM	10/1 fg	10/31 fd	11/29 FR	12/29 FF
2	2/9 RF	3/10 RR	4/9 RF	5/8 mr	6/7 mf	7/6 MH	8/5 MW	9/3 em	10/2 ET	11/1 EM	11/30 fg	12/30 fd
3	2/10 rd	3/11 rg	4/10 rd	5/9 RR	6/8 RF	7/7 mr	8/6 mf	9/4 MH	10/3 et	11/2 em	12/1 ET	12/31 EM
4	2/11 TM	3/12 TT	4/11 TM	5/10 rg	6/9 rd	7/8 RR	8/7 RF	9/5 mr	10/4 MW	11/3 MH	12/2 et	1/1 em
5	2/12 tm	3/13 tt	4/12 tm	5/11 TT	6/10 TM	7/9 rg	8/8 rd	9/6 RR	10/5 mf	11/4 mr	12/3 MW	1/2 MH
6	2/13 FH	3/14 FW	4/13 FH	5/12 tt	6/11 tm	7/10 TT	8/9 TM	9/7 rg	10/6 RF	11/5 RR	12/4 mf	1/3 mr
7	2/14 fr	3/15 ff	4/14 fr	5/13 FW	6/12 FH	7/11 tt	8/10 tm	9/8 TT	10/7 rd	11/6 rg	12/5 RF	1/4 RR
8	2/15 ER	3/16 EF	4/15 ER	5/14 ff	6/13 fr	7/12 FW	8/11 FH	9/9 tt	10/8 TM	11/7 TT	12/6 rd	1/5 rg
9	2/16 eg	3/17 ed	4/16 eg	5/15 EF	6/14 ER	7/13 ff	8/12 fr	9/10 FW	10/9 tm	11/8 tt	12/7 TM	1/6 TT
10	2/17 MT	3/18 MM	4/17 MT	5/16 ed	6/15 eg	7/14 EF	8/13 ER	9/11 ff	10/10 FH	11/9 FW	12/8 tm	1/7 tt
11	2/18 mt	3/19 mm	4/18 mt	5/17 MM	6/16 MT	7/15 ed	8/14 eg	9/12 EF	10/11 fr	11/10 ff	12/9 FH	1/8 FW
12	2/19 RW	3/20 RH	4/19 RW	5/18 mm	6/17 mt	7/16 MM	8/15 MT	9/13 ed	10/12 ER	11/11 EF	12/10 fr	1/9 ff
13	2/20 rf	3/21 rr	4/20 rf	5/19 RH	6/18 RW	7/17 mm	8/16 mt	9/14 MM	10/13 eg	11/12 ed	12/11 ER	1/10 EF
14	2/21 TF	3/22 TR	4/21 TF	5/20 rr	6/19 rf	7/18 RH	8/17 RW	9/15 mm	10/14 MT	11/13 MM	12/12 eg	1/11 ed
15	2/22 td	3/23 tg	4/22 td	5/21 TR	6/20 TF	7/19 rr	8/18 rf	9/16 RH	10/15 mt	11/14 mm	12/13 MT	1/12 MM
16	2/23 FM	3/24 FT	4/23 FM	5/22 tg	6/21 td	7/20 TR	8/19 TF	9/17 rr	10/16 RW	11/15 RH	12/14 mt	1/13 mm
17	2/24 fm	3/25 ft	4/24 fm	5/23 FT	6/22 FM	7/21 tg	8/20 td	9/18 TR	10/17 rf	11/16 rr	12/15 RW	1/14 RH
18	2/25 EH	3/26 EW	4/25 EH	5/24 ft	6/23 fm	7/22 FT	8/21 FM	9/19 tg	10/18 TF	11/17 TR	12/16 rf	1/15 rr
19	2/26 er	3/27 ef	4/26 er	5/25 EW	6/24 EH	7/23 ft	8/22 fm	9/20 FT	10/19 td	11/18 tg	12/17 TF	1/16 TR
20	2/27 MR	3/28 MF	4/27 MR	5/26 ef	6/25 er	7/24 EW	8/23 EH	9/21 ft	10/20 FM	11/19 FT	12/18 td	1/17 tg
21	2/28 mg	3/29 md	4/28 mg	5/27 MF	6/26 MR	7/25 ef	8/24 er	9/22 EW	10/21 fm	11/20 ft	12/19 FM	1/18 FT
22	2/29 RT	3/30 RM	4/29 RT	5/28 md	6/27 mg	7/26 MF	8/25 MR	9/23 ef	10/22 EH	11/21 EW	12/20 fm	1/19 ft
23	3/1 rt	3/31 rm	4/30 rt	5/29 RM	6/28 RT	7/27 md	8/26 mg	9/24 MF	10/23 er	11/22 ef	12/21 EH	1/20 EW
24	3/2 TW	4/1 TH	5/1 TW	5/30 rm	6/29 rt	7/28 RM	8/27 RT	9/25 md	10/24 MR	11/23 MF	12/22 er	1/21 ef
25	3/3 tf	4/2 tr	5/2 tf	5/31 TH	6/30 TW	7/29 rm	8/28 rt	9/26 RM	10/25 mg	11/24 md	12/23 MR	1/22 MF
26	3/4 FF	4/3 FR	5/3 FF	6/1 tr	7/1 tf	7/30 TH	8/29 TW	9/27 rm	10/26 RT	11/25 RM	12/24 mg	1/23 md
27	3/5 fd	4/4 fg	5/4 fd	6/2 FR	7/2 FF	7/31 tr	8/30 tf	9/28 TH	10/27 rt	11/26 rm	12/25 RT	1/24 RM
28	3/6 EM	4/5 ET	5/5 EM	6/3 fg	7/3 fd	8/1 FR	8/31 FF	9/29 tr	10/28 TW	11/27 TH	12/26 rt	1/25 rm
29	3/7 em	4/6 et	5/6 em	6/4 ET	7/4 EM	8/2 fg	9/1 fd	9/30 FR	10/29 tf	11/28 tr	12/27 TW	1/26 TH
30	3/8 MH	4/7 MW		6/5 et		8/3 ET			10/30 FF		12/28 tf	

JAN MT	FEB mt	MAR RW	APR rf	MAY FF	JUN td	JUN td	DAY OF MON	JUL FM	AUG fm	SEP EH	OCT er	NOV MR	DEC mg
9 SPRING	9 WARM	9 CLEAR	11 SUMMER	12 GRAIN	13 HEAT	16 FALL	17 DEW	19 C DEW	20 WINTER	19 SNOW	20 CHILL	19 SPRING	
12:50	7:10	12:25	6:10	10:40	31:03	7:22	9:24	1:43	3:25	19:57	7:03	18:49	
1 27 tr	2 26 tf	3 28 tr	4 26 TW	5 26 TH	6 25 TW	7 24 rm	1	8 23 rt	9 21 RM	10 20 mg	11 19 md	12 18 MR	1 17 MF
1 28 FR	2 27 FF	3 29 FR	4 27 tf	5 27 tr	6 26 tf	7 25 TH	2	8 24 TW	9 22 rm	10 21 RT	11 20 RM	12 19 mg	1 18 md
1 29 fg	2 28 fd	3 30 fg	4 28 FF	5 28 FR	6 27 FF	7 26 tr	3	8 25 tf	9 23 TH	10 22 rt	11 21 rm	12 20 RT	1 19 RM
1 30 ET	3 1 EM	3 31 ET	4 29 fd	5 29 fg	6 28 fd	7 27 FR	4	8 26 FF	9 24 tr	10 23 TW	11 22 TH	12 21 rt	1 20 rm
1 31 et	3 2 em	4 1 et	4 30 ET	5 30 ET	6 29 EM	7 28 fg	5	8 27 fd	9 25 FR	10 24 tf	11 23 tr	12 22 TW	1 21 TH
2 1 MW	3 3 MH	4 2 MW	5 1 em	5 31 et	6 30 em	7 29 ET	6	8 28 EM	9 26 fg	10 25 FF	11 24 FR	12 23 tf	1 22 tr
2 2 mf	3 4 mr	4 3 mf	5 2 MH	6 1 MW	7 1 MH	7 30 et	7	8 29 em	9 27 ET	10 26 fd	11 25 fg	12 24 FF	1 23 FR
2 3 RF	3 5 RR	4 4 RF	5 3 mr	6 2 mf	7 2 mf	7 31 MW	8	8 30 MH	9 28 et	10 27 EM	11 26 ET	12 25 fd	1 24 fg
2 4 rd	3 6 rg	4 5 rd	5 4 RR	6 3 RF	7 3 RF	8 1 mf	9	8 31 mr	9 29 MW	10 28 em	11 27 et	12 26 EM	1 25 ET
2 5 TM	3 7 TT	4 6 TM	5 5 rg	6 4 rd	7 4 rd	8 2 RF	10	9 1 RR	9 30 mf	10 29 MH	11 28 MW	12 27 em	1 26 et
2 6 tm	3 8 tt	4 7 tm	5 6 TT	6 5 TM	7 5 TM	8 3 rd	11	9 2 rg	10 1 RF	10 30 mr	11 29 mf	12 28 MH	1 27 MW
2 7 FH	3 9 FW	4 8 FH	5 7 tt	6 6 tm	7 6 tm	8 4 TM	12	9 3 TT	10 2 rd	10 31 RR	11 30 RF	12 29 mr	1 28 mf
2 8 fr	3 10 ff	4 9 fr	5 8 FW	6 7 FH	7 7 FH	8 5 tm	13	9 4 tt	10 3 TM	11 1 rg	12 1 rd	12 30 RR	1 29 RF
2 9 ER	3 11 EF	4 10 ER	5 9 ff	6 8 fr	7 8 fr	8 6 FH	14	9 5 FW	10 4 tm	11 2 TT	12 2 TM	12 31 rg	2 1 rd
2 10 er	3 12 ed	4 11 ed	5 10 ER	6 9 ER	7 9 ER	8 7 fr	15	9 6 ff	10 5 FH	11 3 tt	12 3 tm	1 1 TT	2 2 TM
2 11 MT	3 13 MM	4 12 MT	5 11 ed	6 10 eg	7 10 ed	8 8 ER	16	9 7 EF	10 6 fr	11 4 FW	12 4 FH	1 2 tt	2 3 tm
2 12 mt	3 14 mm	4 13 mt	5 12 MT	6 11 MT	7 11 MT	8 9 eg	17	9 8 ed	10 7 ER	11 5 ff	12 5 fr	1 3 FW	2 4 FH
2 13 RW	3 15 RH	4 14 RW	5 13 mt	6 12 mt	7 12 mt	8 10 MT	18	9 9 MM	10 8 eg	11 6 EF	12 6 ER	1 4 ff	2 5 fr
2 14 rf	3 16 rr	4 15 rf	5 14 RW	6 13 RW	7 13 RW	8 11 mt	19	9 10 mm	10 9 MT	11 7 ed	12 7 ed	1 5 EF	2 6 ER
2 15 TF	3 17 TR	4 16 TR	5 15 rf	6 14 rf	7 14 rf	8 12 RW	20	9 11 RH	10 10 mm	11 8 MM	12 8 MT	1 6 ed	2 7 eg
2 16 td	3 18 tg	4 17 td	5 16 TR	6 15 TR	7 15 TF	8 13 rf	21	9 12 rr	10 11 RW	11 9 mm	12 9 mt	1 7 MM	2 8 MT
2 17 FM	3 19 FT	4 18 FM	5 17 tg	6 16 tg	7 16 td	8 14 TF	22	9 13 TR	10 12 rf	11 10 RH	12 10 RW	1 8 mm	2 9 mt
2 18 fm	3 20 ft	4 19 fm	5 18 FT	6 17 FT	7 17 FM	8 15 td	23	9 14 tg	10 13 TF	11 11 rr	12 11 rf	1 9 RH	2 10 RW
2 19 EH	3 21 EW	4 20 EH	5 19 ft	6 18 fm	7 18 fm	8 16 FM	24	9 15 FT	10 14 td	11 12 TR	12 12 TF	1 10 rr	2 11 rf
2 20 er	3 22 ef	4 21 ef	5 20 EW	6 19 EW	7 19 EH	8 17 fm	25	9 16 ft	10 15 FM	11 13 tg	12 13 td	1 11 TR	2 12 TF
2 21 MR	3 23 MF	4 22 MR	5 21 ef	6 20 er	7 20 ef	8 18 EH	26	9 17 EW	10 16 fm	11 14 FT	12 14 FM	1 12 tg	2 13 td
2 22 mg	3 24 md	4 23 mg	5 22 MF	6 21 MR	7 21 MF	8 19 er	27	9 18 ef	10 17 EH	11 15 ft	12 15 fm	1 13 FT	2 14 FM
2 23 RT	3 25 RM	4 24 RT	5 23 md	6 22 mg	7 22 md	8 20 MR	28	9 19 MF	10 18 er	11 16 EW	12 16 EH	1 14 ft	2 12 FM
2 24 rt	3 26 rm	4 25 rt	5 24 RM	6 23 RT	7 23 RM	8 21 mg	29	9 20 md	10 19 MR	11 17 ef	12 17 er	1 15 EW	2 13 fm
2 25 TW	3 27 TH		5 25 rm	6 24 rt		8 22 RT	30			11 18 MF		1 16 ef	2 14 EH

1942 RF HORSE

	JAN RT	FEB rt	MAR TW	APR tf	MAY FF	JUN fd	JUL EM	AUG em	SEP MH	OCT mr	NOV RR	DEC rg
Term	20 WARM	20 CLEAR	22 SUMMER	23 GRAIN	25 HEAT	27 FALL	28 DEW	30 C DEW		1 WINTER	1 SNOW	1 CHILL
Time	12:53	18:24	12:07	16:37	3:14	13:10	15:07	7:32		9:12	1:47	13:10

	JAN	FEB	MAR	APR	MAY	JUN	JUL	AUG	SEP	OCT	NOV	DEC
1	2 15 er	3 17 ef	4 15 EH	5 15 EW	6 14 EH	7 13 ft	8 12 fm	9 10 FT	10 10 FM	11 8 tg	12 8 td	1 6 TR
2	2 16 MR	3 18 MF	4 16 er	5 16 ef	6 15 er	7 14 EW	8 13 EH	9 11 ft	10 11 fm	11 9 FT	12 9 FM	1 7 tg
3	2 17 mg	3 19 md	4 17 MR	5 17 MF	6 16 MR	7 15 ef	8 14 er	9 12 EW	10 12 EH	11 10 ft	12 10 fm	1 8 FT
4	2 18 RT	3 20 RM	4 18 mg	5 18 md	6 17 mg	7 16 MF	8 15 MR	9 13 ef	10 13 er	11 11 EW	12 11 EH	1 9 ft
5	2 19 rt	3 21 rm	4 19 RT	5 19 RM	6 18 RT	7 17 md	8 16 mg	9 14 MF	10 14 MR	11 12 ef	12 12 er	1 10 EW
6	2 20 TW	3 22 TH	4 20 rt	5 20 rm	6 19 rt	7 18 RM	8 17 RT	9 15 md	10 15 mg	11 13 MF	12 13 MR	1 11 ef
7	2 21 tf	3 23 tr	4 21 TW	5 21 TH	6 20 TW	7 19 rm	8 18 rt	9 16 RM	10 16 RT	11 14 md	12 14 mg	1 12 MF
8	2 22 FF	3 24 FR	4 22 tf	5 22 tr	6 21 tf	7 20 TH	8 19 TW	9 17 rm	10 17 rt	11 15 RM	12 15 RT	1 13 md
9	2 23 fd	3 25 fg	4 23 FF	5 23 FR	6 22 FF	7 21 tr	8 20 tf	9 18 TH	10 18 TW	11 16 rm	12 16 rt	1 14 RM
10	2 24 EM	3 26 ET	4 24 fd	5 24 fg	6 23 fd	7 22 FR	8 21 FF	9 19 tr	10 19 tf	11 17 TH	12 17 TW	1 15 rm
11	2 25 em	3 27 et	4 25 EM	5 25 ET	6 24 EM	7 23 fg	8 22 fd	9 20 FR	10 20 FF	11 18 tr	12 18 tf	1 16 TH
12	2 26 MH	3 28 MW	4 26 em	5 26 et	6 25 em	7 24 ET	8 23 EM	9 21 fg	10 21 fd	11 19 FR	12 19 FF	1 17 tr
13	2 27 mr	3 29 mf	4 27 MH	5 27 MW	6 26 MH	7 25 et	8 24 em	9 22 ET	10 22 EM	11 20 fg	12 20 fd	1 18 FR
14	2 28 RR	3 30 RF	4 28 mr	5 28 mf	6 27 mr	7 26 MW	8 25 MH	9 23 et	10 23 em	11 21 ET	12 21 EM	1 19 fg
15	3 1 rg	3 31 rd	4 29 RR	5 29 RF	6 28 RR	7 27 mf	8 26 mr	9 24 MW	10 24 MH	11 22 et	12 22 em	1 20 ET
16	3 2 TT	4 1 TM	4 30 rg	5 30 rd	6 29 rg	7 28 RF	8 27 RR	9 25 mf	10 25 mr	11 23 MW	12 23 MH	1 21 et
17	3 3 tt	4 2 tm	5 1 TT	5 31 TM	6 30 TT	7 29 rd	8 28 rg	9 26 RF	10 26 RR	11 24 mf	12 24 mr	1 22 MW
18	3 4 FW	4 3 FH	5 2 tt	6 1 tm	7 1 tt	7 30 TM	8 29 TT	9 27 rd	10 27 rg	11 25 RF	12 25 RR	1 23 mf
19	3 5 ff	4 4 fr	5 3 FW	6 2 FH	7 2 FW	7 31 tm	8 30 tt	9 28 TM	10 28 TT	11 26 rd	12 26 rg	1 24 RF
20	3 6 EF	4 5 ER	5 4 ff	6 3 fr	7 3 ff	8 1 FH	8 31 FW	9 29 tm	10 29 tt	11 27 TM	12 27 TT	1 25 rd
21	3 7 ed	4 6 eg	5 5 EF	6 4 ER	7 4 EF	8 2 fr	9 1 ff	9 30 FH	10 30 FW	11 28 tm	12 28 tt	1 26 TM
22	3 8 MM	4 7 MT	5 6 ed	6 5 eg	7 5 ed	8 3 ER	9 2 EF	10 1 fr	10 31 ff	11 29 FH	12 29 FW	1 27 tm
23	3 9 mm	4 8 mt	5 7 MM	6 6 MT	7 6 MM	8 4 eg	9 3 ed	10 2 ER	11 1 EF	11 30 fr	12 30 ff	1 28 FH
24	3 10 RH	4 9 RW	5 8 mm	6 7 mt	7 7 mm	8 5 MT	9 4 MM	10 3 eg	11 2 ed	12 1 ER	12 31 EF	1 29 fr
25	3 11 rr	4 10 rf	5 9 RH	6 8 RW	7 8 RH	8 6 mt	9 5 mm	10 4 MT	11 3 MM	12 2 eg	1 1 ed	1 30 ER
26	3 12 TR	4 11 TF	5 10 rr	6 9 rf	7 9 rr	8 7 RW	9 6 RH	10 5 mt	11 4 mm	12 3 MT	1 2 MM	1 31 eg
27	3 13 tg	4 12 td	5 11 TR	6 10 TF	7 10 TR	8 8 rf	9 7 rr	10 6 RW	11 5 RH	12 4 mt	1 3 mm	2 1 MT
28	3 14 FT	4 13 FM	5 12 tg	6 11 td	7 11 tg	8 9 TF	9 8 TR	10 7 rf	11 6 rr	12 5 RW	1 4 RH	2 2 mt
29	3 15 ft	4 14 fm	5 13 FT	6 12 FM	7 12 FT	8 10 td	9 9 tg	10 8 TF	11 7 TR	12 6 rf	1 5 rr	2 3 RW
30	3 16 EW		5 14 ft	6 13 fm		8 11 FM		10 9 td		12 7 TF		2 4 rf

1943 rd RAM

	JAN	FEB	MAR	APR	MAY	JUN	JUL	AUG	SEP	OCT	NOV	DEC
Month code	TT	tt	FW	ff	EF	ed	MM	mm	RH	rr	TR	tg
Term	1 SPRING	1 WARM	1 CLEAR	3 SUMMER	4 GRAIN	7 HEAT	8 FALL	9 DEW	11 C DEW	11 WINTER	12 SNOW	11 CHILL
Time	0:41	18:59	23:59	17:54	23:19	9:03	18:19	21:53	13:21	16:06	7:33	19:00

Day grid — each cell shows Gregorian month/day and the day code (DAY OF MON):

Day	JAN	FEB	MAR	APR	MAY	JUN	JUL	AUG	SEP	OCT	NOV	DEC
1	2/5 TF	3/6 rr	4/5 rf	5/4 RH	6/3 RW	7/2 mm	8/1 mt	8/30 MM	9/29 MT	10/29 MM	11/27 eg	12/27 ed
2	2/6 td	3/7 TR	4/6 TF	5/5 rr	6/4 rf	7/3 RH	8/2 RW	8/31 mm	9/30 mt	10/30 mm	11/28 MT	12/28 MM
3	2/7 FM	3/8 tg	4/7 td	5/6 TR	6/5 TF	7/4 rr	8/3 rf	9/1 RH	10/1 RW	10/31 RH	11/29 mt	12/29 mm
4	2/8 fm	3/9 FT	4/8 FM	5/7 tg	6/6 td	7/5 TR	8/4 TF	9/2 rr	10/2 rf	11/1 rr	11/30 RW	12/30 RH
5	2/9 EH	3/10 ft	4/9 fm	5/8 FT	6/7 FM	7/6 tg	8/5 td	9/3 TR	10/3 TF	11/2 TR	12/1 rf	12/31 rr
6	2/10 er	3/11 EW	4/10 EH	5/9 ft	6/8 fm	7/7 FT	8/6 FM	9/4 tg	10/4 td	11/3 tg	12/2 TF	1/1 TR
7	2/11 MR	3/12 ef	4/11 er	5/10 EW	6/9 EH	7/8 ft	8/7 fm	9/5 FT	10/5 FM	11/4 FT	12/3 td	1/2 tg
8	2/12 mg	3/13 MF	4/12 MR	5/11 ef	6/10 er	7/9 EW	8/8 EH	9/6 ft	10/6 fm	11/5 ft	12/4 FM	1/3 FT
9	2/13 RT	3/14 md	4/13 mg	5/12 MF	6/11 MR	7/10 ef	8/9 er	9/7 EW	10/7 EH	11/6 EW	12/5 fm	1/4 ft
10	2/14 rt	3/15 RM	4/14 RT	5/13 md	6/12 mg	7/11 MF	8/10 MR	9/8 ef	10/8 er	11/7 ef	12/6 EH	1/5 EW
11	2/15 TW	3/16 rm	4/15 rt	5/14 RM	6/13 RT	7/12 md	8/11 mg	9/9 MF	10/9 MR	11/8 MF	12/7 er	1/6 ef
12	2/16 tf	3/17 TH	4/16 TW	5/15 rm	6/14 rt	7/13 RM	8/12 RT	9/10 md	10/10 mg	11/9 md	12/8 MR	1/7 MF
13	2/17 FF	3/18 tr	4/17 tf	5/16 TH	6/15 TW	7/14 rm	8/13 rt	9/11 RM	10/11 RT	11/10 RM	12/9 mg	1/8 md
14	2/18 fd	3/19 FR	4/18 FF	5/17 tr	6/16 tf	7/15 TH	8/14 TW	9/12 rm	10/12 rt	11/11 rm	12/10 RT	1/9 RM
15	2/19 EM	3/20 fg	4/19 fd	5/18 FR	6/17 FF	7/16 tr	8/15 tf	9/13 TH	10/13 TW	11/12 TH	12/11 rt	1/10 rm
16	2/20 em	3/21 ET	4/20 EM	5/19 fg	6/18 fd	7/17 FR	8/16 FF	9/14 tr	10/14 tf	11/13 tr	12/12 TW	1/11 TH
17	2/21 MH	3/22 et	4/21 em	5/20 ET	6/19 EM	7/18 fg	8/17 fd	9/15 FR	10/15 FF	11/14 FR	12/13 tf	1/12 tr
18	2/22 mr	3/23 MW	4/22 MH	5/21 et	6/20 em	7/19 ET	8/18 EM	9/16 fg	10/16 fd	11/15 fg	12/14 FF	1/13 FR
19	2/23 RR	3/24 mf	4/23 mr	5/22 MW	6/21 MH	7/20 et	8/19 em	9/17 ET	10/17 EM	11/16 ET	12/15 fd	1/14 fg
20	2/24 rg	3/25 RF	4/24 RR	5/23 mf	6/22 mr	7/21 MW	8/20 MH	9/18 et	10/18 em	11/17 et	12/16 EM	1/15 ET
21	2/25 TT	3/26 rd	4/25 rg	5/24 RF	6/23 RR	7/22 mf	8/21 mr	9/19 MW	10/19 MH	11/18 MW	12/17 em	1/16 et
22	2/26 tt	3/27 TM	4/26 TT	5/25 rd	6/24 rg	7/23 RF	8/22 RR	9/20 mf	10/20 mr	11/19 mf	12/18 MH	1/17 MW
23	2/27 FW	3/28 tm	4/27 tt	5/26 TM	6/25 TT	7/24 rd	8/23 rg	9/21 RF	10/21 RR	11/20 RF	12/19 mr	1/18 mf
24	2/28 ff	3/29 FH	4/28 FW	5/27 tm	6/26 tt	7/25 TM	8/24 TT	9/22 rd	10/22 rg	11/21 rd	12/20 RR	1/19 RF
25	3/1 EF	3/30 fr	4/29 ff	5/28 FH	6/27 FW	7/26 tm	8/25 tt	9/23 TM	10/23 TT	11/22 TM	12/21 rg	1/20 rd
26	3/2 ed	3/31 ER	4/30 EF	5/29 fr	6/28 ff	7/27 FH	8/26 FW	9/24 tm	10/24 tt	11/23 tm	12/22 TT	1/21 TM
27	3/3 MM	4/1 eg	5/1 ed	5/30 ER	6/29 EF	7/28 fr	8/27 ff	9/25 FH	10/25 FW	11/24 FH	12/23 tt	1/22 tm
28	3/4 mm	4/2 MT	5/2 MM	5/31 eg	6/30 ed	7/29 ER	8/28 EF	9/26 fr	10/26 ff	11/25 fr	12/24 FW	1/23 FH
29	3/5 RH	4/3 mt	5/3 mm	6/1 MT	7/1 MM	7/30 eg	8/29 ed	9/27 ER	10/27 EF	11/26 ER	12/25 ff	1/24 fr
30		4/4 RW		6/2 mt		7/31 MT		9/28 eg	10/28 ed		12/26 EF	

1944 TM MONKEY

JAN FT	FEB ft	MAR EW	APR ef	APR ef	MAY MF	JUN md	DAY OF MON	JUL TM	AUG rm	SEP TH	OCT tr	NOV FR	DEC fg
12 SPRING	12 WARM	13 CLEAR	13 SUMMER	16 GRAIN	17 HEAT	20 FALL		21 DEW	22 C DEW	22 WINTER	22 SNOW	23 CHILL	22 SPRING
6:23	0:41	5:54	23:40	4:11	14:37	0:19		3:42	19:10	21:55	13:28	0:35	21:20
1 25 ER	2 24 EF	3 24 fr	4 23 ff	5 22 FH	6 21 FW	7 20 tm	1	8 19 tt	9 17 TM	10 17 TT	11 16 TM	12 15 TT	1 14 rd
1 26 eg	2 25 ed	3 25 ER	4 24 EF	5 23 fr	6 22 ff	7 21 FH	2	8 20 FW	9 18 tm	10 18 tt	11 17 tm	12 16 tt	1 15 TM
1 27 MT	2 26 MM	3 26 eg	4 25 ed	5 24 ER	6 23 EF	7 22 fr	3	8 21 ff	9 19 FH	10 19 FW	11 18 FH	12 17 FW	1 16 tm
1 28 mt	2 27 mm	3 27 MT	4 26 MM	5 25 eg	6 24 eg	7 23 ER	4	8 22 EF	9 20 fr	10 20 ff	11 19 fr	12 18 ff	1 17 FH
1 29 RW	2 28 RH	3 28 mt	4 27 mm	5 26 MT	6 25 MM	7 24 eg	5	8 23 ed	9 21 ER	10 21 EF	11 20 ER	12 19 EF	1 18 fr
1 30 rf	2 29 rr	3 29 RW	4 28 RH	5 27 mt	6 26 mm	7 25 MT	6	8 24 MM	9 22 eg	10 22 ed	11 21 eg	12 20 ed	1 19 ER
1 31 TF	3 1 TR	3 30 rf	4 29 rr	5 28 RW	6 27 RH	7 26 mt	7	8 25 mm	9 23 MT	10 23 MM	11 22 MT	12 21 MM	1 20 eg
2 1 TR	3 2 tg	3 31 TF	4 30 TR	5 29 rf	6 28 rr	7 27 RW	8	8 26 RH	9 24 mt	10 24 mm	11 23 mt	12 22 mm	1 21 MT
2 2 FM	3 3 FT	4 1 tg	5 1 tg	5 30 TF	6 29 TR	7 28 rf	9	8 27 rr	9 25 RW	10 25 RH	11 24 RW	12 23 RH	1 22 mt
2 3 fm	3 4 ft	4 2 FM	5 2 FT	5 31 td	6 30 tg	7 29 TF	10	8 28 TR	9 26 rf	10 26 rr	11 25 rf	12 24 rr	1 23 RW
2 4 EH	3 5 EW	4 3 fm	5 3 ft	6 1 FM	7 1 FT	7 30 td	11	8 29 tg	9 27 TF	10 27 TR	11 26 TF	12 25 TR	1 24 rf
2 5 er	3 6 ef	4 4 EH	5 4 EW	6 2 fm	7 2 ft	7 31 FM	12	8 30 FT	9 28 td	10 28 tg	11 27 td	12 26 tg	1 25 TF
2 6 MR	3 7 MF	4 5 er	5 5 ef	6 3 EH	7 3 EW	8 1 fm	13	8 31 ft	9 29 FM	10 29 FT	11 28 FM	12 27 FT	1 26 td
2 7 mg	3 8 md	4 6 MR	5 6 MF	6 4 er	7 4 ef	8 2 EH	14	9 1 EW	9 30 fm	10 30 ft	11 29 fm	12 28 ft	1 27 FM
2 8 RT	3 9 RM	4 7 mg	5 7 md	6 5 MR	7 5 MF	8 3 er	15	9 2 ef	10 1 EH	10 31 EW	11 30 er	12 29 EW	1 28 fm
2 9 rt	3 10 rm	4 8 RT	5 8 RM	6 6 mg	7 6 md	8 4 MR	16	9 3 MF	10 2 er	11 1 ef	12 1 EH	12 30 ef	1 29 EH
2 10 TW	3 11 TH	4 9 rt	5 9 rm	6 7 RT	7 7 RM	8 5 mg	17	9 4 md	10 3 MR	11 2 MF	12 2 er	12 31 MF	1 30 er
2 11 tf	3 12 tr	4 10 TW	5 10 TH	6 8 rt	7 8 rm	8 6 RT	18	9 5 RM	10 4 mg	11 3 md	12 3 MR	1 1 md	1 31 MR
2 12 FF	3 13 FR	4 11 tf	5 11 tr	6 9 TH	7 9 TH	8 7 rm	19	9 6 rm	10 5 RT	11 4 RM	12 4 mg	1 2 RM	2 1 mg
2 13 fd	3 14 fg	4 12 FF	5 12 FR	6 10 tf	7 10 tr	8 8 TW	20	9 7 TH	10 6 rt	11 5 rm	12 5 RT	1 3 rm	2 2 RT
2 14 EM	3 15 ET	4 13 fd	5 13 fd	6 11 FF	7 11 FR	8 9 tf	21	9 8 tr	10 7 TW	11 6 TH	12 6 rt	1 4 TH	2 3 rt
2 15 em	3 16 et	4 14 EM	5 14 EM	6 12 fd	7 12 fg	8 10 FF	22	9 9 FR	10 8 tf	11 7 tr	12 7 TW	1 5 tr	2 4 TW
2 16 MH	3 17 MW	4 15 em	5 15 em	6 13 EM	7 13 ET	8 11 fd	23	9 10 fg	10 9 FF	11 8 FR	12 8 tf	1 6 FR	2 5 tf
2 17 mr	3 18 mf	4 16 MH	5 16 MH	6 14 em	7 14 et	8 12 ET	24	9 11 ET	10 10 fd	11 9 fg	12 9 FF	1 7 fg	2 6 FF
2 18 RR	3 19 RF	4 17 mr	5 17 mr	6 15 MH	7 15 MW	8 13 em	25	9 12 et	10 11 EM	11 10 ET	12 10 fd	1 8 ET	2 7 fd
2 19 rg	3 20 rd	4 18 RR	5 18 RF	6 16 mr	7 16 mf	8 14 MH	26	9 13 MW	10 12 em	11 11 et	12 11 EM	1 9 et	2 8 EM
2 20 TT	3 21 TM	4 19 rg	5 19 rg	6 17 RR	7 17 RF	8 15 mr	27	9 14 mf	10 13 MH	11 12 MW	12 12 em	1 10 MW	2 9 em
2 21 tt	3 22 tm	4 20 TM	5 20 tt	6 18 rg	7 18 rd	8 16 RR	28	9 15 RF	10 14 mr	11 13 mf	12 13 MH	1 11 mf	2 10 MH
2 22 FW	3 23 FH	4 21 tt		6 19 TM	7 19 TM	8 17 rg	29	9 16 rd	10 15 RR	11 14 RF	12 14 mr	1 12 RF	2 11 mr
2 23 ff		4 22 FW		6 20 tt		8 18 TT	30		10 16 rg	11 15 rd		1 13 rd	2 12 RR

1945 tm ROOSTER

JAN ET	FEB et	MAR MW	APR mf	MAY RF	JUN rd	DAY OF MON	JUL TM	AUG tm	SEP FH	OCT fr	NOV ER	DEC eg
22 WARM	23 CLEAR	25 SUMMER	26 GRAIN	28 HEAT			1 FALL	3 DEW	4 C DEW	4 WINTER	3 SNOW	4 CHILL
6:38	11:52	5:37	10:06	20:27			6:06	9:30	0:59	3:44	19:18	6:17
2 13 rg	3 14 RF	4 12 mr	5 12 mf	6 10 MH	7 9 MH	1	8 8 em	9 6 ET	10 6 EM	11 5 ET	12 5 EM	1 3 fg
2 14 TT	3 15 rd	4 13 RR	5 13 RF	6 11 mr	7 10 mr	2	8 9 MH	9 7 et	10 7 em	11 6 et	12 6 em	1 4 ET
2 15 tt	3 16 TM	4 14 rg	5 14 rd	6 12 RR	7 11 RR	3	8 10 mr	9 8 MW	10 8 MH	11 7 MW	12 7 MH	1 5 et
2 16 FW	3 17 tm	4 15 TT	5 15 TM	6 13 rg	7 12 rg	4	8 11 RR	9 9 mf	10 9 mr	11 8 mf	12 8 mr	1 6 MW
2 17 ff	3 18 FH	4 16 tt	5 16 tm	6 14 TT	7 13 TT	5	8 12 rg	9 10 RF	10 10 RR	11 9 RF	12 9 RR	1 7 mf
2 18 EF	3 19 fr	4 17 FW	5 17 FH	6 15 tt	7 14 tt	6	8 13 TT	9 11 rd	10 11 rg	11 10 rd	12 10 rg	1 8 RF
2 19 ed	3 20 ER	4 18 ff	5 18 fr	6 16 FW	7 15 FW	7	8 14 tt	9 12 TM	10 12 TT	11 11 TM	12 11 TT	1 9 rd
2 20 MM	3 21 eg	4 19 EF	5 19 ER	6 17 ff	7 16 ff	8	8 15 FW	9 13 tm	10 13 tt	11 12 tm	12 12 tt	1 10 TM
2 21 mm	3 22 MT	4 20 ed	5 20 eg	6 18 EF	7 17 EF	9	8 16 ff	9 14 FH	10 14 FW	11 13 FH	12 13 FW	1 11 tm
2 22 RH	3 23 mt	4 21 MM	5 21 MT	6 19 ed	7 18 ed	10	8 17 EF	9 15 fr	10 15 ff	11 14 fr	12 14 ff	1 12 FH
2 23 rr	3 24 RW	4 22 mm	5 22 mt	6 20 MM	7 19 MM	11	8 18 ed	9 16 ER	10 16 EF	11 15 ER	12 15 EF	1 13 fr
2 24 TR	3 25 rf	4 23 RH	5 23 RW	6 21 mm	7 20 mm	12	8 19 MM	9 17 eg	10 17 ed	11 16 eg	12 16 ed	1 14 ER
2 25 tg	3 26 TF	4 24 rr	5 24 rf	6 22 RH	7 21 RH	13	8 20 mm	9 18 MT	10 18 MM	11 17 MT	12 17 MM	1 15 eg
2 26 FT	3 27 td	4 25 TR	5 25 TF	6 23 rr	7 22 rr	14	8 21 RH	9 19 mt	10 19 mm	11 18 mt	12 18 mm	1 16 MT
2 27 td	3 28 FM	4 26 tg	5 26 td	6 24 TR	7 23 TR	15	8 22 rr	9 20 RH	10 20 RH	11 19 RH	12 19 RH	1 17 mt
2 28 EW	3 29 fm	4 27 FT	5 27 FM	6 25 tg	7 24 tg	16	8 23 TR	9 21 rr	10 21 rr	11 20 rr	12 20 rr	1 18 RW
3 1 ef	3 30 EH	4 28 ft	5 28 fm	6 26 FT	7 25 FT	17	8 24 tg	9 22 TR	10 22 TR	11 21 TF	12 21 TR	1 19 rf
3 2 MF	3 31 er	4 29 EW	5 29 EH	6 27 ft	7 26 ft	18	8 25 FT	9 23 td	10 23 tg	11 22 td	12 22 tg	1 20 TF
3 3 md	4 1 MR	4 30 ef	5 30 er	6 28 EW	7 27 EW	19	8 26 ft	9 24 FM	10 24 FT	11 23 FM	12 23 FT	1 21 td
3 4 RM	4 2 mg	5 1 MF	5 31 MR	6 29 ef	7 28 ef	20	8 27 EW	9 25 fm	10 25 ft	11 24 fm	12 24 ft	1 22 FM
3 5 rm	4 3 RT	5 2 md	6 1 mg	6 30 MF	7 29 MF	21	8 28 ef	9 26 EH	10 26 EW	11 25 EH	12 25 EW	1 23 fm
3 6 TH	4 4 rt	5 3 RM	6 2 RT	7 1 md	7 30 md	22	8 29 MF	9 27 er	10 27 ef	11 26 er	12 26 ef	1 24 EH
3 7 tr	4 5 TW	5 4 rm	6 3 rt	7 2 RM	7 31 RM	23	8 30 md	9 28 MR	10 28 MF	11 27 MR	12 27 MF	1 25 er
3 8 FR	4 6 tf	5 5 TH	6 4 TW	7 3 rm	8 1 rm	24	8 31 RM	9 29 mg	10 29 md	11 28 mg	12 28 md	1 26 MR
3 9 fg	4 7 FR	5 6 tr	6 5 th	7 4 TH	8 2 TH	25	9 1 rm	9 30 RM	10 30 RM	11 29 RM	12 29 RM	1 27 mg
3 10 ET	4 8 fd	5 7 FR	6 6 tf	7 5 tr	8 3 tr	26	9 2 TH	10 1 rt	10 31 rt	11 30 rt	12 30 rm	1 28 RT
3 11 et	4 9 EM	5 8 fd	6 7 FF	7 6 FR	8 4 FR	27	9 3 tr	10 2 TW	11 1 TH	12 1 TW	12 31 TH	1 29 rt
3 12 MW	4 10 em	5 9 ET	6 8 fd	7 7 fg	8 5 fg	28	9 4 FR	10 3 tf	11 2 tr	12 2 tf	1 1 tr	1 30 TW
3 13 mf	4 11 MH	5 10 et	6 9 em	7 8 ET	8 6 ET	29	9 5 fg	10 4 FF	11 3 FR	12 3 FF	1 2 FR	1 31 tf
		5 11 MW			8 7 et	30		10 5 fd	11 4 fg	12 4 fd		2 1 FF

190

	JAN MT	FEB mt	MAR RW	APR rf	MAY TF	JUN td	JUL FM	DAY	AUG fm	SEP EH	OCT er	NOV MR	DEC mg
solar term	3 SPRING	3 WARM	4 CLEAR	6 SUMMER	7 GRAIN	10 HEAT	12 FALL	OF	13 DEW	15 C DEW	15 WINTER	15 SNOW	15 CHILL
								MON					
time	18:05	12:25	17:39	11:22	15:49	2:11	11:52		15:18	5:42	9:34	1:01	12:11

Day of Month	JAN MT	FEB mt	MAR RW	APR rf	MAY TF	JUN td	JUL FM	AUG fm	SEP EH	OCT er	NOV MR	DEC mg
1	fd	fg	FF	tr	tf	FH	rt	rm	RT	RM	RT	md
2	EM	ET	fd	FR	FF	tr	TW	FH	rt	rm	rt	RM
3	em	et	EM	fg	fd	FF	tf	tr	TW	FH	TW	rm
4	MH	MW	em	ET	EM	fg	FF	FF	tf	tr	tf	FH
5	mr	mf	MH	et	em	ET	fd	fg	FF	FF	FF	tr
6	RR	RF	mr	MW	MH	et	EM	ET	fd	fg	fd	FF
7	rg	rd	RR	mf	mr	MW	em	et	EM	ET	EM	fg
8	TT	TM	rg	RF	RR	mf	MH	MW	em	et	em	ET
9	tt	tm	TT	rd	rg	RF	mr	mf	MH	MW	MH	et
10	FW	FH	tt	TM	TT	rd	RR	RF	mr	mf	mr	MW
11	ff	fr	FW	tm	tt	TM	rg	rd	RR	RF	RR	mf
12	EF	ER	ff	FH	FW	tm	TT	TM	rg	rd	rg	RF
13	ed	eg	EF	fr	ff	FH	tt	tm	TT	TM	TT	rd
14	MM	MT	ed	ER	EF	fr	FW	FH	tt	tm	tt	TM
15	mm	mt	MM	eg	ed	ER	ff	fr	FW	FH	FW	tm
16	RH	RW	mm	MT	MM	eg	EF	ER	ff	fr	ff	FH
17	rr	rf	RH	mt	mm	MT	ed	eg	EF	ER	EF	fr
18	TR	TF	rr	RW	RH	mt	MM	MT	ed	eg	ed	ER
19	tg	td	TR	rf	rr	RW	mm	mt	MM	MT	MM	eg
20	FT	FM	tg	TF	TR	rf	RH	RW	mm	mt	mm	MT
21	ft	fm	FT	td	tg	TF	rr	rf	RH	RW	RH	mt
22	EW	EH	ft	FM	FT	td	TR	TF	rr	rf	rr	RW
23	ef	er	EW	fm	ft	FM	tg	td	TR	TF	TR	rf
24	MF	MR	ef	EH	EW	fm	FT	FM	tg	td	tg	TF
25	md	mg	MF	er	ef	EH	ft	fm	FT	FM	FT	td
26	RM	RT	md	MR	MF	er	EW	EH	ft	fm	ft	FM
27	rm	rt	RM	mg	md	MR	RM	er	EW	EH	EW	fm
28	TH	TW	rm	RT	rm	RT		MR	ef	er	ef	EH
29	tr	tf	TH	rt				mg	MF	MR	MF	er
30	FR		TW	TW					md	mg		MR

1947 fr BOAR

JAN RT	FEB et	FEB et	MAR TW	APR tf	MAY RF	JUN fd	DAY OF MON	JUL EM	AUG em	SEP MH	OCT mr	NOV RR	DEC rg
14 SPRING	14 WARM	14 CLEAR	16 SUMMER	18 GRAIN	20 HEAT	22 FALL		24 DEW	25 C DEW	26 WINTER	26 SNOW	26 CHILL	26 SPRING
23:55	18:12	23:23	17:05	21:33	7:56	17:39		21:07	11:32	15:23	7:40	18:01	5:43
1 22 mg	2 21 md	3 23 mg	4 21 MF	5 20 er	6 19 ef	7 18 EH	1	8 16 ft	9 15 fm	10 14 FT	11 13 FM	12 12 tg	1 11 td
1 23 RT	2 22 RM	3 24 RT	4 22 md	5 21 MR	6 20 MF	7 19 er	2	8 17 EW	9 16 EH	10 15 ft	11 14 fm	12 13 FT	1 12 FM
1 24 rt	2 23 rm	3 25 rt	4 23 RM	5 22 mg	6 21 md	7 20 MR	3	8 18 ef	9 17 er	10 16 EW	11 15 EH	12 14 ft	1 13 fm
1 25 TW	2 24 TH	3 26 TW	4 24 rm	5 23 RT	6 22 RM	7 21 mg	4	8 19 MF	9 18 MR	10 17 ef	11 16 er	12 15 EW	1 14 EH
1 26 tf	2 25 tr	3 27 tf	4 25 TH	5 24 rt	6 23 rm	7 22 RT	5	8 20 md	9 19 mg	10 18 MF	11 17 MR	12 16 ef	1 15 er
1 27 FF	2 26 FR	3 28 FF	4 26 tr	5 25 TW	6 24 TH	7 23 rt	6	8 21 RM	9 20 RT	10 19 md	11 18 mg	12 17 MF	1 16 MR
1 28 fd	2 27 fg	3 29 fd	4 27 FR	5 26 tf	6 25 tr	7 24 TW	7	8 22 rm	9 21 rt	10 20 RM	11 19 RT	12 18 md	1 17 mg
1 29 EM	2 28 ET	3 30 EM	4 28 fg	5 27 FF	6 26 FR	7 25 tf	8	8 23 TH	9 22 TW	10 21 rm	11 20 rt	12 19 RM	1 18 RT
1 30 em	3 1 et	3 31 em	4 29 ET	5 28 fd	6 27 fg	7 26 FF	9	8 24 tr	9 23 tf	10 22 TH	11 21 TW	12 20 rm	1 19 rt
1 31 MH	3 2 MW	4 1 MH	4 30 et	5 29 EM	6 28 ET	7 27 fd	10	8 25 FR	9 24 FF	10 23 tr	11 22 tf	12 21 TH	1 20 TW
2 1 mr	3 3 mf	4 2 mr	5 1 MW	5 30 em	6 29 et	7 28 EM	11	8 26 fg	9 25 fd	10 24 FR	11 23 FF	12 22 tr	1 21 tf
2 2 RR	3 4 RF	4 3 RR	5 2 mf	5 31 MH	6 30 MW	7 29 em	12	8 27 ET	9 26 EM	10 25 fg	11 24 fd	12 23 FR	1 22 FF
2 3 rg	3 5 rd	4 4 rg	5 3 RF	6 1 mr	7 1 mf	7 30 MH	13	8 28 et	9 27 em	10 26 ET	11 25 EM	12 24 fg	1 23 fd
2 4 TT	3 6 TM	4 5 TT	5 4 rd	6 2 RR	7 2 RF	7 31 mr	14	8 29 MW	9 28 MH	10 27 et	11 26 em	12 25 ET	1 24 EM
2 5 tt	3 7 tm	4 6 tt	5 5 TM	6 3 rg	7 3 rd	8 1 RR	15	8 30 mf	9 29 mr	10 28 MW	11 27 MH	12 26 et	1 25 em
2 6 FW	3 8 FH	4 7 FW	5 6 tm	6 4 TT	7 4 TM	8 2 rg	16	8 31 RF	9 30 RR	10 29 mf	11 28 mr	12 27 MW	1 26 MH
2 7 ff	3 9 fr	4 8 ff	5 7 FH	6 5 tt	7 5 tm	8 3 TT	17	9 1 rd	10 1 rg	10 30 RF	11 29 RR	12 28 mf	1 27 mr
2 8 EF	3 10 ER	4 9 EF	5 8 fr	6 6 FW	7 6 FH	8 4 tt	18	9 2 TM	10 2 TT	10 31 rd	11 30 rg	12 29 RF	1 28 RR
2 9 ed	3 11 eg	4 10 ed	5 9 ER	6 7 ff	7 7 fr	8 5 FW	19	9 3 tm	10 3 tt	11 1 TM	12 1 TT	12 30 rd	1 29 rg
2 10 MM	3 12 MT	4 11 MM	5 10 eg	6 8 EF	7 8 ER	8 6 ff	20	9 4 FH	10 4 FW	11 2 tm	12 2 tt	12 31 TM	1 30 TT
2 11 mm	3 13 mt	4 12 mm	5 11 MT	6 9 ed	7 9 eg	8 7 EF	21	9 5 fr	10 5 ff	11 3 FH	12 3 FW	1 1 tm	1 31 tt
2 12 RH	3 14 RW	4 13 RH	5 12 mt	6 10 MM	7 10 MT	8 8 ed	22	9 6 ER	10 6 EF	11 4 fr	12 4 ff	1 2 FH	2 1 FW
2 13 rr	3 15 rf	4 14 rr	5 13 RW	6 11 mm	7 11 mt	8 9 MM	23	9 7 eg	10 7 ed	11 5 ER	12 5 EF	1 3 fr	2 2 ff
2 14 TR	3 16 TF	4 15 TR	5 14 rf	6 12 RH	7 12 RW	8 10 mm	24	9 8 MT	10 8 MM	11 6 eg	12 6 ed	1 4 ER	2 3 EF
2 15 tg	3 17 td	4 16 tg	5 15 TF	6 13 rr	7 13 rf	8 11 RH	25	9 9 mt	10 9 mm	11 7 MT	12 7 MM	1 5 eg	2 4 ed
2 16 FT	3 18 FM	4 17 FT	5 16 td	6 14 TR	7 14 TF	8 12 rr	26	9 10 RW	10 10 RH	11 8 mt	12 8 mm	1 6 MT	2 5 MM
2 17 ft	3 19 fm	4 18 ft	5 17 FM	6 15 tg	7 15 td	8 13 TR	27	9 11 rf	10 11 rr	11 9 RW	12 9 RH	1 7 mt	2 6 mm
2 18 EW	3 20 EH	4 19 EW	5 18 fm	6 16 FT	7 16 FM	8 14 tg	28	9 12 TF	10 12 TR	11 10 rf	12 10 rr	1 8 RW	2 7 RH
2 19 ef	3 21 er	4 20 ef	5 19 EH	6 17 ft	7 17 fm	8 15 FT	29	9 13 td	10 13 tg	11 11 TF	12 11 TR	1 9 rf	2 8 rr
2 20 MF	3 22 MR			6 18 EW			30	9 14 FM		11 12 td		1 10 TF	2 9 TR

1948 ER RAT

JAN TT	FEB tt	MAR FW	APR ff	MAY EF	JUN ed	DAY	JUL MM	AUG mm	SEP RH	OCT rr	NOV TR	DEC tg
25 WARM	26 CLEAR	27 SUMMER	29 GRAIN		1 HEAT	OF	3 FALL	6 DEW	6 C DEW	7 WINTER	7 SNOW	8 CHILL
23:58	5:10	22:53	3:21		13:44	MON	23:27	2:06	17:21	21:12	13:29	0:08
2/10 tg	3/11 td	4/9 TR	5/9 TF	6/7 rr	7/7 rf	1	8/5 RH	9/3 mt	10/3 mm	11/1 MT	12/1 MM	12/30 eg
2/11 FT	3/12 FM	4/10 tg	5/10 td	6/8 TR	7/8 TF	2	8/6 rr	9/4 RW	10/4 RH	11/2 mt	12/2 mm	12/31 MT
2/12 ft	3/13 fm	4/11 FT	5/11 FM	6/9 tg	7/9 td	3	8/7 TR	9/5 rf	10/5 rr	11/3 RW	12/3 RH	1/1 mt
2/13 EW	3/14 EH	4/12 ft	5/12 fm	6/10 FT	7/10 FM	4	8/8 tg	9/6 TF	10/6 TR	11/4 rf	12/4 rr	1/2 RW
2/14 ef	3/15 er	4/13 EW	5/13 EH	6/11 ft	7/11 fm	5	8/9 FT	9/7 td	10/7 tg	11/5 TF	12/5 TR	1/3 rf
2/15 MF	3/16 MR	4/14 ef	5/14 er	6/12 EW	7/12 EH	6	8/10 ft	9/8 FM	10/8 FT	11/6 td	12/6 tg	1/4 TF
2/16 md	3/17 mg	4/15 MF	5/15 MR	6/13 ef	7/13 er	7	8/11 EW	9/9 fm	10/9 ft	11/7 FM	12/7 FT	1/5 td
2/17 RM	3/18 RT	4/16 md	5/16 mg	6/14 MF	7/14 MR	8	8/12 ef	9/10 EH	10/10 EW	11/8 fm	12/8 ft	1/6 FM
2/18 rm	3/19 rt	4/17 RM	5/17 RT	6/15 md	7/15 mg	9	8/13 MF	9/11 er	10/11 ef	11/9 EH	12/9 EW	1/7 fm
2/19 TH	3/20 TW	4/18 rm	5/18 rt	6/16 RM	7/16 RT	10	8/14 md	9/12 MR	10/12 MF	11/10 er	12/10 ef	1/8 EH
2/20 tr	3/21 tf	4/19 TH	5/19 TW	6/17 rm	7/17 rt	11	8/15 RM	9/13 mg	10/13 md	11/11 MR	12/11 MF	1/9 er
2/21 FR	3/22 FF	4/20 tr	5/20 tf	6/18 TH	7/18 TW	12	8/16 rm	9/14 RT	10/14 RM	11/12 mg	12/12 md	1/10 MR
2/22 fg	3/23 fd	4/21 FR	5/21 FF	6/19 tr	7/19 tf	13	8/17 TH	9/15 rt	10/15 rm	11/13 RT	12/13 RM	1/11 mg
2/23 ET	3/24 EM	4/22 fg	5/22 fd	6/20 FR	7/20 FF	14	8/18 tr	9/16 TH	10/16 TH	11/14 rt	12/14 rm	1/12 RT
2/24 et	3/25 em	4/23 ET	5/23 EM	6/21 fg	7/21 fd	15	8/19 FR	9/17 tf	10/17 tr	11/15 TH	12/15 TH	1/13 rt
2/25 MW	3/26 MH	4/24 et	5/24 em	6/22 ET	7/22 EM	16	8/20 fg	9/18 FF	10/18 FR	11/16 tf	12/16 tr	1/14 TW
2/26 mf	3/27 mr	4/25 MW	5/25 MH	6/23 et	7/23 em	17	8/21 ET	9/19 fd	10/19 fg	11/17 FF	12/17 FR	1/15 tf
2/27 RF	3/28 RR	4/26 mf	5/26 mr	6/24 MW	7/24 MH	18	8/22 et	9/20 EM	10/20 ET	11/18 fd	12/18 fg	1/16 FF
2/28 rd	3/29 rg	4/27 RF	5/27 RR	6/25 mf	7/25 mr	19	8/23 MW	9/21 em	10/21 et	11/19 EM	12/19 ET	1/17 fd
2/29 TM	3/30 TT	4/28 rd	5/28 rg	6/26 RF	7/26 RR	20	8/24 mf	9/22 MH	10/22 MW	11/20 em	12/20 et	1/18 EM
3/1 tm	3/31 tt	4/29 TM	5/29 TT	6/27 rd	7/27 rg	21	8/25 RF	9/23 mr	10/23 mf	11/21 MH	12/21 MW	1/19 em
3/2 FH	4/1 FW	4/30 tm	5/30 tt	6/28 TM	7/28 TT	22	8/26 rd	9/24 RR	10/24 RF	11/22 mr	12/22 mf	1/20 MH
3/3 fr	4/2 ff	5/1 FH	5/31 FW	6/29 tm	7/29 tt	23	8/27 TM	9/25 rg	10/25 rd	11/23 RR	12/23 RF	1/21 mr
3/4 ER	4/3 EF	5/2 fr	6/1 ff	6/30 FH	7/30 FW	24	8/28 tm	9/26 TM	10/26 TM	11/24 rg	12/24 rd	1/22 RR
3/5 eg	4/4 ed	5/3 ER	6/2 EF	7/1 fr	7/31 ff	25	8/29 FH	9/27 tm	10/27 tm	11/25 TM	12/25 TM	1/23 rg
3/6 MT	4/5 MM	5/4 eg	6/3 ed	7/2 ER	8/1 EF	26	8/30 fr	9/28 FH	10/28 FH	11/26 tt	12/26 tm	1/24 TT
3/7 mt	4/6 mm	5/5 MT	6/4 MM	7/3 eg	8/2 ed	27	8/31 ER	9/29 fr	10/29 fr	11/27 FW	12/27 FH	1/25 tt
3/8 RW	4/7 RH	5/6 mt	6/5 mm	7/4 MT	8/3 MM	28	9/1 eg	9/30 ER	10/30 ER	11/28 ff	12/28 fr	1/26 FW
3/9 rf	4/8 rr	5/7 RW	6/6 RH	7/5 mt	8/4 mm	29	9/2 MT	10/1 ed	10/31 eg	11/29 EF	12/29 ER	1/27 ff
3/10 TF		5/8 rf		7/6 RW		30		10/2 MM		11/30 ed		1/28 EF

1949 eg OX

JAN FT	FEB ft	NAR EW	APR ef	MAY MF	JUN md	DAY OF MON	JUL RM	JUL RM	AUG rm	SEP TH	OCT tr	NOV FR	DEC fg
7 SPRING	7 WARM	8 CLEAR	9 SUMMER	10 GRAIN	12 HEAT		14 FALL	16 DEW	18 C DEW	18 WINTER	18 SNOW	18 CHILL	18 SPRING
11:23	5:40	10:52	4:37	9:07	19:32		5:16	7:55	0:15	3:02	19:20	5:39	17:21
1 29 ed	2 28 eg	3 29 EF	4 28 ER	5 28 EF	6 26 fr	1	7 26 ff	8 24 FH	9 22 tt	10 22 tm	11 20 TT	12 20 TM	1 18 rg
1 30 MM	3 1 MT	3 30 ed	4 29 eg	5 29 ed	6 27 ER	2	7 27 EF	8 25 fr	9 23 FW	10 23 FH	11 21 tt	12 21 tm	1 19 TT
1 31 mm	3 2 mt	3 31 MM	4 30 MT	5 30 MM	6 28 eg	3	7 28 ed	8 26 ER	9 24 ff	10 24 fr	11 22 FW	12 22 FH	1 20 tt
2 1 RH	3 3 RW	4 1 mm	5 1 mt	5 31 mm	6 29 MT	4	7 29 MM	8 27 eg	9 25 EF	10 25 ER	11 23 ff	12 23 fr	1 21 FW
2 2 rr	3 4 rf	4 2 RH	5 2 RW	6 1 RH	6 30 mt	5	7 30 mm	8 28 MT	9 26 ed	10 26 eg	11 24 EF	12 24 ER	1 22 ff
2 3 TR	3 5 TF	4 3 rr	5 3 rf	6 2 rr	7 1 RW	6	7 31 RH	8 29 mt	9 27 MM	10 27 MT	11 25 ed	12 25 eg	1 23 EF
2 4 tg	3 6 td	4 4 TR	5 4 TF	6 3 TR	7 2 rf	7	8 1 rr	8 30 RW	9 28 mm	10 28 mt	11 26 MM	12 26 MT	1 24 ed
2 5 FT	3 7 FM	4 5 tg	5 5 td	6 4 tg	7 3 TF	8	8 2 TR	8 31 rf	9 29 RH	10 29 RW	11 27 mm	12 27 mt	1 25 MM
2 6 ft	3 8 fm	4 6 FT	5 6 FM	6 5 FT	7 4 td	9	8 3 tg	9 1 TF	9 30 rr	10 30 rf	11 28 RH	12 28 RW	1 26 mm
2 7 EW	3 9 EH	4 7 ft	5 7 fm	6 6 ft	7 5 FM	10	8 4 FT	9 2 td	10 1 TR	10 31 TF	11 29 rr	12 29 rf	1 27 RH
2 8 ef	3 10 er	4 8 EW	5 8 EH	6 7 EW	7 6 fm	11	8 5 ft	9 3 FM	10 2 tg	11 1 td	11 30 TR	12 30 TF	1 28 rr
2 9 MF	3 11 MR	4 9 ef	5 9 er	6 8 ef	7 7 EH	12	8 6 EW	9 4 fm	10 3 FT	11 2 FM	12 1 tg	12 31 td	1 29 TR
2 10 md	3 12 mg	4 10 MF	5 10 MR	6 9 MF	7 8 er	13	8 7 ef	9 5 EH	10 4 ft	11 3 fm	12 2 FT	1 1 FM	1 30 tg
2 11 RM	3 13 RT	4 11 md	5 11 mg	6 10 md	7 9 MR	14	8 8 MF	9 6 er	10 5 EW	11 4 EH	12 3 ft	1 2 fm	1 31 FT
2 12 rm	3 14 rt	4 12 RM	5 12 RT	6 11 RM	7 10 mg	15	8 9 md	9 7 MR	10 6 ef	11 5 er	12 4 EW	1 3 EH	2 1 ft
2 13 TH	3 15 TW	4 13 rm	5 13 rt	6 12 rm	7 11 RT	16	8 10 RM	9 8 mg	10 7 MF	11 6 MR	12 5 ef	1 4 er	2 2 EW
2 14 tr	3 16 tf	4 14 TH	5 14 TW	6 13 TH	7 12 rt	17	8 11 rm	9 9 RT	10 8 md	11 7 mg	12 6 MF	1 5 MR	2 3 ef
2 15 FR	3 17 FF	4 15 tr	5 15 tf	6 14 tr	7 13 TW	18	8 12 TH	9 10 rt	10 9 RM	11 8 RT	12 7 md	1 6 mg	2 4 MF
2 16 fg	3 18 fd	4 16 FR	5 16 FF	6 15 FR	7 14 tf	19	8 13 tr	9 11 TW	10 10 rm	11 9 rt	12 8 RM	1 7 RT	2 5 md
2 17 ET	3 19 EM	4 17 fg	5 17 fd	6 16 fg	7 15 FF	20	8 14 FR	9 12 tf	10 11 TH	11 10 TW	12 9 rm	1 8 rt	2 6 RM
2 18 et	3 20 em	4 18 ET	5 18 EM	6 17 ET	7 16 fd	21	8 15 fg	9 13 FF	10 12 tr	11 11 tf	12 10 TH	1 9 TW	2 7 rm
2 19 MW	3 21 MH	4 19 et	5 19 em	6 18 et	7 17 EM	22	8 16 ET	9 14 fd	10 13 FR	11 12 FF	12 11 tr	1 10 tf	2 8 TH
2 20 mf	3 22 mr	4 20 MW	5 20 MH	6 19 MW	7 18 em	23	8 17 et	9 15 EM	10 14 fg	11 13 fd	12 12 FR	1 11 FF	2 9 tr
2 21 RF	3 23 RR	4 21 mf	5 21 mr	6 20 mf	7 19 MH	24	8 18 MW	9 16 em	10 15 ET	11 14 EM	12 13 fg	1 12 fd	2 10 FR
2 22 rd	3 24 rg	4 22 RF	5 22 RR	6 21 RF	7 20 mr	25	8 19 mf	9 17 MH	10 16 et	11 15 em	12 14 ET	1 13 EM	2 11 fg
2 23 TM	3 25 TT	4 23 rd	5 23 rg	6 22 rd	7 21 RR	26	8 20 RF	9 18 mr	10 17 MW	11 16 MH	12 15 et	1 14 em	2 12 ET
2 24 tm	3 26 tt	4 24 TM	5 24 TT	6 23 TM	7 22 rg	27	8 21 rd	9 19 RR	10 18 mf	11 17 mr	12 16 MW	1 15 MH	2 13 et
2 25 FH	3 27 FW	4 25 tm	5 25 tt	6 24 tm	7 23 TT	28	8 22 TM	9 20 rg	10 19 RF	11 18 RR	12 17 mf	1 16 mr	2 14 MW
2 26 fr	3 28 ff	4 26 FH	5 26 FW	6 25 FH	7 24 tt	29	8 23 tm	9 21 TT	10 20 rd	11 19 rg	12 18 RF	1 17 RR	2 15 mf
2 27 ER		4 27 fr	5 27 ff		7 25 FW	30			10 21 TM		12 19 rd		2 16 RF

194

JAN ET	FEB ef	MAR MW	APR mf	MAY RF	JUN rd	DAY	JUL TM	AUG tm	SEP FH	OCT fr	NOV ER	DEC eg
18 WARM	19 CLEAR	20 SUMMER	21 GRAIN	24 HEAT	25 FALL	OF	26 DEW	28 C DEW	29 WINTER	29 SNOW	29 CHILL	28 SPRING
11:36	16:45	10:25	15:09	1:14	11:36	MON	13:34	6:04	7:44	1:10	11:31	23:14
2 17 rd	3 18 RR	4 17 RF	5 17 RR	6 15 mf	7 15 mr	1	8 14 mf	9 12 MH	10 11 et	11 10 em	12 9 ET	1 8 EM
2 18 TM	3 19 rg	4 18 rd	5 18 rg	6 16 RF	7 16 RR	2	8 15 RF	9 13 mr	10 12 MW	11 11 MH	12 10 et	1 9 em
2 19 tm	3 20 TT	4 19 TM	5 19 TT	6 17 rd	7 17 rg	3	8 16 rd	9 14 RR	10 13 mf	11 12 mr	12 11 MW	1 10 MH
2 20 FH	3 21 tt	4 20 tm	5 20 tt	6 18 TM	7 18 TT	4	8 17 TM	9 15 rg	10 14 RF	11 13 RR	12 12 mf	1 11 mr
2 21 fr	3 22 FW	4 21 FH	5 21 FW	6 19 tm	7 19 tt	5	8 18 tm	9 16 TT	10 15 rd	11 14 rg	12 13 RF	1 12 RR
2 22 ER	3 23 ff	4 22 fr	5 22 ff	6 20 FH	7 20 FW	6	8 19 FH	9 17 tt	10 16 TM	11 15 TT	12 14 rd	1 13 rg
2 23 eg	3 24 EF	4 23 ER	5 23 EF	6 21 fr	7 21 ff	7	8 20 fr	9 18 FW	10 17 tm	11 16 tt	12 15 TM	1 14 TT
2 24 MT	3 25 ed	4 24 eg	5 24 ed	6 22 ER	7 22 EF	8	8 21 ER	9 19 ff	10 18 FH	11 17 FW	12 16 tm	1 15 tt
2 25 mt	3 26 MM	4 25 MT	5 25 MM	6 23 eg	7 23 ed	9	8 22 eg	9 20 EF	10 19 fr	11 18 ff	12 17 FH	1 16 FW
2 26 RW	3 27 mm	4 26 mt	5 26 mm	6 24 MT	7 24 MM	10	8 23 MT	9 21 ed	10 20 ER	11 19 EF	12 18 fr	1 17 ff
2 27 rf	3 28 RH	4 27 RW	5 27 RH	6 25 mt	7 25 mm	11	8 24 mt	9 22 MM	10 21 eg	11 20 ed	12 19 ER	1 18 EF
2 28 TF	3 29 rr	4 28 rf	5 28 rr	6 26 RW	7 26 RH	12	8 25 RW	9 23 mm	10 22 MT	11 21 MM	12 20 eg	1 19 ed
3 1 td	3 30 TR	4 29 TF	5 29 TR	6 27 rf	7 27 rr	13	8 26 rf	9 24 RH	10 23 mt	11 22 mm	12 21 MT	1 20 MM
3 2 FM	3 31 tg	4 30 td	5 30 tg	6 28 TF	7 28 TR	14	8 27 TF	9 25 rr	10 24 RW	11 23 RH	12 22 mt	1 21 mm
3 3 fm	4 1 FT	5 1 FM	5 31 FT	6 29 td	7 29 tg	15	8 28 td	9 26 TR	10 25 rf	11 24 rr	12 23 RW	1 22 RH
3 4 EH	4 2 ft	5 2 fm	6 1 ft	6 30 FM	7 30 FT	16	8 29 FM	9 27 tg	10 26 TF	11 25 TR	12 24 rf	1 23 rr
3 5 er	4 3 EW	5 3 EH	6 2 EW	7 1 fm	7 31 ft	17	8 30 fm	9 28 FT	10 27 td	11 26 tg	12 25 TF	1 24 TR
3 6 MR	4 4 ef	5 4 er	6 3 ef	7 2 EH	8 1 EW	18	8 31 EH	9 29 ft	10 28 FM	11 27 FT	12 26 td	1 25 tg
3 7 mg	4 5 MF	5 5 MR	6 4 MF	7 3 er	8 2 ef	19	9 1 er	9 30 EW	10 29 fm	11 28 ft	12 27 FM	1 26 FT
3 8 RT	4 6 md	5 6 mg	6 5 md	7 4 MR	8 3 MF	20	9 2 MR	10 1 ef	10 30 EH	11 29 EW	12 28 fm	1 27 ft
3 9 rt	4 7 RM	5 7 RT	6 6 RM	7 5 mg	8 4 md	21	9 3 mg	10 2 MF	10 31 er	11 30 ef	12 29 EH	1 28 EW
3 10 TW	4 8 rm	5 8 rt	6 7 rm	7 6 RT	8 5 RM	22	9 4 RT	10 3 md	11 1 MR	12 1 MF	12 30 er	1 29 ef
3 11 tf	4 9 TH	5 9 TW	6 8 TH	7 7 rt	8 6 rm	23	9 5 rt	10 4 RM	11 2 mg	12 2 md	12 31 MR	1 30 MF
3 12 FF	4 10 tr	5 10 tf	6 9 tr	7 8 TW	8 7 TH	24	9 6 TW	10 5 rm	11 3 RT	12 3 RM	1 1 mg	1 31 md
3 13 fd	4 11 FR	5 11 FF	6 10 FR	7 9 tf	8 8 tr	25	9 7 tf	10 6 TH	11 4 rt	12 4 rm	1 2 RT	2 1 RM
3 14 EM	4 12 fg	5 12 fd	6 11 fg	7 10 FF	8 9 FR	26	9 8 FF	10 7 tr	11 5 TW	12 5 TH	1 3 rt	2 2 rm
3 15 em	4 13 ET	5 13 EM	6 12 ET	7 11 fd	8 10 fg	27	9 9 fd	10 8 FR	11 6 tf	12 6 tr	1 4 TW	2 3 TH
3 16 MH	4 14 et	5 14 em	6 13 et	7 12 EM	8 11 ET	28	9 10 EM	10 9 fg	11 7 FF	12 7 FR	1 5 tf	2 4 tr
3 17 mr	4 15 MW	5 15 MH	6 14 MW	7 13 em	8 12 et	29	9 11 em	10 10 ET	11 8 fd	12 8 fg	1 6 FF	2 5 FR
	4 16 mf	5 16 mr		7 14 MH	8 13 MW	30			11 9 EM		1 7 fd	

1951 mt RABBIT

	JAN MT	FEB mt	MAR RW	APR rf	MAY TF	JUN td	DAY OF MON	JUL FM	AUG fm	SEP EH	OCT er	NOV MR	DEC mg
term	29 WARM	29 CLEAR		1 SUMMER	2 GRAIN	5 HEAT		6 FALL	8 DEW	9 C DEW	10 WINTER	10 SNOW	10 CHILL
time	17:27	22:33		16:10	20:33	7:28		17:24	19:19	11:53	13:27	6:03	17:10

DAY	JAN	FEB	MAR	APR	MAY	JUN	JUL	AUG	SEP	OCT	NOV	DEC
1	2 6 fg	3 8 fd	4 6 FR	5 6 FF	6 6 FR	7 4 tf	8 3 tr	9 1 TW	10 1 TH	10 30 rt	11 29 rm	12 28 RT
2	2 7 ET	3 9 EM	4 7 fg	5 7 fd	6 7 fg	7 5 FF	8 4 FR	9 2 tf	10 2 tr	10 31 TW	11 30 TH	12 29 rt
3	2 8 et	3 10 em	4 8 ET	5 8 EM	6 8 ET	7 6 fd	8 5 fg	9 3 FF	10 3 FR	11 1 tf	12 1 tr	12 30 TW
4	2 9 MW	3 11 MH	4 9 et	5 9 et	6 9 et	7 7 EM	8 6 ET	9 4 fd	10 4 fg	11 2 FR	12 2 FF	12 31 tf
5	2 10 mf	3 12 mr	4 10 MW	5 10 MH	6 10 MW	7 8 et	8 7 et	9 5 EM	10 5 ET	11 3 fg	12 3 fg	1 1 FF
6	2 11 RF	3 13 RR	4 11 mf	5 11 mr	6 11 mf	7 9 MH	8 8 MW	9 6 em	10 6 et	11 4 EM	12 4 ET	1 2 fd
7	2 12 rd	3 14 rg	4 12 RF	5 12 RR	6 12 rd	7 10 mr	8 9 mf	9 7 MH	10 7 MW	11 5 em	12 5 et	1 3 EM
8	2 13 TM	3 15 TT	4 13 rd	5 13 rg	6 13 TM	7 11 RR	8 10 RF	9 8 mr	10 8 mf	11 6 MH	12 6 MW	1 4 et
9	2 14 tm	3 16 tt	4 14 TM	5 14 TT	6 14 tm	7 12 rg	8 11 rd	9 9 RR	10 9 RF	11 7 mr	12 7 mf	1 5 MH
10	2 15 fr	3 17 FW	4 15 tm	5 15 tm	6 15 FH	7 13 TM	8 12 TT	9 10 rg	10 10 rd	11 8 RR	12 8 RF	1 6 mr
11	2 16 ER	3 18 ff	4 16 FH	5 16 FH	6 16 fr	7 14 tm	8 13 tm	9 11 TT	10 11 TM	11 9 rg	12 9 rd	1 7 RR
12	2 17 eg	3 19 EF	4 17 fr	5 17 fr	6 17 ER	7 15 FH	8 14 FH	9 12 tt	10 12 tm	11 10 TT	12 10 TM	1 8 rd
13	2 18 MT	3 20 ed	4 18 ER	5 18 ER	6 18 eg	7 16 fr	8 15 fr	9 13 FW	10 13 FH	11 11 tt	12 11 tm	1 9 rg
14	2 19 mt	3 21 MM	4 19 eg	5 19 eg	6 19 MT	7 17 ER	8 16 ER	9 14 ff	10 14 fr	11 12 FW	12 12 FH	1 10 TT
15	2 20 RW	3 22 mm	4 20 MT	5 20 MT	6 20 mt	7 18 eg	8 17 eg	9 15 EF	10 15 ER	11 13 fr	12 13 fr	1 11 tm
16	2 21 rf	3 23 RH	4 21 mt	5 21 mm	6 21 RW	7 19 MT	8 18 MT	9 16 ed	10 16 eg	11 14 EF	12 14 ER	1 12 FH
17	2 22 TF	3 24 rr	4 22 RW	5 22 RW	6 22 rf	7 20 mt	8 19 mt	9 17 MM	10 17 MT	11 15 ed	12 15 eg	1 13 fr
18	2 23 td	3 25 TR	4 23 rf	5 23 rf	6 23 TF	7 21 RW	8 20 RW	9 18 mm	10 18 mt	11 16 MM	12 16 MT	1 14 EF
19	2 24 FM	3 26 tg	4 24 TF	5 24 TF	6 24 td	7 22 rf	8 21 rf	9 19 RH	10 19 RW	11 17 mt	12 17 mt	1 15 ed
20	2 25 fm	3 27 FT	4 25 td	5 25 td	6 25 FM	7 23 TF	8 22 TF	9 20 rf	10 20 rf	11 18 RH	12 18 RW	1 16 MM
21	2 26 EH	3 28 ft	4 26 FM	5 26 FM	6 26 fm	7 24 td	8 23 td	9 21 TR	10 21 TF	11 19 rr	12 19 rf	1 17 mm
22	2 27 er	3 29 EW	4 27 fm	5 27 ft	6 27 EH	7 25 FM	8 24 FM	9 22 tg	10 22 td	11 20 TR	12 20 TF	1 18 RH
23	2 28 MR	3 30 ef	4 28 EH	5 28 EW	6 28 er	7 26 fm	8 25 fm	9 23 FT	10 23 FM	11 21 tg	12 21 td	1 19 rr
24	3 1 mg	3 31 MF	4 29 er	5 29 er	6 29 MR	7 27 EW	8 26 EH	9 24 ft	10 24 fm	11 22 FT	12 22 FM	1 20 TR
25	3 2 RT	4 1 md	4 30 MR	5 30 MR	6 30 mg	7 28 er	8 27 er	9 25 EH	10 25 EH	11 23 ft	12 23 fm	1 21 tg
26	3 3 rt	4 2 RM	5 1 mg	5 31 md	7 1 RT	7 29 MR	8 28 MR	9 26 er	10 26 er	11 24 EW	12 24 EH	1 22 FT
27	3 4 TW	4 3 rm	5 2 RT	6 1 RM	7 2 rt	7 30 md	8 29 mg	9 27 MF	10 27 MR	11 25 ef	12 25 er	1 23 ft
28	3 5 tf	4 4 TH	5 3 rt	6 2 rm	7 3 TW	7 31 RT	8 30 RT	9 28 mg	10 28 mg	11 26 MF	12 26 MR	1 24 EW
29	3 6 FF	4 5 tr	5 4 TW	6 3 TH		8 1 rt	8 31 rt	9 29 RM	10 29 RT	11 27 md	12 27 mg	1 25 ef
30		4 6 FF	5 5 tf	6 4 tr		8 2 TW		9 30 rm		11 28 RM		1 26 MF
31												1 27 md

196

1952 RW   DRAGON

JAN RT	FEB et	MAR TW	APR tf	MAY FF	MAY FF	JUN fd	DAY OF MON	JUL EM	AUG em	SEP MH	OCT mr	NOV RR	DEC rg SPRING
10 SPRING	10 WARM	11 CLEAR	12 SUMMER	14 GRAIN	16 HEAT	17 FALL		20 DEW	20 C DEW	20 WINTER	21 SNOW	20 CHILL	21 SPRING
4:54	23:08	4:16	21:54	2:21	13:15	23:12		1:14	17:42	19:22	11:56	23:03	10:46
27 RM	25 mg	26 md	24 MR	24 MF	22 er	22 ef	1	20 EH	19 EW	19 EH	17 ft	17 fm	15 FT
28 rm	26 RT	27 RM	25 mg	25 md	23 MR	23 MF	2	21 er	20 ef	20 er	18 EW	18 EH	16 ft
29 TH	27 rt	28 rm	26 RT	26 RM	24 mg	24 md	3	22 MR	21 MF	21 MR	19 ef	19 er	17 EW
30 tr	28 TW	29 TH	27 rt	27 rm	25 RT	25 RM	4	23 mg	22 md	22 mg	20 MF	20 MR	18 ef
31 FR	29 tf	30 tr	28 TW	28 TH	26 rt	26 rm	5	24 RT	23 RM	23 RT	21 md	21 mg	19 MF
1 fg	1 FF	31 FR	29 tf	29 tr	27 TW	27 TH	6	25 rt	24 rm	24 rt	22 RM	22 RT	20 md
2 ET	2 fd	1 fg	30 FF	30 FR	28 tf	28 tr	7	26 TW	25 TH	25 TW	23 rm	23 rt	21 RM
3 et	3 EM	2 ET	1 fd	31 fg	29 FF	29 FR	8	27 tf	26 tr	26 tf	24 TH	24 TW	22 rm
4 MW	4 em	3 et	2 EM	1 ET	30 fd	30 fg	9	28 FF	27 FR	27 FF	25 tr	25 tf	23 TH
5 mf	5 MH	4 MW	3 em	2 et	1 EM	31 ET	10	29 fd	28 fg	28 fd	26 FR	26 FF	24 tr
6 RF	6 mr	5 mf	4 MW	3 MW	2 em	1 et	11	30 EM	29 ET	29 EM	27 fg	27 fd	25 FR
7 rd	7 RR	6 RF	5 mf	4 mf	3 MH	2 MW	12	31 em	30 et	30 em	28 ET	28 EM	26 fg
8 TM	8 rg	7 rd	6 RF	5 RF	4 mr	3 mf	13	1 MH	1 MW	31 MH	29 et	29 em	27 ET
9 tm	9 TT	8 TM	7 rd	6 rd	5 RR	4 RF	14	2 mr	2 mf	1 mr	30 MW	30 MH	28 et
10 FH	10 tt	9 tm	8 TM	7 TM	6 rg	5 rd	15	3 RR	3 RF	2 RR	1 mf	31 mr	29 MW
11 fr	11 FW	10 FH	9 tm	8 tm	7 TT	6 TM	16	4 rg	4 rd	3 rg	2 RF	1 RR	30 mf
12 ER	12 ff	11 fr	10 FH	9 FH	8 tt	7 tm	17	5 TT	5 TM	4 TT	3 rd	2 rg	31 RF
13 eg	13 EF	12 ER	11 fr	10 fr	9 FW	8 FH	18	6 tt	6 tm	5 tt	4 TM	3 TT	1 rd
14 MT	14 ed	13 eg	12 ER	11 ER	10 ff	9 fr	19	7 FW	7 FH	6 FW	5 tm	4 tt	2 TM
15 mt	15 MM	14 MT	13 ed	12 eg	11 EF	10 ER	20	8 ff	8 fr	7 ff	6 FH	5 FW	3 tm
16 RW	16 mm	15 mt	14 MM	13 MT	12 ed	11 eg	21	9 EF	9 EF	8 EF	7 fr	6 ff	4 FH
17 rf	17 RH	16 RW	15 mt	14 mt	13 MM	12 MT	22	10 ed	10 ed	9 ed	8 ER	7 EF	5 fr
18 TF	18 rr	17 rf	16 RW	15 RW	14 mm	13 mt	23	11 MM	11 MM	10 MM	9 eg	8 ed	6 ER
19 td	19 TR	18 TF	17 rf	16 rf	15 RH	14 RW	24	12 mm	12 mt	11 mm	10 MT	9 MM	7 eg
20 FM	20 tg	19 td	18 TR	17 TF	16 rf	15 rf	25	13 RH	13 RW	12 RH	11 mt	10 mm	8 MT
21 fm	21 FT	20 FM	19 tg	18 td	17 TF	16 TF	26	14 rr	14 rf	13 rr	12 RW	11 RH	9 mt
22 EH	22 ft	21 ft	20 FT	19 FM	18 td	17 td	27	15 TR	15 TF	14 TR	13 rf	12 rr	10 RW
23 er	23 EW	22 EH	21 ft	20 fm	19 FM	18 FM	28	16 tg	16 td	15 tg	14 TF	13 TR	11 rf
24 MR	24 ef	23 er	22 EW	21 EH	20 fm	19 fm	29	17 FT	17 FM	16 FT	15 td	14 tg	12 TF
	25 MF		23 ef		21 EW		30	18 ft	18 fm		16 FM		13 td

1953 rf SNAKE

	JAN	FEB	MAR	APR	MAY	JUN	JUL	DAY OF MON	AUG	SEP	OCT	NOV	DEC
pillar	TT	tt	FW	ff	EF	ed	MM		mm	RH	rr	TR	tg
term	21 WARM	22 CLEAR	23 SUMMER	25 GRAIN	27 HEAT	29 FALL			1 DEW	1 C DEW	2 WINTER	2 SNOW	2 CHILL
time	4:56	10:13	3:53	8:17	19:03	5:00			7:59	23:31	1:02	17:38	5:18

DAY	JAN	FEB	MAR	APR	MAY	JUN	JUL	AUG	SEP	OCT	NOV	DEC
1	2 14 FM	3 15 tg	4 14 td	5 13 TR	6 11 rf	7 11 rr	8 9 RW	9 8 RH	10 8 RW	11 6 mm	12 6 mt	1 5 mm
2	2 15 fm	3 16 FT	4 15 FM	5 14 tg	6 12 TF	7 12 TR	8 10 rf	9 9 rr	10 9 rf	11 7 RH	12 7 RW	1 6 RH
3	2 16 EH	3 17 ft	4 16 fm	5 15 FT	6 13 td	7 13 tg	8 11 TF	9 10 TR	10 10 TF	11 8 rr	12 8 rf	1 7 rr
4	2 17 er	3 18 EW	4 17 EH	5 16 ft	6 14 FM	7 14 FT	8 12 td	9 11 tg	10 11 td	11 9 TR	12 9 TF	1 8 TR
5	2 18 MR	3 19 ef	4 18 er	5 17 EW	6 15 fm	7 15 ft	8 13 FM	9 12 FT	10 12 FM	11 10 tg	12 10 td	1 9 tg
6	2 19 mg	3 20 MF	4 19 MR	5 18 ef	6 16 EH	7 16 EW	8 14 fm	9 13 ft	10 13 fm	11 11 FT	12 11 FM	1 10 FT
7	2 20 RT	3 21 md	4 20 mg	5 19 MF	6 17 er	7 17 ef	8 15 EH	9 14 EW	10 14 EH	11 12 ft	12 12 fm	1 11 ft
8	2 21 rt	3 22 RM	4 21 RT	5 20 md	6 18 MR	7 18 MF	8 16 er	9 15 ef	10 15 er	11 13 EW	12 13 EH	1 12 EW
9	2 22 TW	3 23 rm	4 22 rt	5 21 RM	6 19 mg	7 19 md	8 17 MR	9 16 MF	10 16 MR	11 14 ef	12 14 er	1 13 ef
10	2 23 tf	3 24 TH	4 23 TW	5 22 rm	6 20 RT	7 20 RM	8 18 mg	9 17 md	10 17 mg	11 15 MF	12 15 MR	1 14 MF
11	2 24 FF	3 25 tr	4 24 tf	5 23 TH	6 21 rt	7 21 rm	8 19 RT	9 18 RM	10 18 RT	11 16 md	12 16 mg	1 15 md
12	2 25 fd	3 26 FR	4 25 FF	5 24 tr	6 22 TW	7 22 TH	8 20 rt	9 19 rm	10 19 rt	11 17 RM	12 17 RT	1 16 RM
13	2 26 EM	3 27 fg	4 26 fd	5 25 FR	6 23 tf	7 23 tr	8 21 TW	9 20 TH	10 20 TW	11 18 rm	12 18 rt	1 17 rm
14	2 27 em	3 28 ET	4 27 EM	5 26 fg	6 24 FF	7 24 FR	8 22 tf	9 21 tr	10 21 tf	11 19 TH	12 19 TW	1 18 TH
15	2 28 MH	3 29 et	4 28 em	5 27 ET	6 25 fd	7 25 fg	8 23 FF	9 22 FR	10 22 FF	11 20 tr	12 20 tf	1 19 tr
16	3 1 mr	3 30 MW	4 29 MH	5 28 et	6 26 EM	7 26 ET	8 24 fd	9 23 fg	10 23 fd	11 21 FR	12 21 FF	1 20 FR
17	3 2 RR	3 31 mf	4 30 mr	5 29 MW	6 27 em	7 27 et	8 25 EM	9 24 ET	10 24 EM	11 22 fg	12 22 fd	1 21 fg
18	3 3 rg	4 1 RF	5 1 RR	5 30 mf	6 28 MH	7 28 MW	8 26 em	9 25 et	10 25 em	11 23 ET	12 23 EM	1 22 ET
19	3 4 TT	4 2 rd	5 2 rg	5 31 RF	6 29 mr	7 29 mf	8 27 MH	9 26 MW	10 26 MH	11 24 et	12 24 em	1 23 et
20	3 5 tt	4 3 TM	5 3 TT	6 1 rd	6 30 RR	7 30 RF	8 28 mr	9 27 mf	10 27 mr	11 25 MW	12 25 MH	1 24 MW
21	3 6 FW	4 4 tm	5 4 tt	6 2 TM	7 1 rg	7 31 rd	8 29 RR	9 28 RF	10 28 RR	11 26 mf	12 26 mr	1 25 mf
22	3 7 ff	4 5 FH	5 5 FW	6 3 tm	7 2 TT	8 1 TM	8 30 rg	9 29 rd	10 29 rg	11 27 RF	12 27 RR	1 26 RF
23	3 8 EF	4 6 fr	5 6 ff	6 4 FH	7 3 tt	8 2 tm	8 31 TT	9 30 TM	10 30 TT	11 28 rd	12 28 rg	1 27 rd
24	3 9 ed	4 7 ER	5 7 EF	6 5 fr	7 4 FW	8 3 FH	9 1 tt	10 1 tm	10 31 tt	11 29 TM	12 29 TT	1 28 TM
25	3 10 MM	4 8 eg	5 8 ed	6 6 ER	7 5 ff	8 4 fr	9 2 FW	10 2 FH	11 1 FW	11 30 tm	12 30 tt	1 29 tm
26	3 11 mm	4 9 MT	5 9 MM	6 7 eg	7 6 EF	8 5 ER	9 3 ff	10 3 fr	11 2 ff	12 1 FH	12 31 FW	1 30 FH
27	3 12 RH	4 10 mt	5 10 mm	6 8 MT	7 7 ed	8 6 eg	9 4 EF	10 4 ER	11 3 EF	12 2 fr	1 1 ff	1 31 fr
28	3 13 rr	4 11 RW	5 11 RH	6 9 mt	7 8 MM	8 7 MT	9 5 ed	10 5 eg	11 4 ed	12 3 ER	1 2 EF	2 1 ER
29	3 14 TR	4 12 rf	5 12 rr	6 10 RW	7 9 mm	8 8 mt	9 6 MM	10 6 MT	11 5 MM	12 4 eg	1 3 ed	2 2 eg
30		4 13 TF			7 10 RH		9 7 mm	10 7 mt		12 5 MT	1 4 MM	

	JAN FT	FEB ft	MAR EW	APR ef	MAY MF	JUN md	DAY OF MON	JUL RM	AUG rm	SEP TH	OCT tr	NOV FR	DEC fg
Solar term	2 SPRING	2 WARM	3 CLEAR	4 SUMMER	6 GRAIN	9 HEAT	10 FALL	12 DEW	13 C DEW	13 WINTER	14 SNOW	13 CHILL	
Time	16:31	10:29	16:00	9:39	14:02	0:20	10:00	13:47	5:20	8:09	0:28	11:08	
1	2/3 MT	3/5 mm	4/3 eg	5/3 MM	6/1 MT	6/30 mm	1	7/30 mt	8/28 RH	9/27 rf	10/27 rr	11/25 TF	12/25 TR
2	2/4 mt	3/6 RH	4/4 MT	5/4 mm	6/2 mt	7/1 RH	2	8/1 RW	8/29 rr	9/28 TF	10/28 TR	11/26 td	12/26 tg
3	2/5 RW	3/7 rr	4/5 mt	5/5 RH	6/3 RW	7/2 rr	3	8/2 rf	8/30 TR	9/29 td	10/29 tg	11/27 FM	12/27 FT
4	2/6 rf	3/8 TR	4/6 RW	5/6 rr	6/4 rf	7/3 TR	4	8/3 TF	9/1 tg	9/30 FM	10/30 FT	11/28 fm	12/28 ft
5	2/7 TF	3/9 tg	4/7 rf	5/7 TR	6/5 TF	7/4 tg	5	8/4 td	9/2 FT	10/1 fm	11/1 ft	11/29 EH	12/29 EW
6	2/8 td	3/10 FT	4/8 TF	5/8 tg	6/6 td	7/5 FT	6	8/5 FM	9/3 ft	10/2 EH	11/2 EW	11/30 er	12/30 ef
7	2/9 FM	3/11 ft	4/9 td	5/9 FT	6/7 FM	7/6 ft	7	8/6 fm	9/4 EW	10/3 er	11/3 ef	12/1 MR	1/1 MF
8	2/10 fm	3/12 EW	4/10 FM	5/10 ft	6/8 fm	7/7 EW	8	8/7 EH	9/5 ef	10/4 MR	11/4 MF	12/2 mg	1/2 md
9	2/11 EH	3/13 ef	4/11 fm	5/11 EW	6/9 EH	7/8 ef	9	8/8 er	9/6 MF	10/5 mg	11/5 md	12/3 RT	1/3 RM
10	2/12 er	3/14 MF	4/12 EH	5/12 ef	6/10 er	7/9 MF	10	8/9 MR	9/7 md	10/6 RT	11/6 RM	12/4 rt	1/4 rm
11	2/13 MR	3/15 md	4/13 er	5/13 MF	6/11 MR	7/10 md	11	8/10 mg	9/8 RM	10/7 rt	11/7 rm	12/5 TW	1/5 TH
12	2/14 mg	3/16 RM	4/14 MR	5/14 md	6/12 mg	7/11 RM	12	8/11 RT	9/9 rm	10/8 TW	11/8 TH	12/6 tf	1/6 tr
13	2/15 RT	3/17 rm	4/15 mg	5/15 RM	6/13 RT	7/12 rm	13	8/12 rt	9/10 TH	10/9 tf	11/9 tr	12/7 FF	1/7 FR
14	2/16 rt	3/18 TH	4/16 RT	5/16 rm	6/14 rt	7/13 TH	14	8/13 TW	9/11 tr	10/10 FF	11/10 FR	12/8 fd	1/8 fg
15	2/17 TW	3/19 tr	4/17 rt	5/17 TH	6/15 TW	7/14 tr	15	8/14 tf	9/12 FR	10/11 fd	11/11 fg	12/9 EM	1/9 ET
16	2/18 tf	3/20 FR	4/18 TW	5/18 tr	6/16 tf	7/15 FR	16	8/15 FF	9/13 fg	10/12 EM	11/12 ET	12/10 em	1/10 et
17	2/19 FF	3/21 fg	4/19 tf	5/19 FR	6/17 FF	7/16 fg	17	8/16 fd	9/14 ET	10/13 em	11/13 et	12/11 MH	1/11 MW
18	2/20 fd	3/22 ET	4/20 FF	5/20 fg	6/18 fd	7/17 ET	18	8/17 EM	9/15 et	10/14 MH	11/14 MW	12/12 mr	1/12 mf
19	2/21 EM	3/23 et	4/21 fd	5/21 ET	6/19 EM	7/18 et	19	8/18 em	9/16 MW	10/15 mr	11/15 mf	12/13 RR	1/13 RF
20	2/22 em	3/24 MW	4/22 EM	5/22 et	6/20 em	7/19 MW	20	8/19 MH	9/17 mf	10/16 RR	11/16 RF	12/14 rg	1/14 rd
21	2/23 MH	3/25 mf	4/23 em	5/23 MW	6/21 MH	7/20 mf	21	8/20 mr	9/18 RF	10/17 rg	11/17 rd	12/15 TT	1/15 TM
22	2/24 mr	3/26 RF	4/24 MH	5/24 mf	6/22 mr	7/21 RF	22	8/21 RR	9/19 rd	10/18 TT	11/18 TM	12/16 tt	1/16 tm
23	2/25 RR	3/27 rd	4/25 mr	5/25 RF	6/23 RR	7/22 rd	23	8/22 rg	9/20 TM	10/19 tt	11/19 tm	12/17 FW	1/17 FH
24	2/26 rg	3/28 TM	4/26 RR	5/26 rd	6/24 rg	7/23 TM	24	8/23 TT	9/21 tm	10/20 FW	11/20 FH	12/18 ff	1/18 fr
25	2/27 TT	3/29 tm	4/27 rg	5/27 TM	6/25 TT	7/24 tm	25	8/24 tt	9/22 FH	10/21 ff	11/21 fr	12/19 EF	1/19 ER
26	2/28 tt	3/30 FH	4/28 TT	5/28 tm	6/26 tt	7/25 FH	26	8/25 FW	9/23 fr	10/22 EF	11/22 ER	12/20 ed	1/20 eg
27	2/29 FW	4/1 fr	4/29 tt	5/29 FH	6/27 FW	7/26 fr	27	8/26 ff	9/24 ER	10/23 ed	11/23 eg	12/21 MM	1/21 MT
28	2/30 ff	4/2 ER	4/30 FW	5/30 fr	6/28 ff	7/27 ER	28	8/27 EF	9/25 eg	10/24 MM	11/24 MT	12/22 mm	1/22 mt
29	3/1 EF		5/1 ff	6/1 ER	6/29 EF	7/28 eg	29	8/28 ed	9/26 MT	10/25 mm	11/25 mt	12/23 RH	1/23 RW
30	3/2 ed		5/2 EF	6/2 eg	6/30 ed	7/29 MT	30	8/29 MM	9/27 mt	10/26 RH	11/26 RW	12/24 rr	1/24 rf
31	3/3 MM		5/3 ed		7/1 MM			8/30 mm	9/28 RW		11/27 rf		1/25 TF

1955 td RAM

Month	Solar term	Time
JAN ET	12 SPRING	22:18
FEB et	13 WARM	16:32
MAR MW	13 CLEAR	21:39
MAR MW	15 SUMMER	15:18
APR mf	16 GRAIN	19:44
MAY RF	19 HEAT	6:07
JUN rd	21 FALL	15:50
DAY OF MON		
JUL TM	22 DEW	19:36
AUG tm	24 C DEW	11:09
SEP FH	24 WINTER	13:49
OCT fr	25 SNOW	5:23
NOV ER	24 CHILL	16:31
DEC eg	24 SPRING	4:13

JAN ET	FEB et	MAR MW	MAR MW	APR mf	MAY RF	JUN rd	DAY OF MON	JUL TM	AUG tm	SEP FH	OCT fr	NOV ER	DEC eg
1/24 tm	2/22 TT	3/24 TM	4/22 rg	5/22 rd	6/20 RR	7/19 mg	1	8/18 mr	9/16 MW	10/16 MH	11/14 et	12/14 em	1/13 et
1/25 FH	2/23 tt	3/25 tm	4/23 TT	5/23 TM	6/21 rg	7/20 RF	2	8/19 RR	9/17 mg	10/17 mr	11/15 MW	12/15 MH	1/14 MW
1/26 fr	2/24 FW	3/26 FH	4/24 tt	5/24 tm	6/22 TT	7/21 rd	3	8/20 rg	9/18 RF	10/18 RR	11/16 mg	12/16 mr	1/15 mg
1/27 ER	2/25 fr	3/27 fr	4/25 FW	5/25 FH	6/23 tt	7/22 TM	4	8/21 TT	9/19 rd	10/19 rg	11/17 RF	12/17 RR	1/16 RF
1/28 eg	2/26 EF	3/28 ER	4/26 fr	5/26 fr	6/24 FW	7/23 tm	5	8/22 tt	9/20 TM	10/20 TT	11/18 rd	12/18 rg	1/17 rd
1/29 MT	2/27 ed	3/29 eg	4/27 EF	5/27 ER	6/25 fr	7/24 FH	6	8/23 FW	9/21 tm	10/21 tt	11/19 TM	12/19 TT	1/18 TM
1/30 mt	2/28 MM	3/30 MT	4/28 ed	5/28 eg	6/26 EF	7/25 fr	7	8/24 ff	9/22 FH	10/22 FW	11/20 tm	12/20 tt	1/19 tm
1/31 RW	3/1 mm	3/31 mt	4/29 MM	5/29 MT	6/27 ed	7/26 ER	8	8/25 EF	9/23 fr	10/23 ff	11/21 FH	12/21 FW	1/20 FH
2/1 rf	3/2 RH	4/1 RW	4/30 mm	5/30 mt	6/28 MM	7/27 ed	9	8/26 ed	9/24 ER	10/24 EF	11/22 fr	12/22 ff	1/21 fr
2/2 TF	3/3 rr	4/2 rf	5/1 RH	5/31 RW	6/29 mm	7/28 MT	10	8/27 MM	9/25 eg	10/25 ed	11/23 ER	12/23 EF	1/22 ER
2/3 td	3/4 TR	4/3 TF	5/2 rr	6/1 rf	6/30 RH	7/29 mt	11	8/28 mm	9/26 MT	10/26 MM	11/24 eg	12/24 ed	1/23 eg
2/4 FM	3/5 tg	4/4 td	5/3 TR	6/2 TF	7/1 rr	7/30 RW	12	8/29 RH	9/27 mt	10/27 mm	11/25 MT	12/25 MM	1/24 MT
2/5 fm	3/6 FT	4/5 FM	5/4 tg	6/3 td	7/2 TR	7/31 rf	13	8/30 rr	9/28 RW	10/28 RH	11/26 mt	12/26 mm	1/25 mt
2/6 EH	3/7 ft	4/6 fm	5/5 FT	6/4 FM	7/3 tg	8/1 TF	14	8/31 TR	9/29 rf	10/29 rr	11/27 RW	12/27 RH	1/26 RW
2/7 er	3/8 EW	4/7 EH	5/6 ft	6/5 fm	7/4 FT	8/2 td	15	9/1 tg	9/30 TF	10/30 TR	11/28 rf	12/28 rr	1/27 rf
2/8 MR	3/9 ef	4/8 er	5/7 EW	6/6 EH	7/5 ft	8/3 FM	16	9/2 FT	10/1 td	10/31 tg	11/29 TF	12/29 TR	1/28 TF
2/9 mg	3/10 MF	4/9 MR	5/8 ef	6/7 er	7/6 EW	8/4 fm	17	9/3 ft	10/2 FM	11/1 FT	11/30 td	12/30 tg	1/29 td
2/10 RT	3/11 md	4/10 mg	5/9 MF	6/8 MR	7/7 ef	8/5 EH	18	9/4 EW	10/3 fm	11/2 ft	12/1 FM	12/31 FT	1/30 FM
2/11 rt	3/12 RM	4/11 RT	5/10 md	6/9 mg	7/8 MF	8/6 er	19	9/5 ef	10/4 EH	11/3 EW	12/2 fm	1/1 ft	1/31 fm
2/12 TW	3/13 rm	4/12 rt	5/11 RM	6/10 RT	7/9 md	8/7 MR	20	9/6 MF	10/5 er	11/4 ef	12/3 EH	1/2 EW	2/1 EH
2/13 tf	3/14 TH	4/13 TW	5/12 rm	6/11 rt	7/10 RM	8/8 mg	21	9/7 md	10/6 MR	11/5 MF	12/4 er	1/3 ef	2/2 er
2/14 FF	3/15 tr	4/14 tf	5/13 TH	6/12 TW	7/11 rm	8/9 RT	22	9/8 RM	10/7 mg	11/6 md	12/5 MR	1/4 MF	2/3 MR
2/15 fd	3/16 FR	4/15 FF	5/14 tr	6/13 tf	7/12 TH	8/10 rt	23	9/9 rm	10/8 RT	11/7 RM	12/6 mg	1/5 md	2/4 mg
2/16 EM	3/17 fg	4/16 fd	5/15 FR	6/14 FF	7/13 tr	8/11 TW	24	9/10 TH	10/9 rt	11/8 rm	12/7 RT	1/6 RM	2/5 RT
2/17 em	3/18 ET	4/17 EM	5/16 fg	6/15 fd	7/14 FR	8/12 tf	25	9/11 tr	10/10 TW	11/9 TH	12/8 rt	1/7 rm	2/6 rt
2/18 MH	3/19 et	4/18 em	5/17 ET	6/16 EM	7/15 fg	8/13 FF	26	9/12 FR	10/11 tf	11/10 tr	12/9 TW	1/8 TH	2/7 TW
2/19 mr	3/20 MW	4/19 MH	5/18 et	6/17 em	7/16 ET	8/14 fd	27	9/13 fg	10/12 FF	11/11 FR	12/10 tf	1/9 tr	2/8 tf
2/20 RR	3/21 mf	4/20 mr	5/19 MW	6/18 MH	7/17 et	8/15 EM	28	9/14 ET	10/13 fd	11/12 fg	12/11 FF	1/10 FR	2/9 FF
2/21 rg	3/22 RF	4/21 RR	5/20 mf	6/19 mr	7/18 MW	8/16 em	29	9/15 et	10/14 EM	11/13 ET	12/12 fd	1/11 fg	2/10 fd
	3/23 rd		5/21 RF			8/17 MH	30		10/15 em		12/13 EM	1/12 ET	2/11 EM

200

1956 FM MONKEY

JAN MT	FEB mt	MAR RW	APR rf	MAY TF	JUN td	JUL FM	DAY OF MON	AUG fm	SEP EH	OCT er	NOV MR	DEC mg
23 WARM	25 CLEAR	25 SUMMER	28 GRAIN	29 HEAT		2 FALL		4 DEW	5 C DEW	5 WINTER	6 SNOW	5 CHILL
22:25	3:32	21:11	1:36	11:59		21:41		1:24	15:37	19:48	11:03	22:11
2.12 em	3.14 MW	4.13 em	5.15 MW	6.15 MH	7.17 mf	8.17 mr	1	9.19 RF	10.20 rg	11.21 rd	12.22 TT	1.23 TM
2.13 MH	3.15 mf	4.14 MH	5.16 mf	6.16 mr	7.18 RF	8.18 RR	2	9.20 rd	10.21 TT	11.22 TM	12.23 tt	1.24 tm
2.14 mr	3.16 RF	4.15 mr	5.17 RF	6.17 RR	7.19 rd	8.19 rg	3	9.21 TM	10.22 tt	11.23 tm	12.24 FW	1.25 FH
2.15 RR	3.17 rd	4.16 RR	5.18 rd	6.18 rg	7.20 TM	8.20 TT	4	9.22 tm	10.23 FW	11.24 FH	12.25 ff	1.26 fr
2.16 rg	3.18 TM	4.17 rg	5.19 TM	6.19 TT	7.21 tm	8.21 tt	5	9.23 FH	10.24 ff	11.25 fr	12.26 EF	1.27 ER
2.17 TT	3.19 tm	4.18 TT	5.20 tm	6.20 tt	7.22 FH	8.22 FW	6	9.24 fr	10.25 EF	11.26 ER	12.27 ed	1.28 eg
2.18 tt	3.20 FH	4.19 tt	5.21 FH	6.21 FW	7.23 fr	8.23 ff	7	9.25 ER	10.26 ed	11.27 eg	12.28 MM	1.29 MT
2.19 FW	3.21 fr	4.20 FW	5.22 fr	6.22 ff	7.24 ER	8.24 EF	8	9.26 eg	10.27 MM	11.28 MT	12.29 mm	1.30 mt
2.20 ff	3.22 ER	4.21 ff	5.23 ER	6.23 EF	7.25 eg	8.25 ed	9	9.27 MT	10.28 mm	11.29 mt	1.1 RH	2.1 RW
2.21 EF	3.23 eg	4.22 EF	5.24 eg	6.24 ed	7.26 MT	8.26 MM	10	9.28 mt	10.29 RH	11.30 RW	1.2 rr	2.2 rf
2.22 ed	3.24 MT	4.23 ed	5.25 MT	6.25 MM	7.27 mt	8.27 mm	11	9.29 RW	11.1 rr	12.1 rf	1.3 TR	2.3 TF
2.23 MM	3.25 mt	4.24 MM	5.26 mt	6.26 mm	7.28 RW	8.28 RH	12	9.30 rf	11.2 TR	12.2 TF	1.4 tg	2.4 td
2.24 mm	3.26 RW	4.25 mm	5.27 RW	6.27 RH	7.29 rf	8.29 rr	13	10.1 TF	11.3 tg	12.3 td	1.5 FT	2.5 FM
2.25 RH	3.27 rf	4.26 RH	5.28 rf	6.28 rr	7.30 TF	9.1 TR	14	10.2 td	11.4 FT	12.4 FM	1.6 ft	2.6 fm
2.26 rr	3.28 TF	4.27 rr	5.29 TF	6.29 TR	8.1 td	9.2 tg	15	10.3 FM	11.5 ft	12.5 fm	1.7 EW	2.7 EH
2.27 TR	3.29 td	4.28 TR	5.30 td	7.1 tg	8.2 FM	9.3 FT	16	10.4 fm	11.6 EW	12.6 EH	1.8 ef	2.8 er
2.28 tg	3.30 FM	4.29 tg	6.1 FM	7.2 FT	8.3 fm	9.4 ft	17	10.5 EH	11.7 ef	12.7 er	1.9 MF	2.9 MR
2.29 FT	4.1 fm	5.1 FT	6.2 fm	7.3 ft	8.4 EH	9.5 EW	18	10.6 er	11.8 MF	12.8 MR	1.10 md	2.10 mg
3.1 ft	4.2 EH	5.2 ft	6.3 EH	7.4 EW	8.5 er	9.6 ef	19	10.7 MR	11.9 md	12.9 mg	1.11 RM	2.11 RT
3.2 EW	4.3 er	5.3 EW	6.4 er	7.5 ef	8.6 MR	9.7 MF	20	10.8 mg	11.10 RM	12.10 RT	1.12 rm	2.12 rt
3.3 ef	4.4 MR	5.4 ef	6.5 MR	7.6 MF	8.7 mg	9.8 md	21	10.9 RT	11.11 rm	12.11 rt	1.13 TH	2.13 TW
3.4 MF	4.5 mg	5.5 MF	6.6 mg	7.7 md	8.8 RT	9.9 RM	22	10.10 rt	11.12 TH	12.12 TW	1.14 tr	2.14 tf
3.5 md	4.6 RT	5.6 md	6.7 RT	7.8 RM	8.9 rt	9.10 rm	23	10.11 TW	11.13 tr	12.13 tf	1.15 FR	2.15 FF
3.6 RM	4.7 rt	5.7 RM	6.8 rt	7.9 rm	8.10 TW	9.11 TH	24	10.12 tf	11.14 FR	12.14 FF	1.16 fg	2.16 fd
3.7 rm	4.8 TW	5.8 rm	6.9 TW	7.10 TH	8.11 tf	9.12 tr	25	10.13 FF	11.15 fg	12.15 fd	1.17 ET	2.17 EM
3.8 TH	4.9 tf	5.9 TH	6.10 tf	7.11 tr	8.12 FF	9.13 FR	26	10.14 fd	11.16 ET	12.16 EM	1.18 et	2.18 em
3.9 tr	4.10 FF	5.10 tr	6.11 FF	7.12 FR	8.13 fd	9.14 fg	27	10.15 EM	11.17 et	12.17 em	1.19 MW	2.19 MH
3.10 FR	4.11 fd	5.11 FR	6.12 fd	7.13 fg	8.14 EM	9.15 ET	28	10.16 em	11.18 MW	12.18 MH	1.20 mf	2.20 mr
3.11 fg	4.12 EM	5.12 fg	6.13 EM	7.14 ET	8.15 em	9.16 et	29	10.17 MH	11.19 mf	12.19 mr	1.21 RF	2.21 RR
3.12 ET		5.13 ET	6.14 em	7.15 et	8.16 MH	9.17 MW	30	10.18 mr	11.20 RF	12.20 RR	1.22 rd	2.22 rg
3.13 et		5.14 et		7.16 MW		9.18 mf	31	10.19 RR		12.21 rg		2.23 TT

1957 fm ROOSTER

#	JAN RT · SPRING 9:55	FEB rt · WARM 4:11	MAR TW · CLEAR 9:19	APR tf · SUMMER 3:11	MAY FF · GRAIN 7:25	JUN fd · HEAT 17:49	DAY OF MON	JUL EM · FALL 3:33	AUG em · DEW 7:03	AUG em · C DEW 21:31	SEP MH · WINTER 1:37	OCT mr · SNOW 17:57	NOV RR · CHILL 4:05	DEC rg · SPRING 15:50
							5	13	15	15	17	16	17	16
1	31 rt	3 2 TW	4 3 RT	5 4 RM	6 5 mg	7 6 md	1	7 27 MR	8 25 ef	8 24 er	10 23 EW	11 22 EH	12 21 ft	1 20 fm
2	1 TW	3 3 TH	4 4 rt	5 5 rm	6 5 RT	7 6 RM	2	7 28 mg	8 26 MR	8 25 MR	10 24 ef	11 22 er	12 22 EW	1 21 EH
3	2 tf	3 4 tr	4 5 tw	5 5 TH	6 5 RT	7 6 rm	3	7 29 RT	8 27 mg	8 26 mg	10 25 MF	11 23 MR	12 23 MW	1 22 er
4	3 FF	3 5 FR	4 6 tf	5 5 tr	6 6 tf	7 1 TH	4	7 30 RT	8 28 md	8 27 RT	10 26 mg	11 24 ef	12 24 ef	1 23 ef
5	4 fd	3 6 fg	4 7 FF	5 5 FR	6 6 FF	7 2 tr	5	7 31 tw	8 29 RT	8 28 RT	10 27 RM	11 25 MF	12 25 MF	1 24 MF
6	5 EM	3 7 ET	4 8 fd	5 5 fg	6 6 fd	7 3 FR	6	8 1 tf	8 30 tw	8 29 tw	10 28 rm	11 26 RM	12 26 md	1 25 RT
7	6 em	3 8 et	4 9 EM	5 6 ET	6 6 EM	7 4 fg	7	8 2 FF	8 31 tf	8 30 tf	10 29 TH	11 27 rm	12 27 RM	1 26 RT
8	7 MH	3 9 MW	4 10 et	5 6 et	6 6 et	7 5 ET	8	8 3 fd	9 1 FF	9 1 FF	10 30 tr	11 28 TH	12 28 rm	1 27 tw
9	8 mr	3 10 em	4 11 em	5 7 MH	6 7 em	7 5 et	9	8 4 EM	9 2 fd	9 2 fd	10 31 FR	11 29 tr	12 29 TH	1 28 tf
10	9 RR	3 11 mf	4 12 mr	5 8 mr	6 7 mr	7 6 em	10	8 5 em	9 3 EM	9 3 EM	11 1 fg	11 30 FR	12 30 tr	1 29 FF
11	10 rg	3 12 RF	4 13 RR	5 9 RR	6 7 RR	7 7 MH	11	8 6 MH	9 4 em	9 4 em	11 2 ET	12 1 fg	12 31 FR	1 30 fd
12	11 TT	3 13 rd	4 14 rg	5 10 rg	6 7 rg	7 8 mf	12	8 7 mr	9 5 MH	9 5 MW	11 3 et	12 2 ET	1 1 fg	2 1 EM
13	12 tt	3 14 TM	4 15 TT	5 11 TT	6 7 TT	7 9 RF	13	8 8 RR	9 6 mr	9 6 mf	11 4 MW	12 3 et	1 2 ET	2 2 em
14	13 FW	3 15 tm	4 16 tm	5 12 tm	6 7 tt	7 10 rd	14	8 9 rg	9 7 RR	9 7 RR	11 5 mf	12 4 MW	1 3 et	2 3 mr
15	14 ff	3 16 FH	4 17 FW	5 13 FW	6 7 FW	7 11 TM	15	8 10 TT	9 8 rg	9 8 rg	11 6 RF	12 5 mf	1 4 MW	2 4 RR
16	15 EF	3 17 fr	4 18 fr	5 14 fr	6 7 ff	7 12 tm	16	8 11 tt	9 9 TT	9 9 TM	11 7 rd	12 6 RF	1 5 mf	2 5 rg
17	16 ed	3 18 ER	4 19 ER	5 15 EF	6 7 EF	7 13 FH	17	8 12 FW	9 10 tt	9 10 tm	11 8 TM	12 7 rd	1 6 RF	2 6 TT
18	17 MM	3 19 eg	4 20 eg	5 16 ed	6 7 ed	7 14 fr	18	8 13 ff	9 11 FW	9 11 FH	11 9 tm	12 8 TM	1 7 rd	2 7 tt
19	18 mm	3 20 MT	4 21 MT	5 17 MM	6 7 MM	7 15 ER	19	8 14 EF	9 12 ff	9 12 fr	11 10 FH	12 9 tm	1 8 TM	2 8 FW
20	19 RH	3 21 mt	4 22 mm	5 18 mt	6 7 mm	7 16 eg	20	8 15 ed	9 13 EF	9 13 ER	11 11 fr	12 10 FH	1 9 tm	2 9 ff
21	20 rr	3 22 RW	4 23 RW	5 19 RW	6 7 RH	7 17 MM	21	8 16 MM	9 14 eg	9 14 eg	11 12 ER	12 11 fr	1 10 FH	2 10 EF
22	21 TR	3 23 rf	4 24 rf	5 20 rf	6 7 rf	7 18 mm	22	8 17 mm	9 15 MT	9 15 MT	11 13 eg	12 12 ER	1 11 fr	2 11 ed
23	22 tg	3 24 TF	4 25 TR	5 21 TF	6 7 TF	7 19 RH	23	8 18 RH	9 16 mt	9 16 mt	11 14 MT	12 13 eg	1 12 ER	2 12 MM
24	23 FT	3 25 td	4 26 td	5 22 TF	6 7 td	7 20 rf	24	8 19 rr	9 17 RW	9 17 RW	11 15 mt	12 14 MT	1 13 eg	2 13 mm
25	24 ft	3 26 FM	4 27 FM	5 23 td	6 7 tg	7 21 TR	25	8 20 TR	9 18 rf	9 18 rr	11 16 RW	12 15 mt	1 14 MT	2 14 RH
26	25 EW	3 27 fm	4 28 fm	5 24 FM	6 7 FT	7 22 tg	26	8 21 tg	9 19 TF	9 19 TR	11 17 rf	12 16 RW	1 15 mt	2 15 rr
27	26 ef	3 28 EH	4 29 EH	5 25 EW	6 7 ft		27	8 22 FT	9 20 td	9 20 tg	11 18 TF	12 17 rf	1 16 RW	2 16 TR
28	27 MF	3 29 er	4 30 er	5 26 ef			28	8 23 ft	9 21 FM	9 21 FT	11 19 td	12 18 TF	1 17 rf	2 17 TF
29	28 md	3 30 mg	4 31 MF	5 27 MF			29	8 24 EW	9 22 EH	9 22 ft	11 20 FM	12 19 td	1 18 TF	2 18 td
30			4 29 md				30		9 23 EH	9 23 EH	11 21 fm	12 20 FM	1 19 FM	
31	3 1 RM													

1958 EH DOG

JAN TT	FEB tt	MAR FW	APR ff	MAY EF	JUN ed	DAY OF MON	JUL MM	AUG mm	SEP RH	OCT rr	NOV TR	DEC tg
17 WARM	17 CLEAR	18 SUMMER	19 GRAIN	22 HEAT	23 FALL		25 DEW	27 C DEW	27 WINTER	27 SNOW	27 CHILL	27 SPRING
10:06	15:13	9:01	13:13	0:03	9:18		13:01	3:20	7:26	23:47	9:59	21:43
2 18 FT	3 20 FM	4 19 FT	5 19 FM	6 17 tg	7 17 td	1	8 15 TR	9 13 rf	10 13 rr	11 11 RW	12 11 RH	1 9 mt
2 19 ft	3 21 fm	4 20 ft	5 20 fm	6 18 FT	7 18 FM	2	8 16 tg	9 14 TF	10 14 TR	11 12 rf	12 12 rr	1 10 RW
2 20 EW	3 22 EH	4 21 EW	5 21 EH	6 19 ft	7 19 fm	3	8 17 FT	9 15 td	10 15 tg	11 13 TF	12 13 TR	1 11 rf
2 21 ef	3 23 er	4 22 ef	5 22 er	6 20 EW	7 20 EH	4	8 18 ft	9 16 FM	10 16 FT	11 14 td	12 14 tg	1 12 TF
2 22 MF	3 24 MR	4 23 MF	5 23 MR	6 21 ef	7 21 er	5	8 19 EW	9 17 fm	10 17 ft	11 15 FM	12 15 FT	1 13 td
2 23 md	3 25 mg	4 24 md	5 24 mg	6 22 MF	7 22 MR	6	8 20 ef	9 18 EH	10 18 EW	11 16 fm	12 16 ft	1 14 FM
2 24 RM	3 26 RT	4 25 RM	5 25 RT	6 23 md	7 23 mg	7	8 21 MF	9 19 er	10 19 ef	11 17 EH	12 17 EW	1 15 fm
2 25 rm	3 27 rt	4 26 rm	5 26 rt	6 24 RM	7 24 RT	8	8 22 md	9 20 MR	10 20 MF	11 18 er	12 18 ef	1 16 EH
2 26 TH	3 28 TW	4 27 TH	5 27 TW	6 25 rm	7 25 rt	9	8 23 RM	9 21 mg	10 21 md	11 19 MR	12 19 MF	1 17 er
2 27 tr	3 29 tf	4 28 tr	5 28 tf	6 26 TH	7 26 TW	10	8 24 rm	9 22 RT	10 22 RM	11 20 mg	12 20 md	1 18 MR
2 28 FR	3 30 FF	4 29 FR	5 29 FF	6 27 tr	7 27 tf	11	8 25 TH	9 23 rt	10 23 rm	11 21 RT	12 21 RM	1 19 mg
3 1 fg	3 31 fd	4 30 fg	5 30 fd	6 28 FR	7 28 FF	12	8 26 tr	9 24 TW	10 24 TH	11 22 rt	12 22 rm	1 20 RT
3 2 ET	4 1 EM	5 1 ET	5 31 EM	6 29 fg	7 29 fd	13	8 27 FR	9 25 tf	10 25 tr	11 23 TW	12 23 TH	1 21 rt
3 3 et	4 2 em	5 2 et	6 1 em	6 30 ET	7 30 EM	14	8 28 fg	9 26 FF	10 26 FR	11 24 tf	12 24 tr	1 22 TW
3 4 MW	4 3 MH	5 3 MW	6 2 MH	7 1 et	7 31 em	15	8 29 ET	9 27 fd	10 27 fg	11 25 FF	12 25 FR	1 23 tf
3 5 mf	4 4 mr	5 4 mf	6 3 mr	7 2 MW	8 1 MH	16	8 30 et	9 28 EM	10 28 ET	11 26 fd	12 26 fg	1 24 FF
3 6 RF	4 5 RR	5 5 RF	6 4 RR	7 3 mf	8 2 mr	17	8 31 MW	9 29 em	10 29 et	11 27 EM	12 27 ET	1 25 fd
3 7 rd	4 6 rg	5 6 rd	6 5 rg	7 4 RF	8 3 RR	18	9 1 mf	9 30 MH	10 30 MW	11 28 em	12 28 et	1 26 EM
3 8 TM	4 7 TT	5 7 TM	6 6 TT	7 5 rd	8 4 rg	19	9 2 RF	10 1 mr	10 31 mf	11 29 MH	12 29 MW	1 27 em
3 9 tm	4 8 tt	5 8 tm	6 7 tt	7 6 TM	8 5 TT	20	9 3 rd	10 2 RR	11 1 RF	11 30 mr	12 30 mf	1 28 MH
3 10 FH	4 9 FW	5 9 FH	6 8 FW	7 7 tm	8 6 tt	21	9 4 TM	10 3 rg	11 2 rd	12 1 RR	12 31 mr	1 29 mr
3 11 fr	4 10 ff	5 10 fr	6 9 ff	7 8 FH	8 7 FW	22	9 5 tm	10 4 TT	11 3 TM	12 2 rg	1 1 RF	1 30 RR
3 12 ER	4 11 EF	5 11 ER	6 10 EF	7 9 fr	8 8 ff	'23	9 6 FH	10 5 tt	11 4 tm	12 3 TT	1 2 rd	1 31 rg
3 13 eg	4 12 ed	5 12 eg	6 11 ed	7 10 ER	8 9 EF	24	9 7 fr	10 6 FW	11 5 FH	12 4 tt	1 3 TM	2 1 TT
3 14 MT	4 13 MM	5 13 MT	6 12 MM	7 11 eg	8 10 ed	25	9 8 ER	10 7 ff	11 6 fr	12 5 FW	1 4 tm	2 2 tt
3 15 mt	4 14 mm	5 14 mt	6 13 mm	7 12 MT	8 11 MM	26	9 9 eg	10 8 EF	11 7 ER	12 6 ff	1 5 FH	2 3 FW
3 16 RW	4 15 RH	5 15 RW	6 14 RH	7 13 mt	8 12 mm	27	9 10 MT	10 9 ed	11 8 eg	12 7 EF	1 6 fr	2 4 ff
3 17 rf	4 16 rr	5 16 rf	6 15 rr	7 14 RW	8 13 RH	28	9 11 mt	10 10 MM	11 9 MT	12 8 ed	1 7 ER	2 5 EF
3 18 TF	4 17 TR	5 17 TF	6 16 TR	7 15 rf	8 14 rr	29	9 12 RW	10 11 mm	11 10 mt	12 9 MM	1 8 MT	2 6 ed
3 19 td	4 18 tg	5 18 td		7 16 TF		30		10 12 RH		12 10 mm		2 7 MM

1959 er BOAR

	JAN	FEB	MAR	APR	MAY	JUN	DAY	JUL	AUG	SEP	OCT	NOV	DEC
pillar	FT	ft	EW	ef	MF	md	OF	RM	rm	TH	tr	FR	fg
term	27 WARM	28 CLEAR	29 SUMMER		1 GRAIN	3 HEAT	MON	5 FALL	6 DEW	8 C DEW	8 WINTER	9 SNOW	8 CHILL
time	15:57	21:04	14:39		19:01	5:21		15:05	17:49	9:11	13:16	5:37	15:43
1	2/8 mm	3/9 MT	4/8 MM	5/8 MT	6/6 ed	7/6 eg	1	8/4 EF	9/3 ER	10/2 ff	11/1 fr	11/30 FW	12/30 FH
2	2/9 RH	3/10 mt	4/9 mm	5/9 mt	6/7 MM	7/7 MT	2	8/5 ed	9/4 eg	10/3 EF	11/2 ER	12/1 ff	12/31 fr
3	2/10 rr	3/11 RW	4/10 RH	5/10 RW	6/8 mm	7/8 mt	3	8/6 MM	9/5 MT	10/4 eg	11/3 ed	12/2 EF	1/1 ER
4	2/11 TR	3/12 rf	4/11 rr	5/11 rf	6/9 RH	7/9 RW	4	8/7 mm	9/6 mt	10/5 MT	11/4 MT	12/3 ed	1/2 eg
5	2/12 tg	3/13 TF	4/12 TR	5/12 TF	6/10 rr	7/10 rf	5	8/8 RH	9/7 RW	10/6 mt	11/5 mt	12/4 MM	1/3 MT
6	2/13 FT	3/14 td	4/13 tg	5/13 td	6/11 TR	7/11 TF	6	8/9 rr	9/8 rf	10/7 RW	11/6 RW	12/5 mm	1/4 mt
7	2/14 ft	3/15 FM	4/14 FT	5/14 FM	6/12 tg	7/12 td	7	8/10 TR	9/9 TF	10/8 rf	11/7 rf	12/6 RH	1/5 RW
8	2/15 EW	3/16 fm	4/15 ft	5/15 fm	6/13 FT	7/13 FM	8	8/11 tg	9/10 td	10/9 TF	11/8 TF	12/7 rr	1/6 rf
9	2/16 em	3/17 EH	4/16 EW	5/16 EH	6/14 ft	7/14 fm	9	8/12 FT	9/11 FM	10/10 td	11/9 td	12/8 TR	1/7 TF
10	2/17 MF	3/18 er	4/17 ef	5/17 er	6/15 EW	7/15 EH	10	8/13 ft	9/12 fm	10/11 FM	11/10 FM	12/9 tg	1/8 td
11	2/18 md	3/19 MR	4/18 MF	5/18 MR	6/16 ef	7/16 er	11	8/14 EW	9/13 EH	10/12 fm	11/11 fm	12/10 FT	1/9 FM
12	2/19 RM	3/20 mg	4/19 md	5/19 mg	6/17 MF	7/17 MR	12	8/15 ef	9/14 er	10/13 EH	11/12 EH	12/11 ft	1/10 fm
13	2/20 RT	3/21 RT	4/20 RM	5/20 RT	6/18 md	7/18 mg	13	8/16 MF	9/15 MR	10/14 er	11/13 er	12/12 EW	1/11 EH
14	2/21 TH	3/22 TW	4/21 rm	5/21 rt	6/19 RM	7/19 RT	14	8/17 md	9/16 mg	10/15 MR	11/14 MR	12/13 ef	1/12 er
15	2/22 tr	3/23 tf	4/22 TH	5/22 TW	6/20 rm	7/20 rt	15	8/18 RM	9/17 RT	10/16 mg	11/15 mg	12/14 MF	1/13 MR
16	2/23 FR	3/24 FF	4/23 tr	5/23 tf	6/21 TH	7/21 TW	16	8/19 rm	9/18 rt	10/17 RT	11/16 RT	12/15 md	1/14 mg
17	2/24 fg	3/25 fd	4/24 FR	5/24 FF	6/22 tr	7/22 tr	17	8/20 TH	9/19 TW	10/18 rt	11/17 rt	12/16 RM	1/15 RT
18	2/25 ET	3/26 EM	4/25 fg	5/25 fd	6/23 FR	7/23 FF	18	8/21 tr	9/20 tf	10/19 TW	11/18 TW	12/17 rm	1/16 rt
19	2/26 et	3/27 em	4/26 ET	5/26 EM	6/24 fg	7/24 fd	19	8/22 FR	9/21 FF	10/20 tf	11/19 tf	12/18 TH	1/17 TW
20	2/27 MW	3/28 MH	4/27 et	5/27 em	6/25 ET	7/25 EM	20	8/23 fg	9/22 fd	10/21 FF	11/20 FF	12/19 tr	1/18 tf
21	2/28 mf	3/29 mr	4/28 MW	5/28 MH	6/26 et	7/26 em	21	8/24 ET	9/23 EM	10/22 fd	11/21 fd	12/20 FR	1/19 FF
22	3/1 RF	3/30 RR	4/29 mf	5/29 mr	6/27 MW	7/27 MH	22	8/25 et	9/24 em	10/23 EM	11/22 EM	12/21 fg	1/20 fd
23	3/2 rd	3/31 rg	4/30 RF	5/30 RR	6/28 mf	7/28 mf	23	8/26 MH	9/25 MH	10/24 em	11/23 em	12/22 ET	1/21 EM
24	3/3 TM	4/1 TT	5/1 rd	5/31 rg	6/29 RF	7/29 RR	24	8/27 mf	9/26 mf	10/25 MW	11/24 MH	12/23 et	1/22 em
25	3/4 tm	4/2 tt	5/2 TM	6/1 TT	6/30 rd	7/30 rg	25	8/28 RR	9/27 RR	10/26 mr	11/25 mr	12/24 MW	1/23 MH
26	3/5 FH	4/3 FW	5/3 tm	6/2 tt	7/1 TM	7/31 TT	26	8/29 rd	9/28 rg	10/27 RF	11/26 RR	12/25 mf	1/24 mr
27	3/6 fr	4/4 FH	5/4 FH	6/3 FW	7/2 tm	8/1 tt	27	8/30 TM	9/29 TT	10/28 rd	11/27 rg	12/26 RF	1/25 RR
28	3/7 ER	4/5 ff	5/5 fr	6/4 ff	7/3 FW	8/2 FW	28	8/31 tm	9/30 tt	10/29 TM	11/28 TT	12/27 rd	1/26 rg
29	3/8 eg	4/6 EF	5/6 ER	6/5 EF	7/4 fr	8/3 ff	29	9/1 FH	10/1 FW	10/30 tm	11/29 tt	12/28 TM	1/27 TT
30		4/7 ed	5/7 eg		7/5 ER		30	9/2 fr		10/31 FH		12/29 tm	

204

JAN ET	FEB et	MAR MW	APR mf	MAY RF	JUN rd	JUN rd	DAY OF MON	JUL TM	AUG tm	SEP FH	OCT fr	NOV ER	DEC eg
9 SPRING	8 WARM	10 CLEAR	10 SUMMER	13 GRAIN	14 HEAT	15 FALL		18 DEW	18 C DEW	19 WINTER	19 SNOW	19 CHILL	19 SPRING
3:23	21:36	2:44	20:23	1:11	11:13	21:00		0:39	15:09	19:06	11:26	21:43	9:23
1 28 tt	2 27 tm	3 27 TT	4 26 TM	5 25 rg	6 24 rd	7 24 rg	1	8 22 RF	9 21 RR	10 20 mf	11 19 mr	12 18 MW	1 17 MH
1 29 FW	2 28 FH	3 28 tt	4 27 tm	5 26 TT	6 25 TM	7 25 TT	2	8 23 rd	9 22 rg	10 21 RF	11 20 RR	12 19 mf	1 18 mr
1 30 ff	2 29 fr	3 29 FW	4 28 FH	5 27 tt	6 26 tm	7 26 tt	3	8 24 TM	9 23 TT	10 22 rd	11 21 rg	12 20 RF	1 19 RR
1 31 EF	3 1 ER	3 30 ff	4 29 fr	5 28 FW	6 27 FH	7 27 FW	4	8 25 tm	9 24 tt	10 23 TM	11 22 TT	12 21 rd	1 20 rg
2 1 ed	3 2 eg	3 31 EF	4 30 ER	5 29 ff	6 28 fr	7 28 ff	5	8 26 FH	9 25 FW	10 24 tm	11 23 tt	12 22 TM	1 21 TT
2 2 MM	3 3 MT	4 1 ed	5 1 eg	5 30 EF	6 29 ER	7 29 EF	6	8 27 fr	9 26 ff	10 25 FH	11 24 FW	12 23 tm	1 22 tt
2 3 mm	3 4 mt	4 2 MM	5 2 MT	5 31 ed	6 30 eg	7 30 ed	7	8 28 ER	9 27 EF	10 26 fr	11 25 ff	12 24 FH	1 23 FW
2 4 RH	3 5 RW	4 3 mm	5 3 mt	6 1 MM	7 1 MT	7 31 MM	8	8 29 eg	9 28 ed	10 27 ER	11 26 EF	12 25 fr	1 24 ff
2 5 rr	3 6 rf	4 4 RH	5 4 RW	6 2 mm	7 2 mt	8 1 mm	9	8 30 MT	9 29 MM	10 28 eg	11 27 ed	12 26 ER	1 25 EF
2 6 TR	3 7 TF	4 5 rr	5 5 rf	6 3 RH	7 3 RW	8 2 RH	10	8 31 mt	9 30 mm	10 29 MT	11 28 MM	12 27 eg	1 26 ed
2 7 tg	3 8 td	4 6 TR	5 6 TF	6 4 rr	7 4 rf	8 3 rr	11	9 1 RW	10 1 RH	10 30 mt	11 29 mm	12 28 MT	1 27 MM
2 8 FT	3 9 FM	4 7 tg	5 7 td	6 5 TR	7 5 TF	8 4 TR	12	9 2 rf	10 2 rr	10 31 RW	11 30 RH	12 29 mt	1 28 mm
2 9 ft	3 10 fm	4 8 FT	5 8 FM	6 6 tg	7 6 td	8 5 tg	13	9 3 TF	10 3 TR	11 1 rf	12 1 rr	12 30 RW	1 29 RH
2 10 EW	3 11 EH	4 9 ft	5 9 fm	6 7 FT	7 7 FM	8 6 FT	14	9 4 td	10 4 tg	11 2 TF	12 2 TR	12 31 rf	1 30 rr
2 11 ef	3 12 er	4 10 EW	5 10 EH	6 8 ft	7 8 fm	8 7 ft	15	9 5 FM	10 5 FT	11 3 td	12 3 tg	1 1 TF	2 1 TR
2 12 MF	3 13 MR	4 11 ef	5 11 er	6 9 EW	7 9 EH	8 8 EW	16	9 6 fm	10 6 ft	11 4 FM	12 4 FT	1 2 td	2 2 tg
2 13 md	3 14 mg	4 12 MF	5 12 MR	6 10 ef	7 10 er	8 9 ef	17	9 7 EH	10 7 EW	11 5 fm	12 5 ft	1 3 FM	2 3 FT
2 14 RM	3 15 RT	4 13 md	5 13 mg	6 11 MF	7 11 MR	8 10 MF	18	9 8 er	10 8 ef	11 6 EH	12 6 EW	1 4 fm	2 4 ft
2 15 rm	3 16 rt	4 14 RM	5 14 RT	6 12 md	7 12 mg	8 11 md	19	9 9 MR	10 9 MF	11 7 er	12 7 ef	1 5 EH	2 5 EW
2 16 TH	3 17 TW	4 15 rm	5 15 rt	6 13 RM	7 13 RT	8 12 RM	20	9 10 mg	10 10 md	11 8 MR	12 8 MF	1 6 er	2 6 ef
2 17 tr	3 18 tf	4 16 TH	5 16 TW	6 14 rm	7 14 rt	8 13 rm	21	9 11 RT	10 11 RM	11 9 mg	12 9 md	1 7 MR	2 7 MF
2 18 FR	3 19 FF	4 17 tr	5 17 tf	6 15 TH	7 15 TW	8 14 TH	22	9 12 rt	10 12 rm	11 10 RT	12 10 RM	1 8 mg	2 8 md
2 19 fg	3 20 fd	4 18 FR	5 18 FF	6 16 tr	7 16 tf	8 15 tr	23	9 13 TW	10 13 TH	11 11 rt	12 11 rm	1 9 RT	2 9 RM
2 20 ET	3 21 EM	4 19 fg	5 19 fd	6 17 FR	7 17 FF	8 16 FR	24	9 14 tf	10 14 tr	11 12 TW	12 12 TH	1 10 rt	2 10 rm
2 21 et	3 22 em	4 20 ET	5 20 EM	6 18 fg	7 18 fd	8 17 fg	25	9 15 FF	10 15 FR	11 13 tf	12 13 tr	1 11 TW	2 11 TH
2 22 MW	3 23 MH	4 21 et	5 21 em	6 19 ET	7 19 EM	8 18 ET	26	9 16 fd	10 16 fg	11 14 FF	12 14 FR	1 12 tf	2 12 tr
2 23 mf	3 24 mr	4 22 MW	5 22 MH	6 20 et	7 20 em	8 19 et	27	9 17 EM	10 17 ET	11 15 fd	12 15 fg	1 13 FF	2 13 FR
2 24 RF	3 25 RR	4 23 mf	5 23 mr	6 21 MW	7 21 MH	8 20 MW	28	9 18 em	10 18 et	11 16 EM	12 16 ET	1 14 fd	2 14 ET
2 25 rd	3 26 rg	4 24 RF	5 24 RR	6 22 mf	7 22 mr	8 21 mf	29	9 19 MH	10 19 MW	11 17 em	12 17 et	1 15 EM	
2 26 TM		4 25 rd		6 23 RF	7 23 RR		30	9 20 mr		11 18 MH		1 16 em	

Solar-term / subheader line for each month:

Month	Term	Time	Term 2	Time 2
JAN MT	20 WARM	3:35		
FEB mt	20 CLEAR	8:42		
MAR RW	22 SUMMER	2:21		
APR rf	23 GRAIN	6:46		
MAY TF	25 HEAT	17:07		
JUN td	27 FALL	3:27		
JUL FM	29 DEW	5:29		
AUG fm	29 C DEW	22:03		
SEP EH				
OCT er	1 WINTER	0:55	30 SNOW	17:16
NOV MR				
DEC mg	1 CHILL	3:35	30 SPRING	15:18

DAY OF MON column value/code: MON 5:29

DAY OF MON	JAN MT	FEB mt	MAR RW	APR rf	MAY TF	JUN td	JUL FM	AUG fm	SEP EH	OCT er	NOV MR	DEC mg
1	2 15 et	3 17 em	4 15 ET	5 15 EM	6 13 fg	7 13 fd	8 11 FR	9 10 FF	10 10 FR	11 8 tf	12 8 tf	1 6 TW
2	2 16 MW	3 18 MH	4 16 et	5 16 em	6 14 ET	7 14 EM	8 12 fg	9 11 fd	10 11 fg	11 9 FF	12 9 FR	1 7 tf
3	2 17 mf	3 19 mr	4 17 MW	5 17 MH	6 15 em	7 15 em	8 13 ET	9 12 EM	10 12 ET	11 10 fd	12 10 fd	1 8 FF
4	2 18 RF	3 20 RR	4 18 mf	5 18 mr	6 16 MW	7 16 MH	8 14 et	9 13 em	10 13 et	11 11 EM	12 11 EM	1 9 fd
5	2 19 rd	3 21 rg	4 19 RF	5 19 RR	6 17 mf	7 17 mr	8 15 MW	9 14 MH	10 14 MW	11 12 em	12 12 em	1 10 EM
6	2 20 TM	3 22 TT	4 20 rd	5 20 rg	6 18 RF	7 18 RR	8 16 mf	9 15 mr	10 15 mf	11 13 MH	12 13 MW	1 11 em
7	2 21 tm	3 23 tt	4 21 TM	5 21 TT	6 19 rd	7 19 rg	8 17 RF	9 16 RR	10 16 RF	11 14 mr	12 14 mf	1 12 MH
8	2 22 FH	3 24 FW	4 22 tm	5 22 tt	6 20 TM	7 20 TT	8 18 rd	9 17 rg	10 17 rd	11 15 RM	12 15 RF	1 13 mr
9	2 23 fr	3 25 ff	4 23 FH	5 23 FW	6 21 tm	7 21 tt	8 19 TM	9 18 TT	10 18 TM	11 16 rg	12 16 rd	1 14 RF
10	2 24 ER	3 26 EF	4 24 fr	5 24 ff	6 22 FH	7 22 FW	8 20 tm	9 19 tt	10 19 tm	11 17 TT	12 17 TM	1 15 rd
11	2 25 eg	3 27 ed	4 25 ER	5 25 EF	6 23 fr	7 23 ff	8 21 FH	9 20 FW	10 20 FH	11 18 tt	12 18 tm	1 16 RR
12	2 26 MT	3 28 MM	4 26 eg	5 26 ed	6 24 ER	7 24 EF	8 22 fr	9 21 ff	10 21 fr	11 19 FW	12 19 FH	1 17 rg
13	2 27 mt	3 29 mm	4 27 MT	5 27 MM	6 25 eg	7 25 ed	8 23 ER	9 22 EF	10 22 ER	11 20 ff	12 20 fr	1 18 TT
14	2 28 RW	3 30 RH	4 28 mt	5 28 mm	6 26 MT	7 26 MM	8 24 eg	9 23 ed	10 23 eg	11 21 EF	12 21 ER	1 19 tt
15	3 1 rf	3 31 rr	4 29 RW	5 29 RH	6 27 mt	7 27 mm	8 25 MT	9 24 MM	10 24 MT	11 22 ed	12 22 eg	1 20 FW
16	3 2 TF	4 1 TR	4 30 rf	5 30 rr	6 28 RW	7 28 RH	8 26 mt	9 25 mm	10 25 mt	11 23 MM	12 23 MT	1 21 ff
17	3 3 td	4 2 tg	5 1 TF	5 31 TR	6 29 rf	7 29 rr	8 27 RW	9 26 RH	10 26 RW	11 24 mm	12 24 mt	1 22 EF
18	3 4 FM	4 3 FT	5 2 td	6 1 tg	6 30 TR	7 30 TR	8 28 rf	9 27 rf	10 27 rf	11 25 RH	12 25 RW	1 23 ed
19	3 5 fm	4 4 ft	5 3 FM	6 2 FT	7 1 td	7 31 tg	8 29 TF	9 28 TR	10 28 TF	11 26 rr	12 26 rf	1 24 MM
20	3 6 EH	4 5 EW	5 4 fm	6 3 ft	7 2 FM	8 1 FT	8 30 td	9 29 tg	10 29 td	11 27 TR	12 27 TF	1 25 mm
21	3 7 er	4 6 ef	5 5 EH	6 4 EW	7 3 fm	8 2 ft	8 31 FM	9 30 FT	10 30 FM	11 28 tg	12 28 td	1 26 RH
22	3 8 MR	4 7 MF	5 6 er	6 5 ef	7 4 EH	8 3 EW	9 1 fm	10 1 ft	10 31 fm	11 29 FT	12 29 FM	1 27 rr
23	3 9 mg	4 8 md	5 7 MR	6 6 MF	7 5 er	8 4 ef	9 2 EH	10 2 EW	11 1 EH	11 30 ft	12 30 fm	1 28 TR
24	3 10 RT	4 9 RM	5 8 mg	6 7 md	7 6 MR	8 5 MR	9 3 er	10 3 ef	11 2 er	12 1 EW	12 31 EH	1 29 tg
25	3 11 rt	4 10 rm	5 9 RT	6 8 RM	7 7 mg	8 6 mg	9 4 MR	10 4 MF	11 3 MR	12 2 ef	1 1 er	1 30 FT
26	3 12 TW	4 11 TH	5 10 rt	6 9 rm	7 8 RT	8 7 RT	9 5 mg	10 5 md	11 4 mg	12 3 MF	1 2 MR	1 31 ft
27	3 13 tf	4 12 tr	5 11 TW	6 10 TH	7 9 rt	8 8 rt	9 6 RT	10 6 RM	11 5 RT	12 4 md	1 3 mg	2 1 EW
28	3 14 FF	4 13 tf	5 12 tf	6 11 tf	7 10 TW	8 9 TH	9 7 rt	10 7 rt	11 6 rt	12 5 RM	1 4 RT	2 2 ef
29	3 15 fd	4 14 fg	5 13 FF	6 12 FR	7 11 tf	8 10 tr	9 8 TW	10 8 TH	11 7 TW	12 6 rm	1 5 rt	2 3 MF
30	3 16 EM		5 14 fd		7 12 FF		9 9 tf	10 9 tr		12 7 TH		2 4 rm

1962 RT TIGER

JAN RT	FEB rt	MAR TW	APR tf	MAY FF	JUN fd	DAY OF MON	JUL EM	AUG em	SEP MH	OCT mr	NOV RR	DEC rg
	1 WARM	1 CLEAR	3 SUMMER	5 GRAIN	6 HEAT		9 FALL	10 DEW	11 C DEW	12 WINTER	11 SNOW	11 CHILL
	9:30	14:34	8:10	12:31	23:16		9:34	11:16	3:57	5:35	23:06	9:27
2 5 TH	3 6 rt	4 5 rm	5 4 RT	6 2 md	7 2 mg	1	7 31 MF	8 30 MR	9 29 MF	10 28 er	11 27 ef	12 27 er
2 6 tr	3 7 TW	4 6 TH	5 5 rt	6 3 RM	7 3 RT	2	8 1 md	8 31 mg	9 30 md	10 29 MR	11 28 MF	12 28 MR
2 7 FR	3 8 tf	4 7 tr	5 6 TW	6 4 rm	7 4 rt	3	8 2 RM	9 1 RT	10 1 RM	10 30 mg	11 29 md	12 29 mg
2 8 fg	3 9 FF	4 8 FR	5 7 tf	6 5 TH	7 5 TW	4	8 3 rm	9 2 rt	10 2 rm	10 31 RT	11 30 RM	12 30 RT
2 9 ET	3 10 fd	4 9 fg	5 8 FF	6 6 tr	7 6 tf	5	8 4 TH	9 3 TW	10 3 TH	11 1 rt	12 1 rm	12 31 rt
2 10 et	3 11 EM	4 10 ET	5 9 fd	6 7 FR	7 7 FF	6	8 5 tr	9 4 tf	10 4 tr	11 2 TW	12 2 TH	1 1 TW
2 11 MW	3 12 em	4 11 et	5 10 EM	6 8 fg	7 8 fd	7	8 6 FR	9 5 FF	10 5 FR	11 3 tf	12 3 tr	1 2 tf
2 12 mf	3 13 MH	4 12 MW	5 11 em	6 9 ET	7 9 EM	8	8 7 fg	9 6 fd	10 6 fg	11 4 FF	12 4 FR	1 3 FF
2 13 RF	3 14 mr	4 13 mf	5 12 MH	6 10 et	7 10 em	9	8 8 ET	9 7 EM	10 7 ET	11 5 fd	12 5 fg	1 4 fd
2 14 rd	3 15 RR	4 14 RF	5 13 mr	6 11 MW	7 11 MH	10	8 9 et	9 8 em	10 8 et	11 6 EM	12 6 ET	1 5 EM
2 15 TM	3 16 rg	4 15 rd	5 14 RR	6 12 mf	7 12 mr	11	8 10 MW	9 9 MH	10 9 MW	11 7 em	12 7 et	1 6 em
2 16 tm	3 17 TT	4 16 TM	5 15 rg	6 13 RF	7 13 RR	12	8 11 mf	9 10 mr	10 10 mf	11 8 MH	12 8 MW	1 7 MH
2 17 FH	3 18 tt	4 17 tm	5 16 TT	6 14 rd	7 14 rg	13	8 12 RF	9 11 RR	10 11 RF	11 9 mr	12 9 mf	1 8 mr
2 18 fr	3 19 FW	4 18 FH	5 17 tt	6 15 TM	7 15 TT	14	8 13 rd	9 12 rg	10 12 rd	11 10 RR	12 10 RF	1 9 RR
2 19 ER	3 20 ff	4 19 fr	5 18 FW	6 16 tm	7 16 tt	15	8 14 TM	9 13 TT	10 13 TM	11 11 rg	12 11 rd	1 10 rg
2 20 eg	3 21 EF	4 20 ER	5 19 ff	6 17 FH	7 17 FW	16	8 15 tm	9 14 tt	10 14 tm	11 12 TT	12 12 TM	1 11 TT
2 21 MT	3 22 ed	4 21 eg	5 20 EF	6 18 fr	7 18 ff	17	8 16 FH	9 15 FW	10 15 FH	11 13 tt	12 13 tm	1 12 tt
2 22 mt	3 23 MM	4 22 MT	5 21 ed	6 19 ER	7 19 EF	18	8 17 fr	9 16 ff	10 16 fr	11 14 FW	12 14 FH	1 13 FW
2 23 RW	3 24 mm	4 23 mt	5 22 MM	6 20 eg	7 20 ed	19	8 18 ER	9 17 EF	10 17 ER	11 15 ff	12 15 fr	1 14 ff
2 24 rf	3 25 RH	4 24 RW	5 23 mm	6 21 MT	7 21 MM	20	8 19 eg	9 18 ed	10 18 eg	11 16 EF	12 16 ER	1 15 EF
2 25 TF	3 26 rr	4 25 rf	5 24 RH	6 22 mt	7 22 mm	21	8 20 MT	9 19 MM	10 19 MT	11 17 ed	12 17 eg	1 16 ed
2 26 td	3 27 TR	4 26 TF	5 25 rr	6 23 RW	7 23 RH	22	8 21 mt	9 20 mm	10 20 mt	11 18 MM	12 18 MT	1 17 MM
2 27 FM	3 28 tg	4 27 td	5 26 TR	6 24 rf	7 24 rr	23	8 22 RW	9 21 RH	10 21 RW	11 19 mm	12 19 mt	1 18 mm
2 28 fm	3 29 FT	4 28 FM	5 27 tg	6 25 TF	7 25 TR	24	8 23 rf	9 22 rr	10 22 rf	11 20 RH	12 20 RW	1 19 RH
3 1 EH	3 30 ft	4 29 fm	5 28 FT	6 26 td	7 26 tg	25	8 24 TF	9 23 TR	10 23 TF	11 21 rr	12 21 rf	1 20 rr
3 2 er	3 31 EW	4 30 EH	5 29 ft	6 27 FM	7 27 FT	26	8 25 td	9 24 tg	10 24 td	11 22 TR	12 22 TF	1 21 TR
3 3 MR	4 1 ef	5 1 er	5 30 EW	6 28 fm	7 28 ft	27	8 26 FM	9 25 FT	10 25 FM	11 23 tg	12 23 td	1 22 tg
3 4 mg	4 2 MF	5 2 MR	5 31 ef	6 29 EH	7 29 EW	28	8 27 fm	9 26 ft	10 26 fm	11 24 FT	12 24 FM	1 23 FT
3 5 RT	4 3 md	5 3 mg	6 1 MF	6 30 er	7 30 ef	29	8 28 EH	9 27 EW	10 27 EH	11 25 ft	12 25 fm	1 24 ft
	4 4 RM			7 1 MR		30	8 29 er	9 28 ef		11 26 EW	12 26 EH	

1963 rt RABBIT

	JAN TT	FEB tt	MAR FW	APR ff	APR ff	MAY EF	JUN ed	DAY OF MON	JUL MM	AUG mm	SEP RH	OCT rr	NOV TR	DEC tg
	11 SPRING	11 WARM	12 CLEAR	13 SUMMER	15 GRAIN	18 HEAT	19 FALL		21 DEW	22 C DEW	23 WINTER	23 SNOW	22 CHILL	22 SPRING
	21:08	15:17	20:19	13:52	18:15	5:05	15:18		17:12	9:41	11:32	4:13	15:22	2:56
1	1 25 EW	2 24 EH	3 25 ft	4 24 fm	5 23 FT	6 21 td	7 21 tg	1	8 19 TF	9 18 TR	10 17 rf	11 16 rr	12 16 rf	1 15 rr
2	2 26 ef	2 25 er	3 26 EW	4 25 EH	5 24 ft	6 22 FM	7 22 FT	2	8 20 td	9 19 tg	10 18 TF	11 17 TR	12 17 TF	1 16 TR
3	2 27 MF	2 26 MR	3 27 ef	4 26 er	5 25 EW	6 23 fm	7 23 ft	3	8 21 FM	9 20 FT	10 19 td	11 18 tg	12 18 td	1 17 tg
4	2 28 md	2 27 mg	3 28 MF	4 27 MR	5 26 ef	6 24 EH	7 24 EW	4	8 22 fm	9 21 ft	10 20 FM	11 19 FT	12 19 FM	1 18 FT
5	2 29 RM	2 28 RT	3 29 md	4 28 mg	5 27 MF	6 25 er	7 25 ef	5	8 23 EH	9 22 EW	10 21 fm	11 20 ft	12 20 fm	1 19 ft
6	3 30 rm	3 1 rt	4 30 RM	4 29 RT	5 28 md	6 26 MR	7 26 MF	6	8 24 er	9 23 ef	10 22 EH	11 21 EW	12 21 EH	1 20 EW
7	3 31 TH	3 2 TW	4 31 rm	4 30 rt	5 29 RM	6 27 mg	7 27 md	7	8 25 MR	9 24 MF	10 23 er	11 22 ef	12 22 er	1 21 ef
8	3 1 TW	3 3 tf	4 1 TH	5 1 TW	5 30 rm	6 28 RT	7 28 RM	8	8 26 mg	9 25 md	10 24 MR	11 23 MF	12 23 MR	1 22 MF
9	3 2 tf	3 4 FF	4 2 tr	5 2 tf	5 31 TH	6 29 rt	7 29 rm	9	8 27 RT	9 26 RM	10 25 mg	11 24 md	12 24 mg	1 23 md
10	4 3 FF	3 5 fd	4 3 FR	5 3 FF	6 1 tr	6 30 TW	7 30 TH	10	8 28 rt	9 27 rm	10 26 RT	11 25 RM	12 25 RT	1 24 RM
11	4 4 fd	3 6 EM	4 4 fg	5 4 fd	6 2 FR	7 1 tf	7 31 tr	11	8 29 TW	9 28 TH	10 27 rt	11 26 rm	12 26 rt	1 25 rm
12	4 5 EM	3 7 em	4 5 ET	5 5 EM	6 3 fg	7 2 FF	8 1 FR	12	8 30 tf	9 29 tr	10 28 TW	11 27 TH	12 27 TW	1 26 TH
13	4 6 em	3 8 MH	4 6 et	5 6 em	6 4 ET	7 3 fd	8 2 fg	13	8 31 FF	9 30 FR	10 29 tf	11 28 tr	12 28 tf	1 27 tr
14	4 7 MH	3 9 mr	4 7 MW	5 7 MH	6 5 et	7 4 EM	8 3 ET	14	9 1 fd	10 1 fg	10 30 FF	11 29 FR	12 29 FF	1 28 FR
15	4 8 mr	3 10 RR	4 8 mf	5 8 mr	6 6 MW	7 5 em	8 4 et	15	9 2 EM	10 2 ET	10 31 fd	11 30 fg	12 30 fd	1 29 fg
16	4 9 RR	3 11 rg	4 9 RF	5 9 RR	6 7 mf	7 6 MH	8 5 MW	16	9 3 em	10 3 et	11 1 EM	12 1 ET	12 31 EM	1 30 ET
17	4 10 rg	3 12 TT	4 10 rd	5 10 rg	6 8 RF	7 7 mr	8 6 mf	17	9 4 MH	10 4 MW	11 2 em	12 2 et	1 1 em	1 31 et
18	4 11 TT	3 13 tt	4 11 TT	5 11 TT	6 9 rd	7 8 RR	8 7 RF	18	9 5 mr	10 5 mf	11 3 MH	12 3 MW	1 2 MH	2 1 MW
19	4 12 tt	3 14 FW	4 12 tm	5 12 tt	6 10 TM	7 9 rg	8 8 rd	19	9 6 RR	10 6 RF	11 4 mr	12 4 mf	1 3 mr	2 2 mf
20	4 13 FW	3 15 ff	4 13 FH	5 13 FW	6 11 tm	7 10 TT	8 9 TM	20	9 7 rg	10 7 rd	11 5 RR	12 5 RF	1 4 RR	2 3 RF
21	4 14 ff	3 16 EF	4 14 fr	5 14 ff	6 12 FH	7 11 tt	8 10 tm	21	9 8 TT	10 8 TM	11 6 rg	12 6 rd	1 5 rg	2 4 rd
22	4 15 EF	3 17 ed	4 15 ER	5 15 EF	6 13 fr	7 12 FW	8 11 FH	22	9 9 tt	10 9 tm	11 7 TT	12 7 TM	1 6 TT	2 5 TM
23	4 16 eg	3 18 MM	4 16 eg	5 16 ed	6 14 ER	7 13 ff	8 12 fr	23	9 10 FW	10 10 FH	11 8 tt	12 8 tm	1 7 tt	2 6 tm
24	4 17 MT	3 19 mm	4 17 MT	5 17 MM	6 15 eg	7 14 EF	8 13 ER	24	9 11 ff	10 11 fr	11 9 FW	12 9 FH	1 8 FW	2 7 FH
25	4 18 RW	3 20 RH	4 18 mt	5 18 mm	6 16 MT	7 15 ed	8 14 eg	25	9 12 EF	10 12 ER	11 10 ff	12 10 fr	1 9 ff	2 8 fr
26	4 19 rf	3 21 rr	4 19 RW	5 19 RH	6 17 mt	7 16 MM	8 15 MT	26	9 13 ed	10 13 eg	11 11 EF	12 11 ER	1 10 EF	2 9 ER
27	4 20 TF	3 22 TR	4 20 rr	5 20 rr	6 18 RW	7 17 mm	8 16 mt	27	9 14 MM	10 14 MT	11 12 eg	12 12 eg	1 11 eg	2 10 eg
28	4 21 td	3 23 td	4 21 TF	5 21 TF	6 19 rf	7 18 RW	8 17 RW	28	9 15 mt	10 15 mt	11 13 MT	12 13 MT	1 12 MT	2 11 MT
29	4 22 FM	3 24 FT	4 22 td	5 22 tg	6 20 TF	7 19 rr	8 18 rr	29	9 16 RH	10 16 RH	11 14 mm	12 14 mt	1 13 mm	2 12 mt
30	4 23 fm		4 23 FM			7 20 TR	8 19 TR	30	9 17 rr	10 17 rr	11 15 RH	12 15 RW	1 14 RH	

JAN FT	FEB ft	MAR EW	APR ef	MAY MF	JUN md	DAY OF MON	JUL RM	AUG rm	SEP TH	OCT tr	NOV FR	DEC fg
22 WARM	23 CLEAR	24 SUMMER	26 GRAIN	28 HEAT	30 FALL			2 DEW	3 C DEW	4 WINTER	4 SNOW	3 CHILL
20:58	2:18	19:51	0:12	10:32	20:16			p	15:30	17:15	9:53	21:02
2 13 RW	3 14 RH	4 12 mt	5 12 mm	6 10 MT	7 9 ed	1	8 8 eg	9 6 EF	10 6 ER	11 4 ff	12 4 fr	1 3 ff
2 14 rf	3 15 rr	4 13 RW	5 13 RH	6 11 mt	7 10 MM	2	8 9 MT	9 7 eg	10 7 eg	11 5 EF	12 5 ER	1 4 EF
2 15 TF	3 16 TR	4 14 rf	5 14 rr	6 12 RW	7 11 mm	3	8 10 mt	9 8 MM	10 8 MT	11 6 ed	12 6 eg	1 5 ed
2 16 td	3 17 tg	4 15 TF	5 15 TR	6 13 rf	7 12 RH	4	8 11 RW	9 9 mm	10 9 mt	11 7 MM	12 7 MT	1 6 MM
2 17 FM	3 18 FT	4 16 td	5 16 tg	6 14 TF	7 13 rr	5	8 12 rf	9 10 RH	10 10 RW	11 8 mm	12 8 mt	1 7 mm
2 18 fm	3 19 ft	4 17 FM	5 17 FT	6 15 td	7 14 TR	6	8 13 TF	9 11 rf	10 11 rf	11 9 RH	12 9 RW	1 8 RH
2 19 EH	3 20 EW	4 18 fm	5 18 ft	6 16 FM	7 15 td	7	8 14 td	9 12 TF	10 12 TR	11 10 rf	12 10 rf	1 9 rr
2 20 er	3 21 ef	4 19 EH	5 19 EW	6 17 fm	7 16 TF	8	8 15 FM	9 13 td	10 13 td	11 11 TR	12 11 TF	1 10 TR
2 21 MR	3 22 MF	4 20 er	5 20 ef	6 18 EH	7 17 FM	9	8 16 fm	9 14 FM	10 14 FM	11 12 tg	12 12 td	1 11 tg
2 22 mg	3 23 md	4 21 MR	5 21 MF	6 19 er	7 18 fm	10	8 17 EH	9 15 fm	10 15 ft	11 13 FT	12 13 FM	1 12 FT
2 23 RT	3 24 RM	4 22 mg	5 22 md	6 20 MR	7 19 EH	11	8 18 er	9 16 EH	10 16 EW	11 14 ft	12 14 fm	1 13 ft
2 24 rm	3 25 rm	4 23 RT	5 23 RM	6 21 mg	7 20 er	12	8 19 MR	9 17 er	10 17 ef	11 15 EW	12 15 EH	1 14 EW
2 25 TW	3 26 TH	4 24 rt	5 24 rm	6 22 RT	7 21 MR	13	8 20 mg	9 18 MF	10 18 MF	11 16 ef	12 16 er	1 15 ef
2 26 tf	3 27 tr	4 25 TW	5 25 TH	6 23 rt	7 22 mg	14	8 21 RT	9 19 md	10 19 md	11 17 MF	12 17 MR	1 16 MF
2 27 FF	3 28 FR	4 26 tf	5 26 tr	6 24 TW	7 23 RT	15	8 22 rt	9 20 RM	10 20 RT	11 18 md	12 18 mg	1 17 md
2 28 fd	3 29 fg	4 27 FF	5 27 FR	6 25 tf	7 24 rt	16	8 23 TW	9 21 rt	10 21 rt	11 19 RM	12 19 RT	1 18 RM
2 29 EM	3 30 ET	4 28 fd	5 28 fg	6 26 FF	7 25 TW	17	8 24 tf	9 22 TH	10 22 TW	11 20 rm	12 20 rt	1 19 rm
3 1 em	3 31 et	4 29 EM	5 29 ET	6 27 fd	7 26 tf	18	8 25 FF	9 23 tr	10 23 tf	11 21 TH	12 21 TW	1 20 TH
3 2 MH	4 1 MW	4 30 em	5 30 et	6 28 EM	7 27 FR	19	8 26 fd	9 24 FR	10 24 FR	11 22 tr	12 22 tf	1 21 tr
3 3 mr	4 2 mf	5 1 MH	5 31 MW	6 29 em	7 28 fd	20	8 27 EM	9 25 fg	10 25 fd	11 23 FR	12 23 FF	1 22 FR
3 4 RR	4 3 RF	5 2 mr	6 1 mf	6 30 MH	7 29 EM	21	8 28 em	9 26 EM	10 26 EM	11 24 fd	12 24 fd	1 23 fg
3 5 rg	4 4 rd	5 3 RF	6 2 RF	7 1 mr	7 30 em	22	8 29 MH	9 27 em	10 27 em	11 25 EM	12 25 EM	1 24 ET
3 6 TT	4 5 TM	5 4 rg	6 3 rd	7 2 RR	8 1 MH	23	8 30 mr	9 28 MH	10 28 MH	11 26 em	12 26 em	1 25 et
3 7 tt	4 6 tm	5 5 TT	6 4 TM	7 3 rg	8 2 mf	24	9 1 RR	9 29 mr	10 29 mr	11 27 MW	12 27 MH	1 26 MW
3 8 FW	4 7 FH	5 6 tt	6 5 tm	7 4 TT	8 3 RF	25	9 2 rg	9 30 RR	10 30 RR	11 28 mf	12 28 mr	1 27 mf
3 9 ff	4 8 fr	5 7 FW	6 6 FH	7 5 tt	8 4 rd	26	9 3 TT	10 1 rg	10 31 rg	11 29 RF	12 29 RR	1 28 RF
3 10 EF	4 9 ER	5 8 ff	6 7 fr	7 6 FW	8 5 TM	27	9 4 tt	10 2 TT	11 1 TT	11 30 rd	12 30 rg	1 29 rd
3 11 ed	4 10 eg	5 9 EF	6 8 ER	7 7 ff	8 6 tm	28	9 5 FW	10 3 tt	11 2 tt	12 1 TT	12 31 TT	1 30 TM
3 12 MM	4 11 MT	5 10 ed	6 9 eg	7 8 EF	8 7 EF	29		10 4 FH	11 3 FW	12 2 tm	1 1 tt	1 31 tm
3 13 mm		5 11 MM				30		10 5 ff		12 3 FH	1 2 FW	2 1 FW
												2 2 FH

1965 tf SNAKE

	JAN ET	FEB et	MAR MW	APR mf	MAY RF	JUN rd	DAY OF MON	JUL TM	AUG tm	SEP FH	OCT tr	NOV ER	DEC eg
Term	3 SPRING	4 WARM	4 CLEAR	6 SUMMER	7 GRAIN	9 HEAT		12 FALL	13 DEW	14 C DEW	16 WINTER	15 SNOW	15 CHILL
Time	8:46	2:48	8:07	1:42	6:02	16:22		2:05	5:41	21:19	0:13	15:46	3:16

JAN (ET): 2 fr, 3 ER, 4 eg, 5 MT, 6 mt, 7 RW, 8 rf, 9 TF, 10 td, 11 FM, 12 fm, 14 er, 15 MR, 16 mg, 17 RT, 18 rt, 19 TW, 20 tf, 21 FF, 22 fd, 24 em, 25 MH, 26 mr, 27 RR, 28 rg, 1 TT, 2 tt

FEB (et): 3 FW, 4 ff, 5 EF, 6 ed, 7 MM, 8 mm, 9 RH, 10 rr, 11 TR, 12 tg, 13 FT, 14 ft, 15 EW, 16 ef, 17 MF, 18 md, 19 RM, 20 rm, 21 TH, 22 tr, 23 FR, 24 fg, 25 ET, 26 et, 27 MW, 28 mf, 29 RR, 30 rd, 31 TM, 1 tm

MAR (MW): 2 FH, 3 fr, 4 ER, 5 eg, 6 MT, 7 mt, 8 RW, 9 rf, 10 TF, 11 td, 12 FM, 13 fm, 14 EH, 15 er, 16 MR, 17 mg, 18 RT, 19 rt, 20 TW, 21 tf, 22 FF, 23 fd, 24 EM, 25 em, 26 MH, 27 mr, 28 RR, 29 rg, 30 TT, 1 tm

APR (mf): 1 tt, 2 FW, 3 ff, 4 EF, 5 ed, 6 MM, 7 mm, 8 RH, 9 rr, 10 TR, 11 tg, 12 FT, 13 ft, 14 EW, 15 er, 16 MR, 17 mg, 18 RM, 19 rm, 20 TH, 21 tr, 22 FR, 23 fg, 24 ET, 25 et, 26 MW, 27 mr, 28 RF, 29 rd, 30 TM

MAY (RF): 31 tm, 1 FH, 2 fr, 3 ER, 4 eg, 5 MT, 6 mt, 7 RW, 8 rf, 9 TF, 10 td, 11 FM, 12 fm, 13 EH, 14 er, 15 MR, 16 mg, 17 RT, 18 rt, 19 TH, 20 tr, 21 FF, 22 fd, 23 ET, 24 et, 25 MW, 26 mr, 27 RR, 28 rg

JUN (rd): 29 TT, 30 tt, 1 FW, 2 ff, 3 EF, 4 eg, 5 MM, 6 mm, 7 RH, 8 rr, 9 TR, 10 tg, 11 FT, 12 ft, 13 EH, 14 ef, 15 MR, 16 mg, 17 RT, 18 rt, 19 TW, 20 tf, 21 FF, 22 fd, 23 EM, 24 em, 25 MH, 26 mr, 27 RR

JUL (TM): 28 rd, 29 TM, 30 tm, 31 FH, 1 fr, 2 ER, 3 ed, 4 MT, 5 mt, 6 RW, 7 rf, 8 TF, 9 td, 10 FM, 11 fm, 12 EH, 13 er, 14 MR, 15 mg, 16 RT, 17 rt, 18 TH, 19 tr, 20 FF, 21 fd, 22 EM, 23 em, 24 MH, 25 mr, 26 RR

AUG (tm): 27 rd, 28 TM, 29 tm, 30 FW, 31 ff, 1 fr, 2 ER, 3 eg, 4 MT, 5 mt, 6 RW, 7 rf, 8 TF, 9 td, 10 FM, 11 fm, 12 EH, 13 er, 14 MR, 15 mg, 16 RM, 17 rm, 18 TH, 19 tr, 20 FR, 21 fd, 22 EM, 23 em, 24 MH, 25 mr, 26 RR

SEP (FH): 25 RF, 26 rd, 27 TM, 28 tm, 29 FH, 30 fr, 1 ER, 2 eg, 3 MM, 4 mm, 5 RW, 6 rf, 7 TR, 8 td, 9 FM, 10 fm, 11 EH, 12 er, 13 MR, 14 mg, 15 RT, 16 rt, 17 TW, 18 tf, 19 FF, 20 fd, 21 EM, 22 em, 23 MH

OCT (tr): 24 mr, 25 RR, 26 rg, 27 TT, 28 tt, 29 FW, 30 ff, 31 EF, 1 ed, 2 MM, 3 mm, 4 RH, 5 rr, 6 TR, 7 tg, 8 FT, 9 ft, 10 EW, 11 ef, 12 MF, 13 md, 14 EW, 15 er, 16 MR, 17 rm, 18 TH, 19 tr, 20 ET, 21 et, 22 MW

NOV (ER): 23 mf, 24 RF, 25 rd, 26 TM, 27 tm, 28 FH, 29 fr, 30 ER, 1 eg, 2 MT, 3 mt, 4 RW, 5 rf, 6 TF, 7 td, 8 FM, 9 fm, 10 EH, 11 er, 12 MR, 13 mg, 14 RT, 15 rt, 16 TW, 17 tf, 18 FF, 19 fd, 20 EM, 21 em, 22 MH

DEC (eg): 23 mr, 24 RR, 25 rg, 26 TT, 27 tt, 28 FW, 29 ff, 30 EF, 31 ed, 1 MM, 2 mm, 3 RH, 4 rr, 5 TR, 6 tg, 7 FT, 8 ft, 9 EW, 10 ef, 11 MF, 12 md, 13 RM, 14 rm, 15 TH, 16 tr, 17 FR, 18 fg, 19 ET, 20 et

1966 FF HORSE

JAN MT	FEB mt	MAR RW	MAR RW	APR rf	MAY FF	JUN td	DAY OF MON	JUL FM	AUG fm	SEP EH	OCT er	NOV MR	DEC mg
15 SPRING	15 WARM	15 CLEAR	16 SUMMER	18 GRAIN	19 HEAT	22 FALL		24 DEW	25 C DEW	26 WINTER	26 SNOW	26 CHILL	25 SPRING
14:38	8:51	13:57	7:31	11:50	22:07	7:49	MON	11:30	3:08	6:02	21:38	9:06	20:31
1 21 MW	2 20 MH	3 22 MW	4 21 MH	5 20 et	6 19 em	7 18 ET	1	8 16 fd	9 15 fg	10 14 FF	11 12 tr	12 12 tf	1 11 tr
1 22 mg	2 21 mr	3 23 mr	4 22 mr	5 21 MW	6 20 MH	7 19 et	2	8 17 EM	9 16 ET	10 15 fd	11 13 FR	12 13 FF	1 12 FR
1 23 RF	2 22 RR	3 24 RF	4 23 RR	5 22 mf	6 21 mr	7 20 MW	3	8 18 em	9 17 et	10 16 EM	11 14 fg	12 14 fd	1 13 fg
1 24 rd	2 23 rg	3 25 rd	4 24 rg	5 23 RF	6 22 RR	7 21 mf	4	8 19 MH	9 18 MW	10 17 em	11 15 ET	12 15 EM	1 14 ET
1 25 TM	2 24 TT	3 26 TM	4 25 TT	5 24 rd	6 23 rg	7 22 RF	5	8 20 mr	9 19 mf	10 18 MH	11 16 et	12 16 em	1 15 et
1 26 tm	2 25 tt	3 27 tm	4 26 tt	5 25 TM	6 24 tm	7 23 rd	6	8 21 RR	9 20 RF	10 19 mr	11 17 MW	12 17 MH	1 16 MW
1 27 FH	2 26 FW	3 28 FH	4 27 FW	5 26 tm	6 25 tt	7 24 TM	7	8 22 rg	9 21 rd	10 20 RR	11 18 mf	12 18 mr	1 17 mf
1 28 fr	2 27 ff	3 29 fr	4 28 ff	5 27 FH	6 26 FW	7 25 tm	8	8 23 TT	9 22 TM	10 21 rg	11 19 RF	12 19 RR	1 18 RF
1 29 ER	2 28 EF	3 30 ER	4 29 EF	5 28 fr	6 27 ff	7 26 FH	9	8 24 tt	9 23 tm	10 22 TT	11 20 rd	12 20 rg	1 19 rd
1 30 eg	3 1 ed	3 31 eg	4 30 ed	5 29 ER	6 28 EF	7 27 fr	10	8 25 FW	9 24 FH	10 23 tt	11 21 TM	12 21 TT	1 20 TM
1 31 MT	3 2 MM	4 1 MT	5 1 MT	5 30 eg	6 29 ed	7 28 ER	11	8 26 ff	9 25 fr	10 24 FW	11 22 tm	12 22 tt	1 21 tm
2 1 mt	3 3 mm	4 2 mm	5 2 mm	5 31 MT	6 30 MM	7 29 eg	12	8 27 EF	9 26 ER	10 25 ff	11 23 FH	12 23 FW	1 22 FH
2 2 RW	3 4 RH	4 3 RW	5 3 RW	6 1 mt	7 1 mt	7 30 MT	13	8 28 ed	9 27 eg	10 26 EF	11 24 fr	12 24 ff	1 23 fr
2 3 rf	3 5 rr	4 4 rf	5 4 rf	6 2 RW	7 2 RW	7 31 mt	14	8 29 MM	9 28 MT	10 27 ed	11 25 ER	12 25 EF	1 24 ER
2 4 TF	3 6 TR	4 5 TF	5 5 TF	6 3 rf	7 3 rf	8 1 RW	15	8 30 mm	9 29 mt	10 28 MM	11 26 eg	12 26 ed	1 25 eg
2 5 td	3 7 tg	4 6 td	5 6 td	6 4 TR	7 4 TF	8 2 rf	16	8 31 RH	9 30 RW	10 29 mm	11 27 MT	12 27 MM	1 26 MT
2 6 FM	3 8 FT	4 7 FM	5 7 FM	6 5 td	7 5 td	8 3 TR	17	9 1 rr	10 1 rf	10 30 RH	11 28 mt	12 28 mm	1 27 mt
2 7 fm	3 9 ft	4 8 fm	5 8 fm	6 6 FM	7 6 FM	8 4 td	18	9 2 TR	10 2 TR	10 31 rr	11 29 RW	12 29 RH	1 28 RW
2 8 EH	3 10 EW	4 9 EH	5 9 EH	6 7 fm	7 7 fm	8 5 FM	19	9 3 tg	10 3 td	11 1 TR	11 30 rf	12 30 rr	1 29 rf
2 9 er	3 11 ef	4 10 er	5 10 ef	6 8 EH	7 8 EH	8 6 fm	20	9 4 FT	10 4 FM	11 2 tg	12 1 TF	12 31 TR	1 30 TF
2 10 MR	3 12 MF	4 11 MR	5 11 MR	6 9 ef	7 9 ef	8 7 EW	21	9 5 ft	10 5 fm	11 3 FT	12 2 td	1 1 tg	1 31 td
2 11 md	3 13 md	4 12 md	5 12 md	6 10 MR	7 10 MF	8 8 ef	22	9 6 EW	10 6 EW	11 4 ft	12 3 FM	1 2 FT	2 1 FM
2 12 RT	3 14 RM	4 13 RT	5 13 RT	6 11 mg	7 11 md	8 9 MF	23	9 7 ef	10 7 ef	11 5 EW	12 4 fm	1 3 ft	2 2 fm
2 13 rt	3 15 rm	4 14 rt	5 14 rt	6 12 RT	7 12 RM	8 10 md	24	9 8 MF	10 8 MF	11 6 ef	12 5 EH	1 4 EW	2 3 EH
2 14 TW	3 16 TH	4 15 TW	5 15 TW	6 13 rt	7 13 rm	8 11 RM	25	9 9 md	10 9 mg	11 7 MF	12 6 er	1 5 ef	2 4 er
2 15 tf	3 17 tr	4 16 tf	5 16 tf	6 14 TW	7 14 TH	8 12 rm	26	9 10 RM	10 10 RM	11 8 md	12 7 MR	1 6 MF	2 5 MR
2 16 FF	3 18 FR	4 17 FF	5 17 FF	6 15 tf	7 15 tr	8 13 TW	27	9 11 rm	10 11 rm	11 9 RM	12 8 mg	1 7 md	2 6 mg
2 17 fd	3 19 fg	4 18 fd	5 18 fd	6 16 FF	7 16 FR	8 14 tf	28	9 12 TH	10 12 TW	11 10 rm	12 9 RT	1 8 RM	2 7 RT
2 18 EM	3 20 ET	4 19 EM	5 19 EM	6 17 fd	7 17 fg	8 15 FF	29	9 13 tr	10 13 tf	11 11 TH	12 10 rt	1 9 rm	2 8 rt
2 19 em	3 21 et	4 20 em	5 20 em	6 18 EM			30	9 14 FR			12 11 TW	1 10 TH	

211

1967 fd RAM

JAN RT	FEB rt	MAR TW	APR tf	MAY FF	JUN fd	JUL EM	DAY OF MON	AUG em	SEP MH	OCT mr	NOV RR	DEC rg
26 WARM	26 CLEAR	27 SUMMER	29 GRAIN		1 HEAT	3 FALL		5 DEW	6 C DEW	7 WINTER	7 SNOW	7 CHILL
14:42	19:42	13:18	17:36		3:54	13:35		17:18	7:42	11:52	3:18	14:26
2 9 TW	3 11 TH	4 10 TW	5 9 rm	6 8 rt	7 8 rm	8 6 RT	1	9 4 RT	10 4 mg	11 2 MF	12 2 MR	12 31 ef
2 10 FF	3 12 tr	4 11 tf	5 10 TH	6 9 TW	7 9 TH	8 7 rt	2	9 5 RM	10 5 RT	11 3 md	12 3 mg	1 1 MF
2 11 FF	3 13 FR	4 12 FF	5 11 tr	6 10 tf	7 10 tr	8 8 TW	3	9 6 rm	10 6 rm	11 4 RM	12 4 RT	1 2 md
2 12 fd	3 14 fg	4 13 fd	5 12 FR	6 11 FF	7 11 FR	8 9 tf	4	9 7 TH	10 7 TW	11 5 rm	12 5 rt	1 3 RM
2 13 EM	3 15 ET	4 14 EM	5 13 fg	6 12 fd	7 12 fg	8 10 FF	5	9 8 tr	10 8 tf	11 6 TH	12 6 TW	1 4 rm
2 14 em	3 16 et	4 15 em	5 14 ET	6 13 EM	7 13 ET	8 11 fd	6	9 9 FR	10 9 FF	11 7 tr	12 7 tf	1 5 TH
2 15 MH	3 17 MW	4 16 MH	5 15 et	6 14 em	7 14 et	8 12 EM	7	9 10 fg	10 10 fd	11 8 FR	12 8 FF	1 6 tr
2 16 mr	3 18 mf	4 17 mr	5 16 MW	6 15 MH	7 15 MW	8 13 em	8	9 11 ET	10 11 EM	11 9 fg	12 9 fd	1 7 FR
2 17 RR	3 19 RF	4 18 RF	5 17 mf	6 16 mr	7 16 mf	8 14 MH	9	9 12 et	10 12 em	11 10 ET	12 10 EM	1 8 fg
2 18 rg	3 20 rd	4 19 rg	5 18 RF	6 17 RR	7 17 RF	8 15 mr	10	9 13 MW	10 13 MH	11 11 et	12 11 em	1 9 ET
2 19 TT	3 21 TM	4 20 TT	5 19 rd	6 18 rg	7 18 rd	8 16 RR	11	9 14 mf	10 14 mr	11 12 MW	12 12 MH	1 10 et
2 20 FW	3 22 FH	4 21 tm	5 20 TM	6 19 TT	7 19 TM	8 17 rg	12	9 15 RF	10 15 RR	11 13 mf	12 13 mr	1 11 MW
2 21 FW	3 23 fr	4 22 FH	5 21 FH	6 20 tm	7 20 tm	8 18 TT	13	9 16 rd	10 16 rg	11 14 RF	12 14 RR	1 12 mf
2 22 ff	3 24 ER	4 23 fr	5 22 FH	6 21 FW	7 21 FH	8 19 tm	14	9 17 TM	10 17 TT	11 15 rd	12 15 rg	1 13 RF
2 23 EF	3 25 eg	4 24 ER	5 23 fr	6 22 ff	7 22 fr	8 20 FW	15	9 18 tm	10 18 tt	11 16 TM	12 16 TT	1 14 rd
2 24 ed	3 26 MT	4 25 ed	5 24 ER	6 23 EF	7 23 ER	8 21 FH	16	9 19 FH	10 19 FW	11 17 tm	12 17 tt	1 15 TM
2 25 MM	3 27 mt	4 26 MM	5 25 eg	6 24 ed	7 24 eg	8 22 fr	17	9 20 fr	10 20 ff	11 18 FH	12 18 FW	1 16 tm
2 26 mm	3 28 RW	4 27 mt	5 26 MT	6 25 MM	7 25 MT	8 23 ER	18	9 21 EF	10 21 EF	11 19 fr	12 19 ff	1 17 FH
2 27 RH	3 29 rf	4 28 RH	5 27 mt	6 26 mm	7 26 mt	8 24 eg	19	9 22 eg	10 22 ed	11 20 ER	12 20 EF	1 18 fr
2 28 rr	3 30 rf	4 29 rr	5 28 RW	6 27 RH	7 27 RW	8 25 MT	20	9 23 MM	10 23 MM	11 21 eg	12 21 ed	1 19 ER
3 1 TR	3 31 TF	4 30 TR	5 29 rf	6 28 rr	7 28 rf	8 26 mt	21	9 24 mm	10 24 mm	11 22 MT	12 22 MM	1 20 eg
3 2 tg	4 1 tg	5 1 tg	5 30 TF	6 29 TR	7 29 TF	8 27 RW	22	9 25 RH	10 25 RH	11 23 mt	12 23 mm	1 21 ER
3 3 FT	4 2 FM	5 2 FT	6 1 ft	6 30 tg	7 30 TR	8 28 rf	23	9 26 rr	10 26 rf	11 24 RW	12 24 RH	1 22 eg
3 4 ft	4 3 fm	5 3 ft	6 2 fm	7 1 FT	7 31 tg	8 29 TF	24	9 27 TF	10 27 TR	11 25 rf	12 25 rr	1 23 MT
3 5 EW	4 4 EH	5 4 EW	6 3 EH	7 2 ft	8 1 FM	8 30 tg	25	9 28 tg	10 28 tg	11 26 TF	12 26 TR	1 24 mt
3 6 ef	4 5 er	5 5 ef	6 4 ef	7 3 EW	8 2 fm	8 31 FT	26	9 29 FM	10 29 FT	11 27 td	12 27 tg	1 25 RW
3 7 MF	4 6 MR	5 6 MF	6 5 MR	7 4 ft	8 3 EH	9 1 ft	27	9 30 fm	10 30 ft	11 28 FM	12 28 FT	1 26 td
3 8 md	4 7 mr	5 7 mf	6 6 mg	7 5 EW	8 4 er	9 2 EW	28	9 31 EH	10 31 EW	11 29 fm	12 29 ff	1 27 FM
3 9 RM	4 8 RT	5 8 RM	6 7 RT	7 6 ef	8 5 MF	9 3 ef	29	10 1 er	11 1 ef	11 30 EH	12 30 EW	1 28 fm
3 10 rm	4 9 rt			7 7		9 3	30	10 2	11 1 er	12 1 er		1 29 EH
								10 3 MR				

1968 EM MONKEY

JAN TT	FEB tt	MAR FW	APR ff	MAY EF	JUN ed	DAY OF MON	JUL MM	JUL MM	AUG mm	SEP RH	OCT rr	NOV TR	DEC tg
7 SPRING	7 WARM	8 CLEAR	9 SUMMER	10 GRAIN	12 HEAT		14 FALL	15 DEW	17 C DEW	17 WINTER	18 SNOW	17 CHILL	18 SPRING
2:08	20:18	1:21	19:50	23:19	9:42		19:27	23:07	13:35	17:41	9:09	20:17	7:59
1 30 er	2 28 EW	3 29 EH	4 27 ft	5 27 fm	6 26 ft	1	7 25 FM	8 24 FT	9 23 FM	10 22 tg	11 21 td	12 21 tg	1 18 rf
1 31 MR	2 29 ef	3 30 er	4 28 EW	5 28 EH	6 27 EW	2	7 26 fm	8 25 ft	9 24 fm	10 23 FT	11 22 FM	12 22 FT	1 19 TF
2 1 mg	3 1 MF	3 31 MR	4 29 ef	5 29 er	6 28 ef	3	7 27 EH	8 26 EW	9 25 EH	10 24 ft	11 23 fm	12 23 ft	1 20 td
2 2 RT	3 2 md	4 1 mg	4 30 MF	5 30 MR	6 29 MF	4	7 28 er	8 27 ef	9 26 er	10 25 EW	11 24 EH	12 24 EW	1 21 FM
2 3 rt	3 3 RM	4 2 RT	5 1 md	5 31 mg	6 30 md	5	7 29 MR	8 28 MF	9 27 MR	10 26 ef	11 25 er	12 25 ef	1 22 fm
2 4 TW	3 4 rm	4 3 rt	5 2 RM	6 1 RT	7 1 RM	6	7 30 mg	8 29 md	9 28 mg	10 27 MF	11 26 MR	12 26 MF	1 23 EH
2 5 tf	3 5 TH	4 4 TW	5 3 rm	6 2 rt	7 2 rm	7	7 31 RT	8 30 RM	9 29 RT	10 28 md	11 27 mg	12 27 md	1 24 er
2 6 FF	3 6 tr	4 5 tf	5 4 TH	6 3 TW	7 3 TH	8	8 1 rt	8 31 rm	9 30 rt	10 29 RM	11 28 RT	12 28 RM	1 25 MR
2 7 fd	3 7 FR	4 6 FF	5 5 tr	6 4 tf	7 4 tr	9	8 2 TW	9 1 TH	10 1 TW	10 30 rm	11 29 rt	12 29 rm	1 26 mg
2 8 EM	3 8 fg	4 7 fd	5 6 FR	6 5 FF	7 5 FR	10	8 3 tf	9 2 tr	10 2 tf	10 31 TH	11 30 TW	12 30 TH	1 27 RT
2 9 em	3 9 ET	4 8 EM	5 7 fg	6 6 fd	7 6 fg	11	8 4 FF	9 3 FR	10 3 FF	11 1 tr	12 1 tf	12 31 tr	1 28 rt
2 10 MH	3 10 et	4 9 em	5 8 ET	6 7 EM	7 7 ET	12	8 5 fd	9 4 fg	10 4 fd	11 2 FR	12 2 FF	1 1 FR	1 29 TW
2 11 mr	3 11 MW	4 10 MH	5 9 et	6 8 em	7 8 et	13	8 6 EM	9 5 ET	10 5 EM	11 3 fg	12 3 fd	1 2 fg	1 30 tf
2 12 RR	3 12 mf	4 11 mr	5 10 MW	6 9 MH	7 9 MW	14	8 7 em	9 6 et	10 6 em	11 4 ET	12 4 EM	1 3 ET	1 31 FF
2 13 rg	3 13 RF	4 12 RR	5 11 mf	6 10 mr	7 10 mf	15	8 8 MH	9 7 MW	10 7 MH	11 5 et	12 5 em	1 4 et	2 1 fd
2 14 TT	3 14 rd	4 13 rg	5 12 RF	6 11 RR	7 11 RF	16	8 9 mr	9 8 mf	10 8 mr	11 6 MW	12 6 MH	1 5 MW	2 2 EM
2 15 tt	3 15 TM	4 14 TT	5 13 rd	6 12 rg	7 12 rd	17	8 10 RR	9 9 RF	10 9 RR	11 7 mf	12 7 mr	1 6 mf	2 3 em
2 16 FW	3 16 tm	4 15 tt	5 14 TM	6 13 TT	7 13 TM	18	8 11 rg	9 10 rd	10 10 rg	11 8 RF	12 8 RR	1 7 RF	2 4 MH
2 17 ff	3 17 FH	4 16 FW	5 15 tm	6 14 tt	7 14 tm	19	8 12 TT	9 11 TM	10 11 TT	11 9 rd	12 9 rg	1 8 rd	2 5 mr
2 18 EF	3 18 fr	4 17 ff	5 16 FH	6 15 FW	7 15 FH	20	8 13 tt	9 12 tm	10 12 tt	11 10 TM	12 10 TT	1 9 TM	2 6 RR
2 19 ed	3 19 ER	4 18 EF	5 17 fr	6 16 ff	7 16 fr	21	8 14 FW	9 13 FH	10 13 FW	11 11 tm	12 11 tt	1 10 tm	2 7 rg
2 20 MM	3 20 eg	4 19 ed	5 18 ER	6 17 EF	7 17 ER	22	8 15 ff	9 14 fr	10 14 ff	11 12 FH	12 12 FW	1 11 FH	2 8 TT
2 21 mm	3 21 MT	4 20 MM	5 19 eg	6 18 ed	7 18 eg	23	8 16 EF	9 15 ER	10 15 EF	11 13 fr	12 13 ff	1 12 fr	2 9 tt
2 22 RH	3 22 mt	4 21 mm	5 20 MT	6 19 MM	7 19 MT	24	8 17 ed	9 16 eg	10 16 ed	11 14 ER	12 14 EF	1 13 ER	2 10 FW
2 23 rr	3 23 RW	4 22 RH	5 21 mt	6 20 mm	7 20 mt	25	8 18 MM	9 17 MT	10 17 MM	11 15 eg	12 15 ed	1 14 eg	2 11 ff
2 24 TR	3 24 rf	4 23 rr	5 22 RW	6 21 RH	7 21 RW	26	8 19 mm	9 18 mt	10 18 mm	11 16 MT	12 16 MM	1 15 MT	2 12 EF
2 25 tg	3 25 TF	4 24 TR	5 23 rf	6 22 rr	7 22 rf	27	8 20 RH	9 19 RW	10 19 RH	11 17 mt	12 17 mm	1 16 mt	2 13 ed
2 26 FT	3 26 td	4 25 tg	5 24 TF	6 23 TR	7 23 TF	28	8 21 rr	9 20 rf	10 20 rr	11 18 RW	12 18 RH	1 17 RW	2 14 MM
2 27 ft	3 27 FM	4 26 FT	5 25 td	6 24 tg	7 24 td	29	8 22 TR	9 21 TF	10 21 TR	11 19 rf	12 19 rr		2 15 mm
	3 28 fm		5 26 FM	6 25 FT		30	8 23 tg	9 22 td		11 20 TF	12 20 TR		2 16 RH
						31							

JAN FT 18 WARM 2:11	FEB ft 19 CLEAR 7:15	MAR EW 20 SUMMER 0:50	APR ef 22 GRAIN 5:12	MAY MF 23 HEAT 15:32	JUN md 26 FALL 1:14	DAY OF MON	JUL RM 27 DEW 3:56	AUG rm 27 C DEW 19:17	SEP TH 28 WINTER 23:31	OCT tr 28 SNOW 15:54	NOV FR 29 CHILL 1:59	DEC fg 28 SPRING 13:46
2 17 rr	3 18 RW	4 17 RH	5 16 mt	6 16 mm	7 17 RW	1	8 13 MM	9 12 MT	10 11 ed	11 10 eg	12 9 EF	1 8 ER
2 18 TR	3 19 rf	4 18 rr	5 17 RW	6 17 RH	7 18 rf	2	8 14 mm	9 13 mt	10 12 MM	11 11 MT	12 10 ed	1 9 eg
2 19 tg	3 20 TF	4 19 TR	5 18 rf	6 18 rr	7 19 TF	3	8 15 RH	9 14 RW	10 13 mm	11 12 mt	12 11 MM	1 10 MT
2 20 FT	3 21 td	4 20 tg	5 19 TF	6 19 TR	7 20 td	4	8 16 rr	9 15 rf	10 14 RH	11 13 RW	12 12 mm	1 11 mt
2 21 ft	3 22 FM	4 21 FT	5 20 td	6 20 tg	7 21 FM	5	8 17 TR	9 16 TF	10 15 rr	11 14 rf	12 13 RH	1 12 RW
2 22 EW	3 23 fm	4 22 ft	5 21 FM	6 21 FT	7 22 fm	6	8 18 tg	9 17 td	10 16 TR	11 15 TF	12 14 rr	1 13 rf
2 23 ef	3 24 EH	4 23 EW	5 22 fm	6 22 ft	7 23 EH	7	8 19 FT	9 18 FM	10 17 tg	11 16 td	12 15 TR	1 14 TF
2 24 MF	3 25 er	4 24 ef	5 23 EH	6 23 EW	7 24 er	8	8 20 ft	9 19 fm	10 18 FT	11 17 FM	12 16 tg	1 15 td
2 25 md	3 26 MR	4 25 MF	5 24 er	6 24 ef	7 25 MR	9	8 21 EW	9 20 EH	10 19 ft	11 18 fm	12 17 FT	1 16 FM
2 26 RM	3 27 mg	4 26 md	5 25 MR	6 25 MF	7 26 mg	10	8 22 ef	9 21 er	10 20 EW	11 19 EH	12 18 ft	1 17 fm
2 27 rm	3 28 RT	4 27 RM	5 26 mg	6 26 md	7 27 RT	11	8 23 MF	9 22 MR	10 21 ef	11 20 er	12 19 EW	1 18 EH
2 28 TH	3 29 rt	4 28 rm	5 27 RT	6 27 RM	7 28 rt	12	8 24 md	9 23 mg	10 22 MF	11 21 MR	12 20 ef	1 19 er
3 1 tr	3 30 TW	4 29 TH	5 28 rt	6 28 rm	7 29 TW	13	8 25 RM	9 24 RT	10 23 md	11 22 mg	12 21 MF	1 20 MR
3 2 FR	4 1 tf	4 30 tr	5 29 TW	6 29 TH	7 30 tf	14	8 26 rm	9 25 rt	10 24 RM	11 23 RT	12 22 md	1 21 mg
3 3 fg	4 2 FF	5 1 FR	5 30 tf	6 30 tr	8 1 FF	15	8 27 TH	9 26 TW	10 25 rm	11 24 rt	12 23 RM	1 22 RT
3 4 ET	4 3 fd	5 2 fg	6 1 FF	7 1 FR	8 2 fd	16	8 28 tr	9 27 tf	10 26 TH	11 25 TW	12 24 rm	1 23 rt
3 5 et	4 4 EM	5 3 ET	6 2 fd	7 2 fg	8 3 EM	17	8 29 FR	9 28 FF	10 27 tr	11 26 tf	12 25 TH	1 24 TW
3 6 MW	4 5 em	5 4 et	6 3 EM	7 3 ET	8 4 em	18	8 30 fg	9 29 fd	10 28 FR	11 27 FF	12 26 tr	1 25 tf
3 7 mf	4 6 MH	5 5 MW	6 4 em	7 4 et	8 5 MH	19	9 1 ET	9 30 EM	10 29 fg	11 28 fd	12 27 FR	1 26 FF
3 8 RF	4 7 mr	5 6 mf	6 5 MH	7 5 MW	8 6 mr	20	9 2 et	10 1 em	10 30 ET	11 29 EM	12 28 fg	1 27 fd
3 9 rd	4 8 RR	5 7 RF	6 6 mr	7 6 mf	8 7 RR	21	9 3 MW	10 2 MH	11 1 et	11 30 em	12 29 ET	1 28 EM
3 10 TM	4 9 rg	5 8 rd	6 7 RR	7 7 RF	8 8 rg	22	9 4 mf	10 3 mr	11 2 MW	12 1 MH	12 30 et	1 29 em
3 11 tm	4 10 TT	5 9 TM	6 8 rg	7 8 rd	8 9 TT	23	9 5 RF	10 4 RR	11 3 mf	12 2 mr	1 1 MW	1 30 MH
3 12 FH	4 11 tt	5 10 tm	6 9 TT	7 9 TM	8 10 tt	24	9 6 rd	10 5 rg	11 4 RF	12 3 RR	1 2 mf	2 1 mr
3 13 fr	4 12 FW	5 11 FH	6 10 tt	7 10 tm	8 11 FW	25	9 7 TM	10 6 TT	11 5 rd	12 4 rg	1 3 RF	2 2 RR
3 14 ER	4 13 ff	5 12 fr	6 11 FW	7 11 FH	8 12 ff	26	9 8 tm	10 7 tt	11 6 TM	12 5 TT	1 4 rd	2 3 rg
3 15 eg	4 14 EF	5 13 ER	6 12 ff	7 12 fr	8 13 EF?	27	9 9 FH	10 8 FW	11 7 tm	12 6 tt	1 5 TM	2 4 TT
3 16 MT	4 15 ed	5 14 eg	6 13 EF	7 13 ER	8 14 ed?	28	9 10 fr	10 9 ff	11 8 FH	12 7 FW	1 6 tm	2 5 tt
3 17 mt		5 15 MT	6 14 ed	7 14 eg	8 15 MM?	29	9 11 ER	10 10 EF	11 9 fr	12 8 ff	1 7 FH	2 6 FW
3 18 RW		5 16 mt	6 15 MM	7 15 MT	8 16 mm?	30	9 12 eg	10 11 ed	11 10 ER	12 9 EF	1 8 fr	2 7 ff
3 19 rf		5 17 RW		7 16 mt		31	9 13 MT	10 12 MM		12 10 ed		2 8 EF

214

A perpetual-calendar grid for the Year of the Dog (1970). The twelve columns are lunar months (JAN–DEC), each headed by a two-letter cyclic code, a solar-term note, and a time. The centre column (DAY OF MON) is the lunar day-of-month ruler (1–30). Each cell gives the Gregorian month/day and its cyclic two-letter code.

	JAN — ET	FEB — et	MAR — MW	APR — mf	MAY — RF	JUN — rd	DAY OF MON	JUL — TM	AUG — tm	SEP — FH	OCT — fr	NOV — ER	DEC — eg
	29 WARM	29 CLEAR		2 SUMMER	3 GRAIN	5 HEAT		7 FALL	8 DEW	10 C DEW	10 WINTER	9 SNOW	10 CHILL
	7:51	13:00		6:28	11:13	21:14		7:20	9:42	1:06	5:20	21:43	7:45
1	2/6 ff	3/8 fr	4/6 FW	5/5 tm	6/4 tt	7/3 TM	1	8/2 TT	9/1 TM	9/30 rg	10/30 rd	11/29 rg	12/28 RF
2	2/7 EF	3/9 ER	4/7 ff	5/6 FH	6/5 FW	7/4 tm	2	8/3 tt	9/2 tm	10/1 TT	10/31 TM	11/30 TT	12/29 rd
3	2/8 ed	3/10 eg	4/8 EF	5/7 fr	6/6 ff	7/5 FH	3	8/4 FW	9/3 FH	10/2 tt	11/1 tm	12/1 tt	12/30 TM
4	2/9 MM	3/11 MT	4/9 ed	5/8 ER	6/7 EF	7/6 fr	4	8/5 ff	9/4 fr	10/3 FW	11/2 FH	12/2 FW	12/31 tm
5	2/10 mm	3/12 mt	4/10 MM	5/9 eg	6/8 ed	7/7 ER	5	8/6 EF	9/5 ER	10/4 ff	11/3 fr	12/3 ff	1/1 FH
6	2/11 RH	3/13 RW	4/11 mm	5/10 MT	6/9 MM	7/8 eg	6	8/7 ed	9/6 eg	10/5 EF	11/4 ER	12/4 EF	1/2 fr
7	2/12 rr	3/14 rf	4/12 RH	5/11 mt	6/10 mm	7/9 MT	7	8/8 MM	9/7 MT	10/6 ed	11/5 eg	12/5 ed	1/3 ER
8	2/13 TR	3/15 TF	4/13 rr	5/12 RW	6/11 RH	7/10 mt	8	8/9 mm	9/8 mt	10/7 MM	11/6 MT	12/6 MM	1/4 eg
9	2/14 tg	3/16 td	4/14 TR	5/13 rf	6/12 rr	7/11 RW	9	8/10 RH	9/9 RW	10/8 mm	11/7 mt	12/7 mm	1/5 MT
10	2/15 FT	3/17 FM	4/15 tg	5/14 TF	6/13 TR	7/12 rf	10	8/11 rr	9/10 rf	10/9 RH	11/8 RW	12/8 RH	1/6 mt
11	2/16 ft	3/18 fm	4/16 FT	5/15 td	6/14 tg	7/13 TF	11	8/12 TR	9/11 TF	10/10 rr	11/9 rf	12/9 rr	1/7 RW
12	2/17 EW	3/19 EH	4/17 ft	5/16 FM	6/15 FT	7/14 td	12	8/13 tg	9/12 td	10/11 TR	11/10 TF	12/10 TR	1/8 rf
13	2/18 ef	3/20 er	4/18 EW	5/17 fm	6/16 ft	7/15 FM	13	8/14 FT	9/13 FM	10/12 tg	11/11 td	12/11 tg	1/9 TF
14	2/19 MF	3/21 MR	4/19 ef	5/18 EH	6/17 EW	7/16 fm	14	8/15 ft	9/14 fm	10/13 FT	11/12 FM	12/12 FT	1/10 td
15	2/20 md	3/22 mg	4/20 MF	5/19 er	6/18 ef	7/17 EH	15	8/16 EW	9/15 EH	10/14 ft	11/13 fm	12/13 ft	1/11 FM
16	2/21 RM	3/23 RT	4/21 md	5/20 MR	6/19 MF	7/18 er	16	8/17 ef	9/16 er	10/15 EW	11/14 EH	12/14 EW	1/12 fm
17	2/22 rm	3/24 rt	4/22 RM	5/21 mg	6/20 md	7/19 MR	17	8/18 MF	9/17 MR	10/16 ef	11/15 er	12/15 ef	1/13 EH
18	2/23 TH	3/25 TW	4/23 rm	5/22 RT	6/21 RM	7/20 mg	18	8/19 md	9/18 mg	10/17 MF	11/16 MR	12/16 MF	1/14 er
19	2/24 tr	3/26 tf	4/24 TH	5/23 rt	6/22 rm	7/21 RT	19	8/20 RM	9/19 RT	10/18 md	11/17 mg	12/17 md	1/15 MR
20	2/25 FR	3/27 FF	4/25 tr	5/24 TW	6/23 TH	7/22 rt	20	8/21 rm	9/20 rt	10/19 RM	11/18 RT	12/18 RM	1/16 mg
21	2/26 fg	3/28 fd	4/26 FR	5/25 tf	6/24 tr	7/23 TW	21	8/22 TH	9/21 TW	10/20 rm	11/19 rt	12/19 rm	1/17 RT
22	2/27 ET	3/29 EM	4/27 fg	5/26 FF	6/25 FR	7/24 tf	22	8/23 tr	9/22 tf	10/21 TH	11/20 TW	12/20 TH	1/18 rt
23	2/28 et	3/30 em	4/28 ET	5/27 fd	6/26 fg	7/25 FF	23	8/24 FR	9/23 FF	10/22 tr	11/21 tf	12/21 tr	1/19 TW
24	3/1 MW	3/31 MH	4/29 et	5/28 EM	6/27 ET	7/26 fd	24	8/25 fg	9/24 fd	10/23 FR	11/22 FF	12/22 FR	1/20 tf
25	3/2 mf	4/1 mr	4/30 MW	5/29 em	6/28 et	7/27 EM	25	8/26 ET	9/25 EM	10/24 fg	11/23 fd	12/23 fg	1/21 FF
26	3/3 RF	4/2 RR	5/1 mf	5/30 MH	6/29 MW	7/28 em	26	8/27 et	9/26 em	10/25 ET	11/24 EM	12/24 ET	1/22 fd
27	3/4 rd	4/3 rg	5/2 RF	5/31 mr	6/30 mf	7/29 MH	27	8/28 MW	9/27 MH	10/26 et	11/25 em	12/25 et	1/23 EM
28	3/5 TM	4/4 TT	5/3 rd	6/1 RR	7/1 RF	7/30 mr	28	8/29 mf	9/28 mr	10/27 MW	11/26 MH	12/26 MW	1/24 em
29	3/6 tm	4/5 tt	5/4 TM	6/2 rg	7/2 rd	7/31 RR	29	8/30 RF	9/29 RR	10/28 mf	11/27 mr	12/27 mf	1/25 MH
30	3/7 FH			6/3 TT		8/1 rg	30	8/31 rd		10/29 RF	11/28 RR		1/26 mr

1971   mr   BOAR

JAN MT	FEB mt	MAR RW	APR rf	MAY TF	MAY TF	JUN td	DAY OF MON	JUL FM	AUG fm	SEP EH	OCT er	NOV MR	DEC mg
9 SPRING	10 WARM	:0 CLEAR	12 SUMMER	14 GRAIN	16 HEAT	18 FALL		19 DEW	21 C DEW	21 WINTER	21 SNOW	20 CHILL	21 SPRING
19:26	13:35	:8:36	12:08	17:00	3:29	13:29		17:30	8:13	11:10	3:33	13:43	1:20
1 27 RR	2 25 mf	3 27 mr	4 25 MW	5 24 em	6 23 et	7 22 EM	1	8 21 ET	9 19 fd	10 19 fg	11 18 fd	12 18 fg	1 16 FF
1 28 rg	2 26 RF	3 28 RR	4 26 mf	5 25 MH	6 24 MW	7 23 em	2	8 22 et	9 20 EM	10 20 ET	11 19 EM	12 19 ET	1 17 fd
1 29 tt	2 27 rd	3 29 rg	4 27 RF	5 26 mr	6 25 mf	7 24 MH	3	8 23 MW	9 21 em	10 21 et	11 20 em	12 20 et	1 18 EM
1 30 tt	2 28 TM	3 30 TT	4 28 rd	5 27 RR	6 26 RF	7 25 mr	4	8 24 mf	9 22 mr	10 22 MH	11 21 mr	12 21 MW	1 19 em
1 31 FW	3 1 tm	3 31 tt	4 29 TM	5 28 rg	6 27 rd	7 26 RR	5	8 25 RF	9 23 RR	10 23 mf	11 22 RR	12 22 mf	1 20 MH
2 1 ff	3 2 FH	4 1 FW	4 30 tm	5 29 TT	6 28 TM	7 27 rg	6	8 26 rd	9 24 rg	10 24 RF	11 23 rg	12 23 RF	1 21 mr
2 2 EF	3 3 fr	4 2 ff	5 1 FH	5 30 tt	6 29 tm	7 28 TT	7	8 27 TM	9 25 TT	10 25 rd	11 24 TT	12 24 rd	1 22 RR
2 3 ed	3 4 ER	4 3 EF	5 2 fr	5 31 FW	6 30 FH	7 29 tt	8	8 28 tm	9 26 tt	10 26 TM	11 25 tt	12 25 TM	1 23 rg
2 4 MM	3 5 eg	4 4 ed	5 3 ER	6 1 ff	7 1 fr	7 30 FW	9	8 29 FH	9 27 FW	10 27 tm	11 26 FW	12 26 tm	1 24 TT
2 5 mm	3 6 MT	4 5 MM	5 4 eg	6 2 EF	7 2 ER	7 31 ff	10	8 30 fr	9 28 ff	10 28 FH	11 27 ff	12 27 FH	1 25 tt
2 6 RH	3 7 mt	4 6 mm	5 5 MT	6 3 ed	7 3 eg	8 1 EF	11	8 31 ER	9 29 EF	10 29 fr	11 28 EF	12 28 fr	1 26 FW
2 7 rr	3 8 RW	4 7 RH	5 6 mt	6 4 MM	7 4 MT	8 2 ed	12	9 1 eg	9 30 ed	10 30 ER	11 29 ed	12 29 ER	1 27 ff
2 8 TR	3 9 rf	4 8 rr	5 7 RW	6 5 mm	7 5 mt	8 3 MM	13	9 2 MT	10 1 MM	10 31 eg	11 30 MM	12 30 eg	1 28 EF
2 9 tg	3 10 TF	4 9 TR	5 8 rf	6 6 RH	7 6 RW	8 4 mm	14	9 3 mt	10 2 mm	11 1 MT	12 1 mm	12 31 MT	1 29 ed
2 10 FT	3 11 td	4 10 tg	5 9 TF	6 7 rr	7 7 rf	8 5 RH	15	9 4 RW	10 3 RH	11 2 mt	12 2 RH	1 1 mt	1 30 MM
2 11 ft	3 12 FM	4 11 FT	5 10 td	6 8 TR	7 8 TF	8 6 rr	16	9 5 rf	10 4 rr	11 3 RW	12 3 rr	1 2 RW	1 31 mm
2 12 EW	3 13 fm	4 12 ft	5 11 FM	6 9 tg	7 9 td	8 7 TR	17	9 6 TF	10 5 TR	11 4 rf	12 4 TR	1 3 rf	2 1 RH
2 13 ef	3 14 EH	4 13 EW	5 12 fm	6 10 FT	7 10 FM	8 8 tg	18	9 7 td	10 6 tg	11 5 TF	12 5 tg	1 4 TF	2 2 rr
2 14 MF	3 15 er	4 14 ef	5 13 EH	6 11 ft	7 11 fm	8 9 FT	19	9 8 FM	10 7 FT	11 6 td	12 6 FT	1 5 td	2 3 TR
2 15 md	3 16 MR	4 15 MF	5 14 er	6 12 EW	7 12 EH	8 10 ft	20	9 9 fm	10 8 ft	11 7 FM	12 7 ft	1 6 FM	2 4 tg
2 16 RM	3 17 mg	4 16 md	5 15 MR	6 13 ef	7 13 er	8 11 EW	21	9 10 EH	10 9 EW	11 8 fm	12 8 EW	1 7 fm	2 5 FT
2 17 rm	3 18 RT	4 17 RM	5 16 mg	6 14 MF	7 14 MR	8 12 ef	22	9 11 er	10 10 ef	11 9 EH	12 9 ef	1 8 EH	2 6 ft
2 18 TH	3 19 rt	4 18 rm	5 17 RT	6 15 md	7 15 mg	8 13 MF	23	9 12 MR	10 11 MF	11 10 er	12 10 MF	1 9 er	2 7 EW
2 19 tr	3 20 TW	4 19 TH	5 18 rt	6 16 RM	7 16 RT	8 14 md	24	9 13 mg	10 12 md	11 11 MR	12 11 md	1 10 MR	2 8 ef
2 20 FR	3 21 tf	4 20 tr	5 19 TW	6 17 rm	7 17 rt	8 15 RM	25	9 14 RT	10 13 RM	11 12 mg	12 12 RM	1 11 mg	2 9 MF
2 21 fg	3 22 FF	4 21 FR	5 20 tf	6 18 TH	7 18 TW	8 16 rm	26	9 15 rt	10 14 rm	11 13 RT	12 13 rm	1 12 RT	2 10 md
2 22 ET	3 23 fd	4 22 fg	5 21 FF	6 19 tr	7 19 tf	8 17 TH	27	9 16 TW	10 15 TH	11 14 rt	12 14 TH	1 13 rt	2 11 RM
2 23 et	3 24 ET	4 23 ET	5 22 fd	6 20 FR	7 20 FF	8 18 tr	28	9 17 tf	10 16 tr	11 15 TW	12 15 tr	1 14 TW	2 12 rm
2 24 MW	3 25 em	4 24 et	5 23 EM	6 21 fg	7 21 fd	8 19 FR	29	9 18 FF	10 17 TH	11 16 tf	12 16 TF	1 15 tf	2 13 TH
	3 26 MH			6 22 ET		8 20 fg	30		10 18 FR	11 17 FF	12 17 FR		2 14 tr

216

1972 RR RAT

JAN RT	FEB rt	MAR TW	APR tf	MAY FF	JUN fd	DAY OF MON	JUL EM	AUG em	SEP MH	OCT mr	NOV RR	DEC rg
20 WARM	22 CLEAR	22 SUMMER	24 GRAIN	27 HEAT	28 FALL		30 DEW		2 C DEW	2 WINTER	2 SNOW	2 CHILL
19:28	0:36	18:26	22:22	9:17	19:17		21:15		14:02	15:40	9:23	19:26
2 15 FR	3 15 tf	4 14 tr	5 13 TW	6 11 rm	7 11 rt	1	8 8 RM	9 8 RT	10 7 md	11 6 mg	12 6 md	1 4 MR
2 16 fg	3 16 FF	4 15 FR	5 14 tf	6 12 TH	7 12 TW	2	8 9 rm	9 9 rt	10 8 RM	11 7 RT	12 7 RM	1 5 mg
2 17 ET	3 17 fd	4 16 fg	5 15 FF	6 13 tr	7 13 tf	3	8 10 TH	9 10 TW	10 9 rm	11 8 rt	12 8 rm	1 6 RT
2 18 et	3 18 EM	4 17 ET	5 16 fd	6 14 FR	7 14 FF	4	8 11 tr	9 11 tf	10 10 TH	11 9 TW	12 9 TH	1 7 rt
2 19 MW	3 19 em	4 18 et	5 17 EM	6 15 fd	7 15 fd	5	8 12 FR	9 12 FF	10 11 tr	11 10 tf	12 10 tr	1 8 TW
2 20 mf	3 20 MH	4 19 MW	5 18 em	6 16 ET	7 16 EM	6	8 13 fd	9 13 fd	10 12 FR	11 11 FF	12 11 FR	1 9 tf
2 21 RF	3 21 mr	4 20 mf	5 19 MH	6 17 et	7 17 em	7	8 14 ET	9 14 EM	10 13 fg	11 12 fd	12 12 fg	1 10 FF
2 22 rd	3 22 RR	4 21 RF	5 20 mr	6 18 MW	7 18 MH	8	8 15 et	9 15 em	10 14 ET	11 13 EM	12 13 ET	1 11 fd
2 23 TM	3 23 rg	4 22 rd	5 21 RR	6 19 mf	7 19 mr	9	8 16 MW	9 16 MH	10 15 et	11 14 em	12 14 et	1 12 EM
2 24 tm	3 24 TT	4 23 TM	5 22 rg	6 20 RF	7 20 RR	10	8 17 mr	9 17 mr	10 16 MW	11 15 MH	12 15 MW	1 13 em
2 25 FH	3 25 tt	4 24 TT	5 23 TT	6 21 rd	7 21 rg	11	8 18 RF	9 18 RR	10 17 mf	11 16 mr	12 16 mf	1 14 MH
2 26 fr	3 26 FW	4 25 FH	5 24 tt	6 22 TM	7 22 TT	12	8 19 rd	9 19 rg	10 18 RF	11 17 RR	12 17 RF	1 15 mr
2 27 ER	3 27 ff	4 26 fr	5 25 FW	6 23 tm	7 23 tt	13	8 20 TM	9 20 TT	10 19 rd	11 18 rg	12 18 rd	1 16 RR
2 28 eg	3 28 EF	4 27 ER	5 26 ff	6 24 FH	7 24 FW	14	8 21 tm	9 21 tm	10 20 TM	11 19 TT	12 19 TM	1 17 rg
2 29 MT	3 29 ed	4 28 eg	5 27 EF	6 25 fr	7 25 ff	15	8 22 FH	9 22 FW	10 21 tm	11 20 tt	12 20 tm	1 18 TT
3 1 mt	3 30 MM	4 29 MT	5 28 ed	6 26 ER	7 26 EF	16	8 23 fr	9 23 ff	10 22 FH	11 21 FW	12 21 FH	1 19 tt
3 2 RW	3 31 mm	4 30 mt	5 29 MM	6 27 eg	7 27 ed	17	8 24 ER	9 24 EF	10 23 fr	11 22 ff	12 22 fr	1 20 FW
3 3 rf	4 1 RH	5 1 RW	5 30 mm	6 28 MT	7 28 MM	18	8 25 eg	9 25 ed	10 24 ER	11 23 EF	12 23 ER	1 21 ff
3 4 TF	4 2 rr	5 2 rf	5 31 RH	6 29 mt	7 29 mt	19	8 26 MT	9 26 MM	10 25 eg	11 24 ed	12 24 eg	1 22 EF
3 5 tf	4 3 TR	5 3 TF	6 1 rr	6 30 RW	7 30 RH	20	8 27 mt	9 27 mm	10 26 MT	11 25 MM	12 25 MT	1 23 ed
3 6 FM	4 4 tg	5 4 td	6 2 TR	7 1 rf	7 31 rr	21	8 28 RW	9 28 RH	10 27 mt	11 26 mt	12 26 mt	1 24 MM
3 7 fm	4 5 FT	5 5 FM	6 3 tg	7 2 TF	8 1 TR	22	8 29 rf	9 29 rr	10 28 RW	11 27 RH	12 27 RW	1 25 mm
3 8 EH	4 6 ft	5 6 fm	6 4 FT	7 3 td	8 2 tg	23	8 30 TF	9 30 TR	10 29 rf	11 28 rr	12 28 rf	1 26 RH
3 9 er	4 7 EH	5 7 EH	6 5 ft	7 4 FT	8 3 FT	24	9 1 td	10 1 tg	10 30 TF	11 29 TR	12 29 TF	1 27 rr
3 10 MR	4 8 er	5 8 er	6 6 EW	7 5 fm	8 4 ft	25	9 2 FM	10 2 FT	10 31 td	11 30 td	12 30 td	1 28 TR
3 11 mg	4 9 MF	5 9 MR	6 7 ef	7 6 EH	8 5 EW	26	9 3 fm	10 3 ft	11 1 FM	12 1 FT	12 31 FM	1 29 tg
3 12 RT	4 10 md	5 10 mg	6 8 MF	7 7 er	8 6 ef	27	9 4 EH	10 4 EW	11 2 fm	12 2 ft	1 1 fm	1 30 FT
3 13 rt	4 11 RM	5 11 RT	6 9 md	7 8 MF	8 7 MF	28	9 5 er	10 5 ef	11 3 EH	12 3 EW	1 2 EH	1 31 ft
3 14 TW	4 12 rm	5 12 rt	6 10 RM	7 9 mg	8 8 md	29	9 6 MR	10 6 MF	11 4 er	12 4 ef	1 3 er	2 1 EW
	4 13 TH			7 10 RT		30	9 7 mg		11 5 MR	12 5 MF		2 2 ef

JAN TT SPRING 7:04	FEB tt WARM 1:13	MAR FW CLEAR 6:14	APR ff SUMMER 0:08	MAY EF GRAIN 4:C7	JUN ed HEAT 15:05	JUL MM FALL 1:05	DAY OF MON	AUG mm DEW 3:00	SEP RH C DEW 22:48	OCT rr WINTER 21:28	NOV TR SNOW 15:13	DEC tg CHILL 1:20
2 3 MF	4 5 MR	4 3 ef	5 3 er	6 1 EW	7 30 fm	8 30 ft	1	8 28 FM	9 26 tg	10 26 td	11 25 tg	12 24 TF
2 4 md	4 6 mg	4 4 MF	5 4 MF	6 2 ef	7 1 EH	8 31 EW	2	8 29 fm	9 27 FT	10 27 FM	11 26 FT	12 25 td
2 5 RM	4 7 RT	4 5 md	5 5 md	6 3 MF	7 2 er	8 1 ef	3	8 30 EH	9 28 ft	10 28 fm	11 27 ft	12 26 FM
2 6 rm	4 8 rt	4 6 RM	5 6 RM	6 4 md	7 3 MF	8 2 MF	4	8 31 er	9 29 ef	10 29 EH	11 28 ef	12 27 fm
2 7 TH	4 9 TW	4 7 rm	5 7 rm	6 5 RM	7 4 mg	8 3 md	5	9 1 MR	9 30 MF	10 30 er	11 29 MF	12 28 EH
2 8 tr	4 10 tf	4 8 TH	5 8 TH	6 6 rm	7 5 RT	8 4 RM	6	9 2 mg	10 1 md	10 31 MR	11 30 md	12 29 er
2 9 FR	4 11 FF	4 9 tr	5 9 tr	6 7 TH	7 6 rt	8 5 rm	7	9 3 RT	10 2 RM	11 1 mg	12 1 RM	12 30 MR
2 10 fg	4 12 fd	4 10 FR	5 10 FR	6 8 tr	7 7 TW	8 6 TH	8	9 4 rt	10 3 rm	11 2 RT	12 2 rm	12 31 mg
2 11 ET	4 13 EM	4 11 fg	5 11 fg	6 9 FR	7 8 tr	8 7 tr	9	9 5 TH	10 4 TH	11 3 rt	12 3 TH	1 1 RT
2 12 et	4 14 em	4 12 ET	5 12 ET	6 10 fg	7 9 FR	8 8 FR	10	9 6 tr	10 5 tr	11 4 TW	12 4 tr	1 2 rt
2 13 MW	4 15 MH	4 13 et	5 13 et	6 11 ET	7 10 fd	8 9 fg	11	9 7 FR	10 6 FR	11 5 tf	12 5 FR	1 3 TW
2 14 mf	4 16 mr	4 14 MW	5 14 MW	6 12 et	7 11 EM	8 10 ET	12	9 8 fd	10 7 fg	11 6 FF	12 6 fg	1 4 tf
2 15 RF	4 17 RR	4 15 mf	5 15 mf	6 13 MW	7 12 em	8 11 et	13	9 9 ET	10 8 ET	11 7 fd	12 7 ET	1 5 FF
2 16 rd	4 18 rr	4 16 RF	5 16 RF	6 14 mf	7 13 mf	8 12 MW	14	9 10 em	10 9 et	11 8 EM	12 8 et	1 6 fd
2 17 TM	4 19 TT	4 17 rd	5 17 rd	6 15 RF	7 14 mr	8 13 mf	15	9 11 MH	10 10 MW	11 9 em	12 9 MW	1 7 EM
2 18 tm	4 20 tt	4 18 TM	5 18 TM	6 16 rd	7 15 RR	8 14 RF	16	9 12 mr	10 11 mf	11 10 MH	12 10 mf	1 8 em
2 19 FH	4 21 FW	4 19 tm	5 19 tm	6 17 TM	7 16 rg	8 15 rd	17	9 13 RR	10 12 RF	11 11 mr	12 11 RF	1 9 MH
2 20 fr	4 22 ff	4 20 FH	5 20 FW	6 18 tm	7 17 TT	8 16 TM	18	9 14 rg	10 13 rd	11 12 RR	12 12 rd	1 10 mr
2 21 ER	4 23 EF	4 21 fr	5 21 fr	6 19 FW	7 18 tt	8 17 tm	19	9 15 TT	10 14 TM	11 13 rr	12 13 TM	1 11 RR
2 22 eg	4 24 ed	4 22 ER	5 22 ER	6 20 fr	7 19 FW	8 18 FH	20	9 16 tt	10 15 tm	11 14 TT	12 14 tm	1 12 rg
2 23 MT	4 25 MM	4 23 eg	5 23 eg	6 21 ER	7 20 ff	8 19 fr	21	9 17 FW	10 16 FH	11 15 tt	12 15 FH	1 13 TT
2 24 mt	4 26 mm	4 24 MT	5 24 MT	6 22 eg	7 21 EF	8 20 ER	22	9 18 ff	10 17 fr	11 16 FW	12 16 fr	1 14 tt
2 25 RW	4 27 RH	4 25 mt	5 25 mt	6 23 MT	7 22 ed	8 21 eg	23	9 19 EF	10 18 ER	11 17 ff	12 17 ER	1 15 FW
2 26 rf	4 28 rr	4 26 RW	5 26 RW	6 24 mt	7 23 mm	8 22 MT	24	9 20 ed	10 19 eg	11 18 EF	12 18 eg	1 16 ff
2 27 TF	4 29 TR	4 27 rf	5 27 rf	6 25 RW	7 24 mm	8 23 mt	25	9 21 MM	10 20 MT	11 19 ed	12 19 MT	1 17 EF
2 28 td	4 30 tg	4 28 TF	5 28 TF	6 26 rf	7 25 RH	8 24 RW	26	9 22 mm	10 21 mt	11 20 MM	12 20 mt	1 18 ed
3 1 FM	4 31 FT	4 29 td	5 29 td	6 27 TF	7 26 rr	8 25 rf	27	9 23 RH	10 22 RW	11 21 mm	12 21 RW	1 19 MM
3 2 fm	5 1 ft	4 30 FM	5 30 FM	6 28 td	7 27 TR	8 26 TF	28	9 24 rr	10 23 rf	11 22 RH	12 22 rf	1 20 mm
3 3 EH	5 2 EH	4 31 fm	6 1 fm	6 29 FM	7 28 tg	8 27 td	29	9 25 TR	10 24 TF	11 23 rr	12 23 TF	1 21 RH
3 4 er		5 1 EH	6 2 EH	6 30 fm	7 29 FT		30		10 25 TF	11 24 TR		1 22 rr
3 5 MR		5 2 er		6 31 EH								

218

JAN FT	FEB ft	MAR EW	APR ef	APR ef	MAY MF	JUN md	DAY OF MON	JUL RM	AUG rm	SEP TH	OCT tr	NOV FR	DEC fg
13 SPRING	13 WARM	13 CLEAR	15 SUMMER	16 GRAIN	18 HEAT	21 FALL	MON	22 DEW	24 C DEW	25 WINTER	24 SNOW	24 CHILL	24 SPRING
13:00	7:07	12:05	5:34	9:52	20:13	5:57		9:58	1:40	3:18	21:02	0:36	19:02
1 23 TR	2 22 TF	3 24 TR	4 22 rf	5 22 rr	6 20 RW	7 19 mm	1	8 18 mt	9 16 MM	10 15 eg	11 14 ed	12 14 eg	1 12 EF
1 24 tg	2 23 td	3 25 tg	4 23 TF	5 23 TR	6 21 rf	7 20 RH	2	8 19 RW	9 17 mm	10 16 MT	11 15 MM	12 15 MT	1 13 ed
1 25 FT	2 24 FM	3 26 FT	4 24 td	5 24 tg	6 22 TF	7 21 rr	3	8 20 rf	9 18 RH	10 17 mt	11 16 mm	12 16 mt	1 14 MM
1 26 ft	2 25 fm	3 27 ft	4 25 FM	5 25 FT	6 23 td	7 22 TR	4	8 21 TF	9 19 rr	10 18 RW	11 17 RH	12 17 RW	1 15 mm
1 27 EW	2 26 EH	3 28 EW	4 26 fm	5 26 ft	6 24 FM	7 23 tg	5	8 22 td	9 20 TR	10 19 rf	11 18 rr	12 18 rf	1 16 RH
1 28 ef	2 27 er	3 29 ef	4 27 EH	5 27 EW	6 25 fm	7 24 FT	6	8 23 FM	9 21 tg	10 20 TF	11 19 TR	12 19 TF	1 17 rr
1 29 MF	2 28 MR	3 30 MF	4 28 er	5 28 ef	6 26 EH	7 25 ft	7	8 24 fm	9 22 FT	10 21 td	11 20 tg	12 20 td	1 18 TR
1 30 md	3 1 mg	3 31 md	4 29 MR	5 29 MF	6 27 er	7 26 EW	8	8 25 EH	9 23 ft	10 22 FM	11 21 FT	12 21 FM	1 19 tg
1 31 RM	3 2 RT	4 1 RM	4 30 mg	5 30 md	6 28 MR	7 27 ef	9	8 26 er	9 24 EW	10 23 fm	11 22 ft	12 22 fm	1 20 FT
2 1 rm	3 3 rt	4 2 rm	5 1 RT	5 31 RM	6 29 mg	7 28 MF	10	8 27 MR	9 25 ef	10 24 EH	11 23 EW	12 23 EH	1 21 ft
2 2 TH	3 4 TW	4 3 TH	5 2 rt	6 1 rm	6 30 RT	7 29 md	11	8 28 mg	9 26 MF	10 25 er	11 24 ef	12 24 er	1 22 EW
2 3 tr	3 5 tf	4 4 tr	5 3 TW	6 2 TH	7 1 rt	7 30 RM	12	8 29 RT	9 27 md	10 26 MR	11 25 MF	12 25 MR	1 23 ef
2 4 FR	3 6 FF	4 5 FR	5 4 tf	6 3 tr	7 2 TW	7 31 rm	13	8 30 rt	9 28 RM	10 27 mg	11 26 md	12 26 mg	1 24 MF
2 5 fg	3 7 fd	4 6 fg	5 5 FF	6 4 FR	7 3 tf	8 1 TH	14	8 31 TW	9 29 rm	10 28 RT	11 27 RM	12 27 RT	1 25 md
2 6 ET	3 8 EM	4 7 ET	5 6 fd	6 5 fg	7 4 FF	8 2 tr	15	9 1 tf	9 30 TH	10 29 rt	11 28 rm	12 28 rt	1 26 RM
2 7 et	3 9 em	4 8 et	5 7 EM	6 6 ET	7 5 fd	8 3 FR	16	9 2 FF	10 1 tr	10 30 TW	11 29 TH	12 29 TW	1 27 rm
2 8 MW	3 10 MH	4 9 MW	5 8 em	6 7 et	7 6 EM	8 4 fg	17	9 3 fd	10 2 FR	11 1 tf	11 30 tr	12 30 tf	1 28 TH
2 9 mf	3 11 mr	4 10 mf	5 9 MH	6 8 MW	7 7 em	8 5 ET	18	9 4 EM	10 3 fg	11 2 FF	12 1 FR	12 31 FF	1 29 tr
2 10 RF	3 12 RR	4 11 RF	5 10 mr	6 9 mf	7 8 MH	8 6 et	19	9 5 em	10 4 ET	11 3 fd	12 2 fg	1 1 fd	1 30 FR
2 11 rd	3 13 rg	4 12 rd	5 11 RF	6 10 RF	7 9 mr	8 7 MW	20	9 6 MH	10 5 et	11 4 EM	12 3 ET	1 2 EM	1 31 fg
2 12 TM	3 14 TT	4 13 TM	5 12 rd	6 11 rd	7 10 RR	8 8 mf	21	9 7 mr	10 6 MW	11 5 em	12 4 et	1 3 em	2 1 ET
2 13 tm	3 15 tt	4 14 tm	5 13 TM	6 12 TM	7 11 rg	8 9 RF	22	9 8 RR	10 7 mf	11 6 MH	12 5 MW	1 4 MH	2 2 et
2 14 FH	3 16 FW	4 15 FH	5 14 tm	6 13 tm	7 12 TT	8 10 rd	23	9 9 rg	10 8 RF	11 7 mr	12 6 mf	1 5 mr	2 3 MW
2 15 fr	3 17 fw	4 16 fr	5 15 FH	6 14 FH	7 13 tt	8 11 TM	24	9 10 TT	10 9 rd	11 8 RR	12 7 RF	1 6 RR	2 4 mf
2 16 ER	3 18 EF	4 17 ER	5 16 fr	6 15 fr	7 14 FW	8 12 tm	25	9 11 tt	10 10 TM	11 9 rg	12 8 rd	1 7 rg	2 5 RF
2 17 eg	3 19 ed	4 18 ed	5 17 ER	6 16 ER	7 15 fw	8 13 FH	26	9 12 FW	10 11 tm	11 10 TT	12 9 TM	1 8 TT	2 6 rd
2 18 MT	3 20 MM	4 19 MM	5 18 ed	6 17 eg	7 16 EF	8 14 fr	27	9 13 fw	10 12 FH	11 11 tt	12 10 tm	1 9 tt	2 7 TM
2 19 mt	3 21 mm	4 20 mt	5 19 MM	6 18 MT	7 17 ed	8 15 ER	28	9 14 EF	10 13 fr	11 12 FW	12 11 FH	1 10 FW	2 8 tm
2 20 RW	3 22 RH	4 21 RW	5 20 mm	6 19 mt	7 18 MM	8 16 eg	29	9 15 ed	10 14 ER	11 13 fw	12 12 fr	1 11 fw	2 9 FH
2 21 rf	3 23 rr		5 21 RH			8 17 MT	30				12 13 ER		2 10 fr

219

1975 tt RABBIT

DAY	JAN ET	FEB et	MAR MW	APR mf	MAY RF	JUN rd	JUL TM	AUG tm	SEP FH	OCT fr	NOV ER	DEC eg
	24 WARM	24 CLEAR	25 SUMMER	27 GRAIN	29 HEAT		2 FALL	3 DEW	5 C DEW	6 WINTER	6 SNOW	6 CHILL
	13:07	18:02	11:27	15:42	2:00		11:45	15:47	7:29	9:03	1:46	13:34
1	2 11 ER	3 13 EF	4 12 ER	5 11 ff	6 10 fr	7 9 FW	8 7 tm	9 6 tt	10 5 TM	11 3 rg	12 3 rd	1 1 RR
2	2 12 eg	3 14 ed	4 13 eg	5 12 EF	6 11 ER	7 10 ff	8 8 FH	9 7 FW	10 6 tm	11 4 TT	12 4 TM	1 2 rg
3	2 13 MT	3 15 MM	4 14 MT	5 13 ed	6 12 EF	7 11 EF	8 9 fr	9 8 fr	10 7 FH	11 5 tt	12 5 tm	1 3 TT
4	2 14 mt	3 16 mm	4 15 mt	5 14 MT	6 13 MT	7 12 MT	8 10 ER	9 9 EF	10 8 fr	11 6 FH	12 6 FH	1 4 tt
5	2 15 RW	3 17 RH	4 16 RW	5 15 mm	6 14 mt	7 13 MM	8 11 eg	9 10 ed	10 9 ER	11 7 fr	12 7 fr	1 5 FW
6	2 16 rf	3 18 rr	4 17 rf	5 16 RH	6 15 RW	7 14 mm	8 12 MT	9 11 MM	10 10 eg	11 8 ff	12 8 ER	1 6 ff
7	2 17 TF	3 19 TR	4 18 TF	5 17 rr	6 16 rf	7 15 RH	8 13 mt	9 12 mm	10 11 MT	11 9 EF	12 9 eg	1 7 EF
8	2 18 td	3 20 tg	4 19 td	5 18 TR	6 17 TF	7 16 rr	8 14 RW	9 13 RH	10 12 mt	11 10 MM	12 10 MT	1 8 ed
9	2 19 fm	3 21 FT	4 20 fm	5 19 td	6 18 td	7 17 TR	8 15 rf	9 14 rr	10 13 RW	11 11 mm	12 11 mt	1 9 MM
10	2 20 FM	3 22 ft	4 21 fm	5 20 FT	6 19 FM	7 18 tg	8 16 TF	9 15 TR	10 14 rf	11 12 RH	12 12 RW	1 10 mm
11	2 21 EH	3 23 EW	4 22 EH	5 21 ft	6 20 fm	7 19 FT	8 17 td	9 16 tg	10 15 TF	11 13 rr	12 13 rf	1 11 RH
12	2 22 er	3 24 ef	4 23 er	5 22 EW	6 21 EH	7 20 ft	8 18 FM	9 17 FT	10 16 td	11 14 TR	12 14 TF	1 12 RR
13	2 23 MR	3 25 MF	4 24 MR	5 23 ef	6 22 er	7 21 EW	8 19 fm	9 18 fm	10 17 FM	11 15 tg	12 15 td	1 13 TR
14	2 24 mg	3 26 md	4 25 mg	5 24 MF	6 23 MR	7 22 ef	8 20 EH	9 19 EH	10 18 fm	11 16 FM	12 16 FM	1 14 tg
15	2 25 RT	3 27 RM	4 26 RT	5 25 md	6 24 mg	7 23 MF	8 21 er	9 20 ef	10 19 EH	11 17 ft	12 17 fm	1 15 FT
16	2 26 rt	3 28 rm	4 27 rt	5 26 RM	6 25 RT	7 24 md	8 22 MR	9 21 MF	10 20 er	11 18 EW	12 18 EH	1 16 ft
17	2 27 TW	3 29 TH	4 28 TW	5 27 rm	6 26 rt	7 25 RM	8 23 mg	9 22 md	10 21 MR	11 19 ef	12 19 er	1 17 EW
18	2 28 tf	3 30 tr	4 29 tf	5 28 TH	6 27 TW	7 26 rm	8 24 RT	9 23 RM	10 22 mg	11 20 MF	12 20 MR	1 18 ef
19	3 1 FF	3 31 FR	4 30 FF	5 29 tr	6 28 tf	7 27 TH	8 25 rt	9 24 rm	10 23 RT	11 21 md	12 21 mg	1 19 MF
20	3 2 fd	4 1 fg	5 1 fd	5 30 FF	6 29 FF	7 28 tr	8 26 TW	9 25 TH	10 24 rt	11 22 RM	12 22 RT	1 20 md
21	3 3 EM	4 2 ET	5 2 EM	5 31 fg	7 1 EM	7 29 FF	8 27 tf	9 26 tr	10 25 TW	11 23 rm	12 23 rt	1 21 RM
22	3 4 em	4 3 et	5 3 em	6 1 ET	7 2 em	7 30 fd	8 28 FF	9 27 FR	10 26 tf	11 24 TH	12 24 TW	1 22 rm
23	3 5 MH	4 4 MW	5 4 MH	6 2 et	7 3 MH	8 1 EM	8 29 fd	9 28 fd	10 27 FR	11 25 tr	12 25 tf	1 23 TH
24	3 6 mr	4 5 mf	5 5 mr	6 3 MW	7 4 mr	8 2 em	8 30 EM	9 29 EM	10 28 fd	11 26 FR	12 26 FF	1 24 tr
25	3 7 RR	4 6 RF	5 6 RR	6 4 mf	7 5 RR	8 3 MH	8 31 em	9 30 et	10 29 EM	11 27 fg	12 27 fd	1 25 FR
26	3 8 rg	4 7 rd	5 7 rg	6 5 RF	7 6 rg	8 4 mr	9 1 MH	10 1 MW	10 30 em	11 28 ET	12 28 EM	1 26 fg
27	3 9 TT	4 8 TM	5 8 TT	6 6 rd	7 7 TT	8 5 RR	9 2 mr	10 2 mf	10 31 MH	11 29 et	12 29 em	1 27 ET
28	3 10 tt	4 9 tm	5 9 tt	6 7 TM	7 8 tt	8 6 rg	9 3 RR	10 3 RR	11 1 mr	11 30 MW	12 30 MH	1 28 et
29	3 11 FW	4 10 FH	5 10 FW	6 8 tm			9 4 rg	10 4 rd	11 2 RR	12 1 mf	12 31 mr	1 29 MW
30	3 12 ff	4 11 fr		6 9 FH			9 5 TT			12 2 RF		1 30 mf

220

1976 FW DRAGON

JAN MT	FEB mt	MAR RW	APR rf	MAY TF	JUN td	DAY OF MON	JUL FM	AUG fm	AUG fm	SEP EH	OCT er	NOV MR	DEC mg
6 SPRING	5 WARM	5 CLEAR	7 SUMMER	8 GRAIN	11 HEAT		12 FALL	14 DEW	15 C DEW	16 WINTER	17 SNOW	16 CHILL	17 SPRING
0:40	18:48	23:47	17:15	21:31	7:51		17:38	21:36	13:18	16:17	7:41	19:24	6:34
31 RF	1 RR	31 RF	29 mr	29 mf	27 MH	1	27 MW	25 em	24 et	23 EM	21 fg	21 fd	19 FR
1 rd	2 rg	1 rd	30 RR	30 RF	28 mr	2	28 mf	26 MH	25 MW	24 em	22 ET	22 EM	20 fg
2 TM	3 TT	2 TM	1 rg	31 rd	29 RR	3	29 RF	27 mr	26 mf	25 MH	23 et	23 em	21 ET
3 tm	4 tg	3 tm	2 tt	1 TM	30 rg	4	30 rd	28 RR	27 RF	26 mr	24 MW	24 MH	22 et
4 FH	5 FW	4 FH	3 tm	2 tm	1 TT	5	31 TM	29 rg	28 rd	27 RR	25 mf	25 mr	23 MW
5 fr	6 ff	5 fr	4 FW	3 FH	2 tt	6	1 tm	30 TT	29 TM	28 rg	26 RF	26 RR	24 mf
6 ER	7 EF	6 ER	5 ff	4 fr	3 FW	7	2 FH	31 tt	30 tm	29 TT	27 rd	27 rg	25 RF
7 eg	8 ed	7 eg	6 EF	5 ER	4 ff	8	3 fr	1 FW	1 FH	30 tt	28 TM	28 TT	26 rd
8 MT	9 MM	8 MM	7 eg	6 eg	5 EF	9	4 ER	2 ff	2 fr	31 FW	29 tm	29 tt	27 TM
9 mt	10 mm	9 mt	8 MM	7 MT	6 ed	10	5 eg	3 EF	3 ER	1 ff	30 FH	30 FW	28 tm
10 RW	11 RH	10 RW	9 mm	8 mt	7 MT	11	6 MT	4 ed	4 eg	2 EF	1 fr	31 ff	29 FH
11 rf	12 rr	11 rf	10 RH	9 RW	8 mt	12	7 mt	5 MM	5 MT	3 ed	2 ER	1 EF	30 fr
12 TF	13 TR	12 TF	11 rr	10 rf	9 RW	13	8 RW	6 mm	6 mt	4 MM	3 eg	2 ed	31 ER
13 FM	14 tg	13 tg	12 TR	11 TF	10 rf	14	9 rf	7 RH	7 RW	5 mm	4 MT	3 MM	1 eg
14 fm	15 FT	14 FM	13 tg	12 td	11 TF	15	10 TF	8 rr	8 rf	6 RH	5 mt	4 mm	2 MT
15 EH	16 ft	15 fm	14 FM	13 FM	12 tg	16	11 td	9 TR	9 TF	7 rr	6 RW	5 RH	3 mt
16 er	17 EW	16 EH	15 ft	14 fm	13 FT	17	12 FM	10 tg	10 td	8 TR	7 rf	6 rr	4 RW
17 MR	18 ef	17 er	16 EH	15 EH	14 ft	18	13 fm	11 FT	11 FM	9 tg	8 TF	7 TR	5 rf
18 mg	19 MF	18 MR	17 er	16 er	15 EH	19	14 EH	12 ft	12 fm	10 FT	9 td	8 tg	6 TF
19 RT	20 md	19 mg	18 MR	17 MR	16 ef	20	15 er	13 EW	13 EH	11 ft	10 FM	9 FT	7 td
20 rt	21 RM	20 RT	19 mg	18 mg	17 MR	21	16 MR	14 ef	14 er	12 EW	11 fm	10 ft	8 FM
21 TW	22 rm	21 rt	20 RT	19 RT	18 md	22	17 mg	15 MF	15 MR	13 ef	12 EW	11 EW	9 fm
22 tf	23 TH	22 TW	21 rt	20 rt	19 RM	23	18 RT	16 md	16 mg	14 MF	13 MF	12 ef	10 EH
23 FF	24 tf	23 tf	22 TW	21 TW	20 rm	24	19 rt	17 RM	17 RT	15 md	14 md	13 MF	11 er
24 fd	25 FR	24 FF	23 tf	22 tf	21 TH	25	20 TW	18 rm	18 rt	16 RM	15 mg	14 md	12 MR
25 EM	26 fg	25 fd	24 FF	23 FF	22 tr	26	21 tf	19 TH	19 TW	17 rm	16 RM	15 RM	13 mg
26 em	27 ET	26 EM	25 fd	24 fd	23 FR	27	22 FF	20 tr	20 tf	18 TH	17 rt	16 rm	14 RT
27 MH	28 et	27 em	26 EM	25 EM	24 fg	28	23 fd	21 FR	21 FF	19 tr	18 TW	17 TH	15 rt
28 mr	29 MW	28 MH	27 em	26 em	25 ET	29	24 EM	22 fd	22 fd	20 FR	19 tf	18 tr	16 TW
29 mr	30 mf		28 MW		26 et	30		23 ET			20 FF		17 tf

221

1977 ff SNAKE

	JAN	FEB	MAR	APR	MAY	JUN	DAY OF MON	JUL	AUG	SEP	OCT	NOV	DEC
	RT	rt	Tw	tf	FF	fd		EM	em	MH	mr	RR	rg
	17 WARM	17 CLEAR	18 SUMMER	20 GRAIN	21 HEAT	24 FALL		25 DEW	26 C DEW	26 WINTER	27 SNOW	27 CHILL	27 SPRING
	0:44	5:40	23:16	3:32	13:48	0:18		3:24	19:07	22:06	13:31	1:13	12:27
1	2 18 FF	3 20 FR	4 18 tf	5 18 tr	6 17 tf	7 16 TH	1	8 15 TW	9 13 rm	10 13 rt	11 11 RM	12 11 RT	1 9 md
2	2 19 fd	3 21 fg	4 19 FF	5 19 FR	6 18 FF	7 17 tr	2	8 16 tf	9 14 TH	10 14 TW	11 12 rm	12 12 rt	1 10 RM
3	2 20 EM	3 22 ET	4 20 EM	5 20 fg	6 19 fd	7 18 FR	3	8 17 FF	9 15 tr	10 15 tf	11 13 TH	12 13 TW	1 11 rm
4	2 21 em	3 23 et	4 21 ET	5 21 ET	6 20 EM	7 19 fg	4	8 18 fd	9 16 FR	10 16 FF	11 14 tr	12 14 tf	1 12 TH
5	2 22 MH	3 24 MW	4 22 MW	5 22 et	6 21 em	7 20 ET	5	8 19 EM	9 17 fg	10 17 FF	11 15 FR	12 15 FF	1 13 tr
6	2 23 mr	3 25 mf	4 23 MH	5 23 MW	6 22 MH	7 21 et	6	8 20 em	9 18 ET	10 18 EM	11 16 fg	12 16 fd	1 14 FR
7	2 24 RR	3 26 RF	4 24 mr	5 24 mf	6 23 mr	7 22 MW	7	8 21 MH	9 19 et	10 19 em	11 17 ET	12 17 EM	1 15 fg
8	2 25 rg	3 27 rd	4 25 RF	5 25 RF	6 24 RR	7 23 mf	8	8 22 mr	9 20 MW	10 20 MH	11 18 et	12 18 em	1 16 ET
9	2 26 TT	3 28 TM	4 26 rd	5 26 rd	6 25 rg	7 24 RR	9	8 23 RR	9 21 mf	10 21 mr	11 19 MW	12 19 MH	1 17 et
10	2 27 tt	3 29 tm	4 27 TM	5 27 TM	6 26 TT	7 25 rg	10	8 24 rg	9 22 RF	10 22 RR	11 20 mf	12 20 mr	1 18 MW
11	2 28 FW	3 30 FH	4 28 tm	5 28 tm	6 27 tt	7 26 TM	11	8 25 TT	9 23 rd	10 23 rg	11 21 RF	12 21 RR	1 19 mf
12	3 1 ff	4 1 fr	4 29 FH	5 29 FH	6 28 FW	7 27 tm	12	8 26 tt	9 24 TM	10 24 TT	11 22 rd	12 22 rg	1 20 RF
13	3 2 EF	4 2 ER	4 30 fr	5 30 fr	6 29 ff	7 28 FW	13	8 27 FW	9 25 tm	10 25 tt	11 23 TM	12 23 TT	1 21 rd
14	3 3 ed	4 3 eg	5 1 ER	6 1 ER	6 30 EF	7 29 ff	14	8 28 ff	9 26 FH	10 26 FW	11 24 tm	12 24 tt	1 22 TM
15	3 4 MM	4 4 MT	5 2 eg	6 2 MT	7 1 ed	7 30 EF	15	8 29 EF	9 27 fr	10 27 ff	11 25 FH	12 25 FW	1 23 tm
16	3 5 mm	4 5 mt	5 3 MT	6 3 mt	7 2 MM	8 1 ed	16	8 30 ed	9 28 ER	10 28 EF	11 26 fr	12 26 ff	1 24 FH
17	3 6 RH	4 6 RW	5 4 mt	6 4 RW	7 3 mm	8 2 MM	17	9 1 MM	9 29 eg	10 29 ed	11 27 ER	12 27 EF	1 25 fr
18	3 7 rr	4 7 rf	5 5 RW	6 5 rf	7 4 RH	8 3 mm	18	9 2 mm	9 30 MT	10 30 MM	11 28 eg	12 28 ed	1 26 ER
19	3 8 TR	4 8 TF	5 6 rf	6 6 TF	7 5 rr	8 4 RH	19	9 3 RH	10 1 mt	10 31 mm	11 29 MT	12 29 MM	1 27 eg
20	3 9 tg	4 9 td	5 7 TF	6 7 td	7 6 TR	8 5 rr	20	9 4 rr	10 2 RW	11 1 RH	11 30 mt	12 30 mm	1 28 MT
21	3 10 FT	4 10 FM	5 8 td	6 8 FM	7 7 tg	8 6 TR	21	9 5 TR	10 3 rf	11 2 rr	12 1 RW	12 31 RH	1 29 mt
22	3 11 ft	4 11 fm	5 9 FM	6 9 fm	7 8 FT	8 7 tg	22	9 6 tg	10 4 TF	11 3 TR	12 2 rf	1 1 rr	2 1 RW
23	3 12 EW	4 12 EH	5 10 fm	6 10 EH	7 9 ft	8 8 FT	23	9 7 FT	10 5 tg	11 4 tg	12 3 TF	1 2 TR	2 2 rf
24	3 13 ef	4 13 er	5 11 EH	6 11 er	7 10 EW	8 9 ft	24	9 8 ft	10 6 FT	11 5 FT	12 4 tg	1 3 tg	2 3 TF
25	3 14 MF	4 14 MR	5 12 er	6 12 MR	7 11 ef	8 10 er	25	9 9 EW	10 7 ft	11 6 ft	12 5 FM	1 4 FT	2 4 td
26	3 15 md	4 15 mg	5 13 MR	6 13 mg	7 12 MF	8 11 MR	26	9 10 ef	10 8 EH	11 7 EW	12 6 fm	1 5 ft	2 5 FM
27	3 16 RM	4 16 RT	5 14 mg	6 14 RT	7 13 md	8 12 mg	27	9 11 MF	10 9 er	11 8 ef	12 7 EH	1 6 EW	2 6 fm
28	3 17 rm	4 17 rt	5 15 RT	6 15 rt	7 14 RM	8 13 RT	28	9 12 md	10 10 MR	11 9 MF	12 8 er	1 7 ef	2 7 EH
29	3 18 TH		5 16 rt	6 16 TH	7 15 rm	8 14 rt	29	10 1 RM	10 11 mg	11 10 md	12 9 MR	1 8 MF	2 8 er
30	3 19 tr		5 17 TW				30		10 12 RT		12 10 mg		
31			5 18 TH										

222

1978 EF HORSE

JAN TT	FEB tt	MAR FW	APR ff	MAY EF	JUN ed	DAY OF MON	JUL MM	AUG mm	SEP RH	OCT rr	NOV TR	DEC tg
28 WARM	28 CLEAR	30 SUMMER		1 GRAIN	3 HEAT		5 FALL	7 DEW	8 C DEW	8 WINTER	8 :SNOW	8 CHILL
6:38	11:39	5:09		9:23	19:37		5:18	8:08	23:31	2:34	19:20	6:32
2/7 MR	3/9 MF	4/7 er	5/7 ef	6/5 EH	7/5 EW	1	8/4 EH	9/3 EW	10/2 fm	11/1 ft	11/30 FM	12/30 FT
2/8 mg	3/10 md	4/8 MR	5/8 MF	6/6 er	7/6 ef	2	8/5 er	9/4 ef	10/3 EH	11/2 EW	12/1 fm	12/31 ft
2/9 RT	3/11 RM	4/9 mg	5/9 md	6/7 MR	7/7 MF	3	8/6 MR	9/5 MF	10/4 er	11/3 ef	12/2 EH	1/1 EW
2/10 rt	3/12 rm	4/10 RT	5/10 RM	6/8 mg	7/8 md	4	8/7 mg	9/6 md	10/5 MR	11/4 MF	12/3 er	1/2 ef
2/11 TW	3/13 TH	4/11 rt	5/11 rm	6/9 RT	7/9 RM	5	8/8 RT	9/7 RM	10/6 mg	11/5 md	12/4 MR	1/3 MF
2/12 tf	3/14 tr	4/12 TW	5/12 TH	6/10 rt	7/10 rm	6	8/9 rt	9/8 rm	10/7 RT	11/6 RM	12/5 mg	1/4 md
2/13 FF	3/15 FR	4/13 tf	5/13 tr	6/11 TW	7/11 TH	7	8/10 TW	9/9 TH	10/8 rt	11/7 rm	12/6 RT	1/5 RM
2/14 fd	3/16 fg	4/14 FF	5/14 FR	6/12 tf	7/12 tr	8	8/11 tf	9/10 tr	10/9 TW	11/8 TH	12/7 rt	1/6 rm
2/15 EM	3/17 ET	4/15 fd	5/15 fg	6/13 FF	7/13 FR	9	8/12 FF	9/11 FR	10/10 tf	11/9 tr	12/8 TW	1/7 TH
2/16 em	3/18 et	4/16 EM	5/16 ET	6/14 fd	7/14 fg	10	8/13 fd	9/12 fg	10/11 FF	11/10 FR	12/9 tf	1/8 tr
2/17 MH	3/19 MW	4/17 em	5/17 et	6/15 EM	7/15 ET	11	8/14 EM	9/13 ET	10/12 fd	11/11 fg	12/10 FF	1/9 FR
2/18 mr	3/20 mf	4/18 MH	5/18 MW	6/16 em	7/16 et	12	8/15 em	9/14 et	10/13 EM	11/12 ET	12/11 fd	1/10 fg
2/19 RR	3/21 RF	4/19 mr	5/19 mf	6/17 MH	7/17 MW	13	8/16 MH	9/15 MW	10/14 em	11/13 et	12/12 EM	1/11 ET
2/20 rg	3/22 rd	4/20 RR	5/20 RF	6/18 mr	7/18 mf	14	8/17 mr	9/16 mf	10/15 MH	11/14 MW	12/13 em	1/12 et
2/21 TT	3/23 TM	4/21 rg	5/21 rd	6/19 RR	7/19 RF	15	8/18 RR	9/17 RF	10/16 mr	11/15 mf	12/14 MH	1/13 MW
2/22 tt	3/24 tm	4/22 TT	5/22 TM	6/20 rg	7/20 rd	16	8/19 rg	9/18 rd	10/17 RR	11/16 RF	12/15 mr	1/14 mf
2/23 FW	3/25 FH	4/23 tt	5/23 tm	6/21 TT	7/21 TM	17	8/20 TT	9/19 TM	10/18 rg	11/17 rd	12/16 RR	1/15 RF
2/24 ff	3/26 fr	4/24 FW	5/24 FH	6/22 tt	7/22 tm	18	8/21 tt	9/20 tm	10/19 TT	11/18 TM	12/17 rg	1/16 rd
2/25 EF	3/27 ER	4/25 ff	5/25 fr	6/23 FW	7/23 FH	19	8/22 FW	9/21 FH	10/20 tt	11/19 tm	12/18 TT	1/17 TM
2/26 ed	3/28 eg	4/26 EF	5/26 ER	6/24 ff	7/24 fr	20	8/23 ff	9/22 fr	10/21 FW	11/20 FH	12/19 tt	1/18 tm
2/27 MM	3/29 MT	4/27 ed	5/27 eg	6/25 EF	7/25 ER	21	8/24 EF	9/23 ER	10/22 ff	11/21 fr	12/20 FW	1/19 FH
2/28 mm	3/30 mt	4/28 MM	5/28 MT	6/26 ed	7/26 eg	22	8/25 ed	9/24 eg	10/23 EF	11/22 ER	12/21 ff	1/20 fr
3/1 RH	3/31 RW	4/29 mm	5/29 mt	6/27 MM	7/27 MT	23	8/26 MM	9/25 MT	10/24 ed	11/23 eg	12/22 EF	1/21 ER
3/2 rr	4/1 rf	4/30 RH	5/30 RW	6/28 mm	7/28 mt	24	8/27 mm	9/26 mt	10/25 MM	11/24 MT	12/23 ed	1/22 eg
3/3 TR	4/2 TF	5/1 rr	5/31 rf	6/29 RH	7/29 RW	25	8/28 RH	9/27 RW	10/26 mm	11/25 mt	12/24 MM	1/23 MT
3/4 tg	4/3 td	5/2 TR	6/1 TF	6/30 rr	7/30 rf	26	8/29 rr	9/28 rf	10/27 RH	11/26 RW	12/25 mm	1/24 mt
3/5 FT	4/4 FM	5/3 tg	6/2 td	7/1 TR	7/31 TF	27	8/30 TR	9/29 TF	10/28 rr	11/27 rf	12/26 RH	1/25 RW
3/6 ft	4/5 fm	5/4 FT	6/3 FM	7/2 tg	8/1 td	28	8/31 tg	9/30 td	10/29 TR	11/28 TF	12/27 rr	1/26 rf
3/7 EW	4/6 EH	5/5 ft	6/4 fm	7/3 FT	8/2 FM	29	9/1 FT	10/1 FM	10/30 tg	11/29 td	12/28 TR	1/27 TF
3/8 ef		5/6 EW		7/4 ft	8/3 fm	30	9/2 ft		10/31 FT		12/29 tg	

1979 ed RAM

JAN	FT	8 SPRING	18:13	
FEB	ft	8 WARM	12:20	
MAR	EW	9 CLEAR	17:18	
APR	ef	11 SUMMER	10:47	
MAY	MF	12 GRAIN	15:05	
JUN	md	15 HEAT	1:25	
JUN	md	16 FALL	11:11	
DAY OF MON				
JUL	RM	17 DEW	15:01	
AUG	rm	19 C DEW	5:30	
SEP	TH	19 WINTER	9:45	
OCT	tr	19 SNOW	1:18	
NOV	FR	19 CHILL	12:29	
DEC	fg	19 SPRING	0:10	

JAN
1 28 td · 1 29 FM · 1 30 fm · 1 31 EH · 2 1 er · 2 2 MR · 2 3 mg · 2 4 RT · 2 5 rt · 2 6 TW · 2 7 tf · 2 8 FF · 2 9 fd · 2 10 EM · 2 11 em · 2 12 MH · 2 13 mr · 2 14 RR · 2 15 rg · 2 16 tt · 2 17 tt · 2 18 FW · 2 19 ff · 2 20 EF · 2 21 ed · 2 22 MM · 2 23 mm · 2 24 RH · 2 25 rr · 2 26 TR

FEB
2 27 tg · 2 28 FT · 3 1 ft · 3 2 EW · 3 3 ef · 3 4 MF · 3 5 md · 3 6 RM · 3 7 rm · 3 8 TH · 3 9 tr · 3 10 FR · 3 11 fg · 3 12 ET · 3 13 et · 3 14 MW · 3 15 mf · 3 16 RF · 3 17 rd · 3 18 TM · 3 19 tm · 3 20 FH · 3 21 fr · 3 22 ER · 3 23 eg · 3 24 MT · 3 25 mt · 3 26 RW · 3 27 rf

MAR
3 28 TF · 3 29 td · 3 30 FM · 3 31 EM · 4 1 EH · 4 2 er · 4 3 MR · 4 4 mg · 4 5 RT · 4 6 rt · 4 7 TW · 4 8 tf · 4 9 FF · 4 10 fg · 4 11 EM · 4 12 em · 4 13 MH · 4 14 mr · 4 15 RR · 4 16 rg · 4 17 TT · 4 18 tt · 4 19 FW · 4 20 ff · 4 21 EF · 4 22 ed · 4 23 MM · 4 24 mm · 4 25 RH

APR
4 26 rr · 4 27 TR · 4 28 tg · 4 29 FT · 4 30 ft · 5 1 EW · 5 2 ef · 5 3 MF · 5 4 md · 5 5 RM · 5 6 rm · 5 7 TH · 5 8 tr · 5 9 FR · 5 10 fg · 5 11 ET · 5 12 et · 5 13 MW · 5 14 mf · 5 15 RF · 5 16 rd · 5 17 TM · 5 18 tm · 5 19 FH · 5 20 fr · 5 21 ER · 5 22 eg · 5 23 MT · 5 24 mt · 5 25 RW

MAY
5 26 rf · 5 27 TF · 5 28 td · 5 29 FM · 5 30 fm · 5 31 EH · 6 1 er · 6 2 MR · 6 3 mg · 6 4 RT · 6 5 rt · 6 6 TW · 6 7 tf · 6 8 FF · 6 9 fd · 6 10 EM · 6 11 em · 6 12 MH · 6 13 mr · 6 14 RR · 6 15 rg · 6 16 TT · 6 17 tt · 6 18 FW · 6 19 ff · 6 20 EF · 6 21 ed · 6 22 MM · 6 23 mm

JUN (HEAT)
6 24 RH · 6 25 rr · 6 26 TR · 6 27 tg · 6 28 FT · 6 29 ft · 6 30 EW · 7 2 ef · 7 3 MF · 7 4 md · 7 5 RM · 7 6 rm · 7 7 TH · 7 7 tr · 7 8 FR · 7 8 fg · 7 9 ET · 7 10 et · 7 11 MW · 7 12 mf · 7 13 RF · 7 14 rd · 7 15 TM · 7 16 tm · 7 17 FH · 7 18 fr · 7 19 ER · 7 20 ed · 7 21 MM · 7 22 mt · 7 23 mt

JUN (FALL)
7 24 RW · 7 25 rf · 7 26 TF · 7 27 td · 7 28 FM · 7 29 fm · 7 30 EH · 7 31 er · 8 1 MR · 8 2 mg · 8 3 RT · 8 4 rt · 8 5 TW · 8 6 tf · 8 7 FF · 8 8 fd · 8 9 EM · 8 10 em · 8 11 MH · 8 12 mr · 8 13 RR · 8 14 rg · 8 15 TT · 8 16 tt · 8 17 FW · 8 18 ff · 8 19 EF · 8 20 ed · 8 21 MM · 8 22 mm

DAY OF MON
1 · 2 · 3 · 4 · 5 · 6 · 7 · 8 · 9 · 10 · 11 · 12 · 13 · 14 · 15 · 16 · 17 · 18 · 19 · 20 · 21 · 22 · 23 · 24 · 25 · 26 · 27 · 28 · 29 · 30

JUL
8 23 RH · 8 24 rr · 8 25 TR · 8 26 tg · 8 27 FT · 8 28 ft · 8 29 EW · 8 30 ef · 8 31 MF · 9 1 md · 9 2 RM · 9 3 rm · 9 4 TH · 9 5 tr · 9 6 FR · 9 7 fg · 9 8 ET · 9 9 et · 9 10 MW · 9 11 mf · 9 12 RF · 9 13 rd · 9 14 TM · 9 15 tm · 9 16 FH · 9 17 fr · 9 18 ER · 9 19 ed · 9 20 MT

AUG
9 21 mt · 9 22 RW · 9 23 rf · 9 24 TF · 9 25 td · 9 26 FM · 9 27 fm · 9 28 EH · 9 29 er · 9 30 MR · 10 1 mg · 10 2 RT · 10 3 rt · 10 4 TW · 10 5 tf · 10 6 FF · 10 7 fd · 10 8 EM · 10 9 em · 10 10 MH · 10 11 mr · 10 12 RR · 10 13 rg · 10 14 TT · 10 15 tt · 10 16 FW · 10 17 ff · 10 18 EF · 10 19 ed · 10 20 MM

SEP
10 21 mm · 10 22 RH · 10 23 rr · 10 24 TR · 10 25 tg · 10 26 FT · 10 27 ft · 10 28 EW · 10 29 ef · 10 30 MF · 10 31 md · 11 1 RM · 11 2 rm · 11 3 TH · 11 4 tr · 11 5 FR · 11 6 fg · 11 7 ET · 11 8 et · 11 9 MW · 11 10 mf · 11 11 RF · 11 12 rd · 11 13 TM · 11 14 tm · 11 15 FH · 11 16 fr · 11 17 ER · 11 18 eg · 11 19 MT

OCT
11 20 mt · 11 21 RW · 11 22 rf · 11 23 TF · 11 24 td · 11 25 FM · 11 26 fm · 11 27 EH · 11 28 er · 11 29 MR · 11 30 mg · 12 1 RT · 12 2 rt · 12 3 TW · 12 4 tf · 12 5 FF · 12 6 fd · 12 7 EM · 12 8 em · 12 9 MH · 12 10 mr · 12 11 RR · 12 12 rg · 12 13 TT · 12 14 tt · 12 15 FW · 12 16 ff · 12 17 EF · 12 18 ed

NOV
12 19 MM · 12 20 mm · 12 21 RH · 12 22 rr · 12 23 TR · 12 24 tg · 12 25 FT · 12 26 ft · 12 27 EW · 12 28 ef · 12 29 MF · 12 30 md · 12 31 RM · 1 2 rm · 1 2 TH · 1 3 tr · 1 4 FR · 1 5 fg · 1 6 ET · 1 7 et · 1 8 MW · 1 9 mf · 1 10 RF · 1 11 rd · 1 12 TM · 1 13 tm · 1 14 FH · 1 15 fr · 1 16 ER · 1 17 eg

DEC
1 18 MT · 1 19 mt · 1 20 RW · 1 21 rf · 1 22 TF · 1 23 td · 1 24 FM · 1 25 fm · 1 26 EH · 1 27 er · 1 28 MR · 1 29 mg · 1 30 RT · 1 31 rt · 2 1 TW · 2 2 tf · 2 3 FF · 2 4 fd · 2 5 EM · 2 6 em · 2 7 MH · 2 8 mr · 2 9 RR · 2 10 rg · 2 11 TT · 2 12 tt · 2 13 FW · 2 14 ff · 2 15 EF

224

1980　MM　MONKEY

	JAN ET	FEB et	MAR MW	APR mf	MAY RF	JUN rd	DAY OF MON	JUL TM	AUG tm	SEP FH	OCT fr	NOV ER	DEC eg
	19 WARM	19 CLEAR	21 SUMMER	23 GRAIN	25 HEAT	27 FALL		28 DEW	30 C DEW	30 WINTER		1 SNOW	30 SPRING
	18:17	23:15	16:45	21:14	7:24	17:09		19:54	11:20	15:35		7:02	5:56
												30 CHILL	
												18:13	
1	2 16 ed	3 17 eg	4 15 EF	5 14 fr	6 13 ff	7 12 FH	1	8 11 FW	9 9 tm	10 9 tt	11 8 tm	12 7 TT	1 6 TM
2	2 17 MM	3 18 MT	4 16 ed	5 15 ER	6 14 EF	7 13 fr	2	8 12 ff	9 10 FH	10 10 FW	11 9 FH	12 8 tt	1 7 tm
3	2 18 mm	3 19 mt	4 17 MM	5 16 eg	6 15 ed	7 14 ER	3	8 13 EF	9 11 fr	10 11 ff	11 10 fr	12 9 FW	1 8 FH
4	2 19 RH	3 20 RW	4 18 mm	5 17 MT	6 16 MM	7 15 eg	4	8 14 ed	9 12 ER	10 12 EF	11 11 ER	12 10 ff	1 9 fr
5	2 20 rr	3 21 rf	4 19 RH	5 18 mt	6 17 mm	7 16 MT	5	8 15 MM	9 13 eg	10 13 ed	11 12 eg	12 11 EF	1 10 ER
6	2 21 TR	3 22 TF	4 20 rr	5 19 RW	6 18 RH	7 17 mt	6	8 16 mm	9 14 MT	10 14 MM	11 13 MT	12 12 ed	1 11 eg
7	2 22 tg	3 23 td	4 21 TR	5 20 rf	6 19 rr	7 18 RW	7	8 17 RH	9 15 mt	10 15 mm	11 14 mt	12 13 MM	1 12 MT
8	2 23 FT	3 24 FM	4 22 tg	5 21 TF	6 20 TR	7 19 rf	8	8 18 rr	9 16 RW	10 16 RH	11 15 RW	12 14 mm	1 13 mt
9	2 24 ft	3 25 fm	4 23 FT	5 22 td	6 21 tg	7 20 TR	9	8 19 TR	9 17 rf	10 17 rr	11 16 rf	12 15 RH	1 14 RW
10	2 25 EW	3 26 EH	4 24 ft	5 23 FM	6 22 FT	7 21 td	10	8 20 tg	9 18 TF	10 18 TR	11 17 TR	12 16 rr	1 15 rf
11	2 26 ef	3 27 er	4 25 EW	5 24 fm	6 23 ft	7 22 FM	11	8 21 FT	9 19 td	10 19 tg	11 18 td	12 17 TR	1 16 TF
12	2 27 MF	3 28 MR	4 26 ef	5 25 EH	6 24 EW	7 23 fm	12	8 22 ft	9 20 FM	10 20 FT	11 19 FM	12 18 tg	1 17 td
13	2 28 md	3 29 mg	4 27 MF	5 26 er	6 25 ef	7 24 EH	13	8 23 EW	9 21 fm	10 21 ft	11 20 fm	12 19 FT	1 18 FM
14	2 29 rm	3 30 RT	4 28 md	5 27 MR	6 26 MF	7 25 ef	14	8 24 ef	9 22 EH	10 22 EW	11 21 EH	12 20 ft	1 19 fm
15	3 1 TH	3 31 rt	4 29 RM	5 28 mg	6 27 md	7 26 MR	15	8 25 MF	9 23 er	10 23 ef	11 22 ef	12 21 EW	1 20 EH
16	3 2 tr	4 1 TW	4 30 rm	5 29 RT	6 28 RM	7 27 mg	16	8 26 md	9 24 MR	10 24 MF	11 23 MR	12 22 ef	1 21 er
17	3 3 FR	4 2 tf	5 1 TH	5 30 rt	6 29 rm	7 28 RT	17	8 27 rm	9 25 mg	10 25 md	11 24 mg	12 23 MF	1 22 MR
18	3 4 fg	4 3 TF	5 2 tr	5 31 TW	6 30 TH	7 29 rt	18	8 28 rt	9 26 RT	10 26 RM	11 25 RT	12 24 md	1 23 mg
19	3 5 ET	4 4 td	5 3 FR	6 1 tf	7 1 tr	7 30 TH	19	8 29 TW	9 27 rm	10 27 rm	11 26 rm	12 25 RM	1 24 RT
20	3 6 et	4 5 EM	5 4 fg	6 2 TF	7 2 FR	8 1 tf	20	8 30 tr	9 28 TW	10 28 TH	11 27 TW	12 26 rm	1 25 rt
21	3 7 MW	4 6 et	5 5 ET	6 3 td	7 3 fg	8 2 td	21	8 31 FR	9 29 tf	10 29 tr	11 28 tf	12 27 TH	1 26 TW
22	3 8 mf	4 7 MH	5 6 et	6 4 EM	7 4 ET	8 3 EM	22	9 1 fg	9 30 TF	10 30 FR	11 29 TF	12 28 tr	1 27 tf
23	3 9 mr	4 8 mr	5 7 MW	6 5 em	7 5 et	8 4 et	23	9 2 ET	10 1 td	10 31 fg	11 30 td	12 29 FR	1 28 TF
24	3 10 RF	4 9 RR	5 8 mf	6 6 MH	7 6 MW	8 5 MH	24	9 3 et	10 2 em	11 1 ET	12 1 em	12 30 fg	1 29 td
25	3 11 rd	4 10 rg	5 9 RF	6 7 mr	7 7 mf	8 6 mr	25	9 4 MW	10 3 MH	11 2 et	12 2 MH	12 31 ET	1 30 EM
26	3 12 TM	4 11 TT	5 10 rd	6 8 RR	7 8 RF	8 7 RR	26	9 5 mf	10 4 mr	11 3 MW	12 3 mr	1 1 et	1 31 em
27	3 13 tm	4 12 tt	5 11 TT	6 9 rg	7 9 rd	8 8 rg	27	9 6 RF	10 5 RR	11 4 mf	12 4 RR	1 2 MW	2 1 MH
28	3 14 FH	4 13 FW	5 12 tt	6 10 TT	7 10 TM	8 9 TM	28	9 7 rd	10 6 rd	11 5 RF	12 5 rd	1 3 mf	2 2 mr
29	3 15 fr	4 14 ff	5 13 FW	6 11 tt	7 11 tm	8 10 tm	29	9 8 TM	10 7 rd	11 6 rd	12 6 rg	1 4 RF	2 3 RR
30	3 16 ER			6 12 FW			30		10 8 TM	11 7 TM		1 5 rd	2 4 rg

JAN MT	FEB mt	MAR RW	APR rf	MAY TF	JUN td	DAY OF MON	JUL FM	AUG fm	SEP EH	OCT er	NOV MR	DEC mg
29 WARM		1 CLEAR	2 SUMMER	5 GRAIN	6 HEAT		8 FALL	11 DEW	11 C DEW	11 WINTER	12 SNOW	12 CHILL
23:58		4:59	22:35	3:03	13:12		23:31	1:43	17:10	21:24	13:51	0:02
2 5 TT	3 6 rd	4 5 rg	5 4 RF	6 2 mr	7 2 mf	1	7 31 MH	8 29 et	9 28 em	10 28 et	11 26 EM	12 26 ET
2 6 tt	3 7 TM	4 6 TT	5 5 rd	6 3 RR	7 3 RF	2	8 1 mr	8 30 MW	9 29 MH	10 29 MW	11 27 em	12 27 et
2 7 FW	3 8 tm	4 7 tt	5 6 TM	6 4 rg	7 4 rd	3	8 2 RR	8 31 mf	9 30 mr	10 30 mf	11 28 MH	12 28 MW
2 8 ff	3 9 FH	4 8 FW	5 7 tm	6 5 TT	7 5 TM	4	8 3 rg	9 1 RF	10 1 RR	11 1 RF	11 29 mr	12 29 mf
2 9 EF	3 10 fr	4 9 ff	5 8 FH	6 6 tt	7 6 tm	5	8 4 TT	9 2 rd	10 2 rg	11 2 rd	11 30 RR	12 30 RF
2 10 ed	3 11 ER	4 10 EF	5 9 fr	6 7 FW	7 7 FH	6	8 5 tt	9 3 TM	10 3 TT	11 3 TM	12 1 rg	1 1 rd
2 11 MM	3 12 eg	4 11 ed	5 10 ER	6 8 ff	7 8 fr	7	8 6 FW	9 4 tm	10 4 tt	11 4 tm	12 2 TT	1 2 TM
2 12 mm	3 13 MT	4 12 MM	5 11 eg	6 9 EF	7 9 ER	8	8 7 ff	9 5 FH	10 5 FW	11 5 FH	12 3 tt	1 3 tm
2 13 RH	3 14 mt	4 13 mm	5 12 MT	6 10 ed	7 10 eg	9	8 8 EF	9 6 fr	10 6 ff	11 6 fr	12 4 FW	1 4 FH
2 14 rr	3 15 RW	4 14 RH	5 13 mt	6 11 MM	7 11 MT	10	8 9 ed	9 7 ER	10 7 EF	11 7 ER	12 5 ff	1 5 fr
2 15 TR	3 16 rf	4 15 rr	5 14 RW	6 12 mm	7 12 mt	11	8 10 MM	9 8 eg	10 8 ed	11 8 eg	12 6 EF	1 6 ER
2 16 tg	3 17 TF	4 16 TR	5 15 rf	6 13 RH	7 13 RW	12	8 11 mm	9 9 MT	10 9 MM	11 9 MT	12 7 ed	1 7 eg
2 17 FT	3 18 td	4 17 tg	5 16 TF	6 14 rr	7 14 rf	13	8 12 RH	9 10 mt	10 10 mm	11 10 mt	12 8 MM	1 8 MT
2 18 ft	3 19 FM	4 18 FT	5 17 td	6 15 TR	7 15 TF	14	8 13 rr	9 11 RW	10 11 RH	11 11 RW	12 9 mm	1 9 mt
2 19 EW	3 20 fm	4 19 ft	5 18 FM	6 16 tg	7 16 td	15	8 14 TR	9 12 rf	10 12 rr	11 12 rf	12 10 RH	1 10 RW
2 20 ef	3 21 EH	4 20 EW	5 19 fm	6 17 FT	7 17 FM	16	8 15 tg	9 13 TF	10 13 TR	11 13 TF	12 11 rr	1 11 rf
2 21 MF	3 22 er	4 21 ef	5 20 EH	6 18 ft	7 18 fm	17	8 16 FT	9 14 td	10 14 tg	11 14 td	12 12 TR	1 12 TF
2 22 md	3 23 MR	4 22 MF	5 21 er	6 19 EW	7 19 EH	18	8 17 ft	9 15 FM	10 15 FT	11 15 FM	12 13 tg	1 13 td
2 23 RM	3 24 mg	4 23 md	5 22 MR	6 20 ef	7 20 er	19	8 18 EW	9 16 fm	10 16 ft	11 16 fm	12 14 FT	1 14 FM
2 24 rm	3 25 RT	4 24 RM	5 23 mg	6 21 MF	7 21 MR	20	8 19 ef	9 17 EH	10 17 EW	11 17 EH	12 15 ft	1 15 fm
2 25 TH	3 26 rt	4 25 rm	5 24 RT	6 22 md	7 22 mg	21	8 20 MF	9 18 er	10 18 ef	11 18 er	12 16 EW	1 16 EH
2 26 tr	3 27 TW	4 26 TH	5 25 rt	6 23 RM	7 23 RT	22	8 21 md	9 19 MR	10 19 MF	11 19 MR	12 17 ef	1 17 er
2 27 FR	3 28 tf	4 27 tr	5 26 TW	6 24 rm	7 24 rt	23	8 22 RM	9 20 mg	10 20 md	11 20 mg	12 18 MF	1 18 MR
2 28 fg	3 29 FF	4 28 FR	5 27 tf	6 25 TH	7 25 TW	24	8 23 rm	9 21 RT	10 21 RM	11 21 RT	12 19 md	1 19 mg
3 1 ET	3 30 fd	4 29 fg	5 28 FF	6 26 tr	7 26 tf	25	8 24 TH	9 22 rt	10 22 rm	11 22 rt	12 20 RM	1 20 RT
3 2 et	3 31 EM	4 30 ET	5 29 fd	6 27 FR	7 27 FR	26	8 25 tr	9 23 TW	10 23 TH	11 23 TW	12 21 rm	1 21 rt
3 3 MW	4 1 em	5 1 et	5 30 EM	6 28 fg	7 28 fg	27	8 26 FR	9 24 tf	10 24 tr	11 24 tf	12 22 TH	1 22 TW
3 4 mf	4 2 MH	5 2 MW	5 31 em	6 29 ET	7 29 ET	28	8 27 fg	9 25 FF	10 25 FR	11 25 FF	12 23 tr	1 23 tf
3 5 RF	4 3 mr	5 3 mf	6 1 MH	6 30 et	7 30 em	29	8 28 ET	9 26 fd	10 26 fg	11 25. fd	12 24 FR	1 24 FF
	4 4 RR			7 1 MW		30		9 27 EM	10 27 ET		12 25 fg	

226

1982 RH DOG

JAN RT 11 SPRING 11:46	FEB rt 11 WARM 5:57	MAR TW 12 CLEAR 10:54	APR tf 13 SUMMER 4:21	APR tf 15 GRAIN 8:36	MAY FF 17 HEAT 19:19	JUN fd 19 FALL 5:19	DAY OF MON	JUL EM 21 DEW 7:32	AUG em 23 C DEW 0:12	SEP MH 23 WINTER 3:13	OCT mr 23 SNOW 19:40	NOV RR 23 CHILL 5:59	DEC rg 22 SPRING 17:40
1 25 EM	2 24 ET	3 25 fd	4 24 fg	5 23 FF	6 21 tr	7 21 tf	1	8 19 TH	9 17 rt	10 17 rm	11 15 RT	12 15 RM	1 14 RT
1 26 em	2 25 et	3 26 EM	4 25 ET	5 24 fd	6 22 FR	7 22 FF	2	8 20 tr	9 18 TW	10 18 TH	11 16 rt	12 16 rm	1 15 rt
1 27 MH	2 26 MW	3 27 em	4 26 et	5 25 EM	6 23 fg	7 23 fd	3	8 21 FR	9 19 tf	10 19 tr	11 17 TW	12 17 TH	1 16 TW
1 28 mr	2 27 mf	3 28 MH	4 27 MW	5 26 em	6 24 ET	7 24 EM	4	8 22 fr	9 20 FF	10 20 FR	11 18 tf	12 18 tr	1 17 tf
1 29 RR	2 28 RF	3 29 mr	4 28 mf	5 27 MH	6 25 et	7 25 em	5	8 23 ET	9 21 fd	10 21 fg	11 19 FF	12 19 FR	1 18 FF
1 30 rg	3 1 rd	3 30 RR	4 29 RF	5 28 mr	6 26 MW	7 26 MH	6	8 24 et	9 22 EM	10 22 ET	11 20 fd	12 20 fg	1 19 fd
1 31 TT	3 2 TM	3 31 rg	4 30 rd	5 29 RR	6 27 mf	7 27 mr	7	8 25 MW	9 23 em	10 23 et	11 21 EM	12 21 ET	1 20 EM
2 1 tt	3 3 tm	4 1 TT	5 1 TM	5 30 rg	6 28 RF	7 28 RR	8	8 26 mf	9 24 MH	10 24 MW	11 22 em	12 22 et	1 21 em
2 2 FW	3 4 FH	4 2 tt	5 2 tm	5 31 TT	6 29 rd	7 29 rg	9	8 27 RF	9 25 mf	10 25 mf	11 23 MH	12 23 MW	1 22 MH
2 3 ff	3 5 fr	4 3 FW	5 3 FH	6 1 tt	6 30 TM	7 30 TT	10	8 28 rd	9 26 RR	10 26 RF	11 24 mr	12 24 mf	1 23 mr
2 4 EF	3 6 ER	4 4 ff	5 4 fr	6 2 FW	7 1 tm	7 31 tt	11	8 29 TM	9 27 rg	10 27 rd	11 25 RR	12 25 RF	1 24 RR
2 5 ed	3 7 eg	4 5 EF	5 5 ER	6 3 ff	7 2 FH	8 1 FW	12	8 30 tm	9 28 TT	10 28 TM	11 26 rg	12 26 rd	1 25 rg
2 6 mm	3 8 MT	4 6 ed	5 6 eg	6 4 EF	7 3 fr	8 2 ff	13	8 31 FH	9 29 tt	10 29 tm	11 27 TT	12 27 TM	1 26 TT
2 7 RH	3 9 mt	4 7 MM	5 7 MT	6 5 ed	7 4 ER	8 3 EF	14	9 1 fr	9 30 FW	10 30 FH	11 28 tt	12 28 tm	1 27 tt
2 8 rr	3 10 RW	4 8 mm	5 8 mt	6 6 MM	7 5 eg	8 4 ed	15	9 2 ER	10 1 ff	10 31 fr	11 29 FW	12 29 FH	1 28 FW
2 9 TR	3 11 rf	4 9 RH	5 9 RW	6 7 mm	7 6 MT	8 5 MM	16	9 3 eg	10 2 EF	11 1 ER	11 30 ff	12 30 fr	1 29 ff
2 10 tg	3 12 TF	4 10 rr	5 10 rf	6 8 RH	7 7 mt	8 6 mm	17	9 4 MT	10 3 ed	11 2 eg	12 1 EF	12 31 ER	1 30 EF
2 11 FT	3 13 td	4 11 TR	5 11 TF	6 9 rr	7 8 RW	8 7 RH	18	9 5 mt	10 4 MM	11 3 MT	12 2 ed	1 1 eg	1 31 ed
2 12 ft	3 14 FM	4 12 tg	5 12 td	6 10 TR	7 9 rf	8 8 rr	19	9 6 RW	10 5 mm	11 4 mt	12 3 MM	1 2 MT	2 1 MM
2 13 EW	3 15 fm	4 13 FT	5 13 FM	6 11 tg	7 10 TF	8 9 TR	20	9 7 rf	10 6 RH	11 5 RW	12 4 mm	1 3 mt	2 2 mm
2 14 ef	3 16 EH	4 14 ft	5 14 fm	6 12 FT	7 11 td	8 10 tg	21	9 8 TF	10 7 rr	11 6 rf	12 5 RH	1 4 RW	2 3 RH
2 15 MF	3 17 er	4 15 EW	5 15 EH	6 13 ft	7 12 FM	8 11 FT	22	9 9 td	10 8 TR	11 7 TF	12 6 rr	1 5 rf	2 4 rr
2 16 md	3 18 MR	4 16 ef	5 16 er	6 14 EW	7 13 fm	8 12 ft	23	9 10 FM	10 9 tg	11 8 td	12 7 TR	1 6 TF	2 5 TR
2 17 RM	3 19 mg	4 17 MF	5 17 MF	6 15 ef	7 14 EH	8 13 EW	24	9 11 fm	10 10 FT	11 9 FM	12 8 tg	1 7 td	2 6 tg
2 18 rm	3 20 RT	4 18 md	5 18 mg	6 16 MF	7 15 er	8 14 ef	25	9 12 EH	10 11 ft	11 10 fm	12 9 FT	1 8 FM	2 7 FT
2 19 TH	3 21 rt	4 19 RM	5 19 RT	6 17 md	7 16 MR	8 15 MF	26	9 13 er	10 12 EW	11 11 EH	12 10 ft	1 9 fm	2 8 ft
2 20 tf	3 22 TW	4 20 rm	5 20 rt	6 18 RM	7 17 mg	8 16 md	27	9 14 MR	10 13 ef	11 12 er	12 11 EW	1 10 EH	2 9 EW
2 21 FR	3 23 tf	4 21 TH	5 21 TW	6 19 rm	7 18 RT	8 17 RM	28	9 15 mg	10 14 MF	11 13 MR	12 12 ef	1 11 er	2 10 ef
2 22 fg	3 24 FF	4 22 tr	5 22 tf	6 20 TW	7 19 rt	8 18 rm	29	9 16 RT	10 15 md	11 14 mg	12 13 MF	1 12 MR	2 11 MF
		4 23 FR			7 20 TW		30		10 16 RM		12 14 md	1 13 mg	2 12 md

JAN TT	FEB tt	MAR FW	APR ff	MAY EF	JUN ed	DAY OF MON	JUL MM	AUG mm	SEP RH	OCT rr	NOV TR	DEC tg
22 WARM	22 CLEAR	24 SUMMER	25 GRAIN	28 HEAT	30 FALL			2 DEW	4 C DEW	4 WINTER	5 SNOW	4 CHILL
11:48	16:45	10:12	14:27	1:06	11:07			13:21	6:01	9:03	1:30	11:42
2 13 RM	3 15 RT	4 13 md	5 13 mg	6 11 MF	7 10 er	1	8 9 ef	9 7 EH	10 6 ft	11 5 fm	12 4 FT	1 3 FM
2 14 rm	3 16 rt	4 14 RM	5 14 RT	6 12 md	7 11 MR	2	8 10 MF	9 8 er	10 7 EW	11 6 EH	12 5 ft	1 4 fm
2 15 TH	3 17 TW	4 15 rm	5 15 rt	6 13 RM	7 12 mg	3	8 11 md	9 9 MR	10 8 ef	11 7 er	12 6 EW	1 5 EH
2 16 tr	3 18 tf	4 16 TH	5 16 TW	6 14 rm	7 13 RT	4	8 12 RM	9 10 mg	10 9 MF	11 8 MR	12 7 ef	1 6 er
2 17 FR	3 19 FF	4 17 tr	5 17 tf	6 15 TH	7 14 rt	5	8 13 rm	9 11 RT	10 10 md	11 9 mg	12 8 MF	1 7 MR
2 18 fg	3 20 fd	4 18 FR	5 18 FF	6 16 tr	7 15 TW	6	8 14 TH	9 12 rt	10 11 RM	11 10 RT	12 9 md	1 8 mg
2 19 ET	3 21 EM	4 19 fg	5 19 fd	6 17 FR	7 16 tf	7	8 15 tr	9 13 TW	10 12 rm	11 11 rt	12 10 RM	1 9 RT
2 20 et	3 22 em	4 20 ET	5 20 EM	6 18 fg	7 17 FF	8	8 16 FR	9 14 tf	10 13 TH	11 12 TW	12 11 rm	1 10 rt
2 21 MW	3 23 MH	4 21 et	5 21 em	6 19 ET	7 18 fd	9	8 17 fg	9 15 FF	10 14 tr	11 13 tf	12 12 TH	1 11 TW
2 22 mf	3 24 mr	4 22 MW	5 22 MH	6 20 et	7 19 EM	10	8 18 ET	9 16 fd	10 15 FR	11 14 FF	12 13 tr	1 12 tf
2 23 RF	3 25 RR	4 23 mf	5 23 mr	6 21 MW	7 20 em	11	8 19 et	9 17 EM	10 16 fg	11 15 fd	12 14 FR	1 13 FF
2 24 rd	3 26 rg	4 24 RF	5 24 RR	6 22 mf	7 21 MH	12	8 20 MW	9 18 em	10 17 ET	11 16 EM	12 15 fg	1 14 fd
2 25 TM	3 27 TT	4 25 rd	5 25 rg	6 23 RF	7 22 mr	13	8 21 mf	9 19 MH	10 18 et	11 17 em	12 16 ET	1 15 EM
2 26 tm	3 28 tt	4 26 TM	5 26 TT	6 24 rd	7 23 RR	14	8 22 RF	9 20 mr	10 19 MW	11 18 MH	12 17 et	1 16 em
2 27 FH	3 29 FW	4 27 tm	5 27 tt	6 25 TM	7 24 rg	15	8 23 rd	9 21 RR	10 20 mf	11 19 mr	12 18 MW	1 17 MH
2 28 fr	3 30 ff	4 28 FH	5 28 FW	6 26 tm	7 25 TT	16	8 24 TM	9 22 rg	10 21 RF	11 20 RR	12 19 mf	1 18 mr
3 1 ER	3 31 EF	4 29 fr	5 29 ff	6 27 FH	7 26 tt	17	8 25 tm	9 23 TT	10 22 rd	11 21 rg	12 20 RF	1 19 RR
3 2 eg	4 1 ed	4 30 ER	5 30 EF	6 28 fr	7 27 FW	18	8 26 FH	9 24 tt	10 23 TM	11 22 TT	12 21 rd	1 20 rg
3 3 MT	4 2 MM	5 1 eg	5 31 ed	6 29 ER	7 28 ff	19	8 27 fr	9 25 FW	10 24 tm	11 23 tt	12 22 TM	1 21 TT
3 4 mt	4 3 mm	5 2 MT	6 1 MM	6 30 eg	7 29 EF	20	8 28 ER	9 26 ff	10 25 FH	11 24 FW	12 23 tm	1 22 tt
3 5 RW	4 4 RH	5 3 mt	6 2 mm	7 1 MT	7 30 ed	21	8 29 eg	9 27 EF	10 26 fr	11 25 ff	12 24 FH	1 23 FW
3 6 rf	4 5 rr	5 4 RW	6 3 RH	7 2 mt	7 31 MM	22	8 30 MT	9 28 ed	10 27 ER	11 26 EF	12 25 fr	1 24 ff
3 7 TF	4 6 TR	5 5 rf	6 4 rr	7 3 RW	8 1 mm	23	8 31 mt	9 29 MM	10 28 eg	11 27 ed	12 26 ER	1 25 EF
3 8 td	4 7 tg	5 6 TF	6 5 TR	7 4 rf	8 2 RH	24	9 1 RW	9 30 mm	10 29 MT	11 28 MM	12 27 eg	1 26 ed
3 9 FM	4 8 FT	5 7 td	6 6 tg	7 5 TF	8 3 rr	25	9 2 rf	10 1 RH	10 30 mt	11 29 mm	12 28 MT	1 27 MM
3 10 fm	4 9 ft	5 8 FM	6 7 FT	7 6 td	8 4 TR	26	9 3 TF	10 2 rr	10 31 RW	11 30 RH	12 29 mt	1 28 mm
3 11 EH	4 10 EW	5 9 fm	6 8 ft	7 7 FM	8 5 tg	27	9 4 td	10 3 TR	11 1 rf	12 1 rr	12 30 RW	1 29 RH
3 12 er	4 11 ef	5 10 EH	6 9 EW	7 8 fm	8 6 FT	28	9 5 FM	10 4 tg	11 2 TF	12 2 TR	12 31 rf	1 30 rr
3 13 MR	4 12 MF	5 11 er	6 10 ef	7 9 EH	8 7 ft	29	9 6 fm	10 5 FT	11 3 td	12 3 tg	1 1 TF	1 31 TR
3 14 mg		5 12 MR			8 8 EW	30			11 4 FM		1 2 td	2 1 tg

1984 TR RAT

JAN	FEB	MAR	APR	MAY	JUN	JUL	AUG	SEP	OCT	OCT	NOV	DEC
FT	ft	EW	ef	MF	md	RM	rm	TH	tr	tr	FR	fg
3 SPRING	3 WARM	4 CLEAR	5 SUMMER	6 GRAIN	9 HEAT	11 FALL	12 DEW	14 C DEW	15 WINTER	15 SNOW	15 CHILL	15 SPRING
23:19	17:25	22:23	15:51	20:09	6:29	16:18	19:10	11:50	13:46	7:20	18:36	6:12
2 2 FT	3 3 FM	4 1 tg	5 1 td	5 31 tg	6 29 TF	7 28 rr	8 27 rf	9 25 RH	10 24 mt	11 23 mm	12 22 MT	1 21 MM
2 3 ft	3 4 fm	4 2 FT	5 2 FM	6 1 FT	6 30 td	7 29 TR	8 28 TR	9 26 rr	10 25 RW	11 24 RH	12 23 mt	1 22 mm
2 4 et	3 5 EH	4 3 ft	5 3 fm	6 2 ft	7 1 FM	7 30 tg	8 29 td	9 27 TR	10 26 rf	11 25 rr	12 24 RH	1 23 RH
2 5 ef	3 6 eh	4 4 EW	5 4 EH	6 3 EW	7 2 fm	7 31 FT	8 30 FM	9 28 tg	10 27 TF	11 26 TR	12 25 rf	1 24 rr
2 6 MF	3 7 MR	4 5 ef	5 5 er	6 4 ef	7 3 EH	8 1 ft	8 31 fm	9 29 FT	10 28 td	11 27 tg	12 26 TF	1 25 TR
2 7 md	3 8 mg	4 6 MF	5 6 MR	6 5 MF	7 4 er	8 2 EW	9 1 EH	9 30 ft	10 29 FM	11 28 FT	12 27 td	1 26 tg
2 8 RM	3 9 RT	4 7 md	5 7 mg	6 6 md	7 5 MR	8 3 ef	9 2 er	10 1 EW	10 30 fm	11 29 ft	12 28 FM	1 27 FT
2 9 rm	3 10 rt	4 8 RM	5 8 RT	6 7 RM	7 6 mg	8 4 MF	9 3 MR	10 2 er	10 31 EH	11 30 EW	12 29 fm	1 28 ft
2 10 TH	3 11 TH	4 9 rm	5 9 rm	6 8 rm	7 7 RT	8 5 md	9 4 mg	10 3 MR	11 1 er	12 1 ef	12 30 EH	1 29 EW
2 11 tr	3 12 tf	4 10 TH	5 10 TH	6 9 TH	7 8 rt	8 6 RM	9 5 RT	10 4 mg	11 2 MR	12 2 MF	12 31 er	1 30 ef
2 12 FR	3 13 FR	4 11 tr	5 11 tr	6 10 tr	7 9 TW	8 7 rm	9 6 rt	10 5 RT	11 3 mg	12 3 md	1 1 MR	1 31 MF
2 13 fg	3 14 fd	4 12 FR	5 12 FR	6 11 FR	7 10 tf	8 8 TH	9 7 TW	10 6 rm	11 4 RT	12 4 RM	1 2 mg	2 1 md
2 14 ET	3 15 EM	4 13 fd	5 13 fd	6 12 fg	7 11 FF	8 9 tr	9 8 tr	10 7 TH	11 5 rt	12 5 rm	1 3 RT	2 2 RM
2 15 et	3 16 em	4 14 ET	5 14 EM	6 13 ET	7 12 fd	8 10 FR	9 9 FF	10 8 tr	11 6 TW	12 6 TH	1 4 rt	2 3 rm
2 16 MW	3 17 MH	4 15 et	5 15 em	6 14 et	7 13 ET	8 11 fg	9 10 fd	10 9 FR	11 7 tf	12 7 tr	1 5 TW	2 4 TH
2 17 mf	3 18 mr	4 16 MW	5 16 MH	6 15 MW	7 14 et	8 12 ET	9 11 EM	10 10 fg	11 8 FF	12 8 FR	1 6 tf	2 5 tr
2 18 RF	3 19 RR	4 17 mf	5 17 mr	6 16 mf	7 15 MW	8 13 et	9 12 em	10 11 ET	11 9 fd	12 9 fg	1 7 FF	2 6 FR
2 19 rd	3 20 rg	4 18 RF	5 18 RR	6 17 RF	7 16 mf	8 14 MW	9 13 MH	10 12 et	11 10 EM	12 10 ET	1 8 fd	2 7 fg
2 20 TM	3 21 TT	4 19 rd	5 19 rd	6 18 rg	7 17 RF	8 15 mf	9 14 mr	10 13 MW	11 11 em	12 11 et	1 9 EM	2 8 ET
2 21 tm	3 22 tt	4 20 TM	5 20 TT	6 19 TM	7 18 rg	8 16 RF	9 15 RR	10 14 mf	11 12 MH	12 12 MW	1 10 em	2 9 et
2 22 FH	3 23 FW	4 21 tm	5 21 tt	6 20 tm	7 19 TM	8 17 rd	9 16 rg	10 15 RF	11 13 mr	12 13 mf	1 11 MH	2 10 MW
2 23 fr	3 24 ff	4 22 FH	5 22 FW	6 21 FH	7 20 tm	8 18 TM	9 17 TT	10 16 rd	11 14 RR	12 14 RF	1 12 mr	2 11 mf
2 24 ER	3 25 EF	4 23 fr	5 23 ff	6 22 fr	7 21 FH	8 19 tm	9 18 tt	10 17 TM	11 15 rg	12 15 rd	1 13 RR	2 12 RF
2 25 eg	3 26 ef	4 24 ER	5 24 EF	6 23 ER	7 22 fr	8 20 FH	9 19 FW	10 18 tm	11 16 TT	12 16 TM	1 14 rg	2 13 rd
2 26 MT	3 27 MM	4 25 eg	5 25 ed	6 24 eg	7 23 ER	8 21 fr	9 20 ff	10 19 FH	11 17 tt	12 17 tm	1 15 TT	2 14 TM
2 27 mt	3 28 mm	4 26 MT	5 26 MM	6 25 MT	7 24 eg	8 22 ER	9 21 EF	10 20 fr	11 18 FW	12 18 FH	1 16 tt	2 15 tm
2 28 RW	3 29 RH	4 27 mt	5 27 mm	6 26 mt	7 25 MT	8 23 eg	9 22 ed	10 21 ER	11 19 ff	12 19 fr	1 17 FW	2 16 FH
2 29 rf	3 30 rr	4 28 RW	5 28 RH	6 27 RW	7 26 mt	8 24 MT	9 23 MM	10 22 eg	11 20 EF	12 20 ER	1 18 ff	2 17 fr
3 1 TF	3 31 TR	4 29 rf	5 29 rf	6 28 rf	7 27 RW	8 25 mt	9 24 mm	10 23 MT	11 21 ed	12 21 eg	1 19 EF	2 18 ER
3 2 td		4 30 TF	5 30 TR			8 26 RW			11 22 MM		1 20 ed	2 19 eg

229

```
                                                            1985  tg  OX

| JAN ET   | FEB et    | MAR MW    | APR mf    | MAY RF   | JUN rd   | DAY OF MON | JUL TM   | AUG tm     | SEP FH    | OCT fr   | NOV ER    | DEC eg    |
| 14 WARM  | 16 CLEAR  | 16 SUMMER | 18 GRAIN  | 20 HEAT  | 21 FALL  |            | 24 DEW   | 24 C DEW   | 25 WINTER | 26 SNOW  | 25 CHILL  | 26 SPRING |
| 23:16    | 4:14      | 21:43     | 2:00      | 12:19    | 22:04    |            | 1:53     | 17:39      | 19:29     | 13:09    | 23:21     | 11:03     |
```

JAN	FEB	MAR	APR	MAY	JUN	DAY OF MON	JUL	AUG	SEP	OCT	NOV	DEC
2 20 MT	3 21 ed	4 20 eg	5 20 ed	6 18 ER	7 18 EF	1	8 16 fr	9 15 ff	10 14 FH	11 12 tt	12 12 tm	1 10 TT
2 21 mt	3 22 MM	4 21 MT	5 21 MM	6 19 eg	7 19 ed	2	8 17 ER	9 16 EF	10 15 fr	11 13 FW	12 13 FH	1 11 tt
2 22 RW	3 23 mm	4 22 mt	5 22 mm	6 20 MT	7 20 MM	3	8 18 eg	9 17 ed	10 16 ER	11 14 ff	12 14 fr	1 12 FW
2 23 rf	3 24 RH	4 23 RW	5 23 RH	6 21 mt	7 21 mm	4	8 19 MT	9 18 MM	10 17 eg	11 15 EF	12 15 ER	1 13 ff
2 24 TF	3 25 rf	4 24 rf	5 24 rf	6 22 RW	7 22 RH	5	8 20 mt	9 19 mm	10 18 mt	11 16 ed	12 16 eg	1 14 EF
2 25 fd	3 26 TR	4 25 TF	5 25 TR	6 23 rf	7 23 rr	6	8 21 RW	9 20 RH	10 19 mt	11 17 MM	12 17 MT	1 15 ed
2 26 FM	3 27 tg	4 26 fd	5 26 tg	6 24 TF	7 24 TR	7	8 22 rf	9 21 rf	10 20 RW	11 18 mm	12 18 mt	1 16 MM
2 27 fm	3 28 FT	4 27 FM	5 27 FT	6 25 fd	7 25 tg	8	8 23 TF	9 22 TR	10 21 rf	11 19 RH	12 19 RW	1 17 mm
2 28 EH	3 29 ft	4 28 fm	5 28 ft	6 26 FM	7 26 FT	9	8 24 fd	9 23 tg	10 22 TF	11 20 rf	12 20 rf	1 18 RH
3 1 er	3 30 EW	4 29 EH	5 29 EH	6 27 fm	7 27 ft	10	8 25 FM	9 24 FT	10 23 fd	11 21 TR	12 21 TF	1 19 rr
3 2 MR	3 31 ef	4 30 er	5 30 ef	6 28 EH	7 28 EW	11	8 26 fm	9 25 ft	10 24 FM	11 22 tg	12 22 FM	1 20 TR
3 3 mg	4 1 MF	5 1 MR	5 31 MF	6 29 er	7 29 ef	12	8 27 EH	9 26 EW	10 25 fm	11 23 FT	12 23 fm	1 21 tg
3 4 RT	4 2 md	5 2 mg	6 1 md	6 30 MR	7 30 MF	13	8 28 er	9 27 ef	10 26 EH	11 24 ft	12 24 EH	1 22 FT
3 5 rt	4 3 RM	5 3 RT	6 2 RM	7 1 mg	7 31 md	14	8 29 MR	9 28 MF	10 27 er	11 25 EW	12 25 EH	1 23 ft
3 6 TW	4 4 rm	5 4 rt	6 3 rt	7 2 RM	8 1 RM	15	8 30 mr	9 29 md	10 28 er	11 26 er	12 26 er	1 24 EW
3 7 tf	4 5 TH	5 5 TW	6 4 TH	7 3 rt	8 2 rm	16	8 31 RT	9 30 RM	10 29 mg	11 27 MF	12 27 MR	1 25 ef
3 8 FF	4 6 tr	5 6 tf	6 5 tr	7 4 TW	8 3 TH	17	9 1 rt	10 1 rm	10 30 RT	11 28 md	12 28 mg	1 26 MF
3 9 fd	4 7 FR	5 7 FF	6 6 FR	7 5 tf	8 4 tr	18	9 2 TW	10 2 TH	10 31 rt	11 29 RM	12 29 RT	1 27 md
3 10 EM	4 8 fg	5 8 fd	6 7 fg	7 6 FF	8 5 FR	19	9 3 tf	10 3 tr	11 1 TW	11 30 rm	12 30 rt	1 28 RM
3 11 em	4 9 EM	5 9 EM	6 8 et	7 7 fd	8 6 fd	20	9 4 FF	10 4 FR	11 2 tf	12 1 TH	12 31 TW	1 29 rm
3 12 MH	4 10 et	5 10 em	6 9 EM	7 8 EM	8 7 ET	21	9 5 fd	10 5 fg	11 3 FF	12 2 tr	1 1 tf	1 30 TH
3 13 mr	4 11 MW	5 11 MH	6 10 MW	7 9 em	8 8 et	22	9 6 EM	10 6 ET	11 4 fd	12 3 FR	1 2 FF	1 31 tr
3 14 RR	4 12 mf	5 12 mr	6 11 mf	7 10 MH	8 9 MW	23	9 7 em	10 7 et	11 5 EM	12 4 fg	1 3 fd	2 1 FR
3 15 rg	4 13 RF	5 13 RR	6 12 RF	7 11 mr	8 10 mf	24	9 8 MH	10 8 MW	11 6 em	12 5 ET	1 4 EM	2 2 fg
3 16 TT	4 14 rd	5 14 rg	6 13 rd	7 12 RR	8 11 RF	25	9 9 mr	10 9 mf	11 7 MH	12 6 et	1 5 em	2 3 ET
3 17 tt	4 15 TM	5 15 TT	6 14 TM	7 13 rg	8 12 rd	26	9 10 RR	10 10 RF	11 8 mr	12 7 MW	1 6 MH	2 4 et
3 18 FW	4 16 tm	5 16 tt	6 15 tm	7 14 TT	8 13 TM	27	9 11 rg	10 11 rd	11 9 RR	12 8 mf	1 7 mr	2 5 MW
3 19 ff	4 17 FH	5 17 FW	6 16 FH	7 15 tt	8 14 tm	28	9 12 TT	10 12 TM	11 10 rg	12 9 RF	1 8 RR	2 6 mf
3 20 EF	4 18 fr	5 18 ff	6 17 fr	7 16 FW	8 15 FH	29	9 13 tt	10 13 tm	11 11 TT	12 10 rd	1 9 rg	2 7 RF
	4 19 ER	5 19 EF		7 17 ff		30	9 14 FW			12 11 TM		2 8 rd

1986 FT TIGER

	JAN	FEB	MAR	APR	MAY	JUN	JUL	AUG	SEP	OCT	NOV	DEC
Month pillar	MT	mt	RW	rf	TF	td	FM	fm	EH	er	MR	mg
Solar term	26 WARM	27 CLEAR	28 SUMMER	29 GRAIN		1 HEAT	3 FALL	5 DEW	5 C DEW	7 WINTER	6 SNOW	7 CHILL
Time	5:13	10:16	3:50	8:12		18:35	4:17	7:10	23:28	1:20	18:01	5:09

(center stacked label: DAY OF MON)

Day	JAN	FEB	MAR	APR	MAY	JUN	JUL	AUG	SEP	OCT	NOV	DEC
1	2/9 TM	3/10 rg	4/9 rd	5/9 rg	6/7 RF	7/7 RR	8/6 RF	9/4 mr	10/4 mf	11/2 MH	12/2 MW	12/31 em
2	2/10 tm	3/11 TT	4/10 TM	5/10 TT	6/8 rd	7/8 rg	8/7 rd	9/5 RR	10/5 RF	11/3 mr	12/3 mf	1/1 MH
3	2/11 FH	3/12 tt	4/11 tm	5/11 tt	6/9 TM	7/9 TT	8/8 TM	9/6 rg	10/6 rd	11/4 RR	12/4 RF	1/2 mr
4	2/12 fr	3/13 FW	4/12 FH	5/12 FW	6/10 tm	7/10 tt	8/9 tm	9/7 TT	10/7 TM	11/5 rg	12/5 rd	1/3 RR
5	2/13 ER	3/14 ff	4/13 fr	5/13 ff	6/11 FH	7/11 FW	8/10 FH	9/8 tt	10/8 tm	11/6 TT	12/6 TM	1/4 rg
6	2/14 eg	3/15 EF	4/14 ER	5/14 EF	6/12 fr	7/12 ff	8/11 fr	9/9 FW	10/9 FH	11/7 tt	12/7 tm	1/5 TT
7	2/15 MT	3/16 ed	4/15 eg	5/15 ed	6/13 ER	7/13 EF	8/12 ER	9/10 ff	10/10 fr	11/8 FW	12/8 FH	1/6 tt
8	2/16 mt	3/17 MM	4/16 MT	5/16 MM	6/14 eg	7/14 ed	8/13 eg	9/11 EF	10/11 ER	11/9 ff	12/9 fr	1/7 FW
9	2/17 RW	3/18 mm	4/17 mt	5/17 mm	6/15 MT	7/15 MM	8/14 MT	9/12 ed	10/12 eg	11/10 EF	12/10 ER	1/8 ff
10	2/18 rf	3/19 RH	4/18 RW	5/18 RH	6/16 mt	7/16 mm	8/15 mt	9/13 MM	10/13 MT	11/11 ed	12/11 eg	1/9 EF
11	2/19 TF	3/20 rr	4/19 rf	5/19 rr	6/17 RW	7/17 RH	8/16 RW	9/14 mm	10/14 mt	11/12 MM	12/12 MT	1/10 ed
12	2/20 td	3/21 TR	4/20 TF	5/20 TR	6/18 rf	7/18 rr	8/17 rf	9/15 RH	10/15 RW	11/13 mm	12/13 mt	1/11 MM
13	2/21 FM	3/22 tg	4/21 td	5/21 tg	6/19 TF	7/19 TR	8/18 TF	9/16 rr	10/16 rf	11/14 RH	12/14 RW	1/12 mm
14	2/22 fm	3/23 FT	4/22 FM	5/22 FT	6/20 td	7/20 tg	8/19 td	9/17 TR	10/17 TF	11/15 rr	12/15 rf	1/13 RH
15	2/23 EH	3/24 ft	4/23 fm	5/23 ft	6/21 FM	7/21 FT	8/20 FM	9/18 tg	10/18 td	11/16 TR	12/16 TF	1/14 rr
16	2/24 er	3/25 EW	4/24 EH	5/24 EW	6/22 fm	7/22 ft	8/21 fm	9/19 FT	10/19 FM	11/17 tg	12/17 td	1/15 TR
17	2/25 MR	3/26 ef	4/25 er	5/25 ef	6/23 EH	7/23 EW	8/22 EH	9/20 ft	10/20 fm	11/18 FT	12/18 FM	1/16 tg
18	2/26 mg	3/27 MF	4/26 MR	5/26 MF	6/24 er	7/24 ef	8/23 er	9/21 EW	10/21 EH	11/19 ft	12/19 fm	1/17 FT
19	2/27 RT	3/28 md	4/27 mg	5/27 md	6/25 MR	7/25 MF	8/24 MR	9/22 ef	10/22 er	11/20 EW	12/20 EH	1/18 ft
20	2/28 rt	3/29 RM	4/28 RT	5/28 RM	6/26 mg	7/26 md	8/25 mg	9/23 MF	10/23 MR	11/21 ef	12/21 er	1/19 EW
21	3/1 TW	3/30 rm	4/29 rt	5/29 rm	6/27 RT	7/27 RM	8/26 RT	9/24 md	10/24 mg	11/22 MF	12/22 MR	1/20 ef
22	3/2 tf	3/31 TH	4/30 TW	5/30 TH	6/28 rt	7/28 rm	8/27 rt	9/25 RM	10/25 RT	11/23 md	12/23 mg	1/21 MF
23	3/3 FF	4/1 tr	5/1 tf	5/31 tr	6/29 TW	7/29 TH	8/28 TW	9/26 rm	10/26 rt	11/24 RM	12/24 RT	1/22 md
24	3/4 fd	4/2 FR	5/2 FF	6/1 FR	6/30 tf	7/30 tr	8/29 tf	9/27 TH	10/27 TW	11/25 rm	12/25 rt	1/23 RM
25	3/5 EM	4/3 fg	5/3 fd	6/2 fg	7/1 FF	7/31 FR	8/30 FF	9/28 tr	10/28 tf	11/26 TH	12/26 TW	1/24 rm
26	3/6 em	4/4 ET	5/4 EM	6/3 ET	7/2 fd	8/1 fg	8/31 fd	9/29 FR	10/29 FF	11/27 tr	12/27 tf	1/25 TH
27	3/7 MH	4/5 et	5/5 em	6/4 et	7/3 EM	8/2 ET	9/1 EM	9/30 fg	10/30 fd	11/28 FR	12/28 FF	1/26 tr
28	3/8 mr	4/6 MW	5/6 MH	6/5 MW	7/4 em	8/3 et	9/2 em	10/1 ET	10/31 EM	11/29 fg	12/29 fd	1/27 FR
29	3/9 RR	4/7 mf	5/7 mr	6/6 mf	7/5 MH	8/4 MW	9/3 MH	10/2 et	11/1 em	11/30 ET	12/30 EM	1/28 fg
30		4/8 RF	5/8 RR		7/6 mr	8/5 mf		10/3 MW		12/1 et		

1987 ft RAT

JAN RT	FEB rt	MAR TW	APR tf	MAY FF	JUN fd	JUN fd	DAY	JUL EM	AUG em	SEP MH	OCT mr	NOV RR	DEC rg
7 SPRING	7 WARM	8 CLEAR	9 SUMMER	11 GRAIN	13 HEAT	14 FALL	OF	16 DEW	17 C DEW	17 WINTER	18 SNOW	17 CHILL	17 SPRING
16:50	10:59	16:03	9:37	13:59	0:22	10:04	MON	13:33	5:17	7:07	0:49	11:32	22:38
2 29 ET	2 28 EM	3 29 fg	4 28 fd	5 27 FR	6 26 FF	7 26 FR	1	8 24 tf	9 23 tr	10 23 tf	11 21 TH	12 21 TW	1 19 rm
2 30 et	3 1 em	3 30 ET	4 29 EM	5 28 fg	6 27 fd	7 27 fg	2	8 25 FF	9 24 FR	10 24 FF	11 22 tr	12 22 tf	1 20 TH
2 31 MW	3 2 MH	3 31 et	4 30 em	5 29 ET	6 28 EM	7 28 ET	3	8 26 fd	9 25 fg	10 25 fd	11 23 FR	12 23 FF	1 21 tr
2 1 mf	3 3 mr	4 1 MW	5 1 MH	5 30 et	6 29 et	7 29 et	4	8 27 EM	9 26 ET	10 26 EM	11 24 fg	12 24 fd	1 22 FR
2 2 RF	3 4 RR	4 2 mf	5 2 mr	5 31 MW	6 30 MW	7 30 MW	5	8 28 em	9 27 et	10 27 em	11 25 ET	12 25 EM	1 23 fg
2 3 rd	3 5 rg	4 3 RF	5 3 RF	6 1 mf	7 1 mr	8 1 mf	6	8 29 MH	9 28 MW	10 28 MH	11 26 et	12 26 em	1 24 ET
2 4 TM	3 6 TT	4 4 rd	5 4 rd	6 2 RF	7 2 RR	8 2 RF	7	8 30 mr	9 29 mf	10 29 mr	11 27 MW	12 27 MH	1 25 et
2 5 tm	3 7 tt	4 5 TM	5 5 TM	6 3 rd	7 3 rg	8 3 rd	8	8 31 RR	9 30 RF	10 30 RR	11 28 mf	12 28 mr	1 26 MW
2 6 FH	3 8 FW	4 6 tm	5 6 tm	6 4 TM	7 4 TM	8 4 TM	9	9 1 rg	9 31 rd	10 31 rg	11 29 RF	12 29 RR	1 27 mf
2 7 fr	3 9 ff	4 7 FH	5 7 FH	6 5 tm	7 5 tm	8 5 tm	10	9 2 TT	10 1 TM	11 1 TT	11 30 rd	12 30 rg	1 28 RF
2 8 ER	3 10 EF	4 8 ff	5 8 ff	6 6 FH	7 6 FH	8 6 FH	11	9 3 tt	10 2 tm	11 2 tt	12 1 TM	12 31 TT	1 29 rd
2 9 eg	3 11 ed	4 9 ER	5 9 ER	6 7 fr	7 7 fr	8 7 fr	12	9 4 FW	10 3 FH	11 3 FW	12 2 tm	1 1 tt	1 30 TM
2 10 MT	3 12 MM	4 10 ed	5 10 ed	6 8 ER	7 8 ER	8 8 ER	13	9 5 ff	10 4 fr	11 4 ff	12 3 FH	1 2 FW	1 31 tm
2 11 mt	3 13 mm	4 11 MT	5 11 MM	6 9 eg	7 9 eg	8 9 eg	14	9 6 EF	10 5 ER	11 5 EF	12 4 fr	1 3 ff	2 1 FH
2 12 RW	3 14 RH	4 12 mt	5 12 mm	6 10 MT	7 10 MT	8 10 MM	15	9 7 ed	10 6 eg	11 6 ed	12 5 ER	1 4 EF	2 2 fr
2 13 rf	3 15 rr	4 13 RW	5 13 RH	6 11 mt	7 11 mt	8 11 mm	16	9 8 MM	10 7 MT	11 7 MM	12 6 eg	1 5 ed	2 3 ER
2 14 TF	3 16 TR	4 14 rf	5 14 rr	6 12 RW	7 12 RW	8 12 RH	17	9 9 mm	10 8 mt	11 8 mm	12 7 MT	1 6 MM	2 4 eg
2 15 td	3 17 tg	4 15 TF	5 15 TR	6 13 rf	7 13 rf	8 13 rr	18	9 10 RH	10 9 RW	11 9 RH	12 8 mt	1 7 mm	2 5 MT
2 16 FM	3 18 FT	4 16 td	5 16 tg	6 14 TF	7 14 TF	8 14 TR	19	9 11 rr	10 10 rf	11 10 rr	12 9 RW	1 8 RH	2 6 mt
2 17 fm	3 19 ft	4 17 FM	5 17 FT	6 15 td	7 15 td	8 15 tg	20	9 12 TR	10 11 TF	11 11 TR	12 10 rf	1 9 rr	2 7 RW
2 18 EH	3 20 EW	4 18 fm	5 18 ft	6 16 FM	7 16 FM	8 16 FT	21	9 13 tg	10 12 td	11 12 tg	12 11 TF	1 10 TR	2 8 rf
2 19 er	3 21 ef	4 19 EH	5 19 EW	6 17 fm	7 17 fm	8 17 ft	22	9 14 FT	10 13 FM	11 13 FT	12 12 td	1 11 tg	2 9 TF
2 20 MR	3 22 MF	4 20 er	5 20 ef	6 18 EH	7 18 EH	8 18 EH	23	9 15 ft	10 14 fm	11 14 ft	12 13 FM	1 12 FT	2 10 td
2 21 mg	3 23 md	4 21 MR	5 21 MF	6 19 er	7 19 er	8 19 ef	24	9 16 EW	10 15 EH	11 15 EW	12 14 fm	1 13 ft	2 11 FM
2 22 RT	3 24 RM	4 22 mg	5 22 md	6 20 MR	7 20 MR	8 20 MF	25	9 17 ef	10 16 er	11 16 ef	12 15 EH	1 14 EW	2 12 fm
2 23 rt	3 25 rm	4 23 RM	5 23 RM	6 21 mg	7 21 mg	8 21 md	26	9 18 MF	10 17 MR	11 17 MF	12 16 er	1 15 ef	2 13 EH
2 24 TW	3 26 TH	4 24 rt	5 24 rm	6 22 RT	7 22 RT	8 22 RM	27	9 19 md	10 18 mg	11 18 md	12 17 MR	1 16 MF	2 14 er
2 25 tf	3 27 tr	4 25 TW	5 25 TH	6 23 rt	7 23 rt	8 23 rm	28	9 20 RM	10 19 RT	11 19 RM	12 18 mg	1 17 md	2 15 MR
2 26 FF	3 28 FR	4 26 tf	5 26 tr	6 24 TW	7 24 TW	8 24 TH	29	9 21 rm	10 20 rt	11 20 rm	12 19 RT	1 18 RM	2 16 mg
2 27 fd		4 27 FF		6 25 tf	7 25 tf	8 25 tr	30	9 22 TH	10 21 TW		12 20 rt		
									10 22 TW				

1988 EW DRAGON

	JAN	FEB	MAR	APR	MAY	JUN	JUL	DAY OF MON	AUG	SEP	OCT	NOV	DEC
	TT	tt	FW	ff	EF	ed	MM		mm	RH	rr	TR	tg
	18 WARM	18 CLEAR	20 SUMMER	21 GRAIN	24 HEAT	25 FALL	27 DEW		28 C DEW	28 WINTER	29 SNOW	28 CHILL	28 SPRING
	16:48	21:51	15:25	19:47	6:10	15:52	19:18		11:06	14:10	5:35	17:21	4:36
	17 RT	18 RM	16 mg	16 md	14 MR	14 MF	12 er	1	11 ef	11 er	9 EW	9 EH	8 EW
	18 rt	19 rm	17 RT	17 RM	15 mg	15 md	13 MR	2	12 MF	12 MR	10 ef	10 er	9 ef
	19 TW	20 TH	18 tr	18 rm	16 RT	16 RM	14 mg	3	13 md	13 mg	11 MF	11 MR	10 MF
	20 tf	21 tr	19 TW	19 TH	17 rt	17 rm	15 RT	4	14 RM	14 RT	12 md	12 mg	11 md
	21 FF	22 FR	20 tf	20 tr	18 TW	18 TH	16 rt	5	15 rm	15 rt	13 RM	13 RT	12 RM
	22 fd	23 fg	21 FF	21 FR	19 tf	19 tr	17 TW	6	16 TH	16 TW	14 rm	14 rt	13 rm
	23 EM	24 ET	22 fd	22 fg	20 FF	20 FR	18 tf	7	17 tr	17 tf	15 TH	15 TW	14 TH
	24 em	25 em	23 EM	23 ET	21 fd	21 fg	19 FR	8	18 FR	18 FF	16 tf	16 tf	15 tr
	25 MH	26 MW	24 em	24 et	22 EM	22 ET	20 fd	9	19 fd	19 fd	17 FF	17 FF	16 FR
	26 mr	27 mf	25 MW	25 MW	23 em	23 et	21 EM	10	20 ET	20 EM	18 fd	18 fd	17 fg
	27 RR	28 RF	26 mr	26 mf	24 MH	24 MW	22 em	11	21 et	21 em	19 ET	19 EM	18 ET
	28 rg	29 rd	27 RR	27 RF	25 mr	25 mf	23 MH	12	22 MW	22 MH	20 et	20 em	19 et
	29 tt	30 TM	28 rg	28 rg	26 RR	26 RF	24 mr	13	23 mr	23 mr	21 MW	21 MH	20 MW
	1 FW	31 tm	29 TT	29 TM	27 rg	27 rd	25 RR	14	24 RF	24 RR	22 mr	22 mr	21 mf
	2 ff	1 FH	30 tt	30 tm	28 TT	28 TM	26 rg	15	25 rd	25 rg	23 RF	23 RR	22 RF
	3 EF	2 fr	31 FW	31 FH	29 tt	29 tm	27 TT	16	26 TM	26 TT	24 rd	24 rg	23 rd
	4 ef	3 ER	1 FW	1 fr	30 FW	30 FH	28 tt	17	27 tm	27 tt	25 TM	25 TT	24 TM
	5 MM	4 ed	2 ff	2 ER	31 ff	31 FF	29 FW	18	28 FH	28 FW	26 TM	26 tt	25 tm
	6 mm	5 MT	3 EF	3 ER	1 ER	1 ER	30 ff	19	29 FH	29 ff	27 TM	27 FW	26 FH
	7 RH	6 mt	4 ed	4 MT	2 EF	2 EF	31 ER	20	30 ER	30 EF	28 fr	28 ff	27 fr
	8 rr	7 RW	5 MM	5 mt	3 ed	3 ed	1 ER	21	1 eg	31 ed	29 ER	29 EF	28 ER
	9 TR	8 rf	6 mm	6 RW	4 MM	4 MM	2 eg	22	2 MT	1 MM	30 eg	30 ed	29 eg
	10 tg	9 TF	7 RH	7 rf	5 mm	5 mt	3 MT	23	3 mt	2 mm	1 MT	31 MM	30 eg
	11 FT	10 td	8 rf	8 TF	6 RH	6 RH	4 mt	24	4 RH	3 mm	2 mt	1 mm	31 mt
	12 ft	11 FM	9 TR	9 td	7 rf	7 rf	5 RH	25	5 rf	4 RH	3 RW	2 RH	1 RW
	13 EW	12 fm	10 tg	10 FM	8 TR	8 TF	6 rr	26	6 TF	5 rr	4 rf	3 rr	2 rf
	14 ew	13 EH	11 FT	11 fm	9 tg	9 tg	7 TR	27	7 td	6 TR	5 TF	4 TR	3 TF
	15 ef	14 er	12 ft	12 EH	10 FT	10 FT	8 tg	28	8 FM	7 tg	6 td	5 tg	4 td
	16 MF	15 MR	13 EW	13 er	11 ft	11 fm	9 ft	29	9 fm	8 FT	7 FM	6 FT	5 FM
	17 md		14 ef		12 EH	11 EH	9 fm	30	10 EH		8 fm	7 ft	
			15 MF		13 ef		10 EW	31					

233

1989 ef SNAKE

JAN FT	FEB ft	MAR EW	APR ef	MAY MF	JUN md	JUL RM	AUG rm	SEP TH	OCT tr	NOV FR	DEC fg
28 WARM	29 CLEAR		1 SUMMER	3 GRAIN	5 HEAT	7 FALL	9 DEW	9 C DEW	10 WINTER	10 SNOW	9 CHILL
22:36	3:39		21:13	1:35	11:58	21:41	1:07	15:49	19:59	11:24	23:12

JAN FT	FEB ft	MAR EW	APR ef	MAY MF	JUN md	JUL RM	AUG rm	SEP TH	OCT tr	NOV FR	DEC fg
2 6 fm	3 8 ft	4 6 tg	5 5 tg	6 4 td	7 3 TR	8 1 rf	9 31 rr	9 30 rf	10 29 RH	11 28 RW	12 28 RH
2 7 EH	3 9 EW	4 7 FT	5 6 FT	6 5 FM	7 4 tg	8 2 TF	9 1 TR	10 1 TF	10 30 rr	11 29 rf	12 29 rr
2 8 er	3 10 ef	4 8 ft	5 7 ft	6 6 fm	7 5 FT	8 3 td	9 2 tg	10 2 td	10 31 TR	11 30 TF	12 30 TR
2 9 MR	3 11 MF	4 9 EW	5 8 EW	6 7 EH	7 6 ft	8 4 FM	9 3 FT	10 3 FM	11 1 tg	12 1 td	12 31 tg
2 10 mg	3 12 md	4 10 er	5 9 ef	6 8 er	7 7 EW	8 5 fm	9 4 ft	10 4 fm	11 2 FT	12 2 FM	1 1 FT
2 11 RT	3 13 RM	4 11 mg	5 10 MR	6 9 EH	7 8 er	8 6 EH	9 5 EH	10 5 EH	11 3 td	12 3 fm	1 2 ft
2 12 tr	3 14 RM	4 12 RT	5 11 md	6 10 mg	7 9 MF	8 7 er	9 6 ef	10 6 er	11 4 EW	12 4 EH	1 3 EW
2 13 TW	3 15 TH	4 13 rt	5 12 RM	6 11 RT	7 10 md	8 8 MR	9 7 MF	10 7 MR	11 5 ef	12 5 er	1 4 ef
2 14 tf	3 16 tr	4 14 TW	5 13 rm	6 12 rt	7 11 RM	8 9 mg	9 8 md	10 8 mg	11 6 MF	12 6 MR	1 5 MF
2 15 FF	3 17 FR	4 15 tf	5 14 TH	6 13 TW	7 12 rm	8 10 RT	9 9 RM	10 9 RT	11 7 md	12 7 mg	1 6 md
2 16 fd	3 18 fg	4 16 FF	5 15 tr	6 14 tf	7 13 tr	8 11 rt	9 10 RT	10 10 rm	11 8 RT	12 8 RT	1 7 RM
2 17 EM	3 19 ET	4 17 fd	5 16 FR	6 15 FF	7 14 tr	8 12 TW	9 11 TW	10 11 TH	11 9 rm	12 9 rt	1 8 rm
2 18 em	3 20 et	4 18 EM	5 17 fg	6 16 fd	7 15 FR	8 13 tf	9 12 tf	10 12 tr	11 10 TH	12 10 TW	1 9 TH
2 19 MH	3 21 MW	4 19 em	5 18 ET	6 17 EM	7 16 fg	8 14 FF	9 13 FR	10 13 FR	11 11 tr	12 11 tf	1 10 tr
2 20 mr	3 22 mf	4 20 MH	5 19 et	6 18 em	7 17 ET	8 15 fd	9 14 fg	10 14 fd	11 12 FR	12 12 FF	1 11 FR
2 21 RR	3 23 RF	4 21 mr	5 20 MH	6 19 MH	7 18 et	8 16 EM	9 15 EM	10 15 EM	11 13 fd	12 13 fd	1 12 fg
2 22 rg	3 24 rd	4 22 RR	5 21 mf	6 20 mr	7 19 MW	8 17 em	9 16 em	10 16 ET	11 14 ET	12 14 ET	1 13 ET
2 23 TT	3 25 TM	4 23 rg	5 22 RF	6 21 RR	7 20 mf	8 18 MH	9 17 MH	10 17 et	11 15 em	12 15 et	1 14 et
2 24 tt	3 26 tm	4 24 TT	5 23 rd	6 22 rg	7 21 RF	8 19 mr	9 18 mf	10 18 MW	11 16 MH	12 16 MW	1 15 MW
2 25 FW	3 27 FH	4 25 tt	5 24 TM	6 23 TT	7 22 rd	8 20 RR	9 19 mr	10 19 mf	11 17 mr	12 17 mf	1 16 mf
2 26 ff	3 28 fr	4 26 FW	5 25 tm	6 24 tm	7 23 rg	8 21 rg	9 20 RR	10 20 RF	11 18 RR	12 18 RR	1 17 RF
2 27 EF	3 29 ER	4 27 ff	5 26 FH	6 25 FW	7 24 tm	8 22 TT	9 21 rg	10 21 rd	11 19 mr	12 19 mr	1 18 RF
2 28 ed	3 30 eg	4 28 EF	5 27 fr	6 26 ff	7 25 FH	8 23 tt	9 22 TT	10 22 TM	11 20 rg	12 20 rd	1 19 TM
3 1 MM	3 31 MT	4 29 ed	5 28 ER	6 27 EF	7 26 fr	8 24 FW	9 23 tt	10 23 tm	11 21 TT	12 20 TT	1 20 tm
3 2 mm	4 1 mt	4 30 MM	5 29 eg	6 28 ed	7 27 ER	8 25 ff	9 24 FW	10 24 FH	11 22 tt	12 21 tt	1 21 FH
3 3 RH	4 2 RW	5 1 mm	5 30 MT	6 29 MM	7 28 eg	8 26 EF	9 25 ff	10 25 fr	11 23 FW	12 22 FW	1 22 FH
3 4 rr	4 3 rf	5 2 RH	5 31 mt	6 30 mm	7 29 MT	8 27 ed	9 26 EF	10 26 ER	11 24 ff	12 23 ff	1 23 ER
3 5 TR	4 4 TF	5 3 rr	6 1 RW	7 1 RH	7 30 mt	8 28 MM	9 27 ed	10 27 eg	11 25 EF	12 24 EF	1 24 eg
3 6 tg	4 5 td	5 4 TR	6 2 rf	7 2 rr	7 31 RW	8 29 mm	9 28 MM	10 28 MT	11 26 ed	12 25 ed	1 25 MT
3 7 FT			6 3 TF			8 30 RH	9 29 mm		11 27 mt	12 26 MM	1 26 mt

234

JAN ET	FEB et	MAR MW	APR mf	MAY RF	MAY RF	JUN rd	DAY OF MON	JUL TM	AUG fm	SEP FH	OCT fr	NOV ER	DEC eg
9 SPRING	10 WARM	10 CLEAR	12 SUMMER	14 GRAIN	15 HEAT	18 FALL		20 DEW	20 C DEW	22 WINTER	21 SNOW	21 CHILL	20 SPRING
10:15	4:25	9:28	2:53	7:24	17:47	3:30		6:14	21:38	1:49	17:13	5:01	16:04
1 27 RW	2 25 mm	3 27 mt	4 25 MM	5 24 eg	6 23 ed	7 22 ER	1	8 20 ff	9 19 fr	10 18 FW	11 17 FH	12 17 FW	1 16 FH
1 28 rf	2 26 RH	3 28 RW	4 26 mm	5 25 MT	6 24 MM	7 23 eg	2	8 21 EF	9 20 ER	10 19 ff	11 18 fr	12 18 ff	1 17 fr
1 29 TF	2 27 rr	3 29 rf	4 27 RH	5 26 mt	6 25 mm	7 24 MT	3	8 22 ed	9 21 eg	10 20 EF	11 19 ER	12 19 EF	1 18 ER
1 30 td	2 28 TR	3 30 TF	4 28 rr	5 27 RW	6 26 RH	7 25 mt	4	8 23 MM	9 22 MT	10 21 ed	11 20 eg	12 20 ed	1 19 eg
1 31 FM	3 1 tg	3 31 td	4 29 TR	5 28 rf	6 27 rr	7 26 RW	5	8 24 mm	9 23 mt	10 22 MM	11 21 MT	12 21 MM	1 20 MT
2 1 fm	3 2 FT	4 1 FM	4 30 tg	5 29 TF	6 28 TR	7 27 rf	6	8 25 RH	9 24 RW	10 23 mm	11 22 mt	12 22 mm	1 21 mt
2 2 EH	3 3 ft	4 2 fm	5 1 FT	5 30 td	6 29 tg	7 28 TF	7	8 26 rr	9 25 rf	10 24 RH	11 23 RW	12 23 RH	1 22 RW
2 3 er	3 4 EW	4 3 EH	5 2 ft	5 31 FM	6 30 FT	7 29 td	8	8 27 TR	9 26 TF	10 25 rr	11 24 rf	12 24 rr	1 23 rf
2 4 MR	3 5 ef	4 4 er	5 3 EW	6 1 fm	7 1 ft	7 30 FM	9	8 28 tg	9 27 td	10 26 TR	11 25 TF	12 25 TR	1 24 TF
2 5 mg	3 6 MF	4 5 MR	5 4 ef	6 2 EH	7 2 EW	7 31 fm	10	8 29 FT	9 28 FM	10 27 tg	11 26 td	12 26 tg	1 25 td
2 6 RT	3 7 md	4 6 mg	5 5 MF	6 3 er	7 3 ef	8 1 EH	11	8 30 ft	9 29 fm	10 28 FT	11 27 FM	12 27 FT	1 26 FM
2 7 rt	3 8 RM	4 7 RT	5 6 md	6 4 MR	7 4 MF	8 2 er	12	8 31 EW	9 30 EH	10 29 ft	11 28 fm	12 28 ft	1 27 fm
2 8 TW	3 9 rm	4 8 rt	5 7 RM	6 5 mg	7 5 md	8 3 MR	13	9 1 ef	10 1 er	10 30 EW	11 29 EH	12 29 EW	1 28 EH
2 9 tf	3 10 TH	4 9 TW	5 8 rm	6 6 RT	7 6 RM	8 4 mg	14	9 2 MF	10 2 MR	10 31 ef	11 30 er	12 30 ef	1 29 er
2 10 FF	3 11 tr	4 10 tf	5 9 TH	6 7 rt	7 7 rm	8 5 RT	15	9 3 md	10 3 mg	11 1 MF	12 1 MR	12 31 MF	1 30 MR
2 11 fd	3 12 FR	4 11 FF	5 10 tr	6 8 TW	7 8 TH	8 6 rt	16	9 4 RM	10 4 RT	11 2 md	12 2 mg	1 1 md	1 31 mg
2 12 EM	3 13 fg	4 12 fd	5 11 FR	6 9 tf	7 9 tr	8 7 TW	17	9 5 rm	10 5 rt	11 3 RM	12 3 RT	1 2 RM	2 1 RT
2 13 em	3 14 ET	4 13 EM	5 12 fg	6 10 FF	7 10 FR	8 8 tf	18	9 6 TH	10 6 TW	11 4 rm	12 4 rt	1 3 rm	2 2 rt
2 14 MH	3 15 et	4 14 em	5 13 ET	6 11 fd	7 11 fg	8 9 FF	19	9 7 tr	10 7 tf	11 5 TH	12 5 TW	1 4 TH	2 3 TW
2 15 mr	3 16 MW	4 15 MH	5 14 et	6 12 EM	7 12 ET	8 10 fd	20	9 8 FR	10 8 FF	11 6 tr	12 6 tf	1 5 tr	2 4 tf
2 16 RR	3 17 mf	4 16 mr	5 15 MW	6 13 em	7 13 et	8 11 EM	21	9 9 fg	10 9 fd	11 7 FR	12 7 FF	1 6 FR	2 5 FF
2 17 rg	3 18 RF	4 17 RR	5 16 mf	6 14 MH	7 14 MW	8 12 em	22	9 10 ET	10 10 EM	11 8 fg	12 8 fd	1 7 fg	2 6 fd
2 18 TT	3 19 rd	4 18 rg	5 17 RF	6 15 mr	7 15 mf	8 13 MH	23	9 11 et	10 11 em	11 9 ET	12 9 EM	1 8 ET	2 7 EM
2 19 tt	3 20 TM	4 19 TT	5 18 rd	6 16 RR	7 16 RF	8 14 mr	24	9 12 MW	10 12 MH	11 10 et	12 10 em	1 9 et	2 8 em
2 20 FW	3 21 tm	4 20 tt	5 19 TM	6 17 rg	7 17 rd	8 15 RR	25	9 13 mf	10 13 mr	11 11 MW	12 11 MH	1 10 MW	2 9 MH
2 21 ff	3 22 FH	4 21 FW	5 20 tm	6 18 TT	7 18 TM	8 16 rg	26	9 14 RF	10 14 RR	11 12 mf	12 12 mr	1 11 mf	2 10 mr
2 22 EF	3 23 fr	4 22 ff	5 21 FH	6 19 tt	7 19 tm	8 17 TT	27	9 15 rd	10 15 rg	11 13 RF	12 13 RR	1 12 RF	2 11 RR
2 23 ed	3 24 ER	4 23 EF	5 22 fr	6 20 FW	7 20 FH	8 18 tt	28	9 16 TM	10 16 TT	11 14 rd	12 14 rg	1 13 rd	2 12 rg
2 24 MM	3 25 eg	4 24 ed	5 23 ER	6 21 ff	7 21 fr	8 19 FW	29	9 17 tm	10 17 tt	11 15 TM	12 15 TT	1 14 TM	2 13 TT
	3 26 MT			6 22 EF			30	9 18 FH		11 16 tm	12 16 tt	1 15 tm	2 14 tt

1991 md RAM

Month headers and solar-term data:

Month	Code	Term no.	Term	Time
JAN	MT	20	WARM	10:14
FEB	mt	21	CLEAR	15:17
MAR	RW	22	SUMMER	8:51
APR	rf	24	GRAIN	13:14
MAY	TF	26	HEAT	23:37
JUN	td	28	FALL	9:20
JUL	FM		DAY OF MON	
AUG	fm	1	DEW	12:04
SEP	EH	2	C DEW	3:28
OCT	er	3	WINTER	7:39
NOV	MR	3	SNOW	0:08
DEC	mg	2	CHILL	10:12

Calendar grid (each cell: lunar-month / lunar-day / code):

#	JAN	FEB	MAR	APR	MAY	JUN	DAY OF MON	JUL	AUG	SEP	OCT	NOV	DEC
1	2 15 FW	3 16 tm	4 15 tt	5 14 TM	6 12 rg	7 12 rd	1	8 10 RR	9 8 mf	10 8 mr	11 6 MW	12 6 MH	1 5 MW
2	2 16 ff	3 17 FH	4 16 FW	5 15 tm	6 13 TT	7 13 TM	2	8 11 rg	9 9 RF	10 9 RR	11 7 mf	12 7 mr	1 6 mf
3	2 17 EF	3 18 fr	4 17 ff	5 16 FH	6 14 tt	7 14 tm	3	8 12 TT	9 10 rd	10 10 rg	11 8 RF	12 8 RR	1 7 RF
4	2 18 ed	3 19 ER	4 18 EF	5 17 fr	6 15 FW	7 15 FH	4	8 13 tt	9 11 TM	10 11 TT	11 9 rd	12 9 rg	1 8 rd
5	2 19 MM	3 20 eg	4 19 ed	5 18 ER	6 16 ff	7 16 fr	5	8 14 FW	9 12 tm	10 12 tt	11 10 TM	12 10 TT	1 9 TT
6	2 20 mm	3 21 MT	4 20 MM	5 19 eg	6 17 EF	7 17 ER	6	8 15 ff	9 13 FW	10 13 FW	11 11 tm	12 11 tt	1 10 tm
7	2 21 RH	3 22 mt	4 21 mt	5 20 MM	6 18 ed	7 18 eg	7	8 16 EF	9 14 fr	10 14 ff	11 12 FH	12 12 FW	1 11 FH
8	2 22 rr	3 23 RW	4 22 RH	5 21 mt	6 19 MM	7 19 MT	8	8 17 ed	9 15 ER	10 15 EF	11 13 fr	12 13 ff	1 12 fr
9	2 23 TR	3 24 rf	4 23 rr	5 22 RW	6 20 mm	7 20 mt	9	8 18 MM	9 16 eg	10 16 ed	11 14 ER	12 14 EF	1 13 ER
10	2 24 tg	3 25 TF	4 24 TR	5 23 rf	6 21 RH	7 21 RW	10	8 19 mm	9 17 MT	10 17 MM	11 15 eg	12 15 ed	1 14 eg
11	2 25 FT	3 26 td	4 25 tg	5 24 TR	6 22 rf	7 22 rf	11	8 20 RH	9 18 mt	10 18 mm	11 16 MT	12 16 MM	1 15 MT
12	2 26 ft	3 27 FM	4 26 FT	5 25 tg	6 23 TF	7 23 TF	12	8 21 rr	9 19 RW	10 19 RH	11 17 mt	12 17 mm	1 16 mt
13	2 27 EW	3 28 fm	4 27 ft	5 26 FT	6 24 tg	7 24 tg	13	8 22 TR	9 20 rf	10 20 rr	11 18 RW	12 18 RH	1 17 RW
14	2 28 ef	3 29 EH	4 28 EW	5 27 ft	6 25 FT	7 25 FT	14	8 23 tg	9 21 TF	10 21 TR	11 19 rf	12 19 rr	1 18 rf
15	3 1 MF	3 30 er	4 29 ef	5 28 EW	6 26 ft	7 26 fm	15	8 24 FT	9 22 td	10 22 tg	11 20 TR	12 20 TR	1 19 TF
16	3 2 md	3 31 MR	4 30 MF	5 29 ef	6 27 FM	7 27 EH	16	8 25 ft	9 23 FT	10 23 FT	11 21 td	12 21 tg	1 20 td
17	3 3 RM	4 1 mg	5 1 md	5 30 MF	6 28 EH	7 28 er	17	8 26 EW	9 24 fm	10 24 ft	11 22 FM	12 22 FT	1 21 FM
18	3 4 rm	4 2 RT	5 2 RM	5 31 er	6 29 er	7 29 MR	18	8 27 ef	9 25 EH	10 25 EW	11 23 fm	12 23 ft	1 22 fm
19	3 5 TH	4 3 rt	5 3 rm	6 1 RT	6 30 md	7 30 mg	19	8 28 MF	9 26 er	10 26 ef	11 24 EH	12 24 EW	1 23 EH
20	3 6 tr	4 4 TW	5 4 TH	6 2 rt	7 1 RM	7 31 RT	20	8 29 md	9 27 MR	10 27 MF	11 25 ef	12 25 ef	1 24 er
21	3 7 FR	4 5 tf	5 5 tr	6 3 TH	7 2 rm	8 1 rt	21	8 30 RM	9 28 md	10 28 md	11 26 MR	12 26 MF	1 25 MR
22	3 8 fg	4 6 FR	5 6 FR	6 4 tf	7 3 TH	8 2 TW	22	8 31 rm	9 29 RM	10 29 RM	11 27 mg	12 27 md	1 26 mg
23	3 9 ET	4 7 fd	5 7 fg	6 5 FF	7 4 tf	8 3 tf	23	9 1 TH	9 30 rm	10 30 rm	11 28 RT	12 28 RM	1 27 RT
24	3 10 et	4 8 EM	5 8 ET	6 6 fd	7 5 FR	8 4 FF	24	9 2 tr	10 1 TW	10 31 TH	11 29 rt	12 29 rm	1 28 rt
25	3 11 MW	4 9 em	5 9 et	6 7 EM	7 6 fg	8 5 fd	25	9 3 FR	10 2 tf	11 1 tr	11 30 tr	12 30 TH	1 29 TW
26	3 12 mf	4 10 MH	5 10 MW	6 8 em	7 7 ET	8 6 EM	26	9 4 fg	10 3 FR	11 2 tf	12 1 tf	12 31 tr	1 30 tf
27	3 13 RF	4 11 mr	5 11 mf	6 9 MH	7 8 et	8 7 em	27	9 5 ET	10 4 fd	11 3 FF	12 2 FR	1 2 FR	1 31 FF
28	3 14 rd	4 12 RR	5 12 RF	6 10 mr	7 9 MW	8 8 MH	28	9 6 et	10 5 ET	11 4 fd	12 3 fg	1 3 fg	2 1 fd
29	3 15 TM	4 13 rg	5 13 rd	6 11 RR	7 10 mf	8 9 mr	29	9 7 MW	10 6 et	11 5 et	12 4 ET	1 4 ET	2 2 EM
30		4 14 TT			7 11 RF		30		10 7 MW		12 5 et	1 5 et	2 3 em

1992 RM MONKEY

JAN RT	FEB rt	MAR TW	APR tf	MAY FF	JUN fd	DAY OF MON	JUL EM	AUG em	SEP MH	OCT mr	NOV RR	DEC rg
1 SPRING	2 WARM	2 CLEAR	3 SUMMER	5 GRAIN	8 HEAT	9 FALL	11 DEW	13 C DEW	13 WINTER	14 SNOW	13 CHILL	
21:54	16:04	20:57	14:41	18:52	5:26	15:09	17:53	9:17	13:28	5:58	16:01	
2 4 MH	2 4 et	4 3 em	5 3 et	6 1 EM	6 30 fg	1	7 30 fd	8 28 FR	9 26 tf	10 26 tr	11 24 TW	12 24 TH
2 5 mr	2 5 MW	4 4 MH	5 4 MW	6 2 em	7 1 ET	2	8 31 EM	8 29 fg	9 27 FF	10 27 FR	11 25 tf	12 25 tr
2 6 RR	2 6 mf	4 5 mr	5 5 mf	6 3 MH	7 2 et	3	8 1 em	8 30 ET	9 28 fd	10 28 fg	11 26 FF	12 26 FR
2 7 rg	2 7 RF	4 6 RR	5 6 RF	6 4 mr	7 3 MW	4	8 2 MH	8 31 et	9 29 EM	10 29 ET	11 27 fd	12 27 fg
2 8 TT	2 8 rd	4 7 rg	5 7 rd	6 5 RR	7 4 mf	5	8 3 mr	9 1 MW	9 30 em	10 30 et	11 28 EM	12 28 ET
2 9 tt	2 9 TM	4 8 TT	5 8 TM	6 6 rg	7 5 RF	6	8 4 RR	9 2 mf	10 1 MH	10 31 MW	11 29 em	12 29 et
2 10 FW	2 10 tm	4 9 tt	5 9 tm	6 7 TT	7 6 rd	7	8 5 rg	9 3 RF	10 2 mr	11 1 mf	11 30 MH	12 30 MW
2 11 ff	2 11 FH	4 10 FW	5 10 FH	6 8 tt	7 7 TM	8	8 6 TT	9 4 rd	10 3 RR	11 2 RF	12 1 mr	12 31 mf
2 12 EF	2 12 fr	4 11 ff	5 11 fr	6 9 FW	7 8 tm	9	8 7 tt	9 5 TM	10 4 rg	11 3 rd	12 2 RR	1 1 RF
2 13 ed	2 13 ER	4 12 EF	5 12 ER	6 10 ff	7 9 FH	10	8 8 FW	9 6 tm	10 5 TT	11 4 TM	12 3 rg	1 2 rd
2 14 MM	2 14 eg	4 13 ed	5 13 eg	6 11 EF	7 10 fr	11	8 9 ff	9 7 FH	10 6 tt	11 5 tm	12 4 TT	1 3 TM
2 15 mm	2 15 MT	4 14 MM	5 14 MT	6 12 ed	7 11 ER	12	8 10 EF	9 8 fr	10 7 FW	11 6 FH	12 5 tt	1 4 tm
2 16 RH	2 16 mt	4 15 mm	5 15 mt	6 13 MM	7 12 eg	13	8 11 ed	9 9 ER	10 8 ff	11 7 fr	12 6 FW	1 5 FH
2 17 rr	2 17 RW	4 16 RH	5 16 RW	6 14 mm	7 13 MT	14	8 12 MM	9 10 eg	10 9 EF	11 8 ER	12 7 ff	1 6 fr
2 18 TR	2 18 rf	4 17 rr	5 17 rf	6 15 RH	7 14 mt	15	8 13 mm	9 11 MT	10 10 ed	11 9 eg	12 8 EF	1 7 ER
2 19 tg	2 19 TF	4 18 TR	5 18 TF	6 16 rr	7 15 RW	16	8 14 RH	9 12 mt	10 11 MM	11 10 MT	12 9 ed	1 8 eg
2 20 FT	2 20 td	4 19 tg	5 19 td	6 17 TR	7 16 rr	17	8 15 rr	9 13 RW	10 12 mm	11 11 mt	12 10 MM	1 9 MT
2 21 ft	2 21 FM	4 20 FT	5 20 FM	6 18 tg	7 17 TR	18	8 16 TR	9 14 rf	10 13 RH	11 12 RW	12 11 mm	1 10 mt
2 22 EW	2 22 fm	4 21 ft	5 21 fm	6 19 FT	7 18 tg	19	8 17 tg	9 15 TF	10 14 rr	11 13 rr	12 12 RH	1 11 RW
2 23 ef	2 23 EH	4 22 EW	5 22 EH	6 20 ft	7 19 FM	20	8 18 FT	9 16 td	10 15 TR	11 14 TF	12 13 rr	1 12 rr
2 24 MF	2 24 er	4 23 ef	5 23 er	6 21 EW	7 20 fm	21	8 19 ft	9 17 FM	10 16 tg	11 15 td	12 14 TR	1 13 TF
2 25 md	2 25 MR	4 24 MF	5 24 MR	6 22 ef	7 21 EH	22	8 20 EW	9 18 fm	10 17 FT	11 16 FM	12 15 tg	1 14 td
2 26 RM	2 26 mg	4 25 md	5 25 mg	6 23 MF	7 22 er	23	8 21 ef	9 19 EH	10 18 ft	11 17 fm	12 16 FT	1 15 FM
2 27 rm	2 27 RT	4 26 RM	5 26 RT	6 24 md	7 23 MR	24	8 22 MF	9 20 er	10 19 EW	11 18 EH	12 17 ft	1 16 fm
2 28 TH	2 28 rt	4 27 rm	5 27 rt	6 25 RM	7 24 mg	25	8 23 md	9 21 MR	10 20 ef	11 19 er	12 18 EW	1 17 EH
2 29 tr	2 29 TW	4 28 TH	5 28 TW	6 26 rm	7 25 RT	26	8 24 RM	9 22 mg	10 21 MF	11 20 MR	12 19 ef	1 18 er
3 1 FR	2 30 tf	4 29 tr	5 29 tf	6 27 TH	7 26 rt	27	8 25 rm	9 23 RT	10 22 md	11 21 mg	12 20 MF	1 19 MR
3 2 fg	2 31 FF	4 30 FR	5 30 FF	6 28 tr	7 27 TW	28	8 26 TH	9 24 rt	10 23 RM	11 22 RT	12 21 md	1 20 mg
3 3 ET	4 1 fd	5 1 fg	5 31 fd	6 29 FR	7 28 tf	29	8 27 tr	9 25 TW	10 24 rm	11 23 rt	12 22 RM	1 21 RT
	4 2 EM	5 2 ET			7 29 FF	30			10 25 TH		12 23 rm	1 22 rt

237

	JAN	FEB	MAR	MAR	APR	MAY	JUN	JUL	AUG	SEP	OCT	NOV	DEC
Code	TT	tt	FW	FW	ff	EF	ed	MM	mm	RH	rr	TR	tg
Term	13 SPRING	13 WARM	14 CLEAR	14 SUMMER	17 GRAIN	18 HEAT	20 FALL	22 DEW	23 C DEW	24 WINTER	24 SNOW	24 CHILL	24 SPRING
Time	3:43	21:53	2:56	20:30	23:40	11:15	21:10	0:20	15:07	19:17	11:47	21:57	9:33

DAY OF MON

Day	JAN	FEB	MAR	MAR	APR	MAY	JUN	JUL	AUG	SEP	OCT	NOV	DEC
1	1 23 TW	2 21 rm	3 23 rt	4 22 rm	5 21 RT	6 20 RM	7 19 mg	8 18 md	9 16 MR	10 15 ef	11 14 er	12 13 EW	1 12 EH
2	1 24 tf	2 22 TH	3 24 TW	4 23 TH	5 22 rt	6 21 rm	7 20 RT	8 19 RM	9 17 mg	10 16 MF	11 15 MR	12 14 ef	1 13 er
3	1 25 FF	2 23 tr	3 25 tf	4 24 tr	5 23 TW	6 22 TH	7 21 rt	8 20 rm	9 18 RT	10 17 md	11 16 mg	12 15 MF	1 14 MR
4	1 26 fd	2 24 FR	3 26 FF	4 25 FR	5 24 tf	6 23 tr	7 22 TW	8 21 TH	9 19 rt	10 18 RM	11 17 RT	12 16 md	1 15 mg
5	1 27 EM	2 25 fg	3 27 fd	4 26 fg	5 25 FF	6 24 FR	7 23 tf	8 22 tr	9 20 TW	10 19 rm	11 18 rt	12 17 RM	1 16 RT
6	1 28 em	2 26 ET	3 28 EM	4 27 ET	5 26 fd	6 25 fg	7 24 FF	8 23 FR	9 21 tf	10 20 TH	11 19 TW	12 18 rm	1 17 rt
7	1 29 MH	2 27 et	3 29 em	4 28 et	5 27 EM	6 26 ET	7 25 fd	8 24 fg	9 22 FF	10 21 tr	11 20 tf	12 19 TH	1 18 TW
8	1 30 mr	2 28 MW	3 30 MH	4 29 MW	5 28 em	6 27 et	7 26 EM	8 25 ET	9 23 fd	10 22 FR	11 21 FF	12 20 tr	1 19 tf
9	1 31 RR	3 1 mf	3 31 mr	4 30 mf	5 29 MH	6 28 MW	7 27 em	8 26 et	9 24 EM	10 23 fg	11 22 fd	12 21 FR	1 20 FF
10	2 1 rg	3 2 RF	4 1 RR	5 1 RF	5 30 mr	6 29 mf	7 28 MH	8 27 MW	9 25 em	10 24 ET	11 23 EM	12 22 fg	1 21 fd
11	2 2 TT	3 3 rd	4 2 rg	5 2 rd	5 31 RR	6 30 RF	7 29 mr	8 28 mf	9 26 MH	10 25 et	11 24 em	12 23 ET	1 22 EM
12	2 3 tt	3 4 TM	4 3 TT	5 3 TM	6 1 rg	7 1 rd	7 30 RR	8 29 RF	9 27 mr	10 26 MW	11 25 MH	12 24 et	1 23 em
13	2 4 FW	3 5 tm	4 4 tt	5 4 tm	6 2 TT	7 2 TM	7 31 rg	8 30 rd	9 28 RR	10 27 mf	11 26 mr	12 25 MW	1 24 MH
14	2 5 ff	3 6 FH	4 5 FW	5 5 FH	6 3 tt	7 3 tm	8 1 TT	8 31 TM	9 29 rg	10 28 RF	11 27 RR	12 26 mf	1 25 mr
15	2 6 EF	3 7 fr	4 6 ff	5 6 fr	6 4 FW	7 4 FH	8 2 tt	9 1 tm	9 30 TT	10 29 rd	11 28 rg	12 27 RF	1 26 RR
16	2 7 ed	3 8 ER	4 7 EF	5 7 ER	6 5 ff	7 5 fr	8 3 FW	9 2 FH	10 1 tt	10 30 TM	11 29 TT	12 28 rd	1 27 rg
17	2 8 MM	3 9 eg	4 8 ed	5 8 eg	6 6 EF	7 6 ER	8 4 ff	9 3 fr	10 2 FW	10 31 tm	11 30 tt	12 29 TM	1 28 TT
18	2 9 mm	3 10 MT	4 9 MM	5 9 MT	6 7 ed	7 7 eg	8 5 EF	9 4 ER	10 3 ff	11 1 FH	12 1 FW	12 30 tm	1 29 tt
19	2 10 RH	3 11 mt	4 10 mm	5 10 mt	6 8 MM	7 8 MT	8 6 ed	9 5 eg	10 4 EF	11 2 fr	12 2 ff	12 31 FH	1 30 FW
20	2 11 rr	3 12 RW	4 11 RH	5 11 RW	6 9 mm	7 9 mt	8 7 MM	9 6 MT	10 5 ed	11 3 ER	12 3 EF	1 1 fr	1 31 ff
21	2 12 TR	3 13 rf	4 12 rr	5 12 rf	6 10 RH	7 10 RW	8 8 mm	9 7 mt	10 6 MM	11 4 eg	12 4 ed	1 2 ER	2 1 EF
22	2 13 tg	3 14 TF	4 13 TR	5 13 TF	6 11 rr	7 11 rf	8 9 RH	9 8 RW	10 7 mm	11 5 MT	12 5 MM	1 3 eg	2 2 ed
23	2 14 FT	3 15 td	4 14 tg	5 14 td	6 12 TR	7 12 TF	8 10 rr	9 9 rf	10 8 RH	11 6 mt	12 6 mm	1 4 MT	2 3 MM
24	2 15 ft	3 16 FM	4 15 FT	5 15 FM	6 13 tg	7 13 td	8 11 TR	9 10 TF	10 9 rr	11 7 RW	12 7 RH	1 5 mt	2 4 mm
25	2 16 EW	3 17 fm	4 16 ft	5 16 fm	6 14 FT	7 14 FM	8 12 tg	9 11 td	10 10 TR	11 8 rf	12 8 rr	1 6 RW	2 5 RH
26	2 17 ef	3 18 EH	4 17 EW	5 17 EH	6 15 ft	7 15 fm	8 13 FT	9 12 FM	10 11 tg	11 9 TF	12 9 TR	1 7 rf	2 6 rr
27	2 18 MF	3 19 er	4 18 ef	5 18 er	6 16 EW	7 16 EH	8 14 ft	9 13 fm	10 12 FT	11 10 td	12 10 tg	1 8 TF	2 7 TR
28	2 19 md	3 20 MR	4 19 MF	5 19 MR	6 17 ef	7 17 er	8 15 EW	9 14 EH	10 13 ft	11 11 FM	12 11 FT	1 9 td	2 8 tg
29	2 20 RM	3 21 mg	4 20 md	5 20 mg	6 18 MF	7 18 MR	8 16 ef	9 15 er	10 14 EW	11 12 fm	12 12 ft	1 10 FM	2 9 FT
30		3 22 RT	4 21 RM		6 19 md		8 17 MF			11 13 EH		1 11 fm	

1994 TH DOG

Day	JAN (FT)	FEB (ft)	MAR (EW)	APR (ef)	MAY (MF)	JUN (md)	JUL (RM)	AUG (rm)	SEP (TH)	OCT (tr)	NOV (FR)	DEC (fg)
term	25 WARM 3:43	25 CLEAR 8:46	26 SUMMER 2:20	27 GRAIN 6:43	29 HEAT 16:55		2 FALL 2:50	3 DEW 5:34	4 C DEW 22:00	6 WINTER 1:06	5 SNOW 17:36	6 CHILL 3:42
1	11/20 ft	12/21 EH	1/20 FT	2/21 fm	3/21 ft	4/22 EH	5/23 EW	6/24 er	7/26 MF	8/26 MR	9/28 md	10/29 mg
2	11/21 EW	12/22 er	1/21 ft	2/22 EH	3/22 EW	4/23 er	5/24 ef	6/25 MR	7/27 md	8/27 mg	9/29 RM	10/30 RT
3	11/22 ef	12/23 MR	1/22 EW	2/23 er	3/23 ef	4/24 MR	5/25 MF	6/26 mg	7/28 RM	8/28 RT	10/1 rm	11/1 rt
4	11/23 MF	12/24 mg	1/23 ef	2/24 MR	3/24 MF	4/25 mg	5/26 md	6/27 RT	7/29 rm	8/29 rt	10/2 TH	11/2 TW
5	11/24 md	12/25 RT	1/24 MF	2/25 mg	3/25 md	4/26 RT	5/27 RM	6/28 rt	7/30 TH	9/1 TW	10/3 tr	11/3 tf
6	11/25 RM	12/26 rt	1/25 md	2/26 RT	3/26 RM	4/27 rt	5/28 rm	6/29 TW	8/1 tr	9/2 tf	10/4 FR	11/4 FF
7	11/26 rm	12/27 TW	1/26 RM	2/27 rt	3/27 rm	4/28 TW	5/29 TH	7/1 tf	8/2 FR	9/3 FF	10/5 fg	11/5 fd
8	11/27 TH	12/28 tf	1/27 rm	2/28 TW	3/28 TH	4/29 tf	5/30 tr	7/2 FF	8/3 fg	9/4 fd	10/6 ET	11/6 EM
9	11/28 tr	12/29 FF	1/28 TH	2/29 tf	3/29 tr	5/1 FF	6/1 FR	7/3 fd	8/4 ET	9/5 EM	10/7 et	11/7 em
10	11/29 FR	1/1 fd	1/29 tr	2/30 FF	3/30 FR	5/2 fd	6/2 fg	7/4 EM	8/5 et	9/6 em	10/8 MW	11/8 MH
11	11/30 fg	1/2 EM	1/30 FR	3/1 fd	4/1 fg	5/3 EM	6/3 ET	7/5 em	8/6 MW	9/7 MH	10/9 mf	11/9 mr
12	12/1 ET	1/3 em	2/1 fg	3/2 EM	4/2 ET	5/4 em	6/4 et	7/6 MH	8/7 mf	9/8 mr	10/10 RF	11/10 RR
13	12/2 et	1/4 MH	2/2 ET	3/3 em	4/3 et	5/5 MH	6/5 MW	7/7 mr	8/8 RF	9/9 RR	10/11 rd	11/11 rg
14	12/3 MW	1/5 mr	2/3 et	3/4 MH	4/4 MW	5/6 mr	6/6 mf	7/8 RR	8/9 rd	9/10 rg	10/12 TM	11/12 TT
15	12/4 mf	1/6 RR	2/4 MW	3/5 mr	4/5 mf	5/7 RR	6/7 RF	7/9 rg	8/10 TM	9/11 TT	10/13 tm	11/13 tt
16	12/5 RF	1/7 rg	2/5 mf	3/6 RR	4/6 RF	5/8 rg	6/8 rd	7/10 TT	8/11 tm	9/12 tt	10/14 FH	11/14 FW
17	12/6 rd	1/8 TT	2/6 RF	3/7 rg	4/7 rd	5/9 TT	6/9 TM	7/11 tt	8/12 FH	9/13 FW	10/15 fr	11/15 ff
18	12/7 TM	1/9 tt	2/7 rd	3/8 TT	4/8 TM	5/10 tt	6/10 tm	7/12 FW	8/13 fr	9/14 ff	10/16 ER	11/16 EF
19	12/8 tm	1/10 FW	2/8 TM	3/9 tt	4/9 tm	5/11 FW	6/11 FH	7/13 ff	8/14 ER	9/15 EF	10/17 eg	11/17 ed
20	12/9 FH	1/11 ff	2/9 tm	3/10 FW	4/10 FH	5/12 ff	6/12 fr	7/14 EF	8/15 eg	9/16 ed	10/18 MT	11/18 MM
21	12/10 fr	1/12 EF	2/10 FH	3/11 ff	4/11 fr	5/13 EF	6/13 ER	7/15 ed	8/16 MT	9/17 MM	10/19 mt	11/19 mm
22	12/11 ER	1/13 ed	2/11 fr	3/12 EF	4/12 ER	5/14 ed	6/14 eg	7/16 MM	8/17 mt	9/18 mm	10/20 RW	11/20 RH
23	12/12 eg	1/14 MM	2/12 ER	3/13 ed	4/13 eg	5/15 MM	6/15 MT	7/17 mm	8/18 RW	9/19 RH	10/21 rf	11/21 rr
24	12/13 MT	1/15 mm	2/13 eg	3/14 MM	4/14 MT	5/16 mm	6/16 mt	7/18 RH	8/19 rf	9/20 rr	10/22 TF	11/22 TR
25	12/14 mt	1/16 RH	2/14 MT	3/15 mm	4/15 mt	5/17 RH	6/17 RW	7/19 rr	8/20 TF	9/21 TR	10/23 td	11/23 tg
26	12/15 RW	1/17 rr	2/15 mt	3/16 RH	4/16 RW	5/18 rr	6/18 rf	7/20 TR	8/21 td	9/22 tg	10/24 FM	11/24 FT
27	12/16 rf	1/18 TR	2/16 RW	3/17 rr	4/17 rf	5/19 TR	6/19 TF	7/21 tg	8/22 FM	9/23 FT	10/25 fm	11/25 ft
28	12/17 TF	1/19 tg	2/17 rf	3/18 TR	4/18 TF	5/20 tg	6/20 td	7/22 FT	8/23 fm	9/24 ft	10/26 EH	11/26 EW
29	12/18 td		2/18 TF	3/19 tg	4/19 td	5/21 FT	6/21 FM	7/23 ft	8/24 EH	9/25 EW	10/27 er	11/27 ef
30	12/19 FM		2/19 td	3/20 FT	4/20 FM	5/22 ft	6/22 fm	7/24 EW	8/25 er	9/26 ef	10/28 MR	11/28 MF
31	12/20 fm		2/20 FM		4/21 fm		6/23 EH	7/25 ef		9/27 MF		11/29 md

1995 tr BOAR

JAN ET	FEB et	MAR MW	APR mf	MAY RF	JUN rd	DAY OF MON	JUL TM	AUG tm	AUG tm	SEP FH	OCT fr	NOV RR	DEC eg
5 SPRING	6 WARM	5 CLEAR	7 SUMMER	9 GRAIN	10 HEAT		13 FALL	14 DEW	15 C DEW	16 WINTER	16 SNOW	16 CHILL	16 SPRING
15:24	9:34	14:37	8:11	12:34	22:57		22:57	11:25	3:50	5:44	23:27	9:23	3:26

DAY	JAN	FEB	MAR	APR	MAY	JUN	JUL	AUG	AUG	SEP	OCT	NOV	DEC
1	31 RH	3 RF	31 mm	30 mt	29 MM	28 MT	7 27 ed	8 26 tm	9 25 ed	10 24 ER	11 22 ff	12 22 fr	1 20 FW
2	1 rr	3 rd	1 RM	1 RW	30 mm	29 mt	7 28 MM	8 27 MT	9 26 MM	10 35 eg	11 23 EF	12 23 ER	1 21 ff
3	2 TR	3 mr	2 rm	2 rf	31 RH	30 RW	7 29 mm	8 28 mt	9 27 mm	10 26 MT	11 24 ed	12 24 eg	1 22 EF
4	3 tg	3 RR	3 TH	3 TF	1 rr	1 rf	7 30 RH	8 29 RW	9 28 RH	10 27 MT	11 25 MM	12 25 MT	1 23 ed
5	4 FT	3 rg	4 tr	4 td	6 TF	7 rf	7 31 rr	8 30 rf	9 29 rf	10 28 RW	11 26 mm	12 26 mt	1 24 MM
6	5 td	3 TT	5 TW	5 tg	6 rr	7 tf	8 1 TR	8 31 TF	9 30 TR	10 29 rf	11 27 RH	12 27 RW	1 25 mm
7	6 EW	3 tt	6 tf	6 FM	6 tg	7 TR	8 2 tg	9 1 td	10 1 tg	10 30 TF	11 28 rr	12 28 rf	1 26 RH
8	7 ef	3 FH	7 FF	7 fm	6 FT	7 tg	8 3 FT	9 2 FM	10 2 FT	10 31 td	11 29 TR	12 29 TF	1 27 rr
9	8 MF	3 fr	8 fd	8 EH	6 ft	7 FT	8 4 ft	9 3 fm	10 3 ft	11 1 TF	11 30 tg	12 30 td	1 28 TR
10	9 md	3 ER	9 EM	9 er	6 EW	7 ft	8 5 EW	9 4 EH	10 4 EW	11 2 fm	11 31 FM	12 31 FM	1 29 tg
11	10 RM	3 eg	10 md	10 MR	6 MF	7 EW	8 6 ef	9 5 er	10 5 ef	11 3 EH	12 2 ft	1 1 fm	1 30 FT
12	11 rm	3 MT	11 RM	10 md	6 md	7 ef	8 7 MF	9 6 MR	10 6 MF	11 4 er	12 3 EW	2 1 EH	1 31 ft
13	12 TH	3 mt	12 rm	11 RT	6 RM	7 MF	8 8 md	9 7 mg	10 7 md	11 5 MF	12 4 ef	3 2 er	1 1 EW
14	13 tr	3 RW	13 TH	12 rm	6 rm	7 md	8 9 RM	9 8 RT	10 8 RM	11 6 mg	12 5 MF	4 3 MR	2 2 ef
15	14 TW	3 rf	14 tr	13 TH	6 TW	7 RM	8 10 rm	9 9 rt	10 9 rm	11 7 RT	12 6 md	5 4 mg	3 3 MF
16	15 tf	3 TF	15 FR	14 tr	6 tf	7 rm	8 11 TH	9 10 TW	10 10 TH	11 8 rt	12 7 RM	6 5 RT	4 4 md
17	16 FR	3 td	16 fg	15 FR	6 FF	7 TH	8 12 tr	9 11 tf	10 11 tr	11 9 TW	12 8 rm	7 6 rt	5 5 RM
18	17 fd	3 FM	17 ET	16 fg	6 fd	7 tr	8 13 FR	9 12 FF	10 12 FR	11 10 tf	12 9 TH	8 7 TW	6 6 rm
19	18 EM	3 fm	18 et	17 ET	6 EM	7 FR	8 14 fg	9 13 fd	10 13 fg	11 11 tf	12 10 tr	9 8 tf	7 7 TH
20	19 mf	3 EH	19 MW	18 em	6 ET	7 fg	8 15 EM	9 14 FR	10 14 EM	11 12 FR	12 11 FR	10 9 TW	8 8 tr
21	20 RF	3 er	20 RF	19 MH	6 mf	7 ET	8 16 em	9 15 fd	10 15 em	11 13 fg	12 12 fg	11 10 FF	9 9 FR
22	21 rd	3 MR	21 RF	20 mr	6 RF	7 et	8 17 MH	9 16 EM	10 16 MH	11 14 ET	12 13 ET	12 11 fd	10 10 fg
23	22 TM	3 mg	22 rd	21 RR	6 rd	7 MW	8 18 mr	9 17 mr	10 17 mf	11 15 et	12 14 et	13 12 EM	11 11 ET
24	23 tm	3 RT	23 TM	22 rg	6 TM	7 mf	8 19 RR	9 18 RF	10 18 RF	11 16 MW	12 15 MW	14 13 MH	12 12 et
25	24 FH	3 rt	24 tm	23 TT	6 tm	7 RF	8 20 rg	9 19 rd	10 19 rd	11 17 mf	12 16 mf	15 14 mr	13 13 MW
26	25 fr	3 TW	25 FH	24 tt	6 FH	7 rd	8 21 TT	9 20 rd	10 20 TM	11 18 RF	12 17 RF	16 15 mr	14 14 mf
27	26 ER	3 tf	26 fr	25 FW	6 fr	7 TM	8 22 tm	9 21 TT	10 21 tm	11 19 rg	12 18 rd	17 16 RR	15 15 RF
28	27 eg	3 FR	27 ER	26 ff	6 ER	7 tt	8 23 tt	9 22 FH	10 22 FH	11 20 TT	12 19 ET	18 17 rg	16 16 rd
29	28 MT		28 eg	27 EF	6 EF	7 TT	8 24 FW	9 23 fr	10 23 fr	11 21 tt	12 20 tm	19 18 TT	17 17 TM
30			29 MM	28 ed	6 ed	7 ER	8 25 fr	9 24 ER			12 21 FH		18 tm
31					6 eg								

1996 FR RAT

JAN MT	FEB mt	MAR RW	APR rf	MAY TF	JUN td	DAY OF MON	JUL FM	AUG fm	SEP MH	OCT er	NOV MR	DEC mg
16 WARM	17 CLEAR	17 SUMMER	20 GRAIN	22 HEAT	23 FALL		25 DEW	26 C DEW	27 WINTER	27 SNOW	26 CHILL	27 SPRING
15:25	20:28	14:02	18:14	4:47	14:30		17:14	9:38	11:32	5:17	15:22	3:04
2 19 FH	3 19 tt	4 18 tm	5 17 TT	6 16 TM	7 16 TT	1	8 14 rd	9 13 rg	10 12 RF	11 11 RR	12 11 RF	1 9 mr
2 20 fr	3 20 FW	4 19 FH	5 18 tt	6 17 tm	7 17 tt	2	8 15 TM	9 14 TT	10 13 rd	11 12 rg	12 12 rd	1 10 RR
2 21 ER	3 21 ff	4 20 fr	5 19 FW	6 18 FH	7 18 FW	3	8 16 tm	9 15 tt	10 14 TM	11 13 TT	12 13 TM	1 11 rg
2 22 eg	3 22 EF	4 21 ER	5 20 ff	6 19 fr	7 19 ff	4	8 17 FH	9 16 FW	10 15 tm	11 14 tt	12 14 tm	1 12 TT
2 23 MT	3 23 ed	4 22 eg	5 21 EF	6 20 ER	7 20 EF	5	8 18 fr	9 17 ff	10 16 FH	11 15 FW	12 15 FH	1 13 tt
2 24 mt	3 24 MM	4 23 MT	5 22 ed	6 21 eg	7 21 ed	6	8 19 ER	9 18 EF	10 17 fr	11 16 ff	12 16 fr	1 14 FW
2 25 RW	3 25 mm	4 24 mt	5 23 MM	6 22 MT	7 22 MM	7	8 20 eg	9 19 ed	10 18 ER	11 17 EF	12 17 ER	1 15 ff
2 26 rf	3 26 RH	4 25 RW	5 24 mm	6 23 mt	7 23 mm	8	8 21 MT	9 20 MM	10 19 eg	11 18 ed	12 18 eg	1 16 EF
2 27 TF	3 27 rr	4 26 rf	5 25 RH	6 24 RW	7 24 RH	9	8 22 mt	9 21 mm	10 20 MT	11 19 MM	12 19 MT	1 17 ed
2 28 td	3 28 TR	4 27 TF	5 26 rr	6 25 rf	7 25 rr	10	8 23 RW	9 22 RH	10 21 mt	11 20 mm	12 20 mt	1 18 MM
2 29 FM	3 29 tg	4 28 td	5 27 TR	6 26 TF	7 26 TR	11	8 24 rf	9 23 rr	10 22 RW	11 21 RH	12 21 RW	1 19 mm
3 1 fm	3 30 FT	4 29 FM	5 28 tg	6 27 td	7 27 tg	12	8 25 TF	9 24 TR	10 23 rf	11 22 rr	12 22 rf	1 20 RH
3 2 EH	3 31 ft	4 30 fm	5 29 FT	6 28 FM	7 28 FT	13	8 26 td	9 25 tg	10 24 TF	11 23 TR	12 23 TF	1 21 rr
3 3 er	4 1 EW	5 1 EH	5 30 ft	6 29 fm	7 29 ft	14	8 27 FM	9 26 FT	10 25 td	11 24 tg	12 24 td	1 22 TR
3 4 MR	4 2 ef	5 2 er	5 31 EW	6 30 EH	7 30 EW	15	8 28 fm	9 27 ft	10 26 FM	11 25 FT	12 25 FM	1 23 tg
3 5 mg	4 3 MF	5 3 MR	6 1 ef	7 1 er	7 31 ef	16	8 29 EH	9 28 EW	10 27 fm	11 26 ft	12 26 fm	1 24 FT
3 6 RT	4 4 md	5 4 mg	6 2 MF	7 2 MR	8 1 MF	17	8 30 er	9 29 ef	10 28 EH	11 27 EW	12 27 EH	1 25 ft
3 7 rt	4 5 RM	5 5 RT	6 3 md	7 3 mg	8 2 md	18	8 31 MR	9 30 MF	10 29 er	11 28 ef	12 28 er	1 26 EW
3 8 TW	4 6 rm	5 6 rt	6 4 RM	7 4 RT	8 3 RM	19	9 1 mg	10 1 md	10 30 MR	11 29 MF	12 29 MR	1 27 ef
3 9 tf	4 7 TH	5 7 TW	6 5 rm	7 5 rt	8 4 rm	20	9 2 RT	10 2 RM	10 31 mg	11 30 md	12 30 mg	1 28 MF
3 10 FF	4 8 tr	5 8 tf	6 6 TH	7 6 TW	8 5 TH	21	9 3 rt	10 3 rm	11 1 RT	12 1 RM	12 31 RT	1 29 md
3 11 fd	4 9 FR	5 9 FF	6 7 tr	7 7 tf	8 6 tr	22	9 4 TW	10 4 TH	11 2 rt	12 2 rm	1 1 rt	1 30 RM
3 12 EM	4 10 fg	5 10 fd	6 8 FR	7 8 FF	8 7 FR	23	9 5 tf	10 5 tr	11 3 TW	12 3 TH	1 2 TW	1 31 rm
3 13 em	4 11 ET	5 11 EM	6 9 fg	7 9 fd	8 8 fg	24	9 6 FF	10 6 FR	11 4 tf	12 4 tr	1 3 tf	2 1 TH
3 14 MH	4 12 et	5 12 em	6 10 ET	7 10 EM	8 9 ET	25	9 7 fd	10 7 fg	11 5 FF	12 5 FR	1 4 FF	2 2 tr
3 15 mr	4 13 MW	5 13 MH	6 11 et	7 11 em	8 10 et	26	9 8 EM	10 8 ET	11 6 fd	12 6 fg	1 5 fd	2 3 FR
3 16 RR	4 14 mf	5 14 mr	6 12 MW	7 12 MH	8 11 MW	27	9 9 em	10 9 et	11 7 EM	12 7 ET	1 6 EM	2 4 fg
3 17 rg	4 15 RF	5 15 RR	6 13 mf	7 13 mr	8 12 mf	28	9 10 MH	10 10 MW	11 8 em	12 8 et	1 7 em	2 5 ET
3 18 TT	4 16 rd	5 16 rg	6 14 RF	7 14 RR	8 13 RF	29	9 11 mr	10 11 mf	11 9 MH	12 9 MW	1 8 MH	2 6 et
	4 17 TM		6 15 rd	7 15 rg		30	9 12 RR		11 10 mr	12 10 mf		

1997 fg OX

JAN	FEB	MAR	APR	MAY	JUN	DAY	JUL	AUG	SEP	OCT	NOV	DEC
RT	rt	TW	tf	FF	fd	OF	EM	em	MH	mr	RR	rg
27 WARM	28 CLEAR	29 SUMMER		1 GRAIN	3 HEAT	MON	5 FALL	6 DEW	7 C DEW	8 WINTER	8 SNOW	7 CHILL
21:14	2:17	19:50		23:53	10:36		20:19	23:03	15:27	17:22	11:05	21:11
2/7 MW	3/9 MH	4/7 et	5/7 em	6/5 ET	7/5 EM	1	8/3 fg	9/2 fd	10/2 fg	10/31 FF	11/30 FR	12/30 FF
2/8 mf	3/10 mr	4/8 MW	5/8 MH	6/6 et	7/6 em	2	8/4 ET	9/3 EM	10/3 ET	11/1 fd	12/1 fg	12/31 fd
2/9 RF	3/11 RR	4/9 mf	5/9 mr	6/7 MW	7/7 MH	3	8/5 et	9/4 em	10/4 et	11/2 EM	12/2 ET	1/1 EM
2/10 rd	3/12 rg	4/10 RF	5/10 RR	6/8 mf	7/8 mr	4	8/6 MW	9/5 MH	10/5 MW	11/3 em	12/3 et	1/2 em
2/11 TM	3/13 TT	4/11 rd	5/11 rg	6/9 RF	7/9 RR	5	8/7 mf	9/6 mr	10/6 mf	11/4 MH	12/4 MW	1/3 MH
2/12 tm	3/14 tt	4/12 TM	5/12 TT	6/10 rd	7/10 rg	6	8/8 RF	9/7 RR	10/7 RF	11/5 mr	12/5 mf	1/4 mr
2/13 FH	3/15 FW	4/13 tm	5/13 tt	6/11 TM	7/11 TT	7	8/9 rd	9/8 rg	10/8 rd	11/6 RR	12/6 RF	1/5 RR
2/14 fr	3/16 ff	4/14 FH	5/14 FW	6/12 tm	7/12 tt	8	8/10 TM	9/9 TT	10/9 TM	11/7 rg	12/7 rd	1/6 rg
2/15 ER	3/17 EF	4/15 fr	5/15 ff	6/13 FH	7/13 FW	9	8/11 tm	9/10 tt	10/10 tm	11/8 TT	12/8 TM	1/7 TT
2/16 eg	3/18 ed	4/16 ER	5/16 EF	6/14 fr	7/14 ff	10	8/12 FH	9/11 FW	10/11 FH	11/9 tt	12/9 tm	1/8 tt
2/17 MT	3/19 MM	4/17 eg	5/17 ed	6/15 ER	7/15 EF	11	8/13 fr	9/12 ff	10/12 fr	11/10 FW	12/10 FH	1/9 FW
2/18 mt	3/20 mm	4/18 MT	5/18 MM	6/16 eg	7/16 ed	12	8/14 ER	9/13 EF	10/13 ER	11/11 ff	12/11 fr	1/10 ff
2/19 RW	3/21 RH	4/19 mt	5/19 mm	6/17 MT	7/17 MM	13	8/15 eg	9/14 ed	10/14 eg	11/12 EF	12/12 ER	1/11 EF
2/20 rf	3/22 rr	4/20 RW	5/20 RH	6/18 mt	7/18 mm	14	8/16 MT	9/15 MM	10/15 MT	11/13 ed	12/13 eg	1/12 ed
2/21 TF	3/23 TR	4/21 rf	5/21 rr	6/19 RW	7/19 RH	15	8/17 mt	9/16 mm	10/16 mt	11/14 MM	12/14 MT	1/13 MM
2/22 td	3/24 tg	4/22 TF	5/22 TR	6/20 rf	7/20 rr	16	8/18 RW	9/17 RH	10/17 RW	11/15 mm	12/15 mt	1/14 mm
2/23 FM	3/25 FT	4/23 td	5/23 tg	6/21 TF	7/21 TR	17	8/19 rf	9/18 rr	10/18 rf	11/16 RH	12/16 RW	1/15 RH
2/24 fm	3/26 ft	4/24 FM	5/24 FT	6/22 td	7/22 tg	18	8/20 TF	9/19 TR	10/19 TF	11/17 rr	12/17 rf	1/16 rr
2/25 EH	3/27 EW	4/25 fm	5/25 ft	6/23 FM	7/23 FT	19	8/21 td	9/20 tg	10/20 td	11/18 TR	12/18 TF	1/17 TR
2/26 er	3/28 ef	4/26 EH	5/26 EW	6/24 fm	7/24 ft	20	8/22 FM	9/21 FT	10/21 FM	11/19 tg	12/19 td	1/18 tg
2/27 MR	3/29 MF	4/27 er	5/27 ef	6/25 EH	7/25 EW	21	8/23 fm	9/22 ft	10/22 fm	11/20 FT	12/20 FM	1/19 FT
2/28 mg	3/30 md	4/28 MR	5/28 MF	6/26 er	7/26 ef	22	8/24 EH	9/23 EW	10/23 EH	11/21 ft	12/21 fm	1/20 ft
3/1 RT	3/31 RM	4/29 mg	5/29 md	6/27 MR	7/27 MF	23	8/25 er	9/24 ef	10/24 er	11/22 EW	12/22 EH	1/21 EW
3/2 rt	4/1 rm	4/30 RT	5/30 RM	6/28 mg	7/28 md	24	8/26 MR	9/25 MF	10/25 MR	11/23 ef	12/23 er	1/22 ef
3/3 TW	4/2 TH	5/1 rt	5/31 rm	6/29 RT	7/29 RM	25	8/27 mg	9/26 md	10/26 mg	11/24 MF	12/24 MR	1/23 MF
3/4 tf	4/3 tr	5/2 TW	6/1 TH	6/30 rt	7/30 rm	26	8/28 RT	9/27 RM	10/27 RT	11/25 md	12/25 mg	1/24 md
3/5 FF	4/4 FR	5/3 tf	6/2 tr	7/1 TW	7/31 TH	27	8/29 rt	9/28 rm	10/28 rt	11/26 RM	12/26 RT	1/25 RM
3/6 fd	4/5 fg	5/4 FF	6/3 FR	7/2 tf	8/1 tr	28	8/30 TW	9/29 TH	10/29 TW	11/27 rm	12/27 rt	1/26 rm
3/7 EM	4/6 ET	5/5 fd	6/4 fg	7/3 FF	8/2 FR	29	8/31 tf	9/30 tr	10/30 tf	11/28 TH	12/28 TW	1/27 TH
3/8 em		5/6 EM		7/4 fd		30	9/1 FF	10/1 FR		11/29 tr	12/29 tf	

1998 ET TIGER

JAN TT	FEB tt	MAR FW	APR ff	MAY EF	MAY EF	JUN ed	DAY OF MON	JUL MM	AUG mm	SEP RH	OCT r=	NOV TR	DEC tg
8 SPRING	8 WARM	9 CLEAR	11 SUMMER	12 GRAIN	14 HEAT	17 FALL		18 DEW	18 C DEW	20 WINTER	19 SNOW	19 CHILL	19 SPRING
9:05	2:57	8:06	1:40	6:02	22:44	16:25		5:24	21:16	0:24	15:51	3:00	14:42
1 28 tr	2 27 tf	3 28 TH	4 26 rt	5 26 rm	7 24 RT	8 23 md	1	9 22 mg	10 21 md	11 20 MR	12 19 MF	1 19 MR	2 17 ef
1 29 FR	2 28 FF	3 29 tr	4 27 TW	5 27 TH	7 25 rt	8 24 RM	2	9 23 RT	10 22 RM	11 21 mg	12 20 md	1 20 mg	2 18 MF
1 30 fg	3 1 fd	3 30 FR	4 28 tf	5 28 tr	7 26 TW	8 25 rm	3	9 24 rt	10 23 rm	11 22 RT	12 21 RM	1 21 RT	2 19 md
1 31 ET	3 2 EM	3 31 fg	4 29 FF	5 29 FR	7 27 tf	8 26 TH	4	9 25 TW	10 24 TH	11 23 rt	12 22 rm	1 22 rt	2 20 RM
2 1 et	3 3 em	4 1 ET	4 30 fd	5 30 fg	7 28 FF	8 27 tr	5	9 26 tf	10 25 tr	11 24 TW	12 23 TH	1 23 TW	2 21 rm
2 2 MW	3 4 MH	4 2 et	5 1 EM	5 31 ET	7 29 fd	8 28 FR	6	9 27 FF	10 26 FR	11 25 tf	12 24 tr	1 24 tf	2 22 TH
2 3 mf	3 5 mr	4 3 MW	5 2 em	6 1 et	7 30 EM	8 29 fg	7	9 28 fd	10 27 fg	11 26 FF	12 25 FR	1 25 FF	2 23 tr
2 4 RF	3 6 RR	4 4 mf	5 3 MH	6 2 MW	8 1 MH	8 30 ET	8	9 29 EM	10 28 ET	11 27 fd	12 26 fg	1 26 fd	2 24 FR
2 5 rd	3 7 rg	4 5 RF	5 4 mr	6 3 mf	8 2 mr	8 31 et	9	9 30 em	10 29 et	11 28 EM	12 27 ET	1 27 EM	2 25 fg
2 6 TM	3 8 TT	4 6 rd	5 5 RR	6 4 RF	8 3 RR	9 1 MW	10	9 1 MH	10 30 MW	11 29 em	12 28 et	1 28 em	2 26 ET
2 7 tm	3 9 tt	4 7 TM	5 6 rg	6 5 rd	8 4 rg	9 2 mf	11	9 2 mr	11 1 mf	11 30 MH	12 29 em	1 29 MH	2 27 et
2 8 FH	3 10 FW	4 8 tm	5 7 TT	6 6 TM	8 5 TT	9 3 RF	12	9 3 RR	11 2 RF	11 31 mr	12 30 MW	1 30 mr	2 28 MW
2 9 fr	3 11 ff	4 9 FH	5 8 tt	6 7 tm	8 6 tt	9 4 rd	13	9 4 rg	11 3 rd	11 1 RR	12 1 mf	1 1 RR	2 29 mf
2 10 ER	3 12 EF	4 10 fr	5 9 FW	6 8 FH	8 7 FW	9 5 TM	14	9 5 TT	11 4 TM	11 2 rg	12 2 RF	1 2 rg	2 30 RF
2 11 eg	3 13 ed	4 11 ER	5 10 ff	6 9 fr	8 8 ff	9 6 tm	15	9 6 tt	11 5 tm	11 3 TT	12 3 rd	1 3 TT	2 31 rd
2 12 MT	3 14 MM	4 12 eg	5 11 EF	6 10 ER	8 9 EF	9 7 FH	16	9 7 FW	11 6 FH	11 4 tt	12 4 TM	1 4 tt	2 1 TM
2 13 mt	3 15 mm	4 13 MT	5 12 ed	6 11 eg	8 10 ed	9 8 fr	17	9 8 ff	11 7 fr	11 5 FW	12 5 tm	1 5 FW	2 2 tm
2 14 RW	3 16 RH	4 14 mt	5 13 MM	6 12 MT	8 11 MM	9 9 ER	18	9 9 EF	11 8 ER	11 6 ff	12 6 FH	1 6 ff	2 3 FH
2 15 rf	3 17 rr	4 15 RW	5 14 mm	6 13 mt	8 12 mm	9 10 eg	19	9 10 ed	11 9 eg	11 7 EF	12 7 fr	1 7 EF	2 4 fr
2 16 TF	3 18 TR	4 16 rf	5 15 RH	6 14 RW	8 13 RH	9 11 MT	20	9 11 MM	11 10 MT	11 8 ed	12 8 ER	1 8 ed	2 5 ER
2 17 td	3 19 tg	4 17 TF	5 16 rr	6 15 rf	8 14 rr	9 12 mt	21	9 12 mm	11 11 mt	11 9 eg	12 9 eg	1 9 eg	2 6 eg
2 18 FM	3 20 FT	4 18 td	5 17 TR	6 16 TF	8 15 TR	9 13 RW	22	9 13 RH	11 12 RW	11 10 MT	12 10 MT	1 10 MM	2 7 MT
2 19 fm	3 21 ft	4 19 FM	5 18 tg	6 17 td	8 16 tg	9 14 rf	23	9 14 rr	11 13 rf	11 11 mt	12 11 mt	1 11 mm	2 8 mt
2 20 EH	3 22 EW	4 20 fm	5 19 FT	6 18 FM	8 17 TF	9 15 TF	24	9 15 TR	11 14 TF	11 12 RW	12 12 RW	1 12 RH	2 9 RW
2 21 er	3 23 ef	4 21 EH	5 20 ft	6 19 fm	8 18 ft	9 16 td	25	9 16 tg	11 15 td	11 13 rf	12 13 rf	1 13 rr	2 10 rf
2 22 MR	3 24 MF	4 22 er	5 21 EW	6 20 EH	8 19 EW	9 17 FM	26	9 17 FT	11 16 FM	11 14 TF	12 14 TF	1 14 TR	2 11 TF
2 23 mg	3 25 md	4 23 MR	5 22 ef	6 21 er	8 20 ef	9 18 fm	27	9 18 ft	11 17 fm	11 15 td	12 15 td	1 15 tg	2 12 td
2 24 RM	3 26 RM	4 24 mg	5 23 MF	6 22 MR	8 21 MF	9 19 EH	28	9 19 EW	11 18 EH	11 16 FM	12 16 FM	1 16 FT	2 13 FM
2 25 rt	3 27 rm	4 25 RT	5 24 md	6 23 mg		9 20 er	29	9 20 ef	11 19 er	11 17 fm	12 17 fm	1 17 ft	2 14 fm
2 26 TW			5 25 RM			9 21 MR	30	9 21 MF		11 18 EH	12 18 er		2 15 EH

243

1999 et RABBIT

JAN FT	FEB ft	MAR EW	APR ef	MAY MF	JUN md	DAY OF MON	JUL RM	AUG rm	SEP TH	OCT tr	NOV FR	DEC fg
19 WARM	19 CLEAR	21 SUMMER	23 GRAIN	24 HEAT	27 FALL	29 DEW	29 DEW		1 C DEW	1 WINTER	30 CHILL	29 SPRING
8:52	13:55	7:29	11:51	22:14	7:57		11:13		3:06	6:14 / 21:14	9:30	20:32

Header (per lunar-month column)

	JAN	FEB	MAR	APR	MAY	JUN	JUL	AUG	SEP	OCT	NOV	DEC
Code	ET	et	MW	mf	RF	rd	TM	tm	FH	fr	ER	eg
Term	30 WARM	30 CLEAR		2 SUMMER	4 GRAIN	6 HEAT	8 FALL	10 DEW	11 C DEW	12 WINTER	12 SNOW	11 CHILL
Time	14:42	19:45		12:58	17:41	4:04	13:36	17:01	7:56	12:03	3:29	3:19

Data (Gregorian month / day + code)

DAY OF MON	JAN	FEB	MAR	APR	MAY	JUN	JUL	AUG	SEP	OCT	NOV	DEC
1	2 5 rf	3 6 rr	4 5 rf	5 4 RH	6 2 mt	7 2 mm	7 31 MT	8 29 ed	9 27 ER	10 27 EF	11 26 ER	12 26 EF
2	2 6 TF	3 7 TR	4 6 TF	5 5 rr	6 3 RW	7 3 RH	8 1 mt	8 30 MM	9 28 eg	10 28 ed	11 27 eg	12 27 ed
3	2 7 td	3 8 tg	4 7 td	5 6 TR	6 4 rf	7 4 rr	8 2 RW	8 31 mm	9 29 MT	10 29 MM	11 28 MT	12 28 MM
4	2 8 FM	3 9 FT	4 8 FM	5 7 tg	6 5 TF	7 5 TR	8 3 rf	9 1 RH	9 30 mt	10 30 mm	11 29 mt	12 29 mm
5	2 9 fm	3 10 ft	4 9 fm	5 8 FT	6 6 td	7 6 tg	8 4 TF	9 2 rr	10 1 RW	10 31 RH	11 30 RW	12 30 RH
6	2 10 EH	3 11 EW	4 10 EH	5 9 ft	6 7 FM	7 7 FT	8 5 td	9 3 TR	10 2 rf	11 1 rr	12 1 rf	12 31 rr
7	2 11 er	3 12 ef	4 11 er	5 10 EW	6 8 fm	7 8 ft	8 6 FM	9 4 tg	10 3 TF	11 2 TR	12 2 TF	1 1 TR
8	2 12 MR	3 13 MF	4 12 MR	5 11 ef	6 9 EH	7 9 EW	8 7 fm	9 5 FT	10 4 td	11 3 tg	12 3 td	1 2 tg
9	2 13 mg	3 14 md	4 13 mg	5 12 MF	6 10 er	7 10 ef	8 8 EH	9 6 ft	10 5 FM	11 4 FT	12 4 FM	1 3 FT
10	2 14 RT	3 15 RM	4 14 RT	5 13 md	6 11 MR	7 11 MF	8 9 er	9 7 EW	10 6 fm	11 5 ft	12 5 fm	1 4 ft
11	2 15 rt	3 16 rm	4 15 rt	5 14 RM	6 12 mg	7 12 md	8 10 MR	9 8 ef	10 7 EH	11 6 EW	12 6 EH	1 5 EW
12	2 16 TW	3 17 TH	4 16 TW	5 15 rm	6 13 RT	7 13 RM	8 11 mg	9 9 MF	10 8 er	11 7 ef	12 7 er	1 6 ef
13	2 17 tf	3 18 tr	4 17 tf	5 16 TH	6 14 rt	7 14 rm	8 12 RT	9 10 md	10 9 MR	11 8 MF	12 8 MR	1 7 MF
14	2 18 FF	3 19 FR	4 18 FF	5 17 tr	6 15 TW	7 15 TH	8 13 rt	9 11 RM	10 10 mg	11 9 md	12 9 mg	1 8 md
15	2 19 fd	3 20 fg	4 19 fd	5 18 FR	6 16 tf	7 16 tr	8 14 TW	9 12 rm	10 11 RT	11 10 RM	12 10 RT	1 9 RM
16	2 20 EM	3 21 ET	4 20 EM	5 19 fg	6 17 FF	7 17 FR	8 15 tf	9 13 TH	10 12 rt	11 11 rm	12 11 rt	1 10 rm
17	2 21 em	3 22 et	4 21 em	5 20 ET	6 18 fd	7 18 fg	8 16 FF	9 14 tr	10 13 TW	11 12 TH	12 12 TW	1 11 TH
18	2 22 MH	3 23 MW	4 22 MH	5 21 et	6 19 EM	7 19 ET	8 17 fd	9 15 FR	10 14 tf	11 13 tr	12 13 tf	1 12 tr
19	2 23 mr	3 24 mf	4 23 mr	5 22 MW	6 20 em	7 20 et	8 18 EM	9 16 fg	10 15 FF	11 14 FR	12 14 FF	1 13 FR
20	2 24 RR	3 25 RF	4 24 RR	5 23 mf	6 21 MH	7 21 MW	8 19 em	9 17 ET	10 16 fd	11 15 fg	12 15 fd	1 14 fg
21	2 25 rg	3 26 rd	4 25 rg	5 24 RF	6 22 mr	7 22 mf	8 20 MH	9 18 et	10 17 EM	11 16 ET	12 16 EM	1 15 ET
22	2 26 TT	3 27 TM	4 26 TT	5 25 rd	6 23 RR	7 23 RF	8 21 mr	9 19 MW	10 18 em	11 17 et	12 17 em	1 16 et
23	2 27 tt	3 28 tm	4 27 tt	5 26 TM	6 24 rg	7 24 rd	8 22 RR	9 20 mf	10 19 MH	11 18 MW	12 18 MH	1 17 MW
24	2 28 FW	3 29 FH	4 28 FW	5 27 tm	6 25 TT	7 25 TM	8 23 rg	9 21 RF	10 20 mr	11 19 mf	12 19 mr	1 18 mf
25	2 29 ff	3 30 fr	4 29 ff	5 28 FH	6 26 tt	7 26 tm	8 24 TT	9 22 rd	10 21 RR	11 20 RF	12 20 RR	1 19 RF
26	3 1 EF	3 31 ER	4 30 EF	5 29 fr	6 27 FW	7 27 FH	8 25 tt	9 23 TM	10 22 rg	11 21 rd	12 21 rg	1 20 rd
27	3 2 ed	4 1 eg	5 1 ed	5 30 ER	6 28 ff	7 28 fr	8 26 FW	9 24 tm	10 23 TT	11 22 TM	12 22 TT	1 21 TM
28	3 3 MM	4 2 MT	5 2 MM	5 31 eg	6 29 EF	7 29 ER	8 27 ff	9 25 FH	10 24 tt	11 23 tm	12 23 tt	1 22 tm
29	3 4 mm	4 3 mt	5 3 mm	6 1 MT	6 30 ed	7 30 eg	8 28 EF	9 26 fr	10 25 FW	11 24 FH	12 24 FW	1 23 FH
30	3 5 RH	4 4 RW			7 1 MM				10 26 ff	11 25 fr	12 25 ff	

2001 mf SNAKE

	JAN MT	FEB mt	MAR RW	APR rf	APR rf	MAY TF	DAY OF MON	JUN td	JUL FM	AUG fm	SEP EH	OCT er	NOV MR	DEC mg
	12 SPRING	11 WARM	12 CLEAR	13 SUMMER	14 GRAIN	17 HEAT		18 FALL	20 DEW	22 C DEW	22 WINTER	23 SNOW	22 CHILL	23 SPRING
	2:20	20:30	1:33	18:46	23:29	9:52		19:34	22:18	13:42	17:53	9:17	21:10	8:08
1	1 24 fr	2 23 ff	3 25 fr	4 23 FW	4 23 FH	6 21 tt	1	6 21 tm	8 19 TT	9 17 rd	9 17 rg	10 15 RF	11 15 RR	12 13 mf
2	1 25 ER	2 24 EF	3 26 ER	4 24 ff	4 24 fr	6 22 FW	2	6 22 FH	8 20 tt	9 18 TM	9 18 TT	10 16 rd	11 16 rg	12 14 RF
3	1 26 eg	2 25 ed	3 27 eg	4 25 EF	4 25 ER	6 23 ff	3	6 23 fr	8 21 FW	9 19 tm	9 19 tt	10 17 TM	11 17 TT	12 15 rd
4	1 27 MT	2 26 MM	3 28 MT	4 26 ed	4 26 eg	6 24 EF	4	6 24 ER	8 22 ff	9 20 FH	9 20 FW	10 18 tm	11 18 tt	12 16 TM
5	1 28 mt	2 27 mm	3 29 mt	4 27 MM	4 27 MT	6 25 ed	5	6 25 eg	8 23 EF	9 21 fr	9 21 ff	10 19 FH	11 19 FW	12 17 tm
6	1 29 RW	2 28 RH	3 30 RW	4 28 mm	4 28 mt	6 26 MM	6	6 26 MT	8 24 ed	9 22 ER	9 22 EF	10 20 fr	11 20 ff	12 18 FH
7	1 30 rf	3 1 rr	3 31 rf	4 29 RH	4 29 RW	6 27 mm	7	6 27 mt	8 25 MM	9 23 eg	9 23 ed	10 21 ER	11 21 EF	12 19 fr
8	1 31 TF	3 2 TR	4 1 TF	4 30 rr	4 30 rf	6 28 RH	8	6 28 RW	8 26 mm	9 24 MT	9 24 MM	10 22 eg	11 22 ed	12 20 ER
9	2 1 td	3 3 tg	4 2 td	5 1 TR	5 1 TF	6 29 rr	9	6 29 rf	8 27 RH	9 25 mt	9 25 mm	10 23 MT	11 23 MM	12 21 eg
10	2 2 FM	3 4 FT	4 3 FM	5 2 tg	5 2 td	6 30 TR	10	6 30 TF	8 28 rr	9 26 RW	9 26 RH	10 24 mt	11 24 mm	12 22 MT
11	2 3 fm	3 5 ft	4 4 fm	5 3 FT	5 3 FM	7 1 tg	11	7 1 td	8 29 TR	9 27 rf	9 27 rr	10 25 RW	11 25 RH	12 23 mt
12	2 4 EH	3 6 EW	4 5 EH	5 4 ft	5 4 fm	7 2 FT	12	7 2 FM	8 30 tg	9 28 TF	9 28 TR	10 26 rf	11 26 rr	12 24 RW
13	2 5 er	3 7 ef	4 6 er	5 5 EW	5 5 EH	7 3 ft	13	7 3 fm	8 31 FT	9 29 td	9 29 tg	10 27 TF	11 27 TR	12 25 rf
14	2 6 MR	3 8 MF	4 7 MR	5 6 ef	5 6 er	7 4 EW	14	7 4 EH	9 1 ft	9 30 FM	9 30 FT	10 28 td	11 28 tg	12 26 TF
15	2 7 mg	3 9 md	4 8 mg	5 7 MF	5 7 MR	7 5 ef	15	7 5 er	9 2 EW	10 1 fm	10 1 ft	10 29 FM	11 29 FT	12 27 td
16	2 8 RT	3 10 RM	4 9 RT	5 8 md	5 8 mg	7 6 MF	16	7 6 MR	9 3 ef	10 2 EH	10 2 EW	10 30 fm	11 30 ft	12 28 FM
17	2 9 rt	3 11 rm	4 10 rt	5 9 RM	5 9 RT	7 7 md	17	7 7 mg	9 4 MF	10 3 er	10 3 ef	10 31 EH	12 1 EW	12 29 fm
18	2 10 TW	3 12 TH	4 11 TW	5 10 rm	5 10 rt	7 8 RM	18	7 8 RT	9 5 md	10 4 MR	10 4 MF	11 1 er	12 2 ef	12 30 EH
19	2 11 tf	3 13 tr	4 12 tf	5 11 TH	5 11 TW	7 9 rm	19	7 9 rt	9 6 RM	10 5 mg	10 5 md	11 2 MR	12 3 MF	12 31 er
20	2 12 FF	3 14 FR	4 13 FF	5 12 tr	5 12 tf	7 10 TH	20	7 10 TW	9 7 rm	10 6 RT	10 6 RM	11 3 mg	12 4 md	1 1 MR
21	2 13 fd	3 15 fg	4 14 fd	5 13 FR	5 13 FF	7 11 tr	21	7 11 tf	9 8 TH	10 7 rt	10 7 rm	11 4 RT	12 5 RM	1 2 mg
22	2 14 EM	3 16 ET	4 15 EM	5 14 fg	5 14 fd	7 12 FR	22	7 12 FF	9 9 tr	10 8 TW	10 8 TH	11 5 rt	12 6 rm	1 3 RT
23	2 15 em	3 17 et	4 16 em	5 15 ET	5 15 EM	7 13 fg	23	7 13 fd	9 10 FR	10 9 tf	10 9 tr	11 6 TW	12 7 TH	1 4 rt
24	2 16 MH	3 18 MW	4 17 MH	5 16 et	5 16 em	7 14 ET	24	7 14 EM	9 11 fg	10 10 FF	10 10 FR	11 7 tf	12 8 tr	1 5 TW
25	2 17 mr	3 19 mf	4 18 mr	5 17 MW	5 17 MH	7 15 et	25	7 15 em	9 12 ET	10 11 fd	10 11 fg	11 8 FF	12 9 FR	1 6 tf
26	2 18 RR	3 20 RF	4 19 RR	5 18 mf	5 18 mr	7 16 MW	26	7 16 MH	9 13 et	10 12 EM	10 12 ET	11 9 fd	12 10 fg	1 7 FF
27	2 19 rg	3 21 rd	4 20 rg	5 19 RF	5 19 RR	7 17 mf	27	7 17 mr	9 14 MW	10 13 em	10 13 et	11 10 EM	12 11 ET	1 8 fd
28	2 20 TT	3 22 TM	4 21 TT	5 20 rd	5 20 rg	7 18 RR	28	7 18 RR	9 15 mf	10 14 MH	10 14 MW	11 11 em	12 12 et	1 9 EM
29	2 21 tt	3 23 tm	4 22 tt	5 21 TM		7 19 rg	29		9 16 RR	10 15 mr		11 12 MH		1 10 em
30	2 22 FW	3 24 FH		5 22 tm		7 20 TT	30			10 16 RR				1 11 MH

2002 RF HORSE

	JAN	FEB	MAR	APR	MAY	JUN	DAY OF MON	JUL	AUG	SEP	OCT	NOV	DEC
code	RF	rt	TW	tf	FF	fd	OF	EM	em	MH	mr	RR	rg
term	23 WARM	23 CLEAR	24 SUMMER	26 GRAIN	27 HEAT	30 FALL	MON		2 DEW	18 C DEW	3 WINTER	4 SNOW	4 CHILL
time	2:18	7:21	0:55	4:54	15:40	1:23		4:07	19:31	23:43	15:16	2:15
1	2 12 mr	3 14 mf	4 13 mr	5 12 MW	6 11 MH	7 10 et	1	8 9 em	9 7 ET	10 6 fd	11 5 fg	12 4 FF	1 3 FR
2	2 13 RR	3 15 RF	4 14 RR	5 13 mf	6 12 mr	7 11 MW	2	8 10 MH	9 8 et	10 7 EM	11 6 ET	12 5 fd	1 4 fg
3	2 14 rg	3 16 rd	4 15 rg	5 14 RF	6 13 RR	7 12 mf	3	8 11 mr	9 9 MW	10 8 em	11 7 et	12 6 EM	1 5 ET
4	2 15 TT	3 17 TM	4 16 TT	5 15 rd	6 14 rg	7 13 RF	4	8 12 RR	9 10 mf	10 9 MH	11 8 MW	12 7 em	1 6 et
5	2 16 tt	3 18 tm	4 17 tt	5 16 TM	6 15 TT	7 14 rd	5	8 13 rg	9 11 RF	10 10 mr	11 9 mf	12 8 MH	1 7 MW
6	2 17 FW	3 19 FH	4 18 FW	5 17 tm	6 16 tt	7 15 TM	6	8 14 TT	9 12 rd	10 11 RR	11 10 RF	12 9 mr	1 8 mf
7	2 18 ff	3 20 fr	4 19 ff	5 18 FH	6 17 FW	7 16 tm	7	8 15 tt	9 13 TM	10 12 rg	11 11 rd	12 10 RR	1 9 RF
8	2 19 EF	3 21 ER	4 20 EF	5 19 fr	6 18 ff	7 17 FH	8	8 16 FW	9 14 tm	10 13 TT	11 12 TM	12 11 rg	1 10 rd
9	2 20 ed	3 22 eg	4 21 ed	5 20 ER	6 19 EF	7 18 fr	9	8 17 ff	9 15 FH	10 14 tt	11 13 tm	12 12 TT	1 11 TM
10	2 21 MM	3 23 MT	4 22 MM	5 21 eg	6 20 ed	7 19 ER	10	8 18 EF	9 16 fr	10 15 FW	11 14 FH	12 13 tt	1 12 tm
11	2 22 mm	3 24 mt	4 23 mm	5 22 MT	6 21 MM	7 20 eg	11	8 19 ed	9 17 ER	10 16 ff	11 15 fr	12 14 FW	1 13 FH
12	2 23 RH	3 25 RW	4 24 RH	5 23 mt	6 22 mm	7 21 MT	12	8 20 MM	9 18 eg	10 17 EF	11 16 ER	12 15 ff	1 14 fr
13	2 24 rr	3 26 rf	4 25 rr	5 24 RW	6 23 RH	7 22 mt	13	8 21 mm	9 19 MT	10 18 ed	11 17 eg	12 16 EF	1 15 ER
14	2 25 TR	3 27 TF	4 26 TR	5 25 rf	6 24 rr	7 23 RW	14	8 22 RH	9 20 mt	10 19 MM	11 18 MT	12 17 ed	1 16 eg
15	2 26 tg	3 28 td	4 27 tg	5 26 TF	6 25 TR	7 24 rf	15	8 23 rr	9 21 RW	10 20 mm	11 19 mt	12 18 MM	1 17 MT
16	2 27 FT	3 29 FM	4 28 FT	5 27 td	6 26 tg	7 25 TF	16	8 24 TR	9 22 rf	10 21 RH	11 20 RW	12 19 mm	1 18 mt
17	2 28 ft	3 30 fm	4 29 ft	5 28 FM	6 27 FT	7 26 td	17	8 25 tg	9 23 TF	10 22 rr	11 21 rf	12 20 RH	1 19 RW
18	3 1 EW	3 31 EH	4 30 EW	5 29 fm	6 28 ft	7 27 FM	18	8 26 FT	9 24 td	10 23 TR	11 22 TF	12 21 rr	1 20 rf
19	3 2 ef	4 1 er	5 1 ef	5 30 EH	6 29 EW	7 28 fm	19	8 27 ft	9 25 FM	10 24 tg	11 23 td	12 22 TR	1 21 TF
20	3 3 MF	4 2 MR	5 2 MF	5 31 er	6 30 ef	7 29 EH	20	8 28 EW	9 26 fm	10 25 FT	11 24 FM	12 23 tg	1 22 td
21	3 4 md	4 3 mg	5 3 md	6 1 MR	7 1 MF	7 30 er	21	8 29 ef	9 27 EH	10 26 ft	11 25 fm	12 24 FT	1 23 FM
22	3 5 RM	4 4 RT	5 4 RM	6 2 mg	7 2 md	7 31 MR	22	8 30 MF	9 28 er	10 27 EW	11 26 EH	12 25 ft	1 24 fm
23	3 6 rm	4 5 rt	5 5 rm	6 3 RT	7 3 RM	8 1 mg	23	8 31 md	9 29 MR	10 28 ef	11 27 er	12 26 EW	1 25 EH
24	3 7 TH	4 6 TW	5 6 TH	6 4 rt	7 4 rm	8 2 RT	24	9 1 RM	9 30 mg	10 29 MF	11 28 MR	12 27 ef	1 26 er
25	3 8 tr	4 7 tf	5 7 tr	6 5 TW	7 5 TH	8 3 rt	25	9 2 rm	10 1 RT	10 30 md	11 29 mg	12 28 MF	1 27 MR
26	3 9 FR	4 8 FF	5 8 FR	6 6 tf	7 6 tr	8 4 TW	26	9 3 TH	10 2 rt	11 1 RM	11 30 RT	12 29 md	1 28 mg
27	3 10 fg	4 9 fd	5 9 fg	6 7 FF	7 7 FR	8 5 tf	27	9 4 tr	10 3 TW	11 2 rm	12 1 rt	12 30 RM	1 29 RT
28	3 11 ET	4 10 EM	5 10 ET	6 8 fd	7 8 fg	8 6 FF	28	9 5 FR	10 4 tf	11 3 TH	12 2 TW	12 31 rm	1 30 rt
29	3 12 et	4 11 em	5 11 et	6 9 EM	7 9 ET	8 7 fd	29	9 6 fg	10 5 FF	11 4 tr	12 3 tf	1 1 TH	1 31 TW
30	3 13 MW	4 12 MH		6 10 em		8 8 EM	30			11 4 FR		1 2 tr	2 1 tf

2003 rd RAM

	JAN TT	FEB tt	MAR FW	APR ff	MAY EF	JUN ed	DAY OF MON	JUL MM	AUG mm	SEP RH	OCT rr	NOV TR	DEC tg
Term	4 SPRING	4 WARM	4 CLEAR	6 SUMMER	7 GRAIN	8 HEAT	11 FALL	11 FALL	12 DEW	14 C DEW	15 WINTER	14 SNOW	15 CHILL
Time	13:57	8:07	12:55	6:44	10:42	21:29	7:12	7:12	9:56	1:20	5:31	22:04	8:04

Day	JAN	FEB	MAR	APR	MAY	JUN	JUL	AUG	SEP	OCT	NOV	DEC
1	tf	tr	TH	TH	TW	TH	rt	rm	RT	md	mg	MF
2	FF	FR	tr	FF	tf	FR	TW	TH	rt	RM	RT	md
3	fd	fg	FR	fd	FF	fg	tf	tr	TW	rm	rt	RM
4	EM	ET	fg	EM	fd	ET	FF	FR	tf	TH	TW	rm
5	em	et	ET	em	EM	et	fd	fg	FF	tr	tf	TH
6	MH	MW	et	MH	em	MW	EM	ET	fd	FR	FF	tr
7	mr	mf	MW	mr	MH	mf	em	et	EM	fg	fd	FR
8	RF	RF	mf	RF	mr	RR	MH	MW	em	ET	EM	fg
9	RR	RR	RR	rd	RF	rg	mr	mf	MH	et	em	ET
10	rg	rd	rd	TT	RR	TT	RR	RF	mr	MW	MH	et
11	TT	TM	TM	tt	rd	tt	rg	RR	RR	mf	mr	MW
12	tt	tt	tm	FW	TM	FW	TT	rd	rg	RF	RR	mf
13	FW	FW	FH	ff	tm	ff	tt	TM	TT	rd	rg	RF
14	ff	fr	fr	ed	FH	EF	FW	tm	tt	TM	TT	rd
15	EF	ER	ER	ER	fr	ed	ff	FH	FW	tm	tt	TM
16	ed	eg	eg	eg	ER	MM	EF	fr	ff	FH	FW	tm
17	MM	MT	MT	MT	eg	mm	ed	ER	EF	fr	ff	FH
18	mm	mt	mt	mt	MT	RH	MM	eg	ed	ER	EF	fr
19	RH	RW	RW	RW	mt	rr	mm	MT	MM	eg	ed	ER
20	rr	rf	rf	rf	RW	TR	RH	mt	mm	MT	MM	eg
21	TR	TF	TF	TF	rf	tg	rr	RW	RH	mt	mm	MT
22	tg	td	td	td	TF	FT	TR	rf	rr	RW	RH	mt
23	FT	FM	FM	FM	td	ft	tg	TF	TR	rf	rr	RW
24	ft	fm	fm	fm	FM	EW	FT	td	tg	TF	TR	rf
25	EW	EH	EH	EH	fm	ef	ft	FM	FT	td	tg	TF
26	ef	er	er	er	EH	MF	EW	fm	ft	FM	FT	td
27	MF	MR	MR	MR	er	md	ef	EH	EW	fm	ft	FM
28	md	mg	mg	mg	MR	RM	MF	er	ef	EH	EW	fm
29	RM		RM	RM	mg	rm	md	MR	MF	er	ef	EH
30	rm		rm	rm	RM		RM	mg	md	MR	MF	er
31	TH		rt		rm		rm	RM		mg		MR

248

2004 TM MONKEY

JAN FT 14 SPRING 19:46	FEB ft 15 WARM 13:56	FEB ft 15 CLEAR 18:59	MAR EW 17 SUMMER 12:33	APR ef 18 GRAIN 16:55	MAY MF 20 HEAT 2:56	DAY OF MON	JUN md 22 FALL 13:00	JUL RM 23 DEW 15:44	AUG rm 25 C DEW 7:08	SEP TH 25 WINTER 11:21	OCT tr 26 SNOW 3:54	NOV FR 25 CHILL 13:52	DEC fg 26 SPRING 1:34
1/22 MR	2/20 ef	3/21 er	4/19 EW	5/19 EH	6/18 EW	1	7/17 fm	8/16 ft	9/14 FM	10/14 FT	11/12 td	12/12 tg	1/10 TF
1/23 mg	2/21 MF	3/22 MR	4/20 ef	5/20 er	6/19 ef	2	7/18 EH	8/17 EW	9/15 fm	10/15 ft	11/13 FM	12/13 FT	1/11 td
1/24 RT	2/22 md	3/23 mg	4/21 MF	5/21 MR	6/20 MF	3	7/19 er	8/18 ef	9/16 EH	10/16 EW	11/14 fm	12/14 ft	1/12 FM
1/25 rt	2/23 RM	3/24 RT	4/22 md	5/22 mg	6/21 md	4	7/20 MR	8/19 MF	9/17 er	10/17 ef	11/15 EH	12/15 EW	1/13 fm
1/26 TW	2/24 rm	3/25 rt	4/23 RM	5/23 RT	6/22 RM	5	7/21 mg	8/20 md	9/18 MR	10/18 MF	11/16 er	12/16 ef	1/14 EH
1/27 tf	2/25 TH	3/26 TW	4/24 rm	5/24 rt	6/23 rm	6	7/22 RT	8/21 RM	9/19 mg	10/19 md	11/17 MR	12/17 MF	1/15 er
1/28 FF	2/26 tr	3/27 tf	4/25 TH	5/25 TW	6/24 TH	7	7/23 rt	8/22 rm	9/20 RT	10/20 RM	11/18 mg	12/18 md	1/16 MR
1/29 fd	2/27 FR	3/28 FF	4/26 tr	5/26 tf	6/25 tr	8	7/24 TW	8/23 TH	9/21 rt	10/21 rm	11/19 RT	12/19 RM	1/17 mg
1/30 EM	2/28 fg	3/29 fd	4/27 FR	5/27 FF	6/26 FR	9	7/25 tf	8/24 tr	9/22 TW	10/22 TH	11/20 rt	12/20 rm	1/18 RT
1/31 em	2/29 ET	3/30 EM	4/28 fg	5/28 fd	6/27 fg	10	7/26 FF	8/25 FR	9/23 tf	10/23 tr	11/21 TW	12/21 TH	1/19 rt
2/1 MH	3/1 et	3/31 em	4/29 ET	5/29 EM	6/28 ET	11	7/27 fd	8/26 fg	9/24 FF	10/24 FR	11/22 tf	12/22 tr	1/20 TW
2/2 mr	3/2 MW	4/1 MH	4/30 et	5/30 em	6/29 et	12	7/28 EM	8/27 fd	9/25 fd	10/25 fg	11/23 FF	12/23 FR	1/21 tf
2/3 RR	3/3 mf	4/2 mr	5/1 MW	5/31 MH	6/30 MW	13	7/29 em	8/28 EM	9/26 EM	10/26 ET	11/24 fd	12/24 fg	1/22 FF
2/4 rg	3/4 RF	4/3 RR	5/2 mf	6/1 mr	7/1 mf	14	7/30 MH	8/29 em	9/27 em	10/27 et	11/25 EM	12/25 ET	1/23 fd
2/5 TT	3/5 rd	4/4 rg	5/3 RF	6/2 RR	7/2 RF	15	7/31 mr	8/30 MH	9/28 MH	10/28 MW	11/26 em	12/26 et	1/24 EM
2/6 tt	3/6 TM	4/5 TT	5/4 rd	6/3 rg	7/3 rd	16	8/1 RR	8/31 mr	9/29 mr	10/29 mf	11/27 MH	12/27 MW	1/25 em
2/7 FW	3/7 tm	4/6 tt	5/5 TM	6/4 TT	7/4 TM	17	8/2 rg	9/1 RR	9/30 RR	10/30 RF	11/28 mr	12/28 mf	1/26 MH
2/8 ff	3/8 FH	4/7 FW	5/6 tm	6/5 tt	7/5 tm	18	8/3 TT	9/2 rg	10/1 rg	10/31 rd	11/29 RR	12/29 RF	1/27 mr
2/9 EF	3/9 fr	4/8 ff	5/7 FH	6/6 FW	7/6 FH	19	8/4 tt	9/3 TT	10/2 TT	11/1 TM	11/30 rg	12/30 rd	1/28 RR
2/10 ed	3/10 ER	4/9 EF	5/8 fr	6/7 ff	7/7 fr	20	8/5 FW	9/4 tt	10/3 tt	11/2 tm	12/1 TT	12/31 TM	1/29 rg
2/11 MM	3/11 eg	4/10 ed	5/9 ER	6/8 EF	7/8 ER	21	8/6 ff	9/5 FW	10/4 FW	11/3 FH	12/2 tt	1/1 tm	1/30 TT
2/12 mm	3/12 MT	4/11 MM	5/10 eg	6/9 ed	7/9 eg	22	8/7 EF	9/6 ff	10/5 ff	11/4 fr	12/3 FW	1/2 FH	1/31 tt
2/13 RH	3/13 mt	4/12 mm	5/11 MT	6/10 MM	7/10 MT	23	8/8 ed	9/7 EF	10/6 EF	11/5 ER	12/4 ff	1/3 fr	2/1 FW
2/14 rr	3/14 RW	4/13 RH	5/12 mt	6/11 mm	7/11 mt	24	8/9 MM	9/8 ed	10/7 ed	11/6 eg	12/5 EF	1/4 ER	2/2 ff
2/15 TR	3/15 rf	4/14 rr	5/13 RW	6/12 RH	7/12 RW	25	8/10 mm	9/9 MM	10/8 MM	11/7 MT	12/6 ed	1/5 eg	2/3 EF
2/16 tg	3/16 TF	4/15 TR	5/14 rf	6/13 rr	7/13 rf	26	8/11 RH	9/10 mm	10/9 mm	11/8 mt	12/7 MM	1/6 MT	2/4 ed
2/17 FT	3/17 td	4/16 tg	5/15 TF	6/14 TR	7/14 TF	27	8/12 rr	9/11 RH	10/10 RH	11/9 RW	12/8 mm	1/7 mt	2/5 MM
2/18 ft	3/18 FM	4/17 FT	5/16 td	6/15 tg	7/15 td	28	8/13 TR	9/12 rr	10/11 rr	11/10 rf	12/9 RH	1/8 RW	2/6 mm
2/19 EW	3/19 fm	4/18 ft	5/17 FM	6/16 FT	7/16 FM	29	8/14 tg	9/13 td	10/12 TR	11/11 TF	12/10 rr	1/9 rf	2/7 RH
	3/20 EH		5/18 fm	6/17 ft		30	8/15 FT		10/13 tg		12/11 TR		2/8 rr

DAY OF MON	JAN ET 25 WARM 19:45	FEB et 27 CLEAR 0:48	MAR MW 27 SUMMER 18:23	APR mf 29 GRAIN 22:45	MAY RF	JUN rd 2 HEAT 8:44	JUL TM 3 FALL 18:51	AUG tm 4 DEW 21:35	SEP FH 6 C DEW 13:59	OCT fr 6 WINTER 17:10	NOV ER 7 SNOW 9:44	DEC eg 6 CHILL 20:29
1	2 9 TR	3 12 td	4 9 rr	5 8 RW	6 7 RH	7 6 mt	8 5 mm	9 4 mt	10 3 MM	11 2 MT	12 1 ed	12 31 eg
2	2 10 tg	3 13 ft	4 10 TR	5 9 rf	6 8 rr	7 7 RW	8 6 RH	9 5 RW	10 4 mm	11 3 mt	12 2 MM	1 1 MT
3	2 11 FT	3 14 fm	4 11 tg	5 10 TF	6 9 TR	7 8 rf	8 7 rr	9 6 rf	10 5 RH	11 4 RW	12 3 mm	1 2 mt
4	2 12 ft	3 15 EH	4 12 FT	5 11 td	6 10 tg	7 9 TF	8 8 TR	9 7 TF	10 6 rr	11 5 rf	12 4 RH	1 3 RW
5	2 13 EW	3 16 er	4 13 ft	5 12 FM	6 11 FT	7 10 td	8 9 tg	9 8 td	10 7 TR	11 6 TF	12 5 rr	1 4 RH
6	2 14 ef	3 17 MR	4 14 EW	5 13 fm	6 12 ft	7 11 FM	8 10 FT	9 9 FM	10 8 tg	11 7 td	12 6 TR	1 5 rf
7	2 15 MF	3 18 mg	4 15 ef	5 14 EH	6 13 EW	7 12 fm	8 11 ft	9 10 fm	10 9 FT	11 8 FM	12 7 tg	1 6 TF
8	2 16 md	3 19 RT	4 16 MF	5 15 ef	6 14 ef	7 13 EH	8 12 EW	9 11 EH	10 10 ft	11 9 fm	12 8 FT	1 7 td
9	2 17 RM	3 20 rt	4 17 md	5 16 MF	6 15 MF	7 14 er	8 13 ef	9 12 er	10 11 EW	11 10 EH	12 9 ft	1 8 FM
10	2 18 rm	3 21 TW	4 18 RM	5 17 mg	6 16 md	7 15 MR	8 14 MF	9 13 MR	10 12 ef	11 11 er	12 10 EW	1 9 fm
11	2 19 TH	3 22 tf	4 19 rm	5 18 RT	6 17 RM	7 16 mg	8 15 md	9 14 mg	10 13 MF	11 12 MR	12 11 ef	1 10 EH
12	2 20 tr	3 23 fd	4 20 TH	5 19 rt	6 18 rm	7 17 RT	8 16 RM	9 15 RT	10 14 md	11 13 mg	12 12 MF	1 11 er
13	2 21 FR	3 24 EM	4 21 tr	5 20 TW	6 19 TH	7 18 rt	8 17 rm	9 16 rt	10 15 RM	11 14 RT	12 13 md	1 12 MR
14	2 22 fg	3 25 em	4 22 FR	5 21 tf	6 20 tr	7 19 TH	8 18 TH	9 17 TW	10 16 rm	11 15 rt	12 14 RM	1 13 mg
15	2 23 ET	3 26 MH	4 23 fg	5 22 FF	6 21 FR	7 20 tf	8 19 tr	9 18 tf	10 17 TH	11 16 TW	12 15 rm	1 14 RT
16	2 24 et	3 27 mr	4 24 ET	5 23 fd	6 22 fg	7 21 FR	8 20 FR	9 19 FF	10 18 tr	11 17 tf	12 16 TH	1 15 rt
17	2 25 MW	3 28 RR	4 25 et	5 24 EM	6 23 ET	7 22 fg	8 21 fg	9 20 fd	10 19 FR	11 18 FF	12 17 tr	1 16 TW
18	2 26 mf	3 29 rg	4 26 MW	5 25 em	6 24 et	7 23 ET	8 22 ET	9 21 EM	10 20 fg	11 19 fd	12 18 FR	1 17 tf
19	2 27 RF	3 30 TT	4 27 mf	5 26 MH	6 25 MW	7 24 et	8 23 et	9 22 em	10 21 ET	11 20 EM	12 19 fg	1 18 FF
20	2 28 rd	3 31 tt	4 28 RF	5 27 mr	6 26 mf	7 25 MH	8 24 MW	9 23 MH	10 22 et	11 21 em	12 20 ET	1 19 fd
21	3 1 TM	4 1 FW	4 29 rd	5 28 RR	6 27 RF	7 26 mr	8 25 mf	9 24 mr	10 23 MW	11 22 MH	12 21 et	1 20 EM
22	3 2 tm	4 2 ff	4 30 TM	5 29 rg	6 28 rd	7 27 RR	8 26 RF	9 25 RR	10 24 mf	11 23 mr	12 22 MW	1 21 em
23	3 3 FH	4 3 EF	5 1 tm	5 30 TT	6 29 TM	7 28 rg	8 27 rd	9 26 rg	10 25 RF	11 24 RR	12 23 mf	1 22 MH
24	3 4 fr	4 4 ed	5 2 FH	5 31 tt	6 30 tm	7 29 TM	8 28 TM	9 27 TT	10 26 rd	11 25 rg	12 24 RF	1 23 mr
25	3 5 ER	4 5 MM	5 3 fr	6 1 FW	7 1 FH	7 30 tm	8 29 tm	9 28 tt	10 27 TM	11 26 TT	12 25 rd	1 24 RR
26	3 6 eg	4 6 mm	5 4 ER	6 2 ff	7 2 fr	7 31 FH	8 30 FH	9 29 FW	10 28 tm	11 27 tt	12 26 TM	1 25 rg
27	3 7 MT	4 7 RH	5 5 eg	6 3 EF	7 3 ER	8 1 fr	8 31 fr	9 30 ff	10 29 FH	11 28 FW	12 27 tm	1 26 TT
28	3 8 mt	4 8 rr	5 6 MT	6 4 ed	7 4 eg	8 2 ER	9 1 ER	10 1 EF	10 30 fr	11 29 ff	12 28 FH	1 27 tt
29	3 9 RW		5 7 mt	6 5 MM	7 5 MT	8 3 eg	9 2 eg	10 2 ed	10 31 ER	11 30 EF	12 29 fr	1 28 FW
30	3 10 rf		5 8 RW	6 6 mm	7 6 mt	8 4 MT	9 3 MT	10 3 MM	11 1 eg	12 1 ed	12 30 ER	1 29 ff
31	3 11 TF		5 9 rf		7 7 RW		9 4 mt	10 4 mm		12 2 MM		1 30 EF

JAN MT	FEB mt	MAR RW	APR rf	MAY TF	JUN td	JUL FM	JUL FM	DAY OF	AUG fm	SEP EH	OCT er	NOV MR	DEC mg
7 SPRING	7 WARM	8 CLEAR	8 SUMMER	11 GRAIN	12 HEAT	15 FALL	16 DEW	MON	17 C DEW	17 WINTER	17 SNOW	18 CHILL	17 SPRING
7:25	1:35	6:38	23:49	4:34	14:57	0:40	3:32		19:48	23:00	15:33	1:32	13:14

2007 fr BOAR

JAN RT	FEB rt	MAR TW	APR tf	MAY FF	JUN fd	DAY OF MON	JUL EM	AUG em	SEP MH	OCT mr	NOV RR	DEC rg
17 WARM	18 CLEAR	20 SUMMER	21 GRAIN	23 HEAT	26 FALL		27 DEW	29 C DEW	29 WINTER	28 SNOW	28 CHILL	28 SPRING
7:24	12:27	6:01	10:23	20:46	6:29		9:13	1:37	3:32	21:23	7:21	19:03
2 18 rd	3 19 RR	4 17 mf	5 17 mr	6 15 MW	7 14 em	1	8 13 et	9 11 EM	10 11 ET	11 10 EM	12 10 ET	1 8 fd
2 19 TM	3 20 rg	4 18 RF	5 18 RR	6 16 mf	7 15 MH	2	8 14 MW	9 12 em	10 12 et	11 11 em	12 11 et	1 9 EM
2 20 tm	3 21 TT	4 19 rd	5 19 rg	6 17 RF	7 16 mr	3	8 15 mf	9 13 MH	10 13 MW	11 12 MH	12 12 MW	1 10 em
2 21 FH	3 22 tt	4 20 TM	5 20 TT	6 18 rd	7 17 RR	4	8 16 RF	9 14 mr	10 14 mf	11 13 mr	12 13 mf	1 11 MH
2 22 FW	3 23 FF	4 21 tm	5 21 tt	6 19 TM	7 18 rg	5	8 17 rd	9 15 RR	10 15 RF	11 14 RR	12 14 RF	1 12 mr
2 23 ER	3 24 ff	4 22 FH	5 22 FW	6 20 tm	7 19 TT	6	8 18 TM	9 16 rg	10 16 rd	11 15 rg	12 15 rd	1 13 RR
2 24 eg	3 25 EF	4 23 fr	5 23 ff	6 21 FH	7 20 tt	7	8 19 tm	9 17 TT	10 17 TM	11 16 TT	12 16 TM	1 14 rg
2 25 MT	3 26 ed	4 24 ER	5 24 EF	6 22 fr	7 21 FW	8	8 20 FH	9 18 tt	10 18 tm	11 17 tt	12 17 tm	1 15 TT
2 26 mt	3 27 MM	4 25 eg	5 25 ed	6 23 ER	7 22 ff	9	8 21 fr	9 19 FW	10 19 FH	11 18 FW	12 18 FH	1 16 tt
2 27 RW	3 28 mm	4 26 MT	5 26 MM	6 24 eg	7 23 EF	10	8 22 ER	9 20 ff	10 20 fr	11 19 ff	12 19 fr	1 17 FW
2 28 rf	3 29 RH	4 27 mt	5 27 mm	6 25 MT	7 24 ed	11	8 23 eg	9 21 EF	10 21 ER	11 20 EF	12 20 ER	1 18 ff
3 1 TF	3 30 rr	4 28 RW	5 28 RH	6 26 mt	7 25 MM	12	8 24 MT	9 22 ed	10 22 eg	11 21 ed	12 21 eg	1 19 EF
3 2 td	3 31 TR	4 29 rf	5 29 rr	6 27 RW	7 26 mm	13	8 25 mt	9 23 MM	10 23 MT	11 22 MM	12 22 MT	1 20 ed
3 3 FM	4 1 tg	4 30 TF	5 30 TR	6 28 rf	7 27 RH	14	8 26 RW	9 24 mm	10 24 mt	11 23 mm	12 23 mt	1 21 MM
3 4 fm	4 2 FT	5 1 td	5 31 tg	6 29 TF	7 28 rr	15	8 27 rf	9 25 RH	10 25 RW	11 24 RH	12 24 RW	1 22 mm
3 5 EH	4 3 ft	5 2 FM	6 1 FT	6 30 td	7 29 TR	16	8 28 TF	9 26 rr	10 26 rf	11 25 rr	12 25 rf	1 23 RH
3 6 er	4 4 EW	5 3 fm	6 2 ft	7 1 FM	7 30 tg	17	8 29 td	9 27 TR	10 27 TF	11 26 TR	12 26 TF	1 24 rr
3 7 MR	4 5 ef	5 4 EH	6 3 EW	7 2 fm	7 31 FT	18	8 30 FM	9 28 tg	10 28 td	11 27 tg	12 27 td	1 25 TR
3 8 mg	4 6 MF	5 5 er	6 4 ef	7 3 EH	8 1 ft	19	8 31 fm	9 29 FT	10 29 FM	11 28 FT	12 28 FM	1 26 tg
3 9 RT	4 7 md	5 6 MR	6 5 MF	7 4 er	8 2 EW	20	9 1 EH	9 30 ft	10 30 fm	11 29 ft	12 29 fm	1 27 FT
3 10 rt	4 8 RM	5 7 mg	6 6 md	7 5 MR	8 3 ef	21	9 2 er	10 1 EW	10 31 EH	11 30 EW	12 30 EH	1 28 ft
3 11 TW	4 9 rm	5 8 RT	6 7 RM	7 6 mg	8 4 MF	22	9 3 MR	10 2 ef	11 1 er	12 1 ef	12 31 er	1 29 EW
3 12 tf	4 10 TH	5 9 rt	6 8 rm	7 7 RT	8 5 md	23	9 4 mg	10 3 MF	11 2 MR	12 2 MF	1 1 MR	1 30 ef
3 13 FF	4 11 tr	5 10 TW	6 9 TH	7 8 rt	8 6 RM	24	9 5 RT	10 4 md	11 3 mg	12 3 md	1 2 mg	1 31 MF
3 14 fd	4 12 FR	5 11 tf	6 10 tr	7 9 TW	8 7 rm	25	9 6 rt	10 5 RM	11 4 RT	12 4 RM	1 3 RT	2 1 md
3 15 EM	4 13 fg	5 12 FF	6 11 FR	7 10 tf	8 8 TH	26	9 7 TW	10 6 rm	11 5 rt	12 5 rm	1 4 rt	2 2 RM
3 16 em	4 14 ET	5 13 fd	6 12 fg	7 11 FF	8 9 tr	27	9 8 tf	10 7 TH	11 6 TW	12 6 TH	1 5 TW	2 3 rm
3 17 MH	4 15 et	5 14 EM	6 13 ET	7 12 fd	8 10 FR	28	9 9 FF	10 8 tr	11 7 tf	12 7 tr	1 6 tf	2 4 TH
3 18 mr	4 16 MW	5 15 em	6 14 et	7 13 EM	8 11 fg	29	9 10 fd	10 9 FR	11 8 FF	12 8 FR	1 7 FF	2 5 tr
		5 16 MH			8 12 ET	30		10 10 fg	11 9 fd	12 9 fg		2 6 FR

Month column headers (month name, month code, solar term with day, and time):

Column	JAN	FEB	MAR	APR	MAY	JUN	DAY OF MON	JUL	AUG	SEP	OCT	NOV	DEC
Code	TT	tt	FW	ff	EF	ed		MM	mm	RH	rr	TR	tg
Term	28 WARM	28 CLEAR		1 SUMMER	2 GRAIN	5 HEAT		7 FALL	8 DEW	10 C DEW	10 WINTER	10 SNOW	10 CHILL
Time	13:13	28:16		11:50	16:12	2:35		12:18	15:02	7:26	9:21	3:13	13:10

Day-pillar grid (day of month × month):

Day	JAN	FEB	MAR	APR	MAY	JUN	JUL	AUG	SEP	OCT	NOV	DEC
1	FR	fd	FR	fd	fg	EM	ET	em	MW	MH	mf	mr
2	fg	EM	fg	EM	ET	em	et	MH	mf	mr	RF	RR
3	ET	em	ET	em	et	MH	MW	mr	RF	RR	rd	rg
4	et	MH	et	MH	MW	mr	mf	RR	rd	rg	TM	TT
5	MW	mr	MW	mr	mf	RR	RF	rg	TM	TT	tm	tt
6	mf	RR	mf	RR	RF	rg	rd	TT	tm	tt	FH	FW
7	RF	rg	RF	rg	rd	TT	TM	tt	FH	FW	fr	ff
8	rd	TT	rd	TT	TM	tt	tm	FW	fr	ff	ER	EF
9	TM	tt	TM	tt	tm	FW	FH	ff	ER	EF	eg	ed
10	tm	FW	tm	FW	FH	ff	fr	EF	eg	ed	MT	MM
11	FH	ff	FH	ff	fr	EF	ER	ed	MT	MM	mt	mm
12	fr	EF	fr	EF	ER	ed	eg	MM	mt	mm	RW	RH
13	ER	ed	ER	ed	eg	MM	MT	mm	RW	RH	rf	rr
14	eg	MM	eg	MM	MT	mm	mt	RH	rf	rr	TF	TR
15	MT	mm	MT	mm	mt	RH	RW	rr	TF	TR	td	tg
16	mt	RH	mt	RH	RW	rr	rf	TR	td	tg	FM	FT
17	RW	rr	RW	rr	rf	TR	TF	tg	FM	FT	fm	ft
18	rf	TR	rf	TR	TF	tg	td	FT	fm	ft	EH	EW
19	TF	tg	TF	tg	td	FT	FM	ft	EH	EW	er	ef
20	td	FT	td	FT	FM	ft	fm	EW	er	ef	MR	MF
21	FM	ft	FM	ft	fm	EW	EH	ef	MR	MF	mg	md
22	fm	EW	fm	EW	EH	ef	er	MF	mg	md	RT	RM
23	EH	ef	EH	ef	er	MF	MR	md	RT	RM	rt	rm
24	er	MF	er	MF	MR	md	mg	RM	rt	rm	TW	TH
25	MR	md	MR	md	mg	RM	RT	rm	TW	TH	tf	tr
26	mg	RM	mg	RM	RT	rm	rt	TH	tf	tr	FF	FR
27	RT	rm	RT	rm	rt	TH	TW	tr	FF	FR	fd	fg
28	rt	TH	rt	TH	TW	tr	tf	FR	fd	fg	EM	ET
29	TW	tr	TW	tr	tf	FR	FF	fg	EM	ET	em	et
30	tf		tf	FR	FF	fg	fd	ET	em	et	MH	MW
31	FF		FF		fd		EM	et		MW		mf

2009 eg OX

Day	JAN FT	FEB ft	MAR EW	APR ef	MAY MF	MAY MF	JUN md	JUL RM	AUG rm	SEP TH	OCT tr	NOV FR	DEC fg
	12 SPRING	9 WARM	5 CLEAR	11 SUMMER	13 GRAIN	15 HEAT	17 FALL	19 DEW	20 C DEW	21 WINTER	21 SNOW	21 CHILL	21 SPRING
	1:12	19:02	23:49	17:39	22:01	8:24	18:07	21:18	13:15	15:10	9:03	19:00	7:01
1	1 26 md	2 25 mg	3 27 md	4 25 MR	5 24 ef	6 23 er	7 22 EW	8 20 fm	9 19 ft	10 18 FM	11 17 FT	12 16 td	1 15 tg
2	1 27 RM	2 26 RT	3 28 RM	4 26 mg	5 25 MF	6 24 MR	7 23 ef	8 21 EH	9 20 EW	10 19 fm	11 18 ft	12 17 FM	1 16 FT
3	1 28 rm	2 27 rt	3 29 rm	4 27 RT	5 26 md	6 25 mg	7 24 MF	8 22 er	9 21 er	10 20 EH	11 19 EW	12 18 fm	1 17 ft
4	1 29 TH	2 28 TH	3 30 TH	4 28 rt	5 27 RM	6 26 RT	7 25 md	8 23 MR	9 22 MF	10 21 er	11 20 ef	12 19 EH	1 18 EW
5	1 30 tr	3 1 tf	3 31 tr	4 29 TH	5 28 rm	6 27 rt	7 26 RM	8 24 mg	9 23 md	10 22 MR	11 21 MF	12 20 er	1 19 ef
6	1 31 FR	3 2 FF	4 1 FR	4 30 tf	5 29 TH	6 28 TW	7 27 rm	8 25 RT	9 24 RM	10 23 mg	11 22 md	12 21 MR	1 20 MF
7	2 1 ET	3 3 fd	4 2 ET	5 1 FF	5 30 tr	6 29 tf	7 28 TH	8 26 rt	9 25 rm	10 24 RT	11 23 RM	12 22 mg	1 21 md
8	2 2 et	3 4 EM	4 3 et	5 2 fd	5 31 FR	6 30 FF	7 29 tr	8 27 TW	9 26 TH	10 25 rt	11 24 rm	12 23 RT	1 22 RM
9	2 3 et	3 5 em	4 4 em	5 3 EM	6 1 fg	7 1 fd	7 30 FR	8 28 tf	9 27 tr	10 26 TW	11 25 TH	12 24 rt	1 23 rm
10	2 4 MW	3 6 MH	4 5 MH	5 4 em	6 2 ET	7 2 EM	7 31 fg	8 29 FF	9 28 FR	10 27 tf	11 26 tr	12 25 TW	1 24 TH
11	2 5 mf	3 7 mr	4 6 mr	5 5 MW	6 3 et	7 3 em	8 1 ET	8 30 fd	9 29 fg	10 28 FF	11 27 FR	12 26 tf	1 25 tr
12	2 6 RF	3 8 RR	4 7 RR	5 6 mf	6 4 MW	7 4 MH	8 2 et	8 31 EM	9 30 ET	10 29 fd	11 28 fg	12 27 FF	1 26 FR
13	2 7 rd	3 9 rg	4 8 rd	5 7 RF	6 5 mf	7 5 mr	8 3 MW	9 1 em	10 1 et	10 30 EM	11 29 ET	12 28 fd	1 27 fg
14	2 8 TM	3 10 TT	4 9 TM	5 8 rd	6 6 RF	7 6 RR	8 4 mf	9 2 MH	10 2 MW	10 31 em	11 30 et	12 29 EM	1 28 ET
15	2 9 tm	3 11 tt	4 10 tm	5 9 TM	6 7 rd	7 7 rg	8 5 RF	9 3 mr	10 3 mf	11 1 MH	12 1 MW	12 30 em	1 29 et
16	2 10 FH	3 12 FW	4 11 FH	5 10 tm	6 8 TM	7 8 TT	8 6 rd	9 4 RR	10 4 RF	11 2 mr	12 2 mf	12 31 MH	1 30 et
17	2 11 fr	3 13 ff	4 12 fr	5 11 FH	6 9 tm	7 9 tt	8 7 TM	9 5 rg	10 5 rd	11 3 RR	12 3 RF	1 1 mr	1 31 MW
18	2 12 ER	3 14 EF	4 13 ER	5 12 ff	6 10 FH	7 10 FW	8 8 tm	9 6 TT	10 6 TM	11 4 rg	12 4 rd	1 2 RF	2 1 mf
19	2 13 eg	3 15 ed	4 14 eg	5 13 EF	6 11 ff	7 11 ff	8 9 FH	9 7 tt	10 7 tm	11 5 TT	12 5 TM	1 3 rg	2 2 RF
20	2 14 MT	3 16 MM	4 15 MT	5 14 ed	6 12 ER	7 12 EF	8 10 fr	9 8 FW	10 8 FW	11 6 tt	12 6 tm	1 4 TT	2 3 rd
21	2 15 mt	3 17 mm	4 16 mt	5 15 MM	6 13 eg	7 13 ed	8 11 ER	9 9 ff	10 9 ff	11 7 FW	12 7 FH	1 5 tt	2 4 TM
22	2 16 RW	3 18 RH	4 17 RW	5 16 mt	6 14 MT	7 14 MM	8 12 eg	9 10 EF	10 10 EF	11 8 ff	12 8 fr	1 6 FW	2 5 tm
23	2 17 rf	3 19 rr	4 18 rf	5 17 RH	6 15 mt	7 15 mt	8 13 MT	9 11 ed	10 11 ed	11 9 EF	12 9 ER	1 7 ff	2 6 FH
24	2 18 TF	3 20 TR	4 19 TF	5 18 rr	6 16 RH	7 16 RH	8 14 mt	9 12 MT	10 12 MT	11 10 ed	12 10 eg	1 8 EF	2 7 ER
25	2 19 td	3 21 tg	4 20 td	5 19 TR	6 17 rf	7 17 rf	8 15 RW	9 13 mm	10 13 mm	11 11 MM	12 11 MT	1 9 ed	2 8 eg
26	2 20 FM	3 22 FT	4 21 FM	5 20 tg	6 18 TF	7 18 TF	8 16 rf	9 14 RH	10 14 RW	11 12 mm	12 12 mt	1 10 MM	2 9 MT
27	2 21 fm	3 23 ft	4 22 fm	5 21 FT	6 19 td	7 19 td	8 17 TF	9 15 rr	10 15 rf	11 13 RH	12 13 RW	1 11 mm	2 10 mt
28	2 22 EH	3 24 EH	4 23 EH	5 22 ft	6 20 FT	7 20 FT	8 18 td	9 16 TR	10 16 TF	11 14 rr	12 14 rf	1 12 RH	2 11 RW
29	2 23 ef	3 25 ef	4 24 er	5 23 EW	6 21 fm	7 21 ft	8 19 FM	9 17 tg	10 17 td	11 15 TR	12 15 TF	1 13 rr	2 12 rf
30	2 24 MR	3 26 MF			6 22 EH			9 18 FT		11 16 tg	12 tg	1 14 TR	2 13 TF

254

2010 MT TIGER

Month headers / solar terms

Month	Pillar	Solar term	Time
JAN	ET	21 WARM	0:35
FEB	et	21 CLEAR	5:55
MAR	MW	22 SUMMER	23:29
APR	mf	24 GRAIN	3:51
MAY	RF	26 HEAT	14:14
JUN	rd	27 FALL	23:57
JUL	TM		
AUG	tm	1 DEW	3:04
SEP	FH	1 C DEW	19:04
OCT	tr	2 WINTER	21:01
NOV	ER	2 SNOW	13:41
DEC	eg	3 CHILL	1:38

Calendar (DAY OF MON = lunar day of month)

DAY OF MON	JAN	FEB	MAR	APR	MAY	JUN	JUL	AUG	SEP	OCT	NOV	DEC
1	2/14 td	3/16 tg	4/14 TF	5/14 TR	6/12 rf	7/12 rr	8/10 RW	9/8 mm	10/8 mt	11/6 MM	12/6 MT	1/4 ed
2	2/15 FM	3/17 FT	4/15 td	5/15 tg	6/13 TF	7/13 TR	8/11 rf	9/9 RH	10/9 RW	11/7 mm	12/7 mt	1/5 MM
3	2/16 fm	3/18 ft	4/16 FM	5/16 FT	6/14 td	7/14 tg	8/12 TF	9/10 rr	10/10 rf	11/8 RH	12/8 RW	1/6 mm
4	2/17 EH	3/19 EW	4/17 fm	5/17 ft	6/15 FM	7/15 FT	8/13 td	9/11 TR	10/11 TF	11/9 rr	12/9 rf	1/7 RH
5	2/18 er	3/20 ef	4/18 EH	5/18 EW	6/16 fm	7/16 ft	8/14 FM	9/12 tg	10/12 td	11/10 TR	12/10 TF	1/8 rr
6	2/19 MR	3/21 MF	4/19 er	5/19 ef	6/17 EH	7/17 EW	8/15 fm	9/13 FT	10/13 FM	11/11 tg	12/11 td	1/9 TR
7	2/20 mg	3/22 md	4/20 MR	5/20 MF	6/18 er	7/18 ef	8/16 EH	9/14 ft	10/14 fm	11/12 FT	12/12 FM	1/10 tg
8	2/21 RT	3/23 RM	4/21 mg	5/21 md	6/19 MR	7/19 MF	8/17 er	9/15 EW	10/15 EH	11/13 ft	12/13 fm	1/11 FT
9	2/22 rt	3/24 rm	4/22 RT	5/22 RM	6/20 mg	7/20 md	8/18 MR	9/16 ef	10/16 er	11/14 EW	12/14 EH	1/12 ft
10	2/23 TW	3/25 TH	4/23 rt	5/23 rm	6/21 RT	7/21 RM	8/19 mg	9/17 MF	10/17 MR	11/15 ef	12/15 er	1/13 EW
11	2/24 tf	3/26 tr	4/24 TW	5/24 TH	6/22 rt	7/22 rm	8/20 RT	9/18 md	10/18 mg	11/16 MF	12/16 MR	1/14 ef
12	2/25 FF	3/27 FR	4/25 tf	5/25 tr	6/23 TW	7/23 TH	8/21 rt	9/19 RM	10/19 RT	11/17 md	12/17 mg	1/15 MF
13	2/26 fd	3/28 fg	4/26 FF	5/26 FR	6/24 tf	7/24 tr	8/22 TW	9/20 rm	10/20 rt	11/18 RM	12/18 RT	1/16 md
14	2/27 EM	3/29 ET	4/27 fd	5/27 fg	6/25 FF	7/25 FR	8/23 tf	9/21 TH	10/21 TW	11/19 rm	12/19 rt	1/17 RM
15	2/28 em	3/30 et	4/28 EM	5/28 ET	6/26 fd	7/26 fg	8/24 FF	9/22 tr	10/22 tf	11/20 TH	12/20 TW	1/18 rm
16	3/1 MH	3/31 MW	4/29 em	5/29 et	6/27 EM	7/27 ET	8/25 fd	9/23 FR	10/23 FF	11/21 tr	12/21 tf	1/19 TH
17	3/2 mr	4/1 mf	4/30 MH	5/30 MW	6/28 em	7/28 et	8/26 EM	9/24 fg	10/24 fd	11/22 FR	12/22 FF	1/20 tr
18	3/3 RR	4/2 RF	5/1 mr	5/31 mf	6/29 MH	7/29 MW	8/27 em	9/25 ET	10/25 EM	11/23 fg	12/23 fd	1/21 FR
19	3/4 rg	4/3 rd	5/2 RR	6/1 RF	6/30 mr	7/30 mf	8/28 MH	9/26 et	10/26 em	11/24 ET	12/24 EM	1/22 fg
20	3/5 TT	4/4 TM	5/3 rg	6/2 rd	7/1 RR	7/31 RF	8/29 mr	9/27 MW	10/27 MH	11/25 et	12/25 em	1/23 ET
21	3/6 tt	4/5 tm	5/4 TT	6/3 TM	7/2 rg	8/1 rd	8/30 RR	9/28 mf	10/28 mr	11/26 MW	12/26 MH	1/24 et
22	3/7 FW	4/6 FH	5/5 tt	6/4 tm	7/3 TT	8/2 TM	8/31 rg	9/29 RF	10/29 RR	11/27 mf	12/27 mr	1/25 MW
23	3/8 ff	4/7 fr	5/6 FW	6/5 FH	7/4 tt	8/3 tm	9/1 TT	9/30 rd	10/30 rg	11/28 RF	12/28 RR	1/26 mf
24	3/9 EF	4/8 ER	5/7 ff	6/6 fr	7/5 FW	8/4 FH	9/2 tt	10/1 TM	10/31 TT	11/29 rd	12/29 rg	1/27 RF
25	3/10 ed	4/9 eg	5/8 EF	6/7 ER	7/6 ff	8/5 fr	9/3 FW	10/2 tm	11/1 tt	11/30 TM	12/30 TT	1/28 rd
26	3/11 MM	4/10 MT	5/9 ed	6/8 eg	7/7 EF	8/6 ER	9/4 ff	10/3 FH	11/2 FW	12/1 tm	12/31 tt	1/29 TM
27	3/12 mm	4/11 mt	5/10 MM	6/9 MT	7/8 ed	8/7 eg	9/5 EF	10/4 fr	11/3 ff	12/2 FH	1/1 FW	1/30 tm
28	3/13 RH	4/12 RW	5/11 mm	6/10 mt	7/9 MM	8/8 MT	9/6 ed	10/5 ER	11/4 EF	12/3 fr	1/2 ff	1/31 FH
29	3/14 rr	4/13 rf	5/12 RH	6/11 RW	7/10 mm	8/9 mt	9/7 MM	10/6 eg	11/5 ed	12/4 ER	1/3 EF	2/1 fr
30	3/15 TR		5/13 rr		7/11 RH			10/7 MT		12/5 eg		2/2 ER

JAN MT	FEB mt	MAR RW	APR rf	MAY TF	JUN td	DAY OF MON	JUL FM	AUG fm	SEP FH	OCT er	NOV MR	DEC mg
2 SPRING	2 WARM	3 CLEAR	4 SUMMER	5 GRAIN	7 HEAT		9 FALL	11 DEW	13 C DEW	13 WINTER	13 SNOW	13 CHILL
12:32	6:43	11:46	4:51	9:43	20:06		5:49	8:33	0:54	4:07	19:32	7:27
2 3 eg	3 5 ed	3 3 ER	5 3 EF	6 2 ER	7 1 ff	1	7 31 fr	8 29 FW	9 27 tm	10 27 tt	11 25 TM	12 25 TT
2 4 MT	3 6 MM	4 4 eg	5 4 ed	6 3 eg	7 2 EF	2	8 1 ER	8 30 ff	9 28 FH	10 28 FW	11 26 tm	12 26 tt
2 5 mt	3 7 mm	4 5 MT	5 5 md	6 4 mt	7 3 eg	3	8 2 eg	8 31 EF	9 29 fr	10 29 fr	11 27 FH	12 27 FW
2 6 RW	3 8 RH	4 6 mm	5 6 MM	6 5 RW	7 4 MM	4	8 3 mt	9 1 ed	9 30 ER	10 30 ed	11 28 fr	12 28 ff
2 7 rf	3 9 rr	4 7 RW	5 7 RH	6 6 rf	7 5 mm	5	8 4 mt	9 2 MM	10 1 eg	10 31 EF	11 29 ER	12 29 EF
2 8 TF	3 10 TR	4 8 rf	5 8 rr	6 7 TF	7 6 RH	6	8 5 RW	9 3 mm	10 2 MT	11 1 ed	11 30 eg	12 30 ed
2 9 td	3 11 tg	4 9 TF	5 9 TR	6 8 td	7 7 rr	7	8 6 rf	9 4 RH	10 3 mt	11 2 mm	12 1 MT	12 31 MM
2 10 FM	3 12 FT	4 10 td	5 10 tg	6 9 FM	7 8 TR	8	8 7 TF	9 5 rf	10 4 RW	11 3 mt	12 2 mt	1 1 mm
2 11 fm	3 13 ft	4 11 FM	5 11 FT	6 10 fm	7 9 tg	9	8 8 td	9 6 TF	10 5 rf	11 4 RW	12 3 RW	1 2 RH
2 12 EH	3 14 fm	4 12 fm	5 12 ft	6 11 EH	7 10 FT	10	8 9 FM	9 7 EW	10 6 TF	11 5 TR	12 4 rf	1 3 rr
2 13 er	3 15 ef	4 13 EH	5 13 EW	6 12 er	7 11 ft	11	8 10 fm	9 8 fm	10 7 td	11 6 tg	12 5 TF	1 4 TR
2 14 MR	3 16 MF	4 14 er	5 14 ef	6 13 MR	7 12 EW	12	8 11 er	9 9 MF	10 8 FM	11 7 FT	12 6 td	1 5 tg
2 15 mg	3 17 md	4 15 MR	5 15 MF	6 14 mg	7 13 ef	13	8 12 MR	9 10 md	10 9 fm	11 8 ft	12 7 FT	1 6 FT
2 16 RT	3 18 RM	4 16 mg	5 16 RM	6 15 RT	7 14 MF	14	8 13 mg	9 11 RM	10 10 EH	11 9 EW	12 8 fm	1 7 ft
2 17 rt	3 19 rm	4 17 RT	5 17 rm	6 16 rt	7 15 md	15	8 14 RT	9 12 rm	10 11 er	11 10 ef	12 9 EH	1 8 EW
2 18 TW	3 20 TH	4 18 rt	5 18 TH	6 17 TW	7 16 RM	16	8 15 rt	9 13 RT	10 12 MR	11 11 MF	12 10 er	1 9 ef
2 19 tf	3 21 tr	4 19 TW	5 19 tr	6 18 tf	7 17 rm	17	8 16 TW	9 14 TW	10 13 mg	11 12 md	12 11 MR	1 10 MF
2 20 FF	3 22 FR	4 20 tf	5 20 FR	6 19 FF	7 18 TH	18	8 17 tf	9 15 tf	10 14 RM	11 13 RM	12 12 mg	1 11 md
2 21 fd	3 23 fg	4 21 FF	5 21 fg	6 20 fd	7 19 tr	19	8 18 FF	9 16 FF	10 15 rt	11 14 rm	12 13 RT	1 12 RM
2 22 EM	3 24 ET	4 22 fd	5 22 ET	6 21 EM	7 20 FR	20	8 19 fd	9 17 fd	10 16 TW	11 15 TH	12 14 rt	1 13 rm
2 23 em	3 25 et	4 23 EM	5 23 et	6 22 em	7 21 fg	21	8 20 EM	9 18 EM	10 17 tf	11 16 tr	12 15 TW	1 14 TH
2 24 MH	3 26 MW	4 24 et	5 24 MW	6 23 MH	7 22 ET	22	8 21 em	9 19 em	10 18 FF	11 17 FR	12 16 tf	1 15 tr
2 25 mr	3 27 mf	4 25 MH	5 25 mf	6 24 mr	7 23 et	23	8 22 MH	9 20 MH	10 19 fd	11 18 fg	12 17 FF	1 16 FR
2 26 RR	3 28 RF	4 26 mr	5 26 RF	6 25 RR	7 24 MW	24	8 23 mr	9 21 mr	10 20 EM	11 19 ET	12 18 fd	1 17 fg
2 27 rg	3 29 rd	4 27 RR	5 27 rd	6 26 rg	7 25 mf	25	8 24 RR	9 22 RR	10 21 em	11 20 et	12 19 EM	1 18 ET
2 28 TT	3 30 TM	4 28 rg	5 28 TM	6 27 TT	7 26 RF	26	8 25 rg	9 23 rd	10 22 MH	11 21 MW	12 20 em	1 19 et
3 1 tt	3 31 tm	4 29 TT	5 29 tm	6 28 tt	7 27 rd	27	8 26 TT	9 24 TM	10 23 mr	11 22 mf	12 21 MH	1 20 MW
3 2 FW	4 1 FH	4 30 tt	5 30 FW	6 29 FW	7 28 TM	28	8 27 tt	9 25	10 24 RR	11 23 RF	12 22 mr	1 21 mf
3 3 ff	4 2 fr	4 31 FH	5 31 fr	6 30	7 29 tm	29	8 28	9 26	10 25 rd	11 24 rd	12 23 RR	1 22 RF
3 4 EF		5 1 fr	6 1 fr		7 30 FH	30			10 26 TT		12 24 rg	
	5 2											

2012 RW DRAGON

JAN RT	FEB rt	MAR Tw	APR tf	APR tf	MAY FF	DAY OF MON	JUN fd	JUL EM	AUG em	SEP MH	OCT mr	NOV RR	DEC rg
13 SPRING	13 WARM	14 CLEAR	15 SUMMER	16 GRAIN	19 HEAT	20 FALL	20 FALL	22 DEW	23 C DEW	24 WINTER	24 SNOW	24 CHILL	24 SPRING
18:40	12:28	17:16	10:40	14:50	1:21	11:26		14:44	6:42	9:56	2:32	13:16	0:31
1/23 rd	2/22 rg	3/22 RF	4/21 RR	5/21 RF	6/19 mr	1	7/19 mf	8/17 MH	9/16 MW	10/15 em	11/14 et	12/13 EM	1/12 ET
1/24 TM	2/23 TT	3/23 rd	4/22 rg	5/22 rd	6/20 RR	2	7/20 RF	8/18 mr	9/17 mf	10/16 MH	11/15 MW	12/14 em	1/13 et
1/25 tm	2/24 tt	3/24 TM	4/23 TT	5/23 TM	6/21 rg	3	7/21 rd	8/19 RR	9/18 RF	10/17 mr	11/16 mf	12/15 MH	1/14 MW
1/26 FH	2/25 FW	3/25 tm	4/24 tt	5/24 tm	6/22 TT	4	7/22 TM	8/20 rg	9/19 rd	10/18 RR	11/17 RF	12/16 mr	1/15 mf
1/27 fr	2/26 ff	3/26 FH	4/25 FW	5/25 FH	6/23 tt	5	7/23 tm	8/21 TT	9/20 TM	10/19 rg	11/18 rd	12/17 RR	1/16 RF
1/28 ER	2/27 EF	3/27 fr	4/26 ff	5/26 fr	6/24 FW	6	7/24 FH	8/22 tt	9/21 tm	10/20 TT	11/19 TM	12/18 rg	1/17 rd
1/29 eg	2/28 ed	3/28 ER	4/27 EF	5/27 ER	6/25 ff	7	7/25 fr	8/23 FW	9/22 FH	10/21 tt	11/20 tm	12/19 TT	1/18 TM
1/30 MT	2/29 MM	3/29 eg	4/28 ed	5/28 eg	6/26 EF	8	7/26 ER	8/24 ff	9/23 fr	10/22 FW	11/21 TT	12/20 tt	1/19 tm
1/31 mt	3/1 mm	3/30 MT	4/29 MM	5/29 MT	6/27 ed	9	7/27 eg	8/25 EF	9/24 ER	10/23 ff	11/22 tt	12/21 FW	1/20 FH
2/1 RW	3/2 RH	3/31 mt	4/30 mm	5/30 mt	6/28 MM	10	7/28 MT	8/26 ed	9/25 eg	10/24 EF	11/23 FW	12/22 ff	1/21 fr
2/2 rf	3/3 rr	4/1 RW	5/1 RH	5/31 RW	6/29 mm	11	7/29 mt	8/27 MM	9/26 MT	10/25 ed	11/24 ff	12/23 EF	1/22 ER
2/3 TF	3/4 TR	4/2 rf	5/2 rr	6/1 rf	6/30 RH	12	7/30 RW	8/28 mm	9/27 mt	10/26 MM	11/25 EF	12/24 ed	1/23 eg
2/4 td	3/5 tg	4/3 TF	5/3 TR	6/2 TF	7/1 rr	13	7/31 rf	8/29 RH	9/28 RW	10/27 mm	11/26 ed	12/25 MM	1/24 MT
2/5 FM	3/6 FT	4/4 td	5/4 tg	6/3 td	7/2 TR	14	8/1 TF	8/30 rr	9/29 rf	10/28 RH	11/27 MM	12/26 mm	1/25 mt
2/6 fm	3/7 ft	4/5 FM	5/5 FT	6/4 FM	7/3 tg	15	8/2 td	8/31 TR	9/30 TF	10/29 rr	11/28 mm	12/27 RH	1/26 RW
2/7 EH	3/8 EW	4/6 fm	5/6 ft	6/5 fm	7/4 FT	16	8/3 FM	9/1 tg	10/1 td	10/30 TR	11/29 RH	12/28 rr	1/27 rf
2/8 er	3/9 ef	4/7 EH	5/7 EW	6/6 EH	7/5 ft	17	8/4 fm	9/2 FT	10/2 FM	10/31 tg	11/30 rr	12/29 TR	1/28 TF
2/9 MR	3/10 MF	4/8 er	5/8 ef	6/7 er	7/6 EW	18	8/5 EH	9/3 ft	10/3 fm	11/1 FT	12/1 TR	12/30 tg	1/29 td
2/10 mg	3/11 md	4/9 MR	5/9 MF	6/8 MR	7/7 ef	19	8/6 er	9/4 EW	10/4 EH	11/2 ft	12/2 tg	12/31 FT	1/30 FM
2/11 RT	3/12 RM	4/10 mg	5/10 md	6/9 mg	7/8 MF	20	8/7 MR	9/5 ef	10/5 er	11/3 EW	12/3 FT	1/1 ft	1/31 fm
2/12 rt	3/13 rm	4/11 RT	5/11 RM	6/10 RT	7/9 md	21	8/8 mg	9/6 MF	10/6 MR	11/4 ef	12/4 ft	1/2 EW	2/1 EH
2/13 TW	3/14 TH	4/12 rt	5/12 rm	6/11 rt	7/10 RM	22	8/9 RT	9/7 md	10/7 mg	11/5 MF	12/5 EW	1/3 ef	2/2 er
2/14 tf	3/15 tr	4/13 TW	5/13 TH	6/12 TW	7/11 rm	23	8/10 rt	9/8 RM	10/8 RT	11/6 md	12/6 ef	1/4 MF	2/3 MR
2/15 FF	3/16 FR	4/14 tf	5/14 tr	6/13 tf	7/12 TH	24	8/11 TW	9/9 rm	10/9 rt	11/7 RM	12/7 MF	1/5 md	2/4 mg
2/16 fd	3/17 fg	4/15 FF	5/15 FR	6/14 FF	7/13 tr	25	8/12 tf	9/10 TH	10/10 TW	11/8 rm	12/8 md	1/6 RM	2/5 RT
2/17 EM	3/18 ET	4/16 fd	5/16 fg	6/15 fd	7/14 FR	26	8/13 FF	9/11 tr	10/11 tf	11/9 TH	12/9 RM	1/7 rm	2/6 rt
2/18 em	3/19 et	4/17 EM	5/17 ET	6/16 EM	7/15 fg	27	8/14 fd	9/12 FR	10/12 FF	11/10 tr	12/10 rm	1/8 TH	2/7 TW
2/19 MH	3/20 MW	4/18 em	5/18 et	6/17 em	7/16 ET	28	8/15 EM	9/13 fg	10/13 fd	11/11 FR	12/11 TH	1/9 tr	2/8 tf
2/20 mr	3/21 mf	4/19 MH	5/19 MW	6/18 MH	7/17 et	29	8/16 em	9/14 ET	10/14 EM	11/12 fg	12/12 tr	1/10 FR	2/9 FF
2/21 RR		4/20 mr	5/20 mf		7/18 MW	30		9/15 et		11/13 ET		1/11 fg	

2013 rf SNAKE

Month	Code	Solar term	Time
JAN	TT	24 WARM	18:19
FEB	tt	24 CLEAR	23:05
MAR	FW	26 SUMMER	16:28
APR	ff	27 GRAIN	20:44
MAY	EF	29 HEAT	7:09
JUN	ed		
JUL	MM	1 FALL	17:14
AUG	mm	3 DEW	20:33
SEP	RH	4 C DEW	12:31
OCT	rr	5 WINTER	15:45
NOV	TR	5 SNOW	8:21
DEC	tr	5 CHILL	20:07

DAY OF MON | FALL

#	JAN	FEB	MAR	APR	MAY	JUN	JUL	AUG	SEP	OCT	NOV	DEC
1	2 10 fd	3 12 fg	4 10 FF	5 10 FR	6 9 FF	7 8 tr	8 7 tf	9 5 TH	10 5 TW	11 3 rm	12 3 rt	1 1 RM
2	2 11 EM	3 13 ET	4 11 fd	5 11 fg	6 10 fd	7 9 FR	8 8 FF	9 6 tr	10 6 tf	11 4 TH	12 4 TW	1 2 rm
3	2 12 em	3 14 et	4 12 EM	5 12 ET	6 11 EM	7 10 fg	8 9 fd	9 7 FR	10 7 FF	11 5 tr	12 5 tf	1 3 TH
4	2 13 MH	3 15 MW	4 13 em	5 13 et	6 12 em	7 11 ET	8 10 EM	9 8 fg	10 8 fd	11 6 FR	12 6 FF	1 4 tr
5	2 14 mr	3 16 mf	4 14 MH	5 14 MW	6 13 MH	7 12 et	8 11 em	9 9 ET	10 9 EM	11 7 fg	12 7 fd	1 5 FR
6	2 15 RR	3 17 RF	4 15 mr	5 15 mf	6 14 mr	7 13 MW	8 12 MH	9 10 et	10 10 em	11 8 ET	12 8 EM	1 6 fg
7	2 16 rg	3 18 rd	4 16 RR	5 16 RF	6 15 RR	7 14 mf	8 13 mr	9 11 MW	10 11 MH	11 9 et	12 9 em	1 7 ET
8	2 17 TT	3 19 TM	4 17 rd	5 17 rd	6 16 rg	7 15 RF	8 14 RR	9 12 mr	10 12 mr	11 10 MW	12 10 MH	1 8 et
9	2 18 tt	3 20 tm	4 18 TT	5 18 TM	6 17 TT	7 16 rd	8 15 rg	9 13 RF	10 13 RR	11 11 mf	12 11 mr	1 9 MW
10	2 19 FW	3 21 FH	4 19 tt	5 19 tm	6 18 tt	7 17 TM	8 16 TT	9 14 rd	10 14 rg	11 12 RF	12 12 RR	1 10 mf
11	2 20 ff	3 22 fr	4 20 FW	5 20 FH	6 19 FW	7 18 tm	8 17 tt	9 15 TM	10 15 TT	11 13 rd	12 13 rg	1 11 RF
12	2 21 EF	3 23 ER	4 21 ff	5 21 fr	6 20 ff	7 19 FH	8 18 FW	9 16 tm	10 16 tt	11 14 TM	12 14 TT	1 12 rd
13	2 22 ed	3 24 eg	4 22 EF	5 22 ER	6 21 EF	7 20 fr	8 19 ff	9 17 FW	10 17 FW	11 15 tm	12 15 tt	1 13 TM
14	2 23 MM	3 25 MT	4 23 ed	5 23 eg	6 22 ed	7 21 ER	8 20 EF	9 18 fr	10 18 ff	11 16 FH	12 16 FW	1 14 tm
15	2 24 mm	3 26 mt	4 24 MM	5 24 MT	6 23 MM	7 22 eg	8 21 ed	9 19 ER	10 19 EF	11 17 fr	12 17 ff	1 15 FH
16	2 25 RH	3 27 RW	4 25 mm	5 25 mt	6 24 mm	7 23 MT	8 22 MM	9 20 eg	10 20 ed	11 18 ER	12 18 EF	1 16 fr
17	2 26 rr	3 28 rf	4 26 RH	5 26 RW	6 25 RH	7 24 mt	8 23 mm	9 21 MT	10 21 MM	11 19 eg	12 19 ed	1 17 ER
18	2 27 TR	3 29 TF	4 27 rr	5 27 rf	6 26 rr	7 25 RW	8 24 RH	9 22 mm	10 22 mm	11 20 MT	12 20 MM	1 18 ed
19	2 28 tg	3 30 td	4 28 TR	5 28 TF	6 27 TR	7 26 rr	8 25 rr	9 23 RW	10 23 RH	11 21 mt	12 21 mm	1 19 MT
20	3 1 FT	3 31 FM	4 29 tg	5 29 td	6 28 tg	7 27 TR	8 26 TR	9 24 rf	10 24 rr	11 22 RW	12 22 RH	1 20 mt
21	3 2 ft	4 1 fm	4 30 FT	5 30 FM	6 29 FT	7 28 td	8 27 tg	9 25 TF	10 25 TR	11 23 rf	12 23 rr	1 21 RW
22	3 3 EW	4 2 EH	5 1 ft	5 31 fm	6 30 ft	7 29 FM	8 28 FT	9 26 td	10 26 tg	11 24 TF	12 24 TR	1 22 rf
23	3 4 MF	4 3 er	5 2 EW	6 1 EH	7 1 EW	7 30 fm	8 29 ft	9 27 FT	10 27 FT	11 25 tg	12 25 tg	1 23 TF
24	3 5 MF	4 4 MR	5 3 ef	6 2 er	7 2 ef	8 1 EH	8 30 EW	9 28 ft	10 28 ft	11 26 FM	12 26 FT	1 24 td
25	3 6 md	4 5 mg	5 4 MF	6 3 MR	7 3 MF	8 2 er	8 31 ef	9 29 EW	10 29 EW	11 27 fm	12 27 ft	1 25 FM
26	3 7 RM	4 6 RT	5 5 md	6 4 mg	7 4 md	8 3 MR	9 1 MF	9 30 ef	10 30 ef	11 28 EH	12 28 EW	1 26 fm
27	3 8 rm	4 7 rt	5 6 RM	6 5 RT	7 5 RM	8 4 mg	9 2 md	10 1 MF	10 31 MF	11 29 er	12 29 ef	1 27 EH
28	3 9 TH	4 8 TW	5 7 rm	6 6 rm	7 6 rm	8 5 rt	9 3 RM	10 2 md	11 1 md	11 30 MR	12 30 MF	1 28 er
29	3 10 tr	4 9 tf	5 8 TH	6 7 TW	7 7 TH	8 6 TW	9 4 rm	10 3 RT	11 2 RM	12 1 mg	12 31 md	1 29 MR
30	3 11 FR		5 9 tr	6 8 tf				10 4 rt		12 2 RT		1 30 mg

2014 TF HORSE

JAN FT	FEB ft	MAR EW	APR ef	MAY MF	JUN md	JUL RM	DAY	AUG rm	SEP TH	SEP TH	OCT tr	NOV FR	DEC fg
5 SPRING	6 WARM	6 CLEAR	7 SUMMER	9 GRAIN	11 HEAT	12 FALL	OF	15 DEW	15 C DEW	15 WINTER	16 SNOW	16 CHILL	16 SPRING
6:21	0:07	4:50	22:16	2:32	12:57	23:02	MON	2:21	18:20	21:36	14:11	0:57	12:09
1/31 RT	3/1 md	3/31 mg	4/29 MF	5/29 MR	6/27 ef	7/27 er	1	8/25 EW	9/24 EH	10/24 EW	11/22 fm	12/22 ft	1/20 FM
2/1 rt	3/2 RM	4/1 RT	4/30 md	5/30 mg	6/28 MF	7/28 MR	2	8/26 ef	9/25 er	10/25 ef	11/23 EH	12/23 EW	1/21 fm
2/2 TW	3/3 rm	4/2 rt	5/1 RM	5/31 RT	6/29 md	7/29 mg	3	8/27 MF	9/26 MR	10/26 MF	11/24 er	12/24 ef	1/22 EH
2/3 tf	3/4 TH	4/3 TW	5/2 rm	6/1 rt	6/30 RM	7/30 RT	4	8/28 md	9/27 mg	10/27 md	11/25 MR	12/25 MF	1/23 er
2/4 FF	3/5 tr	4/4 tf	5/3 TH	6/2 TW	7/1 rm	7/31 rt	5	8/29 RM	9/28 RT	10/28 RM	11/26 mg	12/26 md	1/24 MR
2/5 fd	3/6 FR	4/5 FF	5/4 tr	6/3 tf	7/2 TH	8/1 TW	6	8/30 rm	9/29 rt	10/29 rm	11/27 RT	12/27 RM	1/25 mg
2/6 EM	3/7 fg	4/6 fd	5/5 FR	6/4 FF	7/3 tr	8/2 tf	7	8/31 TH	9/30 TW	10/30 TH	11/28 rt	12/28 rm	1/26 RT
2/7 em	3/8 ET	4/7 EM	5/6 fg	6/5 fd	7/4 FR	8/3 FF	8	9/1 tr	10/1 tf	10/31 tr	11/29 TW	12/29 TH	1/27 rt
2/8 MH	3/9 et	4/8 em	5/7 ET	6/6 EM	7/5 fg	8/4 fd	9	9/2 FR	10/2 FF	11/1 FR	11/30 tf	12/30 tr	1/28 TW
2/9 mr	3/10 MW	4/9 MH	5/8 et	6/7 em	7/6 ET	8/5 EM	10	9/3 fg	10/3 fd	11/2 fg	12/1 FF	12/31 FR	1/29 tf
2/10 RR	3/11 mf	4/10 mr	5/9 MW	6/8 MH	7/7 et	8/6 em	11	9/4 ET	10/4 EM	11/3 ET	12/2 fd	1/1 fg	1/30 FF
2/11 rg	3/12 RF	4/11 RR	5/10 mf	6/9 mr	7/8 MW	8/7 MH	12	9/5 et	10/5 em	11/4 et	12/3 EM	1/2 ET	1/31 fd
2/12 TT	3/13 rd	4/12 rg	5/11 RF	6/10 RR	7/9 mf	8/8 mr	13	9/6 MW	10/6 MH	11/5 MW	12/4 em	1/3 et	2/1 EM
2/13 tt	3/14 TM	4/13 TT	5/12 rd	6/11 rg	7/10 RF	8/9 RR	14	9/7 mf	10/7 mr	11/6 mf	12/5 MH	1/4 MW	2/2 em
2/14 FW	3/15 tm	4/14 tt	5/13 TM	6/12 TT	7/11 rd	8/10 rg	15	9/8 RF	10/8 RR	11/7 RF	12/6 mr	1/5 mf	2/3 MH
2/15 ff	3/16 FH	4/15 FW	5/14 tm	6/13 tt	7/12 TM	8/11 TT	16	9/9 rd	10/9 rg	11/8 rd	12/7 RR	1/6 RF	2/4 mr
2/16 EF	3/17 fr	4/16 ff	5/15 FH	6/14 FW	7/13 tm	8/12 tt	17	9/10 TM	10/10 TT	11/9 TM	12/8 rg	1/7 rd	2/5 RR
2/17 ed	3/18 ER	4/17 EF	5/16 fr	6/15 ff	7/14 FH	8/13 FW	18	9/11 tm	10/11 tt	11/10 tm	12/9 TT	1/8 TM	2/6 rg
2/18 MM	3/19 eg	4/18 ed	5/17 ER	6/16 EF	7/15 fr	8/14 ff	19	9/12 FH	10/12 FW	11/11 FH	12/10 tt	1/9 tm	2/7 TT
2/19 mm	3/20 MT	4/19 MM	5/18 eg	6/17 ed	7/16 ER	8/15 EF	20	9/13 fr	10/13 ff	11/12 fr	12/11 FW	1/10 FH	2/8 tt
2/20 RH	3/21 mt	4/20 mm	5/19 MT	6/18 MM	7/17 eg	8/16 ed	21	9/14 ER	10/14 EF	11/13 ER	12/12 ff	1/11 fr	2/9 FW
2/21 rr	3/22 RW	4/21 RH	5/20 mt	6/19 mm	7/18 MT	8/17 MM	22	9/15 eg	10/15 ed	11/14 eg	12/13 EF	1/12 ER	2/10 ff
2/22 TR	3/23 rf	4/22 rr	5/21 RW	6/20 RH	7/19 mt	8/18 mm	23	9/16 MT	10/16 MM	11/15 MT	12/14 ed	1/13 eg	2/11 EF
2/23 tg	3/24 TF	4/23 TR	5/22 rf	6/21 rr	7/20 RW	8/19 RH	24	9/17 mt	10/17 mm	11/16 mt	12/15 MM	1/14 MT	2/12 ed
2/24 FT	3/25 td	4/24 tg	5/23 TF	6/22 TR	7/21 rf	8/20 rr	25	9/18 RW	10/18 RH	11/17 RW	12/16 mm	1/15 mt	2/13 MM
2/25 ft	3/26 FM	4/25 FT	5/24 td	6/23 tg	7/22 TF	8/21 TR	26	9/19 rf	10/19 rr	11/18 rf	12/17 RH	1/16 RW	2/14 mm
2/26 EW	3/27 fm	4/26 ft	5/25 FM	6/24 FT	7/23 td	8/22 tg	27	9/20 TF	10/20 TR	11/19 TF	12/18 rr	1/17 rf	2/15 RH
2/27 ef	3/28 EH	4/27 EW	5/26 fm	6/25 ft	7/24 FM	8/23 FT	28	9/21 td	10/21 tg	11/20 td	12/19 TR	1/18 TF	2/16 rr
2/28 MF	3/29 er	4/28 ef	5/27 EH	6/26 EW	7/25 fm	8/24 ft	29	9/22 FM	10/22 FT	11/21 FM	12/20 tg	1/19 td	2/17 TR
	3/30 MR		5/28 er		7/26 EH		30	9/23 fm	10/23 ft		12/21 FT		2/18 tg

2015 td RAM

JAN ET	FEB et	MAR MW	APR mf	MAY RF	JUN rd	DAY OF MON	JUL TM	AUG tm	SEP FH	OCT tr	NOV ER	DEC eg
16 WARM	17 CLEAR	18 SUMMER	20 GRAIN	22 HEAT	24 FALL		26 DEW	27 C DEW	27 WINTER	26 SNOW	27 CHILL	26 SPRING
5:56	10:58	4:00	8:20	18:30	4:51		8:10	0:09	3:25	20:01	6:47	18:00
2 19 FT	2 20 td	4 19 tg	5 18 TF	6 16 rr	7 16 rf	1	8 14 RH	9 13 RW	10 13 RH	11 12 RW	12 11 mm	1 10 mt
2 20 ft	2 21 FM	4 20 FT	5 19 td	6 17 TR	7 17 TF	2	8 15 rr	9 14 rf	10 14 rf	11 13 rf	12 12 RH	1 11 RW
2 21 EW	2 22 fm	4 21 ft	5 20 FM	6 18 tg	7 18 td	3	8 16 TR	9 15 TF	10 15 TR	11 14 TF	12 13 rr	1 12 rf
2 22 ef	2 23 EH	4 22 EW	5 21 fm	6 19 FT	7 19 FM	4	8 17 tg	9 16 td	10 16 tg	11 15 td	12 14 TR	1 13 TF
2 23 MF	2 24 er	4 23 ef	5 22 EH	6 20 ft	7 20 ft	5	8 18 FT	9 17 FM	10 17 FT	11 16 FM	12 15 tg	1 14 td
2 24 md	2 25 MR	4 24 MF	5 23 er	6 21 EW	7 21 EH	6	8 19 ft	9 18 fm	10 18 ft	11 17 fm	12 16 FT	1 15 FM
2 25 RM	2 26 md	4 25 md	5 24 MF	6 22 ef	7 22 er	7	8 20 EH	9 19 EH	10 19 EW	11 18 EH	12 17 ft	1 16 fm
2 26 rm	2 27 RT	4 26 RM	5 25 md	6 23 MF	7 23 MR	8	8 21 ef	9 20 ef	10 20 ef	11 19 er	12 18 EW	1 17 EH
2 27 TH	2 28 rt	4 27 rm	5 26 RT	6 24 md	7 24 mg	9	8 22 MF	9 21 MR	10 21 MF	11 20 MR	12 19 ef	1 18 er
2 28 tr	2 29 TW	4 28 TH	5 27 rt	6 25 RM	7 25 RT	10	8 23 md	9 22 mg	10 22 md	11 21 mg	12 20 MF	1 19 MR
3 1 FR	3 30 tf	4 29 tr	5 28 TW	6 26 rm	7 26 rt	11	8 24 RM	9 23 RT	10 23 RM	11 22 RT	12 21 md	1 20 mg
3 2 fg	3 31 FF	4 30 FR	5 29 tf	6 27 TH	7 27 TW	12	8 25 rm	9 24 rm	10 24 rm	11 23 rt	12 22 RM	1 21 RT
3 3 ET	3 1 fd	4 31 fg	5 30 FR	6 28 tr	7 28 tf	13	8 26 TW	9 25 TW	10 25 TH	11 24 TW	12 23 rm	1 22 rt
3 4 et	3 2 EM	5 1 ET	6 31 fd	6 29 FR	7 29 FR	14	8 27 tr	9 26 tf	10 26 tr	11 25 tf	12 24 TH	1 23 TW
3 5 MW	3 3 em	5 2 et	6 1 EM	6 30 fg	7 30 fd	15	8 28 FR	9 27 FF	10 27 FR	11 26 FF	12 25 tr	1 24 tf
3 6 mr	3 4 MH	5 3 MW	6 2 et	7 1 ET	7 31 ET	16	8 29 fd	9 28 fd	10 28 fg	11 27 fd	12 26 FR	1 25 FF
3 7 RF	3 5 mr	5 4 mf	6 3 MH	7 2 em	8 1 em	17	8 30 ET	9 29 EM	10 29 ET	11 28 EM	12 27 fg	1 26 fd
3 8 rd	3 6 RR	5 5 RF	6 4 mr	7 3 MW	8 2 MW	18	8 31 et	9 30 em	10 30 em	11 29 em	12 28 ET	1 27 EM
3 9 TM	3 7 rg	5 6 rd	6 5 RR	7 4 mf	8 3 mf	19	9 1 MW	10 1 MH	10 31 MW	11 30 MH	12 29 et	1 28 em
3 10 tm	3 8 TT	5 7 TM	6 6 rg	7 5 RF	8 4 RF	20	9 2 mf	10 2 mr	11 1 mf	12 1 mr	12 30 MW	1 29 MH
3 11 FH	3 9 tt	5 8 tm	6 7 TT	7 6 rd	8 5 rd	21	9 3 RF	10 3 RR	11 2 RF	12 2 RR	12 31 mf	1 30 mr
3 12 fr	3 10 FW	5 9 FH	6 8 tt	7 7 TT	8 6 TM	22	9 4 rd	10 4 rg	11 3 rd	12 3 rg	1 1 RF	1 31 RR
3 13 ER	3 11 ff	5 10 fr	6 9 FW	7 8 tm	8 7 tm	23	9 5 TM	10 5 TM	11 4 TM	12 4 TT	1 2 rd	2 1 TT
3 14 eg	3 12 EF	5 11 ER	6 10 ff	7 9 FH	8 8 FH	24	9 6 tm	10 6 tm	11 5 tm	12 5 tt	1 3 TM	2 2 tt
3 15 MT	3 13 ed	5 12 eg	6 11 EF	7 10 fr	8 9 fr	25	9 7 FH	10 7 FH	11 6 FH	12 6 FW	1 4 tm	2 3 FW
3 16 mt	3 14 MM	5 13 MT	6 12 ed	7 11 ER	8 10 EF	26	9 8 fr	10 8 fr	11 7 fr	12 7 ff	1 5 FH	2 4 ff
3 17 RW	3 15 mt	5 14 mt	6 13 MM	7 12 er	8 11 ed	27	9 9 ER	10 9 EF	11 8 ER	12 8 EF	1 6 fr	2 5 EF
3 18 rf	3 16 RH	5 15 RW	6 14 mm	7 13 MT	8 12 MM	28	9 10 eg	10 10 eg	11 9 er	12 9 ed	1 7 ER	2 6 ed
3 19 TF	3 17 rr	5 16 rf	6 15 RH	7 14 mt	8 13 mm	29	9 11 MT	10 11 MM	11 10 MT	12 10 MM	1 8 eg	2 7 ed
	3 18 TR	5 17 TF		7 15 RW		30	9 12 mt	10 12 mm	11 11 mt		1 9 MT	

2016 FM MONKEY

JAN MT	FEB mt	MAR RW	APR rf	MAY TF	JUN td	DAY OF MON	JUL FM	AUG fm	SEP EH	OCT er	NOV MR	DEC mg
27 WARM	27 CLEAR	29 SUMMER		1 GRAIN	4 HEAT		5 FALL	7 DEW	8 C DEW	8 WINTER	9 SNOW	8 CHILL
11:46	16:32	9:54		14:09	0:33		10:39	13:48	5:59	9:14	1:54	12:36
2 8 MM	3 9 MT	4 7 ed	5 7 eg	6 5 EF	7 4 fr	1	8 3 ff	9 1 FH	10 1 FW	10 31 FH	11 29 tt	12 29 tm
2 9 mm	3 10 mt	4 8 MM	5 8 MT	6 6 ed	7 5 ER	2	8 4 EF	9 2 fr	10 2 ff	11 1 fr	11 30 FW	12 30 FH
2 10 RH	3 11 RW	4 9 mm	5 9 mt	6 7 MM	7 6 eg	3	8 5 ed	9 3 ER	10 3 EF	11 2 ER	12 1 ff	12 31 fr
2 11 rr	3 12 rf	4 10 RH	5 10 RW	6 8 mm	7 7 MT	4	8 6 MM	9 4 eg	10 4 ed	11 3 eg	12 2 EF	1 1 ER
2 12 TR	3 13 TF	4 11 rr	5 11 rf	6 9 RH	7 8 mt	5	8 7 mm	9 5 MT	10 5 MM	11 4 MT	12 3 ed	1 2 eg
2 13 tg	3 14 td	4 12 TR	5 12 TF	6 10 rr	7 9 RW	6	8 8 RH	9 6 mt	10 6 mm	11 5 mt	12 4 MM	1 3 MT
2 14 FT	3 15 FM	4 13 tg	5 13 td	6 11 TR	7 10 rf	7	8 9 rr	9 7 RW	10 7 RH	11 6 RW	12 5 mm	1 4 mt
2 15 ft	3 16 fm	4 14 FT	5 14 FM	6 12 tg	7 11 TF	8	8 10 TR	9 8 rf	10 8 rr	11 7 rf	12 6 RH	1 5 RW
2 16 EW	3 17 EH	4 15 ft	5 15 fm	6 13 FT	7 12 td	9	8 11 tg	9 9 TF	10 9 TR	11 8 TF	12 7 rr	1 6 rf
2 17 ef	3 18 er	4 16 EW	5 16 EH	6 14 ft	7 13 FM	10	8 12 FT	9 10 td	10 10 tg	11 9 td	12 8 TR	1 7 TF
2 18 MF	3 19 MR	4 17 ef	5 17 er	6 15 EW	7 14 fm	11	8 13 ft	9 11 FM	10 11 FT	11 10 FM	12 9 tg	1 8 td
2 19 md	3 20 mg	4 18 MF	5 18 MR	6 16 ef	7 15 EH	12	8 14 EW	9 12 fm	10 12 ft	11 11 fm	12 10 FT	1 9 FM
2 20 RM	3 21 RT	4 19 md	5 19 mg	6 17 MF	7 16 er	13	8 15 ef	9 13 EH	10 13 EW	11 12 EH	12 11 ft	1 10 fm
2 21 rm	3 22 rt	4 20 RM	5 20 RT	6 18 md	7 17 MR	14	8 16 MF	9 14 er	10 14 ef	11 13 er	12 12 EW	1 11 EH
2 22 TH	3 23 TW	4 21 rm	5 21 rt	6 19 RM	7 18 mg	15	8 17 md	9 15 MR	10 15 MF	11 14 MR	12 13 ef	1 12 er
2 23 tr	3 24 tf	4 22 TH	5 22 TW	6 20 rm	7 19 RT	16	8 18 RM	9 16 mg	10 16 md	11 15 mg	12 14 MF	1 13 MR
2 24 FR	3 25 FF	4 23 tr	5 23 tf	6 21 TH	7 20 rt	17	8 19 rm	9 17 RT	10 17 RM	11 16 RT	12 15 md	1 14 mg
2 25 fg	3 26 fd	4 24 FR	5 24 FF	6 22 tr	7 21 TW	18	8 20 TH	9 18 rt	10 18 rm	11 17 rt	12 16 RM	1 15 RT
2 26 ET	3 27 EM	4 25 fg	5 25 fd	6 23 FR	7 22 tf	19	8 21 tr	9 19 TW	10 19 TH	11 18 TW	12 17 rm	1 16 rt
2 27 et	3 28 em	4 26 ET	5 26 EM	6 24 fg	7 23 FF	20	8 22 FR	9 20 tf	10 20 tr	11 19 tf	12 18 TH	1 17 TW
2 28 MW	3 29 MH	4 27 et	5 27 em	6 25 ET	7 24 fd	21	8 23 fg	9 21 FF	10 21 FR	11 20 FF	12 19 tr	1 18 tf
2 29 mf	3 30 mr	4 28 MW	5 28 MH	6 26 et	7 25 EM	22	8 24 ET	9 22 fd	10 22 fg	11 21 fd	12 20 FR	1 19 FF
3 1 RF	3 31 RR	4 29 mf	5 29 mr	6 27 MW	7 26 em	23	8 25 et	9 23 EM	10 23 ET	11 22 EM	12 21 fg	1 20 fd
3 2 rd	4 1 rg	4 30 RF	5 30 RR	6 28 mf	7 27 MH	24	8 26 MW	9 24 em	10 24 et	11 23 em	12 22 ET	1 21 EM
3 3 TM	4 2 TT	5 1 rd	5 31 rg	6 29 RF	7 28 mr	25	8 27 mf	9 25 MH	10 25 MW	11 24 MH	12 23 et	1 22 em
3 4 tm	4 3 tt	5 2 TM	6 1 TT	6 30 rd	7 29 RR	26	8 28 RF	9 26 mr	10 26 mf	11 25 mr	12 24 MW	1 23 MH
3 5 FH	4 4 FW	5 3 tm	6 2 tt	7 1 TM	7 30 rg	27	8 29 rd	9 27 RR	10 27 RF	11 26 RR	12 25 mf	1 24 mr
3 6 fr	4 5 ff	5 4 FH	6 3 FW	7 2 tm	7 31 TT	28	8 30 TM	9 28 rg	10 28 rd	11 27 rg	12 26 RF	1 25 RR
3 7 ER	4 6 EF	5 5 fr	6 4 ff	7 3 FH	8 1 tt	29	8 31 tm	9 29 TT	10 29 TM	11 28 TT	12 27 rd	1 26 rg
3 8 eg		5 6 ER			8 2 FW	30		9 30 tt	10 30 tm		12 28 TM	1 27 TT

2017 fm ROOSTER

JAN RT	FEB rt	MAR Tw	APR ff	MAY FF	JUN fd	JUN fd	DAY	JUL EM	AUG em	SEP MH	OCT mr	NOV RR	DEC rg
7 SPRING	8 WARM	8 CLEAR	10 SUMMER	11 GRAIN	14 HEAT	16 FALL	OF MON	17 DEW	19 C DEW	19 WINTER	20 SNOW	19 CHILL	19 SPRING
23:49	17:36	22:20	15:42	19:46	6:21	16:27		19:46	11:47	15:03	7:40	18:26	5:38

JAN	FEB	MAR	APR	MAY	JUN	JUN	DAY	JUL	AUG	SEP	OCT	NOV	DEC
1 28 tt	2 26 TM	3 28 TT	4 26 rd	5 26 rg	6 24 RF	7 23 mr	1	8 22 mf	9 20 MH	10 20 MW	11 18 em	12 18 et	1 17 em
1 29 FW	2 27 tm	3 29 tt	4 27 TM	5 27 TT	6 25 rd	7 24 RR	2	8 23 RF	9 21 mr	10 21 mf	11 19 MH	12 19 MW	1 18 MH
1 30 fr	2 28 FH	3 30 FW	4 28 tm	5 28 tm	6 26 TM	7 25 TM	3	8 24 rd	9 22 RR	10 22 RF	11 20 mr	12 20 mf	1 19 mr
1 31 EF	3 1 fr	3 31 ff	4 29 FH	5 29 FW	6 27 tm	7 26 TT	4	8 25 TM	9 23 rg	10 23 rd	11 21 RR	12 21 RF	1 20 RR
2 1 ed	3 2 ER	4 1 EF	4 30 fr	5 30 ff	6 28 FH	7 27 tt	5	8 26 tm	9 24 TT	10 24 TM	11 22 rg	12 22 rd	1 21 rg
2 2 MM	3 3 eg	4 2 ed	5 1 ER	5 31 EF	6 29 fr	7 28 FW	6	8 27 FH	9 25 tt	10 25 tm	11 23 TT	12 23 TM	1 22 TT
2 3 mm	3 4 MT	4 3 MM	5 2 eg	6 1 ed	6 30 ER	7 29 ff	7	8 28 fr	9 26 FW	10 26 FH	11 24 tt	12 24 tm	1 23 tt
2 4 RH	3 5 mt	4 4 mm	5 3 MT	6 2 MM	7 1 eg	7 30 EF	8	8 29 ER	9 27 ff	10 27 fr	11 25 FW	12 25 FH	1 24 FW
2 5 rr	3 6 RW	4 5 RH	5 4 mt	6 3 mm	7 2 MT	7 31 ed	9	8 30 eg	9 28 EF	10 28 ER	11 26 ff	12 26 fr	1 25 ff
2 6 TR	3 7 rf	4 6 rr	5 5 RW	6 4 RH	7 3 mt	8 1 MM	10	8 31 MT	9 29 ed	10 29 eg	11 27 EF	12 27 ER	1 26 EF
2 7 tg	3 8 TF	4 7 TR	5 6 rf	6 5 rr	7 4 RW	8 2 mm	11	9 1 mt	9 30 MM	10 30 MT	11 28 ed	12 28 eg	1 27 ed
2 8 ft	3 9 td	4 8 tg	5 7 TF	6 6 TR	7 5 rf	8 3 RH	12	9 2 RW	10 1 mm	10 31 mt	11 29 MM	12 29 MT	1 28 MM
2 9 FM	3 10 FM	4 9 FT	5 8 td	6 7 tg	7 6 TF	8 4 rr	13	9 3 rf	10 2 RH	11 1 RW	11 30 mm	12 30 mt	1 29 mm
2 10 EW	3 11 fm	4 10 ft	5 9 FM	6 8 FT	7 7 td	8 5 TR	14	9 4 TF	10 3 rr	11 2 rf	12 1 RH	1 1 RW	1 30 RH
2 11 ef	3 12 EH	4 11 EW	5 10 fm	6 9 ft	7 8 FM	8 6 tg	15	9 5 td	10 4 TR	11 3 TF	12 2 rr	1 2 rf	1 31 rr
2 12 MF	3 13 er	4 12 ef	5 11 EH	6 10 EW	7 9 fm	8 7 FT	16	9 6 FM	10 5 tg	11 4 td	12 3 TR	1 3 TF	2 1 TR
2 13 md	3 14 MR	4 13 MF	5 12 er	6 11 ef	7 10 EH	8 8 ft	17	9 7 fm	10 6 FT	11 5 FM	12 4 tg	1 4 td	2 2 tg
2 14 RM	3 15 mg	4 14 md	5 13 MR	6 12 MF	7 11 er	8 9 EW	18	9 8 EH	10 7 ft	11 6 fm	12 5 FT	1 5 FM	2 3 FT
2 15 rm	3 16 RT	4 15 RM	5 14 mg	6 13 md	7 12 MR	8 10 ef	19	9 9 er	10 8 EW	11 7 EH	12 6 ft	1 6 fm	2 4 ft
2 16 TH	3 17 rt	4 16 rm	5 15 RT	6 14 RM	7 13 mg	8 11 MF	20	9 10 MR	10 9 ef	11 8 er	12 7 EW	1 7 EH	2 5 EW
2 17 tr	3 18 TW	4 17 TH	5 16 rt	6 15 rm	7 14 RT	8 12 md	21	9 11 mg	10 10 MF	11 9 MR	12 8 ef	1 8 er	2 6 ef
2 18 FR	3 19 tf	4 18 tr	5 17 TW	6 16 TH	7 15 rt	8 13 RM	22	9 12 RT	10 11 md	11 10 mg	12 9 MF	1 9 MR	2 7 MF
2 19 fg	3 20 FF	4 19 FR	5 18 tf	6 17 tr	7 16 TW	8 14 rm	23	9 13 rt	10 12 RM	11 11 RT	12 10 md	1 10 mg	2 8 md
2 20 ET	3 21 fd	4 20 fg	5 19 FR	6 18 FR	7 17 tf	8 15 TH	24	9 14 TW	10 13 rm	11 12 rt	12 11 RM	1 11 RT	2 9 RM
2 21 et	3 22 EM	4 21 ET	5 20 fd	6 19 fg	7 18 FF	8 16 tr	25	9 15 tf	10 14 TH	11 13 TW	12 12 rm	1 12 rt	2 10 rm
2 22 MW	3 23 em	4 22 et	5 21 EM	6 20 ET	7 19 fd	8 17 FR	26	9 16 FF	10 15 tr	11 14 tf	12 13 TH	1 13 TW	2 11 TH
2 23 mf	3 24 MH	4 23 MW	5 22 em	6 21 et	7 20 EM	8 18 fg	27	9 17 fd	10 16 FR	11 15 FF	12 14 tr	1 14 tf	2 12 tr
2 24 RF	3 25 mf	4 24 mf	5 23 MH	6 22 MW	7 21 em	8 19 ET	28	9 18 EM	10 17 fg	11 16 fd	12 15 FR	1 15 FF	2 13 FR
2 25 rd	3 26 RR	4 25 RF	5 24 mr	6 23 mf	7 22 MH	8 20 et	29	9 19 em	10 18 ET	11 17 EM	12 16 fg	1 16 fd	2 14 fd
	3 27 rg		5 25 RR			8 21 MW	30		10 19 et		12 17 ET		2 15 ET

2018 EH DOG

	JAN TT	FEB tt	MAR FW	APR ff	MAY EF	JUN ed	DAY OF MON	JUL MM	AUG mm	SEP RH	OCT rr	NOV TR	DEC tg
solar term	18 WARM	21 CLEAR	20 SUMMER	23 GRAIN	24 HEAT	26 FALL	—	29 DEW	29 C DEW	30 WINTER	—	1 SNOW	1 CHILL · 30 SPRING
time	23:25	4:20	21:31	1:29	12:09	22:15	—	1:35	17:36	20:54	—	13:30	0:16 · 11:28

Daily grid (lunar-month · lunar-day · code)

DAY OF MON	JAN TT	FEB tt	MAR FW	APR ff	MAY EF	JUN ed	JUL MM	AUG mm	SEP RH	OCT rr	NOV TR	DEC tg
1	2 16 et	3 17 EM	4 16 ET	5 15 fd	6 14 fg	7 13 FF	8 11 tr	9 10 tf	10 9 TH	11 8 TW	12 7 rm	1 6 rt
2	2 17 MW	3 18 em	4 17 et	5 16 EM	6 15 ET	7 14 fd	8 12 FR	9 11 FF	10 10 tr	11 9 tf	12 8 TH	1 7 TW
3	2 18 mf	3 19 MH	4 18 MW	5 17 em	6 16 et	7 15 EM	8 13 fg	9 12 fd	10 11 FR	11 10 FF	12 9 tr	1 8 tf
4	2 19 RF	3 20 mr	4 19 mf	5 18 MH	6 17 MW	7 16 em	8 14 ET	9 13 EM	10 12 fg	11 11 fd	12 10 FR	1 9 FF
5	2 20 rd	3 21 RR	4 20 RF	5 19 mr	6 18 mf	7 17 MH	8 15 et	9 14 em	10 13 ET	11 12 EM	12 11 fg	1 10 fd
6	2 21 TM	3 22 rg	4 21 rd	5 20 RR	6 19 RF	7 18 mr	8 16 MW	9 15 MH	10 14 et	11 13 em	12 12 ET	1 11 EM
7	2 22 tm	3 23 TT	4 22 TM	5 21 rg	6 20 rd	7 19 RR	8 17 mf	9 16 mr	10 15 MW	11 14 MH	12 13 et	1 12 em
8	2 23 FH	3 24 tt	4 23 tm	5 22 TT	6 21 TM	7 20 rg	8 18 RF	9 17 RR	10 16 mf	11 15 mr	12 14 MW	1 13 MH
9	2 24 fr	3 25 FW	4 24 FH	5 23 tt	6 22 tm	7 21 TM	8 19 rd	9 18 rg	10 17 RF	11 16 RR	12 15 mf	1 14 mr
10	2 25 ER	3 26 ff	4 25 fr	5 24 FW	6 23 FH	7 22 tt	8 20 TM	9 19 TT	10 18 rd	11 17 rg	12 16 RF	1 15 RR
11	2 26 eg	3 27 EF	4 26 ER	5 25 ff	6 24 fr	7 23 FW	8 21 tm	9 20 tt	10 19 TM	11 18 TT	12 17 rd	1 16 rg
12	2 27 MT	3 28 ed	4 27 eg	5 26 EF	6 25 ER	7 24 ff	8 22 FH	9 21 FW	10 20 tm	11 19 tt	12 18 TM	1 17 TT
13	2 28 mt	3 29 MM	4 28 MT	5 27 ed	6 26 eg	7 25 EF	8 23 fr	9 22 ff	10 21 FH	11 20 FW	12 19 tm	1 18 tt
14	3 1 RW	3 30 mm	4 29 mt	5 28 MM	6 27 MT	7 26 ed	8 24 ER	9 23 EF	10 22 fr	11 21 ff	12 20 FH	1 19 FW
15	3 2 rf	3 31 RH	4 30 RW	5 29 mm	6 28 mt	7 27 MM	8 25 eg	9 24 ed	10 23 ER	11 22 EF	12 21 fr	1 20 ff
16	3 3 TF	4 1 rr	5 1 rf	5 30 RH	6 29 RW	7 28 mm	8 26 MT	9 25 MT	10 24 eg	11 23 ed	12 22 ER	1 21 EF
17	3 4 td	4 2 TR	5 2 TF	5 31 rr	6 30 rf	7 29 RH	8 27 mt	9 26 mt	10 25 MT	11 24 MM	12 23 eg	1 22 ed
18	3 5 FM	4 3 tg	5 3 td	6 1 TR	7 1 TF	7 30 rr	8 28 RW	9 27 RH	10 26 mt	11 25 mm	12 24 MT	1 23 MM
19	3 6 fm	4 4 FT	5 4 FM	6 2 tg	7 2 td	7 31 TR	8 29 rf	9 28 rr	10 27 RW	11 26 RH	12 25 mt	1 24 mm
20	3 7 EH	4 5 ft	5 5 fm	6 3 FT	7 3 FM	8 1 tg	8 30 TF	9 29 TR	10 28 rf	11 27 rr	12 26 RW	1 25 RH
21	3 8 er	4 6 EH	5 6 EH	6 4 ft	7 4 fm	8 2 FT	8 31 td	9 30 tg	10 29 TF	11 28 TR	12 27 rf	1 26 rr
22	3 9 MR	4 7 ef	5 7 er	6 5 EW	7 5 EH	8 3 ft	9 1 FM	10 1 FT	10 30 td	11 29 tg	12 28 TF	1 27 TR
23	3 10 mg	4 8 MF	5 8 MR	6 6 ef	7 6 er	8 4 EW	9 2 fm	10 2 ft	10 31 FM	11 30 FT	12 29 td	1 28 tg
24	3 11 RT	4 9 md	5 9 mg	6 7 MF	7 7 MR	8 5 ef	9 3 EH	10 3 EW	11 1 fm	12 1 ft	12 30 FM	1 29 FT
25	3 12 rt	4 10 RT	5 10 RT	6 8 md	7 8 mg	8 6 MF	9 4 er	10 4 ef	11 2 EH	12 2 EW	12 31 fm	1 30 ft
26	3 13 TW	4 11 rm	5 11 rt	6 9 RM	7 9 RT	8 7 md	9 5 MR	10 5 MF	11 3 er	12 3 ef	1 1 EH	2 1 EW
27	3 14 tf	4 12 TH	5 12 TW	6 10 rm	7 10 rt	8 8 RM	9 6 mg	10 6 md	11 4 MR	12 4 MF	1 2 er	2 2 MF
28	3 15 FF	4 13 tr	5 13 tf	6 11 TH	7 11 TW	8 9 rm	9 7 RT	10 7 RT	11 5 mg	12 5 md	1 3 MR	2 3 md
29	3 16 fd	4 14 FR	5 14 FF	6 12 tr	7 12 tf	8 10 TH	9 8 rt	10 8 rm	11 6 RT	12 6 RM	1 4 mg	2 4 RM
30	—	—	—	6 13 FR	—	—	9 9 TW	—	11 7 rt	—	1 5 md	—
31	—	—	—	—	—	—	—	—	—	—	—	—

2019 er BOAR

JAN FT	FEB ft	MAR EW	APR ef	MAY MF	JUN md	JUL RM	AUG rm	SEP TH	OCT tr	NOV FR	DEC fg
	1 WARM	1 CLEAR	2 SUMMER	4 GRAIN	5 HEAT	8 FALL	10 DEW	10 C DEW	12 WINTER	12 SNOW	12 CHILL
	5:14	9:59	3:20	7:33	17:57	4:03	7:24	23:25	2:42	19:20	6:06
2 5 rm	3 6 RT	4 5 RM	5 5 RT	6 3 md	7 3 mg	8 1 MF	8 30 er	9 29 ef	10 28 EH	11 26 ft	12 26 fm
2 6 TH	3 7 rt	4 6 rm	5 6 rt	6 4 RM	7 4 RT	8 2 md	8 31 MR	9 30 MF	10 29 er	11 27 EW	12 27 EH
2 7 tr	3 8 TW	4 7 TH	5 7 TW	6 5 rr	7 5 rr	8 3 RM	9 1 mg	10 1 md	10 30 MR	11 28 ef	12 28 er
2 8 FR	3 9 tf	4 8 tr	5 8 tf	6 6 TH	7 6 TW	8 4 rm	9 2 RM	10 2 rm	10 31 RT	11 29 MF	12 29 MR
2 9 fg	3 10 FF	4 9 FR	5 9 FF	6 7 tr	7 7 tf	8 5 TH	9 3 rt	10 3 rm	11 1 rt	11 30 md	12 30 mg
2 10 ET	3 11 fd	4 10 fg	5 10 fd	6 8 FF	7 8 FR	8 6 tr	9 4 TW	10 4 TH	11 2 RT	12 1 RM	12 31 RT
2 11 et	3 12 EM	4 11 ET	5 11 EM	6 9 fg	7 9 fd	8 7 FR	9 5 tf	10 5 tr	11 3 rt	12 2 rm	12 1 rt
2 12 MW	3 13 em	4 12 et	5 12 em	6 10 ET	7 10 EM	8 8 fg	9 6 FF	10 6 FR	11 4 TW	12 3 TH	12 1 TW
2 13 mf	3 14 MH	4 13 MW	5 13 MH	6 11 em	7 11 et	8 9 ET	9 7 fd	10 7 fg	11 5 tf	12 4 tr	12 1 tf
2 14 RF	3 15 mr	4 14 mr	5 14 mr	6 12 MH	7 12 MW	8 10 et	9 8 EM	10 8 ET	11 6 FR	12 5 FR	12 1 FF
2 15 rd	3 16 RR	4 15 RR	5 15 RF	6 13 mr	7 13 mf	8 11 MW	9 9 em	10 9 et	11 7 fg	12 6 fg	12 1 fd
2 16 TM	3 17 rg	4 16 rg	5 16 rd	6 14 RR	7 14 RF	8 12 mf	9 10 MW	10 10 MW	11 8 ET	12 7 ET	12 6 EM
2 17 tm	3 18 TT	4 17 TM	5 17 rg	6 15 rg	7 15 rd	8 13 RF	9 11 mf	10 11 mf	11 9 et	12 8 et	12 7 em
2 18 FH	3 19 tt	4 18 tm	5 18 TM	6 16 TT	7 16 TM	8 14 rd	9 12 RR	10 12 RF	11 10 MH	12 9 MW	12 8 MH
2 19 fr	3 20 FW	4 19 FH	5 19 tm	6 17 tt	7 17 tm	8 15 TM	9 13 rg	10 13 rd	11 11 mr	12 10 mf	12 9 mr
2 20 ER	3 21 ff	4 20 fr	5 20 FH	6 18 FW	7 18 TT	8 16 tm	9 14 TT	10 14 TM	11 12 RR	12 11 RF	12 10 RR
2 21 eg	3 22 EF	4 21 ER	5 21 ff	6 19 ff	7 19 tt	8 17 FH	9 15 tt	10 15 tm	11 13 rg	12 12 rd	12 11 rg
2 22 MT	3 23 ed	4 22 eg	5 22 EF	6 20 EF	7 20 FW	8 18 fr	9 16 FW	10 16 FH	11 14 TT	12 13 TM	12 12 TT
2 23 mt	3 24 MM	4 23 MT	5 23 ed	6 21 ed	7 21 ff	8 19 ER	9 17 ff	10 17 fr	11 15 tt	12 14 tm	12 13 tt
2 24 RW	3 25 mm	4 24 mt	5 24 MM	6 22 MM	7 22 EF	8 20 eg	9 18 EF	10 18 ER	11 16 FH	12 15 FW	12 14 FW
2 25 rf	3 26 RH	4 25 RW	5 25 mm	6 23 mm	7 23 ed	8 21 MT	9 19 ed	10 19 eg	11 17 fr	12 16 ff	12 15 ff
2 26 TF	3 27 rr	4 26 rf	5 26 RH	6 24 RH	7 24 MM	8 22 mt	9 20 MM	10 20 MT	11 18 ER	12 17 EF	12 16 EF
2 27 td	3 28 TR	4 27 TR	5 27 rr	6 25 rr	7 25 mt	8 23 RW	9 21 mm	10 21 mt	11 19 eg	12 18 ed	12 17 ed
2 28 FM	3 29 tg	4 28 td	5 28 TR	6 26 TR	7 26 RW	8 24 rf	9 22 RH	10 22 RW	11 20 MT	12 19 MM	12 18 MM
3 1 fm	3 30 FT	4 29 FT	5 29 tg	6 27 TF	7 27 rf	8 25 TF	9 23 rr	10 23 rf	11 21 mt	12 20 mt	12 19 mm
3 2 EH	3 31 ft	4 30 ft	5 30 FT	6 28 PM	7 28 TF	8 26 td	9 24 TR	10 24 TF	11 22 RW	12 21 RW	12 20 RH
3 3 er	4 1 EW	5 1 EW	5 31 ft	6 29 fm	7 29 td	8 27 FM	9 25 tg	10 25 td	11 23 rf	12 22 rf	12 21 rr
3 4 MR	4 2 ef	5 2 er	6 1 EW	6 30 EH	7 30 FM	8 28 fm	9 26 FT	10 26 TR	11 24 TF	12 23 TF	12 22 TR
3 5 mg		5 3 MR	6 2 er	7 1 er	7 31 fm	8 29 EH	9 27 ft	10 27 tg	11 25 td	12 24 tg	12 23 tg
		5 4 mg		7 2 MR			9 28 EW			12 25 FM	12 24 FT

264

2020 MR   RAT

JAN ET	FEB et	MAR MW	APR mf	APR mf	MAY RF	JUN rd	DAY OF MON	JUL TM	AUG tm	SEP FH	OCT fr	NOV ER	DEC eg
11 SPRING	12 WARM	12 CLEAR	13 SUMMER	14 GRAIN	16 HEAT	18 FALL		20 DEW	22 C DEW	22 WINTER	23 SNOW	22 CHILL	22 SPRING
17:18	11:03	15:48	9:48	13:22	23:46	9:51		13:12	5:15	8:31	1:09	11:55	23:08
1 25 ft	2 23 FM	3 24 FT	4 23 FM	5 23 FT	6 21 td	7 21 tg	1	8 19 TF	9 17 rr	10 17 rf	11 15 RH	12 14 mt	1 13 mm
1 26 EW	2 24 fm	3 25 ft	4 24 fm	5 24 ft	6 22 FM	7 22 FT	2	8 20 td	9 18 TR	10 18 TF	11 16 rr	12 15 RW	1 14 RH
1 27 ef	2 25 EH	3 26 EW	4 25 EH	5 25 EW	6 23 fm	7 23 ft	3	8 21 FM	9 19 tg	10 19 td	11 17 TR	12 16 rf	1 15 rr
1 28 MF	2 26 er	3 27 ef	4 26 er	5 26 ef	6 24 EH	7 24 EW	4	8 22 fm	9 20 FT	10 20 FM	11 18 tg	12 17 TF	1 16 TR
1 29 md	2 27 MR	3 28 MF	4 27 MR	5 27 MF	6 25 er	7 25 ef	5	8 23 EH	9 21 ft	10 21 fm	11 19 FT	12 18 td	1 17 tg
1 30 RM	2 28 mg	3 29 md	4 28 mg	5 28 md	6 26 MR	7 26 MF	6	8 24 er	9 22 EW	10 22 EH	11 20 ft	12 19 FM	1 18 FT
1 31 rm	2 29 RT	3 30 RM	4 29 RT	5 29 RM	6 27 mg	7 27 md	7	8 25 MR	9 23 ef	10 23 er	11 21 EW	12 20 fm	1 19 ft
2 1 TH	3 1 rt	3 31 rm	4 30 rt	5 30 rm	6 28 RT	7 28 RM	8	8 26 mg	9 24 MF	10 24 MR	11 22 ef	12 21 EH	1 20 EW
2 2 tr	3 2 TW	4 1 TH	5 1 TW	5 31 TH	6 29 rt	7 29 rm	9	8 27 RT	9 25 md	10 25 mg	11 23 MF	12 22 er	1 21 ef
2 3 FR	3 3 tf	4 2 tr	5 2 tf	6 1 tr	6 30 TW	7 30 TH	10	8 28 rt	9 26 RM	10 26 RT	11 24 md	12 23 MR	1 22 MF
2 4 fg	3 4 FF	4 3 FR	5 3 FF	6 2 FR	7 1 tf	7 31 tr	11	8 29 TW	9 27 rm	10 27 rt	11 25 RM	12 24 mg	1 23 md
2 5 ET	3 5 fd	4 4 fg	5 4 fd	6 3 fg	7 2 FF	8 1 FR	12	8 30 tf	9 28 TH	10 28 TW	11 26 rm	12 25 RT	1 24 RM
2 6 et	3 6 EM	4 5 ET	5 5 EM	6 4 ET	7 3 fd	8 2 fg	13	8 31 FF	9 29 tr	10 29 tf	11 27 TH	12 26 rt	1 25 rm
2 7 MW	3 7 em	4 6 et	5 6 em	6 5 et	7 4 EM	8 3 ET	14	9 1 fd	9 30 FR	10 30 FF	11 28 tr	12 27 TW	1 26 TH
2 8 mf	3 8 MH	4 7 MW	5 7 MH	6 6 MW	7 5 em	8 4 et	15	9 2 EM	10 1 fg	10 31 fd	11 29 FR	12 28 tf	1 27 tr
2 9 RF	3 9 mr	4 8 mf	5 8 mr	6 7 mf	7 6 MH	8 5 MW	16	9 3 em	10 2 ET	11 1 EM	11 30 fg	12 29 FF	1 28 FR
2 10 rd	3 10 RR	4 9 RF	5 9 RR	6 8 RF	7 7 mr	8 6 mf	17	9 4 MH	10 3 et	11 2 em	12 1 ET	12 30 fd	1 29 fg
2 11 TM	3 11 rg	4 10 rd	5 10 rg	6 9 rd	7 8 RR	8 7 RF	18	9 5 mr	10 4 MW	11 3 MH	12 2 et	12 31 EM	1 30 ET
2 12 tm	3 12 TT	4 11 TM	5 11 TT	6 10 TM	7 9 rg	8 8 rd	19	9 6 RR	10 5 mf	11 4 mr	12 3 MW	1 1 em	1 31 et
2 13 FH	3 13 tt	4 12 tm	5 12 tt	6 11 tm	7 10 TT	8 9 TM	20	9 7 rg	10 6 RF	11 5 RR	12 4 mf	1 2 MH	2 1 MW
2 14 fr	3 14 FW	4 13 FH	5 13 FW	6 12 FH	7 11 tt	8 10 tm	21	9 8 TT	10 7 rd	11 6 rg	12 5 RF	1 3 mr	2 2 mf
2 15 ER	3 15 ff	4 14 fr	5 14 ff	6 13 fr	7 12 FW	8 11 FH	22	9 9 tt	10 8 TM	11 7 TT	12 6 rd	1 4 RR	2 3 RF
2 16 eg	3 16 EF	4 15 ER	5 15 EF	6 14 ER	7 13 ff	8 12 fr	23	9 10 FW	10 9 tm	11 8 tt	12 7 TM	1 5 rg	2 4 rd
2 17 MT	3 17 ed	4 16 eg	5 16 ed	6 15 eg	7 14 EF	8 13 ER	24	9 11 ff	10 10 FH	11 9 FW	12 8 tm	1 6 TT	2 5 TM
2 18 mt	3 18 MM	4 17 MT	5 17 MM	6 16 MT	7 15 ed	8 14 eg	25	9 12 EF	10 11 fr	11 10 ff	12 9 FH	1 7 tt	2 6 tm
2 19 RW	3 19 mm	4 18 mt	5 18 mm	6 17 mt	7 16 MM	8 15 MT	26	9 13 ed	10 12 ER	11 11 EF	12 10 fr	1 8 FW	2 7 FH
2 20 rf	3 20 RH	4 19 RW	5 19 RH	6 18 RW	7 17 mm	8 16 mt	27	9 14 MM	10 13 eg	11 12 ed	12 11 ER	1 9 ff	2 8 fr
2 21 TF	3 21 rr	4 20 rf	5 20 rr	6 19 rf	7 18 RH	8 17 RW	28	9 15 mm	10 14 MT	11 13 MM	12 12 eg	1 10 EF	2 9 ER
2 22 td	3 22 TR	4 21 TF	5 21 TR	6 20 TF	7 19 rr	8 18 rf	29	9 16 RH	10 15 mt	11 14 mm	12 13 MT	1 11 ed	2 10 eg
	3 23 tg	4 22 td	5 22 tg		7 20 TR		30		10 16 RW			1 12 MM	2 11 MT

JAN MT	FEB mt	MAR RW	APR rf	MAY TF	JUN td	DAY OF MON	JUL FM	AUG fm	SEP EH	OCT er	NOV MR	DEC mg
22 WARM	23 CLEAR	24 SUMMER	25 GRAIN	28 HEAT	29 FALL			1 DEW	3 C DEW	3 WINTER	4 SNOW	3 CHILL
16:54	21:37	14:57	19:09	5:33	15:40			19:01	11:04	14:21	7:00	17:46
2 12 mt	4 13 MM	4 12 MT	5 12 MM	6 10 eg	7 10 ed	1	8 8 ER	9 7 EF	10 6 fr	11 5 ff	12 4 FH	1 3 FW
2 13 RW	4 14 mm	4 13 mt	5 13 mm	6 11 MT	7 11 MM	2	8 9 eg	9 8 ed	10 7 ER	11 6 EF	12 5 fr	1 4 ff
2 14 rf	4 15 RH	4 14 RW	5 14 RH	6 12 mm	7 12 mm	3	8 10 MT	9 9 MM	10 8 eg	11 7 ed	12 6 ER	1 5 EF
2 15 TF	4 16 rr	4 15 rf	5 15 rr	6 13 RW	7 13 RH	4	8 11 mt	9 10 mm	10 9 MT	11 8 MM	12 7 ed	1 6 eg
2 16 td	4 17 TR	4 16 TF	5 16 TR	6 14 rf	7 14 rr	5	8 12 RW	9 11 RH	10 10 mt	11 9 mm	12 8 MT	1 7 MM
2 17 FM	4 18 tg	4 17 td	5 17 tg	6 15 TF	7 15 TR	6	8 13 rf	9 12 rr	10 11 RW	11 10 RH	12 9 mt	1 8 mm
2 18 fm	4 19 FT	4 18 FM	5 18 FT	6 16 td	7 16 tg	7	8 14 TF	9 13 TR	10 12 rf	11 11 rr	12 10 RW	1 9 RH
2 19 EH	4 20 ft	4 19 fm	5 19 ft	6 17 FM	7 17 FT	8	8 15 td	9 14 TF	10 13 TR	11 12 TR	12 11 rf	1 10 rr
2 20 er	4 21 EW	4 20 EH	5 20 EW	6 18 fm	7 18 ft	9	8 16 FM	9 15 td	10 14 TF	11 13 td	12 12 TF	1 11 TR
2 21 MR	4 22 ef	4 21 er	5 21 ef	6 19 EH	7 19 EW	10	8 17 fm	9 16 FM	10 15 td	11 14 FT	12 13 td	1 12 tg
2 22 mg	4 23 MF	4 22 MR	5 22 MF	6 20 er	7 20 ef	11	8 18 EH	9 17 fm	10 16 FM	11 15 ft	12 14 FM	1 13 FT
2 23 RT	4 24 md	4 23 mg	5 23 md	6 21 MR	7 21 MF	12	8 19 er	9 18 ef	10 17 EH	11 16 EW	12 15 fm	1 14 ft
2 24 rt	4 25 rm	4 24 RT	5 24 RM	6 22 mg	7 22 md	13	8 20 MR	9 19 MF	10 18 er	11 17 er	12 16 EH	1 15 EW
2 25 TW	4 26 TH	4 25 rt	5 25 TH	6 23 RT	7 23 RM	14	8 21 rm	9 20 md	10 19 MR	11 18 MF	12 17 er	1 16 ef
2 26 tf	4 27 tr	4 26 TW	5 26 tr	6 24 rt	7 24 rm	15	8 22 RT	9 21 RM	10 20 mg	11 19 md	12 18 MR	1 17 MF
2 27 FF	4 28 FR	4 27 tf	5 27 FR	6 25 TW	7 25 TH	16	8 23 rt	9 22 rm	10 21 RT	11 20 RM	12 19 mg	1 18 md
2 28 fd	4 29 fd	4 28 FF	5 28 fd	6 26 tf	7 26 tr	17	8 24 TW	9 23 TH	10 22 rt	11 21 rm	12 20 RT	1 19 RM
3 1 EM	4 30 ET	4 29 fd	5 29 ET	6 27 FF	7 27 FR	18	8 25 tf	9 24 tr	10 23 TW	11 22 TH	12 21 rt	1 20 rm
3 2 em	4 31 et	4 30 ET	5 30 et	6 28 fd	7 28 fg	19	8 26 FF	9 25 TW	10 24 TH	11 23 tr	12 22 TW	1 21 TH
3 3 MH	5 1 MW	5 1 em	5 31 EM	6 29 EM	7 29 ET	20	8 27 fd	9 26 tf	10 25 FF	11 24 FR	12 23 tr	1 22 tr
3 4 mr	5 2 mf	5 2 MH	6 1 et	6 30 em	7 30 et	21	8 28 EM	9 27 FF	10 26 fd	11 25 fg	12 24 FR	1 23 FR
3 5 RR	5 3 RF	5 3 mr	6 2 MW	7 1 MH	7 31 MW	22	8 29 em	9 28 fd	10 27 ET	11 26 ET	12 25 fg	1 24 fg
3 6 rg	5 4 rd	5 4 RR	6 3 mr	7 2 mf	8 1 mf	23	8 30 MH	9 29 ET	10 28 et	11 27 et	12 26 EM	1 25 ET
3 7 TT	5 5 TM	5 5 rg	6 4 RF	7 3 RR	8 2 mr	24	8 31 mr	9 30 et	10 29 em	11 28 MW	12 27 em	1 26 et
3 8 tt	5 6 tm	5 6 TT	6 5 rg	7 4 rg	8 3 RF	25	9 1 RR	10 1 MW	10 30 mr	11 29 mf	12 28 MH	1 27 MW
3 9 FW	5 7 FH	5 7 tt	6 6 TM	7 5 TT	8 4 rd	26	9 2 rg	10 2 mf	10 31 RR	11 30 mr	12 29 mr	1 28 mf
3 10 ff	5 8 ff	5 8 FW	6 7 tm	7 6 tt	8 5 TM	27	9 3 TT	10 3 RF	11 1 rg	12 1 RF	12 30 RR	1 29 RF
3 11 EF	5 9 fr	5 9 ff	6 8 FH	7 7 FW	8 6 tm	28	9 4 tt	10 4 rd	11 2 TM	12 2 TT	12 31 rg	1 30 rd
3 12 ed	5 10 ER	5 10 EF	6 9 ER	7 8 ff	8 7 FH	29	9 5 FW	10 5 TM	11 3 tt	12 3 tm	1 1 rg	1 31 TM
	5 11 eg	5 11 ed		7 9 EF		30	9 6 ff		11 4 FW		1 2 tt	

2022 RT TIGER

	JAN RT	FEB rt	MAR TW	APR tf	MAY FF	JUN fd	DAY OF MON	JUL EM	AUG em	SEP MH	OCT mr	NOV RR	DEC rg
	4 SPRING	3 WARM	5 CLEAR	5 SUMMER	8 GRAIN	9 HEAT		10 FALL	13 DEW	13 C DEW	14 WINTER	14 SNOW	14 CHILL
	4:58	22:42	3:22	20:45	0:58	11:52		21:28	0:50	16:53	20:11	12:49	23:35
1	2 1 tm	3 3 tt	4 1 TM	5 1 TT	5 30 rd	6 29 rg	1	7 29 rd	8 27 RR	9 26 RF	10 25 mr	11 24 mf	12 23 MH
2	2 2 FH	3 4 FW	4 2 tm	5 2 tt	5 31 TM	6 30 TT	2	7 30 TM	8 28 rg	9 27 rd	10 26 RR	11 25 RF	12 24 mr
3	2 3 fr	3 5 ff	4 3 FH	5 3 FW	6 1 tm	7 1 tt	3	7 31 tm	8 29 TT	9 28 TM	10 27 rg	11 26 rd	12 25 RR
4	2 4 ER	3 6 EF	4 4 fr	5 4 ff	6 2 FW	7 2 FW	4	8 1 fr	8 30 tt	9 29 tm	10 28 TT	11 27 TM	12 26 rg
5	2 5 eg	3 7 ed	4 5 ER	5 5 EF	6 3 fr	7 3 fr	5	8 2 FH	8 31 FW	9 30 FH	10 29 tt	11 28 tm	12 27 TT
6	2 6 MT	3 8 MM	4 6 eg	5 6 ed	6 4 ER	7 4 ER	6	8 3 ER	9 1 ff	10 1 fr	10 30 FW	11 29 FH	12 28 tt
7	2 7 mt	3 9 mm	4 7 MT	5 7 MM	6 5 eg	7 5 eg	7	8 4 eg	9 2 EF	10 2 ER	10 31 ff	11 30 fr	12 29 FW
8	2 8 RW	3 10 RH	4 8 mt	5 8 mm	6 6 MT	7 6 MT	8	8 5 MT	9 3 ed	10 3 eg	11 1 EF	12 1 ER	12 30 ff
9	2 9 rf	3 11 rr	4 9 RW	5 9 RH	6 7 mt	7 7 mt	9	8 6 mt	9 4 MM	10 4 MT	11 2 eg	12 2 eg	12 31 EF
10	2 10 td	3 12 tg	4 10 rf	5 10 TR	6 8 RW	7 8 rr	10	8 7 RW	9 5 mm	10 5 mt	11 3 MM	12 3 MT	1 2 ed
11	2 11 FM	3 13 FT	4 11 TF	5 11 tg	6 9 rf	7 9 TF	11	8 8 rf	9 6 RH	10 6 RW	11 4 mm	12 4 mt	2 3 MM
12	2 12 fm	3 14 ft	4 12 td	5 12 FT	6 10 TF	7 10 td	12	8 9 TF	9 7 rr	10 7 rf	11 5 RH	12 5 RW	3 mm
13	2 13 EH	3 15 EW	4 13 FM	5 13 ft	6 11 td	7 11 FM	13	8 10 td	9 8 TR	10 8 TF	11 6 rr	12 6 rf	4 RH
14	2 14 ef	3 16 ef	4 14 fm	5 14 EH	6 12 FM	7 12 fm	14	8 11 FM	9 9 tg	10 9 td	11 7 TR	12 7 TF	5 RH
15	2 15 MR	3 17 MF	4 15 EH	5 15 er	6 13 fm	7 13 FT	15	8 12 fm	9 10 FM	10 10 FM	11 8 TR	12 8 td	6 rr
16	2 16 mg	3 18 md	4 16 er	5 16 MF	6 14 EH	7 14 ft	16	8 13 EH	9 11 ft	10 11 fm	11 9 ft	12 9 FM	7 tg
17	2 17 RT	3 19 RM	4 17 MF	5 17 md	6 15 er	7 15 EH	17	8 14 er	9 12 EW	10 12 EH	11 10 ft	12 10 fm	8 FT
18	2 18 rt	3 20 rm	4 18 mg	5 18 RM	6 16 MR	7 16 er	18	8 15 MR	9 13 ef	10 13 er	11 11 EW	12 11 EH	9 ft
19	2 19 TW	3 21 tr	4 19 RM	5 19 RM	6 17 mg	7 17 MR	19	8 16 mg	9 14 MF	10 14 MR	11 12 ef	12 12 er	10 EW
20	2 20 tf	3 22 TH	4 20 rt	5 20 TH	6 18 RM	7 18 mg	20	8 17 rt	9 15 md	10 15 mg	11 13 MF	12 13 MR	11 ef
21	2 21 FF	3 23 tf	4 21 TW	5 21 tr	6 19 rt	7 19 rm	21	8 18 TW	9 16 RM	10 16 RT	11 14 md	12 14 mg	12 MF
22	2 22 fd	3 24 FR	4 22 tf	5 22 FR	6 20 TW	7 20 rt	22	8 19 tf	9 17 rm	10 17 rt	11 15 RM	12 15 RT	13 md
23	2 23 ET	3 25 fg	4 23 FF	5 23 FF	6 21 tf	7 21 TW	23	8 20 PF	9 18 TH	10 18 TW	11 16 rm	12 16 rt	14 RM
24	2 24 em	3 26 ET	4 24 fd	5 24 fg	6 22 FR	7 22 tf	24	8 21 FF	9 19 tr	10 19 TH	11 17 TH	12 17 TW	15 rm
25	2 25 MH	3 27 et	4 25 ET	5 25 et	6 23 fd	7 23 FF	25	8 22 fd	9 20 FR	10 20 PF	11 18 tr	12 18 tf	16 TH
26	2 26 mr	3 28 EM	4 26 em	5 26 MW	6 24 EM	7 24 fd	26	8 23 EM	9 21 fg	10 21 fd	11 19 FR	12 19 tf	17 tr
27	2 27 RR	3 29 MW	4 27 MH	5 27 mf	6 25 em	7 25 EM	27	8 24 em	9 22 ET	10 22 EM	11 20 fg	12 20 FF	18 FR
28	3 1 rg	3 30 mf	4 28 mr	5 28 mf	6 26 MH	7 26 mr	28	8 25 MH	9 23 et	10 23 em	11 21 ET	12 21 fd	19 fg
29	3 2 TT	3 31 RF	4 29 RR	5 29 RF	6 27 mr	7 27 RR	29		8 24 MW	10 24 MH	11 22 et	12 22 EM	20 ET
30		rd	4 30 rg		6 28 RR		30		9 25 mf		11 23 MW		21 et

JAN TT 14 SPRING 10:47	FEB tt 15 WARM 4:31	FEB tt 15 CLEAR 9:14	MAR FW 17 SUMMER 2:33	APR ff 18 GRAIN 6:46	MAY EF 20 HEAT 18:10	DAY OF MON 22 FALL 3:16	JUN ed	JUL MM 24 DEW 6:38	AUG mm 24 C DEW 22:41	SEP RH 25 WINTER 2:00	OCT rr 25 SNOW 18:38	NOV TR 25 CHILL 5:25	DEC tg 25 SPRING 16:37
1 22 MW	2 20 em	3 22 et	4 20 EM	5 20 ET	6 18 fd	1	7 18 fg	8 16 FF	9 15 FR	10 15 FF	11 13 tr	12 13 tf	1 11 TH
1 23 mf	2 21 MH	3 23 MW	4 21 em	5 21 et	6 19 EM	2	7 19 ET	8 17 fd	9 16 fg	10 16 fd	11 14 FR	12 14 FF	1 12 tr
1 24 RF	2 22 mr	3 24 mf	4 22 MH	5 22 MW	6 20 em	3	7 20 et	8 18 EM	9 17 ET	10 17 EM	11 15 fg	12 15 fd	1 13 FR
1 25 rd	2 23 rg	3 25 RF	4 23 mf	5 23 mf	6 21 MH	4	7 21 MW	8 19 em	9 18 et	10 18 em	11 16 ET	12 16 EM	1 14 fg
1 26 TM	2 24 TT	3 26 rd	4 24 RR	5 24 RF	6 22 mr	5	7 22 mf	8 20 MH	9 19 MW	10 19 MH	11 17 et	12 17 em	1 15 ET
1 27 tm	2 25 tt	3 27 TM	4 25 rg	5 25 rd	6 23 RR	6	7 23 RF	8 21 mr	9 20 mf	10 20 mr	11 18 MW	12 18 MH	1 16 et
1 28 FH	2 26 FW	3 28 tm	4 26 TT	5 26 TM	6 24 rg	7	7 24 rd	8 22 RR	9 21 RF	10 21 RR	11 19 mf	12 19 mr	1 17 MW
1 29 fr	2 27 ff	3 29 FH	4 27 tt	5 27 tm	6 25 TT	8	7 25 TM	8 23 rg	9 22 rd	10 22 rg	11 20 RF	12 20 RR	1 18 mf
1 30 ER	2 28 EF	3 30 fr	4 28 FW	5 28 FH	6 26 tt	9	7 26 tm	8 24 TT	9 23 TM	10 23 TT	11 21 rd	12 21 rg	1 19 RF
1 31 eg	3 1 ed	3 31 ER	4 29 ff	5 29 fr	6 27 FW	10	7 27 FH	8 25 tt	9 24 tm	10 24 tt	11 22 TM	12 22 TT	1 20 rd
2 1 MT	3 2 MM	4 1 eg	4 30 EF	5 30 ER	6 28 ff	11	7 28 fr	8 26 FW	9 25 FH	10 25 FW	11 23 tm	12 23 tt	1 21 TM
2 2 mt	3 3 mm	4 2 MT	5 1 ed	5 31 eg	6 29 EF	12	7 29 ER	8 27 ff	9 26 fr	10 26 ff	11 24 FH	12 24 FW	1 22 tm
2 3 RW	3 4 RH	4 3 mt	5 2 MM	6 1 MT	6 30 ed	13	7 30 eg	8 28 EF	9 27 ER	10 27 EF	11 25 fr	12 25 ff	1 23 FH
2 4 rf	3 5 rr	4 4 RW	5 3 mm	6 2 mt	7 1 MM	14	7 31 MT	8 29 ed	9 28 eg	10 28 ed	11 26 ER	12 26 EF	1 24 fr
2 5 TF	3 6 TR	4 5 rf	5 4 RH	6 3 RW	7 2 mm	15	8 1 mt	8 30 MM	9 29 MT	10 29 MM	11 27 eg	12 27 ed	1 25 ER
2 6 td	3 7 tg	4 6 TF	5 5 rr	6 4 rf	7 3 RH	16	8 2 RW	8 31 mm	9 30 mt	10 30 mm	11 28 MT	12 28 MM	1 26 eg
2 7 FM	3 8 FT	4 7 td	5 6 TR	6 5 TF	7 4 rr	17	8 3 rf	9 1 RH	10 1 RW	10 31 RH	11 29 mt	12 29 mm	1 27 MT
2 8 fm	3 9 ft	4 8 FM	5 7 tg	6 6 td	7 5 TR	18	8 4 TF	9 2 rr	10 2 rf	11 1 rr	11 30 RW	12 30 RH	1 28 mt
2 9 EH	3 10 EW	4 9 fm	5 8 FT	6 7 FM	7 6 tg	19	8 5 td	9 3 TR	10 3 TF	11 2 TR	12 1 rf	12 31 rr	1 29 RW
2 10 er	3 11 ef	4 10 EH	5 9 ft	6 8 fm	7 7 FT	20	8 6 FM	9 4 tg	10 4 td	11 3 tg	12 2 TF	1 1 TR	1 30 rf
2 11 MR	3 12 MF	4 11 er	5 10 EW	6 9 EH	7 8 ft	21	8 7 fm	9 5 FT	10 5 FM	11 4 FT	12 3 td	1 2 tg	1 31 TF
2 12 mg	3 13 md	4 12 MR	5 11 ef	6 10 er	7 9 EW	22	8 8 EH	9 6 ft	10 6 fm	11 5 ft	12 4 FM	1 3 FT	2 1 td
2 13 RT	3 14 RM	4 13 mg	5 12 MF	6 11 MR	7 10 ef	23	8 9 er	9 7 EW	10 7 EH	11 6 EW	12 5 fm	1 4 ft	2 2 FM
2 14 rt	3 15 rm	4 14 RT	5 13 md	6 12 mg	7 11 MF	24	8 10 MR	9 8 ef	10 8 er	11 7 ef	12 6 EH	1 5 EW	2 3 fm
2 15 TW	3 16 TH	4 15 rt	5 14 RM	6 13 RT	7 12 md	25	8 11 mg	9 9 MF	10 9 MR	11 8 MF	12 7 er	1 6 ef	2 4 EH
2 16 tf	3 17 tr	4 16 TW	5 15 rm	6 14 rt	7 13 RM	26	8 12 RT	9 10 md	10 10 mg	11 9 md	12 8 MR	1 7 MF	2 5 er
2 17 FF	3 18 FR	4 17 tf	5 16 TH	6 15 TW	7 14 rm	27	8 13 rt	9 11 RM	10 11 RT	11 10 RM	12 9 mg	1 8 md	2 6 MR
2 18 fd	3 19 fg	4 18 FF	5 17 tr	6 16 tf	7 15 TH	28	8 14 TW	9 12 rm	10 12 rt	11 11 rm	12 10 RT	1 9 RM	2 7 mg
2 19 EM	3 20 ET	4 19 fd	5 18 FR	6 17 FF	7 16 tr	29	8 15 tf	9 13 TH	10 13 TW	11 12 TH	12 11 rt	1 10 rm	2 8 RT
	3 21 et		5 19 fg		7 17 FF	30		9 14 tr	10 14 tf		12 12 TW		2 9 rt

268

2024   TW   DRAGON

JAN FT	FEB ft	MAR EW	APR ef	MAY MF	JUN md	JUL RM	DAY OF MON	AUG rm	SEP TH	OCT tr	NOV FR	DEC fg
25 WARM	26 CLEAR	27 SUMMER	29 GRAIN		1 HEAT	4 FALL		5 DEW	6 C DEW	7 WINTER	7 SNOW	6 CHILL
10:21	15:03	8:22	12:34		22:58	9:05		12:27	4:31	7:49	0:29	11:15
2 10 TW	3 10 rm	4 9 rt	5 8 RM	6 6 mg	7 6 md	8 4 MR	1	9 3 MF	10 3 MR	11 1 ef	12 1 er	12 31 ef
2 11 tf	3 11 TH	4 10 TW	5 9 rm	6 7 RT	7 7 RM	8 5 mg	2	9 4 md	10 4 mg	11 2 MF	12 2 MR	1 1 MF
2 12 FF	3 12 tr	4 11 tf	5 10 TH	6 8 rt	7 8 rm	8 6 RT	3	9 5 RM	10 5 RT	11 3 md	12 3 mg	1 2 md
2 13 fd	3 13 FR	4 12 FF	5 11 tr	6 9 TW	7 9 TH	8 7 rt	4	9 6 rm	10 6 rt	11 4 RM	12 4 RT	1 3 RM
2 14 EM	3 14 fg	4 13 fd	5 12 FR	6 10 tf	7 10 tr	8 8 TW	5	9 7 TH	10 7 TW	11 5 rm	12 5 rt	1 4 rm
2 15 em	3 15 ET	4 14 EM	5 13 fg	6 11 FF	7 11 FR	8 9 tf	6	9 8 tr	10 8 tf	11 6 TH	12 6 TW	1 5 TH
2 16 MH	3 16 et	4 15 em	5 14 ET	6 12 fd	7 12 fg	8 10 FF	7	9 9 FR	10 9 FF	11 7 tr	12 7 tf	1 6 tr
2 17 mr	3 17 MW	4 16 MH	5 15 et	6 13 EM	7 13 ET	8 11 fd	8	9 10 fg	10 10 fd	11 8 FR	12 8 FF	1 7 FR
2 18 RR	3 18 mf	4 17 mr	5 16 MW	6 14 em	7 14 et	8 12 EM	9	9 11 ET	10 11 EM	11 9 fg	12 9 fd	1 8 fg
2 19 rg	3 19 RF	4 18 RR	5 17 mf	6 15 MH	7 15 MW	8 13 em	10	9 12 et	10 12 em	11 10 ET	12 10 EM	1 9 ET
2 20 TT	3 20 rd	4 19 rg	5 18 RF	6 16 mr	7 16 mf	8 14 MH	11	9 13 MW	10 13 MH	11 11 et	12 11 em	1 10 et
2 21 tt	3 21 TM	4 20 TT	5 19 rd	6 17 RR	7 17 RF	8 15 mr	12	9 14 mf	10 14 mr	11 12 MW	12 12 MH	1 11 MW
2 22 FW	3 22 tm	4 21 tt	5 20 TM	6 18 rg	7 18 rd	8 16 RR	13	9 15 RF	10 15 RR	11 13 mf	12 13 mr	1 12 mf
2 23 ff	3 23 FH	4 22 FW	5 21 tm	6 19 TT	7 19 TM	8 17 rg	14	9 16 rd	10 16 rg	11 14 RF	12 14 RR	1 13 RF
2 24 EF	3 24 fr	4 23 ff	5 22 FH	6 20 tt	7 20 tm	8 18 TT	15	9 17 TM	10 17 TT	11 15 rd	12 15 rg	1 14 rd
2 25 ed	3 25 ER	4 24 EF	5 23 fr	6 21 FW	7 21 FH	8 19 tt	16	9 18 tm	10 18 tt	11 16 TM	12 16 TT	1 15 TM
2 26 MM	3 26 eg	4 25 ed	5 24 ER	6 22 ff	7 22 fr	8 20 FW	17	9 19 FH	10 19 FW	11 17 tm	12 17 tt	1 16 tm
2 27 mm	3 27 MT	4 26 MM	5 25 eg	6 23 EF	7 23 ER	8 21 ff	18	9 20 fr	10 20 ff	11 18 FH	12 18 FW	1 17 FH
2 28 RH	3 28 mt	4 27 mm	5 26 MT	6 24 ed	7 24 eg	8 22 EF	19	9 21 ER	10 21 EF	11 19 fr	12 19 ff	1 18 fr
2 29 rr	3 29 RW	4 28 RH	5 27 mt	6 25 MM	7 25 MT	8 23 ed	20	9 22 eg	10 22 ed	11 20 ER	12 20 EF	1 19 ER
3 1 TR	3 30 rf	4 29 rr	5 28 RW	6 26 mm	7 26 mt	8 24 MM	21	9 23 MT	10 23 MM	11 21 eg	12 21 ed	1 20 eg
3 2 tg	3 31 TF	4 30 TR	5 29 rf	6 27 RH	7 27 RW	8 25 mm	22	9 24 mt	10 24 mm	11 22 MT	12 22 MM	1 21 MT
3 3 FT	4 1 td	5 1 tg	5 30 TF	6 28 rr	7 28 rf	8 26 RH	23	9 25 RW	10 25 RH	11 23 mt	12 23 mm	1 22 mt
3 4 ft	4 2 FM	5 2 FT	5 31 td	6 29 TR	7 29 TF	8 27 rr	24	9 26 rf	10 26 rr	11 24 RW	12 24 RH	1 23 RW
3 5 EW	4 3 fm	5 3 ft	6 1 FM	6 30 tg	7 30 td	8 28 TR	25	9 27 TF	10 27 TR	11 25 rf	12 25 rr	1 24 rf
3 6 ef	4 4 EH	5 4 EW	6 2 fm	7 1 FT	7 31 FM	8 29 tg	26	9 28 td	10 28 tg	11 26 TF	12 26 TR	1 25 TF
3 7 MF	4 5 er	5 5 ef	6 3 EH	7 2 ft	8 1 fm	8 30 FT	27	9 29 FM	10 29 FT	11 27 td	12 27 tg	1 26 td
3 8 md	4 6 MR	5 6 MF	6 4 er	7 3 EW	8 2 EH	8 31 ft	28	9 30 fm	10 30 ft	11 28 FM	12 28 FT	1 27 FM
3 9 RM	4 7 mg	5 7 md	6 5 MR	7 4 ef	8 3 er	9 1 EW	29	10 1 EH	10 31 EW	11 29 fm	12 29 ft	1 28 fm
	4 8 RT			7 5 MF		9 2 ef	30	10 2 er		11 30 EH	12 30 EW	

2025 tf SNAKE

JAN ET 6 SPRING 22:27	FEB et 6 WARM 16:11	MAR MW 7 CLEAR 20:52	APR mf 8 SUMMER 14:11	MAY RF 10 GRAIN 18:22	JUN rd 13 HEAT 4:46	JUN rd 14 FALL 14:53	DAY OF MON	JUL TM 16 DEW 18:15	AUG tm 17 C DEW 10:19	SEP FH 18 WINTER 13:40	OCT fr 18 SNOW 6:18	NOV ER 17 CHILL 17:05	DEC eg 17 SPRING 4:16
1/29 EH	2/28 EW	3/29 fm	4/28 ft	5/27 FM	6/25 tg	7/25 td	1	8/23 TR	9/22 TF	10/21 rr	11/20 rf	12/20 rr	1/19 rf
1/30 er	3/1 ef	3/30 EH	4/29 EW	5/28 fm	6/26 FT	7/26 FM	2	8/24 tg	9/23 td	10/22 TR	11/21 TF	12/21 TR	1/20 TF
1/31 MR	3/2 MF	3/31 er	4/30 ef	5/29 EH	6/27 ft	7/27 fm	3	8/25 FT	9/24 FM	10/23 tg	11/22 td	12/22 tg	1/21 td
2/1 mg	3/3 md	4/1 MR	5/1 MF	5/30 er	6/28 EW	7/28 EH	4	8/26 ft	9/25 fm	10/24 FT	11/23 FM	12/23 FT	1/22 FM
2/2 RT	3/4 RM	4/2 mg	5/2 md	5/31 MR	6/29 ef	7/29 er	5	8/27 EW	9/26 EH	10/25 ft	11/24 fm	12/24 ft	1/23 fm
2/3 rt	3/5 rm	4/3 RT	5/3 RM	6/1 mg	6/30 MF	7/30 MR	6	8/28 ef	9/27 er	10/26 EW	11/25 EH	12/25 EW	1/24 EH
2/4 TW	3/6 TH	4/4 rt	5/4 rm	6/2 RT	7/1 md	7/31 mg	7	8/29 MF	9/28 MR	10/27 ef	11/26 er	12/26 ef	1/25 er
2/5 tf	3/7 tr	4/5 TW	5/5 TH	6/3 rt	7/2 RM	8/1 RT	8	8/30 md	9/29 mg	10/28 MF	11/27 MR	12/27 MF	1/26 MR
2/6 FF	3/8 FR	4/6 tf	5/6 tr	6/4 TW	7/3 rm	8/2 rt	9	8/31 RM	9/30 RT	10/29 md	11/28 mg	12/28 md	1/27 mg*
2/7 fd	3/9 fg	4/7 FF	5/7 FR	6/5 tf	7/4 TH	8/3 TW	10	9/1 rm	10/1 rt	10/30 RM	11/29 RT	12/29 RM	1/28 RT
2/8 EM	3/10 ET	4/8 fd	5/8 fg	6/6 FF	7/5 tr	8/4 tf	11	9/2 TH	10/2 TW	10/31 rm	11/30 rt	12/30 rm	1/29 rt
2/9 em	3/11 et	4/9 EM	5/9 ET	6/7 fd	7/6 FR	8/5 FF	12	9/3 tr	10/3 tf	11/1 TH	12/1 TW	12/31 TH	1/30 TW
2/10 MH	3/12 MW	4/10 em	5/10 et	6/8 EM	7/7 fg	8/6 fd	13	9/4 FR	10/4 FF	11/2 tr	12/2 tf	1/1 tr	1/31 tf
2/11 mr	3/13 mf	4/11 MH	5/11 MW	6/9 em	7/8 ET	8/7 EM	14	9/5 fg	10/5 fd	11/3 FR	12/3 FF	1/2 FR	2/1 FF
2/12 RR	3/14 RF	4/12 mr	5/12 mf	6/10 MH	7/9 et	8/8 em	15	9/6 ET	10/6 EM	11/4 fg	12/4 fd	1/3 fg	2/2 fd
2/13 rg	3/15 rd	4/13 RR	5/13 RF	6/11 mr	7/10 MW	8/9 MH	16	9/7 et	10/7 em	11/5 ET	12/5 EM	1/4 ET	2/3 EM
2/14 TT	3/16 TM	4/14 rg	5/14 rd	6/12 RR	7/11 mf	8/10 mr	17	9/8 MW	10/8 MH	11/6 et	12/6 em	1/5 et	2/4 em
2/15 tt	3/17 tm	4/15 TT	5/15 TM	6/13 rg	7/12 RF	8/11 RR	18	9/9 mf	10/9 mr	11/7 MW	12/7 MH	1/6 MW	2/5 MH
2/16 FW	3/18 FH	4/16 tt	5/16 tm	6/14 TT	7/13 rd	8/12 rg	19	9/10 RF	10/10 RR	11/8 mf	12/8 mr	1/7 mf	2/6 mr
2/17 ff	3/19 fr	4/17 FW	5/17 FH	6/15 tt	7/14 TM	8/13 TT	20	9/11 rd	10/11 rg	11/9 RF	12/9 RR	1/8 RF	2/7 RR
2/18 EF	3/20 ER	4/18 ff	5/18 fr	6/16 FW	7/15 tm	8/14 tt	21	9/12 TM	10/12 TT	11/10 rd	12/10 rg	1/9 rd	2/8 rg
2/19 ed	3/21 eg	4/19 EF	5/19 ER	6/17 ff	7/16 FH	8/15 FW	22	9/13 tm	10/13 tt	11/11 TM	12/11 TT	1/10 TM	2/9 TT
2/20 MM	3/22 MT	4/20 ed	5/20 eg	6/18 EF	7/17 fr	8/16 ff	23	9/14 FH	10/14 FW	11/12 tm	12/12 tt	1/11 tm	2/10 tt
2/21 mm	3/23 mt	4/21 MM	5/21 MT	6/19 ed	7/18 ER	8/17 EF	24	9/15 fr	10/15 ff	11/13 FH	12/13 FW	1/12 FH	2/11 FW
2/22 RH	3/24 RW	4/22 mm	5/22 mt	6/20 MM	7/19 eg	8/18 ed	25	9/16 ER	10/16 EF	11/14 fr	12/14 ff	1/13 fr	2/12 ff
2/23 rr	3/25 rf	4/23 RH	5/23 RW	6/21 mm	7/20 MT	8/19 MM	26	9/17 eg	10/17 ed	11/15 ER	12/15 EF	1/14 ER	2/13 EF
2/24 TR	3/26 TF	4/24 rr	5/24 rf	6/22 RH	7/21 mt	8/20 mm	27	9/18 MT	10/18 MM	11/16 eg	12/16 ed	1/15 eg	2/14 ed
2/25 tg	3/27 td	4/25 TR	5/25 TF	6/23 rr	7/22 RW	8/21 RH	28	9/19 mt	10/19 mm	11/17 MT	12/17 MM	1/16 MT	2/15 MM
2/26 FT	3/28 FM	4/26 tg	5/26 td	6/24 TR	7/23 rf	8/22 rr	29	9/20 RW	10/20 RH	11/18 mt	12/18 mm	1/17 mt	2/16 mm
2/27 ft		4/27 FT			7/24 TF		30	9/21 rf		11/19 RW	12/19 RH	1/18 RW	

2026 FT HORSE

	JAN MT	FEB mt	MAR RW	APR rf	MAY TF	JUN td	JUL FM	AUG fm	SEP EH	OCT er	NOV MR	DEC mg
Term	WARM	CLEAR	SUMMER	GRAIN	HEAT	FALL	DEW	C DEW	WINTER	SNOW	CHILL	SPRING
Day	17 WARM	18 CLEAR	19 SUMMER	21 GRAIN	23 HEAT	25 FALL	27 DEW	28 C DEW	29 WINTER	29 SNOW	28 CHILL	28 SPRING
Time	22:00	2:41		0:11	10:34	20:41	0:04	16:08	19:29	12:08	22:55	10:06

DAY OF MON

Day	JAN	FEB	MAR	APR	MAY	JUN	JUL	AUG	SEP	OCT	NOV	DEC
1	2/17 RH	3/19 RW	4/17 mm	5/17 mt	6/15 MM	7/14 eg	8/13 ed	9/11 ER	10/10 ff	11/9 fr	12/9 ff	1/8 fr
2	2/18 rr	3/20 rf	4/18 RH	5/18 RW	6/16 mm	7/15 MT	8/14 MM	9/12 eg	10/11 EF	11/10 ER	12/10 EF	1/9 ER
3	2/19 TR	3/21 TF	4/19 rr	5/19 rf	6/17 RH	7/16 mt	8/15 mm	9/13 MT	10/12 ed	11/11 eg	12/11 ed	1/10 eg
4	2/20 tg	3/22 td	4/20 TR	5/20 TF	6/18 rr	7/17 RW	8/16 RH	9/14 mt	10/13 MM	11/12 MT	12/12 MM	1/11 MT
5	2/21 FT	3/23 FM	4/21 tg	5/21 td	6/19 TR	7/18 rf	8/17 rr	9/15 RW	10/14 mm	11/13 mt	12/13 mm	1/12 mt
6	2/22 ft	3/24 fm	4/22 FT	5/22 FM	6/20 tg	7/19 TF	8/18 TR	9/16 rf	10/15 RH	11/14 RW	12/14 RH	1/13 RW
7	2/23 EW	3/25 EH	4/23 ft	5/23 fm	6/21 FT	7/20 td	8/19 tg	9/17 TF	10/16 rr	11/15 rf	12/15 rr	1/14 rf
8	2/24 ef	3/26 er	4/24 EW	5/24 EH	6/22 ft	7/21 FM	8/20 FT	9/18 td	10/17 TR	11/16 TF	12/16 TR	1/15 TF
9	2/25 MF	3/27 MR	4/25 ef	5/25 er	6/23 EW	7/22 fm	8/21 ft	9/19 FM	10/18 tg	11/17 td	12/17 tg	1/16 td
10	2/26 md	3/28 mg	4/26 MF	5/26 MR	6/24 ef	7/23 EH	8/22 EW	9/20 fm	10/19 FT	11/18 FM	12/18 FT	1/17 FM
11	2/27 RM	3/29 RT	4/27 md	5/27 mg	6/25 MF	7/24 er	8/23 ef	9/21 EH	10/20 ft	11/19 fm	12/19 ft	1/18 fm
12	2/28 rm	3/30 rt	4/28 RM	5/28 RT	6/26 md	7/25 MR	8/24 MF	9/22 er	10/21 EW	11/20 EH	12/20 EW	1/19 EH
13	3/1 TH	3/31 TW	4/29 rm	5/29 rt	6/27 RM	7/26 mg	8/25 md	9/23 MR	10/22 ef	11/21 er	12/21 ef	1/20 er
14	3/2 tr	4/1 tf	4/30 TH	5/30 TW	6/28 rm	7/27 RT	8/26 RM	9/24 mg	10/23 MF	11/22 MR	12/22 MF	1/21 MR
15	3/3 FR	4/2 FF	5/1 tr	5/31 tf	6/29 TH	7/28 rt	8/27 rm	9/25 RT	10/24 md	11/23 mg	12/23 md	1/22 mg
16	3/4 fg	4/3 fd	5/2 FR	6/1 FF	6/30 tr	7/29 TW	8/28 TH	9/26 rt	10/25 RM	11/24 RT	12/24 RM	1/23 RT
17	3/5 ET	4/4 EM	5/3 fg	6/2 fd	7/1 FR	7/30 tf	8/29 tr	9/27 TW	10/26 rm	11/25 rt	12/25 rm	1/24 rt
18	3/6 et	4/5 em	5/4 ET	6/3 EM	7/2 fg	7/31 FF	8/30 FR	9/28 tf	10/27 TH	11/26 TW	12/26 TH	1/25 TW
19	3/7 MW	4/6 MH	5/5 et	6/4 em	7/3 ET	8/1 fd	8/31 fg	9/29 FF	10/28 tr	11/27 tf	12/27 tr	1/26 tf
20	3/8 mf	4/7 mr	5/6 MW	6/5 MH	7/4 et	8/2 EM	9/1 ET	9/30 fd	10/29 FR	11/28 FF	12/28 FR	1/27 FF
21	3/9 RF	4/8 RR	5/7 mf	6/6 mr	7/5 MW	8/3 em	9/2 et	10/1 EM	10/30 fg	11/29 fd	12/29 fg	1/28 fd
22	3/10 rd	4/9 rg	5/8 RF	6/7 RR	7/6 mf	8/4 MH	9/3 MW	10/2 em	10/31 ET	11/30 EM	12/30 ET	1/29 EM
23	3/11 TM	4/10 TT	5/9 rd	6/8 rg	7/7 RF	8/5 mr	9/4 mf	10/3 MH	11/1 et	12/1 em	12/31 et	1/30 em
24	3/12 tm	4/11 tt	5/10 TM	6/9 TT	7/8 rd	8/6 RR	9/5 RF	10/4 mr	11/2 MW	12/2 MH	1/1 MW	1/31 MH
25	3/13 FH	4/12 FW	5/11 tm	6/10 tt	7/9 TM	8/7 rg	9/6 rd	10/5 RR	11/3 mf	12/3 mr	1/2 mf	2/1 mr
26	3/14 fr	4/13 ff	5/12 FH	6/11 FW	7/10 tm	8/8 TT	9/7 TM	10/6 rg	11/4 RF	12/4 RR	1/3 RF	2/2 RR
27	3/15 ER	4/14 EF	5/13 fr	6/12 ff	7/11 FH	8/9 tt	9/8 tm	10/7 TT	11/5 rd	12/5 rg	1/4 rd	2/3 rg
28	3/16 eg	4/15 ed	5/14 ER	6/13 EF	7/12 fr	8/10 FW	9/9 FH	10/8 tt	11/6 TM	12/6 TT	1/5 TM	2/4 TT
29	3/17 MT	4/16 MM	5/15 eg	6/14 ed	7/13 ER	8/11 ff	9/10 fr	10/9 FW	11/7 tm	12/7 tt	1/6 tm	2/5 tt
30	3/18 mt		5/16 MT			8/12 EF			11/8 FH	12/8 FW	1/7 FH	

	JAN RT	FEB rt	MAR Tw	APR tf	MAY FF	JUN fd	JUL EM	AUG em	SEP MH	OCT mr	NOV RR	DEC rg
	29 WARM	29 CLEAR	.	1 SUMMER	2 GRAIN	4 HEAT	7 FALL	8 DEW	9 C DEW	1 WINTER	10 SNOW	10 CHILL
	3:49	8:31		1:46	5:58	16:22	2:30	5:52	21:56	1:18	17:58	4:44

DAY OF MON	JAN	FEB	MAR	APR	MAY	JUN	JUL	AUG	SEP	OCT	NOV	DEC
1	2 6 FW	3 8 FH	4 7 FW	5 6 tm	6 5 tt	7 4 TM	8 2 rg	9 1 rd	9 30 RR	10 29 mf	11 28 mr	12 28 mf
2	2 7 ff	3 9 fr	4 8 ff	5 7 FH	6 6 FW	7 5 tm	8 3 TT	9 2 TM	10 1 rg	10 30 RF	11 29 RR	12 29 RF
3	2 8 EF	3 10 ER	4 9 EF	5 8 fr	6 7 ff	7 6 FH	8 4 tt	9 3 tm	10 2 TT	10 31 rd	11 30 rg	12 30 rd
4	2 9 ed	3 11 eg	4 10 ed	5 9 ER	6 8 EF	7 7 fr	8 5 FW	9 4 FH	10 3 tt	11 1 TM	12 1 TT	12 31 TM
5	2 10 MM	3 12 MT	4 11 MM	5 10 eg	6 9 ed	7 8 ER	8 6 ff	9 5 fr	10 4 FW	11 2 tm	12 2 tt	1 1 tm
6	2 11 mm	3 13 mt	4 12 mm	5 11 MT	6 10 MM	7 9 eg	8 7 EF	9 6 ER	10 5 ff	11 3 FH	12 3 FW	1 2 FH
7	2 12 RH	3 14 RW	4 13 RH	5 12 mt	6 11 mm	7 10 MT	8 8 ed	9 7 eg	10 6 EF	11 4 fr	12 4 ff	1 3 fr
8	2 13 rr	3 15 rf	4 14 rr	5 13 RW	6 12 RH	7 11 mt	8 9 MM	9 8 MT	10 7 ed	11 5 ER	12 5 EF	1 4 ER
9	2 14 TR	3 16 TF	4 15 TR	5 14 rf	6 13 rr	7 12 RW	8 10 mm	9 9 mt	10 8 MM	11 6 eg	12 6 ed	1 5 eg
10	2 15 tg	3 17 td	4 16 tg	5 15 TF	6 14 TR	7 13 rf	8 11 RH	9 10 RW	10 9 mm	11 7 MT	12 7 MM	1 6 MT
11	2 16 FT	3 18 FM	4 17 FT	5 16 td	6 15 tg	7 14 TF	8 12 rr	9 11 rf	10 10 RH	11 8 mt	12 8 mm	1 7 mt
12	2 17 ft	3 19 fm	4 18 ft	5 17 FM	6 16 FT	7 15 td	8 13 TR	9 12 TF	10 11 rr	11 9 RW	12 9 RH	1 8 RW
13	2 18 EW	3 20 EH	4 19 EW	5 18 fm	6 17 ft	7 16 FM	8 14 tg	9 13 td	10 12 TR	11 10 rf	12 10 rr	1 9 rf
14	2 19 ef	3 21 er	4 20 ef	5 19 EH	6 18 EW	7 17 fm	8 15 FT	9 14 FM	10 13 tg	11 11 TF	12 11 TR	1 10 TF
15	2 20 MF	3 22 MR	4 21 MF	5 20 er	6 19 ef	7 18 EH	8 16 ft	9 15 fm	10 14 FT	11 12 td	12 12 tg	1 11 td
16	2 21 md	3 23 mg	4 22 md	5 21 MR	6 20 MF	7 19 er	8 17 EW	9 16 EH	10 15 ft	11 13 FM	12 13 FT	1 12 FM
17	2 22 RM	3 24 RT	4 23 RM	5 22 mg	6 21 md	7 20 MR	8 18 ef	9 17 er	10 16 EW	11 14 fm	12 14 ft	1 13 fm
18	2 23 rm	3 25 rt	4 24 rm	5 23 RT	6 22 RM	7 21 mg	8 19 MF	9 18 MR	10 17 ef	11 15 EH	12 15 EW	1 14 EH
19	2 24 TH	3 26 TW	4 25 TH	5 24 rt	6 23 rm	7 22 RT	8 20 md	9 19 mg	10 18 MF	11 16 er	12 16 ef	1 15 er
20	2 25 tr	3 27 tf	4 26 tr	5 25 TW	6 24 TH	7 23 rt	8 21 RM	9 20 RT	10 19 md	11 17 MR	12 17 MF	1 16 MR
21	2 26 FR	3 28 FF	4 27 FR	5 26 tf	6 25 tr	7 24 TW	8 22 rm	9 21 rt	10 20 RM	11 18 mg	12 18 md	1 17 mg
22	2 27 fg	3 29 fd	4 28 fg	5 27 FF	6 26 FR	7 25 tf	8 23 TH	9 22 TW	10 21 rm	11 19 RT	12 19 RM	1 18 RT
23	2 28 ET	3 30 EM	4 29 ET	5 28 fd	6 27 fg	7 26 FF	8 24 tr	9 23 tf	10 22 TH	11 20 rt	12 20 rm	1 19 rt
24	3 1 et	3 31 em	4 30 et	5 29 EM	6 28 ET	7 27 fd	8 25 FR	9 24 FF	10 23 tr	11 21 TW	12 21 TH	1 20 TW
25	3 2 MW	4 1 MH	5 1 MW	5 30 em	6 29 et	7 28 EM	8 26 fg	9 25 fd	10 24 FR	11 22 tf	12 22 tr	1 21 tf
26	3 3 mf	4 2 mr	5 2 mf	5 31 MH	6 30 MW	7 29 em	8 27 ET	9 26 EM	10 25 fg	11 23 FF	12 23 FR	1 22 FF
27	3 4 RF	4 3 RR	5 3 RF	6 1 mr	7 1 mf	7 30 MH	8 28 et	9 27 em	10 26 ET	11 24 fd	12 24 fg	1 23 fd
28	3 5 rd	4 4 rg	5 4 rd	6 2 RR	7 2 RF	7 31 mr	8 29 MW	9 28 MH	10 27 et	11 25 EM	12 25 ET	1 24 EM
29	3 6 TM	4 5 TT	5 5 TM	6 3 rg	7 3 rd	8 1 RR	8 30 mf	9 29 mr	10 28 MW	11 26 em	12 26 et	1 25 em
30	3 7 tm	4 6 tt		6 4 TT			8 31 RF			11 27 MH	12 27 MW	

2028 EM MONKEY

JAN TT	FEB tt	MAR FW	APR ff	MAY EF	MAY EF	DAY OF	JUN ed	JUL MM	AUG mm	SEP RH	OCT rr	NOV TT	DEC tg
10 SPRING	10 WARM	10 CLEAR	11 SUMMER	13 GRAIN	14 HEAT	MON	17 FALL	19 DEW	20 C DEW	21 WINTER	21 SNOW	21 CHILL	20 SPRING
15:56	9:38	14:19	7:36	11:47			8:17	11:41	3:46	7:07	23:47	10:34	21:45

JAN	FEB	MAR	APR	MAY(GRAIN)	MAY(HEAT)	DAY OF MON	JUN	JUL	AUG	SEP	OCT	NOV	DEC
1 26 MH	2 25 MW	3 26 MH	4 25 MW	5 24 em	6 23 et	1	7 22 EM	8 20 fg	9 19 fd	10 18 FR	11 16 FR	12 16 tr	15 tf
1 27 mr	2 26 mf	3 27 mr	4 26 mf	5 25 MH	6 24 MW	2	7 23 em	8 21 ET	9 20 EM	10 19 fg	11 17 fg	12 17 FR	16 FF
1 28 RR	2 27 RF	3 28 RR	4 27 RF	5 26 mr	6 25 mf	3	7 24 MH	8 22 et	9 21 em	10 20 ET	11 18 ET	12 18 fg	17 fd
1 29 rg	2 28 rd	3 29 rg	4 28 rd	5 27 RR	6 26 RF	4	7 25 mr	8 23 MW	9 22 MH	10 21 et	11 19 et	12 19 ET	18 EM
1 30 tt	2 29 tm	3 30 tg	4 29 tm	5 28 TT	6 27 RR	5	7 26 rg	8 24 MM	9 23 mr	10 22 em	11 20 em	12 20 et	19 em
1 31 FW	2 1 tt	3 31 tt	4 30 FH	5 29 TT	6 28 rg	6	7 27 rg	8 25 mm	9 24 RR	10 23 MT	11 21 MH	12 21 MW	20 MH
2 1 ff	3 2 FH	4 1 FW	5 1 fr	5 30 FW	6 29 TT	7	7 28 TM	8 26 MT	9 25 rg	10 24 tt	11 22 mr	12 22 mf	21 mr
2 2 EF	3 3 fr	4 2 ff	5 2 ER	5 31 ff	6 30 tt	8	7 29 tm	8 27 tm	9 26 TT	10 25 rd	11 23 RF	12 23 RF	22 RR
2 3 ed	3 4 ER	4 3 EF	5 3 eg	6 1 EF	6 31 FW	9	7 30 FH	8 28 FW	9 27 tt	10 26 TM	11 24 rd	12 24 rd	23 rg
2 4 mm	3 5 eg	4 4 ed	5 4 MT	6 2 ed	7 1 ff	10	7 31 fr	8 29 ff	9 28 FH	10 27 tm	11 25 TM	12 25 TM	24 TT
2 5 RH	3 6 MT	4 5 MM	5 5 mt	6 3 MM	7 2 EF	11	8 1 ER	8 30 EF	9 29 fr	10 28 FH	11 26 tm	12 26 tm	25 tt
2 6 rr	3 7 mt	4 6 mm	5 6 RW	6 4 mm	7 3 ed	12	8 2 eg	8 31 ed	9 30 ER	10 29 fr	11 27 FH	12 27 FH	26 FW
2 7 TR	3 8 RW	4 7 RH	5 7 rf	6 5 RH	7 4 MM	13	8 3 MM	9 1 MM	10 1 eg	10 30 ER	11 28 fr	12 28 fr	27 ff
2 8 tg	3 9 rf	4 8 rr	5 8 TF	6 6 rr	7 5 mm	14	8 4 mm	9 2 mm	10 2 MM	10 31 eg	11 29 ER	12 29 ER	28 EF
2 9 FT	3 10 TF	4 9 TR	5 9 tg	6 7 rr	7 6 RH	15	8 5 RH	9 3 mt	10 3 mm	11 1 MM	11 30 eg	12 30 ed	29 ed
2 10 ft	3 11 FM	4 10 td	5 10 FT	6 8 TR	7 7 rr	16	8 6 rr	9 4 RW	10 4 RH	11 2 mm	12 1 MM	12 31 MT	30 MM
2 11 EW	3 12 fm	4 11 FT	5 11 ft	6 9 tg	7 8 TR	17	8 7 TR	9 5 rf	10 5 rr	11 3 RH	12 2 mm	1 1 mt	31 mm
2 12 ef	3 13 EH	4 12 ft	5 12 EW	6 10 FT	7 9 td	18	8 8 tg	9 6 TF	10 6 TR	11 4 rr	12 3 RH	1 2 RW	1 RH
2 13 md	3 14 er	4 13 EW	5 13 ef	6 11 ft	7 10 FM	19	8 9 FT	9 7 tg	10 7 tg	11 5 TR	12 4 rf	1 3 rf	2 rr
2 14 RM	3 15 MR	4 14 ef	5 14 MF	6 12 EW	7 11 fm	20	8 10 ft	9 8 FT	10 8 FT	11 6 TF	12 5 TR	1 4 TF	3 TR
2 15 rm	3 16 mg	4 15 MF	5 15 md	6 13 ef	7 12 EH	21	8 11 EW	9 9 ft	10 9 ft	11 7 tg	12 6 td	1 5 tg	4 tg
2 16 TH	3 17 RT	4 16 md	5 16 RM	6 14 MF	7 13 er	22	8 12 ef	9 10 EW	10 10 EW	11 8 FT	12 7 FM	1 6 FT	5 FT
2 17 FR	3 18 rt	4 17 RM	5 17 rt	6 15 md	7 14 MR	23	8 13 MF	9 11 ef	10 11 ef	11 9 ft	12 8 fm	1 7 ft	6 ft
2 18 fg	3 19 TW	4 18 rm	5 18 TH	6 16 RM	7 15 mg	24	8 14 md	9 12 MF	10 12 MF	11 10 EW	12 9 EH	1 8 EW	7 EW
2 19 ET	3 20 tf	4 19 TH	5 19 tr	6 17 rm	7 16 RM	25	8 15 RM	9 13 md	10 13 md	11 11 ef	12 10 er	1 9 ef	8 ef
2 20 et	3 21 FF	4 20 tr	5 20 FF	6 18 TH	7 17 rm	26	8 16 rm	9 14 RT	10 14 RM	11 12 MF	12 11 MR	1 10 MF	9 MF
2 21 fg	3 22 fd	4 21 FR	5 21 fd	6 19 tr	7 18 TW	27	8 17 TH	9 15 rt	10 15 rm	11 13 md	12 12 mg	1 11 md	10 md
2 22 ET	3 23 ET	4 22 fg	5 22 EM	6 20 FR	7 19 tf	28	8 18 tr	9 16 TW	10 16 TH	11 14 RT	12 13 RT	1 12 RT	11 RM
2 23 et	3 24 em	4 23 ET		6 21 fg	7 20 FF	29	8 19 FR	9 17 tf	10 17 tr	11 15 rt	12 14 rt	1 13 rt	12 rm
2 24 et		4 24 et		6 22 ET	7 21 fd	30		9 18 FF			12 15 TW	1 14 TW	

273

JAN FT	FEB ft	MAR EW	APR ef	MAY MF	JUN md	JUL RM	AUG rm	SEP TH	OCT tr	NOV FR	DEC fg
21 WARM	21 CLEAR	22 SUMMER	24 GRAIN	26 HEAT	28 FALL	29 DEW		1 C DEW	2 WINTER	3 SNOW	2 CHILL
15:29	20:08	13:26	17:35	3:58	14:06	17:29		9:35	12:57	5:37	16:24

(DAY OF MON)

JAN	FEB	MAR	APR	MAY	JUN	JUL	AUG	SEP	OCT	NOV	DEC
2/13 TH	3/15 TW	4/14 TH	5/13 rt	6/12 rm	7/11 RT	8/10 RM	9/8 mg	10/8 md	11/6 MR	12/5 MF	12/4 er
2/14 tr	3/16 tf	4/15 tr	5/14 TW	6/13 TH	7/12 rt	8/11 rm	9/9 RT	10/9 RM	11/7 mg	12/6 MF	12/5 MR
2/15 FR	3/17 FF	4/16 FR	5/15 tf	6/14 tr	7/13 TW	8/12 TH	9/10 rt	10/10 rm	11/8 RT	12/7 md	12/6 mg
2/16 fg	3/18 fd	4/17 fg	5/16 FF	6/15 FR	7/14 tf	8/13 tr	9/11 TW	10/11 TH	11/9 rt	12/8 RM	12/7 RT
2/17 ET	3/19 EM	4/18 ET	5/17 fd	6/16 fg	7/15 FF	8/14 FR	9/12 tf	10/12 tr	11/10 TW	12/9 rm	12/8 rt
2/18 et	3/20 em	4/19 et	5/18 EM	6/17 ET	7/16 fd	8/15 fg	9/13 FF	10/13 FR	11/11 tf	12/10 TH	12/9 TW
2/19 MW	3/21 MH	4/20 MW	5/19 em	6/18 et	7/17 EM	8/16 ET	9/14 fd	10/14 fg	11/12 FF	12/11 tr	12/10 tf
2/20 mf	3/22 mr	4/21 mf	5/20 MH	6/19 MW	7/18 em	8/17 et	9/15 EM	10/15 ET	11/13 fd	12/12 FR	12/11 FF
2/21 RF	3/23 RR	4/22 RF	5/21 mr	6/20 mf	7/19 MH	8/18 MW	9/16 em	10/16 et	11/14 EM	12/13 fg	12/12 fd
2/22 rd	3/24 rg	4/23 rd	5/22 RR	6/21 RF	7/20 mr	8/19 mf	9/17 MH	10/17 MW	11/15 em	12/14 ET	12/13 EM
2/23 TM	3/25 TT	4/24 TM	5/23 rg	6/22 rd	7/21 RR	8/20 RF	9/18 mr	10/18 mf	11/16 MH	12/15 et	12/14 em
2/24 tm	3/26 tt	4/25 tm	5/24 TT	6/23 TM	7/22 rg	8/21 rd	9/19 RR	10/19 RF	11/17 mr	12/16 MW	12/15 MH
2/25 FH	3/27 FW	4/26 FH	5/25 tt	6/24 tm	7/23 TM	8/22 TM	9/20 rg	10/20 rd	11/18 RR	12/17 mf	12/16 mr
2/26 fr	3/28 ff	4/27 fr	5/26 FW	6/25 FH	7/24 tt	8/23 tm	9/21 TT	10/21 TM	11/19 rg	12/18 RF	12/17 RR
2/27 ER	3/29 EF	4/28 ER	5/27 ff	6/26 fr	7/25 FW	8/24 FH	9/22 tt	10/22 tm	11/20 TT	12/19 rd	12/18 rg
2/28 eg	3/30 ed	4/29 eg	5/28 EF	6/27 ER	7/26 ff	8/25 fr	9/23 FW	10/23 FH	11/21 tt	12/20 TM	12/19 TT
3/1 MT	4/1 MM	4/30 MT	5/29 ed	6/28 eg	7/27 EF	8/26 ER	9/24 ff	10/24 fr	11/22 FW	12/21 tm	12/20 tt
3/2 mt	4/2 mm	5/1 mt	5/30 MM	6/29 MT	7/28 ed	8/27 eg	9/25 EF	10/25 ER	11/23 ff	12/22 FH	12/21 FW
3/3 RW	4/3 RH	5/2 RW	6/1 mm	6/30 mt	7/29 MM	8/28 MT	9/26 ed	10/26 eg	11/24 EF	12/23 fr	12/22 ff
3/4 rf	4/4 rr	5/3 rf	6/2 RH	7/1 RW	7/30 mt	8/29 mt	9/27 MM	10/27 MT	11/25 ER	12/24 fr	12/23 EF
3/5 TF	4/5 TR	5/4 TF	6/3 rr	7/2 rf	7/31 RW	8/30 RW	9/28 mm	10/28 mt	11/26 eg	12/25 fr	12/24 ed
3/6 td	4/6 tg	5/5 td	6/4 TR	7/3 TF	8/1 rf	9/1 rf	9/29 RH	10/29 RW	11/27 MT	12/26 ER	12/25 MM
3/7 FM	4/7 FT	5/6 FM	6/5 tg	7/4 td	8/2 TF	9/2 TF	9/30 rr	10/30 rf	11/28 mt	12/27 eg	12/26 mm
3/8 fm	4/8 ft	5/7 fm	6/6 FT	7/5 FM	8/3 td	9/3 td	10/1 TR	10/31 TF	11/29 MM	12/28 MT	12/27 RH
3/9 EH	4/9 EW	5/8 EH	6/7 ft	7/6 fm	8/4 FM	9/4 FM	10/2 tg	11/1 td	11/30 mm	12/29 mt	12/28 rr
3/10 er	4/10 ef	5/9 er	6/8 EW	7/7 EH	8/5 fm	9/5 fm	10/3 FT	11/2 FM	12/1 RH	12/30 RW	12/29 TR
3/11 MR	4/11 MF	5/10 MR	6/9 ef	7/8 er	8/6 EH	9/6 EH	10/4 ft	11/3 fm	12/2 rr	1/1 rf	12/30 tg
3/12 mg	4/12 md	5/11 mg	6/10 MF	7/9 MR	8/7 er	9/7 er	10/5 EW	11/4 EH	12/3 TR	1/2 TF	12/31 FT
3/13 RT		5/12 RT	6/11 md	7/10 mg	8/8 MR		10/6 ef	11/5 er	12/4 tg	1/2 td	1/1 ft
3/14 rt					8/9 mg		10/7 MF			1/3 FM	

274

JAN ET	FEB et	MAR MW	APR mf	MAY RF	JUN rd		DAY	JUL TM	AUG tm	SEP FH	OCT fr	NOV ER	DEC eg
3 SPRING	2 WARM	3 CLEAR	4 SUMMER	5 GRAIN	7 HEAT		OF	9 FALL	10 DEW	12 C DEW	12 WINTER	13 SNOW	12 CHILL
3:35	21:18	1:57	19:13	23:23	9:46		MON	19:54	23:18	15:24	18:47	11:27	22:14

DAY	JAN (ET)	FEB (et)	MAR (MW)	APR (mf)	MAY (RF)	JUN (rd)	JUL (TM)	AUG (tm)	SEP (FH)	OCT (fr)	NOV (ER)	DEC (eg)
1	EW	EH	EW	fm	EW	fm	FT	FM	tg	td	TR	TF
2	ef	er	ef	EH	ef	EH	ft	fm	FT	FM	tg	td
3	MF	MR	MF	er	MF	er	EW	EH	ft	fm	FT	FM
4	md	mg	md	MR	md	MR	ef	er	EW	EH	ft	fm
5	RM	RT	RM	mg	RM	mg	MF	MR	ef	er	EW	EH
6	rm	rt	rm	RT	rm	RT	md	mg	MF	MR	ef	er
7	TH	TW	TH	rt	TH	rt	RM	RT	md	mg	MF	MR
8	tr	tf	tr	TW	tr	TW	rm	rt	RM	RT	md	mg
9	FR	FF	FR	tf	FR	tf	TH	TW	rm	rt	RM	RT
10	fg	fd	fg	FF	fg	FF	tr	tf	TH	TW	rm	rt
11	ET	EM	ET	fd	ET	fd	FR	FF	tr	tf	TH	TW
12	et	em	et	EM	et	EM	fg	fd	FR	FF	tr	tf
13	MW	MH	MW	em	MW	em	ET	EM	fg	fd	FR	FF
14	mf	mr	mf	MH	mf	MH	et	em	ET	EM	fg	fd
15	RF	RR	RF	mr	RF	mr	MW	MH	et	em	ET	EM
16	rd	rg	rd	RR	rd	RR	mf	mr	MW	MH	et	em
17	TM	TT	TM	rg	TM	rg	RF	RR	mf	mr	MW	MH
18	tm	tt	tm	TT	tm	TT	rd	rg	RF	RR	mf	mr
19	FH	FW	FH	tt	FH	tt	TM	TT	rd	rg	RF	RR
20	fr	ff	fr	FW	fr	FW	tm	tt	TM	TT	rd	rg
21	ER	EF	ER	ff	ER	ff	FH	FW	tm	tt	TM	TT
22	eg	ed	eg	EF	eg	EF	fr	ff	FH	FW	tm	tt
23	MT	MM	MT	ed	MT	ed	ER	EF	fr	ff	FH	FW
24	mt	mm	mt	MM	mt	MM	eg	ed	ER	EF	fr	ff
25	RW	RH	RW	mm	RW	mm	MT	MM	eg	ed	ER	EF
26	rf	rr	rf	RH	rf	RH	mt	mm	MT	MM	eg	ed
27	TF	TR	TF	rr	TF	rr	RW	RH	mt	mm	MT	MM
28	td	tg	td	TR	td	TR	rf	rr	RW	RH	mt	mm
29	FM		FM	tg	FM	tg	TF	TR	rf	rr	RW	RH
30	fm		fm	FT		FT	td	tg	TF	TR	rf	rr
31	ft		ft									

Glossary

Alliance. The union of any two branches in the trio group; participating signs lose their original nature and function as one element.

Blooming. A growth cycle including the three most powerful stages of any stem.

Branch. A group of twelve signs denoting the temporal changes of flows; basically the hours of the day and the twelve months in the lunar calendar.

Breed. The process of one element strengthening another element.

Clashing. The interaction between any two signs resulting in the elimination or weakening of one of the pair.

Con-trio. A union of any three signs in any one cardinal direction in the branches; the three become a powerful unit as one element.

Contracting. A growth cycle including the five weakest stages of a stem.

Cosmic Flows. The invisible energy flows in the cosmos that are defined as the five elements. They are responsible for the changing conditions of the cosmos.

Element. Energy flows governing the operation of the cosmos and responsible for its changes.

Equilibrium. A state in which all different energy flows (defined as the five elements) are in perfect balance, each being properly supported or controlled by another, resulting in a perfect moment or perfect life.

Grantor. The element that breeds, strengthens, or encourages the growth of a certain other element, e.g. wood is the grantor of fire because it fuels it.

Growing. The growth cycle that includes the four stages of moderate growth in the stems.

Interbreeding. A process in which all elements encourage the growth of each other in a rotation.

Interruling. A process in which all elements exercise control over each other.

Kin. Signs belonging to the same element.

Lunar month. The month of a lunar calendar used by ancient Chinese; the number of days in each month ranging from twenty-nine to thirty. Each lunar month is thirty to forty-five days behind the western calendar, e.g. lunar January occurs in February of the western calendar.

Meng. A Chinese character meaning life, fate, or destiny.

Money Sign. The element the self controls becomes its possession and is called the money sign, e.g. fire can melt and shape metal into ornaments that can be sold for a profit; thus, metal is the money sign of fire.

Offspring. An element the self breeds, e.g. fire is the offspring of wood because wood fuels fire.

Pairing. The union of two specific signs in either the stem group or the branch group, functioning as one sign after the transformation, depending on the nature of pairing.

Pillar. The combination of one stem and one branch to denote the periodic changes of cosmic conditions. A complete set of cosmic flows consists of sixty pillars rotating continuously in the cosmos.

Rule. Used in connection with a flow. A flow rules when it dominates a situation or an environment at a given period of time.

Ruler. The element controlling the self is the ruler; it symbolizes our driving force, e.g. water is the ruler of fire because it can extinguish it.

Sign. One of a group of specific alphabets used to designate cosmic flows.

Spatial. The distribution of flows in space.

Tao. The operating law of the cosmos that provides guiding light for proper action.

Temporal. Timely rotational changes of comic flows.

Tri-union (Trio). The unity of three specific branch signs transforming into a powerful element.

Universe. The cosmos, including the earth and the other planets in space.

Yang. Lives, beings, forces, and all things that possess the nature of the masculine gender.

Yin. Lives, beings, forces, and all the things that have the characteristics of the feminine gender.

Stay in Touch. . .

Llewellyn publishes hundreds of books on your favorite subjects

On the following pages you will find listed some books now available on related subjects. Your local bookstore stocks most of these and will stock new Llewellyn titles as they become available. We urge your patronage.

Order by Phone

Call toll-free within the U.S. and Canada, **1–800–THE MOON**.
In Minnesota call **(612) 291–1970**.
We accept Visa, MasterCard, and American Express.

Order by Mail

Send the full price of your order (MN residents add 7% sales tax) in U.S. funds to:

> **Llewellyn Worldwide**
> **P.O. Box 64383, Dept. L133–3**
> **St. Paul, MN 55164–0383, U.S.A.**

Postage and Handling

> u $4.00 for orders $15.00 and under
> u $5.00 for orders over $15.00
> u No charge for orders over $100.00

We ship UPS in the continental United States. We cannot ship to P.O. boxes. Orders shipped to Alaska, Hawaii, Canada, Mexico, and Puerto Rico will be sent first-class mail.

International orders: Airmail—add freight equal to price of each book to the total price of order, plus $5.00 for each non-book item (audiotapes, etc.); Surface mail—add $1.00 per item.

Allow 4–6 weeks delivery on all orders. Postage and handling rates subject to change.

Group Discounts

We offer a 20% quantity discount to group leaders or agents. You must order a minimum of 5 copies of the same book to get our special quantity price.

Free Catalog

Get a free copy of our color catalog, *New Worlds of Mind and Spirit*. Subscribe for just $10.00 in the United States and Canada ($20.00 overseas, first-class mail). Many bookstores carry *New Worlds*—ask for it!

**FENG SHUI FOR
BEGINNERS
Successful Living by Design
by Richard Webster**

Not advancing fast enough in your career? Maybe your desk is located in a "negative position." Wish you had a more peaceful family life? Hang a mirror in your dining room and watch what happens. Is money flowing out of your life rather than into it? You may want to look to the construction of your staircase!

For thousands of years, the ancient art of feng shui has helped people harness universal forces and lead lives rich in good health, wealth and happiness. The basic techniques in *Feng Shui for Beginners* are very simple, and you can put them into place immediately in your home and work environments. Gain peace of mind, a quiet confidence, and turn adversity to your advantage with feng shui remedies.

1–56718–803–6, 240 pp., 5¼ x 8, photos, diagrams, softcover $12.95